ABNORMAL PSYCHOLOGY
CHANGING CONCEPTIONS

ABNORMAL PSYCHOLOGY
CHANGING CONCEPTIONS

Second Edition

Melvin Zax and Emory L. Cowen
University of Rochester

HOLT, RINEHART AND WINSTON
New York   Chicago   San Francisco   Atlanta
Dallas   Montreal   Toronto   London   Sydney

Library of Congress Cataloging in Publication Data

Zax, Melvin.
Abnormal psychology.

Bibliography: p. 577
Includes index.
1. Psychiatry.   I. Cowen, Emory L., joint author.
II. Title.   [DNLM: 1. Psychopathology.   WM100   Z41a]
RC454.Z38   1976   616.8′9   75-38894

ISBN: 0-03-089517-0

To the memory of
Joseph and Sadie Zax
and
Philip and Rose Cowen
who would have been proud

Preface

This text is a revision of a book published in 1972. A major purpose of the earlier version was to bring to the student's attention some of the profound changes that were taking place in the mental health fields. These changes were considered important enough by Nicholas Hobbs to be called a "third mental health revolution." In so doing he accorded them the same status as Pinel's sweeping reforms in hospital care during the late eighteenth century and Freud's psychodynamic revolution of the late nineteenth and early twentieth century. Bringing the student of abnormal psychology a feeling for this third mental health revolution remains as a major purpose in this edition.

Another purpose of the first edition, retained here, was to provide a historical framework to use in understanding current changes and anticipating future developments. Major upheavals within a discipline call cherished beliefs into question and alter perspectives on phenomena that have long been taken for granted. Current happenings in abnormal psychology are no exception. New abnormal psychology texts tend to follow the basic structure of earlier ones, doing little more than updating references to the literature within a fixed formal and substantive framework. Changes in the field have carried us to a point where this is no longer valid.

To demonstrate most clearly what is now happening we continue to use the historical approach, which places evolving approaches and ideas within a context that makes these developments understandable. Further, we attempt to stress the evolutionary nature of the field of abnormal psychology itself. The sense of unfolding and development is easily lost in periods of stability. When changes begin to occur rapidly, we are reminded that in the long view, change is more characteristic of any discipline than is stasis. That notion was forgotten for a long time in psychology, as the mental health professions worked to assimilate and evaluate the contributions of Freud and others stimulated by him. Recent developments have changed that equilibrium. This text attempts to describe how and why these changes have come about.

In the process of presenting an all-encompassing view, a fair amount of the traditional material of the abnormal psychology text remains. Hopefully, however, the context within which it is embedded lends perspective to its overall significance. For example, when most of an abnormal psychology text is devoted to describing and discussing syndromes, or clusters of symptoms thought to occur together, the student inevitably comes away thinking that the process of classifying illness is the prime business of the field. We hope to show that although classification is important under some circumstances, it is entirely irrelevant under others. The same is true for many other activities long regarded as fundamental to abnormal psychology. Though some may see this as a bold, presumptuous position to take, we justify it on the basis of the rapidly changing, challenging, and exciting nature of the field, which encourages questioning the old order and virtually demands the testing of new theories and practices.

The organization of the edition differs somewhat from the earlier one. Also, some material has been eliminated, much has been added, and all has been updated to keep up with a rapidly moving field. Case materials have been added to bring life to abstract descriptions, and the format has been enlivened through the use of photographs, illustrations, and various study aids.

The authors acknowledge a considerable intellectual debt to the many students and professionals who have participated with them in developing concepts and programs that challenge the old order. Many of the ideas that shape this book have emerged from such mutual effort. Finally, we are grateful for the editorial assistance provided by Johnna Barto of Holt, Rinehart and Winston, who has proven to be much more than a copy editor.

Rochester, N.Y.   M.Z.
January 1976   E.L.C.

Contents

CHAPTER 11   Personality Disorder: Development of the Concept and Psychopathic Behavior   324

CHAPTER 12   Sexual Disorders   358

CHAPTER 13   Addictions   376

CHAPTER 14   Individual Psychotherapy   406

CHAPTER 15   Group Psychotherapy   434

PART TWO
The Present and The Future   454

CHAPTER 16   A Field in Transition   457

CHAPTER 17   The Prevention of Disordered Behavior   478

CHAPTER 18   Programs in Action: The Schools   513

CHAPTER 1

Introduction

"She's a witch! We must burn her to death," sixteenth-century town fathers pronounced of a woman whose behavior did not conform to their standards. It was a rather drastic therapy to follow.

In the early part of this century, a person who sometimes acted irrationally was assigned to psychoanalysis. Today, a senior citizen who feels lonely and isolated in an urban apartment may be cheered by some special program providing college student companions on a regular basis.

The mental health field has been changing for the past several hundred years. Today is a period of great change, if not advance, for the mental health professions. It is a change that is being felt pervasively. New theories are being proposed to explain the development of behavior disorders, suggesting treatment approaches that are different from those most commonly used during the past thirty or forty years. Many new notions are also being introduced about who can render direct service, with a consequent reevaluation of the role of the highly skilled professional.

All of this seems to have come about because, once again, the mental health profession is redefining the orbit within which it is equipped and willing to operate. More specifically, many of the traditional helping professionals in psychology, psychiatry, and social work are beginning to agree that the large numbers of culturally deprived, impoverished individuals who have rarely been "patients" in the usual sense of the word are legitimate objects of the attention and concern of the specialist in human behavior. The obvious social need for instituting preventive measures aimed

1

The Bettmann Archive

In earlier times unusual behavior was responded to with drastic measures.

at heading off disorders before they become serious enough to require the traditional treatment approaches is also contributing to the present upheaval.

It is the purpose of this book to bring these movements to the attention of the student of abnormal psychology within a framework that can accommodate what is happening as a logical event in an ongoing process. The more popular texts of recent years have been organized around the syndromes as the central concern. They characteristically contain a chapter dealing with the question "What is abnormality?", a chapter tracing the history of significant ideas and events in the field of abnormal psychology, and one or more chapters set-

ting forth a personality theory or theories. Then the heart of the book follows: a series of chapters detailing syndromes and using the personality theory to offer—with varying degrees of certitude—explanations that result in a neatly, if unrealistically, tied package. It is often a package so well tied that it is difficult to squeeze into it ideas and research which are divergent from the theory being emphasized in the book. Furthermore, such a format hardly accommodates differing therapeutic approaches, much less preventive approaches. Often, in deference to recent thinking, authors tack chapters on to the end of the traditional text entitled "The Problem for Society," or "Action for Mental Health," but these seem foreign in a context which has not only been emphasizing a different way of looking at problems of human behavior but has also been focusing on entirely different kinds of problems.

Traditional ideas about psychopathology largely determine what to look for, what to emphasize, what techniques of information-gathering to use, and which therapeutic measures to invoke. Some valiant efforts have been made to broaden psychodynamic models and theory. However, the nature of these models or, more specifically, the personal commitment of their adherents to them often sets limits to the field of vision, interpretation, and hypothesis. On the other hand, as attempts are made to extend psychodynamic models and approaches to more and more areas of human behavior, it is almost inevitable that the feedback from such attempts should raise questions and problems for both theory and practice. When "tried and true" methods fail or fall short, innovations are sometimes attempted that must themselves be accounted for and explained. Since "classical" theories and approaches can be found wanting, other bodies of knowledge and ways of looking at problems may offer an answer, as well as provide the possibility of revisions in the main body of theory. It is our contention that the format which characterizes the currently popular text on abnormal psychology is not flexible enough to incorporate ideas and movements which no longer focus on the patient who comes to the clinic to be diagnosed and treated.

This text will attempt an approach which sees the process of change in man's ideas about abnormal behavior as in large measure a natural consequence of the fact that the specialist in behavior disorder has been willing to accept more and different kinds of problems as falling within his sphere of competence. Beginning with primitive times when only the very dramatically deviant individual was regarded as abnormal and demons were thought to have invaded his being, we hope to demonstrate that the advance in ideas about problems in human behavior has been entwined with our changing view of what constitutes an abnormality which is worthy of scientific attention. In a sense, as problems were confronted which always existed but were simply not seen as being within the province of the mental health worker, theories and clinical practices were altered. Thus, Freud's revolutionary impact in part resulted from his viewing hysteria as a psychological rather than a physical disorder, so that a completely new realm of behavior had to be understood and dealt with. Within such a framework, the significance of the very recent emphasis upon community health and prevention of behavior disorder can be seen as a further broadening of the scope of the mental health worker, to embrace the individual, neither neurotic nor psychotic, whose antisocial or excessively dependent behavior, seemingly growing out of a particular subcultural milieu, poses a serious problem for society.

Preventive emphases, of course, cast an even wider net in that they go beyond the boundaries of subcultures and attempt to deal with vast numbers of individuals struggling to adapt to stressful situations, be they children starting school, mothers having their first child, or adults who are bereaved.

This text is, therefore, historically oriented. It stresses the development of ideas as a function of changes in the way we define the problems we are concerned with. It will attempt to avoid conveying the impression that we have reached the point where all agree on what behavior disorder consists of, much less on what causes it. Rather, it focuses on the development of ideas, and its concluding chapters simply represent the most recent point reached in this process. The syndromes that are traditionally the "guts" of an abnormal psychology text are included but without the emphasis and detailed description they usually receive. The perspective provided by this general approach will, hopefully, allow the reader to distinguish contexts in which syndromes have great relevance from those in which they are insignificant. The remainder of this chapter will elaborate the changes in ideas that are taking place in the mental health field.

THE PROCESS OF SCIENTIFIC ADVANCE

Scientific disciplines proceed through complicated evolutionary processes. At various periods in the development of such disciplines, theories become entrenched, techniques become rigidified, and the role of the scientist becomes stereotyped. Often, such static periods persist until some dramatic breakthrough results in what can be called a scientific revolution. Kuhn

(1962), an historian of science, points out that a "revolution" takes place in the natural sciences when the scientific community rejects a time-honored (and highly influential) theory in favor of a new one which is incompatible with it. This, essentially, has been the significance of the work of men such as Copernicus, Newton, Lavoisier, and Einstein in the physical sciences. Each, within his respective discipline, produced basic changes in the standards for deciding which scientific problems ought to be studied and in the technology for studying them.

This process of change is found in the social sciences as well as in the natural sciences. One essential difference, however, between the way scientific revolutions come about in the natural and the social sciences should be discussed. Kuhn sees the normal activity of a natural science as being very much like solving puzzles. Scientific problems are tests of "ingenuity or skill in solution" in much the same way that puzzles are. Furthermore, both puzzle-solving and normal scientific activity proceed according to rules that limit the nature of acceptable solutions and the means by which one arrives at them. This kind of scientific activity, particularly in the mature natural science, grows out of what may be termed a shared paradigm: essentially, a set of rules and standards of practice based on certain accepted theoretical considerations. Scientific revolutions involve the introduction of theoretical changes that alter the rules of the old paradigm and open up inquiry into a new set of problems through a new type of paradigm. Such alterations are most likely to take place when experiments on natural phenomena fail to turn out the way theories derived from the old paradigm would have predicted.

It is not always accurate to describe scientists in the medical or social sciences as these kinds of puzzle-solvers. They are less likely than natural scientists to engage in research primarily because they feel a need to pit their skill and ingenuity against the intricacies of nature. More often, their work tends to be set in motion by some specific social need. Their raison d'être is not that there is a mystery out there which it would be fun to solve, but that there is a practical problem concerned with human kind's physical or social or emotional vulnerabilty about which something must be done. Zilboorg and Henry (1941, p. 21) make this point very clearly:

> It may be said with considerable certainty that it was not the doctor who by some miracle of spontaneous generation appeared first on the scene and, inspired by a lofty love for suffering humanity, sought to alleviate pain and began to make medical discoveries. Guided from the very beginning by the demands of the patients, the doctor had to respond and to serve; it was his business at all times and at all costs to supply what the patient wanted. This particular type of relationship between patient and doctor was and still is the most potent stimulus to the progress of medicine and surgery.

Jaynes (1966) has compared physics and psychology as scientific pursuits, using a metaphor that highlights differences between the two fields and that supports the distinction we have made. Scientific progress in physics is compared to mountain climbing; its workers are roped together by a common method and push constantly in the same direction. Many paths lead upward but each new generation faces a similar problem: "rope on, test the pitons, follow the leader, look for better lay-backs and footholds to the heights." Thus, one proceeds upward from ledge to ledge. Confusion or uncertainty may arise "on the ledges," but the final goal is always clear. Psychology, on the other hand, is less like a mountain than a dense forest. Some of it is easy to walk through on certain levels, but the directions out of this forest are often unknown, and perhaps nonexistent. At times the student is not even certain that he is meant to find his way out. Here, all manner of wanderers are to be found crossing each other's paths in "happy chaos." This description conforms well to Kuhn's thesis that the medical or social researcher, in attempting to cure cancer or to develop a plan for world peace, may not be dealing with the sorts of puzzles that engage the natural scientist. The challenges of the social scientist may be made up of pieces selected randomly from two different puzzles; in that case they are insoluble in their stated form. Identification of the two separate puzzles may be as near to a solution as the social or medical scientist can come. Only rarely is someone able to point out how the separate puzzles are really only parts of a larger one whose total complex can often only be guessed.

CONCEPTUAL CHANGE
IN ABNORMAL PSYCHOLOGY

Looking closely at one realm of social science, the field of abnormal psychology, it is apparent that those who have worked in the area have been motivated to solve certain practical problems confronting society. Most of the major changes within the field of behavioral abnormality have taken place not because new theories have grown out of old paradigms—thus leading to the development of a new paradigm—but, rather, because problems that had not before been accepted as relevant to the discipline came to be redefined as falling within the scope of the professional community concerned with behavioral abnormality. Work on these new problems often seemed to demand new theories and new practices that have evolved implicitly from the reorientation of the field.

New theories and practices are not, however, readily embraced. Entrenched theories and viewpoints die hard. Particularly where new practices require shifts in the roles played by professionals, they tend to be resisted stubbornly, if subtly. At times professional practices, once initiated, are perpetuated without the benefit of sound theoretical underpinning. Jackson (1962), for example, in his discussion of schizophrenia, points out that the now discredited prefrontal lobotomy, a brain operation in which certain nerve fibers are severed, began to be practiced on schizophrenics because it was noted that lobotomized cats became placid and less excitable following lobotomy. Shock therapy, in which seizures are induced chemically or electrically, was introduced on the strength of the mistaken observation that epileptics do not develop schizophrenia. Seizures were, therefore, thought to have curative effects. Electroconvulsive therapy (the seizure here is induced electrically) is still widely applied to certain types of patients, despite the fact that there are no generally accepted theories to explain its effects. The same has been said of psychedelic therapies in which consciousness-expanding drugs are used (Mogar, 1968; Savage, 1968).

Much of what has been said up to now indicates the complexity of the field of abnormal psychology, especially when compared to the natural sciences. This complexity tends to be compounded by another fact. In the natural sciences, puzzles are solved directly with greater frequency than in the social sciences. Such solutions make for good housekeeping within the science, since they can result in the verification of one theory and the possibility of discarding several competing ones. In abnormal psychology solutions are rarer and the problems one confronts are less likely to have direct or simple solutions. One is rarely able to demonstrate convincingly that anything is true or false. Therefore, theories tend not to be discarded readily. Change in the paradigms of abnormal psychology usually results from the identification of new problems. This in itself neither automatically solves existing problems nor necessarily detracts from the interest of many members of the scientific community in such problems. There is thus a proliferation of theories and a tendency to use a theory developed in connection with one problem to explain a different problem. For example, Freud had much to say about human behavior and its etiology, primarily through his contacts with neurotics. However, many of his ideas have been drawn on by those interested in psychotics, and many applications of his theories have been made in that realm.

Even within a given subarea a group of theories may develop that not only fail to build upon each other but, indeed, may have little or no interrelationship. Jackson's discussion of schizophrenia (1962) illustrates this point. He describes genetic, biochemical, psychological, sociocultural, and family-oriented theories, each of which has been developed independently in an attempt to understand schizophrenia; few of these miniature theories are related to the more prominent treatment approaches for schizophrenia.

Thus, while new theories capture the attention and enthusiasm of many who are concerned with behavioral abnormality, theory in this field proliferates in a manner reminiscent of the attic of a very retentive individual who cannot bear to part with anything because it might prove someday to be worth using. And, as it cannot be proved conclusively that the contents of the attic will *not* be useful, it seems more prudent to put up with the clutter than to be compulsively neat. This condition, however, works a hardship on the student who seeks conclusive answers to fascinating questions about human behavior and, incidentally, on would-be textbook writers who hope to approximate such answers. For the textbook writer the choice is between optimistically providing neat, seemingly conclusive, and informative answers, despite their inaccuracy, or confiding to the student the complexities that preclude pat answers.

THE CHANGING SCOPE OF ABNORMAL PSYCHOLOGY

We have described abnormal psychology as a field within which interest has moved from one problem or class of problems to another. How and why this has come about is part of the history of man's discovery of himself as a psychological being. Einstein once asked, "What does a fish know about the water in which he swims all his life?" In thinking about his own ideas and behavior, man has been in the position of Einstein's fish. Just as the fish is apt to become most aware of the water he swims in when there is not enough of it, so man becomes most sensitive to his behavior when it presents problems. In the absence of serious aberration, we are inclined to believe that we, as individuals, and our fellows develop as human beings according to some predetermined plan which cannot be amended.

Historically, when aberrations appeared the usual tendency was to see them as inspired by evil forces that needed to be curbed. A primitive response has been, and is, to seek a quick and simple remedy to set things right, rather than to attempt to understand the processes that brought about the unhappy situation. Sometimes we fail even to acknowledge that such processes might exist. In addition, the scientist concerned with understanding abnormal behavior has had to compete over the years with others among society's agents who also have concerns about behavior. Traditionally, these agents have included: clergymen, whose interest has been primarily in behavior that may be deemed immoral; legal authorities, who have concentrated on behavior that transgresses the law; and, more recently, physicians, who have often been defined as prime care-agents in all matters pertaining to human health and well-being. The domain of the behavioral scientist has, therefore, been somewhat uncertain and has undergone considerable change over the years.

This movement has perhaps, in the long view, displayed some regularity: a periodic *broadening* of the meaning of the term "abnormal behavior." The earliest concerns of the science were with the relatively few in society who manifested grossly deviant (but not necessarily illegal) behavior. As abnormal psychology has become more inclusive, more attention has been devoted to larger numbers of individuals whose behavior is troublesome in less obvious ways. This number includes many whose problems were formerly seen to be within the exclusive domain of the religious, medical, or legal authorities. As a result, some (for example, Szasz, 1960; Wootton, 1959) have wondered if what we have done is to have taken on a strange mixture of moral, legal, and scientific problems, which itself raises a whole new set of problems.

The towering genius in the study of abnormal psychology has been Sigmund Freud. Conceivably, time and progress may lessen the number of his contributions, but

Sigmund Freud has been credited with starting the second revolution in mental health.

one that will remain is the fact that his work, more than that of any person, has resulted in a redefinition of the scope of his field. Unlike other professionals of his era, Freud worked with the neurotic rather than the grossly psychotic patient. Ultimately he was able to convince his contemporaries that the behavior of such patients was of legitimate concern to the specialist in human behavior. His theories of personality development and mental dynamics, which sought to explain behavioral characteristics of the normal person as well as of the disturbed, paved the way for the development of other theories of personality and led to a concern for behavior that was less dramatic than that seen in psychoneurosis and that involved many more people. Eventually, conditions that had been regarded as purely physical (psychosomatic disorders) and behavior that had been regarded as criminal came to be viewed as objects of legitimate concern for the behavioral scientist. Hand in hand with the confrontation of fresh problems and the unfolding of theories for understanding them came attempts to develop techniques for coping with these problems.

As in the case of the physical sciences, the excitement of discovery in abnormal psychology tends to be followed by periods of stabilization when the new professional roles which have been created become established and professionals set to work practicing the techniques dictated by the new theories. During such periods of calm, orthodoxy prevails and research tends to be directed toward an elaboration and evaluation of the prevailing model. Such a period followed the major discoveries of Freud. The reader, however, should not be misled into believing that extreme role shifts and new theoretical models are warmly received. Freud was regarded as a maverick in his time, and acceptance of the model of the psychoanalytic therapist came only after considerable time and in the face of much resistance. Once they became established though, Freud's theories and techniques, and their practice by professionals, prevailed for the first half of the twentieth century.

The current period in abnormal psychology is one in which another major upheaval seems about to take place. Again, it is being ushered in by a change in focus of the mental health worker, a change brought about by a variety of facts. One important stimulus was a growing dissatisfaction in the 1950s with the results of traditional treatment approaches. Eysenck (1952) pointed out that the effectiveness of psy-chotherapy, a technique that had long been practiced by then, had never been demonstrated. This point was elaborated by further surveys (Eysenck, 1961; Levitt, 1957). Because it was felt that the mental health professions were not adequately meeting the needs of the mentally ill, the United States Congress passed the Mental Health Study Act of 1955, providing for a comprehensive study of the human and economic problems resulting from mental illness and the development of methods for solving them.

The responsibility for carrying out this task was given to a nongovernmental interdisciplinary group from the mental health field, selected by the National Institute of Mental Health with the assistance of the National Mental Health Advisory Council. It consisted of 45 individuals drawn from various mental health professions such as psychiatry, psychology, biology, sociology, nursing, education, occupational therapy, social work, pediatrics, and the church. The name given to this group of experts was the Joint Commission on Mental Illness and Health.

The Joint Commission sponsored a number of comprehensive substudies in all major areas relevant to mental health. One of the most important of these was a survey of manpower trends in the mental health fields (Albee, 1959). The findings of this investigation made it clear that the professional manpower pool will not grow to the extent needed to meet the future needs for mental health services. On the contrary, given our rate of population growth and the fact that pressures for services are constantly increasing in amount and scope, the prospects are that the supply of trained professionals will fall even further behind demand.

Another sobering finding (Joint Commission, 1961) was that a relatively small proportion (18 percent) of Americans with personal problems requiring help turn to mental health professionals. The largest percentage (42) went to their clergymen, and the next largest group consulted their physicians (29 percent). The remaining 10 percent were seen in social agencies. These and other data uncovered in several social psychiatric surveys (Hollingshead & Redlich, 1958; Srole, Langner, Michael, Opler, & Rennie, 1962) suggest that presently overworked mental health professionals are dealing with only a small fraction of those who need help. Consequently, with their limited numbers they cannot hope to be able to deal directly even with those who are willing to seek the help of a professional. Another implication of these facts is that people who turn to their doctor or clergyman might be better helped if such "care-givers" received the kind of training and supervision that the experienced professional can provide.

Thus far we have been speaking of meeting the needs of those people who recognize the existence of personal problems and actively seek help in solving them. What of the even greater numbers of less sophisticated, impoverished, or culturally deprived individuals who do not see themselves as needing the services of the mental health worker (Reiff, 1966)? Many of these eventually develop disorders requiring the attention of the traditional clinician. They pose an even more serious community problem, however, because of their nonproductivity and because they are generally defined as needing to be cared for or controlled by welfare and law-enforcement agencies. Hence, huge government-supported programs are being instituted in the hope that fundamental changes can be brought about in the way these people live their lives and in the environment in which they develop. Although mental health professionals are often seen to have a key part in such programs, to function effectively in them, they may be required to behave in ways that are quite different from their traditional roles.

In these new programs, human behavior specialists are brought into a new arena. The object of their concern is a different and broader segment of the population than the one they have typically dealt with before. It is made up largely of people who do not see themselves as patients. They do not turn up in someone's office seeking help. The professional must come to them and bring something they will perceive as relevant and be willing to accept. Obviously, this state of affairs presents a completely new set of problems for the professional. It has already produced theoretical change, sweeping role shifts, and considerable alteration of the form of interaction between the helper and the person being helped. For example, in some model programs now developing, the helper is not a professional. The later works primarily through a group of paraprofessionals whose numerical superiority brings them in direct contact with far more people than a single professional could ever deal with directly.

Such extreme role shifts and the introduction of new theoretical models do not occur smoothly. These recent movements in the mental health fields face obstacles, two major classes of which must be overcome. The first is the need to break away from the traditions of the mental health profession which specify (a) that one works with a "patient," who (b) should come to the professional motivated by a desire to change some of his behavior, and (c) should possess certain personality characteristics that maximize the likelihood that he will benefit from the type of treatment which the professional, guided by certain theoretical assumptions, is accustomed to providing. This is one part of what is sometimes referred to loosely as "the medical model," a model that implies rejection of those who fail for whatever reason to regard themselves as ill (Reiff, 1966). The second obstacle is the fact that even if broad goals, such as the prevention of emotional disorder and the maximization of human potential, are clear, the means by which these are to be achieved remain obscure. How does one achieve prevention? What does one do to maximize the potential of a youngster from a subculture that has taught him to think primarily of survival and immediate gratification? These problems strain the ingenuity and the scientific skill of the professional who must create program models and establish their effectiveness. The ultimate forms of such programs cannot be predicted, nor can one foresee the direction they will eventually take. What does seem clear now is that the horizon of the mental health professions has been widened and will never again be restricted to the patient in the clinic, hospital, or agency.

THE DEFINITION OF ABNORMALITY

The way in which abnormality is defined is closely related to the kinds of problems the specialist in abnormal behavior chooses to confront. The tautology that abnormal behavior is what is studied by the psychologist interested in abnormality is true if not entirely informative. Were matters simpler, as in pre-Freudian times, most would be content with Foley's (1935) definition of abnormality as simply a deviancy from the statistical norms of a particular cultural group. This concept is still retained by many writers; indeed, the term *abnormal*

itself implies deviation from a norm. Many raise objections to it on the grounds that some "deviancies" are desirable (high intelligence, great wealth) and modify the position to conclude that the term *deviant* should be applied only to behavior which seems to be inappropriate or disabling to the individual (Maher, 1966).

Others have much more fundamental objections to the notion that abnormality can be viewed solely in terms of deviancy. Wegrocki (1939), for example, is concerned with the *purpose* of behavior that seems deviant. If the behavior, however deviant, represents an attempt on the part of the person to cope with an intrapsychic problem, Wegrocki does not consider it abnormal. On the other hand, if the deviancy represents an attempt to flee from conflict, then it is abnormal. The implication here is that coping behavior is an ideal which defines normality, and its absence reflects abnormality. Moving still further in the direction of a definition of abnormality as a failure to live up to certain ideals, Shoben (1957) postulates that normality consists of the fulfillment of one's potentialities as a human being. He describes what he feels should be man's essential goals. This approach has philosophical overtones to which many object, since the ideals espoused by any single writer are necessarily subjective.

One of the dangers in this type of controversy is the possibility that the practical implications of how one defines abnormality will be overlooked. When one focuses on the practical, it is apparent that different definitions relate best to different problems. For the clinician based in an office, serving those who seek his assistance, the relationship between deviancy and abnormality often seems central. His patients present problems that usually take some form of deviance (depression that interferes with eating, sleeping, or ability to work; or anxiety resulting in an inability to relate to others or to perform certain functions). Often the complaint is couched in terms of this deviancy: "I have trouble sleeping," "I have no appetite," "I have no friends," "I never date." Implied in such complaints is a comparison to some standard of how long one should sleep, how much one should eat, or how many friends or dates one should have. The clinician's job in this instance is to make an estimate of the degree of the deviance compared to the norms of the sociocultural group to which the patient belongs. In much the same way that the physician must decide whether a temperature of 104° is a serious deviancy, the psychologist or psychiatrist is obliged to make decisions about his patient's emotional symptoms. His judgment in this matter determines the course of action he takes—outpatient, hospitalization, or no treatment at all. Very often the clinician's diagnostic skills are limited by the amount of information he possesses about the group norms relevant to a particular patient. In special groups where variability in behavior is the rule rather than the exception, diagnosis is indeed a difficult task. Adolescents are such a group; thus, whereas participating in streaking might be a serious deviancy in a middle-aged executive, it could be regarded as a minor aberration in a teenager or college student.

On the other hand, some specialists in human behavior are asked to serve a very different function from the traditional diagnostic and therapeutic one. They may, for example, be called upon to evaluate the executive potential of a candidate for an important business position. In such instances gross deviancies are almost certainly not an issue. The major question revolves about the degree to which the man's skills match the requirements of the job. Likewise, in the massive community programs that are currently being mounted the aim is to create better, more productive citizens. The focus, then, is less on deviancy than it is on the development of certain valued personal qualities like the desire for an education, working regularly, paying taxes, caring for one's family, and so forth. The measures of the success of such programs will more likely be in such terms than in terms of the absence of deviancies.

The import of this discussion is that abnormality can be defined differently depending upon the problem with which one is attempting to deal. This in turn will depend upon the values of a particular society at a particular point in time, so that as man changes in response to a variety of forces, what will be regarded as abnormal will also change. As we have said, there is a crude regularity in the way conceptions of abnormality have changed, generally in the direction of greater inclusiveness. The growing tendency to see the chronic alcoholic, the addict, and even the "criminal psychopath" as psychologically sick and deserving of treatment rather than punishment is part of this trend. Thus it is that at various times in the development of the field of abnormal psychology, it has been convenient, perhaps even important, to define abnormality one way rather than another. As the various historical phases of the field are discussed, this point should become increasingly apparent.

THE CLASSIFICATION OF ABNORMAL BEHAVIOR

In chapters which follow it will be seen that man has devoted considerable effort to classifying the behaviors that he re-

The Museum of Modern Art

This woodcut, *The Shriek*, 1896, by Edvard Munch, vividly illustrates man's inability to react effectively with his environment. (Lithograph, printed in black, 20⅝ x 15¹³⁄₁₆″ sheet. Collection, The Museum of Modern Art, New York. Mathew T. Mellon Fund.)

garded as abnormal. At times zeal for classification superseded efforts to uncover the root causes of disorder. In recent years, standard systems for classifying abnormal behavior have been developed and revised from time to time. These are considered necessary to avoid the chaos of proliferating diagnostic schemata designed to deal with specific problems. Such idiosyncratic designations often filter into different settings and are used to describe conditions for which they had not been intended. This can cause considerable difficulty in the discussion of mental disorder.

In 1917, therefore, a standard nomenclature or diagnostic and statistical manual for mental diseases was formulated by the Commitee on Statistics of the American Psychiatric Association. Periodic revisions have been made, including a major expansion in 1952, to accommodate the experience of psychiatric casualities during World War II (American Psychiatric Association Committee on Nomenclature and Statistics, 1952). The most recent revision of this nomenclature was published in 1968 (American Psychiatric Association Committee on Nomenclature and Statistics, 1968), as part of the development of an international classification of mental diseases. Consequently, the 1968 nosology is an amalgam of. the 1952 revision and the classification of mental disorders in the International Classification of Diseases (World Health Organization, 1968), published by the World Health Organization. Since the standard nomenclature of the American Psychiatric Association (both the 1952 and 1968 versions) is the most widely used of the existing nosologies, it will be adopted here in describing the various organic or psychogenic syndromes. All references in this book to the diagnostic and statistical manuals will use the designation DSM–I (1952) or DSM–II (1968).

One major difference between the 1952 and 1968 nosology should be mentioned. In the 1952 nomenclature virtually all the diagnostic categories were regarded as *reactions*, in keeping with Adolph Meyer's (Lief, 1948) dictum that what passes for mental disorder is best understood as an individual's awkward effort at adjusting to some demand. In effect, therefore, the roots of the disorder are to be found in the multitude of life situations leading up to the development of symptoms in any given individual. The 1968 nomenclature has eliminated the designation "reaction" from most diagnostic labels; for example, the *schizo-phrenic reaction* of 1952 has become simply *schizophrenia* in 1968. This change was made in order "to avoid terms which carry with them *implications* regarding either the nature of a disorder or its causes" (DSM–II, 1968, p. viii, our italics). Apparently, framers of the most recent nomenclature felt that speaking of reaction types led to a bias in favor of psychogenic origins.

THE TROUBLES WITH CLASSIFICATION

A variety of objections and criticisms of taxonomies has appeared over the years and many continue to be prominent in the thinking of contemporary psychologists. These may be roughly classified into two broad categories. The first type of objection is concerned with the process of classification per se. Such critics tend to feel that either classification is altogether unnecessary as part of the clinical enterprise or that its drawbacks are so significant that they seriously hamper the proper conduct of treatment. As such, they do more harm than good. The other class of objections to classifying behavior tends to be leveled at specific classification schemes. This one is most obviously directed toward the most widely used system of classification, the one described in DSM–II (1968) which will be discussed in more detail in succeeding chapters.

A good example of a critique which questions the utility of any classifying scheme was offered many years ago by Patterson (1948). He draws a distinction between behavioral disorders which result from purely or largely physiological causes and those which are rooted primarily in psychological causes. In the case of the former he concedes that diagnosis may play a significant role in the approach to dealing with the problem and, as such, is drawing a distinction between the role of diagnosis in medicine as opposed to psychology. Patterson then advances the view that all psychologically based behavior disorders have similar causes regardless of the external form that the disorder may take. From such a viewpoint he argues that there is no need to be concerned about external symptoms or to attempt to formulate diagnoses concerning the etiology of such disorder. Thus, for Patterson, diagnosis is altogether unessential to the treatment of psychological disorder. This, incidentally, is a viewpoint similar to that expressed in recent years by many who identify themselves as humanistic psychologists. Many humanistic psychologists, for example, see the root cause of all behavior disorder as deriving from a failure to discharge emotions which build up within the individual and thereby lead to a variety of behavioral symptoms. From this viewpoint, which will be further elaborated upon in Chapters 9, 14, and 15, diagnosis has little relevance.

Rogers (1951) offers another viewpoint resulting in the rejection of diagnostic evaluations. His client-centered approach to psychotherapy, which will be described in Chapter 14, emphasizes the client's personal responsibility for changing in psychotherapy. On this basis he feels that the practice of rendering diagnoses is unwise. He sees the very process of diagnosing a case as placing the responsibility of an evaluation in the hands of "the expert" rather than upon the client where it belongs. Such a practice might easily lead the potentially dependent client to believe that the responsibility for understanding and improving his life situation also resides in the hands of the therapist from Rogers' viewpoint. Furthermore, Rogers expresses concern about the long-range implications of an expert being the primary locus of evaluation. This could easily lead to a situation in which social control is exercised by a few people over many.

Harry Stack Sullivan (1956b), with a conception of the therapeutic role—in which he accepts the therapist as an "expert"—that is very different from Rogers' was also wary of the practice of making diagnoses. His concern was that once having attached a label to a set of symptoms, the diagnostician must thereafter fight to defend or justify it. He might do this by responding selectively to data that support his diagnosis and ignoring important data that fail to do so. There is the further danger that once having invested one's professional prestige in a label, the therapist might insidiously influence the patient to behave in ways that the label suggests he might.

Those who criticize the form of existing diagnostic schemes are concerned about various aspects of specific systems. Some studies (Ash, 1949; Mehlman, 1952) have been concerned with the *reliability* of diagnostic schemes. This refers to the degree to which different people using the same system can agree about diagnoses. Obviously, if the particular diagnostic system which is used as a yardstick to apply to patients cannot be used reliably, it is difficult to see how it can be helpful in any overall treatment enterprise. The findings of such studies indicate that the reliability of widely used schemes is not high, particularly when fine differentiations are attempted within major diagnostic categories. Thus, while there may be some agreement among different observers that a given patient suffers from schizophrenia, there is often very little agreement that the disorder is of a paranoid, or a catatonic type.

Another type of concern about the kind of taxonomy that is most widely used in

psychiatry and psychology has been expressed by Maslow (1948). He pointed out that psychological reality consists of elements which are constantly changing and developing, as well as some which remain stable and fixed. Generalizing from this view, the type of diagnostic system most commonly used in psychology seems to be one which focuses on those elements of the individual which allow one to classify him and ignores all others which contribute to his uniqueness. We are thereby led to focus only on what is static and to ignore what is dynamic within the individual. This produces a very limited picture of the person, one too limited to allow us to be truly helpful to the individual who is having problems.

In keeping with this line of thinking, Wallace (1966) has distinguished between a response disposition and a response capability approach in the area of personality assessment. Most current approaches to personality assessment, and those underlying the traditional diagnostic system, take the position that behavioral evidence seen in a given situation, such as a diagnostic testing session, reflects inner predispositions to behave in a certain way. Thus, the patient who makes schizophrenic-like responses to a projective test or in a diagnostic interview is described as suffering from schizophrenia, with the implication that this disposition pervades all of his activities. Test situations are typically left as unstructured as possible in order to allow the patient as much opportunity as possible to reveal his true inner dispositions. Wallace argues, on the other hand, that it is more valuable to think of the patient who manifests schizophrenic responses not as a schizophrenic but as one who is *capable* under certain specifiable circumstances of making such responses. From this viewpoint it becomes necessary for the diagnostician to be concerned with specifying the conditions under which such responses are made by the particular patient, and this process is potentially far more valuable than one which assumes a response disposition. Such an approach conforms better to the reality that few patients display schizophrenic behavior at all times and can lead to a better understanding of the patient's problems and a far better conception of how to deal with them.

Wallace's position is very much in keeping with that of the behavior therapists who have become prominent on the clinical scene in recent years. The behavioral approach is well described by Kanfer and Saslow (1965). These authors point out that in traditional medicine the diagnosis made about a patient has been viewed as an essential prerequisite to all that follows because that diagnosis indicates some knowledge of the origin and future course of the illness. In addition, medical diagnoses often infer a great deal about the pathological process leading to the development of symptoms and the result encountered by others in treating patients manifesting such a disease. While the model of rendering diagnoses has been taken over from medicine in psychology and psychiatry, unfortunately the labels that are used fail to relate necessarily to etiology, or to suggest the optimal treatment course. Kanfer and Saslow illustrate this point with the example of three patients who were diagnosed as schizophrenics. According to these authors,

the first patient eventually gave increasing evidence of an endocrinopathy and when this was recognized and treated, the psychotic symptoms went into remission. The second case had a definite history of seizures and appropriate anticonvulsant medication was effective in relieving his symptoms. In the third case, treatment directed at an uncovering analysis of the patient's adaptive techniques resulted in considerable improvement in the patient's behavior and subsequent relief from psychotic episodes. [Kanfer and Saslow, 1965, p. 532]

The implication of this illustration is that the schizophrenic behavior manifested by each patient was not the result of a disease having a unique etiology but rather a similar outcome of several different types of processes.

Diagnoses based on symptoms are also seen by Kanfer and Saslow often to focus on behaviors which may be relatively trivial in the patient's overall pattern of life. For example, some individuals may be able to function reasonably effectively in spite of the fact that they suffer from mild delusions, the occurrence of which may prompt a clinician to diagnose them as psychotic. Another concern of Kanfer and Saslow is that emphasis on symptoms prompts the focusing of attention on behavior patterns which may be relatively unimportant in themselves but are the consequences of other aspects of the patient's life which are important. Thus, the syndrome orientation prompts the diagnostician to be concerned about the patient's subjective complaints concerning his mood and the way he feels rather than on the conditions of his life which tend to produce and maintain such feelings. In their attempt to develop a diagnostic procedure from which predictions of future behavior and suggestions concerning a course of treatment would flow, Kanfer and Saslow propose an approach based on behavior modification procedures.

Kanfer and Saslow's "functional approach" involves a continuing assessment of the behaviors currently displayed by the patient and of the stimuli in his environment which control these behaviors. In this approach, at the same time that efforts are made to control and change behavior, the patient's life pattern is continually evaluated along with stimuli which control it. This assessment is arrived at through a series of questions aimed at describing the patient's behavior as concretely as possible.

The questions are directed toward seven separate categories of patient behavior. The first is concerned with analyzing the problem situation. Here the patient's complaints are classified in terms of excesses and deficits with dimensions such as frequency, intensity, duration, appropriateness of form, and stimulus conditions being carefully described. The second category involves a clarification of the problem. Here situations and people that tend to sustain the problem behavior are considered along with the consequences of these behaviors both for the patient and for those around him. Thirdly, a motivational analysis is done to determine the people, events, and objects which reinforce the patient's behavior. The fourth category involves a developmental analysis focusing on: (a) the patient's typical behavior at various stages in his life; (b) the stimuli which create noticeable changes from his typical behavior; and (c) the relationship between such behavior changes and the present problem. The fifth category used in assessment involves an analysis of the patient's self-control methods. Concern here is both with the manner and degree to which self-control is exercised in daily life along with the people and events in the patient's life situation which have reinforced such behaviors. The sixth category involves an analysis of social relationships in order to determine how the significant people in the patient's social network influence his problem behaviors and how they in turn are influenced by the patient for his own satisfaction. Informa-

tion gathered in this category may be useful for planning the way in which the people in a patient's social sphere may be used in a treatment program. Finally, the seventh category involves an analysis of the social-cultural-physical environment. Emphasized here is a study of the norms characterizing the patient's natural environment and the degree to which the patient's life conforms or deviates from these norms.

The carrying out of this functional analysis of the patient does not rest entirely on his verbal report or on the way he performs on psychological tests. It requires that observations be made of the stimulus field within which the patient lives and the way in which the patient's behavior changes as a function of change and situational variables. Verbal reports are seen to provide information about the way the patient sees his environment and himself and about the content of his memory and his fantasies. On the other hand, to learn of his behavior, it is necessary to actually observe him in a variety of controlled situations. One of these situations is obviously the interview in which the clinician interacts with the patient. A fuller set of observations however may require obtaining information from people who know the patient in other situations as well as actually to observe him in such typical important situations as his behavior at work. In this approach the patient may also be asked to provide samples of his behavior through the use of tape recordings of interactions with members of his family, fellow workers, or people in other situations in his everyday life. It is felt that only through such an approach can the necessary firsthand information about the way the patient lives his everyday life be collected, and it is only this kind of information which can ultimately be useful in planning for his treatment.

National Institute of Mental Health

Verbal reports provide the therapist with information about how the patient sees himself and his environment.

In their summary and analysis of a variety of criticisms of diagnostic practices Zigler and Phillips (1961) point out the many advantages the taxonomies have, particularly the fact that they convey considerable information in an efficient way. They express concern about many of the fundamental issues raised in the general critiques of diagnostic systems but argue that a poor system can always be revised. They regard the most serious criticism of any system as relating to the fact that the assignment of a phenomenon to a class automatically obscures many individual characteristics of

the phenomenon. Therefore, they point out that the disadvantages of a taxonomy can be minimized by developing diagnostic schemes that take into account most, or all, of the relevant aspects of a phenomenon and obliterate only irrelevant differences. They agree that current taxonomies in the mental health field probably do not approach this ideal. The suggestions of theorists such as Wallace and Kanfer and Saslow obviously point in this direction and merit very serious consideration.

The significant trend in many of the suggestions for revision of diagnostic approaches involves greater concern for factors external to the individual as determinants of his behavior. This concern has invaded the area of psychotherapy and is basic to the developing area of community psychology. A fuller discussion of it should help the reader to understand better the organization of the chapters which follow in this book.

INTERNAL VERSUS EXTERNAL CAUSES OF BEHAVIOR DISORDER

As will be seen in Chapter 2 and many of the chapters which follow, psychology and psychiatry have been dominated for many years by the idea that man's behavior is largely determined by forces within himself. At certain times and in particular places these forces were seen to be largely rooted in his biology. At other times these have been seen to be psychological forces instilled very early in a person's life which have played the role of a guiding force in all that has followed. Thus, it may be only a slight oversimplification to say that when a behavior disorder appeared, the culprit invariably was seen to be human nature, bad protoplasm, genetic weakness, a disease, or a faulty upbringing. This prompted the type of traditional diagnostic approach which focused on the identification of pathological entities and the assumption that similar etiologies characterized all who received a given diagnosis. Likewise, treatment was seen to be a matter between a therapist and a patient with the world outside of the therapy room playing an insignificant role, if any, in the process.

Many of the objections to traditional diagnostic taxonomies have involved a challenge to the idea that the patient's problem has resulted entirely from internal causes. Certainly, the behavioral approach espoused by Kanfer and Saslow represents almost a complete turnabout with respect to the basic assumption about what are the important causes of behavior. Just as this kind of issue has been raised with respect to diagnostic problems, it has also become increasingly prominent with respect to treatment issues.

Furthermore, as will be seen in later chapters, the impetus for the community psychology approach derives in great measure from a concern that many of man's problems, the extreme behavioral deviations as well as the more subtle but widely pervasive problems such as failure to achieve potentials, are in large measure a function of the kind of social conditions under which man must live. The essential reasonableness of this viewpoint makes it surprising that it has been so long in becoming significant within abnormal psychology. The reason that we are only just being taken by such an obvious notion seems to lie in the fact that the field of abnormal psychology grew out of a medical tradition. This factor will be elaborated on in Chapter 3. Several of the chapters which follow will focus on specific syndromes and present material that makes the assumption that man's problems are rooted in factors which are internal to the individual in the same manner that physical diseases result from bacteria and viruses and various breakdowns of the internal physiological system. In reading this material the student is advised to maintain a healthy skepticism toward the validity of this assumption. In some cases it may be an accurate one, but it has very likely been vastly overworked in abnormal psychology.

The material which concludes the book, beginning with Chapter 15, will stress community approaches which make the assumption that most of man's behavior problems derive from forces that he has to contend with that are external to himself. It is an assumption to which man has been drawn as a result of many obvious weaknesses and failures in traditional approaches. Time and experience may conceivably demonstrate that the assumption that most of man's problems are caused by the world in which he must live is overdrawn, but it is currently presented as an important alternative which has received far too little consideration up to the present time.

THE ORGANIZATION OF THIS BOOK

In order to achieve the objectives of this book the historical approach will be combined with description of syndromes, explanatory theories, treatment approaches, and community and preventive programs. It is hoped that the historical background will establish the context out of which current ideas have developed and will, therefore, make these ideas more meaningful. The framework we will attempt to develop will hopefully make the changes taking place within the mental health field understandable as more or less inevitable steps in a process.

Most of the changes in man's ideas about abnormal behavior are direct consequences of the fact that he has been willing to accept more and different kinds of problems as falling within his sphere of competence. This book should therefore begin with a discussion of man's earliest concepts of mental illness and deal with each broadening redefinition of the field as it occurs. To some extent this will be done. Chapter 2 will survey conceptions of mental illnesses and treatment practices that characterize the many hundreds of years of man's earliest history. The third chapter will be some-

thing of a departure from the historical sequencing in order to present a description and critique of the medical model. This is important since many of the chapters which follow it will characterize syndromes which have been conceptualized on the basis of the medical model. Chapter 4 will focus on organic brain defects, which were recognized early in man's history but not well understood until the advances in physiology and medicine of the nineteenth century. Logically, the following chapters should take up the different psychotic disorders as they are currently described. Unfortunately, the complexity of the field dictates a departure at this point from a purely logical order of presentation.

A meaningful discussion of conceptions of schizophrenia and other psychotic illnesses is hardly possible without mention of Freudian theory. Freud's work, however, was done with psychoneurotic patients and it will be pointed out that one of his major contributions, the one that had truly revolutionary impact, was the broadening redefinition that it forced on the mental health field. Thus, because his theories were applied outside the context in which they developed, it will be necessary to discuss Freud's work and the theories of personality and pathology (in Chapter 5) before completing the discussion of disorders that have been the traditional concern of the mental health professional. Chapters 6, 7, and 8 will deal with schizophrenia and other psychoses and Chapter 9 will take up several current views of psychoneurosis along with alternative theoretical approaches to Freud.

Chapters 10 through 13 will resume a logical order of presentation in terms of our overriding theme. The recognition of psychosomatic factors in illness will be described as a further broadening of the mental health field (Chapter 10). The still further broadening impact of the concept of personality disorder will be taken up next (Chapters 11, 12 and 13), and this discussion will begin to serve as a bridge to later chapters devoted to the community psychology approach. Chapters 14 and 15 will be devoted to psychotherapy and group therapy and as such will involve something of a departure from a strict historical sequencing. The authors have elected to take up these topics in individual chapters, rather than in separate chapters scattered throughout the book, for the sake of clarity and to enhance the opportunity for comparison between systems. Chapter 15 will begin to sketch the kind of transition taking place within abnormal psychology, from a focus on traditional problems and traditional treatment methods toward approaches which deal with broader behavioral problems that emphasize preventive approaches. Chapter 16 will describe the preventive model which is the basis for many of the community programs to be taken up in Chapters 17 and 18. These final chapters of the book will elaborate the most recent trends in the mental health field and will point toward future developments.

SUMMARY

1. This is a time of pervasively felt change in the mental health field because a redefinition of its scope is underway.
2. Advance in the natural sciences occurs when new theories prompt rejection of a time-honored approach and reorient the field. In abnormal psychology new orientations have occurred because of periodic redefinitions of the field's scope. These redefinitions have been steadily scope-broadening. The most recent changes have led to the emergence of community approaches.
3. Definitions of behavioral abnormality are a function of the problems with which one wishes to deal. Society's values play a role in that what is considered abnormal in one place or time may not be in other places or times.
4. Systems for classifying abnormal behavior have long existed. Despite their potential convenience, all have serious weaknesses. Many mental health workers feel they are more damaging than they are worth. Most suggestions for revising the currently popular system would give greater weight than has been done to the importance of forces outside the person in shaping his behavior.

PART ONE

THE PAST AND THE PRESENT

FOREWORD

Part One of this volume takes up the "traditional" content of abnormal psychology. Oriented around manifest behavior disorder, this section presents a contemporary view of established syndromes. Beyond that, however, it attempts to provide an historical context within which to understand how current conceptions have emerged, and to suggest directions that might be taken in the future. Uncertainties and controversies that persist today will be highlighted—and these exist even with respect to disorders that have been studied for many centuries. Thus, the reader may well accumulate more questions than answers.

Our purpose in this part of the book is to convey a realistic image of what the field of abnormal psychology has been like in the past and what it is currently. Hopefully, this will serve as a useful prelude to Part Two, which describes very recent developments in a future-oriented way.

CHAPTER 2

The Mentally Abnormal

Some Historical Perspectives

Some years ago, an archeologist exploring a cave discovered several ancient human skulls which had large holes in them. What did these round openings on the surface of the skulls mean? They were obviously intentional drillings made by a surgical procedure we now call trepaning. One author has suggested that the cave dwellers who used this practice were concerned with a condition that is known today as traumatic epilepsy, which is characterized by such symptoms as confusion, headache, melancholy, and seizures. He reasons that the condition was probably attributed to the presence of evil spirits within the skull; the trepan permitted the devil to escape and "incidentally relieved a certain amount of mechanical pressure on the brain." Since many trepaned skulls have been found with signs of healing around the opening, at least some primitives survived this treatment.

It is useful to study various historical views of mental abnormality such as trepaning because it bares the roots of current ideas. More importantly, to observe the tortuous development of ideas and to learn of the obstacles impeding the acquisition of knowledge of any kind (particularly of the human psychological nature) fosters an understanding of the difficulties of making progress in our own time. These historical observations may even suggest how difficult it is to *recognize* progress itself.

MENTAL ILLNESS AS SEEN BY ANCIENT MAN

Even in humankind's early history, people interested in behavioral abnormality have created classifications and described "cases." Whenever this has occurred, discussing the behaviorally aberrant in that period is a simple matter of reporting. More often, however, it is necessary to infer that a particular behavioral phenomenon was of concern at a particular time. Sometimes this evidence is indirect; at other times it is less so, deriving from descriptions of what was regarded as "madness" in some mythological, historical, or fictional figure.

References to behavioral abnormality in early religious writings describe what was regarded as mental disorder in those times and require less speculation on the part of the modern interpreter. The Vedas of the early Hindus viewed alcoholics, those claiming to be God, and those displaying much pride and a hot temper as suffering a mental disorder. Other examples of the mentally disordered, for these people, included the individual who decorated himself with trinkets while singing and dancing, the filthy, and the gluttonous, as well as the person of poor memory who

The University Museum (Philadelphia)

These trepaned skulls are evidence that even cave dwellers tried to relieve mental problems.

moved about in an uneasy manner and refused to wear clothing. The early Hindus, as well as many other ancient peoples, described several types of seizures.

An example of mental disturbance described in the Old Testament is the depression of King Saul, who tried to persuade a servant to kill him and who finally committed suicide. Several other biblical descriptions of what appear to be catatonic excitement (uncontrolled destructive behavior) and epileptic seizures are also to be found. Nebuchadnezzar was described as suffering the unusual psychosis of lycanthropy (the delusion that one is a wolf).

The mythological writings of the Greeks are a rich source of descriptions of what was looked upon as mental disorder in very early times. Homer describes Ulysses as yoking a bull and a horse together, plowing sand instead of the fields, and sowing salt rather than corn, at a time when he was feigning derangement. Ajax, who was mad, killed sheep, mistaking them for his enemies, and when he came to his senses his remorse led him to throw himself on his sword. Orestes experienced hallucinations, seeing furies that his sister could not see. The daughters of Proteus, the king of Argos, condemned to madness by divine powers, believed themselves to be cows and would leave their royal home to run wild in the forest, lowing like beasts. Hercules was described as suffering from epilepsy, and this disorder has been known through the ages as "the disease of Hercules." In addition, as Zilboorg and Henry (1941) point out, much behavior that would be attributed to mental disorder in our own time was not regarded as such in Homer's writings. For example, the Pythias of the Delphian oracle were described as behaving in strange ways that suggest severe mental disturbance.

The classical era in Greek history produced advances in man's knowledge in many areas, including his own behavior. Hippocrates (460–377 B.C.), "the father of medicine," contributed to an understanding of human behavior through his description of mental disorders. He described conditions such as "puerperal insanity," later known as postpartum psychosis (usually a depression following childbirth); the delirious states found in tuberculosis and malaria; memory disturbance in a patient suffering from dysentery; and acute mental confusion resulting from hemorrhage. In addition, he recorded the earliest observations of what we now call a phobia—a specific psychoneurotic disorder in which certain objects or situations must be avoided or considerable anxiety will result. Hippocrates developed one of the earliest classifications of mental disorders, which included epilepsy, mania (excitement and hyperactivity), melancholia (depression), and paranoia. The latter state, for him, involved extreme mental deterioration; this is not the case for the condition presently described as paranoia, which is characterized by systematic persecutory and/or grandiose delusions.

Hippocrates also recognized a disorder known as hysteria. He did not regard it as a mental disorder, believing that it was a physical affliction restricted to women. He theorized that it was caused by the moving of the uterus, which was regarded as an organ free to shift its position within the body if loosened from its mooring in the pelvic cavity. Further, he described an alcoholic delirium in which the patient saw snakes and other animals fighting goblins, with himself in the midst of the struggle. The patient's sleep was disturbed by combat with dreadful, unseen forces. Other writers of the Greek era, Plato and Aristotle, mentioned disorders such as mania, melancholia, stupor or dementia, and imbecility.

More than three centuries later a Roman classified mental disorders into two general categories, acute and chronic. The former included delirium induced by febrile diseases (those involving high fevers). Chronic disorders were regarded as true insanity; these included conditions theretofore labeled melancholia and involving hallucinations. The latter were described in great detail.

Another Roman physician, Arataeus (ca. A.D. 30–90), observed that manic and depressive states often occurred in the same individual and that between disordered periods the patient was lucid. He observed the progress and outcomes of mental disorders and tried to differentiate them on this basis. Prior to his time, the term "mania" was used for a variety of disorders. Arataeus noted that some persons so labeled seemed "stupid, absent and musing," and that such qualities bore little resemblance to another type of mania: "a stupefaction of the sense of reason and other faculties of the mind." The latter "mania" more closely resembles a disorder that came later to be known as schizophrenia (characterized by thought disorder and affective disturbance). Arataeus also noticed that, in the second type of disorder, mental deterioration sometimes occurred: in his words, "it is not rare to see their sensibility and intelligence fall into such a degree of degradation that, plunged into an absolute fatuousness, they forget themselves, pass the remainder of their lives as brute beasts, and the habits of their bodies lose all human dignity." This condition resembles that seen in deteriorated schizophrenics (usually people who have displayed schizophrenic behavior for extended periods of time).

The wealth of thought and observation about problems of abnormality that characterized Greek and Roman civilization diminished during the Middle Ages for reasons that are elaborated in the following section. However, it is clear that many of the mental aberrations first identified during the Greco-Roman era continued to be prevalent during the long period of scientific decline that characterized the Middle Ages. Additionally, new conditions were identified, peculiar to this age. One of these was lycanthropy (first mentioned in the Bible). Persons afflicted with this illness had the delusion that they were wolves and at night would wander about deserted places (not infrequently cemeteries) howling. The clinical picture of this disorder was fully described as early as the third century by Marcellus. In this same epoch, Arabian physicians described a persecutory psychosis resembling what we now term paranoia, and a degenerative disorder associated with the involutional period of life (the time when women experience menopause and men the climacteric).

The Bettmann Archive

David played his harp in an attempt to lessen the depression of King Saul.

Finally, during the Middle Ages, three types of "peculiar" mental reactions appeared, at least two of which appear to be unique to that time. The first was a group phenomenon in which people gathered in large processions, traveling about the countryside doing public penance for their sins and believing that the end of the world was approaching. Known as flagellants, they carried banners, crosses, and candles. Their black clothing was marked with a red cross, and they carried heavy leather whips, often metal-tipped, with which they flogged themselves until blood flowed. Such groups existed in Russia as late as the seventeenth century. The second condition was known as "dance mania." Individuals were impelled to laugh, dance, sing, and make noises until they were exhausted. Similar behavior has reappeared at various points in man's history, and the dance marathons that were popular in the United States in recent times may have been a mild form of it. The third condition was known as "devil possession." The victim was supposedly pushed, pulled, and thrown about by an inner devil to such a degree that he became excited, possibly violent, and would froth at the mouth. Someone with spiritual power was needed to exorcise the demon and, if this were successfully accomplished, the devil would jump out with a sudden jerk.

This sketchy catalogue has been constructed for the purpose of identifying the problems to which those concerned with mental aberrations in man's early history addressed themselves. "Mental disorder" obviously almost always involved dramatic or extreme behavior. These extreme deviancies resemble many of those seen in modern times. What is now termed manic-depressive psychosis was well described by ancient observers, and Arataeus anticipated Kraepelin by many centuries in recognizing that mania and melancholia were part of a single disorder.

To be sure, a few disorders less extreme than current-day psychoses were also noted. Among these, the one recognized earliest and most frequently through the ages has been hysteria, now regarded as a psychoneurotic disorder. This is a condition characterized by physical symptomatology that is often very dramatic and striking (such as paralyses and anesthesias, blindness, and deafness). These symptoms often failed either to respect the physiological facts or to conform to anatomical structures. Thus, although hysterical disorders are now regarded as "milder" than the psychoses, they often appeared to would-be healers as extreme deviancy.

Other disorders more subtle than the psychoses were also sometimes noted in early times, but until recently there seems to have been relatively little interest in them. For example, Cicero spoke, in the middle of the first century, of what we would call psychopathic behavior (grossly antisocial acts performed without evidence of guilt), as did Najab, an Arabian physician of the fifteenth century. Najab also described a disorder characterized by ruminations, anxiety, and doubt, which resembles what is now called an obsessive-compulsive neurosis. Caelius Aurelianus, who lived around 400 A.D., regarded certain sexual perversions, rife at the time, as mental disorders. These insights, however, were largely isolated. Essentially, when early man was concerned about behavior, he had in mind what we now see as extreme psychosis or the dramatic hysterias.

Recognizing man's general reluctance to look into himself and to speculate on his behavior, it is not difficult to appreciate that, in the beginning he approached the task gingerly and looked only where he had to. Of course, the extreme (and therefore threatening) nature of the psychoses demanded the attention of the healers of the day. Furthermore, there may have been some special security achieved in speculating about the peculiarly deranged creature as opposed to the more subtly disturbed, since one could assume discontinuity between the observer's behavior and that of the grossly aberrant individual.

EARLY MAN'S IDEAS ABOUT THE CAUSES OF MENTAL ILLNESS AND ITS TREATMENT

Primitive Man

In any discussion of man's ideas about the cause and cure of mental illness, one must inevitably consider social, political, religious, and economic forces. Scientific progress, especially in the social sciences, takes place in spurts that are strongly influenced by the attitudes of the time. Ideas about human behavior are particularly subject to environmental forces since they are not the exclusive province of the scientist. Legal authorities and theologians also have considerable stakes in this area, and both groups are as ready as scientists to advance theories and to institute practices for shaping or controlling human behavior. In periods when one or the other group has been forceful in asserting views in this domain, the scientist has tended to retreat. Moreover, even the scientist is not a person independent of current social influences, including those of the church and the law; thus, his abdication is, not uncommonly, entirely voluntary.

We have mentioned primitive man's belief that spirits caused mental disorder. How such a view came about is not difficult to comprehend. The primitive used a variety of intuitive, largely concrete, means to maintain his physical equanimity. Injuries or fevers were cooled with water or saliva; foreign matter was removed from the skin; snake bites were sucked to extract venom, and so on. Similarly, the earliest theories to explain mental disease were simple, straightforward ones. When the cause of mental disorder was not obvious, man sought to explain it on the basis of some influence that another human being, or perhaps a spirit, exercised over him. The influence of the former could potentially be combatted by a counterexercise of influence through magic. Superhuman forces were appealed to by the development of magico-religious practices.

Superhuman forces were probably postulated after the recognition of certain temporal sequences such as the coming of day when the sun rose. The assumption was made that the sun *caused* the light to appear. Man recognized, too, that he himself was capable of making light appear by fire. Therefore, just as man could control phenomena such as the presence of light because it was his *intention* to do so, some other being, more powerful and unknown, caused the sun to rise because he intended it to do so. Thus, the belief developed that gods were responsible for all natural phenomena; this view evolved from an extension of the motivational causality of man's own actions to all of nature.

When illnesses involved externally observable symptoms, man did not need to go beyond his intuitive remedies to seek a cure. However, when the disorder was internal, affecting organs that could not be seen, or when its causes were not readily apparent, primitive man applied ideas about his own motivations to unseen powers. These powers were thought to invade the being of the sufferer and to take possession of him. The idea that spirits caused mental disorders held sway for a longer period of time in man's history than any other; through the centuries more sophisticated views, time and again, gave way to that same basic conviction.

Classic Greek and Roman Thought

The earliest recorded changes in man's view of physical and behavior disorder came about in the classical Greek era when a scientific approach was applied to the understanding of all natural phenomena. The early Greek centers of healing had been the Aesculapean temples in which the priests, who were thought to have inherited the secrets of healing, performed religious ceremonies to cure illness. Patients slept near the temple and were encouraged to dream of a god who would cure their affliction. Herbs were administered, depending upon the nature of the dreams. Many who would probably now be thought of as mentally disturbed were not so regarded then and were often chosen to interpret and aid in the treatment of other afflicted individuals. Few questions about the nature of mental disorder were raised in these temples, steeped as they were in the supernaturalism of the time.

Greek genius broke free from this animism. Apparently a certain degree of security and freedom from more immediate problems of existence permitted the slave-owning Greeks of the classic era to develop curiosity about man's physical and psychologic functions and to apply rationality to what they observed. As early as the sixth century B.C. a Greek physician dissected a human body, enucleated an eyeball, and was probably the first to perceive a connection between the senses and the brain. Another advanced a primitive theory of psychopathology, emphasizing that each man was psychologically unique in some

The Bettmann Archive

Hippocrates, known as the father of medicine, insisted that all disorders could be explained by natural causes.

respects and must be understood on that basis. Empedocles (490–430 B.C.) suggested the humoral theory, based on what he regarded as the four elementals (fire, earth, water, and air). These were characterized by four qualities—heat, dryness, moisture, and cold. For each element, a corresponding bodily humor was postulated; blood (in the heart), phlegm (in the brain), yellow bile (in the liver), and black bile (in the spleen). Disease was said to be caused by imbalance among these humors, and cure required the administration of drugs with qualities opposite to heat, dryness, moisture, or cold—whichever was thought to be out of balance.

Hippocrates (460–377 B.C.) lived at a time unique in human history. Among his contemporaries were Pericles, Anaxagoras, Theophrastus, Thucydides, Phidias, Sophocles, Euripides, Aristophanes, and Socrates. This was the age of Hellenic enlightenment, when an eager curiosity achieved new heights in such diverse areas as political science, drama, philosophy, sculpture, and architecture. It is understandable that important advances were made in medicine as well as in other areas. Hippocrates was an excellent observer (witness his descriptions of mental disorders mentioned in the preceding section), and he applied the speculations of earlier philosophers to what he saw. Of his many contributions, perhaps the greatest was his insistence that all illness or mental disorder must be explained on the basis of natural causes. He scornfully refuted those who regarded epilepsy as a "sacred" disease. In one of his medical treatises he wrote, "if you cut open the head, you will find the brain humid, full of sweat and smelling badly. And in this way you may see that it is not a god which injures the body, but disease." It was this unswerving attitude of inquiry and insistence on natural, understandable bases for all disorders that led to his being regarded as the "father of medicine."

Hippocrates' theoretical speculations were few and largely traditional. His treatment techniques were based on Empedocles' humoral theory. Within this framework, temperament was thought to be either choleric, phlegmatic, sanguine, or melancholic—depending on the predominance of one of the four bodily humors. Despite his acceptance of the humoral theory, Hippocrates was eclectic in his view of the causes of mental disorder. For example, as indicated above, he felt the locus of epilepsy to be in the brain and believed that "madness" was due to an excess of bile. In testimony before a court, he expressed the opinion that a pro-

found emotional state in a pregnant woman could affect the skin color of the child she was bearing. Finally, he subscribed at times to an endocrinological theory, when he claimed that certain body juices might cause madness. As a busy clinician, and not a researcher, he was open to many types of natural explanation.

Hippocrates' version of humoral theory, which strongly influenced his work, held that air (the breath) was the source of intelligence and feeling, that it reached the brain through the mouth and was then distributed throughout the body. His psychopathology was largely physiology. For example, unpleasant dreams and anxiety were seen as being caused by a sudden flow of bile to the brain; melancholia was thought to be brought on by an excess of black bile; and a predominance of warmth and dampness in the brain was considered to lead to a feeling of exaltation.

It may be said that Hippocrates wrote the first page of medical history and that he did this with few scientific facts at hand. Although he had relatively little influence on his contemporaries, he remained for centuries the supreme medical authority.

Other Greek thinkers strongly influenced later observers of behavioral abnormality. Two who stand out in this respect were Plato (427–347 B.C.) and his pupil Aristotle (384–322 B.C.). Zilboorg and Henry (1941) regard Plato as having had a retrograde influence on psychology, largely because he reintroduced a mystical element in the explanation of behavior. He saw man as composed of two parts, mind and matter. Mind, the true reality, seated in the brain, was conceived as that to which everything owes its form; it was thought to represent the principle of law and order in the universe. Matter—including the body —was denigrated by Plato as the inferior part, which accepted the impress of mind and was its unwilling servant. Ideas were accepted as the only true realities, and when a sensation led to an idea, it was seen as a recollection of the past rather than as a new notion, since all knowledge was treated as preexistent. In his theory of psychopathology, Plato conceived of two souls —one rational, the other irrational. The rational soul resided in the brain, was immortal, and presided over the mortal irrational soul which was the source of human emotion. These emotions were located in various parts of the body—anger and audacity in the heart, hunger and passion between the navel and the diaphragm. Thus, affect was relegated to a lower, animal plane, and there was no interest in the function of emotions in the behavior of the organism.

One historian has described Plato's psychology as a "kind of phrenology on a large scale." Mental disorder in his scheme resulted when the irrational soul severed its connection with the rational, resulting in excess of happiness, sadness, pleasure-seeking, or pain avoidance. For Plato the reasons for this abandonment of reason were satisfactorily explained by Hippocrates' humoral theory. Further, Plato distinguished between two kinds of madness. One resulted from disease, but the other was divinely inspired and, as such, was unrelated to the irrational soul and endowed the recipient with prophetic powers. The notion of a divinely inspired madness smacks of primitive man's animistic views and well exemplifies Platonian mysticism that diluted Hippocrates' more naturalistic, medical point of view. Many centuries later, during the early part of the Christian era, this same Platonian mysticism exercised much influence over thinking about the etiology of disordered behavior.

Aristotle, though a pupil of Plato, was not his disciple. For him the world was filled with interesting and exciting phenomena meriting study; knowledge was not "reminiscent" as it had been for Plato. Although, like Plato, Aristotle divided the soul into two parts—one rational, the source of wisdom and memory, and the other irrational, the source of temperance and courage—these two were not separable from each other, as in Plato's system, but were thought to function only as a unit, and all psychological reactions were seen as total. Emotions were thought to relate to whether or not a sensation supported or impeded the activity of a bodily function. The former were said to be pleasurable and the latter were conceived of as unpleasant. Man's reason, which was immaterial in his view, was granted the status of immortality and immunity from illness. On the other hand, illness could attack man's material aspect. This orientation led Aristotle to the conclusion that all illness, mental or otherwise, was rooted in man's physical structure. This significant conception was destined to play an important role in the history of medical psychology.

Aristotle's theory of how the body operated held that the soul was partly material and partly immaterial, and that it required warmth in order to function. He did not fully agree with Hippocrates' bile theory. While he accepted the view that an excess of black bile could cause disease, he did not believe that the disease inherently resulted from bile but rather that this bile carried heat or cold. Aristotle believed that very cold bile made man appear cowardly and stupid, moderately cold bile caused vertigo or apprehensiveness, warm bile was the source of gaiety, and very hot bile produced amorous feelings and loquacity.

The brain was not left entirely out of Aristotle's system. It was seen as cold and serving the function of condensing hot vapors emanating from the heart; the dew that resulted was thought to refresh the heart, thus making it more temperate. This is the first suggestion that nervous disorders were due to vapors—a notion which was revived again and again, even as late as the seventeenth century.

The Hellenistic period that followed the time of Hippocrates, Plato, and Aristotle linked Greece with Alexandria, in Egypt, which became a center of learning following the Macedonian victories. Eventually, Rome became an important Mediterranean power and through the Punic Wars (264–146 B.C.) came to dominate much of the civilized world. A practical and politically oriented people, the Romans produced few notable physicians of their own. Instead, they imported Greek physicians for service in their military forces. Around 300 B.C. the Aesculapian cult flourished in Rome and, during the Punic Wars, Greek physicians were used to treat wounded Roman soldiers in hospitals set up along the roads leading to Rome (this was probably the first system of army field hospitals). Eventually, Greek physicians, who had not at first been warmly received by the Roman citizens, began to practice in Rome itself. Many of the advances in Roman thinking about mental disorder therefore came from men trained in the Greek tradition.

Asclepiades (exact dates unknown) was one such person, advancing a theory that opposed Hippocrates' humoral theory. Following Democritus, who conceived of the atom as the basic structure of matter, Asclepiades reasoned that the body was composed of atoms, with space between them, which attracted and repelled each other. At times these spaces were blocked, thereby inhibiting the normal movement of the atoms. Treatment consisted of taking measures to bring the atoms back to proper motility. Specific techniques thus resembled what we would now think of as sim-

ple physical therapy. This appealed to the Romans, who appreciated such experiences as soaking in a warm tub while enjoying a fine wine. Asclepiades is credited with inventing a number of devices for comforting patients, such as a bed that was suspended and swayed so as to produce a sedative effect, and innumerable types of baths. He also regarded "musical harmony and a concert of voices" to be a useful therapeutic tool. An excellent observer, Asclepiades was the first to distinguish between delusions and hallucinations, and regarded mental disorders as stemming from emotional disturbances or, in his terms, "passions of sensations." The popularity of Asclepiades' remedies did much to gain favor for Greek physicians in Rome and in 46 B.C. they were granted full citizenship by Julius Caesar.

From our point of view, perhaps the most significant advances in Roman thought about mental illness were contributed not by a healer but by the philosopher Cicero (106–43 B.C.). In rejecting Hippocrates' bile theory. Cicero expressed the opinion that emotional factors could cause physical illness. "What we call furor they call melancholia, as if the reason were affected only by a black bile, and not disturbed as often by a violent rage, or fear, or grief." He perceived the fundamental difference between physical illness and mental disorder to be that the former may befall one as the result of purely extraneous factors whereas "perturbations of the mind proceed from a neglect of reason." Animals, therefore, fall ill physically but, lacking reason, they are not subject to mental aberration. He also called upon man to participate in his own cure through "philosophy." Substitute the word "psychotherapy" and Cicero would be indistinguishable from most modern practitioners.

Another Roman whose ideas forecast a more modern point of view was Arataeus (ca. A.D. 30–90). Like several of his predecessors, he was a fine clinical observer. He believed that the locus of mental disorder might be either in the head or in the abdomen but that, whichever was primarily affected, the other might be affected secondarily. This view deviated from the traditional notion that each disease was lodged in its own site, affected only by that portion of the anatomy; it pointed to the conclusion that the individual functions as a unitary system. Arataeus' speculations about the premorbid personalities of his patients constituted another significant contribution. Individuals who became manic were characteristically labile in nature, easily irritable, angry, or happy. Those who developed melancholias tended to depression in their premorbid state. Such observations suggested that emotional disorders were merely an extension or exaggeration of normal personality traits—a truly advanced idea for the time. Arataeus' emphasis on detailed observation prompted him to take special note of the specific ideas patients expressed as well as of the course and outcome of the disorder—a method of clinical study that was to be recalled and utilized many centuries later.

Other Roman physicians, although contributing little new thinking about the nature of mental disease, were nevertheless advanced in their humanitarian attitude to treatment procedures. They placed much emphasis on the disturbed individual's comfort and were among the first to consider cultural factors in treating behavior disorders. They prescribed readings for convalescing patients and recommended, for example, that a laborer should be engaged in discussing the cultivation of fields while navigation should be discussed with a sailor.

The flourishing period of the Roman empire was culminated by the work of Galen (A.D. 130–200), who had enormous influence over medical thought for many centuries. The seven centuries between Hippocrates and Galen witnessed subtle cultural changes in the Greco-Roman world. Greek rationalism was gradually infused with a stream of Oriental mysticism, and by Galen's time, breakdown of the classical culture was well advanced and much of the rationality that had typified it had been replaced by unsupported speculation. The scientist of that day, who still respected the Greek tradition, sought to cull out all that was useful from both the contemporary and the ancient world and to combine it into a single system. This eclecticism was compatible with Galen's temperament and he became the leading medical exponent of this approach.

At times Galen displayed the ultimate in empiricism. "Do not go to the gods to make inquiries and thus attempt by soothsaying to discover the nature of the directing soul ... or the principle of the nation of nerves; but go and take instruction on the subject from an anatomist." However, he was also very much a teleologist who, unsatisfied by observation alone, sought to explain why a particular organ was constructed as it was. He followed, quite literally, Aristotle's principle that there is purpose in all that nature does, and attributed the form of anatomical structures to God's wisdom.

One of Galen's most important ideas was very close to Arataeus' belief that symptoms did not always indicate a diseased organ or organ part. He considered it possible that although one part may be primarily affected, by *consensus* other essentially separate parts might also display symptoms. As will be seen, this conception was central to his theory of mental disorder.

The brain was conceived of as the center of psychic functions by Galen, who divided the rational soul into parts controlling internal and external functions. The former include imagination, judgment, memory, apperception, and movement, while the external functions consist of the five senses. Galen considered that there were two irrational (apparently "irrational," for him, meant emotional) souls, located in the heart and the liver.

In Galen's scheme of bodily function, food passed from the stomach to the liver, where it was transformed into chyle and was permeated by *natural spirits*, innate in every living substance. This material was then carried to the heart through the veins. In the meantime, air, which carried the *vital principle*, entered through the lungs and combined with the natural spirits, thereby producing the *vital spirits*. These rose into the brain where they were converted into the *animal spirits*. Mental disease, or disturbance of the animal spirits, therefore arose either because the brain itself was afflicted or because it was, by *consensus*, affected by a disorder in another organ. Specifically, Galen believed that: amentia or imbecility was caused by a diminution of the animal spirits or by the coldness and humidity of the brain; mania and melancholia resulted from direct brain disease; drunkenness resulted when wine filled the entire body with warm vapors, disrupting the function of the two irrational souls (the heart and liver) and, by

consensus, impairing judgment (the brain).

Few of Galen's descriptive ideas or his views about therapy were original, but his system provided a summary of the Greco-Roman period in medicine. The impact of this summary is distinctive, at least partly because of the contrast between the period of medical history that he represented and that which was about to begin.

PSYCHOLOGY DURING THE MIDDLE AGES

Understanding the development of thought about man's psychological functioning requires, as has been repeatedly stressed, a grasp of the tenor of the times. Nowhere is this principle more clearly demonstrated than in a description of the diagnosis and treatment of mental disorders in the Middle Ages.

At the height of its power, Greek civilization was characterized by its drive to acquire new knowledge in diverse areas. The Romans benefited from this heritage and added to it their genius for organization—social, military, legal, and technological. The result was a relatively stable society in which ideas grew freely.

The collapse of the Roman empire has been and undoubtedly will continue to be debated by historians. Clearly, the pres-

TABLE 2.1
Galen's Scheme Concerning the Souls

SOULS	LOCATION	FUNCTION
Rational	Brain	Controls internal and external functions: Internal are imagination, judgment, memory, apperception, movement. External are the five senses.
Irrational	Heart, Liver	Control all emotions.

sures of barbarians moving in from the north and east contributed. The six plague epidemics between the first and fourth centuries A.D., which caused the death of hundreds of thousands of people, also played a part. In troubled times people grasp desperately for security, and a great many find it in supernatural explanations of phenomena that are distressing and difficult to comprehend rationally. In the period of Roman decline, this movement toward the security of mysticism had started by the time of Galen's death. It crystallized around a religious sect, Christianity, which had grown, rather rapidly, from the status of a persecuted minority to the official religion by the fourth century A.D.

It is difficult to overestimate the constructive role that the Christian Church played in bringing consolation to confused, demoralized masses. Some historians feel that only this influence ensured the continuity of civilization and, in that sense, prevented a more serious retrogression. The price humankind paid for this measure of security was the abdication of the scientific attitude.

The Church of the early Middle Ages demanded a faith that did not brook the competition of the rationalism that was essential to science. Furthermore, man's worldly state was deprecated. Human existence they attributed to moral weaknesses and the major concern became not life on earth but in the hereafter. Partly for these reasons interest in the healing arts, in particular, declined. Another reason for this decline was the fact that early Christian doctrine stressed the healing powers of religious symbols. Christ was worshipped as a healer of the body and various saints were regarded as protectors against disease. However, the trend toward establishing saints as lesser gods was not encouraged by early Christian theologians.

For them, as strict monotheists, there was only one mediator between man and God —Christ. Proliferation of mediators went against the basic tenets of the Church.

A gradual infusion of polytheism took place during the first three centuries after the death of Christ. This process represented a throwback to the very primitive ideas of earliest man. The notion of many gods, however, struck a responsive chord in the people of that age and virtually forced its way into Christian theology. Official Christianity attempted to combat the development of superstition and the practice of magic that followed. Its effectiveness in so doing was limited because its opposition was based on the fear that magic represented an impurity in the religion rather than on a denial of the existence of supernatural beings. In other words, the official Church position was one of belief in the supernatural. Thus, repeated proclamations condemning occult practices were made, but to no avail. Ultimately, a Church council in 343 stamped the practice of magic as evidence of communion with demons. As Zilboorg and Henry (1941, p. 103) point out, "Thus, under the guise of combatting the ignorance of the masses, man finally came to the official recognition of the efficacy of magic. It did seem to bring about communion with the unknown and the powerful, but it was a bad communion with a bad power." It was only a matter of time before the differentiation was made, first by religious authorities and eventually by legal ones, between contact with good spirits and contact with evil ones. In 429 magic was officially prohibited by the *Codex Theodosianus* and formally recognized as criminal. Shortly thereafter, for the first time a practitioner of magic was put to death in Spain. The execution of sorcerers was to become a recognized practice of the time.

The earlier rationalism that had led to scientific advance abated. The learning of the Greeks and their Roman followers was preserved only in monastic libraries, which became the sole refuges for those who wished to pursue knowledge. These men retired from life into the monasteries, where they read the early Greek writings and often wrote compilations of them—adding, however, little that was original.

Alexander and Selesnick (1966) cite evidence for the view that there was a more enlightened view of mental illness among laymen than among those of the Middle Ages concerned with mental disturbance. Some basis for this interpretation is found in literary works dating back to the twelfth century in France, when the idea appeared that emotional crises may eventuate in serious emotional disorder.

The phenomenon of mental disturbance puzzled the early Christian authorities. The devil could not always be blamed for behavioral aberrations, since the content of many such disorders seemed to have religious significance. Because it was difficult for the Church authority to decide whether he was dealing with a saint or an agent of Satan, writers of the time weighed these issues and speculated about them. By the beginning of the seventh century a position on this matter began to crystalize. At that time, the devil was accepted as the culprit in all cases of deviant behavior, and the study of his ways predominated. Cures of a celestial nature were sought in this struggle with the devil. Sainted relics were applied to afflicted individuals, and incantations and exorcism became major tools of the healer both for physical illness and for mental disorder.

Demonology became the "psychiatry" of the day. Studies were undertaken to detect signs of the devil's influence; these led inevitably to interest in symptomatology and ultimately to its classification. One technique for identifying those corrupted by the devil was to search for a mark which the devil presumably placed on his agents to identify them himself. One church figure described such marks as pigmented spots or areas of anesthesia. These signs were then called *stigmata diaboli*; later, in the nineteenth century, they were seen by Charcot as part of the clinical picture of hysteria. In the Middle Ages, however, hunters of "the possessed" had assistants whose job it was to prick suspected persons with needles in various parts of the body to locate an insensitive spot. Thus, despite the fact that the theology of the time endowed human beings with free will, they were lost as individuals, facing nothing but a struggle between their own temptations and the harsh requirements of their Church.

The writings of St. Augustine (born A.D. 354) reveal this conflict between human temptation and religious restriction; they serve also as a valuable psychological document by revealing the way psychic forces operate. These writings are a rare example, during that time, of a man's daring to observe a phenomenon closely and to think about it rationally. When one considers that the phenomenon Augustine observed was his own psyche, his writings are all the more remarkable. In his *Confessions* he denied the innocence of infants and recognized their demanding selfishness. He speculated on the means by which speech was acquired. He discussed candidly his reactions as a boy to the demands made of him. His discussion of stealing as a youngster reveals great insight into what can cause such behavior. He also recognized the psychology of the gang, which reinforced forbidden behavior.

The religious transformation of the Bedouins, seminomadic inhabitants of the Arabian desert, by their prophet Mohammed at the end of the sixth century played a significant role in the history of scientific ideas during the Middle Ages. Mohammed inspired his followers to proselytize. Within a century after his death, the Arabs had conquered Babylonia, Persia, Egypt, and Syria, and had penetrated into Europe as far as Spain; they were finally stopped at Tours by Charles Martel. Since they were not interested in changing the cultural habits of their victims (as long as they could collect taxes), and were tolerant of monotheists such as Jews and Christians, the Arabs provided an intellectual oasis for philosophers and persecuted heretics. It was here that the Greek tradition in medicine was kept alive.

By the middle of the eighth century, a group of Nestorian (a religious sect led by the Syrian Nestorius) physicians, who were forced to flee their homeland, settled in Baghdad and soon became prominent healers. A descendant of this group translated the works of Hippocrates, Galen, and Aristotle into Syrian, permitting the Arabs to continue the tradition of Greek medicine. Within a few hundred years medicine among the Arabs reached heights that had not existed since Hellenic times. The Hippocratic tradition was reborn in opposition to widespread medical superstition and a great tenth-century Arabian physician established a section for the mentally disturbed in his hospital.

However, little original work flowed from this reawakening of the Greek medical tradition because the Koran was seen as the authority for all knowledge; thus no schools for higher learning except those teaching the Koran could exist. The psychophysiological theories of Hippocrates and Galen therefore prevailed, and therapies, such as the administration of purgatives, were traditional. A principal psychotherapeutic measure involved argument with the patient, which was seen to be "like stirring of a dead fire to make it burn afresh."

The reappearance of Greek medicine, including a concern with emotional well-being in the Arab world of the eighth and ninth centuries, was nothing more than a glimmer of a new dawn. It had little effect on western Europe where medicine was restricted to bodily disease and where the mentally disturbed were left to the clerics. Instead, such issues as the meaning of the term "transubstantiation" in cases where an animal, and not a man, eats the consecrated host, were debated. Such preoccupations required no tools other than the imagination. The observation and investigation of psychological phenomena were simply disregarded. The study of certain of the natural sciences not held to be within the Church's domain was advanced at this time because the intellectual who wished to avoid accusations of heresy took refuge in noncontroversial pursuits. Surprisingly, despite the prevailing superstitions about devil-possession and mental illness, the victims of illness were not treated harshly. Saints were appealed to in exorcistic rituals, and many religious paintings of the eleventh and twelfth centuries depicted holy church figures in the process of casting out the devils. Torture and execution of the "witch" and the "sorcerer" flourished later —seemingly as the response of the orthodox to the signs of a new intellectual awakening.

THE RENAISSANCE

The appearance of the witch-hunt coincided with the beginnings of the Renaissance spirit in Europe. During this era (the thirteenth, fourteenth, and fifteenth centuries) the feudal system was threatened by the discovery of gunpowder; plague killed half the population of Europe; the printing press was invented and made self-education possible; and the Church found itself under attack for its abuses, a harbinger of the Reformation. Another impetus to the concern about witches was the threat within church ranks created by a special problem. The vows of celibacy which were imposed on monks and nuns were not sufficient to inhibit erotic drives. Some monasteries were connected by underground passageways to nunneries; special steps, also, often had to be taken to protect maidens of towns situated near monasteries. Such threats to the status quo demanded a cause around which the forces of orthodoxy could rally their flocks, and that cause became the witch-hunt.

Since it was assumed that woman stimulated man's licentiousness, it was "logical" to lay the blame for sinful, erotic behavior at her feet. In terminology Freud developed much later, the unsavory impulses of men were *projected* upon women. Since women "tempted man with sin," they were presumed to be the devil's agents. (Indeed, support for this view was derived from the biblical account of the Garden of Eden.) Given such an atmosphere, psychotic women, who openly expressed erotic fantasies and who blasphemed against the Church, became easy targets.

In granting status to the persecution of witches, the Church increased general anxiety about the mentally disturbed. Epidemics of psychotic-like behavior developed in the thirteenth and fourteenth centuries and even the Church was hard put to control them. It was at this time that the flagellants we have mentioned came on the scene. Such was the strength of this organization that it threatened to usurp the Church's hitherto exclusive prerogative of forgiving sinners. Eventually such formal

The Bettmann Archive

During the Middle Ages, religious zealots engaged in flailing as a penance. The flagellants believed that the practice would lighten their emotional distress.

groups were banned by Emperor Charles IV and Pope Clement. This did not prevent the emergence of other less formal group phenomena such as the dance manias in which self-humiliation seemed to relieve guilt over sinful, bodily desires.

By the end of the fifteenth century, "psychological" problems had become entwined with so many abstract theologico-legal issues that it was scarcely possible to consider them alone. The devil was the cause of all ills. Even Galen's humoral theory was rejected. Mental disorder was equated with sin, and the devil's major preoccupation was considered to be sex. As Zilboorg and Henry (1941) observe, "The accusation of pansexualism which was raised against Freud . . . could have been raised with good reason against those of the fifteenth century who fancied devils, *incubi* and *succubi*, indulging the perennial seduction of women and men respectively." A greatly respected scholar of the day wrote as follows:

There is no part in our body that the

witches would not injure. Most of the time they make human beings possessed and thus they are left to the devils to be tortured with unheard of pains. They even get into carnal relations with them. Unfortunately, the number of such witches is very great in every province; more than that, there is no locality too small for a witch to find. Yet Inquisitors and judges who could avenge these open offenses against God and nature are few and far between. Man and beast die as a result of these women and no one thinks of the fact that these things are perpetrated by witches. Many suffer constantly from the most severe diseases and are not even aware that they are bewitched.

A concern about the ineffectiveness of Inquisitors in seeking out witches was shared by two Dominican friars in Germany, Johann Sprenger and Heinrick Kraemer, who founded a movement for the extermination of witches. They wrote a book entitled *Malleus Maleficarum,* "The Hammer of Evildoers," which became the authoritative source on the topic of witches. Written in three parts, the book first presented the argument that witches do indeed exist. Those who denied this were said to be either committing an honest error or heretics. The second part presented case histories of witches and useful methods for identifying them. The final section dealt with the legal techniques for examining a witch and passing sentence. The volume was not a legal treatise but rather an argumentative, threatening, uncompromising polemic. It argued that where doctors could find no cause for a disease and where the patient failed to respond to traditional treatment, the disease was caused by the devil. It also pointed out that "all witchcraft comes from carnal lust which is in women insatiable," and later that "three general vices appear to have special do-

minion over wicked women, namely, infidelity, ambition, and lust. Therefore, they are more than others inclined towards witchcraft who more than others are given to these vices." Many descriptions were included of incubi—male demons who seduce women—and succubi—female demons who capture males and violate them sexually and the book was replete with graphic examples of orgies supposed to have taken place between demons and their human hosts. Sprenger and Kraemer recommended that the witch be stripped, with her pubic hair shaved, before presentation to judges so that demons could not have a place to hide in the pubic area.

This work became a "huntsman's bible" directed against the heretic. With it as a guide, literally hundreds of thousands of women and children were condemned as witches and dealt with as the *Malleus* recommended—burned at the stake. Sprenger and Kraemer were authorized by a papal bull in 1484 by Pope Innocent VIII to embark on their Inquisition, and within the next few years their mission won the support both of Maximilian I, the Holy Roman Emperor, and the theological faculty of the University of Cologne. With such prestigious backing, the book's recommendations were followed with enthusiasm. The *Malleus* went through ten editions before 1669 and through another nine within the next century. In this climate all naturalistic thinking about mental aberration was swept away.

The forcefulness of the movement fostered by the *Malleus* sprang from a reaction of an anxious power structure to signs of growing restlessness. It is one example among many of the way in which authority has reacted to intellectual restlessness. Insofar as new ideas force man into hitherto unexamined realms, the threat of the new unknown is, in almost reflex fashion, coun-

The Bettmann Archive

Unable to explain certain deviant behavior, clergymen in the seventeenth century often cast the blame on demons.

tered by an extreme reassertion of orthodoxy.

The fifteenth century was marked by devaluation of the worth of individual man; the sixteenth century, however, reasserted this value. The early questioning of the established order, which had led to the retrogression represented by the witch-hunt, gained impetus in the sixteenth century. In part this was due to a rise in trading among the Mediterranean countries. In part it may have been due to the reintroduction of Hellenic learning by way of the Arabs. A humanistic movement developed that venerated the writings of the ancients. This movement exemplifies how people, long subjected to religious authority, substituted the wisdom and authority of antiquity for the dogma of the Church. The significance of this development was in part due to the fact that the ancient philosophers disagreed with one another; man was thus encouraged to weigh one against the other and, most importantly, to think, and eventually to trust to his own experience.

In the sixteenth century Machiavelli (1469–1527) described the world of political reality, Copernicus described the reality of geophysics, and Renaissance painters depicted the human body in all its concreteness. Men like Calvin, Knox, and Luther even dared to look closely at the institution of the Church, to criticize it, and to challenge its authority. Eventually, the writings of the Greek philosophers, which, for some, had supplanted that of the Church, came under fire and were rejected. Leonardo da Vinci (1452–1519) was able to assert, "Those who study old authors and not the works of nature are stepsons, not sons of Nature, who is the mother of all good authors."

The newfound reliance on direct observation had its impact on the physicians of the sixteenth century, who began to look at patients closely and to record what they saw. In the field of mental illness, case descriptions and the development of classificatory schemes began to appear. Montaigne (1533–1592) and Machiavelli were particulary important figures in this movement. Montaigne was a psychological realist concerned with character, behavior, and the richness of human feelings. Although he was not a systematic theorist, his writings attempted to understand human behavior in almost "psychodynamic" terms. Machiavelli was a practical student of interpersonal relations. His writings on how to gain and hold power derived from his intuitive grasp of human interactions. Both men concentrated on how men actually behave, without evaluating the behavior. They distinguished between behavior and morals, and in this distinction may lie their most important contribution to the growth of ideas about human behavior.

It would be misleading to suggest that these advances took place in an altogether accommodating climate. The sixteenth century also saw a rise in the popularity of astrology and the derivative belief that celestial bodies controlled events on the earth. Other magic rituals such as sand- or flour-gazing and reading tea leaves became popular. Palm-reading (which dates back to ancient China) and physiognomic study were also widely accepted at this time. Indeed, a number of these practices were used by specialists of the day in describing and foretelling personality configurations. Precursors of this position had already appeared during the thirteenth century. At that time, for example, many felt that man was particularly susceptible to emotional distress when he was alone at night; it was further noted that a prominent heavenly body, the moon, was also present then. From this association had come the term "lunatic" meaning one who is deranged by the presence of the lunar body. This is a prime example of a tendency to cling to animism at a time when a new intellectual freedom is addressing itself to some questions objectively but inevitably raising other vexing ones, discovering new unknowns. As an illustration of this contrast, one scientist responsible for developing three laws relating to planetary motion occasionally drew horoscopes. Although astrology was officially condemned by the Church, the popes were known to consult astrologers.

During the Renaissance it was also believed that "the king's touch" contained healing powers, readily extendible from kings, who were few and not often interested in the practice of medicine, to others who displayed leadership qualities. One such "divinely inspired" person was Valentine Greatrakes (1628–1666), a former soldier in Cromwell's army. He built a "practice" until eventually his patients literally numbered in the thousands. All forms of suffering humanity were housed in his barns and outhouses. This was one of the first extensions to a layman of a healing power heretofore restricted to the ruling class. Many other individuals have appeared, up to the present day, who have claimed healing powers similar to those of Greatrakes.

In addition to the Renaissance figures of the witch-hunter, Machiavelli, Montaigne, the astrologer, Leonardo da Vinci, and Greatrakes, several others warrant mention. Although the latter had less impact on their time, they represented enlightened people whose insistence on a return to reason, careful observation, and rejection of the occult eventually contributed to the advances that were to follow them. The first of these was the humanist, Juan Luis Vives (1492–1540), a social philosopher whose interests ranged from education through social welfare to mental illness. He advocated establishment of hospitals for treating the mentally ill and stressed that "the mentally sick are, first and last, men, human beings, individuals to be saved and to be treated with utmost humaneness." He proposed a psychological theory based on the principles of association through contiguity, similarity, and opposites, thus anticipating the associationist school that flowered in England a century later. He also described a process whereby events register in our minds outside of our conscious awareness, and indicated how later recall took place through a chain of associations. Such advanced thinking foreshadowed the idea of the unconscious. Similarly, he noted that one may be hurt more seriously by a psychological wound than by a physical one. In a manner reminiscent of St. Augustine, Vives also described man's drives and emotions. He recognized that emotions were often mixtures of one kind of feeling and its opposite and, in this, anticipated Freud and Bleuler's formulation of "ambivalence."

Perhaps the most eminent physician of Renaissance times was Johan Weyer (1515–1588). Weyer's professional career was enhanced by the fact that he was the private physician of William, Duke of Cleves. The duke was a chronic depressive, with many relatives who suffered from mental illness. Recognizing that their behavior resembled that of many who were being burned as witches, the duke supported Weyer's rejection of the doctrine of witchcraft and protected him against those who found his ideas heretical. Weyer conducted careful investigations of reported cases of witchcraft and offered naturalistic explanations for them. He provided excellent descriptions of mental disturbances. His primary significance in the history of abnormal psychology lies in his reestablishment and furthering of the Hippocratic tradition.

The later Renaissance era reoriented man toward reality. To be sure, superstition still prevailed, but an opposing tide began to swell during this time which eventually overcame preoccupation with the supernatural and led to the development of fruitful new ideas for understanding man's behavior.

THE SEVENTEENTH CENTURY TO THE BEGINNING OF THE MODERN ERA

This period in the history of man's ideas has been termed "The Era of Reason and Observation" by Alexander and Selesnick (1966), who see in it the establishment of the foundations of modern civilization. This was a time marked by a general, and literal, expansion of man's horizons. Great seafarers like Francis Drake and Walter Raleigh discovered new lands and, through reports of their experiences, stimulated new ideas about the social order. Man came out of the Renaissance with a new respect for the unaided power of his own mind. The Reformation had, by now, successfully challenged the Pope's authority. Man's heritage from the sixteenth century was a sense of liberation, and in this spirit he began to trust himself to observe the phenomena around him openly and to attempt to understand them on a naturalistic basis. His new faith was in an order that was basic to all natural phenomena and susceptible to discovery. Many significant ideas regarding mental functioning were developed during this period by philosophers and literary figures. Physicians of the time looked most actively into physiology in an effort to understand mental disorder.

During the seventeenth century a group of English philosophers developed associational psychology. In essence, they regarded sense perceptions as the only wellspring of psychic life; these perceptions were thought to become associated with each other because of their temporal relationship. John Locke went so far as to conceptualize the mind of man as a *tabula rasa*, a blank page, at birth. For him the building up of perception, through associations, filled the page and resulted in a unique personality. This was a mechanistic approach, inherited from the Greeks of the Cyrenaic and Stoic schools, which elevated man's senses to a state of prime importance.

Other men of the same period studied

the emotions closely and recognized the effect of emotions on the physical organs, particularly the heart. The philosopher Spinoza (1632–1677) wrote systematically on a similar topic, espousing the tenets that mind and body are inseparable and, in fact, identical, and that physical processes are experienced psychologically as emotions, thoughts, and desires. For him physiology and psychology were simply two aspects of the same thing—the living organism. Spinoza also advanced the view that psychological events had causes in the same way that physical events did. This led to rejection of the traditional idea that man possessed an absolutely free will, and in implication was the beginning of a truly psychodynamic approach.

Spinoza regarded self-preservation as the force behind all psychic processes. He believed that man retained consciously those parts of experience which enhanced the body's powers and avoided recognition of whatever decreased the body's power. In this notion he anticipated Freud's idea of repression. Spinoza developed a detailed analysis of emotions, concluding that we "love" whatever enhances our survival and "hate" whatever threatens it. He fully recognized the complex mixture of emotions that one may experience. The impact of Spinoza's work was to elevate psychological phenomena to the same status as material processes.

Two prominent seventeenth-century literary figures also contributed, albeit not systematically, to the analysis and understanding of psychological processes. These were William Shakespeare (1564–1616) and Miguel de Cervantes (1547–1616). Shakespeare produced masterful descriptions of the unconscious conflicts in man. Hamlet is now regarded as a classic literary example of the compulsive neurotic. Falstaff, in *Henry IV*, is a fine characterization

of psychopathic personality; the root of his problem—a deep resistance to growing up —is suggested in the contrasting figure of Prince Hal who had a father with whom to identify. In *King Lear*, Shakespeare recognized the deep attachments that often form between father and daughter, and in *Othello* he offered profound insight into the psychology of jealousy. Cervantes's insight is revealed in his monumental work, *Don Quixote,* in which he portrayed the desire of all men to find excitement in life and to escape from a drab reality through a return to a colorful past. His heroes, Don Quixote and Sancho Panza, personify two aspects of the same personality—wishful fantasizing and stabilizing rationality. One of the profound significances of this work lies in its recognition of a process characterizing all men, sick or well, thus suggesting that no special psychology must be invoked to understand the mentally disturbed. The latter may simply be seen as more vulnerable or less able to control processes that typify us all.

The important contributions in the eighteenth and early nineteenth centuries were in the treatment of behavioral abnormality rather than in theories of its causes. This was an era marked by proliferation of diagnostic systems—a process that appears and reappears through the course of history. This is a reflection of the fact that the form taken by behavioral disorder is a product of the social and cultural structure of the time. Unlike the plant, which remains relatively stable in its basic structure over the years, the mentally disturbed and those who observe them do not. Symptom pictures change, at least superficially, in keeping with cultural changes, and what is regarded as abnormal may also change as the values of society become modified. There is, thus, periodic need for stocktaking; the late eighteenth and early nineteenth centuries were indeed such a time.

During this period physicians were handicapped in developing classificatory schemata by their lack of prime observational data. Many prominent figures of the day, therefore, set to work observing and describing. Neurotic behavior was described as we know it today and it was emphasized that there was nothing shameful about such disorders. Neuroses were divided into hysteria, hypochondriasis, and nervous exhaustion, a condition that later became known as "neurasthenia." Other eighteenth-century physicians became important figures in the history of mental illness because of their humanitarian efforts in connection with the hospital care of the mentally ill.

THE MENTAL HOSPITAL IN EARLY TIMES

The mental hospital as an institution has, understandably, inspired considerable discussion and writing for many years. It appeared in early medieval times and became prominent in Europe by the sixteenth and seventeenth centuries. Foucault (1965) relates both the appearance of mental hospitals and the attitudes of those who placed patients in them to the "public health" measures taken to control leprosy during the Middle Ages.

Leprosy was widespread throughout Europe in the Middle Ages, and its victims were forced to leave their homes for confinement in isolated leprosaria. These leprosaria became quite numerous; indeed, during the thirteenth century it was estimated that there were some 22,000 of them in France alone, at least 43 of which were in Paris. Once confined to a leprosarium, the chances were great that a patient would never leave. Physical exclusion of the leper led, eventually, to elimination of the disease in Europe through strict control of the sources of the infection.

Foucault's convincing thesis is that, although leprosy disappeared and the leper vanished, the idea of segregating those who were ill or undesirable by simply excluding them from organized society was transferred to the mentally disturbed. Zilboorg and Henry (1941) report that during the period of the Inquisition, people simply turned out family members with symptoms of mental disorder. Many, unable to care for themselves, wandered through fields like animals and, eventually, lost all vestiges of human appearance. Another practice cited by Foucault was handing over the insane to seamen who transported them to remote places exactly as one might do with an unwanted animal. In the nineteenth century, places of confinement (the precursors of what we call hospitals) appeared in Europe. Such institutions were sometimes very large—for example, one out of every hundred Parisians was confined to the Hôpital Général in 1656, shortly after its founding. This institution was not set up primarily to treat illness but was rather a place to which a judge could remand anyone who was troublesome to the community.

A network of hospitals like the Hôpital Général developed in Europe in the seventeenth century. In these places, all manner of undesirables were confined: the criminal, the family "black sheep," the idler, the insane. Confinement was also widely used when economic recessions threw people out of work and increased mendicancy. Later the confined were required to work, thus contributing, while institutionalized, to the general prosperity of the community.

The mentally disturbed, comprising about ten percent of those confined to the Hôpital Général in Paris, served a special function. Undoubtedly less useful than the criminal or vagabond as workers, the insane were commonly displayed to the public who paid a nominal fee to see them. This form of "entertainment" assumed an institutional character in Paris and London. As late as 1815 it was reported to the English House of Commons that the Bethlehem hospital made £400 in the preceding year by exhibiting the mentally ill. At the standard fee of one penny per visit, this represents 96,000 visits, a staggering total for the time. Apparently, visits to the mental hospital were made in the same spirit as going to see the animals in the zoo. The insane were looked upon as men apart. They were seen not as unfortunate examples of conditions to which all men were susceptible but as animals, and they were treated as such.

The conditions at La Bicêtre, a hospital in Paris, were described at the end of the eighteenth century (Foucault, 1965, pp. 70–71): "The unfortunate whose entire furniture consisted of this straw pallet, lying with head, feet, and body pressed against the wall, could not enjoy sleep without being soaked by the water that trickled from that mass of stone." Another mental hospital in Paris, La Salpêtrière, had its cells at the level of the sewers that flooded in winter when the Seine rose. At such times "those cells . . . became not only more unhealthy but, worse still, a refuge for a swarm of huge rats which, during the night, attacked the unfortunates confined there and bit them wherever they could reach them; madwomen have been found with feet, hands, and faces torn by bites which are often dangerous and from which several have died" (Foucault, 1965, p. 71). The more dangerous the patient, the more restrictively he was confined, usually by chains to a wall or bed.

Such examples of the way the mentally disturbed were treated reinforce the interpretation that they were regarded not as sick people, but as animals. As animals, they were thought to be insensitive to pain or temperature, to possess the special protection that animals have against the elements, and to be less vulnerable to disease than others. Even the physician and great humanitarian, Pinel, admired "the constancy and the ease with which certain of the insane of both sexes bear the most rigorous and prolonged cold." Mental aberration was not in this epoch firmly tied to medicine nor even to the corrective measures applied to criminals.

It was to such settings that Phillipe Pinel in France, Chiarugi and Pisani in Italy, and Tuke in England brought reforms. The intellectual climate of their time was characterized by stirrings of criticism of the inhumane conditions of mental hospitals. Pinel and Chiarugi were physicians and, as administrators of mental hospitals, opposed unreasonable restraint of patients. Pinel's work is probably the best known because many later and well-known figures followed his practices. The greater freedom introduced in mental hospitals was opposed, in this period, by a fearful public which was then (and remains) uneasy about mental disorder. Many questioned whether the abnormal could or should be trusted with much freedom. However, not all did so, and William Tuke, a Quaker layman, established the York Retreat in 1792, based on the humanitarian thinking of Pinel. He provided a kindly atmosphere for his patients and was able to demonstrate that such a humanitarian approach was efficacious. His son and grandson continued his work at York in the nineteenth century.

The final chapter on mental hospitals as treatment centers has not been written: we will discuss this further when modern-day treatment of severe mental disorders is described. Suffice it to say that there was a strong tendency in earlier periods for the mental hospital, even after reforms had been instituted, to slip back into becoming less a treatment center and more a custodial institution where social misfits were dealt with as animals rather than as sick people. Perhaps conditions never regressed to what they were in the time before Pinel and other contemporary reformers, but they were to arouse the zeal of the reformer again and again.

The work of Dorothea Lynde Dix (1802–1887) in the United States, Canada, and Scotland stimulated the building or remodeling of 32 mental hospitals throughout the world. As a result of her pioneering efforts, conditions were improved in many mental hospitals. For example, St. Elizabeth's Hospital was built in Washington, D.C., by the United States government, as a model to be followed by the states. Around the turn of the twentieth century, Clifford Beers, an ex-mental patient, wrote a book based on his own experiences as an inmate of a state hospital, critical of conditions in mental hospitals in his day. He stimulated hospital reforms and the establishment of the Mental Hygiene movement, which was backed by such eminent figures as Adolph Meyer and William James. In 1955 the Joint Commission on Mental Illness and Health (described in Chapter 1) observed that attitudes of rejection of the mentally ill, resulting in inhumane treatment or substandard living conditions, remain with us today. Indeed, the Commission has identified the problem of coping with major mental illness as the prime problem of the mental health professions today.

The hospital reformers of the late eighteenth and early nineteenth century were not men of genius but rather were dedicated and courageous humanitarians. They provided few new ideas to enrich our understanding of mental illness. Others of their time did develop such ideas, some of which were throwbacks to promising, but dormant, notions from bygone eras.

EIGHTEENTH-CENTURY MOVEMENTS

Most significant in the history of thought about mental illness was the work of Franz Joseph Gall (1758–1828) and Anton Mesmer (1734–1815). Gall, a scholar who made many contributions to medical thought, was greatly influenced in his thinking about brain function by the belief that specific brain areas controlled specific body functions. He went beyond physical functions, however, and reasoned that "character" traits were relatable to the structure of certain localized areas within the brain. He drew up a list of 37 character traits (for example, aggressiveness, cautiousness, benevolence, firmness) which he regarded as localized within 37 different structures in the brain. Gall's further, highly controversial, assumption was that skull shape and, particularly, protuberances accurately reflected brain shape and, with it, over- or underdevelopment of particular character traits. Thus, a direct method for reading character–"phrenology"–was conceived. Gall's lectures on this topic attracted a disciple, Johann Casper Spurzheim (1776–1832), who added the notion that proper moral influence could change the mental characteristics uncovered through phrenology. Spurzheim's thinking attracted the attention and interest of many prominent people of the time, including the forerunners of modern-day psychiatrists.

Mesmer's work, no better founded theoretically than Gall's, attracted considerable attention and stimulated work on the phenomenon of hypnosis. For some time before Mesmer, man had been fascinated by magnets and the forces of attraction and repulsion between them. Such phenomena were vivid examples of unseen forces operating between objects. Respected scientists of the sixteenth and seventeenth centuries had expressed the belief that magnetic powers resided in man as well as in natural objects; they postulated the existence of a "universal fluid" responsible for the influence of man over matter and of man over man. Mesmer expanded these views and formalized them in several propositions. At the core of these propositions was the view that man had a potential ability to influence other men, by powers akin to the magnetic. He called this power "animal magnetism," and saw it as a property that could be intensified by mirrors, and stored, concentrated, and transported. He further believed that animal magnetism could be used to cure mental disorders as well as other disorders, and could even be applied to prevent mental aberration.

At first, Mesmer used magnets in working with patients, but he later discarded them and relied on a "personal" magnetic force presumably transmitted through his hands. The conservative physicians of Vienna, the city where Mesmer lived, forced him to take his practice elsewhere, so he moved to Paris, at the invitation of Louis XVI, and became enormously popular during his five years of practice there. He attracted a great many female patients suffering from hysteria, and treated them with great showmanship. Alexander and Selesnick (1966, p. 128) described one of Mesmer's treatment sessions as follows: "The patients entered a thickly carpeted, dimly lit room that was mirrored so as to reflect every shadow; soft melodies were heard, and there was a fragrance of orange blossoms. The patients held hands in a circle around the baquet, a tub filled with 'magnetized' water. Into this prepared scene would step the healer, clothed in a lilac cloak and waving a yellow wand." In these sessions, tensions rose and Mesmer sought to produce a "crisis"—a dramatic moment when one patient suddenly screamed, broke into a cold sweat, or convulsed. The mass suggestive effects of this supposedly led to similar reactions from others who purportedly responded favorably to the sudden release of tension.

Few contemporary professionals reacted favorably to Mesmer's approach, and, eventually, a distinguished commission was appointed by Louis XVI to study animal magnetism. Part of its conclusion read as follows:

> having finally demonstrated by decisive experience that imagination without magnetism produces convulsions and that magnetism without imagination produces nothing, [the members of the committees] have unanimously concluded in regard to the question of the existence and usefulness of animal magnetic fluid that such fluid does not exist and therefore cannot be useful, that the violent effects seen in public treatments result from the touching [of the patients], from the imagination which is set into action, and from the machine of excitement, which we must admit against our own desire is the only thing which impressed us. [Zilboorg & Henry, 1941, p. 345]

Mesmer sank into oblivion following this setback. Certain aspects of his work, however, attracted the attention of medical workers. Ultimately, mesmerism, as the process came to be known, was used as a form of surgical anesthesia. In the mid-nineteenth century Esdaile used mesmerism, anesthetically, in performing more than 250 operations. In 1843 James Baird, a Manchester surgeon proposed that the trance states experienced in mesmerism were not magical but resulted from physical exhaustion following periods of intense concentration in which muscles became fatigued. He renamed the phenomenon *hypnosis*, from the Greek word meaning sleep. A new air of respectability was thus attached to the phenomenon, and hypnotic techniques soon became a part of medical practice, where they were used by serious scientists to treat hysteria.

EARLY NINETEENTH-CENTURY THOUGHT

The late eighteenth and early nineteenth centuries in Europe saw much political conflict. There were wars, revolutions, and continuous turmoil generated by such social upheavals. After Napoleon's fall, steps were taken by European powers to restore order. The ruling classes, shaken by the threats demonstrated by their own unsettled people, became more interested in reestablishing control over the masses than in international adventure. Suppression was the rule of the day; informers and secret agents were ubiquitous. In such a sociopolitical climate man turned inward, and membership in broad social movements was replaced by a concern about personal destiny. Interpersonal relationships took on exaggerated importance, and the thinking of the day, spearheaded by some physicians and literary figures, turned toward man's inner life.

Among those who were involved in treatment of the mentally ill, the contributions of Reil, Esquirol, Moreau, and Heinroth were especially notable. Reil was a humanitarian dedicated to hospital reform. More importantly, however, he was convinced that mental disorder derived from psycho-logical factors and that it should be treated by psychological methods. In 1803, he published what was probably the first discourse devoted entirely to psychological therapy. His notions were not related to a systematic personality theory and his techniques were naive. For example, he recommended placing the excited patient in a dark, noiseless room or shocking the silent patient with loud noises. He also spoke of the potential efficacy of psychological approaches in ameliorating even physical diseases. This reflected an awareness of the interaction between psychological and physiological phenomena. Reil pioneered in therapeutic methods that are now known as occupational therapy, music therapy, and drama therapy.

Esquirol was a student of Pinel and, like his teacher, published clinical descriptions of syndromes. Esquirol, however, went one step further by looking into the events precipitating the emotional disorder of hundreds of his patients at La Bicêtre and by using statistics to summarize his findings. He described idiocy precisely and warned that this condition should not be assumed automatically in all cases of intellectual defect, since excessive preoccupation with one's own thought and feelings could produce a similar clinical picture. He distinguished between hallucinations (false sensory impressions) and illusions (misinterpretations of accurate sensory impressions) for the first time. Esquirol recognized the force of emotional factors in an individual's life. He pointed out that extreme behavior like that of the criminal could result from emotional factors, in which case treatment, not punishment, was called for.

J. Moreau de Tours, a disciple of Esquirol, was a man of great originality. He and his followers were not content, as Pinel and Esquirol had been, to stop with mere classification of mental disorder. Rather, they wished to understand the individual as a functioning totality. For Moreau, psychological understanding could come only through introspection. To know an emotion, one must feel it himself. Dreams were conceptualized as similar to hallucinations and were, therefore, seen as the connecting link between the healthy person and the insane. Thus, for Moreau, dreaming was a transient form of psychopathology. Moreau further postulated that man existed in two realms, one resulting from his communion with the world outside of him and the other from contact with his own internal sources. The dream represented a bridge between these two realms. The insane, therefore, dreamed while awake, as if the internal world had impinged on the outer. Dreams normally occurred when external stimuli were shut off and inner stirrings had an opportunity to well up into awareness; in the insane person, however, there was an excessive preoccupation with the inner world and an alienation from external affairs. This summary of Moreau's views sounds surprisingly similar to those later formulated by Freud.

Moreau's dynamic emphasis on psychosis as a manifestation of the total personality was reflected in the ideas of Johann Christian Heinroth. Heinroth, however, believed that sin was the causal factor in mental illness. In speaking of sin, he was not referring to sinful acts in the social sense but rather to the fact that an individual's thoughts could offend his moral sense. He was thus referring to internal conflict between unacceptable impulses and conscience. Heinroth developed a theory of psychological processes stressing three levels of functioning. The lowest of these were the instinctual forces that seek pleasure. The second was called *ich* (ego) whose aims were to facilitate security in the external world and to enhance the enjoyment of life. The third level Heinroth called *gewissen*, the conscience. The *ich* developed from the lowest level of psychological organization through recognition of differences between the self and the world around it. The conscience, seen to evolve from the ego, is experienced first as an alien force opposing self-centered ego strivings.

A more highly articulated form of the *gewissen*, which Heinroth came to call the *super-uns*, produced conflict within the ego. The development of the *super-uns* was restricted, in Heinroth's thinking, to relatively few, advanced humans; most people were thought to have little in the way of a conscience. When the development of the conscience took place in a man or woman, he or she became an altruist who lived to serve others. Mental health inhered in a full assimilation of conscience within the ego, and illness resulted from conflict with one's conscience. Heinroth's views about personality, formulated early in the nineteenth century, herald the first truly comprehensive theory of personality and psychotherapy—that of Freud.

In the mid-nineteenth century, the theoreticians of mental disturbance turned toward attempts to understand mental illness largely on an organic basis, and the pioneering ideas described above were eclipsed. When, at the end of the century, Freud's theories burst upon the scene, they were regarded as quite novel. It is unclear just how much direct or indirect contact Freud had with the writings of Moreau and Heinroth. It is certain, however, that he was exposed to the thinking of the literary geniuses of the nineteenth century including Stendahl, Flaubert, Ibsen, Dostoievsky, and de Maupassant, each of whom plumbed the depth of man's psychological functioning in their writings, as Shakespeare and Cervantes had done before them. They wrote of everyday people whose impulses and motivations they carefully dissected. Collectively, their work suggested that behavior was understandable on the basis of psychological processes; furthermore, it elucidated some of these processes, albeit in an unsystematic way.

LATE NINETEENTH-CENTURY PSYCHIATRY: DEMENTIA PRAECOX AND MANIC-DEPRESSIVE PSYCHOSIS

It has already been seen that geographical shifts in the center of productive thought about behavioral disorder have characterized different time periods. For much of the nineteenth century, the most advanced thinking about mental disorder took place in Germany—witness the work of Heinroth, whose earlier theorizing directly anticipated Freud. However, during the latter half of the nineteenth century, psychiatry took on a different emphasis that obscured Heinroth and his contemporaries, who were rejected as romanticists and philosophers.

This was an age when considerable progress was being made in the understanding of medical diseases. The atmosphere was a "hard nosed" scientific one, fostered by the successes of Darwin, Wundt, Helmholtz, and Fechner. Chemistry and physics were being incorporated into medical research; Pasteur established a germ theory of disease. Advances were taking place in embryology, in the understanding of infectious diseases and of diseases of specific organs such as Bright's disease, Addison's disease, and Hodgkin's disease. Closer to psychiatry, brain function was becoming better understood, and efforts were underway to understand general paresis on an organic basis. For those interested in behavior disorder, the climate was ripe to establish psychiatry, the principle mental health profession of the day, as a scientifically respectable medical specialty. The behavior disorders were to be freed of the tampering of philosophers and theologians once and for all. The prime task facing those interested in behavior disorders was to solve the age-old riddle of psychosis on the basis of the scientific advances of the era. Heinroth, with his intuitive-clinical notions formulated in rather vague and unscientific terminology, was discarded, and with him the emphasis on the human factors in psychic disorder disappeared. The psychiatry of this era was to do without psychology entirely. All interest centered in attempts to understand brain processes. This was the era of the pure somatist.

The man who exemplified the spirit of this era was the German psychiatrist William Griesinger (1817–1868). His textbook, published when he was only 25, proclaimed that mental diseases were somatic diseases, diagnoses were adequate only when they specified physiological causes, and so-called psychological reactions were no more than reflex actions of the brain—thus anticipating Pavlov. Griesinger made no distinction between psychiatry and neurology.

Griesinger also reacted to the proliferation of nomenclature that characterized the psychiatry of his time. He argued that because mental disorders took on many nuances, the tender-minded theorist simply invented new names for each, resulting in huge and unnecessarily complex diagnostic schemes. Classification, argued Griesinger, had become all-important primarily because there was little else to lead to a better understanding of the phenomenon.

It was as if the professional of the time felt better for having at least named a phenomenon that he was unable to explain or understand. For Griesinger, there was no need for classifications. He believed that there was only one behavioral disease—insanity—and that its cause was to be found in the brain. His position was an appealing one for his contemporaries in psychiatry. Psychologically oriented theorists had not developed insights or hypotheses that had helped in a practical way and had only muddied already murky waters by offering a succession of short-lived classificatory schemes. The natural sciences seemed to be showing the way to a more fundamental understanding of behavioral processes. They had proved themselves in general medicine and, hopefully, could do so also in psychiatry.

And indeed, the somatic approach led to real progress in certain areas, as, for example, the development of knowledge —to be discussed in the next chapter— about organic brain disorders. General paresis (a progressive disease leading to complete paralysis and eventually to death) was studied energetically; the effects of alcohol on brain function became better understood; the relationship of senile psychoses to vascular (blood-vessel) changes in the brain was established; and extensive studies of the febrile exhaustive states were made. Unfortunately, however, the emphasis on disease processes, the brain, and the spinal cord, so basic to the somatogenic approach, had the effect of relegating to obscurity most of the disturbed individuals who had prompted this activity in the first place. Because the psychiatrist of the day concentrated on the patient's nervous system and its vicissitudes, he failed to see him as a person. This was an approach originating from and best suited to the temperament and

functions of those who were researchers primarily.

Many clinically oriented psychiatrists soon came to recognize a pressing need to develop approaches better suited to their emphases and predilections. There thus ensued a growth of interest in the course of mental disorders. In a sense, the laboratory-oriented worker emphasized one aspect of the Hippocratic tradition, the establishment of the organic basis of mental disease, while the clinician, with his interest in the course and outcome of disease, stressed a different aspect. For the clinician there was no productive alternative, despite the fact that this approach made his position similar to that of his psychologically minded predecessors in the earlier part of the century who simply made observations and multiplied classifications.

Two of the clinicians of this era, Karl Ludwig Kahlbaum (1828–1899) and Ewald Hecker (1843–1909), made contributions that had lasting effects. Kahlbaum set out to observe the forms taken by abnormal *behaviors* (he avoided calling them diseases). He noted, in common with several others, many instances of disorder in which a gradual process of deterioration culminated in general dementia. Some cases followed such a course, manifested by additional "peculiar" symptoms such as muscular spasms, strange postures, and, at times, stuporous states. These are described in some detail and named "catatonia." Hecker, his student, described another patient group that declined rapidly after being stricken with psychosis during puberty. This disorder was called "hebephrenia." Kahlbaum also wrote about a "cyclic insanity," characterized by alternation of mood from mild depression to mild euphoria, and termed it "cyclothymia." These syndromes, together with paranoia—a disorder involving systematized persecutory ideas without mental deterioration—came to be recognized as standard symptom complexes." These descriptive contributions were followed by a period of relative quiescence in German psychiatry until the appearance of Emil Kraepelin (1855–1926), a key figure in the psychiatry of his day.

Kraepelin's work began in the last twenty years of the nineteenth century. He was a faithful follower of the tradition fostered by Griesinger and was devoted to the establishment of relationships between physical causes and mental disturbance. Accordingly, his early attention was directed to the effects of fevers, toxic drugs, injuries, and so forth on mental functioning. At the same time he was interested in a variety of mental disorders, not yet well understood by the somatists. There were, at the time, many classification schemes for mental disorders, and Kraepelin set himself the task of studying clinical phenomena and arriving at significant generalizations about what he saw, in the service of better classification.

Zilboorg and Henry (1941) point out that, as was typical of the psychiatry of the time, Kraepelin lost sight of the individual. He was far less interested in the unique problems of an individual than in what that person had in common with other mentally disturbed people. Detailed case studies were collected, including extensive current as well as historical information about the patient, and these were studied intensively. Comparing masses of data on numerous patients, Kraepelin's search was for commonalities and generalizations, and he did not pay particular attention to peculiarities of individual cases. Perhaps this emphasis was made more acceptable by the fact that Kraepelin lived at a time and in a place when such an approach was commonplace. German technology was advancing rapidly, and its prevailing spirit of nationalized unity considered the individual important only in terms of what he contributed to the overall welfare of the state. People were "statistical elements" in an all-important totality. The work of those concerned with mental disorders reflected this view.

Kraepelin was convinced that the causes of mental disorder were to be understood on purely organic grounds. At first, he leaned strongly toward regarding hereditary factors as the causative factors in mental disorder; later he shifted to a belief in the importance of metabolic processes and factors. However, regardless of the organic determinants of disorder. Kraepelin held to his primary concern in sorting out from the welter of behavioral phenomena manifested by the mentally ill a series of discrete mental disorders.

Kraepelin's long efforts at compiling, organizing, studying, and comparing data on literally thousands of mentally disturbed people led to a relatively simple pair of observations that were the basis for his classifications: (1) some people become psychotic (severely disorganized behaviorally) but recover; and (2) others become psychotic and deteriorate until they reach a demented state and never recover. Prognosis, then, was the principle around which to organize classification. He saw the curable disorder as caused by external conditions while the incurable one was due to internal, constitutional conditions. Actually, to speak of curable and incurable in Kraepelin's system is inaccurate: his attitude of fatalistic predetermination was that some people got better and some just got worse.

Kraepelin's textbook underwent several revisions to accommodate the development of his theories. His system was most fully expressed in the fifth and sixth editions, appearing in 1896 and 1899. In these, he postulated two major groups of mental disorders—*manic-depressive psychosis* and *dementia praecox*. The former was the disorder first recognized in Hippocrates' time and later investigated and described by Roman physicians. It ran a cyclic course of intermittent attacks of elation or depression, with normal intervals intervening. Prognosis for recovery from the individual attack was good and there was no mental deterioration. The term "dementia praecox" (*démence précoce*) was taken from Morel, who used it in 1860 to designate a process of deterioration that set in early in the patient's life, usually around the time of puberty, and progressed to dementia. For Kraepelin, this term captured the essence of the incurable patients he had studied. He eventually included under this rubric the catatonic type described by Kahlbaum, the hebephrenic type of Hecker, and the paranoid type, which had formerly been called *paranoia hallucinatoris* and had been considered a separate disease. These three forms of dementia praecox (later called schizophrenia) are, even today, considered the classic forms of the disorder, along with the simple type that Kraepelin added later.

Many objections were raised to Kraepelin's system, particularly with respect to dementia praecox. As Jung pointed out in 1905, the condition does not always become manifest early in life nor do all cases progress to dementia. A certain percentage of cases, indistinguishable from others at diagnosis, recover without undergoing deterioration. These objections led to a reformulation by Kraepelin which conceded that dementia was not inevitable. Similar objections later led Eugen Bleuler to reconsider the disorder entirely, and even to rename it.

Kraepelin's conception of manic-depressive psychosis was also questioned. Some pointed out that mood swings were also seen in paranoia and catatonia. Kraepelin had also designated the melancholias occurring during menopause and climacteric as separate diseases (involutional melancholia), and some of his colleagues felt these syndromes should have been included with manic-depressive psychosis. Despite these criticisms, Kraepelin's views exerted enormous influence on those interested in severe mental disorders. Indeed, many of his

Melancholia (From *A Psychiatrist's Anthology*, by Louis J. Karnosh, published in 1942 by the Occupational Therapy Press, Cleveland City Hospital. Reprinted with permission of the author.)

classifications are an integral part of present-day psychiatric nomenclature.

Kraepelin's work in the psychoses formed a bridge between a chaotic era when there was no universally accepted way of grouping psychopathological phenomena, and an era which settled upon a way (for better or ill) of codifying these phenomena. Once agreement was reached on how the behavioral pie was to be sliced (following the contributions of Bleuler), research efforts became better focused.

Weaknesses of Kraepelin's work inevitably limited its overall usefulness. We have already pointed to his failure to be concerned with the individual. While Kraepelin had much to say about symptom-commonalities, he had considerably less understanding of the psychology of a given person than did sensitive literary figures of his time, including Ibsen and Dostoievsky. Secondly, his emphasis on prognostic distinctions had the effect of consigning the patient with dementia praecox to a hopeless future and of suggesting that the prime task for professionals was to improve hospital conditions so that patients might experience minimal discomfort. Finally, Kraepelin's approach further encouraged man's long-range inclination to set the mentally disturbed apart from the normal person. One was either sick or he was not; he had an intact constitution or a defective one. As suggested earlier, such views may have been comforting for the masses but they have inevitably made the lot of the mentally disturbed a difficult one and have failed to lead to any positive steps toward solution of the problems of mental disorder. Kraepelin's theory of a somatic basis for mental disorder was not strengthened by his work. Eventually, that theory found a better focus in schizophrenia and, when that topic is discussed, the efforts of present-day somatists will be reconsidered.

CONCLUSION

For virtually the entire period covered by this summary of man's concern with behavior disorder, only extreme, dramatic deviancies were regarded as manifestations of mental illness. Occasional observers described as problems behavior that fell short of what would currently be regarded as psychotic, but these less dramatic behavior disorders were not widely recognized as mental health problems until the twentieth century. Despite the fact that few changes took place in the conception of the nature of mental disorder, a variety of notions were advanced to explain the development of mental illnesses, and an equal variety of treatment approaches were advocated.

Earliest man's belief in the significance of spiritual forces as the cause of mental disorder made the priest the logical person to treat such illness. The Hellenic and Roman eras saw a shift toward a belief in natural, organic causes of mental illness. This resulted in the development of a profession, separate from the clergy, that was devoted to healing. The physician of that day, in keeping with current theories of causation, concentrated on physical therapies—administration of drugs, application of potions, hydrotherapy, and so forth.

The Middle Ages saw a reversion to the primitive belief in spirits or demons. Healing powers were, once again, vested in the Church. Until the rise of concern with witchcraft, most treatment consisted of exorcism or efforts to make the body an uncomfortable habitat for the devil. When demonology became orthodox, the witch, frequently someone who was mentally ill, was executed by burning. All pretense of treatment was abandoned and concern for the protection of those not yet victimized by the devil was paramount.

The Renaissance initiated a return to rationality and a scientific outlook on mental disorder which progressed through the seventeenth, eighteenth, and nineteenth centuries. Once again there was a return to natural causes as an explanation of mental disorder. The medical profession gained prestige and as its members learned more about the functions of the brain and the body as a whole, this knowledge was applied to understanding mental illness. Treatment approaches became once more largely physical and, in addition, hospitals for the mentally disturbed were established. The character of these institutions was such that they appeared to serve the nonhospitalized "normals" better than their patients and in this sense they had something in common with the practice of burning witches and isolating lepers.

Throughout this survey we have cited occasional discussions of the significance of emotional and experiential factors in the development of deviant behavior. These instances represent the insights of percep- tive writers, such as Shakespeare or Cervantes; the penetrating introspection of a St. Augustine; the sensitive concern of a humanitarian such as Vives; or the "romantic" notions of a physician such as Heinroth. Emotional causes of mental disorder were not to be taken seriously by the mental health profession until the modern era.

It is hoped that, in addition to a multitude of facts, the reader will gather from this chapter some feeling of what man has learned in his concerns about abnormal behavior and his efforts to look inside himself. His struggle has clearly been with his own irrational nature, with the framework and limitations imposed on him by his cultural setting, and with his ignorance. These handicaps are more readily recognized and dispassionately evaluated when viewed from a distance and with the perspective offered by an historical overview. To benefit from the experience of others, however, one must be prepared to apply lessons of the past to current situations.

SUMMARY

1. The ancients regarded mental illness as involving largely instances of extreme, dramatic behavior disorder. Occasionally subtle disorders were recognized but relatively little interest was shown in them.
2. Early man attributed the cause of emotional and behavioral disorder to spiritual forces. The first recorded change in this view occurred in classical Greece when a scientific, rational view was introduced. Hippocrates, the father of modern medicine, advanced the idea that natural causes were at work in illnesses of all types. Greek thought influenced Roman physicians and philosophers and many theories were advanced to explain behavior disorders on a rational basis.
3. The Middle Ages saw a reversion to spiritualistic explanations. Religious figures became healers and medical advance was halted.
4. The Renaissance saw an increasing reliance on rationality. The threat this posed to the established church, however, led to a preoccupation with devil possession and witchcraft. Many with mental disorders suf-

fered and died at the hands of religious zealots dedicated to eradicating the devil's influence.

5. The seventeenth century, the beginning of the modern era, saw the development of many ideas about the workings of mental processes. It also marked the rise in prominence of the mental hospital which started as a wastebasket for all of society's undesirables. Over the years successive waves of reform altered living conditions in mental hospitals and turned them into more therapeutic institutions, although society seems never to have given up the concept that the seriously mentally disturbed should be isolated.

6. The eighteenth century gave rise to the work of men like Gall and Mesmer who, while not making solid scientific contributions, were to influence the work of many later scientists.

7. In the early ninteenth century many theories about man's psychology were advanced only to be eclipsed by the successes of the physiologists of that era. The growing understanding of brain physiology encouraged the most influential nineteenth-century psychiatrists to seek purely physiological explanations of behavior disorder. The classification scheme of Kraepelin was developed in the service of this mission.

CHAPTER 3

The Medical Model

A seven-year-old boy with a school phobia; a thirty-four-year-old delusional paranoid schizophrenic; a twenty-eight-year-old acutely depressed mother of two children—these are some of the concrete, urgent situations that the mental health professional must deal with.

The professional's intervention in such cases has been guided by a conceptual model that has long shaped practice in dealing with disordered behavior. The model was not deliberately planned. No one person or group of people suddenly developed "an approach" for viewing and dealing with behavior problems! Rather, at different times, different people who had to engage behavior disorders adapted approaches then in use for dealing with other, seemingly similar problems. Medicine, with already developed rationales and service delivery models for physical problems, offered one handy set of guides for approaching emotional disturbance.

CONCEPTUALIZATION: ITS NATURE AND PLACE

Why a conceptual model in the first place? Simply put, a conceptual model in abnormal psychology offers an orienting guide to how man's emotional problems come about and how best to cope with them. It helps those in positions of social responsibility to select the most useful interventions or programs from many potential activities. It thus helps to shape professional functions. But a conceptual model also has restrictions. Resource or technique gaps limit it as does the fact that any model is hypothetical. As experience accumulates, conceptual frameworks must be changed, especially when their theorizing is not supported by empirical findings from programs they generate.

Acute physical or psychological problems call for immediate solutions by the social agents who must deal with them. This has always been so for abnormal psychology and is still true for today's mental health professional! Current practice and long-term health planning have always been shaped more by immediate needs than by orderly conceptualization. The mental health professional must typically *do* something! If it works, he may reason backwards in trying to clarify its conceptual underpinnings. Thus, there are two types of mental health conceptualization: implicit and systematic. Good social planning demands systematic conceptualization to orient the field broadly. In that way, as new problems and situations are identified, directions for logical, concrete solutions are available. But the practicing mental health professional rarely operates at the level of systematic conceptualization. He deals with the right-now distresses of patients who come to him in clinics and hospitals—agencies that have fixed structures and ways of proceeding. These ways, too, betray implicit conceptualizations about what causes behavior disorders and how to deal with them.

When mental health professionals move into action, their interventon options are limited by their background and knowledge, their effectiveness and comfort with various methods, and the circumstances of the case. Whatever their ideas for dealing with a problem, these options are limited by the urgency of the patient's problems and the circumstances of the encounter. If the latter are less than ideal, no matter how capable the professional, the situation limits what he can do.

Professionals typically ignore the fact that if they don't conceptualize explicitly, then they conceptualize by default. The jobs professionals undertake, how they use their time, and their specific clinical roles reflect either an active seeking or a passive acceptance of a ready-made conceptualization. Even the "snake pit" stereotype of the mental hospital reflects its own implicit conceptualization of disorder—that is, when individuals behave in extreme, bizarre ways

Paranoia (From *A Psychiatrist's Anthology*, by Louis J. Karnosh, published in 1942 by the Occupational Therapy Press, Cleveland City Hospital. Reprinted with permission of the author.)

and are grossly removed from reality there is little hope for them. All that remains is for them to be shunted off to an isolated, custodial institution to vegetate. From this perspective, seriously disturbed persons are seen more as animals than as humans; their physical and psychological states are not matters of serious concern for those who take care of them. Their "keepers" help them to survive physically but that is about all! And doing even that little may be motivated only to our need to avoid feeling "uncivilized" or "barbaric." The point to be underscored is that *some* conceptual stance is reflected in everything the mental health professional does. Decisions to function one way exclude possibilities for doing other things. These choices (not necessarily consciously made) inevitably reflect the professional's concepts of what mental disorder is all about and how best to cope with it.

Implicit conceptualization has two major dangers. The first, already suggested, is that it is narrow. Professionals evaluate what they are doing on the basis of the apparent effectiveness of their actions, ignoring the broader question of whether continuing to do the same will help to solve pressing social problems. For example, if much of our mental health effort consists of doing "the wrong things," so what if they are done well —even with positive effects? The skilled, finely trained analyst, who devotes his entire professional career to the long-term, intensive treatment of 200 highly educated, prosperous patients may successfully "cure" 125 or 150 of them. But his very career choice profoundly restricts the *social* impact of his professional activity! With severe mental health professional manpower shortages, now and in the predictable future, how does such a career choice help the many with emotional problems who cannot find anyone to work with them?

A second danger of implicit conceptual-ization is that it imposes a passive stance on the mental health professions. By failing to establish broad concepts of disordered behavior and its treatment, the mental health professionals, in effect, accept the implicit assumptions of existing approaches. They go about their work from the standpoint of: "that's how the world is" or "that's the ways things must be done," and do their best within that framework. Innovation consists of occasional minor variations on existing themes which, themselves, are far from the best. For example, the hidden assumption that emotional disorders must be treated by mental health professionals (psychiatrists, psychologists, or social workers) has been both influential and restrictive. This assumption has directed attention to refining technology for identifying and coping with disorder. What if it turns out that by the time we identify "abnormal" behaviors, it is too late to treat them effectively? If that is what is happening, mental health workers need to reallocate effort to identifying the social conditions that promote disorder. That would permit intervention to start before disturbances became severe and could possibly prevent many problems that are so difficult to deal with later.

Preventive concepts, focusing on how disorder arises in the first place, direct interest to the structure and effects of such social institutions as: the home, community, and schools. We have much to learn about such institutions from sociologists, urban planners, economists, educators, and political scientists. But the way mental health professionals have generally defined psychological problems has limited use of the knowledge of other social scientists. Thus, we may have doomed ourselves to a long-range pursuit of approaches which, though sometimes effective, and even dramatic, ultimately lead down blind alleys.

Later chapters will clarify many of the

questions that have arisen in recent years about the mental health's failure to deal effectively with pressing problems. Many such concerns come about because abnormal psychology is indeed expanding its scope. This process confronts us with many more issues that we failed to identify before or defined as not belonging to the field. This is why it is important to consider mental health's past basic conceptualizations. Similarly, the social fact that so many mental health problems are unsolved demands a basic re-examination of assumptions and operations.

When this is done, one can, in oversimplified terms, identify two alternative conceptual models: a medical and a preventive model. While it would be handy if these were mutually exclusive, pure forms, that alas just is not the case. Also it would be wrong to assume that the use of the term medical means that the approach is used only by psychiatrists or other medically trained people who work with emotional disturbance. Rather, the term describes a set of assumptions and practices that resemble the typical practice of somatic medicine. Both medical and nonmedical mental health specialists use these approaches in mental health. This chapter deals only with the medical model, because the chapters which follow describe conditions and treatment approaches that rest on the model's assumptions.

THE MEDICAL MODEL

Although the term medical model is widely used (Albee, 1967; Bloom, 1965; Cowen, 1967; Sarason & Ganzer, 1968; Turner & Cumming, 1967), different authors use it in different ways. To evaluate the model properly its many aspects must be clarified.

Perhaps the most central feature of the medical model in mental health, is the assumption that emotional disorders can be viewed structurally just as physical illness. This is not valid! The typical physical illness is brief. It involves temporary disruption of a heretofore well-functioning organism by some noxious agent. The doctor's job is to understand the cause of the dysfunction and to find a remedy that restores normal functioning. Mental health people differ in how literally they accept this view. The most literal, narrowest application of the model assumes that psychological disorders result from specific *diseases* involving biological, chemical, or physiological irritants. This form of the medical model is called the disease or illness model. People who subscribe to it emphasize treatments designed to overcome the physical elements presumed to cause disorders. Historically, this approach has been widely used. Indeed, as the previous chapter suggested, it was a dominant approach for long periods of recorded history.

But we need not literally assume illness or disease to stay within the bounds of the medical model. School phobias, temper tantrums, schizophrenia, character disorders, and many somatic complaints can be seen to result from entirely nonphysical "causes" such as: feelings of insecurity, anxiety, and rejection. So, psychological factors can replace bacteria and viruses as causes. Whether we use physical or psychological explanations of cause in mental disorder, the analogy between the medical model as used in physical medicine and in psychology holds. Either way, we are concerned, because of the presence of manifest pathology, with identifyng sources of dysfunction and selecting treatments that hold the greatest promise for the condition. Szasz (1960) is very critical of the illness model. He believes that the patient's expectation that his problems stem from illnesses or disease is misleading and damaging. He argues that so-called mentally disturbed people really have "problems in living" and that their disorders involve deviation from psychosocial, ethical, and legal, rather than physiological, norms. The illness concept is attractive to people because it helps to avoid facing problems; they can blame their difficulties on a mental *illness*. Thus, Szasz, as a practitioner, while not disputing the broad assumptions of the medical model, is dissatisfied with the limited conception of it that the illness model imposes.

Another concern in extending the medical model to disordered behavior has to do with those to whom it is targeted. The model directs attention almost exclusively to manifest disorder. It assumes that when emotional difficulties reach a certain point, people will either seek help voluntarily or will be sent by others to a professional. Mental health specialists are thus cast in roles similar to physicians. They are seen as people who determine causes of psychological problems and initiate direct cures just as physicians do when people come to them with chicken pox or the flu.

Historical Roots
of the Medical Model

How has the medical model achieved its preeminent position in guiding mental health activities? Historically, it was not the first conceptual framework for understanding and dealing with psychological disturbance. An earlier view, dominant for many centuries, was that supernatural forces—devils, evil spirits, or demons—invaded the disturbed person's body (Alexander & Selesnick, 1966; Cowen & Zax, 1967; Sarason & Ganzer, 1968). Healers tried to cope with disturbance through prayer, incantation, or physical abuse, hoping to coax the mysterious force causing the deviant

behavior to leave the victim. This approach to both physical and emotional disorder yielded slowly to more rational ones. And even the early rational approaches focused first on concrete, tangible physical disorders, not on intangible behavioral ones.

Precursors of a disease model of mental illness, itself a special case of the broader medical model, first appeared in the Middle Ages (Sarason & Ganzer, 1968) and did not reach full development until the eighteenth, nineteenth, and early twentieth centuries. Albee (1967) emphasizes that the disease model was an advanced humanistic substitute for the view that disturbed behavior was caused by sin, taint, and demons. The disease model evolved as part of a broader scientific revolution. It offered a rational basis for understanding and dealing with many human dysfunctions. Medicine was entering a new era of disease conquest. Advances in microbiology, successful applications of germ theory, and medical research had unlocked the mysteries of ravaging physical disorders—plagues, pestilence, smallpox, and typhoid fever. Closer to home for the mental health fields was the discovery of a cure for syphilis, which led to conquest of a significant organic psychosis—general paresis. Bloom (1965) supports Albee's view that advances in germ theory, development of the contagion principle to control infectious disease, and success in coping with nutritional disorders all helped to extend the disease concept to mental health. Both Albee and Bloom, however, argue that generalizing the disease model to mental health was a mistake. Even though it rested on real and important successes in other areas, these were intrinsically irrelevant to mental health.

Medicine's success in conquering serious diseases throughout history added greatly to knowledge about bodily processes, germs, and infections. It also established medicine's territorial right to treat *psychological* disturbances, which still persists today. The human body's disorders were first seen to be the concern of the witch doctor, then the priest, and finally the physician. When the latter inherited the body, he also inherited the mind, as part of the conviction that emotional disorder could best be understood by the same processes that had only recently, with much success, been discovered to solve deep mysteries of physical dysfunction. Why not? The view was logical and consonant with abnormal psychology's scope at the time.

The medical advances of the eighteenth and nineteenth centuries led to the establishment of many medical subareas, a specialization process that continues even today. One such subarea, psychiatry, was charged wtih understanding and treating emotional disorder. Implicit in establishing such a specialty is the assumption that emotional dysfunction is a medical problem. The knowledge and findings—indeed the very approaches—that had so effectively overcome difficult medical problems were now to be applied to the solution of psychological problems. Clearly, psychiatry has expanded both its horizons and its explanatory base since it first started. Yet, its historical roots are evident both in the assumption that abnormal behavior is primarily the concern of the medically trained and in the focus of its activities, which stress, more than other helping professions, the physical aspects of etiology and treatment.

Since the emotions were defined as the province of medical specialists, it is not surprising that early mental health personnel were virtually exclusively medically trained and that most treatment took place in medical facilities—clinics and hospitals. With psychiatry as the core helping profession, and the medical setting as the place for treating the emotionally disturbed, all pro-

fessionals, whatever their discipline, were imprinted in the ways of the medical model. Psychologists and social workers too were trained in psychiatric or medical settings, within the medical model's framework. That certainly shaped their views of mental disorder! This happened largely because there *were* no other types of training settings. As a result, whatever the mental health professional's area of specialization, his practice has reflected the medical model outlook. Small wonder then that the model is pan-professional in its present-day impact.

One unfortunate legacy of the view that emotional problems are medical problems has been interprofessional quarreling. As new nonmedical helping disciplines began to develop, vested interests were challenged. This issue was very clear in the post-World War II period when professional psychiatric associations adamantly opposed the licensing or certification of "newcomer" groups. The medical profession sought to amend existing medical practice legislation so as to rule certain professional activities (for example, psychotherapy) off-limits for nonmedical practitioners. How paradoxical that such power struggles took place at a time of desperate manpower shortages in all mental health fields! That such an illogical situation could have happened reflects the deep roots of the assumption that emotional dysfunction is a medical problem.

A forceful challenge to past prevailing views about mental health "ownership" was raised in the final report of the Joint Commission on Mental Illness and Health (1961). This report, a "magna carta" in mental health planning, recognized the magnitude of the social problems posed by emotional disorder and stressed the compelling need to broaden the base of mental health approaches. While emphasizing that primarily medical and neurological examinations and treatments must continue to be done by medically trained people, the report argued that psychotherapy and related procedures should be practiced by people whose training and experience qualified them for it. The Commission went so far as to propose that some psychological treatments could be carried out by "mental health workers"—people without full professional credentials but with appropriate qualifications, training, and supervision. While more time is needed for final social assessment of the liberalizing effects of this recommendation, some of its consequences are already clear. Professionals are more willing to use new interventions and types of help-agents to meet existing problems. There have been many new and different proposals recently for dealing with mental health problems that bypass the medical model's classic assumptions and ways of operating. Albee's proposal (1966) for establishing psychological service centers is a case in point.

Albee (1967) has identified several motivational factors which, he believes, have sustained the disease model's dominance in mental health. He points out, for example, that one of the model's tacit assumptions is that many disease processes are irreversible. He argues that this view, paradoxically, comforts people whose lives are affected by profound emotional disorder in someone close to them. It also eases society's conscience about isolating the seriously disturbed in poorly supported institutions that offer at best minimal care or treatment. Albee suggests that even the disturbed person himself may welcome the view that his problem is irreversible, because it removes life's struggles and burdens from his shoulders and permits him to withdraw totally into a socially sanctioned private world. This "playing-the-game" conformity-view of what is expected socially of the profoundly disturbed person is consistent with several recently proposed interpretations of the functional psychoses (Braginsky, Braginsky, & Ring, 1967; Goffman, 1961; Sheff, 1966).

Another motivational prop for the disease model view, according to Albee, is that it attracts funds for research and care by emphasizing tangible neurological and chemical determinants. This permits us to attack specific things, as in research and treatment with physical diseases. Finally, Albee argues that families of the disturbed are comforted by physical explanations of emotional disorders. If a loved one is schizophrenic, the condition can be seen with the same sense of blamelessness that one has toward diabetes or cancer.

Up to now we have focused on the disease model of emotional disorder. What about the even broader medical model concept? The successful medical approaches of the eighteenth and nineteenth centuries were first extended to dramatic, highly deviant behavior disorders—the prime conditions then seen to fall within abnormal psychology's scope. But that scope has not remained static. It has moved toward greater inclusiveness, embracing more subtle disorders. Freud played a vital role in moving abnormal psychology away from a specific disease model. He identified potential links between early psychological events in life and later pathology. For some, notably Adolf Meyer, this linkage pointed to the need for preventive approaches. Freud, however, chose instead to extend the disease model to what we are here calling the medical model. Rather than accepting the prior literal quest to identify biological and physical determinants of psychological problems, he sought psychological determinants. This led to important new treatments such as psychoanalysis and, later, psychotherapy. But mental health professionals, even under Freud's in-

fluence, still focused primarily on people already in serious psychological distress. Psychotherapy's goal was to understand the psychological forces that caused the distress and to relieve them. So, psychological events and life experiences joined bacteria and viruses as causes of psychological dysfunction. The sophisticated use of language in patient-therapist interactions was added to chemical and physical curative agents. These changes made it possible to engage a broader spectrum of emotional disorders. Essentially, though, they only transformed a simplistic disease model to a relatively complex, more sophisticated medical model.

Has the twentieth century basically changed this concepiton? Certainly it has witnessed serious efforts to find new ways for delivering services, for deciding how, and to whom, help should be distributed, and for broadening the disease model into a more elastic, inclusive medical model. But the broader model retains many of the fundamental characteristics of its predecessor; that is, it still assumes an analogy of cause between physical and psychological dysfunction; dysfunction is still not seen by the professional until relatively late in the game, and patients still cast professionals in the role of all-knowing authorities who diagnose and treat disorder.

Both the emergence and present influence of the medical model are understandable. Indeed, given abnormal psychology's narrow scope as recently as a century ago, the model may have been suitable and effective.

New challenges arise now primarily because the discipline has expanded, new mandates have been identified, and problems, not well handled within the medical model framework, are more apparent. This requires exploring conceptual alternatives. Continued exclusive adherence to the medical model in mental health is no longer profitable. While the model can still help to deal with some disorders considered in the next several chapters, alternatives are sorely needed if the vital problems identified in the last third of this book are to be engaged meaningfully.

CRITIQUE OF THE MEDICAL MODEL

No one can deny the relationship between biological or physiological factors and certain psychological disorders (Turner & Cumming, 1967). Brain injury, brain tumor, vascular disorders, nutritional avitaminosis, toxic poisoning, anoxia, and arterial changes with age, among others, can all cause severe psychological problems. The psychological consequences of any of these conditions can be serious, including psychosis. Furthermore, many recent studies suggest that heightened vulnerability to some extreme psychotic disorders, for example, schizophrenia, is related to inherited predispositions (Heston & Denney, 1968; Rosenthal, Wender, Kety, Schulsinger, Welner, & Østergaard, 1968).

Physically based psychological disorders

require medical diagnosis and, often, primarily medical treatment. Thus, the medical model cannot be summarily dismissed. It will continue to play a significant role in dealing with certain psychological dysfunctions. At the same time we must be concerned about its adequacy as a *comprehensive* model if we are to develop a clearer understanding of how to supplement it. Physically based psychological disorders are only a small fraction of the many problems that call for psychological help, particularly now that abnormal psychology's scope is so much expanded.

Faulty Assumptions of the Medical Model

The major weakness of a disease or medical model as applied to mental health problems lies in the analogy between the causes of physical and psychological disorder. While the analogy is occasionally valid, it does not apply well for the typical instances of the two types of dysfunction. Most emotional problems do not result from sudden tissue insult or from viruses and bacteria. They are a product of continuous adverse influences over long time-periods. They relate to significant persons in the individual's development and to the impact of key social institutions in his life. This idea is far from novel. In fact, it is central to Freud's theory and position. The problem is not that medical model practitioners fail to recognize it, but rather that the types of services that the model dictates have not sufficiently accommodated to it. One accommodation would be to study, in some detail, how important others and critical social institutions influence human development. Through such studies we might identify influences that maximize emotional growth and build psychological health. Then we could plan helping programs based on such knowledge.

Prevention has not been a major thrust of abnormal psychology despite Freud's recognition of the deeply rooted, complex determinants of behavior disorder. Instead, our emphasis has been on treatments designed to explore relationships between current difficulties and past experiences. Although Freud's discoveries could have been used profitably to challenge the medical model, they were used to strengthen it. Freud put psychotherapy on the map and constructively enlarged our framework for viewing emotional problems. But, his work failed to alter the basic assumption of laymen, or even professionals, that the time to see the "mind" doctor, just as with "body" doctors, is when you are sick. Given the long developmental history of most psychological disorders, this is not an optimal approach for them. Indeed, its potential for satisfactory outcomes is poor.

For example, an initial schizophrenic reaction in a twenty-year-old may involve profound symptoms requiring hospitalization and drastic treatments. The prognosis for his recovery is guarded. Not uncommonly, the final outcome is prolonged hospitalization. In other words, by the time the person has reached an extreme pathological state the options available for treating him are limited (Rappaport, Chinsky, & Cowen, 1971). We can further dramatize the situation facing this hypothetical patient. When his symptoms became manifest he had already had a life experience of some 175,000 hours. Much of this was, doubtless, filled with conflict, anxiety, and human failings as well as an inability to develop the resources needed to cope with life's problems. Why should we expect to be able to intervene successfully when such a condition is so well entrenched and floridly manifest? How can we hope to compensate, in any short range approach, for a lifetime of failure and inadequate development? Indeed, society's poor treatment record with schizophrenics well reflects the hopelessness of our classic approaches (Rappaport, Chinsky, & Cowen, 1971). This hypothetical example highlights the challenge to the medical model's implicit analogy between physical and psychological disorder. Given the frequency of psychological disorders, such as the one just cited, we must eventually face an inescapable question: "In the sense of long range social planning (choice of models) could we not be more optimistic if we were able to orient ourselves to an understanding of the influence systems and social processes that underlie presently observable unfortunate outcomes, to modify such systems and influence processes, and to build positively beforehand rather than being restricted largely to a type of after-the-fact 'counter punching?'" (Cowen, 1967, p. 395).

We have argued, in considering medical model limitations, that the typical cases of physical and psychological dysfunction are quite different. Consideration of some *non*-typical instances, however, may help to establish two important points: (1) that the notion of pure medical or preventive models is illusory, that is, there are clear overlap points between the two; and (2) that for some psychological disorders, with other than biochemical or physiological causes, the medical model is still appropriate and useful. Many, but not all, psychological problems have deep roots and long histories. Exceptions might include bereavement, realistic fear caused by illness or the prospect of dangerous surgery, dejection over failure to achieve important life goals (promotions, academic degrees), and adjustment to new, unknown, and potentially threatening experiences. All these can produce significant, enduring psychological problems. Such problems occur in people whose previous adjustment ranged from reasonably good to excellent, as well as those with less satisfactory adjustment histories. The problems that stem from these situations resemble typical instances of physical illness (that is, acute symptom onset in previously well-functioning individuals). In such cases the classical tools of the medical model, such as psychotherapy, have been quite effective. This point is reflected in the frequently cited irony that psychologically healthy people get the most out of psychotherapy.

The typical physical malfunction involves a previously healthy person who experiences a relatively sudden problem—influenza, pneumonia, an ear infection, a cold, measles, or a broken arm. Causes and cures for many of these conditions are more or less well understood. For wounds or broken bones, the physician knows that the patient's regenerative forces will do the most of the repair work. His role is to maximize the likelihood of effective restoration and to minimize chances of infection. If the disease is caused by bacteria, the physician prescribes the appropriate antibacterial medication. His role as an authoritative diagnostician and cure-agent conforms to reality; it is appropriate. The patient's view of the doctor as a knowledgeable authority is similar to that held by many people experiencing emotional problems when they first come to see a mental health professional. However understandable that perception, it is less warranted in the second case.

Physical medicine's most serious challenges come less from modal instances of cross-sectionally isolated disorder in previously well-functioning organisms and more from ongoing illnesses or processes that stem from underlying bodily malfunctions or sources of trauma. The latter conditions more closely resemble serious psychological disorder in their long-range, cumulative aspects. Diabetes, ulcers, rheumatic heart conditions, and a variety of auto-immune entities exemplify the group. In such cases, the physician does his best to control the disorder's symptoms, to make the patient more comfortable, and to try to prevent permanent damage. His long-term handling seeks to minimize the likelihood that the symptoms will recur.

Some serious medical conditions, as for example certain forms of cancer, have no known cure. Patients thus afflicted eventually reach a terminal stage where little can be done except to minimize pain and discomfort. While medical research continually seeks to discover the causes of, and cures for, cancer, its major thrust for such conditions is preventive. This is based on the reality that, given existing knowledge and technology limits, once a patient reaches a certain point in the disease process he is doomed. There is a good analogy between terminal cancer and certain advanced psychological states. For example, it is probably realistic to consider a concept such as "terminal schizophrenia" wherein once an individual reaches a certain state he too is doomed, in the psychological sense. Such an analogy points strongly to the need to *prevent* the occurrence of schizophrenia rather than accepting the condition as a given and trying valiantly, but ineffectively, to cure it.

Somatic medicine has not been inattentive to prevention's potential. Many major medical triumphs involve the prevention of previously baffling, damaging conditions. The control of typhoid fever through water purification, of malaria through chemical obliteration of its breeding grounds, and of disorders such as whooping cough, smallpox, or polio through immunological procedures are all classic triumphs, within medicine, for the preventive approach. Thus, some psychological dysfunctions can best be understood and treated within the medical model framework, and conversely, the preventive triumphs of physical medicine have much to contribute to a long-range conceptual plan for coping with abnormal behavior.

Another major problem in extending the medical model to mental health concerns what we earlier called its "passive-receptive stance." Given contemporary definitions of mental health helping services, demand for help is enormous and mental health professionals, who are extremely busy people, cannot meet it. They are scarcely in a position to seek out people with psychological problems. More typically, they are "tracked down" by many more people with problems than they can handle. Persons who need professional help must take the initiative for finding it on their own or with the help of someone who is concerned about them. They can seek help from private practitioners, clinics, or hospitals. However, in searching they are often deterred by overcrowded facilities and long waiting lists, professionals who are very difficult to get to, high costs, personal anxieties, or the perceived stigma of having to turn to someone for help. With all these barriers to overcome, by the time the person finds someone who can see him he is often already very upset with a condition that has existed for some time. So the professional is mostly called upon to spin his magic in cases of relatively entrenched, serious pathology. Though this inefficiency in the medical model's operation is, doubtless, an unintended byproduct, it is nevertheless, characteristic of the system.

Insufficient Scope of the Medical Model

Another shortcoming of the medical model in mental health is its limited scope. The model works largely through one-to-one interactions. It is very costly in professional manpower, where society can least afford the expense. Some (Bloom, 1965) see this as a "foolhardy" emphasis and argue that some basic elements of the model, for example, its stress on diagnosis, are wasteful. This view rests on the conviction that since mental health treatment, unlike treatment in physical medicine, is far from being diagnosis-specific, diagnosis simply is not worth the effort. Regardless of one's opinion on this specific matter, as the model now operates, it is clear that we have too few professionals to meet the rising demand for services. Future projections (Albee, 1967) suggest that professional manpower shortages will become more severe. We are faced with the unhappy prospect of running as fast as we can on our present course only to fall behind as slowly as possible!

Another major scope defect of the medical model is that it distributes services unequally. In general, the wealthy, best educated groups get the biggest piece of the pie. One reason for this is the way the rules of the mental health game, both explicit and implicit, have been spelled out. These rules have to do with where, and how often, the professional and the patient meet, what the setting looks like, how the two proceed with their business, and what their objectives are. In the past, these rules, whether spoken or unspoken, have reflected predominant middle-class values. They have not encouraged the flow of other than middle-class clientele. Mental health services have not been effectively transported to cultural and ethnic groups whose status and values differ from those of the American middle-class. Students of this problem (Lorion, 1973, 1974; Reiff, 1967; Reiff & Riessman, 1965; Riessman, 1967; Riessman & Miller, 1964; Turner & Cumming, 1967) argue that the medical model's services, format, and specific procedures are so foreign to the poor that they provide little basis for establishing meaningful contacts with mental health professionals. For those few who do manage to establish an initial contact, lack of common procedures and objectives minimizes the possibility of getting effective help. This limitation in the model's scope has meant, at least until recently, that adequate help for mental health problems, has not been available to the poor.

Limited Effectiveness of the Medical Model

Unlike concerns about the medical model's scope, concerns about its effectiveness are less challenging to the basic model than to how it is being implemented. Weaknesses in the model's assumptions or inadequacies in its scope, demand that alternative or supplementary frameworks be developed. By contrast, even severe effectiveness limits can be tolerated without discarding the model. If it does not work well, maybe it can be improved to make it more useful.

One problem of the model's effectiveness comes from the limited reliability and validity of its diagnostic tools—a point considered in Chapter 1. One study (Nathan et al., 1969) vividly underscores the problem. Thirty-two mental health professionals observed an extensive diagnostic testing of a chronic alcoholic who had been admitted to a hospital for treatment. At the end of the exam the professionals were asked to submit a diagnostic write-up. The procedure yielded 14 different diagnoses! These included a broad range of conditions—for example, depression, temporal lobe epilepsy, and paranoid schizophrenia. This example identifies an important problem in diagnosis—a major activity of mental health professionals. As noted in Chapter 1, both the reliability and validity of classification schemes have been challenged on many counts (Ash, 1949; Jellinek, 1939; Mehlman,

1952; Ward et al., 1962; Zigler & Phillips, 1961a). These include: disagreement about the nature of pathological entities; grouping different symptom patterns under the same diagnostic label; differences in diagnostic bias due to training and experience; and changes in patient status (Masserman & Carmichael, 1938). One thing that seems clear is that diagnostic reliability (but not usefulness) increases with the breadth of the category used.

Limits of diagnostic validity also raise questions about the predictive validity of clinical diagnoses (Holtzman & Sells, 1954; Little & Shneidman, 1959; Taft, 1959). In one major assessment project (Kelley & Fiske, 1951) with poor initial predictive validity, adding new information made it even worse! Equally disconcerting are data indicating that naive, untrained judges are no less accurate, as assessors on some clinical judgmental tasks, than sophisticated professionals (Kelley & Fiske, 1951; Soskin, 1954; Taft, 1955; Weiss, 1953). Smith (1966) reviewed ten studies dealing with the influence of psychological training on the accuracy of clinical judgment. Experimental tasks included matching movies or observations of behavior to personality sketches, and predicting test responses from case history or observations. The results indicated that professional training failed to increase "insight into one's fellows." Subjects ranged from mental health professionals to graduate students to naive undergraduates and to people with absolutely no relation to the mental health fields, for example, actors, musicians, and physical scientists. Smith summed up his review as follows: "Does intensive training designed to increase sensitivity actually do so? No. Indeed, more than one of these studies show that the less well trained do significantly better" (Smith, 1966, p. 8).

While individual clinicians vary in the importance they attach to diagnostic data in choosing among alternative interventions, many do weigh such data heavily. If diagnoses are unreliable or invalid, even if there is diagnosis-treatment specificity (Cameron, 1953), interventions built on shaky premises and irrelevant foundations cannot be maximally effective (Rotter, 1973; Strupp & Bergin, 1969).

Much of this discussion has dealt with the question: "Can we agree on what the problem is?" Even when we can, variables such as gaps in the professional's knowledge, background, training, skills, and biases, and aspects of the patient's personal style and life-circumstances importantly influence treatment decisions. Even with 100 percent diagnostic agreement, the "treatment" selected for a given patient could be: hospitalization, intensive psychotherapy within one of many different frameworks, supportive therapy, chemotherapy, or even doing nothing, depending on who the patient is and the professional consulted. Even when something is known about the patient (young or old, rich or poor, black or white) and the helper (psychiatrist or social worker, Freudian or behavior modifier), treatment possibilities are still extensive. The problem is that we know so little about the comparative effectiveness of different treatments, let alone their differential usefulness for different disorders, personality styles, demographic groups, and patient-therapist combinations (Garfield, 1971; Paul, 1967a). Many decisions about how to treat a patient are governed less by theory, careful clinical observation, or empirical knowledge, as they should be, and more by fortuitous, irrelevant factors.

These assessment and treatment failings obviously limit the effectiveness of the medical model as defined. When we add to that the mental health professional's modest success with specific disorders, the indictment becomes more serious. Success in dealing with schizophrenia for example is often measured in terms of having patients achieve a minimally adequate state, rather than in terms of control or modification of the basic disorder itself (Rappaport, Chinsky, & Cowen, 1971). We have not done appreciably better with delinquency, addiction, antisocial behavior, or criminal acting-out.

RECENT CHANGES IN THE MEDICAL MODEL

Recent developments within a medical model framework seek to correct its weaknesses. The mental health field has gone through a period of considerable self-scrutiny. The impact of its functions has been studied and efforts to increase its effectiveness and extend its reach are in process. One significant thrust is the attempt to identify and treat disorder as early as possible to increase the likelihood of positive outcomes. This development was facilitated by the Joint Commission on Mental Illness and Health's (1961) recommendation that a nationwide network of community mental health centers be established. The Community Mental Health Centers Act of 1963 was the significant step in implementing this important recommendation. Since then, many community mental health centers have been set up, and, although they differ in how they function, they share certain emphases.

The community health center is designed as a buffer between the troubled individual and the mental hospital. Centers try to see patients early in the development of their disorder so that their interventions need not be drastic. They also help patients to stay in the community and to be treated in less stigmatizing ways that isolate them less from their natural environment. In addition to its buffer role, the community mental health center can provide consultation and educative services to the community along with training and research (Glasscote et al., 1964; Smith & Hobbs, 1966), making it a potentially viable force for introducing new approaches to mental health problems. Some have expressed disappointment that the community mental health center concept is not sufficiently innovative (Cowen & Zax, 1967). Still, the mere fact that new roles and functions are recognized appropriately encourages reexamination of the *status quo* and the search for new approaches.

Recognizing the need to engage psychological disorder as early as possible, how have mental centers been innovative? They have set up crisis clinics, suicide centers, short-term "drop-in" clinics, and emergency telephone services. All are designed to bring immediate help to people experiencing problems that could become serious emotional disorders. Another change in the

Volunteers often help staff suicide prevention centers. This man serves as a telephone counselor for the National Save-A-Life League in New York City.

medical model's implementation, seen more often today than a decade ago, is a reaching out to areas in which psychological problems occur with high frequency. This is a step away from the model's traditionally passive-receptive stance. Clinicians no longer restrict their activities exclusively to hospitals, clinics, or consulting rooms. At least in certain agencies they move more freely to "where the action is." Illustratively, mental health people today are more interested than before in schools and educational approaches, and services and research in school settings are increasing correspondingly (Bower & Hollister, 1967; Newman, 1967). More extensive psychological services are now also found in courts, prisons, settlement homes, welfare and enforcement agencies, and other settings which, in their normal everyday function, have to deal with people experiencing emotional troubles. This broadening is both encouraging and responsive to a real need. But, ultimately, the question of *what* we do is more significant than *where* we do it.

These medical model extensions seek to engage dsiorders earlier and/or in their natural settings. As such, they reflect expansion in the model's scope. That is good, but what of the still untold number of people with emotional problems who have not been reached at all? Many of these are found among the poor. Energetic efforts are underway to extend mental health services to this group. The question is whether we can accomplish this simply by changing the locus of service. Probably not. More likely mental health services will have to be rethought and repackaged to make them more meaningful to the poor and the culturally deprived. Such repackaging must consider the life style of the poor, how they see the world and human frailty, as well as where and how they can best accept and profit from mental health services. Professionals

must also examine their own attitudes toward treating the poor. Two excellent reviews (Lorion, 1973, 1974) point out that poor patients who remain in psychotherapy do about as well as higher income patients. However, large numbers of the poor drop out of treatment in the first few sessions— before it really starts. Lorion argues that this attrition is due as much to therapist, as to patient, attitudes. He recommends that professionals adjust treatment goals and formats for the poor "to reflect more accurately patient needs, expectations, and reality problems."

Riessman, Cohen, and Pearl (1964) describe both the problems involved in meeting the mental health needs of the poor and new programs to resolve them. The latter includes setting up treatment units in neighborhood storefronts (Riessman, 1967) and bringing treatment to the home, job, or street corner. Riessman advocates services that have concrete, action-oriented goals consistent with realities of the culture of poverty. But even such informed programming will not solve all the problems of low-income people. Their needs are still more basic: for food, clothing, shelter, jobs, life opportunities, and hope. Meeting these needs will require basic social engineering tailored to the life situation of the poor. This way of thinking certainly transcends the medical model.

Are other scope limitations of the medical model being addressed? Some yes, some no. An example of another serious scope problem is the concentration of mental health services in major urban centers. Rural areas are badly neglected. This problem has received some attention recently leading to the establishment of several innovative programs designed to bring helping services to remote areas. A volume by Huessy (1966) entitled *Mental Health with Limited Resources: Yankee Ingenuity and Low Cost*

Programs describes a network of programs developed to augment scarce mental health resources in rural Vermont. These programs involve consultation, mobile professional personnel, imaginative uses of nonprofessionals, and retooling existing services. Other rural areas are developing similar programs, prompted by the question: Given limited resources, now, and in the foreseeable future, how can we get maximal mileage from them?

Still another development to extend the limited reach of the medical model is the expanding T-group and encounter-group movement (Burton, 1969b), considered in Chapter 15. The force behind this movement does not come primarily from the mental health fields. Yet, it represents a social effort to reduce dysfunction and to enhance adaptation. The movement has spread widely. Not surprisingly, however, its development far outpaces its evaluation (Lieberman, Yalom, & Miles, 1973). Some praise the groups, others damn them. But for the most part, reactions are based on personal experience rather than systematic research.

© Chris Rollins

The appearance of numerous encounter groups has helped to expand the scope of the medical model.

Current efforts to improve treatment effectiveness within the medical model framework are widespread. This is commendable. Anyone who does psychotherapy, for example, should continually be asking himself: "Does what I do with patients produce the results I seek?"; "Is my approach equally effective with all patients?"; "How can I change what I do to produce better outcomes for those who seem not to be profiting from it?" In recent years clinicians have been more willing to examine the effects of their basic functions. Willingness to consider alternatives in the past has, indeed, produced new approaches such as nondirective therapy (Rogers, 1942, 1951).

Many studies of the effectiveness of traditional treatments have yielded disappointing findings. This has led to the development of new, exciting, and more hopeful alternatives. Behavior therapy or behavior modification (Kalish, 1965; Ullmann & Krasner, 1965; Wolpe, 1958, 1968) is among the most significant of these. In this approach laboratory learning principles are applied directly to the modification of behavioral maladjustment. The approach is appealing for several reasons. Its aims are simple and operational and, since its methodology comes from established learning principles, it is easy to teach. Behavioral approaches depart significantly from classical psychoanalysis both in theory and practice. They focus on overt behavior and· how to change it. Historical antecedents and dynamic factors, considered so important by analysts in dealing with current disorder, are largely bypassed. Instead, behavior modifiers focus doggedly on changing current behavior. Hence, treatment is briefer, narrower, and more goal-directed than traditional therapeutic approaches. The fact that behavior modification's theoretical and empirical roots are in the mainstream of traditional psychology makes it both appealing to psychologists and quite researchable. Thus, evaluation of behavioral approaches has been more rapid and extensive than for other treatment approaches. Behavior modification has been applied to a variety of problems ranging from treating autistic children (Lovaas, 1968) to extinguishing snake phobias (Lang, 1968).

Encouraging early results from the use of behavior modification have led to their application to behavior problems not typically handled by psychotherapy in the past. For example, Baer (1968) trained teachers to modify the socially maladaptive behavior of nursery school children. Guerney (1969) has done similar work using parents and peers as reinforcers. The data are still too meager to suggest that behavior modification should replace other forms of psychotherapy. Yet the approach shows promise, clinically and economically, for dealing more effectively with certain conditions than has so far been possible.

Other current developments may also strengthen psychotherapy's contribution within the medical model framework. Stampfl's implosive therapy (Levis & Carrera, 1967; London, 1964; Stampfl & Levis, 1967) is an approach that has attracted recent attention. The implosive therapist accepts the psychodynamic view that anxiety, or unrealistic fear, is at the core of the neuroses and other pathologies. Treatment seeks to teach the patient that he need no longer be afraid. Learning principles are used to do this. The patient's worst fears are first induced through persuasion, imagination, and related techniques, and then are extinguished. If major sources of the patient's anxiety can thus be controlled, it is assumed that anxiety in other areas will also be reduced.

Another illustration of the breadth of the current search for better "medicine" is the fact that nearly a third of the chapters of a major volume on research on psychotherapy (Shlien, 1968) deals with drug therapies. Several chapters (Mogar, 1968; Savage 1968) describe drug-therapy patients with "philosophical" neuroses, characterized by a lack of clear meaning or purpose in life. Such patients differ perceptibly from past, more classic drug-therapy patients.

Efforts to improve psychotherapy involve change in established procedures as well as development of new approaches. Psychotherapy began as a one-to-one approach. As problems were identified that did not respond optimally to that format, group and family therapies developed. Group therapy has gone through many changes (Rosenbaum, 1965; Scheidlinger, 1969). Many of these modifications developed because they seemed to have potential for dealing more effectively with specific problems. The recent growing awareness that many disorders are rooted in the complex social system of the family has led to the development, and rapid acceptance, of family therapies (Sager et al., 1969). Psychotherapy is obviously not standing still (Bergin & Suinn, 1975; Strupp & Bergin, 1969). Much the same can be said for approaches to the care and treatment of the seriously disturbed.

The Joint Commission on Mental Illness and Health (1961, p. iv) stated, as one of its major conclusions, that "major mental illness is the core problem and unfinished business of the mental health movement." This statement has been disputed on many counts (Cowen & Zax, 1967). But one reason why it was made was to challenge the then dominant approach to the care of the profoundly disturbed—that is, confinement to a mental hospital. One of the Joint Commission's task forces specifically considered how the seriously disturbed were treated. It dealt with three separate components of the problem: (1) How can we reduce the likelihood that a person will be hospitalized in the first place?; (2) How can institutions do a better job?; and (3) How can rehabilitation be facilitated after institutionalization?

The community mental health center model was proposed to reduce the need for people to be in mental hospitals for extended time periods. As noted earlier, these centers are designed to provide effective services early in the history of disorder. They broaden the definition of treatment and extend it to more natural community-based settings. Efforts to upgrade the effectiveness of the mental hospital are going on at several levels. Here, the past wide gulf between the hospital and the community must be reduced. The assumption that being sick and being well are unrelated states to be lived in totally different worlds must be laid to rest.

More and more we are aware of important connections between a mental hospital's organization and orientation and its size and location, on the one hand, and the effectiveness of its patient programs, on the other. Such factors fix sharp limits on what can, and cannot, be done for patients. For example, a 3000 bed hospital located 50 miles from the nearest city creates staffing problems, limits therapeutic programs, and isolates patients from the world in which they lived, and to which they should return. Such isolation favors the view that patients are alien beings; it fosters a custodial orientation sometimes mindful of a jail or leper colony. Recognizing this problem, the Joint Commission strongly recommended that all new inpatient facilities: be small; be located in areas that encourage patient participation in community programs; and minimize isolation from the surrounding world.

Many people are now taking a closer look at the quality of life in mental hospitals and, in so doing, they find many standard mental hospital practices far from therapeutic. Some practices, in fact, are seen to dehumanize patients and make their disorders even more chronic (Goffman, 1961; Rubenstein & Lasswell, 1966). Many important questions are heard with growing frequency. For example, "Do such things as having patients wear institutional clothes, live in drab locked wards, isolated from the outside world, make them *less* fit for life than they were *before* they entered the institution?" (Felix, 1967). Other, similar challenges to traditional hospital practices have been stated (Greenblatt & Levinson, 1965; M. Jones, 1953, 1968; Rubenstein & Lasswell, 1966). More and more, locked wards are being opened, patients are encouraged to set up their own ward-governments, nonprofessional socializing and help-agents are being brought into institutions, and hospital aides and nurses are encouraged to be more treatment oriented. Exciting experimental studies (Clark & Yeomans, 1969; Colarelli & Siegel, 1966; Ellsworth, 1968; Fairweather, 1964; Fairweather, Sanders, & Tornatzky, 1974; Rubenstein & Lasswell, 1966; Sanders, Smith, & Weinman, 1967) challenge the traditional ways of the mental hospital. These projects emphasize therapeutic milieus that reduce discontinuities between institutions and the communities, give patients decision-making power and even use them in therapeutic roles.

Facilitating patient readaptation to the community after leaving an institution is an after-care problem that is being dealt with in many ways. All seek to overcome the simplistic view that a person is either sick or well. In the past, many patients have languished full-time in mental hospitals because they were not quite ready to take up a full life outside. Some of those could surely leave the institution and live in the community with the support of someone to help them over rough spots. Several after-care models have been developed that recognize this reality. One is the day hospital where the patient spends five days a week, going home evenings and weekends. The day hospital emphasizes both treatment and acquiring work and social skills. The day hospital patient stays in continuous touch with his home, family, and social surrounding. He is not stigmatized as a mental "in-patient." Another example is the night hospital for patients who can work effectively but who need continuous psychological support and treatment. The latter are provided during evening hours. Treatment does not disrupt employment or many important aspects of social life. And, again, the stigma of being a mental patient is reduced.

Foster family placement is another after-care approach that is more frequently used these days. This approach has a long history. It is designed for patients who do not have a home to return to or who are not welcome in their homes. If viable alternatives to the institution are not available, such patients must remain in the hospital. Foster care provides a sheltered setting in which many patients, who would otherwise not have an opportunity to try their wings, can make a reasonable adjustment.

The half-way house is still another approach to after-care. Several recent examples of such programs have been reported (Fairweather et al, 1969; Raush & Raush, 1969). Half-way houses are transitional facilities in which small groups of former mental patients, who have progressed toward recovery, live communally in a protected setting that usually offers some professional services. Many half-way house residents are well enough to work and manage their affairs with only minimal supervision. Thus, half-way house patients, like foster-home patients, can leave the institution and try various activities, but still be sheltered. For some patients, half-way houses provide more independence and privacy than foster homes. Because half-way houses have only expatients, they offer the comfort, sense of understanding, kinship, and therapeutic atmosphere that come from close association with others who have shared a common stressful experience.

CONCLUSION

Consideration of the current status of the medical model has included a review of the widespread efforts to broaden its scope and to improve its effectiveness. The model is hardly static. Conceivably, recent developments will lead to important breakthroughs that will help to resolve the long-standing problems of emotional disorder. As much as we want to be hopeful, however, the model's history suggests that it is unwise to assume that this will happen.

Measured evaluation of the medical model in mental health suggests that some of its features will surely survive. Manifest emotional disorders will not be eliminated in the foreseeable future, and even the most optimistic person must concede that we are not soon likely to become effective enough in prevention to erase all significant psychological disorders. A portion of the mental health community's effort will continue to be needed to treat dysfunction. Such "repair work" is central to the medical model and we should strive to make it as effective as possible. While the model falls short of solving many of modern society's complex mental health problems, it seeks genuinely to deal with many that must be met on the spot. It is easier to sit on the sidelines in a long-range planner's

© J. Brian King 1975

chair and discredit the model than it is to jump into the clinical breech and really help a suffering human being. We should also keep in mind that some disordered behaviors are best handled by the approaches of the medical model (Lemkau, 1959). Two such examples are psychological dysfunctions resulting directly from known physical causes (toxic poisoning, delirium following fever, tumor, and so forth) and narrowly bounded reactive problems in people who have basically adjusted well. Thus, there are valid reasons for the survival of certain elements of the medical model and for trying to make it as effective as possible. To dismiss the model out-of-hand would be irresponsible.

There will be problems, however, if we bet all our chips on what the medical model can accomplish in mental health. Taking the long view highlights the model's shortcomings. Despite heroic effort, skillful and sincere professionals operating within its framework have not solved the major problem of behavior disorder. Only peripheral battles have been won, and the growth of new approaches has not been matched by improvement in cure rates. Many seemingly promising breakthroughs have simply failed to fulfill their promise. Though there have been periods when it seemed that we were gaining in the struggle, we are scarcely a healthier society today than we were a century ago. Some may consider this argument unfair, both because the strains of modern life may be greater than before, and because the scope of mental health's concerns has so vastly broadened. Still, the fact remains: Progress in mental health has not approximated the conquest of physical disorder. The emergence of a social philosophy emphasizing the rights, dignity, and happiness of all has added to the rising tide of concern about psychological disorder and its control. Such developments along with the problems generated by rapid population expansion lead to the argument (Sanford, 1965) that disordered behavior, psychological suffering, and unhappiness are of far greater concern today than ever before in man's history. Given the best guesses that can be made about the directions of future society, the social burdens created by human psychological problems are likely to increase rather than decrease.

A key failing of the medical model is its longstanding focus on manifest dysfunction rather than on forces that promote adaptation. Thus the model has failed to cut down the flow of disorder. While this emphasis and the view of disordered behavior that it generates can be understood historically, eventually long-range planners must engage the challenge of how to stop disorder. Better yet, the question they should be asking is how to build health!

The material through Chapter 15 details thinking and progress in diverse areas within the medical model framework. The book's final chapters introduce the concept of prevention and describe programs and models that stem from this orientation. It may confuse some readers to begin an abnormal psychology text that covers the traditional core of the field, with a critique of its underlying conceptual base. By so doing, however, we seek to provide a perspective that may help the discerning student to read critically. *Caveat emptor*! This approach can produce both discomfort and skepticism as the student proceeds. He may doubt that he is reading the "gospel." We do not apologize for this. Indeed, if it happens, our purpose will have been well served.

SUMMARY

1. This chapter's aim was to describe and criticize the medical model— a conceptual model that has long determined the practices of those who deal with disordered behavior.

2. The model provides one set of guiding assumptions about how emotional problems develop and how best to cope with them. These conceptualizations are either *systematic* or *implicit*. For most practitioners they are implicit and grow out of the urgent need to treat acutely disturbed individuals, now.

3. The narrowest interpretation of the medical model is as a disease model. Many, however, see it more broadly and recognize that there can be psychological as well as physical determinants of dysfunction.

4. Historically, the medical model was not man's first guide to thinking about emotional disorder. Before it, spiritistic and religious models held sway. Medicine's success in understanding and curing physical disorders led to the model's extension to emotional disorder, notwithstanding many weaknesses in the analogy between physical and emotional disorder.

5. The medical model is criticized for its faulty assumptions, narrow scope, and limited effectiveness.

6. Recent changes in the medical model have been aimed at correcting its weaknesses. The establishment of community mental health centers with their varied emergency and outreach services is one major corrective effort.

7. Efforts are also underway to extend relevant services to previously neglected groups such as the poor and rural dwellers.

8. New therapeutic approaches have been developed hopefully to provide more effective treatment. Questions have also been raised about the structure of the traditional mental hospital and important changes have been implemented.

9. Diverse after-care programs are developing in large numbers.

10. The procedures of the medical model will continue to have a place in mental health in dealing with both manifest and physically caused emotional disorder. However, the model's limited effectiveness and inadequate scope, taken together with mental health's ever-expanding mandate, demand that it be supplemented meaningfully by preventive approaches.

CHAPTER 4

Organic Roots of Behavior Disorder

Giovanni Morgagni earned a medical degree in 1701 and spent his entire career trying to understand disease through his work in pathology. His interest was not so much in the cadaver per se as it was in the relationship between findings at autopsy and the patient's symptom picture. He therefore made the case history a routine part of his autopsy reports. Morgagni made specific contributions to the study of brain pathology through his demonstration that the symptoms of stroke were caused by ruptured blood vessels which only secondarily affected brain tissue, rather than by disease in the tissue itself. He also recognized that stroke-induced paralysis affected the side of the body opposite to that on which hemorrhage had occurred in the brain. His primary impact on later students of behavior disorder lay in his emphasis on relationships between brain function and mental illness, including the view that specific diseases could be localized in specific areas of the brain.

Broadly speaking, there are two approaches to behavior disorder. One holds that physiological or constitutional factors are crucial to the occurrence of mental disturbance; the other emphasizes social, environmental, or psychological forces. Each has its proponents, and throughout the years one or the other has dominated the field and led to important advances. Historically the organic view, which originated with Hippocrates, takes precedence over the environmental, and since significant behavioral effects of known damage to the organic structure can be observed, this viewpoint has received much support.

81

Following the intellectual reawakening during the Renaissance, Morgagni (1682–1771) firmly established the organic theory as a scientific foundation for behavior disorder. Most psychiatrists of the mid-nineteenth century, particularly William Griesinger, whom we have already mentioned, were more favorably impressed by Morgagni's approach than by the more dynamic contemporary position of Moreau and Heinroth. The organicists sought to establish psychiatry solidly within the framework of medicine proper and believed that this could be best accomplished by the scientific verification of Morgagni's hypothesis about mental disease and brain function. For these men, adequacy of psychiatric diagnosis depended on designation of a defect in the brain. Support for such a position was found in several fruitful lines of research during the nineteenth and twentieth centuries.

LOCALIZATION OF BRAIN FUNCTION

The phrenologist Gall has already been cited for his conceptualization of the brain as a relatively simple mechanism compartmentalized into subareas, each subserving specific functions, including mental ones. Boring (1950) believes that Gall's theory exemplifies an essentially wrong idea which was, however, sufficiently correct to advance scientific thought. In establishing the brain as the "organ of the mind," Gall's approach opened the way for progress in the study of brain physiology. Phrenology also made an extreme case for the localization of brain function. While this case was doubtless overstated, Gall stimulated the study of physiological functions of different parts of the brain.

This work led to encouraging discoveries for the localizationists. Rolando (1773–1831) and Flourens (1794–1867), although not strict localizationists themselves, established that the cerebellum was the part of the brain which controlled coordinated movement. Paul Broca (1824–1880) identified a speech center in the cerebral cortex. Shortly thereafter, Wernicke (1848–1905) identified a similar area—the angular transverse temporal gyrus—that presumably subserved the functions of speech reception and understanding. These findings have since been questioned but at the time they were widely accepted. In 1870, Eduard Hitzig (1843–1907) and Theodor Fritsch (1838–1897) localized motor functions in an area of the cerebral cortex. The establishment of the motor centers stimulated a search for sensory centers and, before long, centers for vision, touch, and hearing were established.

Flourens, whose own work had contributed to acceptance of the view that brain function could be localized found such a position to be oversimplified. He felt that, while specific areas of the brain were responsible for certain functions, there remained a unity to the nervous system such that injury to, or removal of, any one part potentially affected other parts. This position was supported by the work of Franz and Lashley in the twentieth century, as summarized by the latter in 1929. Lashley proposed two basic principles of brain function: *equipotentiality* and *mass action*. Equipotentiality held that complex functions such as learning or qualities such as intelligence were affected equally no matter where the cortical damage occurred. The principle of mass action held that all equipotential parts function as a unit and that the magnitude of loss of cortical tissue was more important than its location in determining its behavioral effects.

The conviction that the brain was more

complicated than had been supposed by Gall and other early localizationists was also implicit in the work and thought of the outstanding clinical neurologist of the nineteenth century, J. Hughlings Jackson (1835–1911). He made major contributions both to understanding the ancient disorder of epilepsy and, more generally, to the understanding of psychological functioning and its relationship to brain structure. While some of his findings (for example, that particular brain diseases were related to particular behavioral manifestations) contributed to the localization viewpoint, his basic position on brain function was more complicated and was influenced by Herbert Spencer (1820–1903), a philosopher, and Thomas Laycock (1812–1876), a physician and his former teacher. These men anticipated Darwin in suggesting that the human brain was the product of an evolutionary process. They believed that if the form of the nervous system resulted from gradual development, then the psychological processes, which are correlates of brain structure, must themselves have evolved by degrees.

Jackson described how such an evolutionary process could have taken place in the structure of the nervous system. He pointed out that the oldest levels of the brain and the spinal cord mediated simple reflex actions and were the most primitive structures of the nervous system. The next oldest region of the brain was the cerebellum which controlled motor behavior. Finally, the newest structures from the viewpoint of evolution were the frontal lobes. The frontal lobes are the most complex brain structures and the ones most involved in higher mentation processes, such as thinking abstractly and using symbols. Jackson felt that no matter where the brain was injured, the most profoundly affected centers were the complex ones, which were

the last to evolve. He also believed that the higher centers exercised an inhibiting influence over lower ones; thus, when their function was disrupted, archaic behavior patterns were manifested more readily.

Jackson's theories were based on observations from his clinical work. Some of his theoretical propositions were later verified experimentally by Sherrington (1857–1952). The latter, for example, found that removal of higher brain centers in animals led to greater responsivity in the spinal cord. This demonstrated the inhibitory effects of higher brain centers on lower ones.

Jackson's work was extended in the twentieth century by Kurt Goldstein, whose wide experience as a neurologist with brain-injured soldiers during World War I led him to develop an "organismic approach." At the heart of this position is the view that symptoms result from an unsuccessful struggle, by a sick organism, to adjust in the face of simultaneous pressures deriving from its own limitations and the demands being made upon it. For Goldstein, symptoms were only partially understandable on the basis of the dysfunction of a segment of the brain. He reasoned that one must also consider the person in whom symptoms appear and that such symptoms must be understood as the overall response of a unique and struggling individual.

Goldstein later extended this theorizing to psychopathological processes in general. He stressed that, for the brain-injured person, the most general loss resulting from damage (wherever it occurred) was in the capacity to assume the *abstract attitude*. He distinguished between concrete and abstract attitudes, describing the former as taking cognizance only of the immediate demands of a situation. For example, we enter a dark room and automatically switch on the light. When we think abstractly, however, we transcend immediate demands and assume a broader, reflective viewpoint. For example, on entering the dark room we may consider that putting on the light may disturb someone asleep in the room—so we refrain. The healthy individual uses both attitudes. Much that is done routinely requires only the concrete attitude. On the other hand, in a great many situations one must think abstractly in order to behave most effectively. For Goldstein, the essential defect in the brain-injured is the loss of ability to shift from concrete to abstract forms of thought and behavior. This is because abstraction, the highest and most recently evolved of mental processes, is the first to be affected by nervous system damage.

The specific way in which loss of abstraction will show itself is a function of the uniqueness of the individual and his particular experiences. Where abstract function has been part of a well-learned response pattern, and thus has become routinized, brain damage is less likely to interfere. However, in novel situations requiring the same degree of abstracting ability he is likely to fail.

Goldstein has been criticized for emphasizing symptoms relating to higher level functioning and for largely ignoring more specific sensory defects that are generally thought to derive from the location and extent of a brain lesion. He has countered this criticism by pointing out that his organismic approach does not ignore such lower-level symptoms but, in applying it to special problems like aphasia—which has been regarded primarily as loss of the higher level ability to symbolize—some workers have ignored the contributions of motor and sensory defects to the problem.

One way of evaluating the long-standing controversy between the localizationists and those who see the brain as a more complicated mechanism is to say that both

groups are partly correct. Some relatively simple functions seem to be related to specific areas of the brain while certain more complex functions seem to depend on an intact brain. When specific brain disorders are discussed later in this chapter, the symptoms attributable to the sheer fact of brain injury as well as its locus and extent will be described.

CONQUEST OF GENERAL PARESIS

Another source of reinforcement for the strict organicists was the conquest of a disease known at first as *general paralysis* (a stark description of the symptoms of its extreme state) and, later, as *general paresis*. This disorder first appeared in Europe after Columbus's return from the new world at the end of the fifteenth century. The development of a clinical picture of paresis as a separate disease was rather slow. In 1672 Thomas Willis observed that some patients exhibited "dullness of the mind and forgetfulness" followed by "stupidity and foolishness," and that "they would afterward fall into paralysis." In 1798 Haslam mentioned the same disorder and by the early part of the nineteenth century it was widely noted. Esquirol and his students became interested in general paresis and described its basic features quite accurately. Essentially, it involved a progressive paralysis nearly always accompanied by a deterioration of mental processes.

Three stages of the disorder were carefully described by Bayle in 1826. In the first, patients were characterized as displaying "the peculiar ambitious variety of mental illness." The primary symptoms of the second stage were "a more or less general mental derangement, with predominance of ideas of ambitious character, and a state of excitement, agitation or fury with some more or less obvious traces of incomplete paralysis." Finally, the third stage was depicted thus: ". . . a very considerable enfeeblement of the intellectual facilities, a more or less extensive obliteration of ideas, with a predominance of those relating to wealth and grandeur, and by an incomplete and general paralysis." This description by Bayle stimulated a search for the organic basis of this disorder.

Those who first wrote about general paralysis suspected that syphilis was involved in its etiology. Objections were raised to this view, most notably by Griesinger, the great psychiatric authority of the time, who observed that general paralysis occurred in cases in which there were "no traces of a former syphilitic infection." Griesinger was not troubled by the fact that the disorder occurred more commonly in men than in women, believing that this could just as readily reflect men's "more frequent excesses in spiritous liquors and in venery" and perhaps also their "greater use of strong cigars and strong coffee." Griesinger notwithstanding, the suspicion remained that syphilis was involved. Introduction of the use of the microscope to study brain pathology in the mid-nineteenth century slowly led to an accumulation of evidence substantiating this view. Also, more careful history-taking with paretic patients revealed a higher than normal percentage with earlier syphilitic infections.

In 1897, Krafft-Ebing carried out an important study on the relation of syphilitic infection to paresis by injecting nine paretics, each of whom had failed to report a history of syphilis, with the syphilis-producing virus. When none of the nine patients developed secondary symptoms, Krafft-Ebing concluded that they had,

without question, suffered an earlier infection.

Development of laboratory procedures for diagnosing organic disease also contributed to the eventual solution of the riddle of general paresis. Studies of the cerebrospinal fluid differentiated paresis from other diseases, and, in 1906, Wasserman perfected a blood test for detecting the presence of syphilitic antibodies. When over 90 percent of paretics were found to react positively on the Wasserman test, the link between syphilis and paresis was firmly established. This link was secured completely when the syphilitic organism was discovered and first isolated in the pia of the brains of congenital syphilitics in 1907 and later in the paretic brain itself by Noguchi and Moore in 1913.

Early treatment procedures for paresis were indistinguishable from those applied to other psychological or organic disorders. Prognosis was poor, with death the typical outcome. Bayle recommended procedures that would ameliorate "the inflammation of the meninges." Preventive measures (such as alcoholic abstinence and prohibition from marriage) were suggested for those thought to be hereditarily predisposed to paresis. Specific treatment techniques developed to combat syphilis were increasingly applied to paretics as the etiological relationship between the two conditions was recognized. None of these, however, was effective with paretics.

Eventually, the observation, dating back at least to Hippocrates, that a serious illness could sometimes be alleviated by the contraction of another less serious one was invoked in the treatment of paresis. This approach was stimulated by occasional reports during the nineteenth century of the arrest of paresis following the accidental contraction of a malarial fever. Thus, in 1917, Wagner-Jauregg, 30 years after he had begun working with fever-producing agents in an attempt to cure paresis, undertook a crucial experiment. He infected nine paretics with malaria and found that six received definite benefit from the treatment. Breutsch (1959) has attributed the effectiveness of malaria therapy to the fact that it "stimulates the defensive powers of the host by activating reticuloendothelial cells." This work of Wagner-Jauregg was so highly regarded that he received the Nobel Prize for it in 1927—the only psychiatrist ever to be so honored.

In the 1940s, penicillin was found to act directly on the syphilitic organism and to destroy it. Since then, a very high proportion of paretics have been treated successfully with this drug. Malzberg's (1959) statistics on the steadily declining rate of first admissions to New York State hospitals of patients with general paresis is impressive testimony to the conquest, by an organic approach, of what had been a major mental disorder of its time.

DISCOVERY OF THE CONDITIONED REFLEX

The work of the Russian physiologists of the late nineteenth and early twentieth centuries was an important contribution to the effort to link behavior to neurophysiology. I. M. Sechenov (1825–1905), who is regarded as the father of Russian physiology, believed that the human body, in which the nervous system was the central regulator, could be compared to a machine. For him thinking was dependent upon external stimulation and "all acts of conscious or unconscious life are reflexes." Sechenov was also interested in neural action and, like Jackson, believed that spinal reflexes are normally inhibited in their action by the cerebral cortex.

I. P. Pavlov, discoverer of conditioned reflex.

I. P. Pavlov (1849–1936), best known of the Russian physiologists, was strongly influenced by Sechenov. After discovering the secretory nerves of the pancreas—for which he received the Nobel Prize in 1904 —he began his renowned studies of digestive functions. This work led to the finding that animals secreted digestive fluids in anticipation of food. Discovery of the conditioned reflex followed shortly thereafter when Pavlov observed that an originally neutral stimulus such as a bell could, by itself, elicit salivation (an unconditioned reflex) merely by repetitive association with a stimulus which typically caused salivation (such as food). This was a truly significant finding in that it provided a methodology—other than introspection— for determining what an organism perceived or discriminated. Boring (1950) looked upon this as a language that occurred entirely on the objective level of stimulus, nerve action, and response, thereby bypassing the need to assume anything about consciousness. Pavlov believed that even the higher cerebral processes could be understood as elaborations of conditioned reflexes; hence, the latter were viewed as the building blocks of all psychic processes. Along with Sechenov and J. Hughlings Jackson, Pavlov was persuaded that higher mental processes, like thought, required the inhibition of lower reflexes.

Pavlov ultimately developed a mechanistic theory of personality based on the view that different individuals dealt with noxious stimuli in accord with the structure of their nervous systems. He typed people as melancholic, choleric (exhibiting "both strong excitatory and inhibiting tendencies," with the former predominating), phlegmatic (those who had "rigid" reflexes), and sanguine (those whose nervous systems manifested much lability). This typology is the ancient Hippocratic system cloaked in new mechanistic garb. Pavlov's theory of personality did not gain wide acceptance outside Russia. On the other hand, his work on the conditioned reflex has been highly influential throughout the world, certainly so in the area of learning, to a considerable extent in objective approaches to the study of behavior, and, most recently, in the behavior-modification approach within psychotherapy.

BIOCHEMICAL APPROACHES TO BEHAVIOR DISORDER

Many have felt that behavior disorder could be understood on the basis of biochemical imbalance. In this section, several examples are presented in which such imbalances have been identified and where their rectification has resulted in improved functioning.

Work with diseases stemming from nutritional deficiencies has served as a model for treatment of general mental disorder by organic means. Pellagra, for example, is a disorder in which a variety of mental symptoms may be manifested, depending on the individual. In 1917 a dietary origin of pellagra was discovered and in 1937 it was established that administration of the vitamin niacin relieved the mental symptoms.

Equally impressive has been work done on *phenylpruvic oligophrenia,* a condition of profound intellectual retardation that accounts for about 1 percent of all diagnosed mental defectives. In the mid-1930s, some defective children were found to have a metabolic dysfunction resulting in the urinary excretion of phenylpyruvic acid. This was due to the absence of an enzyme necessary for metabolic processes. Although the precise relationship between the metabolic failure and the retardation has not been established, early treatment with the missing enzyme can successfully arrest further development of phenylpyruvic oligophrenia.

Another disorder characterized by retarded mental and physical development—cretinism—has been found to result from hyposecretion of the thyroid gland. Early hormone treatment for this condition often results in marked physical changes as well as elevations in intelligence. Even with such treatment, however, cretins rarely achieve normal IQs.

This brief survey by no means exhausts the work being done to understand abnormal behavior on an organic basis. It has not included the contributions of organically oriented workers actively attempting to unravel the mysteries of schizophrenia; these will be considered in a later section on schizophrenia so that such work can be viewed in its proper context. The rest of this chapter will consider mental disorders known to be directly caused by impaired brain functioning.

TABLE 4.1
Biochemical Dysfunctions Causing Behavior Disorders

CONDITION	SYMPTOMS	CAUSE	TREATMENT
Phenylpyruvic Oligophrenia	1. Mental and motor retardation 2. Lack of speech 3. EEG abnormalities and sometimes convulsions 4. Dwarfism	Deficiency of an enzyme	Restricted diet and administration of the missing enzyme
Cretinism (Hypothyroidism)	1. Dwarfism 2. Coarse, puffy features 3. Abdominal distention 4. Mental retardation	Undersecretion of thyroid gland	Hormone treatment
Galactosemia	1. Retardation of growth and development 2. Mental retardation	Defect in carbohydrate metabolism	Removal of galactose substances from diet
Gargoylism	1. Enlarged head 2. Protruding forehead 3. Stunted body	Generalized enzyme disease	No known treatment

GENERAL EFFECTS
OF BRAIN DAMAGE

As has already been noted, particularly in higher and more recently evolved brain processes, certain general effects of brain damage are readily observed regardless of the cause or location of the injury. One such general effect is confusion, resulting in impairment of *orientation*. Orientation has been defined as ". . . the process by which one apprehends his environment and locates himself in it" (Noyes & Kolb, 1963, p. 88). When impairment of this function occurs, the individual may lose track of time, be unaware of his specific, or even his general, location, or fail to recognize his relationship to people around him. Accordingly, assessment of the patient's ori-

entation for "time, place, and person" is of particular importance whenever brain damage is suspected. Disorientation is symptomatic of many acute states of cerebral insufficiency, transient conditions of intense emotional conflict, and instances of loss of interest in one's surroundings.

Another higher function often impaired in cases of brain damage is memory. Memory is, of course, a complex process involving the collection, storage, and appropriate recall of information. Its adaptive function is considerable in that it enables the individual to profit from his experiences. Typically in cases of brain damage, it is memory for recent events, tested by such questions as "Why are you in the hospital?" and "What did you have for breakfast?," that is most disrupted. Remote memory, recollection of facts from the distant past, is generally more nearly intact. Brain-damaged patients often try to deny memory loss by confabulation—making up stories to imply that their memory is sound.

Complex intellectual functions, such as the ability to calculate and to comprehend, and the learning of new materials, are also weakened in brain-injured patients. Often, too, such patients find it difficult to exercise "good judgment." This is manifested by the inability to grasp ideas, to understand how ideas interrelate, and to reach accurate conclusions from this process.

Finally, there is a noticeable change in the way the organically impaired react affectively. They often respond emotionally like small children. Their feelings are labile and lacking in depth and intensity. Like the child, they are quick to tears and equally quick in changing from feeling devastated to being extremely pleased and carefree.

These primary symptoms may be mild, moderate, or severe, depending upon the extent of the brain injury. Other less common behavioral symptoms may also be seen, depending upon the patient's personality structure, his life situation, and the nature of the brain damage. Such symptoms may resemble those of neurosis or even psychosis. They represent the psychological reactions that the patient would have had to any stressful stimuli.

The demands posed by the loss of function that follows damage to the nervous system may be looked upon as a form of stress. If the damage occurs gradually enough, the afflicted individual may adapt well, both physiologically and psychologically, without manifesting serious malfunction. This is more likely to be the case for those with a relatively successful history of adaptive coping with stress. Those with histories of marginal adjustment, however, often have difficulty in adapting even

to objectively minor disruptions of brain function. Sudden insult to the nervous system is typically more difficult to accommodate to than is gradual decline. Again, however, it is the flexible, adaptive personality who is better able to adjust to serious loss of function and is less likely to display severe psychological symptoms. A relevant fact that should be remembered in any discussion of the impact of brain injury is the environment in which the individual lives. A supportive environment eases the adaptation that must be made. Thus, both the premorbid personality of the patient and his life circumstances interact with the nature, site, and extent of the brain damage to shape his overall psychological response.

With these general remarks as a prelude, we may now consider the classification of organic syndromes and provide a fuller description of some of the more common ones.

GROSS CLASSIFICATION OF BRAIN DISORDERS

One simple way of categorizing organic brain syndromes is based on whether or not the defect is reversible. Brain tissue does not regenerate or heal as does tissue in other parts of the body. Accordingly, brain lesions (abnormal structural changes) involve permanent damage, and whatever recovery of function takes place requires a reorganization so that intact areas assume functions formerly served by the impaired ones. There are some conditions, however, that interfere with normal brain function without causing permanent damage. Symptoms arising from such conditions are entirely reversible.

To this clearcut differentiation between the two orders of brain dysfunction, a qualification must be added. There are some nervous system dysfunctions with considerable acute symptomatology that clear up substantially with proper treatment, only to leave a chronic residue. Conversely, there are chronic brain conditions with periodic acute flare-ups. Practically, then, the distinction between acute and chronic brain syndromes is often difficult to make, even though differences between these two states are theoretically straightforward.

In DSM-I (1952) the chronic-acute distinction was the prime subdivision of the organic disorders; hence, organic disorders were specified as *chronic brain syndromes* or *acute brain syndromes*. In DSM-II (1968) the emphasis shifted to a different dimension. In the latter source a major distinction is made between *psychotic* and *nonpsychotic conditions*. The acute-chronic dimension is retained through qualifying phrases added to a diagnosis, but the primary differentiation is made between organic disorders resulting in psychosis (defined in terms of the individual's inability to manage the usual demands of life because of mood changes and deficiencies in perception, language, and memory) as opposed to those resulting in a less serious psychological condition. Should a psychotic state arise during a given episode, whether or not it persists, the condition is considered to be a psychotic one.

Below are listed the major diagnostic groups and subgroups of organic brain syndromes of psychotic proportions according to the agents or conditions causing the disorder as given in DSM-II (1968). In each major category prominent examples are discussed in detail.

Classification by Causative Factors

Senile and Presenile Dementia

Senile brain disease is associated with the aging process. This disorder, affecting significant numbers of old people, accounts

---

CASE 4–1:　A CASE OF SENILE PSYCHOSIS

Sarah J., an eighty-one-year-old widow, was admitted to a state hospital on the West Coast by her eldest son, with whose family she had been residing for only four months. Prior to that time she and her husband, a retired banker, resided in the family home that they had moved into when they married.

When she was admitted, Sarah was unable to give a very coherent history, and what little personal background was obtained came from relatives whose knowledge was sketchy. It was known that Sarah was an only child born to an immigrant couple after they had migrated from Central Europe to the West Coast of the United States. Her father was trained as a physician and was able to resume the practice of medicine in America, making a comfortable living. As an only child Sarah received much attention from her parents and never wanted for material objects. Eschewing a college education, Sarah chose to marry a few years after graduating from high school. She chose for a husband a man who was ten years her senior and who was already well established in the business community.

*　　*　　*

For the fifteen years prior to her hospitalization Sarah and her husband lived uneventful lives in retirement. In the few years before admission Sarah displayed occasional memory lapses, as when she would prepare dinner on evenings when she and her husband had agreed to eat at the home of one of their children. About seven months prior to her hospital admission Sarah's husband, by now in his early nineties, suffered a heart attack, and subsequent to this Sarah began to deteriorate noticeably. Her husband seemed to recover for a time, but upon his death four months after the heart attack, Sarah had to be moved to the home of her eldest son, and it was then abundantly apparent that she was generally confused about her whereabouts and very forgetful. Within a few weeks she began insisting that her husband was not dead, but was expecting her to return to him, and that he was awaiting her in the old home they had shared for so many years. She failed to recognize her daughter-in-law or her grandchildren, insisting they were strangers. She occasionally grew very angry with her son because he disagreed with these ideas, and she grew so violent she had to be restrained. Her son and his wife grew particularly concerned when Sarah slipped out of the house on a midwinter evening intending to walk the seven miles to her old home. After this incident the family doctor was consulted and he recommended her hospitalization.

When she was seen in the hospital Sarah appeared relatively comfortable, except when she would inappropriately interject questions like "Have you found out what they did with my china?" She talked freely and was friendly but often was completely incoherent. She could not state the date and, although she knew she was in a hospital, was not aware that it was in the same city where she had lived most of her life. Her memory was poor for both recent and many remote events, so that she could not give her correct age or the year in which she was born. Neither did she know how long she was married, the address of her home, or her phone number. Sarah could not name the then current president of the United States or the doctors or nurses to whom she had just been introduced. When asked to name a large river in the United States she replied the "River William." This disorganization extended to her ability to do even the simplest of calculations, and she was totally unable to grasp the point of proverbs or to form abstractions.

Sarah remained hospitalized for the remaining three years of her life. During this time there was no essential change in her condition.

for a large proportion of first admissions to mental hospitals (up to 40 percent of first admissions to New York State mental hospitals in recent years). Malzberg (1959) points out that the rate of increase of senile patients and cerebral arteriosclerotics is higher than that of individuals 45 years old and over. He argues that previously, when life expectancy was lower, the person who reached middle age was from a constitutionally select group and could better withstand the degenerative processes of later life. Improved medical practices, however, have lengthened the life-span of physically less select people who are, therefore, more susceptible to the disorders of old age. These disorders are not yet well enough understood for effective therapies to have been developed.

In senile brain disease, structural damage is centered in the nerve cells and fibers rather than, as with cerebral arteriosclerosis, in the vascular system. Both types of damage may occur in the same individual but, strictly speaking, senility refers to atrophy of the cerebral cortex in which the frontal lobes of the brain take on a wrinkled appearance and histopathological studies reveal a reduction in the number of brain cells.

The symptoms of senile brain disease are best viewed as exaggerations of behavioral and psychological changes that are seen in many, but far from all, people as they grow older. Memory and the ability to perform mental functions quickly and learn new things may show a gradual decline. Perhaps because of these changes, older people tend to assume a somewhat conservative view of life; they become less tolerant of new ideas than they used to be; they look back at the past a good deal and revere it, and they may become rigid and doctrinaire. Change is difficult for them to accept and the ambition and drive that may have characterized their youth tend to disappear. Not uncommon is an increasing self-centeredness, with a corresponding decrease of warmth and spontaneity toward others. There may be a slowing down so that even routine activities take longer than they once did. As these attributes become markedly accentuated in a given individual, there is increased likelihood that the diagnosis of senile psychosis will be entertained. It is not easy to specify the point in the sequence at which the diagnosis will be made since this depends upon many factors. Rarely, however, is the diagnosis of senile psychosis made before the patient has reached 60.

As the condition progresses, memory, especially for recent events, worsens. The victim dwells on ideas from the past that are overlearned, due either to repetition

Senile Dementia (From *A Psychiatrist's Anthology*, by Louis J. Karnosh, published in 1942 by the Occupational Therapy Press, Cleveland City Hospital. Reprinted with permission of the author.)

or because they are emotionally tinged. Advanced senile deterioration obliterates even such memories and takes the individual further and further back toward his early childhood. Thus such things as the death of a loved one or even the names of one's spouse or children may be forgotten. Orientation becomes progressively poorer and confusion increases. He loses track of time and place or his own age. Because he is unaware of the passage of time, he may arise during the night and wander about. In the dark he is even more confused than normally, and develops illusions about his surroundings. The memory defect coupled with confusion causes him to mistake fantasy and dreams for reality. This intermingling of inner and outer stimuli is aggravated by the fact that the severely senile individual tends to sleep only a few hours at a time, with intermittent periods of wakefulness.

The senile psychotic is often depressed, with self-pity and self-accusatory delusions; anxiety and suicidal impulses are often manifested. Others resent their surroundings, are irritable, feel betrayed by their families, and display frankly paranoid delusions. Senile patients frequently neglect normal personal hygiene, engage in petty thefts, become profane or sexually exhibitionistic, or even attempt to act out sexually.

The onset of senile psychosis is almost always gradual. Sometimes the victim of this condition is able to withstand the physiological changes making for senility until some significant environmental event such as retirement or the death of a spouse undermines the adjustment and sets off more rapid decline. Generally, the healthier the lifetime pattern of adjustment of the individual, the greater is the likelihood of that individual's withstanding the deleterious effects of the aging process.

The category *presenile dementia* includes brain disorders such as Alzhesimer's and Pick's diseases that present clinical pictures similar to those seen in senile dementia. Presenile disorders, however, arise in individuals who are much younger than the typical senile patients and each disorder is attributable to specific brain pathology.

Alcoholic Psychosis

Within this general class, several alcohol-induced disorders are listed as subcategories. These include the following: *delirium tremens; Korsakov's psychosis, other alcoholic hallucinosis; alcohol paranoid state; acute alcohol deterioration;* and *pathological intoxication.*

All disorders in this category involve the disruption of normal cerebral metabolism by toxic substances. In intoxication, however, the toxic substance is neither a virus nor a by-product of another disease but, rather, some substance taken internally. Intoxication may occur as a complication of drug therapy, from instances of incorrect self-medication or attempts to end one's life with drugs. A variety of substances such as barbiturates, bromides, cortisone, sympathomimetic amines (Benzedrine, Dexedrine, and Desoxyn) can affect brain functioning; each produces a specific clinical picture.

By far the most common form of intoxication is that associated with the consumption of alcohol. Later in this book alcoholism is discussed as an addiction; the present attention is on the effects alcohol can have on brain function. The body absorbs alcohol from the gastrointestinal tract more rapidly than it can be broken down and eliminated. It therefore accumulates in the bloodstream in concentrations that can affect all of the body's cells; its effects are most marked, however, on brain functioning. The mechanics of alcohol's influence on the workings of the brain are not well understood, although it is known to act as a depressant rather than a stimulant (as most laymen believe). Brain functions initially depressed by alcohol are those controlled by higher cortical centers: memory, judgment, and learning. Depression of higher centers reduces their inhibitory control over lower ones, thus accounting for the "high" feeling that many people experience after drinking too much. Continued drinking, however, leads to depression of lower brain functions and eventually can result in inhibition of brain centers controlling breathing and the heart-beat.

The two brain disorders most commonly associated with acute alcoholic intoxication are *delirium tremens* and *acute alcoholic hallucinosis*. These conditions result from the direct action of alcohol on the brain rather than from secondary effects mediated by alcohol-associated, nutritional deficiencies. Delirium tremens may arise during, or in the terminal stages of, a drinking bout, and it is characterized by dramatic, disquieting symptomatology. The victim perspires profusely, feels generally weak, and may become delirious even while maintaining partial contact with the environment. Visual hallucinations, often bizarre, are so common to this condition that they have become an identifying hallmark. The victim may see creatures doing terrible things or even trying to kill him, and he may attempt to flee or even to commit suicide. Auditory hallucinations occur only rarely in delirium tremens and consist of threatening words or phrases. Tactual hallucinations, such as feeling insects crawling on one's skin, sometimes also occur.

Acute alcoholic hallucinosis develops gradually during a drinking bout. Its only symptom is auditory hallucinations, in which the victim feels he is being threat-

---

CASE 4–2: A CASE OF ACUTE ALCOHOLIC HALLUCINOSIS

Naomi L., a fifty-year-old married but childless woman, was brought to a large eastern hospital after having passed out in a bar during an alcoholic episode. She and her husband were living in a lower middle class neighborhood in that city.

*   *   *

The binge resulting in the current hospitalization began three weeks prior to admission, after a quarrel between her and her husband, and she drank continually until admission. During this time she had sexual relations for money to support her drinking with "someone"—a man she met in a bar; this made her husband furious. Naomi felt that his anger was unjustified, since she was too drunk to know what she had been doing.

When she entered the hospital she was markedly apprehensive, tremulous, and agitated, even though she had been on heavy dosages of paraldehyde. She spontaneously told the admitting physician that she would not remember his name on the following day, and didn't. She showed a marked startle reaction at the slightest noise and occasionally displayed large jerking movements in her extremities. Naomi heard voices calling her dirty names, and, if she closed her eyes, saw shadowy figures who frightened her. She felt as though people were talking about her and criticizing her, and she accused her husband of wanting to have her committed. However, she was oriented in all spheres, did not display any marked memory loss, and showed no significant physical or neurological findings.

Naomi was treated with paraldehyde and massive vitamin doses, and after her symptoms cleared up, signed herself out of the hospital against medical advice. She rejected all suggestions that she enter an outpatient treatment program, and returned to her husband and bottle.

From Zax & Stricker, 1963, pp. 282–283.

ened and accused of wrongdoings. Since there is no delirium associated with acute alcoholic hallucinosis, the victim often can continue to function adequately while experiencing the condition, and he may be able to hide his difficulties from outsiders indefinitely.

Nutritional deficiencies commonly result from chronic alcoholism. These can lead to serious disruption of brain function and even to permanent brain damage. Heavy drinkers neglect their health, eat irregularly, and nourish themselves poorly. This renders them vulnerable to conditions that may damage the brain. For example, brain metabolism takes place chiefly through the utilization of glucose. Glucose ordinarily breaks down to pyruvate, and this substance, in turn, is catalyzed in the presence of Vitamin B₁. When serious deficiencies of B₁ occur (as is often the case among chronic alcoholics), abnormally high levels of pyruvate collect in the blood. This condition disturbs the function of nerve cells and, unless forestalled, can lead to changes in cellular structure and to the actual destruction of neurons. There is some variation among individuals in the time of onset of such tissue changes, but the reasons for this variability are not well understood. There is also variation in the symptoms

that are manifested during the process of deterioration, probably as a function of which part of the nervous system is most affected.

One of the better known conditions of vitamin and dietary deficit associated with chronic alcoholism is *Korsakov's psychosis*. This condition is characterized by extreme deficiency in recent memory and a marked tendency for the patient, whose judgment is usually very poor, to attempt to cover up for this. Pathetic efforts are made to fill in gaps in order to hide, from oneself and others, the memory loss for recent and obvious events. Patients cannot even recall the stories they have just made up so that, in response to similar questions asked moments apart, they may give entirely different answers. Another prominent feature of this disorder is polyneuritis (inflammation of multiple nerves). Prognosis in Korsakov's psychosis is poor, and full recovery is rare.

Psychosis Associated with Intracranial Infection

Subgroups within this category include the following: *general paralysis; syphilis of the central nervous system; epidemic en-*

CASE 4–3: CHRONIC BRAIN DISORDER DUE TO ALCOHOLISM WITH SOME FEATURES OF KORSAKOV'S PSYCHOSIS

Amanda P., a forty-five-year-old married mother of three children, was referred to a large psychiatric center on the Pacific Coast, after a long history of alcoholism. She, her husband, and their children were living in a well-to-do neighborhood in a small community where he was socially prominent.

Amanda was the only child of an unhappily married couple in a large midwestern city. Her father died while she was still an infant, and her mother, who led a very active social life, did not want to be burdened with a child and gave her up for adoption. The family that reared her relegated her to a servant's role, satisfying all of her physical needs, but few of her emotional ones. From time to time, as she grew, she was visited by her real mother, and hence knew she was adopted. She was a bright student who did well in school, and was planning to enter a specialized secretarial training program when she received a letter from her mother asking her to go and live with her and her newly acquired husband. Although Amanda had not heard from her for over six years, she abandoned all her plans and went to join her mother. She was very unhappy with her mother and stepfather, and, when only eighteen, married an auto racer whom she had known less than a week. They had one child, who was tragically killed when he ran away from Amanda into the street and was run over. Shortly after the child's death, and after five years of a relatively happy marriage, her husband was involved in a crash during a race and was also killed. Amanda was thus left all alone, in California, where she knew nobody; nevertheless, she did not seem to be particularly grieved despite her plight.

Her second marriage to an up-and-coming young businessman was initially very happy, until he began to be involved in a variety of status-producing community activities. As he became more prominent he also became less attentive to Amanda, and this neglect, coupled with a painful operation shortly after the birth of her third child, marked the beginning of Amanda's excessive and repetitive drinking. She rapidly increased her consumption to over a quart of liquor a day, and neglected all responsibilities and other activities. As a result of her neglect of personal hygiene, her husband had not approached her sexually for over two years previous to her hospital admission. She stole money from one of her husband's many enterprises—a large dry cleaning establishment which she previously had helped manage quite successfully—and became involved in so many nasty situations with customers and employees that he had to ask her to remain at home. She also became a habitual liar, was exceedingly sloppy at home and in public, and discontinued all of her community activities. Finally, her husband brought her to the center for treatment.

On admission Amanda was confused, tearful, and almost completely disoriented. She suffered an almost total loss of recent memory, which she attempted to shield by falsifying details to fill in gaps. Upon physical examination she showed abnormal skin sensitivity and an exquisite tenderness of the feet, which suggested peripheral neuritis due to chronic alcoholism. Her liver was definitely damaged and there was strong suspicion that brain damage was present.

In her first few interviews she was unsure of the date, confused about the location of the doctor's office and unable to remember the names of the nurses. When asked to explain the meanings of several proverbs, her responses were somewhat concretistic and, at times, bizarre as when in giving the point behind the saying "Too many cooks spoil the broth," she replied, "Too many people mess in one septic tank; wind up with nothing."

After a period of a few months Amanda's confusion and disorientation had cleared, and when she promised not to drink any more she was released. A follow-up interview one year later disclosed that she had kept her promise, but although she no longer drank, things were very much as before regarding her personal habits and morality. Her memory defects were still prominent and she seemed to suffer from a mild confusion.

From Zax & Stricker, 1963, pp. 287–289.

cephalitis; other and unspecified encephalitis; and *other intracranial infection.*

The category includes a small group of disorders caused by viral or bacterial infections in the brain tissue proper or in some other part of the central nervous system within the cranium. General paralysis and syphilis of the central nervous system are caused by a virus called *Spirochaeta pallida,* the virus associated with syphilis, while the various forms of encephalitis can be caused by many different viruses.

General paralysis is another name for *general paresis,* described earlier as figuring prominently in the history of man's struggle against mental disorder. In general paresis the syphilitic virus attacks brain tissue proper. In other cases it infects the outer coverings (meninges) or blood vessels of the brain. The designation "psychosis with other syphilis of the central nervous system" is used to describe the latter conditions.

Enchephalitis is also caused by viruses that invade brain tissue. The designation "psychosis with epidemic encephalitis" is reserved for infections involving a specific virus responsible for an encephalitis epidemic following World War I. Virtually no cases of this condition (sometimes called von Economo's encephalitis) have been reported since 1926. However, since it has distinct features it has been given a special designation. It is a condition that sometimes leads to acute delirium; on other occasions, however, its outstanding feature is an outward indifference to important events or people, ordinarily of considerable emotional significance to the patient. Sometimes, too, the patient is driven to engage in compulsive behavior.

The designation "psychosis with other and unspecified encephalitis" is used to describe all encephalitic infections other than that causing epidemic encephalitis.

The acute form of the disorder is often characterized by drowsiness and lack of energy; hence the popular term "sleeping sickness." Actually, however, acute encephalitis can also follow an entirely different course marked by restlessness, irritability, inability to sleep, and seizures, both local and generalized. The residuals of encephalitis among survivors vary, and include tremors (trembling) and tics (sudden involuntary muscular contractions), and, at times, athetoid (slow, involuntary, wormlike movements of the fingers, hands, toes, and feet). Typically, however, there is no intellectual impairment.

Encephalitis occurs more frequently among children than adults and the after-effects of the disease tend to be more serious among children. Some children undergo profound character change, with a once well-behaved child becoming a serious behavior problem. They may become overactive and impulsive, lose their inhibitions, or become very irritable. Antisocial behavior such as lying, stealing, and sexual misbehavior is not uncommon, nor is grossly cruel behavior. The relationship between these behaviors and the extent of neurological disorder is not well understood. However, degree of behavioral disorder is not correlated with apparent neurological impairment. Often, very young children contract encephalitis in conjunction with common childhood disorders such as mumps and measles. In such cases, intellectual impairment may be quite evident.

The category "psychosis with other intracranial infection" includes a variety of acute and chronic infections that are not caused by syphilitic or encephalitic viruses. Probably the most common disorder in this category is meningitis, which is caused by bacteria that inflame the meninges, the membranes covering the cerebral cortex. It may lead to a delirious state (described

CASE 4–4: ORGANIC BRAIN SYNDROME ASSOCIATED WITH ENCEPHALITIS

Betty L., a twenty-one-year-old single girl, was admitted to a large mid-western university hospital after an exacerbation of tantrum-like behavior which had been prominent for many years in a more moderate form. She lived with her parents in a middle-class neighborhood in the vicinity of the hospital.

Betty was the youngest of three children born to a socially alert family. Her father was an economics professor at the state university, and her mother, a former social worker, was active in many community betterment organizations. Both took pride in their children's accomplishments and were genuinely concerned over any impediments to their progress. The two older children, both boys, had been successful students and well-accepted members of the community, being active athletically and socially. Betty's oldest brother had recently completed medical school and had married a fine girl. The second of her brothers was a graduate student in sociology at a fine eastern university.

Betty's own social and educational progress was meager indeed when compared to that of her siblings. She had, unfortunately, been a sickly child, and almost from her infancy required a series of surgical operations. These involved the correction of sensory and orthopedic difficulties. By the age of eleven she was making satisfactory progress at school when she developed a severe case of measles. This was accompanied by an inflammation of the middle ear, a skin infection, vertigo, and nausea. Although she did not develop convulsions or meningitis she was diagnosed as having measles encephalitis.

Following this illness Betty began a rather isolated social life. Her academic record became mediocre and she had no friends. She tired very easily and hence was restricted to sedentary activities. During adolescence, when other girls were actively dating, Betty always stayed at home alone, feeling strange and different from the others. Her only companion for the past four years had been a Siamese cat which she constantly fondled, took with her everywhere, and could not tolerate to leave. She developed an intense fear of fire which manifested itself in crying even at the sight of a lighted match or a stove. While she had never been affectionate toward her parents, she cried and had temper tantrums if they left the house, and behaved similarly when strangers came to visit, thus severely restricting their social life. She had been in an almost continuous program of outpatient psychotherapeutic care from the age of fourteen, but this did not seem to affect her behavior in any way.

Shortly before hospitalization Betty began to have increasingly frequent outbursts of crying, screaming, and cursing. She told her parents that she wished they were dead and that the house would burn down. She told her father that she wished he would have a heart attack or die of cancer, hit her mother with a broom, and constantly threatened to run away. This began when she learned her eldest brother was to visit the family, and when she further learned that allergies of the brother's child would necessitate giving her cat to a veterinarian for the visit. From then on her tantrums were continual and uninterrupted.

At the time of hospitalization Betty was crying and agitated. She was tired and angry, and also appeared to be frightened by the hospital and depressed at being there. She was well oriented in all spheres, but very infantile as to her behavior and concerns. She viewed hospitalization as a punishment for being naughty, and expected to be released when she had atoned for her misbehavior. An EEG performed during this hospitalization was severely abnormal, and indicated diffuse brain damage.

After a short period in the hospital Betty had calmed down sufficiently to be released. Later contact with her family showed that this behavior continued unabated over a number of years and eventually required permanent institutionalization.

From Zax & Stricker, 1963, pp. 292–293.

---

below) that progresses to coma and death. In less severe cases, the delirium is milder and is often accompanied by drowsiness and confusion. Upon recovery there may be no residual symptomatology. However, in other cases—even mild ones—varying degrees of sensory impairment, paralysis, or mental defect may remain. Typical mental symptoms include difficulty in concentrating, irritability, and memory defect. When meningitis occurs in infants, it can result in a serious impairment of intellectual development.

Psychosis Associated with Other Cerebral Conditions

The subcategories of this group are as follows: *cerebral arteriosclerosis; other cerebrovascular disturbance; epilepsy; intracranial neoplasm; degenerative disease of the central nervous system;* and *brain trauma.*

As both this diagnostic label and its subgroups indicate, this category groups a number of diverse conditions with widely varying behavioral manifestations. Four of these—cerebral arteriosclerosis, epilepsy, intracranial neoplasm, and brain trauma— will be discussed in some detail. One of

the remaining two, "psychosis with other cerebrovascular disturbance," is applied to circulatory disorders attributable to thrombosis (blood clots), embolisms (occlusion of a blood vessel by undissolved material in the blood), hypertension (high blood pressure), and so forth. The other subcategory, "psychosis with degenerative disease of the central nervous system," is reserved for degenerative diseases the causes of which are uncertain or unknown.

Cerebral arteriosclerosis is a diagnostic label that was applied to 21 percent of the first admissions to New York State mental hospitals in 1950, indicating that it is a highly prevalent disorder. Noyes and Kolb (1963) point out that the term *arteriosclerosis,* referring as it does to a hardening of blood vessel walls, is a misnomer for this disease. The circulatory problem in this condition is caused not by hardening of arteries per se—a relatively benign process —but rather by a thickening of the vessel wall caused by deposits of fatty plaques leading to a narrowing, or complete occlusion, of the passage through which blood must flow. This condition, known as *atherosclerosis,* leads to disturbance in cellular metabolism and to the eventual death of cells. Atherosclerosis most commonly af-

"As the days dwindle down to a precious few,
I say to hell with everybody!"

fects older people (usual onset between ages 50 and 65), not because it results directly from aging but, rather, because it takes many years for the condition to reach a point where the blood circulation is seriously affected. Thus, as man's life span is lengthened by the conquest of diseases that might have caused an early demise, increase in the frequency of occurrence of cerebral arteriosclerosis is to be expected.

The behavioral symptoms of cerebral arteriosclerosis are varied since the condition may either have a gradual, insidious onset or a sudden and dramatic one, as, for example, following a stroke. Where onset is gradual, complaints of fatigue, headache, dizziness, and lessening of the ability to concentrate are typical. The arteriosclerotic may feel drowsy in the afternoon or evening and may show almost imperceptible changes in physical and mental abilities. The latter tend to be recognized only after they have accumulated over a period of time, when the patient is discerned as having undergone a change in personality. His initiative is lost; he is unable to pay attention for prolonged periods; his memory, especially for recent events, becomes poor; and he is affectively labile. He becomes less affectionate, neglects his personal appearance and cleanliness. These characterological changes also include either an exaggeration of psychological mechanisms, normally used to defend against anxiety, or giving in to formerly restrained, unacceptable impulses. Thus, paranoid features may become prominent in one who had formerly been only isolated and cautious, or a person who had shown some dependency may become markedly so.

When cerebral arteriosclerosis arises relatively suddenly, a period of confusion is the first obvious mental symptom. Consciousness is clouded and the victim is restless and incoherent. In advanced cases there may be minor strokes provoking periods of psychosis or delirium, or major strokes accompanied by aphasia or loss of function in the limbs.

Not uncommonly cerebral arteriosclerotics are aware, at least in the early stages of the disorder, of their decline in mental function. Such awareness is less common in those experiencing senile psychosis. This insight into his condition probably accounts for the greater discomfort and anxiety that the arteriosclerotic feels about his deterioration in comparison to the senile patient.

CASE 4–5:   A CASE OF CEREBRAL ARTERIOSCLEROSIS

Leo D., a sixty-eight-year-old father of two sons and one daughter, was admitted to the psychiatric ward of a private hospital in a large eastern metropolis. He was the owner of a very well-known furniture business which he had built up over the years and which he managed with the assistance of his eldest son. He and his second wife resided in a small but comfortable midtown apartment.

*   *   *

The illness which eventuated in Leo's hospitalization began to develop as the result of a combination of factors about six months before his admission. One of these involved a few business setbacks, the like of which had occurred in the past occasionally, but which somehow seemed more threatening at this time. Shortly after being beset by these concerns over business affairs, he suffered a mild stroke. There was some paralysis at first, but it subsided rapidly, leaving some mild residual symptomatology. While in the hospital with this condition he was prevailed upon by his daughter to see the son he had disowned. She indicated that things had gone very badly for the son, and he was barely able to earn a living for his small family. Leo grew anxious and depressed. He also had difficulty sleeping. When he made a partial recovery from his stroke he attemped to return to work, only to find that he tired very easily; he would come home exhausted, only to sleep restlessly. Gradually these symptoms worsened, his appetite diminished to the extent that he lost twenty pounds, and he began to feel quite self-depreciative. He brooded over past indiscretions, cried when alone, and blamed himself for his first wife's death and his son's sorry straits. Eventually he gave up trying to work and began hinting that he had suicidal ideas. At this point his family doctor, who had been following the case, recommended hospitalization.

When he was interviewed, Leo appeared to be a neat, distinguished-looking man who was alert and cooperative. He generally wore a stern expression mixed with occasional hints of sadness. A frequent theme of his remarks was the feeling that he had become old and did not feel capable of coping with situations as he once could. His orientation for time and place was good, but there appeared to be mild lapses of both recent and remote memory. Higher-level mental activities such as grasping the essence of proverbs and forming verbal abstractions were both quite impaired.

During a six-week hospital stay Leo was found to have an EEG pattern suggesting mild brain damage, and a few physical concomitants of that condition, such as an area of numbness on the right hand and an ataxic gait. His depression was treated with a series of five electric shocks, resulting in a marked improvement. He was discharged to the care of his family doctor.

From Zax & Stricker, 1963, pp. 298–300.

Epilepsy has been prominently mentioned in earlier chapters and is perhaps the first mental disorder to have been recognized. Despite this long history, the precise meaning of the term is becoming increasingly difficult to define simply. The concept of epilepsy has undergone much broadening over the years and now embraces considerably more diverse phenomena than it did in earlier times. From a purely behavioral viewpoint, the many forms of epilepsy have in common intermittent and relatively brief periods of disturbed consciousness, often, but not always, accompanied by seizures involving uncontrolled movements.

On a neurophysiological basis a simpler, and perhaps less questionable, definition is possible; epilepsy is a condition characterized by seizures stemming from excessive neuronal discharge within the nervous system. The anatomical pathology in all forms of epilepsy seems to be an area of grey matter in which circulation is defective. This can be caused by a variety of lesions including scar tissue, atrophy, tumor, and inflammation. The term *idiopathic epilepsy* is used to refer to instances in which the cerebral disorder causing epilepsy is unknown. As diagnostic procedures improve, cases labeled "idiopathic" decrease. It is questionable, therefore, whether such a category will continue to be useful as the disorder becomes better understood.

The reasons for the broadening of the concept of epilepsy merit consideration since they help to understand diverse behavioral phenomena now included under the term. Strauss (1959) points out that the first type of epilepsy to be noted was the *grand mal* attack; other phenomena later came to be designated as epileptic if they were related to a *grand mal* seizure in any one of the following ways: (1) if they were commonly seen in people who suffered *grand mal* seizures; (2) if they shared with *grand mal* seizures paroxysmal qualities, sudden onset, and brief duration; (3) if they appeared repeatedly; (4) if they resembled a part of the behavioral manifestation of a generalized seizure; or (5) if they involved manifestations resembling those seen either just before or just after a generalized seizure. This broadening of the concept of epilepsy came to encompass many purely psychiatric disturbances in people who never had seizures simply because their behavior had characteristics commonly seen in epileptics. The development of electroencephalography (EEG), a technique for measuring the electrical discharges given off by various parts of the cerebral cortex, led to further broadening of the concept. Through EEG testing, ab-

The nineteenth-century writer Fedor Dostoievsky was a victim of epilepsy.

normal discharges similar to those of epileptics were also found in some patients with migraine headaches, abdominal pain, psychotic symptoms, or other behavior disorders.

The symptoms of epilepsy are varied since they arise from organic defects in any of a number of areas of the brain. There are commonalities, however, which have prompted many attempts at symptom categorization. One frequent distinction is between focal and generalized seizures. The clinical picture of some seizures—for example, a twitching in an isolated part of the body—suggests that the abnormal electrical discharge in the brain is highly localized. By implication, the very general *grand mal* seizure was originally thought to arise from more general cortical discharge. Recent evidence, however, suggests

that, although the behavioral distinction between generalized and focal seizures may be valid, the etiological distinction between the two is questionable. *Grand mal* seizures themselves are now thought to arise from focal brain disturbances; in that sense, there may be no nonfocal seizures.

Certain prodromal (warning) signs, sometimes called the *aurae*, occur with sufficient frequency among epileptics to warrant citation. These signs, either motor, sensory, or psychic, typically occur before loss of consciousness, but not always soon enough to allow the epileptic to prepare for what is to come. They often involve visceral sensations such as a feeling of pressure moving upward from the pit of the stomach toward the head. Sometimes, the aura is not followed by any more general attack. For this reason many prefer to regard the aura as part of the seizure or as a minor attack in itself, rather than as a warning of an impending attack.

Epileptic seizures are generally classified into four major types. The most dramatic, best known, and most prevalent is the *grand mal* seizure. The frequency of attacks varies widely among individuals. The convulsion itself is a generalized one, sometimes ushered in by a characteristic cry, and starting with a stage in which the body becomes very tense and rigid. Typically, the trunk is extended, the head overextended backwards, the jaws are firmly closed, the fists are clenched tightly, the muscles are quite rigid, the eyes are open wide, and breathing is suspended. The face turns dark blue and the eyes are bloodshot. This stage, often referred to as the "tonic" stage, lasts anywhere from five to thirty seconds, and is followed by a "clonic" stage characterized by rapid alternation between the rigidity of the prior tonic phase and relaxation of the entire musculature. At the beginning of the clonic stage these alternations occur as frequently as twelve to four-teen times per second so that they resemble rapid, generalized tremors. Later, contractions and relaxations alternate only once or twice per second. Breathing becomes more normal during the later clonic stage, and the opening and closing of the jaws may produce a frothy foam around the mouth. The epileptic may be incontinent. Although virtually all patients are completely unconscious during the attack, a variety of patterns are seen at its end. Typically, although the body is covered with perspiration, there is a relaxation of the muscles and the bluish coloring of the face disappears. Whereas some individuals are then able to rise feeling perfectly well, many more sleep for varying periods of time. Some awake with headache and nausea and many have aching muscles for days.

Another classical type of epileptic attack, the *petit mal* seizure, is not typically preceded by an aura; rather, it involves dimming of consciousness in which the patient becomes totally or largely unaware of what is happening around him. Some hear things that are being said but cannot understand them. There is complete immobility except for minor movements such as fluttering of the eyelids. The *petit mal* victim appears pale and stares without fixating on any point. If the seizure has its onset while he is doing something, he stops so that, if eating, he may spill his food or drop the glass he was raising to his lips. *Petit mal* seizures sometimes last no longer than one second and rarely exceed thirty or forty seconds. Thus, at times they are so brief that patients are not aware that they have occurred. In other instances, the victim recognizes the attack but conceals it from observers. As in the case of the *grand mal* seizure, attacks vary considerably in frequency.

The *psychomotor seizure*, also known as

the *twilight state*, is another form of epileptic attack. Some twilight states occur as the aftermath of a *grand mal* seizure; in this condition, the epileptic is confused for anywhere from a few minutes to several days. During such periods of disturbed consciousness, the patient can move about and talk with little sign of impairment. Other twilight states, which are called psychomotor seizures, are not preceded by *grand mal* attacks; in fact, they usually start without prior warning signs. The epileptic is also disoriented during this type of seizure and is either totally oblivious to his surroundings or only partially aware of them. This disorder takes a variety of forms. Some people experience only brief periods (five to ten minutes) during which they either remain quite still or else move about aimlessly or mumble without reacting to outside stimuli. For these individuals, either full and clear consciousness returns quickly or there are several more minutes of drowsiness and difficulty in thinking. Others seem more normal, at least superficially, during the psychomotor seizure. They are able to continue what they were doing before the seizure (such as walking in the street) without appearing "peculiar," even though they may appear somewhat more mechanical. Not uncommonly, upon return to full awareness, they find themselves far from where they were at the onset of the attack without remembering how they got there. Thus, it is possible for seizure victims to take long trips with only the vaguest recollection of how they got where they did. During such a twilight state the patient, despite his normal appearance, may be of some danger to himself or others by causing accidents or committing crimes.

It has been theorized that the psychomotor seizure results from a cerebral disturbance within a center of the brain which is essential for maintaining a normal state of consciousness. When a twilight state follows a paroxysmal discharge, as in *grand mal*, it may result from a paralysis of this system. In the case of pure psychomotor seizures, however, this area is itself thought to be the seat of paroxysmal discharges.

A fourth type of epileptic seizure, *Jacksonian seizure*, is so named because it was first described by the eminent neurologist, J. Hughlings Jackson. Jacksonian seizures originate in and are restricted to certain parts of the body and involve tonic or clonic phenomena as in *grand mal*. They may remain limited to their area of origin or may spread, eventuating in a generalized seizure like *grand mal*.

Treatment of epileptic disorders depends on their specific causes. Where the cause is acute, as in the case of a tumor or syphilitic infection, therapy is directed toward the causative agents. In a majority of cases, however, epilepsy is chronic, in which case it is treated with drugs, and the epileptic is advised to avoid irritants, such as alcohol or fatigue, that can lead to seizures.

An *intracranial neoplasm*, or tumor, is a growth within the cranium. Since the skull is an unyielding container, a new growth in the brain may cause a variety of symptoms. Some are related to the pressure exerted on the entire surface of the brain by the tumor; others result from damage produced in specific brain locations by the pressure that the tumor exerts. Psychological symptoms of tumors vary widely, depending both on the nature of the brain damage and the patient's personality. Typically, there is an exaggeration of the patient's normal defensive style; not infrequently, however, tumor sufferers become uninhibited, ill-mannered, and immoral. Many of the memory and cognitive defects that characterize other brain syndromes are also found among tumor patients. More specific symptomatology is related to the location of the tumor and its rate of growth.

At times the mental symptoms caused by tumors are mistakenly seen as psychoses of psychogenic origin. Accordingly, the death rate in mental hospitals for patients suffering brain tumors is nearly double that in general hospitals. This underscores the importance of prompt and accurate diagnosis in such cases. The treatment of choice in tumor cases is surgery. Residual symptoms, and the form they take, depend on how much brain tissue is removed in the process of removing the tumor, the location of permanent lesions, and the adjustive capacities of the patient.

Physical injury to the brain, or brain trauma, may cause acute or chronic brain syndromes, depending on the nature and extent of the injury. In mild cases of concussion in which cerebral processes are only momentarily interrupted, recovery tends to be rapid and complete. When the brain surface is bruised (contusion) or torn (laceration), acute symptoms are more severe and chronic sequelae are not uncommon.

Acute disorders due to head injury may be grouped in four categories; the first of these is called the *concussion syndrome* (Noyes & Kolb, 1963). This is characterized by a loss of consciousness lasting from a few minutes to a few hours, often followed by memory loss for the events immediately preceding the concussion. There is no apparent relationship between the duration of unconsciousness and the severity of residual symptomatology. Typically, recovery does not take long and is complete. The prize fighter who is knocked out exemplifies the concussion syndrome.

The second category of acute reaction to brain injury is the *traumatic coma*. In this case the victim is unconscious for several hours and possibly for several days,

CASE 4–6:   ORGANIC BRAIN SYNDROME DUE TO BRAIN TRAUMA, WITH RECOVERY

Wayne T., a nineteen-year-old single man, was admitted to a general hospital in the Southwest, four days after having sustained a concussion. He was employed as a laborer in the oil fields and lived with his parents and three siblings in one of the best neighborhoods in the small city in which he grew up.

*   *   *

About four days before his hospitalization, Wayne engaged in a barroom quarrel over a girl and in the course of this was knocked down, striking his head on the hard floor. He was dazed briefly but suffered no other symptoms. When he was brought home his parents insisted upon a physical examination, to which he acquiesced. At that time the findings, including those of the X-rays which were done, were negative. The next day, however, Wayne began complaining of a strange feeling of a change of pressure in his ears such as one experiences upon driving in mountainous regions. This was more a strange and annoying sensation than a painful one. He also complained of feeling foggy and vaguely restless. His ability to concentrate was impaired, so that he tended to lose sight of his goal in dealing with a task and found himself repeating meaningless operations. Finally his time sense was disturbed, and recent events were often subjectively experienced as being from the distant past, while remote ones often seemed as though they had just occurred. When this complex of symptoms failed to subside after three days Wayne's physician prevailed upon him to enter a hospital for observation.

When he was examined Wayne appeared comfortable and cooperative. He seemed able to concentrate on the interview with some effort, but from time to time he had to rub his eyes or pick at his ears and seemed restless. He admitted that he felt "edgy." There seemed to be only mild impairment in superficial intellectual functions but he found it necessary to heighten his effort noticeably to perform many relatively simple memory tasks. Wayne's electroencephalogram was taken the day after his hospital admission and revealed an abnormality which was consistent with a post-traumatic state. During his hospital stay this procedure was repeated three times at four- or five-day intervals. Improvement was noted in each and the last electroencephalogram was essentially normal.

During this stay in the hospital Wayne was treated with sedatives; these allayed his feelings of anxiety and restlessness, and then were withdrawn gradually. His initially seclusive manner and uncooperative attitude toward ward routine improved progressively during the three weeks he was hospitalized. He was then discharged to the care of his private physician.

From Zax & Stricker, 1963, pp. 283–285.

although there may be transient periods when consciousness becomes clearer. The period following coma is characterized by stupor, restlessness, and a lack of orientation. In traumatic coma there is usually evidence that the brain has been bruised or torn.

Another acute condition known to follow brain trauma is *traumatic delirium*. Typically, this state begins as the patient emerges from a coma, and its underlying causes are the same as those leading to the coma. In traumatic delirium the patient's consciousness is cloudy, he is irritable and restless, and mutters unintelligibly. His orientation is poor, he is likely to be frightened, and may even attack those taking care of him because he mistakes them for enemies.

CASE 4–7: ORGANIC BRAIN SYNDROME, CHRONIC, ASSOCIATED WITH TRAUMA

Helen Q., a fifty-three-year-old mother of one child, was committed by her family on the advice of their doctor to a state hospital for a 30-day observation period. This was her second admission to a psychiatric hospital. She had been living with her husband in a small apartment and in the more recent weeks of her illness had been cared for by her husband, her son and her daughter-in-law.

*   *   *

Almost one year before her latest hospital admission, Helen suffered a fall in her home and sustained a severe head injury. She lost consciousness for fifteen days, and an operation to remove fluid causing pressure on the brain was performed. When she recovered Helen had some confusion and suffered amnesia regarding the accident. Soon after the operation she began to experience nausea and vomiting and eventually began to have convulsions on the average of once a week. These seizures were described as being preceded by a numbness in the right side of the face and lips, followed by a loss of consciousness and severe twitching in the mouth region. Gradually the confusion cleared and Helen began resuming her normal activities, bothered only occasionally by vivid nightmares full of bizarre hostile actions. These dreams seeemed so realistic to Helen that it took much reassurance from her husband to calm her. He, incidentally, had to change jobs to have more time at home to look after her.

A few weeks before her admission to the hospital Helen had a cold and some chest pain, and seemed to become quite exhausted after only slight exertion. Once she actually fell before she could reach her bed to lie down. She also began having more difficulty sleeping and her nightmares became even more terrifying and realistic. These changes were so upsetting that she began talking of suicide, and an old pistol that her husband had owned for many years was found under her mattress. About five days before her hospitalization Helen became more difficult to control. She dreamed that her daughter-in-law was feeding raw flesh to a man, and was not convinced of the unreality of this for nearly an hour after waking. She woke her husband in the middle of the night, accusing him of having dated the young daughter of one of their neighbors. She called those people who were trying to care for her obscene names and began threatening to kill them. Finally, she found it difficult to maintain her balance while walking and staggered as though drunk. It was at this stage that she was hospitalized.

When she was examined in the hospital Helen had one eye completely closed and seemed to squint through the other. She talked as though drunk and was confused so that, although she was oriented as to time, she was not fully aware of where she was. Her retention was poor and her calculations only fair. When asked to explain the meaning of the proverb, "A rolling stone gathers no moss," she responded, "A rolling stone does not have moss. This means nothing. If there is no moss, there is none to roll." When she was then asked to give the meaning of "People who live in glass houses shouldn't throw stones," she replied, "It's an old saying meaning nothing. It means exactly what it says. There is the right thing to do, if there is a rolling stone it just doesn't have any moss." When the question was repeated, her answer was, "Who wants an ancient and old bit of physiology? Things that people do can easily be seen and if we throw stones, that which we do isn't right because what we do can be seen." During this interview she cried readily and appeared depressed.

During her one-month stay in the hospital Helen displayed little change in her condition. She was often confused (for example, getting dressed in the middle of the night as if to go out). Frequently, she displayed considerable anger, directed especially toward her husband. The family was advised to commit Helen for an indefinite period but they declined to do this at the time. After keeping her at home for about three months she was recommitted to a state hospital and still remains there.

From Zax & Stricker, 1963, pp. 289–292.

Finally, some victims of brain trauma experience the acute symptoms of *Korsakov's syndrome*. As with the psychosis of the same name, associated with chronic alcoholism, the prominent feature of this disorder is a recent memory loss and the transparent fabrications (often referred to as confabulations) produced to mask it. Unlike Korsakov's psychosis, polyneuritis is rarely seen in Korsakov's syndrome.

Chronic disorders that follow head injury can be divided into two groups: disorders resulting directly from the injury and those only secondarily caused by the trauma. The former involve symptoms that reflect the efforts of the brain-damaged person to adapt to new deficiencies in functioning. Kurt Goldstein's writings about the effects of a loss in abstract attitude and the struggle of the brain-injured to adapt to the breakdown of an earlier, effective psychic organization contain good examples of direct reactions to injury.

Psychosis Associated with Other Physical Conditions

This category includes the following subgroups: *endocrine disorder; metabolic and nutritional disorder; systemic infection; drug or poison intoxication (other than alcohol); childbirth; other and undiagnosed physical condition.*

The overall category includes several *general systemic* disorders (as distinguished from *cerebral* disorders) that have an indirect effect on brain function and hence on behavior. The various subcategories simply differentiate among the possible sources of such disorders. Endocrine disorders include thyroid, pituitary, adrenal, or other glandular dysfunction as well as disorders arising from complications of diabetes. Metabolic and nutritional disorders include pellagra, avitaminosis, and metabolic dysfunction. Drug and poison intoxication can result from some drugs (including the psychedelic drugs), as well as from hormones, heavy metals, gases, and so on. Childbirth is occasionally followed by a systemic upset resulting in a brain syndrome. However, the stress of the postpartum period is more likely to cause a variety of psychogenic disorders which should be differentiated from the organic. "Other and undiagnosed physical condition" is simply a residual category used to cover physical conditions not subsumed under other categories that cause brain syndromes.

Systemic infection is a category used commonly enough to warrant further discussion. It refers to brain syndromes resulting from conditions such as pneumonia, typhoid fever, malaria, and rheumatic fever that are characterized by high fever and consequent *delirium* (each of which has also been mentioned as a component of other disorders).

The earliest sign of delirium is a fluctuating impairment of consciousness in which the patient may range from being mildly confused to being completely stuporous. Recent memory is disturbed and, as the condition progresses, bizarre and frightening hallucinations—most commonly visual or auditory—occur. Delusions of a threatening nature also occur during delirious states. Illusions, in which innocuous stimuli are seen as threatening, are also common; for example, a loud noise may be interpreted as a gun being fired at the patient. Often during the delirium the patient shows emotional lability—weeping at one instant, changing quickly to euphoria. Although patients can answer questions coherently in mild delirious states, in extreme states they tend to mutter unintelligibly. The mildly delirious patient often reacts to frightening hallucinations by becoming active and trying to elude imaginary pursuers; under such circumstances he may injure himself by bumping into things or falling down. In severe states of delirium the patient is more likely to thrash about in bed, mumbling to himself. In virtually all such cases, the patient looks acutely ill as evidenced by flushing, a rapid, fluctuating pulse, excessive perspiring, a rapidly changing breathing rhythm, and, at times, tremors of the hands and lips. Although delirious states may be treated directly, basically they are cleared up through treatment of the infection causing them.

Psychoses can be caused by a variety of organic conditions. These include nervous system changes that come about through aging, the direct and indirect effects of toxic substances, infections attacking the brain or its coverings directly, indirect effects of febrile diseases, the occlusion of blood vessels supplying the brain, direct injury to the brain, chronic malfunction of certain brain areas, new growths within the skull, as well as endocrine or nutritional disorders. Each cause results in general symptoms reflecting disruption of the unity of brain function and the personality of the victim and in specific symptoms related to the location and nature of the organic defect.

Nonpsychotic Organic Brain Syndromes

The subcategories under this major heading are as follows: *intracranial infection; alcohol; other drug, poison, or systemic intoxication; brain trauma; circulatory disturbance; epilepsy; disturbance of metabolism, growth, or nutrition; senile or presenile brain disease; intracranial neoplasm; degenerative disease of the central nervous system; other physical condition.*

This list does not add new syndromes beyond those already described as potentially causing brain syndromes of psychotic proportions. Therefore, cases are classified here if a brain syndrome results in disordered behavior which is not deemed to be as serious as a psychosis.

CONCLUSION

All the disorders described in this chapter result from well established organic defect. Chapter 3 identified such disorders as best fitting the dominant service delivery system of the medical model. In all cases tangible organic damage plays a significant role in producing the disorder. Can we assume, however, that whatever behavioral symptoms arise are attributable exclusively to the nature and extent of brain damage? The answer to that question is clearly "no!"

Organic brain damage from a variety of sources (aging, trauma, infection) obviously causes some behavioral symptoms, but psychological factors play an equally if not more significant role. One such factor is the personality of the afflicted person. Thus, if two people were to suffer precisely the same organic defect, their behavioral reactions would very likely differ. Let us suppose that one has been a very dependent person all his life while the other has been an independent person who has faced much stress and has managed to handle it well. The dependent person would be much more likely than the coper to suffer serious disabling functional impairment.

Another factor bearing on a person's reaction to brain damage is his or her life situation. The person who lives a tranquil life free of pressures will very likely manage far better in the face of brain damage than one whose life is filled with strain and turbulence. Also, since a general effect of brain damage is impairment of recent memory, new learning will be a difficult

challenge for the patient with organic defect. Thus, if the injured persons can go on living in familiar surroundings and with the people they are familiar with, their symptoms will be milder than they might be. If, on the other hand, they must be moved to an unfamiliar place surrounded by strangers, they may well show extreme symptoms.

Case 4–1 (Sarah J.) provides a good example of the significance of psychological factors in the reaction to brain damage. Sarah J. showed some signs of her senile condition in her memory lapses but her dramatic deterioration followed her husband's heart attack and death. Until her husband's illness she was forgetful but capable of caring for herself and for him. In the short space of seven months she went from this state of self-sufficiency to a state of confusion marked by delusions. So extreme were her symptoms, she had to be hospitalized for the rest of her life.

It should also be stressed that the psychological symptoms seen in cases of brain damage are generally exaggerations of the patient's usual personality style. The chronically suspicious person may become paranoid after becoming ill. The generally low-keyed, mildly pessimistic person may become depressed in the face of brain damage. In essence, injury to the brain is a form of stress by virtue of the physical changes and limitations it imposes on a person. The reaction to this stress will resemble the reaction the person might have had to many other types of stress.

Given this view, might not all sorts of serious psychological disorders be caused basically by organic defect? This position is certainly one that many in the mental health field have subscribed to over the years. However, conclusive evidence of organic causes of the so-called functional disorders has not been uncovered. Nonetheless, the efforts that have been made to understand the psychoses and neuroses on organic grounds will be described in later chapters.

SUMMARY

1. Behavior disorder may be seen to result either from physiological or psychological causes. This chapter deals with disorders caused by known damage to the nervous system.
2. As scientists learned about brain function a controversy arose over whether the brain involved a large number of specific functions localized in discrete areas, or whether the brain's function depended upon its over-all organization. Both viewpoints seem partly correct. Many relatively simple functions are associated with specific areas of the brain, whereas many complex functions depend upon the overall organization of an intact brain.
3. The conquest of *general paresis*, the major triumph of the organicists in the mental health field, encouraged the search for physiological bases of behavior disorder.
4. The discovery of the conditioned reflex by Pavlov also promised to link behavior to neurophysiology.
5. Biochemical imbalances have been found to result in some behavior disorders.
6. Damage to the brain results in the following general effects: recent memory loss; impaired orientation; difficulty with new learning, calculations, and comprehension; and affective lability.
7. In DSM-II organic brain syndromes are classified by the agents or condition causing them and by the severity of the resulting behavior disorder. Conditions causing damage include: aging; overuse of alcohol; infections; cerebral conditions such as arteriosclerosis, epilepsy, and brain trauma; and physical conditions such as endocrine disorder, drug or poison intoxication, and systemic infection.
8. Behavioral reactions to brain injury are at least as much a function of psychological factors as they are of the nature and extent of the injury.

CHAPTER 5

Psychodynamic Roots of Behavior Disorder

On an early September morning the child awoke as bright sunshine and the chirping of birds floated through the window with the late summer breeze. It was the day he was to leave for boarding school. The boy sat up in bed and swung his feet to the floor. Suddenly he felt very warm and began to perspire profusely. His legs felt weak and when he tried to stand, they buckled beneath him. He crawled back into bed and began sobbing until his body shook.

    This brief narrative describes a hysteric reaction of an about-to-be schoolboy of the nineteenth century. Chances are his parents bullied him into getting dressed and marching dutifully off to the coach waiting to carry him away from his home to a strange new environment. Hysterical, and more generally neurotic, individuals were not really regarded as sick people. Not commonly, they were perceived as foolish women, in keeping with the traditional misconception that only women were hysterics. Mental hospitals such as the Salpêtrière in Paris housed some patients classed as "non-insane," but rather than neurotics these were typically epileptics who were severely incapacitated by their illness.

    While Kraepelin was preoccupied with the psychoses and psychiatry was struggling to establish itself as a respectable medical specialty based on the new biological understanding, a less conspicuous movement appeared in the mental health field. Its birth was attended by general practitioners rather than by psychiatrists. And, like most new movements within abnormal psychology, it was concerned with a specific problem in human behavior—the age-old disorder of hysteria. Manifestations of this condition had repeatedly been described through the years, but those concerned with behavioral abnormality never included it among the phenomena that they studied and treated. Because of the florid nature of psychosis there was greater pressure on the professional to devote his attention to that problem.

NINETEENTH-CENTURY WORK ON HYSTERIA

Neurotics occasionally found people interested in their problems, sometimes to their serious detriment. During the great witch hunts, many of those burned at the stake were probably neurotics. Early healers such as Greatrakes and Mesmer, who developed immense followings, also dealt primarily with neurotics. During the nineteenth century the neurotic continued to seek help from whomever would attend to his ills and found some general practitioners and neurologists willing to treat him. But psychiatry, engrossed in what it regarded as a more significant mission, was not fundamentally oriented to neurosis.

The few professionals of the time who were interested in hysteria were attracted to the example of Mesmer and the dramatic effects that he achieved using animal magnetism. As we have noted, fascination with this process prompted some practitioners to utilize it even though it was branded as highly disreputable by the great majority of the medical profession. Demonstrations of the successful use of this process (now called hypnotism rather than mesmerism) in surgical anesthesia failed to impress the

orthodox, who simply denied the truth of such reports. As a result, research on hypnotism was carried on in the shadow of disrepute. This notwithstanding, hypnosis was explored further by A. A. Liebeault (1823–1904), a general practitioner in a provincial French town (Nancy), and others who were motivated both by curiosity and a genuine desire to help neurotic or hysterical patients by whatever means seemed feasible.

Liebeault turned to hypnosis in treating hysteria because more orthodox treatment techniques had been unsuccessful in dealing with this disorder. Despite the great medical advances of the era, the peculiar nature of hysterical symptoms made them incomprehensible from a purely medical viewpoint. Although hysterical patients displayed symptoms similar to those found in cases of organic defect, these symptoms characteristically either violated well-established physiological or anatomical principles or resulted in behavior atypical for the defect. For example, areas of body anesthesia failed to follow nerve patterns and paralyzed limbs failed to atrophy as they did in true paralysis. Unlikely the truly blind person, the hysterically blind avoided objects in unfamiliar surroundings that might cause them to trip and hurt themselves.

Liebault sought to treat hysterical disorder with hypnosis. Recognizing that he was traveling over poorly explored terrain, he took no payment for such work. He was sustained materially by those willing to accept only traditional treatment procedures and intellectually by those willing to participate in his studies of hypnosis. His work attracted considerable attention thus enabling him to collect great masses of clinical data. Eventually Liebeault's work came to the attention of Hippolyte-Marie Bernheim (1840–1919), a more academically oriented physician than Liebeault, who undertook

CASE 5–1: A CASE OF CONVERSION HYSTERIA

Inga S., a thirty-four-year-old married mother of four, was brought to the outpatient clinic of a large eastern hospital by her husband. They had been living in a small home in a lower middle class neighborhood.

*   *   *

Inga was a shy, timid girl who had neither the time nor the inclination for the usual adolescent activities. She married a postman in a nearby medium-sized city when she was eighteen years old, at the insistence of her parents. Although she did not love him at the time—indeed she hardly knew him—she felt that she had grown to love him, and that their marriage was a successful one. In further describing this marriage she admitted that at first there was a great deal of difficulty making a satisfactory sexual adjustment, and penetration was not achieved until after the first year of marriage. All of her pregnancies were painful and difficult, and two unplanned children served to reduce Inga's faith in contraceptive devices. In recent years she had acceded to having intercourse only to please her husband, and from the onset of her symptoms had not had relations with him at all. Her husband, described as a patient and good man, was said not to be very attentive to Inga. He often went out to play cards or attend lodge meetings, leaving Inga alone with the children and her housework.

Inga's symptoms dated back to eight weeks prior to her hospitalization. Her husband was out late playing cards that night. Soon after retiring, she noted the onset of a numbing sensation in her feet which gradually rose up both legs as far as her stomach. This was accompanied by heart palpitation and difficulty getting her breath. Her mouth felt dry and she became nauseated. Very quickly after the numbness began, it changed to stiffness of her lower extremities. Inga awoke one of her children who summoned a neighbor, and the latter called an ambulance which took her to the local hospital. Here she found it difficult to talk because of dryness of the mouth, and was again nauseated. She remained overnight and returned home the following morning. At this time she still felt nauseated and her legs were stiff and weak. She was referred to a private psychiatrist, but couldn't see him because of the expense involved.

Two weeks afterward a similar episode occurred. During the day Inga observed a neighbor being forcibly taken by ambulance attendants after an episode of delirium tremens. That night she again had a surging sensation in her feet and legs, and difficulty in breathing. This came and went many times during the night, but the stiffness was not as severe as the first time. The third recurrence was after another two-week interim. That day Inga saw a television program in which a husband was shot by his wife, and experienced an upsetting fantasy of herself in the room depicted. That night she again experienced difficulty with her limbs and in breathing.

Between episodes Inga had an increasing stiffness in her legs, and when she appeared at the hospital could not eat without aid. A sister stayed with her during the day and did the housework, and the youngest child was placed in another sister's home. Because of digestive disturbances Inga was subsisting on a liquid diet.

On admission Inga arrived with one of her brothers, and needed much assistance in getting to the interview room. Only with great reluctance did she agree to be interviewed with her brother absent, and then required assurance that he would return immediately after the interview. She was accepted for therapy and seen for three months by a social worker. Almost immediately her symptoms dramatically disappeared, although no insight was achieved. Before therapy had ended she suffered a recurrence of a mild arthritic complaint which greatly curtailed her activities at home.

From Zax & Stricker, 1963, pp. 160–162.

careful study of his techniques. This fruitful collaboration resulted in many valuable reports and stimulated a constructive controversy between members of the Nancy school and a group, working on similar problems in Salpêtrière, in Paris, led by the most prominent neurologist of the day, Jean-Martin Charcot (1825–1893).

Charcot, early in his career, achieved pre-eminence as a neurologist. In 1862 he was appointed physician-in-charge at the Salpêtrière. During his tenure there he was exposed to great numbers of disordered patients, many of whom, he observed, did not fall into traditional clinical categories. Among these patients was a sizable group

The Bettmann Archive

A clinical lecture by Jean-Martin Charcot at the Salpêtrière.

with symptoms such as paralyses, anesthesias, mutism, and hysterical seizures that were not readily explained on physiological grounds. Even though Charcot himself believed that these conditions (hysterias) were fundamentally diseases of the nervous system, many of his followers and others familiar with his work became increasingly impressed, over time, with the possible role of psychological factors in this type of disordered behavior. With this recognition, there developed a resurgence of interest in problems of hysteria and the potential utility of hypnotic approaches in their treatment.

The clinic at Salpêtrière thus became active in treating hysterics by hypnosis, using a treatment pattern that had been developed by both Liebeault and Charcot. Under hypnosis patients were given direct suggestions aimed at the elimination of their symptoms. An interesting and important observation made by Charcot was that entirely new symptoms could be induced in hysterics through suggestion. Although this demonstration convinced Charcot that mental factors played an important role in hysteria, he could not entirely abandon his organic orientation. It was this latter failure that led to a controversy between him and the group at Nancy under Bernheim.

Charcot believed that hysterics were particularly suggestible people and that they could be hypnotized for precisely that reason. He did not believe that people in general were susceptible to hypnosis. Charcot felt that the excessive susceptibility of the hysteric to suggestion was due to weakness of the nervous system. Thus, for him, suggestibility, hypnotizability, and hysterical symptomatology all had their roots in organic defect. Bernheim, on the other hand, felt that these phenomena were explainable on psychological grounds. He believed that all people, not only hysterics, were suggest-

ible, and that a good deal of behavior, normal and abnormal, social and antisocial, resulted from suggestion, not always apparent, applied by others or even by oneself. Thus for Bernheim suggestion was a basic cause of hysteria. He demonstrated, through posthypnotic suggestion, that behavior was influenced by factors below one's conscious awareness. He further denied that only hysterics could be hypnotized. The tests of time have shown that Bernheim was more correct than Charcot in his thinking about hysteria.

Once led to these views about the effects of suggestion, Bernheim generalized about other "dramatic" forms of behavior. He reasoned that the criminal had little responsibility for his behavior since many of his actions were stimulated by psychic "automatisms," acts that imposed themselves or were imposed on him by his suggestibility. This was an attack on the doctrine of free will, according to which man chooses freely among several courses of action open to him. Such an attack represented a basic challenge to theological and legal tenets that had been handed down for many centuries. It raised significant questions about how aberrant behaviors should be viewed and handled. These issues have been raised again and again as the "psychological viewpoint" gained strength, and in some instances their satisfactory resolution has not yet been attained.

Bernheim's therapeutic approach was equally advanced for its time. His treatment was based on the process of "de-suggestion" in which one first uncovered the suggestion that the patient "unconsciously simulates" and then de-suggested it. In other words, he sought to uncover the unconscious elements leading to the hysterical symptomatology and to remove or alter these elements by using against them the same process of suggestion that created them in the first place.

This approach was similar in important ways to that developed by the young neurologist Sigmund Freud (1856–1939), after familiarizing himself with Charcot's and Bernheim's work and after seeing many hysterical patients in his own practice in Vienna.

DEVELOPMENT OF FREUD'S IDEAS ON PSYCHOPATHOLOGY AND THERAPY

Freud came reluctantly to the practice of medicine after a lengthy period as a medical student. His progress through medical training had been interrupted to pursue research in pure physiology. In the course of this he had entered the laboratory of Ernst Brücke, an eminent physiologist of the day. This was an exciting period for the biological scientist. Great discoveries were being made, and it was felt that many of the profound mysteries of human biology could be uncovered by methods that had already led to the enormous contributions of Darwin and Helmholtz. The following statement, attributed to duBois-Raymond, well expressed the attitudes of many scientists of the time: "Brücke and I pledged a solemn oath to put into power this truth: 'No other forces than the common physical-chemical ones are active within the organism; that, in those cases which cannot at the time be explained by these forces one has either to find the specific way or form of their action by means of the physical-mathematical method, or to assume new forces equal in dignity to the chemical-physical forces inherent in matter, reducible to the force of attraction and repulsion'" (E. Jones, 1953, pp. 40–41).

As a bright, ambitious medical student in this era Freud tried to find a path that would lead to scientific preeminence. Practical matters, such as earning a living, marrying, and raising a family interfered, however, with his ambitions for a career in pure research. In those days an independent income was a prerequisite to an academic career, and Freud did not have such means. So he did the expedient thing and completed his medical degree. After some years of clinical training in several areas, he became interested in neurology, and in the last stages of his training won a fellowship to study in Charcot's laboratory for four months (October 1885 to February 1886). There he learned about hysteria and the ways in which hypnosis was being used in its treatment.

Following his sojourn in Paris, Freud embarked on a neurological practice and on writing on various topics in neurology. His interest in hysteria was further stimulated by his association with Dr. Joseph Breuer (1842–1925) beginning in the 1870s and culminating in a jointly authored book on the topic. Breuer was a Viennese physician of high scientific standing. He also had a lucrative medical practice, numbering among his patients many of the families of the university faculty. He and Freud had similar interests and became very good friends.

Early in their relationship Breuer described to Freud, shortly after its termination, a case of an hysteric, Anna O., whom he had treated for about a year and a half, between 1880 and 1882. The patient was characterized by E. Jones (1953) as having a "museum of symptoms" originating during the time she cared for her father during his terminal illness. She complained of paralyses, anesthesias, disturbances of vision and speech, inability to eat, and a nervous cough that caused great distress. The latter symptom was the one for which she sought Breuer's help. In addition to this collection of symptoms, the patient seemed to have two personalities—a normal twenty-one-year-old and a naughty child. A type of "self-hypnosis" intervened between the dominance of one personality or the other. Breuer visited Anna O. during one such period of "self-hypnosis," and she readily confided in him her displeasure with much that had happened during the day. Surprisingly, she felt some relief from her symptoms after this episode. Breuer made regular visits during which he encouraged the patient to unburden herself. To his amazement he found that when she talked about the circumstances surrounding the formation of

---

CASE 5-2: AN EXCERPT FROM THE CASE OF ANNA O

In July, 1880, the patient's father, of whom she was passionately fond, fell ill of a peripleuritic abscess which failed to clear up and to which he succumbed in April, 1881. During the first months of the illness Anna devoted her whole energy to nursing her father, and no one was much surprised when by degrees her own health greatly deteriorated. No one, perhaps not even the patient herself, knew what was happening to her; but eventually the state of weakness, anaemia and distaste for food became so bad that to her great sorrow she was no longer allowed to continue nursing the patient. The immediate cause of this was a very severe cough, on account of which I examined her for the first time. It was a typical *tussis nervosa*. She soon began to display a marked craving for rest during the afternoon, followed in the evening by a sleep-like state and afterwards a highly excited condition.

At the beginning of December a convergent squint appeared. An ophthalmic surgeon explained this (mistakenly) as being due to paresis of one abducens. On December 11 the patient took to her bed and remained there until April 1.

There developed in rapid succession a series of severe disturbances which were *apparently* quite new: left-sided occipital headache; convergent squint (diplopia), markedly increased by excitement; complaints that the walls of the room seemed to be falling over (affection of the obliquus); disturbances of vision which it was hard to analyse; paresis of the muscles of the front of the neck, so that finally the patient could only move her head by pressing it backwards between her raised shoulders and moving her whole back; contracture and anaesthesia of the right upper, and, after a time, of the right lower extremity. The latter was fully extended, adducted and rotated inwards. Later the same symptom appeared in the left lower extremity and finally in the left arm, of which, however, the fingers to some extent retained the power of movement. So, too, there was no complete rigidity in the shoulder-joints. The contracture reached its maximum in the muscles of the upper arms. In the same way, the region of the elbows turned out to be the most affected by anaesthesia when, at a later stage, it became possible to make a more careful test of this. At the beginning of the illness the anesthesia could not be efficiently tested, owing to the patient's resistance arising from feelings of anxiety.

From Studies on Hysteria, *by Josef Breuer and Sigmund Freud, Translated from the German and edited by James Strachey in collaboration with Anna Freud, Assisted by Alix Strachey and Alan Tyson, Published in the United States by Basic Books, Inc. by arrangement with The Hogarth Press Ltd.*

a symptom, it disappeared. Many of her key symptoms were dislodged in this way and the patient herself began to refer to the process as a "talking cure." Others called it "cathartic therapy."

Breuer was fascinated by this case and began visiting the patient as often as twice a day, inducing hyposis at times. The relationship terminated rather abruptly when Breuer found that it was occupying his thoughts to an inordinate degree and was interrupting his home life. Anna, who had made much progress to that point, at least symptomatically, relapsed dramatically. Breuer was called to her bedside to find her highly excited and in the throes of an hysterical childbirth. He was greatly unnerved by this turn of events, which suggested, even to one resisting the thought, that their relationship had taken on a sexual tinge. Breuer calmed the patient by using hypnosis and then left Vienna on a second honeymoon with his wife. Many of the principles of psychotherapy that Freud later derived were stimulated by Breuer's experiences with Anna O., as will be described below.

During the late 1880s Freud carried on an uneventful neurological practice and busied himself writing on neurological problems such as aphasia. His interest in hysteria persisted and it alienated him from his medical colleagues in Vienna. His reports on many of his experiences at Charcot's laboratory were met with skepticism. For instance, the suggestion that hysteria affected men as well as women, a belief he brought back from Paris, met with a hostile reception from Viennese psychiatric authorities.

Nevertheless, Freud's interest in hysteria continued and he attempted to treat patients having hysterical symptoms using hypnosis. By 1889 he grew quite dissatisfied with his technique because he was not always able to induce hypnosis, or at least a deep enough hypnotic state to effect the changes he considered necessary. He decided, therefore, to visit Nancy where he spent several weeks observing Liebeault and Bernheim at work. There he was deeply impressed with the possibility that powerful mental processes existed which, although not conscious, played a profound role in directing behavior.

Back in Vienna, his practice continued. But Freud was too restless to content himself simply with seeing patients, hypnotizing them, and relieving their symptoms through suggestion, only to find that the symptoms returned and required a repetition of the same hypnotic suggestion if temporary relief was to be achieved. He was certain that symptoms were based on very real but poorly understood forces. Restlessly he strove to gain access to that realm. He used Breuer's cathartic method wherever possible. While this produced interesting material in his quest for the psychological roots of hysterical disorder, it was not a method that he could use with all patients, because it depended on hypnosis. He came to feel that therapeutic progress depended less on the specfic technique of hypnosis than on the personal relationship that developed between the therapist and patient. This view was fostered by the example of Breuer's work with Anna O., and by experience in his own practice where he encountered a similar situation with a female patient who openly communicated affection for him. Such incidents brought him closer to the theories that he ultimately developed about both the sexual basis of neuroses and the special nature of the therapist-patient relationship. Whereas Breuer was so personally stirred as to recoil in horror at the implications of the relationship he was developing with Anna O., Freud maintained objectivity and strove to understand why a sexually tinged attraction formed in psychotherapy.

Gradually Freud came to feel that in order to progress in psychotherapy, hypnosis had to be abandoned altogether, since its formality interfered with the formation of emotional ties between therapist and patient that were central to therapeutic gain. An experience in 1892 with a patient refractory to hypnosis reinforced this conviction. In working with her he recalled a casual remark of Bernheim's that patients who had forgotten events occurring during hypnosis could be induced to remember them if the hypnotist insisted that they could be recalled. Freud reasoned that the same might be true for other experiences occurring outside the hypnotic state that had been forgotten.

His new methodology borrowed three features from hypnosis: the use of a couch; reduction of distracting stimuli; and emphasis on relaxation. However, rather than inducing a trance, he asked his patient to concentrate on a particular symptom and to recall anything that might shed light on its source. Persistence in this approach brought forth useful material, and the patient also observed that she could have produced the same material almost immediately but for the fact that she had regarded it as trivial or irrelevant. This led Freud to insist that the patient offer any thought that came to mind even if it seemed insignificant, embarassing, or inappropriate.

Freud played a very active role in the initial application of this technique, encouraging the patient to produce thoughts. When one patient rebuked him for interfering with her flow of ideas by his badgering, he became more passive. As a result of other similar experiences the technique became progressively freer. At the present time, free association is regarded as a central and powerful technique in classic psychoanalytic therapy.

The use of free association produced much information about the past life of the patient that Freud found of great interest. Imbued as he was from his early training in physiology with the principle of determinism, he found that he was often able to establish relationships between two seemingly disconnected trains of thought. He also observed that patients often had inordinate difficulty bringing unpleasant material to the surface. He called this difficulty *resistance*, and he related it to a process he called repression, which involved the forcing out of consciousness of unpleasant memories.

A synthesis of these ideas and experiences suggested to Freud that disconnected free association of the patient was often simply a manifestation of resistance in the service of maintaining repression. The patient's free associations seemed related to the unpleasant experiences that were repressed, yet the individual failed to establish the obvious connections necessary to make the painful memory apparent. This led Freud to postulate the existence of an *unconscious* psychic realm. It also reinforced for him the need to pay careful attention to the patient's verbal productions in order to gain access to the unconscious which was of such significance to the patient's behavior.

Freud discovered that relevant patient memories rarely stopped at the point where symptoms had first developed but went back to experiences in early life. These memories were typically about distressing events that Freud viewed as "traumatic." Freud came to view symptoms as reactions to events later in life that were related to unhappy attitudes or associations of a much earlier period.

The process of tracing symptoms back to the unpleasant memories at their roots led to many other discoveries that became cornerstones of Freud's theory. In a paper written in 1896 Freud (1963a) observed that although unpleasant prepubertal events relating to a patient's symptoms were often identified, these events lacked either sufficient "determining power" (relevance) or "traumatic power" (significance) to account for the symptom. He therefore assumed that the crucial symptom-determining events had taken place still earlier in life. He thus encouraged patients to search for earlier and earlier memories, going back as far as the first few years of life. Invariably these earliest recollections centered around sexual contacts between the patient and an adult or another child that were both sufficiently traumatic and relevant to current symptomatology to explain it. Thus, he postulated the importance of sexual factors, even in the very young child, in shaping later symptomatology.

Later Freud discovered that many of his patients' sexually tinged reports, which he had accepted literally, were actually fantasies rather than objective descriptions of real encounters. This discovery did not however lead Freud to abandon his theory of the sexual etiology of hysteria. Indeed it reinforced his belief in it, through the assumption that such fantasies constituted powerful, direct evidence that sexual forces were basic to the disorder. Later, as Freud accumulated experience with other neurotic disorders in his clinical practice, he extended his emphasis on sex as an etiological force in the development of neurosis.

DEVELOPMENT OF THE THEORY OF DREAMS

By the late 1890s Freud's work with the psychoanalytic technique and the process of free association led him to extend his theorizing to still another central behavioral phenomenon—the dream. In this case he was less stimulated by clinical contacts with patients than by a project he embarked on to resolve troublesome personal problems: his self-analysis.

Freud recognized that he could not sustain the associative processes necessary to the analytic procedure if he was both patient and analyst at the same time. He therefore began to use his own dreams as jumping-off points for free association. Since he had occasionally worked in this way previously with patients who, spontaneously, brought their dreams to him, he had some experience in applying the free-association technique to dreams and in making interpretations on this basis. He therefore carefully recorded his own dreams upon awakening each morning and free-associated to their various elements until satisfied that he had traced each to its roots. These were recognized when thoughts were arrived at that stirred him with intense emotionality, in marked contrast to the relatively unemotional nature of the dream itself. Also, his individual associative chains often evinced common central threads, revealing a convergence of ideas on a single point that had apparently set the process in motion.

During the course of this self-analysis Freud (1950) wrote *The Interpretation of Dreams*, which many regard as his most important work. In this book Freud attempted to describe the processes that gave dreams their characteristic obscurity, deduce the conflicting and cooperating forces responsible for the production of dreams, and, finally, to demonstrate that the meaning of dreams could be revealed.

Freud theorized that dreams, which often take on the coloring of recent events, consist in reality of one of two types of content or, more commonly, of a composite of both. The two content types are: the *manifest content*, the material that one reports having dreamt, and the *latent content*, the true meaning of the material that is dreamt. The process by which latent content is converted into manifest content he called the *dream work*. Its counterpart is the process by which dreams are analyzed.

Basic to all dreams is the desire to have a wish fulfilled, if only in fantasy. When this wish is acceptable the dream is likely to be a simple and straightforward one—as for example children's dreams of the continuation of a recent pleasurable experience that may for some reason have been cut short. The hungry man's dream of sitting down to a great feast is another example. However, where the wishes are unacceptable the dream work disguises them so that at least symbolic wish fulfillment can be enjoyed without the dreamer's feeling disturbed and having his sleep interrupted, as in a nightmare. Thus, successful dream work protects sleep.

Two "thought-constructing agencies" were hypothesized in man's mental apparatus—the first with free access to consciousness only by way of the first. There is a censor between these two agencies whose job it is to admit what is pleasant and to obstruct what is not. Material rejected by the censor remains repressed. The censor is most effective during the waking state although, even here, occasional slips of the tongue or pen betray its failure and suggest the unwelcome intrusion of unconscious material. In sleep, however, when there are fewer distractions and the censor is more relaxed, the relative strengths of these two agencies change, and unconscious material gains access to consciousness more readily. However, even during sleep the censor remains operative (as demonstrated by the fact that external stimuli are monitored), and alters repressed material (through the dream work) to make it less upsetting. Thus, what appears in the dream is a composite of the forbidden wish and the dis-

guise imposed on it by the censor. When the wish is too powerful and cannot be disguised sufficiently the person becomes upset and awakens, and in the waking state the censor regains its full strength. Even when sleep is not disturbed the common phenomenon of quickly forgetting one's dream is attributed to the censor's having again taken control over the unconscious. Freud's interest in unraveling dream work stemmed from his conviction that this process enables one to trace back into the unconscious the wish that prompted the dream and that presumably plays a central part in directing behavior. His application of free-association techniques to elements of dreams also helped him to identify and describe various processes that were basic to dream work.

SIGNIFICANCE OF FREUD'S EARLY WORK

This account of the development of Freud's ideas has been presented in order to convey a feeling for the way his theory developed. It did not appear "full-blown" as the result of a sudden inspiration, but rather it evolved gradually out of Freud's clinical experience with middle-class, neurotic patients. Also, it is clear that Freud began, not with a conception of what people were like psychologically, but with a technique for dealing with a particular problem. His earliest discoveries prompted him to polish the technique. Only later, as a by-product of the technique, did he gather material which he used to build a theory about how people are constituted psychologically. Thus moving from a therapeutic approach to a particular psychological problem, Freud evolved the first comprehensive theory of personality, which has never really had its final statement. It was added to and modified over the years, as Freud continued to work with patients, and he remained active till the time of his death.

It is appropriate also to speak of the impact of Freud's theorizing on the professions concerned with behavioral disorder. Freud probably compared himself with Darwin, the towering scientific figure of his student days, whose theory of evolution seemed to have answered, in one stroke, many questions about man's biological heritage. It is difficult to resist the speculation that Freud hoped to accomplish in psychology what Darwin had achieved for biology. Freud was certainly not content to limit himself to developing a therapeutic technique for dealing with hysteria or to constructing a theory for understanding the appearance of hysterical symptoms. Rather he was quick to generalize from his experience and to theorize about universals in man's behavior. As a result the theory he built sought to encompass normal as well as abnormal development (that is, to be relevant to the behavior of all men and women, wherever they grew up and whatever their specific experiences). One consequence of this broad orientation and ambitious approach was that his theorizing became burdened with many untested assumptions.

The impact of Freud's work was manifold. If Darwin's theory, postulating that man evolved from lower forms of life rather than springing full-blown in the image of God, was threatening, Freud's was even more so. It was one thing to be stripped of one's divine descent; it was quite another to learn that one's very rationality was illusory. With Freud's deterministic orientation, which in the last analysis is basic to a science of behavior, man could no longer cherish the notion that his will was free. Freud's emphasis on unconscious forces and their usually animal quality forcibly underscored the view that despite man's ostensible biological evolution from animals much of the animal remained in him. Furthermore, Freud's view that normal and abnormal behavior were to be found on the same continuum was an idea that had always been rejected by all but the most perceptive.

On the other hand, Freud's formulations well reflected the thinking of many contemporaries who had become increasingly aware that psychological forces played an important role in man's behavior. Had the latter view not clearly been present at the time Freud might have been dismissed as a harmless quack. However, he was sufficiently correct to vex even his most serious detractors. As an example of this, Meynert, the professor of psychiatry at Vienna in Freud's time, bitterly challenged Freud when he asserted that hysteria was not restricted to females. E. Jones (1953), however, reports that when Meynert was on his death bed, he confessed to Freud that he himself had suffered the classic symptoms of hysteria. Undoubtedly, another feature of Freud's position that was attractive enough to create interest even in those who did not accept his theories unequivocally was that he offered a promising treatment approach at a time when few others did. As has been pointed out, for all of the great hopes engendered by the organic approach with which the psychiatry of Freud's day was imbued, little beyond categorization of disorder and custodial care was being achieved. Although Freud had little explicit to say about psychoses, at least he held out the hope that he could modify behavior. This naturally proved to be exciting for those who hoped that something tangible might be accomplished by a science of psychology.

Perhaps more important than the specific form of his theories was the impact Freud's work had on the scope of the helping professions. It was his work and his theorizing that eventually brought psychoneurotic disorders into the orbit of the psychiatrist and psychologist. This was a redefinition of the limits of their field that caused mental health professionals to attend to a much wider class of behavior than had before been the object of their concern. Furthermore, his willingness to speculate about the experimental forces common to all people, normal or abnormal, paved the way for a still greater broadening of the horizons of the behavioral sciences, as shall be seen.

FREUD'S THEORY
OF PERSONALITY

Before summarizing the basic features of psychoanalytic theory and its application to psychopathology, its biological aspects should be mentioned. Freud had considerable interest and experience in physiology, and his most respected mentors worked in that area. In fact, much of Freud's effort prior to 1900 went to establishing a neurophysiological theory of hysteria. When that failed he shifted to an effort to understand the disorder on psychological grounds. Holt (1965) questions whether Freud really shifted completely. He suggests that Freud was led to his fundamental psychoanalytic principles by assumptions about man's biology that were commonly held in his day and have since been discredited. The fact that they were offered in purely psychological terms has interfered with their being revised, as a better understanding of physiology has emerged. Brenner (1955) has also argued that it was Freud's hope that, eventually, the biological basis of mental phenomena would be firmly established. In the section to follow, evidences of the biological influence on specific aspects of Freud's theory should become clearer.

The Motive Force
in Behavior

Freud saw man as an essentially passive organism, who must monitor a variety of stimuli impinging on him and react to them. Just as he possesses the physical energy to do work, so, too, he possesses a fund of psychic energy available for mental activity. Like physical energy that can be transformed but never lost from the system, psychic energy exists in a closed, internal system. The biology of the individual determines how much of this energy exists within him.

In the ideal state, psychic energy is distributed in a way that creates an optimal balance, so that relatively little need be directed to dealing with any given stimulus. Stimuli create tensions, and psychic energy is required to cope with these tensions. Tension is experienced as unpleasurable, and reduction of tension is subjectively pleasurable. The view that the organism's basic goal is to mediate among stimuli and to maintain a relatively tension-free state is called the *principle of constancy*. This reduction of all tensions has been referred to in the psychoanalytic literature as a Nirvana-like state and the concept of the constancy principle is sometimes used interchangeably with the term *Nirvana principle*.

Although stimuli that create tensions for the organism may derive from external or internal sources, Freud focused primarily on the internal ones. Despite his deterministic inclination, in his early writings, at least, he neglected the possibility that there may have been some consistency in the external stimuli that man experienced as the result of socio-cultural practices. Indeed, he often referred to environmental forces as "accidental factors." The few social regularities he did acknowledge were thought to come about genetically through the inheritance of acquired characteristics so that even the transmission of cultural practices was thought to result from internal rather than external factors.

Freud did not attempt to develop long lists of specific internal forces (*instincts*, as he called them) with which man had to cope but, instead, tried to categorize them in general ways. In his earlier theorizing Freud separated them into the sexual instincts and the self-preservative instincts. The sexual instincts, though forbidden, demanded expression. They were restrained by the self-preservative instincts, and the result of this inhibitory process was often experienced in the form of anxiety, guilt feelings, ethical ideals, and so on. This conflict between two sets of instincts was seen as the essence of anxiety. As other aspects of the theory developed, this distinction was abandoned and for a time only sexual instincts were thought to exist.

Eventually, Freud's observations (in World War I) led to the construction of a new dichotomy which was, in part, a logical extension of the Nirvana principle. If the ideal state was a tensionless one, the ultimate of such a state was death itself. Thus, he felt that there was a class of instincts, subsumed by the death instinct, which, turned outward, prompted destructive behavior and, according to the physical principle of entropy, strove to reunite man with the inorganic matter from which he grew. In this later formulation another class of instincts was seen to be dedicated to seeking stimuli and striving for the opposite of Nirvana. The death instincts were propelled by an aspect of psychic energy which some analysts have named *destrudo* or *thanatos*. The sexual instincts were an expression of a form of psychic energy called *libido*. In any given activity both types of instinct were thought to operate,

with one or the other being more prominent.

This categorization of instincts is one aspect of Freud's theory that has not won universal acceptance, even by orthodox analysts. Fenichel (1945), for example, argues that while the sexual instincts propel one to seek stimulation, at the same time they strive basically for the relaxation of tensions and in this sense do not violate the principle of constancy. Furthermore, while aggressive drives do clearly exist, they need not necessarily be viewed as a turning outward of a destructive urge. In fact, it is argued, they can usually be better understood as an indirect course taken by frustrated sexual instincts.

The Structure of Personality

Freud conceived that personality could be divided into three interconnected aspects, each of which had its own functions and properties. The first of these, called the *id*, is the initial repository of all psychic energy and is the only one present at birth.

All that is inherited and all of the instincts are included in the id. It is the aspect that is in closest touch with the inner world of the individual. The id cannot tolerate stimuli that create tension and seeks to have them reduced immediately and by any means. The principle by which it operates is called the *pleasure principle*.

The id has relatively few resources within itself to achieve tension-reduction. Essentially, it possesses two mechanisms that it can use directly. The first is *reflex action* which is inherent in the organism and involves automatic reactions such as sneezing and blinking in response to irritating stimuli. Many such reflexes exist but they deal with relatively simple irritants. The other device, termed *primary process*, is more psychological in nature; it involves forming a mental image (a fantasy or hallucination) that is used to reduce tension. In essence, primary process is a form of wish-fulfillment. Dreams represent a good example of the way primary process operates in the normal. Obviously, these two techniques are not completely effective in dealing with the myriad stimuli that create tension. However, a second aspect of personality that develops later, the *ego*, also contributes to tension-reduction.

The ego develops, in part at least, because the individual must acquire from the world around him the wherewithal for reducing tensions. When one is hungry he must get food, when thirsty he must get water. The organism must learn the difference between a memory image of food, which has only very limited use, and real food. And so techniques must be developed for obtaining needed food or for getting others to bring it. Thus, some part of the organism must become acquainted with the world outside of it; this is a major job of the ego. To do this successfully, the ego cannot rely on either the pleasure principle or primary process. The alternative principle followed by the ego is the *reality principle*, and the process it uses is called the *secondary process*. Operation in terms of the reality principle prevents discharge of tension until an appropriate object is found. Secondary process involves thinking logically and realistically rather than simply in terms of wish-fulfillment. The effective operation of this realistic approach to tension-reduction is called *reality testing*. This requires an ability to distinguish between what comes from outside in the form of external stimuli and perceptions and what is internally stimulating as a result of id impulses pressing for wish-fulfillment.

The ego, as an organized portion of the id, is dedicated to forwarding the aims of the id, not to frustrating them. At times it may have to divert an impulse or delay its gratification, but essentially it exists to serve the id by mediating between its impulses, the demands and limitations of the environment, and those of the third aspect of personality, the *superego*, which develops later. The ego is aided in its struggle to achieve mastery over the environment by utilizing three functions of the organism. These are: (a) sensory perceptions, which provide information about the environment; (b) the ability to think, compare, and remember, all of which depend upon the secondary process; and (c) motor skills, which are useful when physical means are needed to alter the environment.

Ego growth, which takes place as energy is captured from the id, is a complicated process that bears discussion because of its central role in understanding pathological processes. Essentially, if the ego is to grow, energy formerly attached to a specific drive must become *neutralized* (detached from that drive) and become available for a variety of purposes directed by the ego. One important factor in ego development is the process of *identification*, whereby the organism emulates a person in the environment whom he has *cathected*. The term *cathexis* refers to the investment of psychic energy in the mental representation of a person or thing. Presumably, when people become important to the infant because they are instrumental in reducing tensions, he identifies with them and becomes like them as much as possible. By copying them he can begin to reduce tensions for himself. Thus, imitation of the behavior of others leads to the expansion of the ego.

Another factor that helps the ego to take over id-energy is its role in dealing with anxiety. For Freud, anxiety resulted from any situation that threatened to overwhelm the psyche with stimulation. The prototypical anxiety state was the *birth trauma*, when the neonate is thrust out from a totally sheltered environment into one full of strange stimuli with which it is powerless to cope. One of the ego's prime jobs is to protect the organism against recurrences of such trauma. This function is of sufficient importance to merit considerable energy investment. As the ego takes shape, greater and greater mastery over incoming stimuli should take place and there should be less vulnerability to anxiety. Although in the birth trauma and others to which the individual is subjected in early life, the threatening stimuli come from the environment, later in life most serious ego threats are from stimuli that come from within (from the instincts).

Discussion of the process whereby the ego acquires control over significant segments of neutralized id-energy prompts consideration of how the ego operates to master anxiety. One such technique involves the use of anxiety itself. In this case the anxiety is used as a *signal* (warning) that a situation is potentially traumatic (overwhelming) and that steps must be taken to prevent this outcome. Thus, the

baby may recognize that, with the mother present, tensions are quickly reduced. When she leaves, however, such tensions are not dealt with promptly and are very unpleasant. Thus, the mother's leaving the baby prompts signal-anxiety and mobilizes effort on the part of the baby (such as crying), to bring her back. Therefore, signal anxiety, which is much lower in intensity than traumatic anxiety, is used by the ego to prevent occurrence of the more threatening state.

Generally the ego must act to ward off id impulses, which, if expressed, would produce an influx of stimuli that could not be mastered easily and would result in trauma. For this purpose it can use a variety of techniques such as furthering another id impulse that can compete with a dangerous one but is safer. Through its control of perceptual processes it can avoid stimuli that might provoke the impulse. The ego can also develop temporarily satisfying fantasy gratifications. In addition to these operations, however, the ego utilizes as a prime *modus operandi* a variety of dynamisms, collectively known as *defense mechanisms*, to control id impulses.

TABLE 5.1
Comparison of Freud's Id, Ego, and Superego

	ID	EGO	SUPEREGO
Contents	All psychic energy All instincts	Gains control of cognitive and motor functions	Conscience Ego-ideal
Tools	Reflex action Primary process	Secondary process	Identification with authorities
Principle of Operation	Pleasure principle	Reality principle	Moral principle
Purpose	To relieve tensions	To relieve tensions appropriately	To limit behavior to what is morally acceptable

Lists of defense mechanisms vary in length with the classificatory schema of the classifier. There are some, however, that are widely regarded as basic. Perhaps the most central of all is *repression*, a process used to bar from consciousness any id impulses that threaten to be upsetting. Repression requires a substantial investment of the ego's energy and involves a fairly long-lasting stalemate in which there is a force, or cathexis, emanating from the id and a counterforce, or countercathexis, coming from the ego. Actually, rather than stable equilibrium between such forces, alterations in the relative strengths of the opposing forces are more typical. When the countercathexis weakens, some repressed material emerges into consciousness and, possibly, leads to action. Toxic states, such as alcohol intoxication or sleep, are examples of situations in which countercathexes are weakened. Temptation aroused by objects potentially gratifying to the id impulse may strengthen the cathexis and upset the balance of forces. The ego may react to such disequilibria with signal anxiety as a preliminary to taking steps to restore a balance. Repression takes place on an entirely unconscious level. An analogous process on the conscious level is known as *suppression.*

It is widely held that repression is the most basic of all defense mechanisms and that others are used either as reinforcers of repression or as necessary operations after repression has failed. Some of these are *reaction formation, isolation, denial, projection,* and *sublimation.* Although each will be described only briefly here, they will come up again in later discussion of the psychoanalytic view of specific disorders.

Reaction formation, involving repression of undesirable feelings and overemphasis of more acceptable ones, occurs in situations about which one is ambivalent. Thus, in a situation where one feels both love and hate, the hate, because of its potentially threatening quality, may seem to be entirely replaced by love, although it persists and has its unconscious effects.

Isolation involves a process of partial repression. In this case an idea or a wish-fulfilling fantasy is separated from the feeling that ordinarily accompanies it and the affect is repressed. Thus, the fantasy has access to consciousness but without the affective charge that it would ordinarily have and, therefore, it is not as upsetting as it might be. Individuals who use such a defense extensively often seem to be quite "unfeeling."

Denial is a process in which the external reality goes unrecognized. This is often accomplished through some wish-fulfilling fantasy. Many children's games emphasizing the child's power in relation to the objectively larger and more commanding figures around him exemplify this process. The popularity, with children, of "Popeye"

can be seen to derive from the child's identification with the frail hero who regularly bests his massive antagonist, thereby reinforcing the child's denial of his weakness compared to grown-ups.

Projection is a mechanism whereby one attributes his own unacceptable wish to someone else. The impulse is projected from its internal source onto some person or object in the external world. Often one's own intolerable, violent impulses are projected and the individual finds much danger in people around him or perhaps in the inanimate forces of the environment.

Sublimation is often regarded as a defense mechanism but, in reality, is probably more of a counterpart of such mechanisms. Whereas other mechanisms are invoked to prevent the expression of an id impulse, sublimation fosters the *indirect* expression of such impulses. Thus, the child who wishes to handle his own feces makes mud pies instead and gains some of the gratification that satisfaction of the original wish would have afforded. Normal socialized behavior consists of many such instances of sublimation—of the diversion of an unacceptable impulse into acceptable channels resulting in some degree of primary gratification.

The list of defense mechanisms may be extended well beyond those presented. In fact, as specific neurotic and psychotic disorders are discussed mechanisms other than the few considered will undoubtedly be mentioned. It is also true that much more could, and will in later chapters, be said about the ego. Some attention should be devoted, however, to the third and last of the personality systems to develop according to Freud, the *superego*.

To understand fully how the superego develops, it must be seen in the context of the stages of psychological development to be described. Suffice it to say that the superego is the internal representative of the moral and ethical aspects of the culture as they are transmitted to the child by his parents or parent substitutes. It establishes ideals and standards to which the individual must conform. In so doing, it inhibits those id aims that are unacceptable to the internalized norms of society. The ego seeks to delay direct gratification of an impulse at a particular moment because it anticipates long-range traumatic consequences; it thus seeks suitable substitute gratification. Its concerns are mainly practical. The superego, in contrast, prohibits certain actions entirely—not because of their inappropriateness but because they are morally wrong. On the other hand the superego has the positive function of encouraging forms of behavior valued by the social group. In addition to encouraging certain forms of behavior and discouraging others, the superego observes the self critically and punishes it for improper behavior.

The superego comes into existence through identification with parents who reward certain actions and punish others. That which the child learns to be improper forms the subject-matter of what we have come to think of as *conscience*. That term, however, implying conscious awareness, is slightly misleading when used in connection with the superego since the latter is largely unconscious. Behavior approved by parents is referred to as the *ego-ideal*. More will be said about the building of the superego later.

Psychosexual Stages and Personality Development

With its emphasis upon the importance of early life experiences, psychoanalytic theory understandably includes a systematic elaboration of the significance of the various developmental stages through which the growing child passes. These stages will be surveyed briefly to give an overview and then each will be taken up in some detail.

The developmental stages are differentiated according to the zones of the body that are of particular relevance at given times. For the helpless infant, the mouth is the zone of primary significance. It is only by eating that immediate survival is assured. Consequent growth and increase in strength and independence are achieved in the same way. Because of the centrality of the mouth and eating, this initial stage (the first year or two of life) has been called the *oral* stage. With growth and development of greater independence and capability, attention in the next psychosexual stage turns to the alimentary tract's other terminal, the anus. During this *anal* stage (roughly in the second year of life) eliminative functions assume special significance. This is due particularly to the emphasis placed upon them by important figures in one's life seeking to instill a fixed pattern in the way they are handled. This stage is succeeded by the *phallic* stage (around the third or fourth year of life) during which sensitivity is centered in the sexual organs. These three stages—the oral, anal, and phallic—are referred to as the *pregenital* stages. They are followed by a *latency* period (generally from age five to the onset of puberty), regarded as a quiescent stage when little biological change is occurring. Of great theoretical significance in the phallic stage is the occurrence of the *Oedipal conflict*. Generally, this conflict is resolved prior to the onset of latency, partly because of the fear of castration and partly because of the development of external interests. Its resolution requires much repression which holds most impulses in check during latency. With the onset of adolescence there is a new biological upheaval and a resurgence of pregenital impulses

that must be dealt with by the defense mechanisms and sublimation. If this is done successfully, the individual enters the final period of development, the *genital* stage.

For Freud the prolonged helplessness of the human infant and baby accounts for the significance in the development of human personality of the pregenital stages and the importance of relationships with people during this period. Earliest relationships with people (or objects, as they are referred to in the psychoanalytic literature) are in terms of need gratification. Indeed, in the child's very earliest days only "part-objects" are important. For example, the child does not recognize Mother as a unity. Instead, that part of Mother which gratifies a specific need such as hunger is cathected.

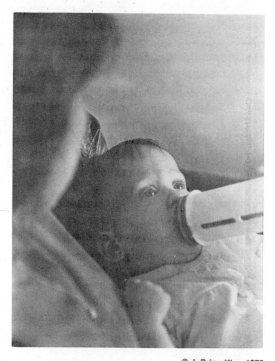

© J. Brian King 1975

If oral requirements are satisfied during the first two years of life, positive feelings toward others usually are evident in adult life.

The earliest part-object to be recognized is, therefore, the breast, or the bottle, or the hand—that part of Mother most closely associated with feeding. During the latter part of the first year, whole objects begin to be perceived. This combining of various parts into a whole is accompanied by the first experience of ambivalence—simultaneous feelings of love and hate. This occurs because different sets of experiences with parts of the object provoke either one or the other feeling and when the object is recognized as a whole, that unity has inevitably been associated with both feelings.

The stages of development are of considerable significance because the adaptations characterizing each stage are thought to be prototypical of important traits that develop later in life. Successful negotiation of a stage results in positive personality characteristics. Failure to have the demands of a psychosexual stage adequately gratified results in a fixation at that stage so that characteristics of that period will persist in the personality, usually in the form of personality traits that are regarded as detriments. Fixations arise for several reasons. These include excessive indulgence, which makes difficult the giving up of gratification; excessive frustration, which makes the organism unwilling to advance because needs have not been adequately met; abrupt shifts from excessive satisfaction to excessive frustration; and, most frequently, the simultaneous satisfaction of an instinctual need and the need to feel secure from anxiety.

The Oral Stage

During the oral stage eating is the principle pleasure and this activity is associated with the mouth. Pleasure for the child derives from tactile stimulation of the lips and oral cavity as well as from swallowing pleasant substances or spitting up unpleasant ones. Eventually teeth are acquired, and biting and chewing become both possible and a source of gratification.

Adequate gratification of oral needs predisposes the adult to feeling positively toward other people, provides a capacity for warmth and closeness, and makes him independent and capable of giving to others. Oral fixation results in a variety of negative traits. The need to incorporate orally, restricted to food in the infant, may, for example, be converted in the adult to a need to incorporate information (gullibility). The impulse to bite, pleasurable for the infant, may become converted in the socialized adult to a verbal aggressiveness (sarcasm, argumentativeness). The pleasure the infant enjoys in being comforted, held, fondled, nursed, and so on, may be sought continually in some adult form later in life (dependency).

The Anal Stage

During the anal stage the baby has adequately gratified his oral demands and thus begins to derive pleasure and relief through elimination of feces from the lower end of the intestinal tract, where their accumula-

© J. Brian King 1975

When a child is treated with patience and tolerance during toilet training, she may be productive and creative in later life.

tion causes discomfort. Toilet training is often the first life situation in which outside agents make demands on the child to regulate an internal impulse. It therefore has important implications for later personality development. In the analytic view, much is thought to depend upon how this training is handled by the parents and how it is reacted to by the child. If the parents are rigid, overly insistent, or harsh, the child may resist the encroachment upon his freedom by becoming constipated, not producing at all, or by expelling his feces at inappropriate times. Generalization of the type of reaction that leads to constipation is believed to result in obstinacy and stinginess or excessive orderliness later in life. Expulsiveness, a form of openly expressed anger, may have its later counterpart in cruelty, destructiveness, studied sloppiness, or temper tantrums. Under ideal conditions the child is treated with patience and tolerance and rewarded with praise for the correct response so that he can derive genuine pleasure from this aspect of socialization. In later life this may be the basis for productivity and creativity in an individual who takes pride in what he can do.

The Phallic Stage and the Oedipal Conflict

This stage comes about as maturation leads to the localization of pleasurable sensations in the genital organs. It is at this time that masturbation becomes frequent in children and physical contact with others is sought. There is an attraction for members of the opposite sex on the part of both boys and girls. The strong attraction that develops for and becomes centered on the parent of the opposite sex may pose serious problems. This results in the appearance of the *Oedipal conflict*, the resolution of which terminates the relatively

eventful pregenital era and ushers in the latency period.

For children of both sexes the Oedipal conflict is thought to be intense, even though, for some, conflicts resulting from earlier stages in life may be of such continuing importance that the Oedipal conflict becomes secondary. This conflict begins with the closeness of the child to the mother, who has gratified most of his important needs until then and who is, therefore, regarded as the potential gratifier of phallic needs. The strength of the child's feelings during this period results in a desire for the exclusive attention of the mother; thus competitors are generally resented. The father is particularly resented because the child senses that he enjoys some special privileges with the mother, such as sharing the privacy of the bedroom, which may be of a sexual nature. While the youngster does not typically have exact knowledge of what such sexual behavior might involve he may have many speculations and fantasies about it.

At this point it is necessary to differentiate the separate forms taken by the Oedipal conflict in males and females.

The young male child becomes attracted to the mother and at the same time resentful of the father, whose elimination from the scene would presumably provide him with the exclusive attention of the mother. The highly aggressive wish to replace the father is, however, also an extremely frightening one, for two reasons. First there is the danger that the seemingly all-powerful father might retaliate. Secondly, such impulses are in conflict with feelings of love, admiration, and dependence which are usually held for the father.

The type of retaliation that the young boy grows to fear is the removal of precisely the organ that is simultaneously the source of so much pleasure and the instigator of the entire problem—the penis. This is the meaning of the concept of *castration anxiety*. For the male this is an acutely intense and uncomfortable feeling, which cannot long be tolerated. For that reason some resolution of the conflict must take place relatively quickly. The only form such resolution can take, given the child's limitations, the father's power, and the mother's apparent preference for the father, is the repression of the Oepidal wish and the holding in check of sexual impulses. Other consequences of the Oedipal conflict will be discussed later.

In the girl the course of the Oedipal struggle is different, and more complicated, than that in the boy. She, like the boy, cathects the mother and wishes to replace the father. She, however, does not come to grief because of castration anxiety since she lacks a penis in the first place. The realization that she is anatomically different from the male results in a mixture of intense feelings, including shame and inferiority over her inadequacy, jealousy of the male (technically referred to as *penis envy*—the female counterpart of castration anxiety—the theory is now being questioned by feminists), and anger toward the mother who is considered responsible for the little girl's "deprivation." This emotional reaction causes the female to turn away from the mother and to draw closer to the father, the possessor of the prized organ. She does what she can to replace the mother in her father's esteem. For the female, the Oedipal conflict tends to be more protracted than for the male since she is not under the immediate pressure that he is to resolve it. For a period of years she can be quite close to the father, can manifest much open affection as "daddy's little girl." By early adolescence, when the girl is more of a grown-up woman than a child, her wish to be the father's sole sexual ob-

ject must terminate because of incest taboos. At this point, the girl's earlier attachment to the mother is reinstituted and she identifies with her as a wife, homemaker, and so on. This allows her to serve her father in some of the ways that her mother does and, at the same time, conditions her for peer heterosexual interactions culminating in marriage. Thus, the original Oedipal wish must eventually be renounced and repressed in the female, as in the male, if a normal development sequence is to ensue.

Another consequence of the Oedipal conflict is the consolidation of the superego. The beginnings of this system are present in the prephallic stages as the demands of significant figures such as parents or parent-substitutes begin to shape behavior. These early demands are relatively simple ones, however, with the most important of them involving responses that must be curbed in connection with toilet training. In these early stages of development parents are obeyed because of the uncomfortable consequences that might follow disobedience and, often, restraint requires the presence of the parent. During the Oedipal period, however, morality and doing the right thing become "inner" matters and the dread punishment for transgression comes more from within than from without.

The factors that produce this transformation are related to repression and abandonment of incestuous Oedipal wishes. In addition to renouncing the Oedipal wish, the child must also identify, in large measure, with the threatening parent. This is a case of "if you can't lick 'em, join 'em." It is this identification associated with the repudiation of the incestuous wish that forms the nucleus of the mature superego.

The development of the superego during the Oedipal phase eases the burden on the ego which, during this period, must hold intense feelings in check. The superego assists in this defensive action of the ego and from that viewpoint it is an asset. On the other hand, the presence of the superego also serves to limit all future actions of the ego. No longer is it sufficient to be concerned with the practical consequences of instinctual release. Henceforth, moral and ethical considerations assume equal importance, thereby making it necessary for the ego to serve "three harsh masters," as Freud once put it: the id, external reality, and the superego.

The person who fails to develop satisfactorily through the phallic period and who never properly resolves the Oedipal conflict may display later personality characteristics reflecting problems basic to this developmental stage. Such individuals may behave recklessly and in what appears to be a self-assured fashion. They may seem especially courageous or may engage in activities that involve great risk. Basically, they must constantly attempt to demonstrate their adequacy because they are driven by unresolved castration anxiety.

The successful resolution of the Oedipal conflict enables the child to develop a model that is an important basis for successfully filling his role as an adult. Assumption of the proper sex role, the role of husband or wife, and eventually of parent will all be facilitated by the experience of having had the Oedipal conflict and having mastered it. In addition, the development of a mature superego provides control over impulses and lessens the burden of the ego, whose organization is thereby strengthened and prepared for further growth.

Latency

The phallic stage is followed by the period of *latency*. This is a period of moratorium between the turbulence of the first three pregenital stages and the turmoil of adolescence. It extends from age six or seven to twelve or thirteen. During latency the instincts are thought to be relatively dormant. According to Fenichel (1945), Freud believed that such a quiescent period characterized the entire human species. The natural weakening of the infantile biological urges was, in fact, seen as a "biological precondition" for repression. A variety of forces, such as shame, that oppose instinctual expression develops during this period.

The Genital Stage

The *genital stage* of development is reached after the Oedipal wishes, which reemerge in early adolescence, have been resolved. Up to this time all cathexes have been narcissistic ones. That is, other people have been important only insofar as they provided pleasure, and the object uppermost in one's concerns has been oneself. In the genital stage altruistic motives take on importance and one finds pleasure in giving to others as well as in receiving. This becomes an important basis for advanced socialization, marriage, and taking one's place as a responsible member of society. During this final phase, the pregenital impulses are not entirely replaced by genital ones, but become fused with the genital impulses.

PSYCHOPATHOLOGY FROM A PSYCHOANALYTIC VIEWPOINT

Freud initially distinguished between neuroses based on physical disturbances of the sexual metabolism and those resulting from psychic conflict. The former were called *actual neuroses* and the latter *psychoneuroses*. He included neurasthenia (listlessness, vague aches and pains, headaches) and anxiety reactions among the actual neuroses. "Unhygienic" sexual practices such as masturbation or coitus interruptus were assumed to lead to biochemical disturbances resulting in symptoms of actual neurosis. Although Freud maintained this distinction throughout his career, he wrote relatively little about the actual neuroses and this topic has not received much attention from other psychoanalytic theorists.

For Freud, the psychoneuroses resulted from internal conflicts between instincts pressing for discharge and counterforces set up by the ego. An understanding of how such conflicts become troublesome can be approached from the point of view of both the ego and the instincts. The ego may fail to develop with sufficient adequacy to manage its many complex obligations effectively. This may occur because it cannot make the identifications or model itself after people who best prepare it for its mediating functions. Failure to identify properly can result from excessive frustration of instincts or their excessive indulgence during any given stage of development. Excessive or insufficient suppression of instincts can have adverse consequences on behavior. Excessive inhibition, for example, results in an incapacity for enjoying life, whereas too little inhibition often results in a poorly socialized personality, ill-suited to normal competition. Related to these over- or underinhibited states may be a superego that is unduly harsh, or lenient, or some inconsistent alternation between the two.

Many instinctual outlets chosen by the ego are based on identification and/or sublimation. One may become a scientist either through identification with a respected person who has followed such a career or because of the sublimation of an intense sexual curiosity deriving from early childhood. Often, however, effective sublimations cannot be engineered by the ego, in which case some of its energy is diverted into keeping the instinct in check. These restrictions can have enormous behavioral consequences, as shown, for example, by the person who subconsciously avoids success in his life work in order to escape a conflict that would cause anxiety or unhappiness.

Sometimes when the personality is confronted by a conflict (such as the Oedipal conflict) it cannot adequately master, there will be an instinctual reversion to an earlier developmental stage at which a fixation had occurred. This process is known as *regression*. In regression the individual unconsciously renounces the potential pleasures of the current stage to which he cannot adapt in favor of the gratifications of an earlier developmental stage where libido remained invested. In another process described earlier as *fixation*, libidinal investment at a particular stage is so intense that relatively little instinctual energy can be invested in later developmental stages. These fixations and regressions result in character traits akin to those described as typifying the various developmental stages.

A typical pattern in the psychoneuroses involves id-ego conflict stemming from early childhood (most commonly the Oedipal stage) which is resolved through the ego's use of identification, regression, repression, and possibly even some partial sublimation. This resolution may be adequate until some later period in life when something occurs to weaken the ego's ability to restrain the instinct. Thus, the instincts or their *derivatives* (instinctual cathexes displaced onto associatively connected objects or ideas that are less objectionable to the ego), threaten to make their way into consciousness. When this occurs symptoms arise reflecting a compromise between the direct instinctual expression and the efforts of the ego to restrain it. Such a compromise is precisely like the one that occurs in many dreams, where manifest content is a resultant of the instinct's efforts to gain access to consciousness and the censor's efforts to prevent this. Thus, the symptoms of psychoneuroses such as hysteria, phobias, and obsessive-compulsive reactions are seen to reflect both the drive-derivative and the ego's defense against it. Also, as in a dream where manifest content is "overdetermined," a given symptom may be rooted in more than a single conflict.

It should be added that constitutional factors are thought to play some part in the development of a psychoneurosis. Such factors may determine the intensity of a given conflict, since the strength of a particular instinct is seen to be related to hereditary factors.

FREUDIAN THEORY IN PERSPECTIVE

Despite its enormous influence over twentieth-century thought, Freudian theory is not without its shortcomings. This was felt even by many of the men who were part of Freud's inner circle in the earliest days of psychoanalysis. Freud's early formulations took the shape they did, undoubtedly, because he worked primarily with hysterical middle-class females in Victorian Vienna. Ford and Urban (1963) speculate that since Freud was known to regard sexuality as an important aspect of life, he may have attracted patients who were willing, perhaps even eager, to stress such matters. Thus, a theory that may have been formulated tentatively at first seemed to be reinforced again and again in his clinical practice. Further, as he became more con-

vinced of the validity of his theory, Freud may well have unwittingly encouraged his patients to make the types of responses he expected. Work done in the 1960s on the social psychology of the experiment by Orne (1962) and on experimenter bias by Rosenthal (1963) supports such an interpretation.

A major problem with analytic theory is in the universality imputed to Freud's constructs. Freud was not content to unravel the problem of hysteria and to find a way to treat it. His ambition was to understand all of human behavior and its vicissitudes. From the patients he actually worked with he drew the principles of human behavior that were then applied to a variety of behavioral phenomena. Two of Freud's classic case studies (one involving phobia in a child and one a serious paranoid disorder) were done on patients he had never even seen and whose problems were quite unlike those of his early patients. As the clinical experience of Freud's early collaborators widened, several (Adler, Jung, and Rank, for example) rejected ideas that Freud felt were central to his theory. Their experience led them to downgrade the importance of sexual forces in shaping behavior in favor of other forces. Adler stressed the significance of certain social forces. Jung became impressed by the possible existence of a "collective unconscious." Rank attempted to base a theory of behavior on the reaction to birth trauma and all later separations.

Many who have trained as psychoanalysts but who rejected basic aspects of its theories have tended to stress the significance of social forces in shaping man's life. In so doing such individuals (for example, Horney, Fromm, Sullivan) are no longer regarded as orthodox psychoanalysts. Perhaps the major modification of Freud's theory that won widespread acceptance even in orthodox circles involved the re-evaluation of his views of ego development by men such as Rudolf Lowenstein, Ernst Kris, David Rapaport, and Erik Erikson. These, so-called ego psychologists, questioned whether all psychic energy resides in the id. Further, they denied that all ego functions depend upon the diversion of psychic energy only to assist the id to adapt to the environment's demands.

Another weakness of psychoanalysis already alluded to in Chapter 3 is in the fact that instead of promoting prevention, it stressed an extraordinarily expensive (in both time and money) treatment model. Admittedly, the duration of treatment became prolonged gradually as experience built up with patients other than hysterics. Still, the current version of the treatment model is most unwieldy and impractical. Even if psychoanalysis were always successful, the time required to train an analyst and the time it takes to work a patient through the process limits its application to a tiny percentage of those needing assistance with psychological problems. Furthermore, since psychoanalysis is suitable only for the relatively bright, psychologically sound, and financially well-fixed, it paradoxically offers the most intensive attention to that segment of the population with psychological problems who seemingly need it the least.

Finally, on scientific grounds psychoanalysis leaves much to be desired. Key concepts are poorly defined, and the theory engages in much circular reasoning. The validity of the theory is, therefore, very difficult to test. Many assertions about prototypical early life situations can only be verified through the revelations of patients in treatment. But how can we be sure that what a patient produces is not elicited by a therapist who expects to receive such material?

CONCLUSION

Despite the shortcomings of psychoanalysis, Freud's contribution to abnormal psychology was monumental. His insistence on *psychic determinism* established a groundwork for a science of human behavior. The concept of the *unconscious* made much puzzling behavior explicable. In addition, his work was "revolutionary" in its impact because it broadened the scope of the helping professions. Because of Freud's work psychoneuroses and, later, other disorders not considered worthy of the mental health professional's concern began to receive attention.

Paradoxically, the framework Freud created may well have impeded further theoretical advance for a time. This is not an uncommon result of a revolutionary upheaval in any field. Freud's insistence that he was uncovering general behavior laws and his ability to win the acceptance of his views probably slowed the development of theoretical modifications. Such modifications were ultimately made by clinicians who had experience with patients different from those Freud saw early in his career.

Freud's work did lead to the development of diagnostic schemes and the recognition of neurotic symptoms quite different from the hysterias that Freud first encountered. Chapter 9 will include a full description of neurotic disorders along with a discussion of current nosology. In addition, recent theoretical outlooks on neurosis differing from Freud's will be presented there.

SUMMARY

1. The study and treatment of hysterics was carried on in the nineteenth century primarily by general practitioners. One major controversy was over whether hysteria resulted from organic or purely psychological causes. Hypnosis was a common method for treating hysteria.
2. Freud was a neurologist who became interested in the problem of hysteria through contact with Breuer, a well-known Viennese physician. He included many hysterics in his medical practice and augmented his early training in Paris with such patients by visiting Liebeault's clinic in Nancy. In Vienna he adopted Breuer's technique of talking to the patient about current problems and eventually abandoned hypnosis.
3. What Freud learned from the discussions with patients led to the theories of *resistance* and the *unconscious*. Dream theory developed as an experiment in the self-analysis of his own unconscious.
4. As his work progressed Freud attempted to build a theory to explain behavior of all kinds.
5. Freud developed a personality theory in which he saw man as constantly motivated to maintain a balance of internal psychic forces. He conceived of three aspects of personality: *id, ego,* and *superego.* A variety of psychological defense mechanisms were described as protecting the person from the damaging effects of acting on impulses.
6. Development was conceived to take place through various psychosexual stages mostly in the first five years of life: the oral, anal, phallic, and genital. Each stage was seen to bear the seeds for adult behavior patterns.
7. Psychopathology was seen to result from inner conflict stemming from a combination of inadequate development and insurmountable current challenges.
8. Weaknesses in Freudian theory are seen to derive largely from the overgeneralization of principles developed from work with a specific patient population.
9. Freud's work is considered revolutionary in its scope-broadening impact.

CHAPTER 6

Schizophrenia

*Description,
Nosology,
and Treatment*

The same hour was the thing fulfilled upon Nebuchadnezzar: and he was driven from men, and did eat grass as oxen, and his body was wet with the dew of heaven, till his hairs were grown like eagle's feathers, and his nails like bird's claws.

Daniel 4:33

Psychotic disorders were described even in biblical times. Schizophrenia is the most highly researched and least well understood of all the psychotic disorders. Only elements of what we know as schizophrenia were described before the nineteenth century. Several nineteenth-century psychiatrists described aspects of schizophrenia. It was not, however, until Kraepelin's work on major disorders that a distinct nosological entity emerged. Kraepelin labeled the disorder *dementia praecox* and stressed its progressively declining course. This view was not acceptable to other contemporary students of behavior disorder. The most noteworthy dissenter was Eugen Bleuler (1857–1939). Bleuler was a Swiss psychiatrist familiar with the work of both Kraepelin and Freud. He gave dementia praecox a new name, schizophrenia, and established a new set of principles for diagnosing the disorder. His work has had great influence over current thinking about schizophrenia. For that reason many of his ideas will be set forth in some detail.

139

BLEULER'S VIEW OF SCHIZOPHRENIA

Bleuler was professor of psychiatry at the Burghölzli, a public mental hospital in Zurich, where his students included Carl Jung, Karl Abraham, and Max Eitingon, each of whom had had extended contact with Freud. For a time Bleuler himself was a member of the International Psychoanalytic Association. Bleuler's central thesis was that patients diagnosed as suffering dementia praecox might have either a good or poor prognosis; he therefore searched for features that distinguished the different types of patients grouped under this diagnostic entity, since he believed that the outcome was related to the specific manifestation of the disorder. His new understanding prompted him to rename the disorder "schizophrenia," a term he believed conveyed more accurately the essence of the illness, regardless of the overt clinical picture—that various psychic functions were split apart. Whereas in the normal there

was a harmony among such functions as thinking, feeling, and relating to the external world, this was not found in the patient with dementia praecox. For the latter there was more or less a loss of unity to the personality, such that at different times different "psychic complexes" predominated. Instead of combining forces toward a single guiding purpose, individual complexes dominate for a time while others are "split off" and play no role in behavior. The resultant behavior is unpredictable and at times bizarre. On the other hand, perception, orientation, and memory may be unaffected—as with other less profound disorders.

In 1911 Bleuler described the precise nature of the schizophrenic disorder as manifested in all of its subcategories (Bleuler, 1950). He distinguished between fundamental symptoms, present to some degree in all cases, and accessory symptoms whose presence was variable and inconsistent, and which were not confined to schizophrenia. When these symptoms were found in schizophrenia, however, they had a distinctive quality in terms either of origin or of their clinical appearance compared to that in a nonschizophrenic patient.

The Bettmann Archive

This William Blake drawing depicts the suffering of the psychotic King Nebuchadnezzar.

SCHIZOPHRENIC SYMPTOMATOLOGY FROM BLEULER'S VIEW

The "Fundamental" Symptoms

The Simple Functions

Association

Basic in schizophrenia, according to Bleuler, is disturbance of the continuity of thought. Thinking is ordinarily guided by thousands of associative threads. In the schizophrenic, single threads or whole groups of thoughts are interrupted so that the normal logic of thought is lost.

One form of this disturbance is the lack of purpose in the remarks of schizophrenics. Purpose, or the desire to make a point, is a central determinant of normal association. Because this is lacking in the schizophrenic, his verbal productions are not held together by a guiding purpose. An example is the following excerpt from a letter written by a schizophrenic (Bleuler, 1950, p. 17):

> DEAR MOTHER: Today I am feeling better than yesterday. I really don't feel much like writing. But I love to write to you. After all, I can tackle it twice. Yesterday, Sunday, I would have been so happy if you and Louise and I could have gone to the park. One has such a lovely view from Stephen's Castle. Actually, it is very lovely in Burghölzli. Louise wrote Burghölzli on her last two letters, I mean to say on the envelope, no, the "couverts" which I received. However, I have written Burghölzli in the spot where I put the date. There are also patients in Burghölzli who call it "Holzliburg." Others talk of a factory. One may also regard it as a health resort.

Where the normal might have engaged in a narrative to describe his surroundings and how he felt about them, this patient was impelled to respond first to one, then to another, idea, as they flashed through consciousness. Side associations intrude, and his thinking is not held together by a central purpose.

In other cases, the thought disorder involves a disruption of so many of the associative threads that virtually no connections can be found. The following passage (Bleuler, 1950, p. 20) exemplifies disconnected association (asterisks indicate points where a sudden shift in ideas has been made):

> One must have arisen sufficiently early and then there is usually the necessary "appetite" present. "L'appetit vient en mangeant," says the Frenchman. *With time and years the individual becomes so lazy in public life that he is not even capable of writing any more. On such a sheet of paper, one can squeeze many letters if one is careful not to transgress by one "square shoe." *In such fine weather one should be able to take a walk in the woods. Naturally, not alone, but with a girl. *At the end of the year one always renders the annual accounting. . . .

Relationships among ideas established by schizophrenics can sometimes be traced to emotional factors. Thus, one patient associated the phrase "that my cousin Max would come to life again" to the word "wood," seemingly in response to the idea that a coffin is made of wood and to a death (which was significant to her because it played a part in her unhappy love affair).

On other occasions, schizophrenics make associations based on the similarity of word sounds, such as "head-bed." These so-called clang-associations are found in manic patients as well as in schizophrenics; however, the sound similarities that bring two words into association are more distant for the schizophrenic than for the manic.

Schizophrenics also string out associations, based on well-known phrases, even though they are entirely out of context. One woman, for example, in enumerating the members of her family, said "father, son," and then added "the holy ghost."

Condensations (contractions) of several ideas into one are also common. One patient associated "steam-sail" to the word "sail" as a combination of the separate ideas of "steam-boat" and "sail-boat." The creation of new words (neologisms), such as "sad-some," as a combination of "sad" and "lonesome," is another example of schizophrenic disruption of language and thought.

A fairly common cause of associative disturbance among schizophrenics is their tendency to remain fixed on a limited cluster of ideas that intrude in a stereotyped way. Occasionally the cue for stereotyped responding is found in a previous response. For example, one patient gave the following reactions to the designated stimulus words: *star*—"that is the greatest of blessings"; *caressing*—"that is perfection"; *wonderful*—"the will"; *child*—"of the deity"; *purple*—"heaven and earth." The first association was a religious one and those that followed continued in a religious vein despite their inappropriateness.

Another associative pattern found in schizophrenics involves simply naming objects in one's view, as for example when stimulus words elicit the names of objects in the room usually quite inappropriately. A related response of schizophrenics is simply to repeat what is heard (*echolalia*).

Yet another characteristic is "blocking" of a train of thought. Here there is an abrupt cessation of associations because the patient finds them unpleasant. For example, a young girl speaks freely of her past life only up to the time when she met her sweetheart.

Affectivity

The basic affective symptom in schizophrenics is a lack of emotional involvement in the things and people that had previously been important. In chronic cases, affective impoverishment is an outstanding feature. Even in less chronic cases, however, it is present, although there are intact areas of affect. Illustrations of this emotional indifference are as follows: a mother has no concern whatever for her family even though she is intellectually aware that good or evil is about to befall them; patients sit, uninvolved, in a ward while one of their fellows kills another; a patient writes home for the first time after six weeks of hospitalization and asks only about the family cat. The patient may be unconcerned about whether he starves or suffers from extreme heat or cold. Bleuler described an occasion when a fire on a ward placed patients in danger of burning to death or suffocating, yet many did nothing to save themselves and had to be led out by others.

Affective impoverishment, however, is not necessarily all-pervasive in all cases. In the early phases of the disorder, there is often an emotional oversensitivity resulting in so much lability that patients must isolate themselves to escape overstimulation. Even in these cases, however, Bleuler believed that affect was shallow and that close observation could show that partial indifference had replaced concern. Still, some schizophrenics do retain considerable affect and genuine involvement about isolated segments of their existence. Bleuler cited some who would be described as "active writers, world improvers, health fanatics, and founders of new religions."

A striking feature of the affective deterioration of schizophrenics is the quick mood-swing that occurs because "pockets" of emotion remain intact. The pain or the joys of a remote love affair, for example, may be experienced vividly as if the feeling had been preserved in its original state. The feelings most often preserved are those of anger or irritability, although they may include parental love or even sympathy for others.

Finally, Bleuler identified two dramatic forms of affective disturbance seen in some schizophrenics—*parathymia* and *paramimia*. The former term describes a reaction to an event that is opposite to the one expected: news of a death in the family elicits laughter, and neutral or slightly pleasant events provoke irritation. This reversal of affect extends to taste and smell so that substances from which one normally recoils in disgust are savored by the schizophrenic. Bleuler described a patient who was questioned about why he drank his own urine. His response was, "Herr Direktor, if you should taste it but once, you would never want to drink anything else" (Bleuler, 1950, p. 52). In paramimia, the patient expresses opposing feelings simultaneously; thus, a patient approached an admired attendant and said, very sweetly, "I really would like to slap your face. People like you are usually called S.O.B.'s" (Bleuler, 1950, p. 52).

Ambivalence

The tendency to endow psychic mechanisms or objects with positive and negative features simultaneously is considered by Bleuler to be a characteristic though not always obvious symptom of schizophrenia. This can involve: *the feelings*, in which, for example, both love and hate for a close relative are expressed; *the will*, in which one both wants and does not want to do something; or *the intellect*, in which one makes an assertion and promptly denies it. The contradictions resulting from such behavior are not usually noticed by the patient.

Intact Simple Functions

Bleuler made a strong point in differentiating schizophrenia from organic psychoses with respect to certain of the so-called simple functions, such as sensation and perception, memory, orientation, consciousness, and motility. Organic defects may disrupt all or some of these functions to various degrees. In contrast, Bleuler held that schizophrenia left these processes essentially unimpaired. Where defects in such functions were found, Bleuler believed that they were secondary effects of schizophrenia. Simple functions such as orientation are difficult to assess in the schizophrenic. For example, a patient may be unable to tell the examiner what year it is, not because he does not know, but rather because he is not interested in the question or because a delusion compels him to respond idiosyncratically.

Another problem in communication arises because the patient with associative difficulties often speaks symbolically while the examiner accepts what he says literally. For example, a schizophrenic's complaint that he is unable to see might not mean that his eyesight is impaired but, rather, that his perception of reality is defective. Bleuler went so far as to say that the schizophrenic engages in "double-entry bookkeeping" in which both realities and their personal falsifications are registered. Depending upon circumstances, one or the other entry, or both, may be used at any given time.

Experiments that seemed to indicate defective sensory processes in schizophrenics were interpreted by Bleuler to reflect only the fact that such patients are inattentive and not motivated to respond appropriately on sensory and perceptual tasks. Bleuler believed that the memory of schizophrenics was, in some respects, *more* acute than that of normals because they registered details dismissed by normals as unessential. Bleuler recognized that frequently schizophrenics seem to have difficulty in reproducing what they experience.

This occurred, he felt, because accurate reproduction depends upon intact associational processes which, in turn, are influenced by the emotions.

The Compound Functions

Autism

By autism Bleuler meant a detachment from reality, resulting in a predominance of the inner life over the external. Schizophrenics are thus taken up largely with their own wishes or fears, which become, for them, more real than stimuli from the outside world. The degree of autism in the schizophrenic varies with the severity of the disorder. Some patients mingle a capacity for relating realistically with autistic tendencies. An example of this is the woman who at a concert suddenly begins singing and continues, quite satisfied, until she is finished, despite the protests of those around her.

Many schizophrenics' autism reaches a total lack of concern with their surroundings, staring at a blank wall or drawing bed clothes over them to shut off their sensory receptors. In others, where autism is less obvious, it is only after extended observation that one notices how little they are affected by outside influences and how much they seek their own way. Normal reactions are possible only in matters that do not touch upon the autisms.

In the same way that autistic feeling is divorced from reality, autistic thought is subjective. Being organized around affective needs, it is not necessarily bound to usual logic. Instead, symbols, analogies, and fragmentary concepts direct the autisms in a schizophrenic, even though he is capable of thinking logically when he turns his attention back to reality. Some patients are believed to sense the difference in these two types of thinking and recognize that their relationship to reality has been changed by the rise of their autism. Others, however, never become aware of how their thought processes have deviated from realistic thinking.

Attention

Because of affective impoverishment in schizophrenia, what Bleuler referred to as "active attention" is diminished. Where emotional involvement remains, the schizophrenic can approach normal attentiveness, but where interest has been withdrawn from the external world he is unmotivated to attend to specific stimuli. However, Bleuler believed that *passive* attention, or reception of stimuli—many of which are normally ignored precisely because attention is focused on a limited sector—is actually enhanced in schizophrenics. Consequently, a remarkable number of events register on the minds of schizophrenics who are quite out of touch with reality. Many years after an event, a patient can reproduce minute details of what had occurred, despite having been apparently entirely self-absorbed at the time.

© Chris Rollins

Autistic schizophrenics sometimes sit for hours completely withdrawn from reality.

The attention span of schizophrenics is variable, ranging from normal to an almost complete inability to concentrate, even with special effort. Fatigue and blocking may cause attention to waver. In cases of blocking, the schizophrenic seems suddenly to be diverted during a conversation and appears to be thinking of something entirely remote, or not thinking at all. Even at such times, however, schizophrenics are capable of monitoring what occurred during the inattentive period and are later able to answer questions that they seemed unable to comprehend at the time.

The Will

Bleuler believed that the will, like attention, is adversely affected by the affective and associative deterioration of the schizophrenic. Since schizophrenics are not interested in doing things, they appear lazy and neglectful, neither motivated by nor responding to the urging of others. There are, however, occasions when "will" in schizophrenics takes an opposite form. Some schizophrenics can neither withstand nor temper internally or externally stimulated impulses. They follow whatever whim arises, either because they fail to consider the consequences or because, though aware of the consequences, they are indifferent to them. Their behavior is, accordingly, unpredictable.

Schizophrenic "Dementia"

Bleuler went to some length to differentiate between the seemingly demented behavior of schizophrenics and that caused by brain deterioration. He pointed out that many schizophrenics score poorly on intelligence tests, not because their abilities have deteriorated as a result of organic processes, but rather because of the associative and affective disturbances that are basic to the disorder. Whereas the mental defective has never been able to form complicated connections between ideas and associations, and the organically damaged patient has lost the ability to do so, the schizophrenic can or cannot do so depending upon specific circumstances. Thus a schizophrenic who has appeared quite demented may, for example, suddenly produce a well-integrated plan to escape from the hospital. Less dramatically, a patient who at one moment cannot add 17 and 14 and at another can solve a difficult arithmetic problem is far more likely to be schizophrenic than mentally defective or suffering from brain damage. Mental defectives and the organically damaged are adequate in simple situations and fail at what is too complicated for them. Not so the schizophrenic. Where the problem, no matter how simple, touches a danger area for him, his performance may be bizarre and inadequate, but with nonthreatening tasks his intellectual powers can operate at their former level of efficiency. Accordingly, schizophrenics cannot properly be compared to organics or to children in terms of intellectual functions. Although their total scores on intelligence tests may be similar, they are likely to achieve them in qualitatively different ways.

Behavior in Mild Schizophrenia

Schizophrenic behavior was seen by Bleuler to vary with the severity of the disorder. The blatantly disturbed patient has already been described as lacking interests, initiative, and goals, and as disregarding reality. The very mild case, on the other hand, may lead an essentially normal life in many respects, and may be regarded as healthy by casual observers. Those with mild forms of schizophrenia can work successfully at a variety of functions ranging from the routine to the highly complicated, although they are likely to be most successful in the former. Outstanding characteristics include their special sensitivities, strong reactions to events that others see as trivial, and an occasional odd "bit" of behavior. Not uncommonly, they are regarded by others as "different" and drift from job to job, thus limiting contacts with the external world.

The "Accessory" Symptoms

Accessory symptoms, though not basic to the disorder, give schizophrenia its "external stamp." Bleuler believed that such symptoms often make institutionalization necessary since their appearance makes the psychosis manifest. These symptoms may be present either throughout the entire schizophrenic disorder or only during certain periods. The most common are *hallucinations, illusions*, and *delusions*.

Hallucinations

Hallucinations, the experiencing of sensations in the absence of external stimuli, are quite common in hospitalized schizophrenics. Auditory hallucinations are most common. Visual hallucinations are common only in patients experiencing acute excitement or a clouding of consciousness. Tactile or taste hallucinations are rare and often difficult to distinguish from *illusions*, in which external stimuli are simply misinterpreted. Occasionally, small animals—such as snakes—are felt crawling over the body.

Bleuler believed that the content of hallucinations, which ranges quite widely, could be generated by anything that a normal person perceived and that it might be determined by the patient's wishes or fears. For example, ambitious patients may hear that they are to achieve power and status, or that their enemies conspire against them. Most commonly, auditory hallucinations

involve speech. "Voices" utter threats and curses from almost anywhere—the walls, the roof, heaven, hell, near or far. The voices may be contradictory, at one moment threatening and at another pleasant. When the patient is confused, the voices may be a babble.

Visual hallucinations become a part of the immediate surroundings of the patient. People are seen walking through the room or standing over someone's head. In some visions people become transparent, so that the room behind them is visible. Where others find a percept vague the schizophrenic may see definite objects. Generally, visual images are seen as both moving about and producing noises.

Hallucinations of taste or smell are characterized less by special characteristics and more by the wide range they assume. Typical complaints are of tasting blood, sperm, feces, or poison in food, or of the odor of corpses, chloroform, tar, or "snake-sweat." Indeed, one patient even claimed he could smell his own masturbation. When the patient is in a "good mood" pleasant smells or tastes may be hallucinated.

Bleuler observed that hallucinations occurred primarily when patients were alone in quiet surroundings: darkness and night maximize their appearance; distractions, by contrast, reduce them.

Illusions

Illusions are misperceptions of real stimuli. They are not always easily distinguished from hallucinations since they may be prompted by vague, external stimuli or even internal ones. Speech that is quite clear to most observers may be entirely misinterpreted by the schizophrenic in keeping with delusional beliefs. Certain types of visual illusions can be quite dangerous to the patient—for example, mistaking a window for a door.

Delusions

Bleuler believed that delusions, misinterpretations of actual events, reflected—as do hallucinations—the patient's wishes and fears. Although they may take any form, most delusions are of the persecutory type. Examples of these are seen in patients who are persuaded that, through the scheming of others, they have lost jobs, been assigned particularly hard jobs, been defamed by neighbors, or been robbed. Freemasons, Jesuits, "black Jews," fellow employees, and so on, are engaged in a conspiracy against them. Rarely does a schizophrenic attempt to determine *how* these persecutions are being carried out; he concentrates on *why* they are. Typical conclusions are jealousy over the patient's commercial or sexual prowess, pleasure derived from torturing the patient, or the desire to use the patient in an experiment.

Many delusions are grandiose in nature. Some have a base of plausibility—a patient with mathematical ability may believe that further study will make him a great mathematician. Most grandiose delusions, however, go far beyond reasonable bounds. One patient insists that he has as much money as there are "snowflakes on the ground." Another regards himself as the King of England, Napoleon, or Christ. One patient of Bleuler's insisted he had invented all the machines made in the past fifty years, although he himself was only twenty.

Schizophrenic delusions usually lack unity. Entirely unconnected or even contradictory ideas may coexist. Furthermore, Bleuler noted that parts of the personality often "recognized" that the delusions did not make good sense. One patient, for example, could laugh at the fact that although he was the Lord, he could not get himself out of the hospital.

Delusions may come about simply because of erroneous interpretations based on inadequate information. When this happens, however, it is probably because they are supported by the patient's affective needs. Bleuler used an example based on *delusions of reference*, in which the patient believes that trivial or routine occurrences have special relevance to him. A schizophrenic was asked by his sister, during a meal, whether he wanted more bread. This simple question precipitated a wild outburst in which the schizophrenic attempted to stab his sister because she had referred to his unemployment (in German, his "breadlessness").

The duration of delusions is quite varied. Many delusional ideas that arise during acute schizophrenic episodes fade away as the acute state passes. In chronic schizophrenia delusions can last a lifetime, although some recede after having been re-

Schizophrenia (From *A Psychiatrist's Anthology*, by Louis J. Karnosh, published in 1942 by the Occupational Therapy Press, Cleveland City Hospital. Reprinted with permission of the author.)

peated monotonously for some time. Bleuler described a woman with chronic schizophrenia who managed to maintain herself outside of a hospital until after her menopause. The woman had developed the delusion, when she was 20, that she would receive 20,000 francs if she remained a virgin for 30 more years. When she reached the age of 50 she tried to collect the money at a bank.

Bleuler believed that schizophrenics never entirely renounce their delusions and that, even when much improved after a period of illness, cannot be objective about earlier delusions. Either they try to dismiss them too lightly or they remain emotionally involved with them. There are times when one can only understand an "improved" patient's thought by assuming that his delusions retain some reality for him. Furthermore, the fact that relapse into schizophrenia often reawakens old delusions makes it seem more likely that the delusions have been preserved rather than abandoned.

Bleuler's Classification of Schizophrenia

Bleuler's categorization was quite similar to Kraepelin's. He adopted the latter's three subgroups—the paranoid, hebephrenic, and catatonic. Kraepelin himself added the category of simple schizophrenia, following Bleuler's suggestion. These have become a part of modern nosologies, including the ones found in DSM-I (1952) and DSM-II (1968).

CURRENT CLASSIFICATION OF SCHIZOPHRENIA

DSM-II (1968) describes schizophrenia as follows: "This large category includes a group of disorders manifested by characteristic disturbances of thinking, mood and behavior. Disturbances in thinking, are marked by alterations of concept formation which may lead to misinterpretation of reality and sometimes to delusions and hallucinations, which frequently appear psychologically self-protective. Corollary mood changes include ambivalent, constricted and inappropriate emotional responsiveness and loss of empathy with others. Behavior may be withdrawn, regressive and bizarre." This description obviously draws much from Bleuler. Schizophrenic subtypes are determined by the predominant symptoms.

Schizophrenia, Simple Type

The most notable symptom of simple schizophrenia is withdrawal from external interests and relationships. Apathy and indifferenece are marked; overt delusions and hallucinations are uncommon. Onset is insidious. Simple schizophrenics function well below their potential level, and this contrast between ability and accomplishment is a striking feature of the disorder. Simple schizophrenics often end up as social isolates in marginal occupations. Frequently, the severity of their symptoms and their mental deterioration increase with time. Dramatically psychotic states, as seen in other schizophrenic types, are, however, not found.

Schizophrenia, Hebephrenic Type

The most prominent feature of hebephrenic schizophrenia is the shallow and inappropriate affect. This includes giggling, "silly" behavior, and tearful periods. Somatic delusions and profound regressive behavior are commonly noted. Hebephrenic patients are rarely able to care for themselves be-

CASE 6-1: A CASE OF SIMPLE SCHIZOPHRENIA

Charleton C., a thirty-six-year-old single man, was committed for the first time to a midwestern state hospital after being arrested for vagrancy.

He was the youngest of eight children born to a struggling farm family in New England. His education was interrupted after the completion of grammar school because of the need to help on the family farm. Although he always related well to members of his family, contact with them was limited, due to the pressing needs of the farm, which occupied the energies of his parents and older siblings. He had virtually no social contact with people outside his family, since his time was spent either working on the farm or doing various odd jobs in the neighborhood. When World War II began he was inducted and served until the end, seeing combat throughout the European theater. When discharged he still had the rank of private, and continued to occupy himself with a series of farming and unskilled labor jobs. He never remained at any job longer than a year, and frequently left otherwise satisfactory jobs because he felt that he had stayed in one place for too long a period of time. He traveled from area to area seeking various migrant and transient employments, and was thus able to support himself, albeit at a rather low level.

Two years before his commitment to the hospital he began to have difficulty with even the minimally demanding jobs he usually obtained. He became suspicious of his co-workers, and rather than isolate himself from them, as he previously had done, began to accuse them of various crimes. In an attempt to avoid contact with others, he neglected any semblance of work unless it became necessary to satisfy his basic needs. In the year before he was committed, Charleton was arrested for vagrancy on nine different occasions in the southwest, the midwest, and the northeast. Finally, when he seemed confused and was unable to follow instructions, the police had him examined, certified, and committed to a state institution.

Upon admission to the hospital, Charleton seemed indifferent to his surroundings, and it was not altogether clear that he realized what had occurred. Upon questioning he was very evasive and underproductive and volunteered almost nothing concerning himself. His relationship with the examiner was quite withdrawn, and when he did respond, it was minimally and with no affect. On the ward he did not participate in any activity, and his only contact with other patients was to express suspicion about their activities. Charleton was discharged in the custody of one of his sisters when she agreed to provide a home for him, and he seemed content to live with her and again help with farm chores.

From Zax & Stricker, 1963, pp. 57–58.

cause of their gross personality deterioration and are virtually always placed in institutions. Indeed, of the various schizophrenic subtypes, hebephrenics are perhaps the easiest group for the layman to recognize as profoundly ill, and they conform well to stereotypes of aberrant behavior.

CASE 6-2:   A CASE OF HEBEPHRENIC SCHIZOPHRENIA

Gertrude B., an unmarried woman who had been living with her family in the same New England city in which she was born, entered a state hospital for the second time when she was twenty-nine years old.

*   *   *

At the age of twenty-six Gertrude announced that it was no longer neces-, sary for her to work, as she would surely be provided for, although she was not entirely clear as to her potential source of support. She grew indifferent to others around her, and began to neglect many of her old friends. She constantly complained of headaches and other physical ailments, and would become very frightened at night. She thought that someone would kill her, although she did not know who it would be. When Gertrude began to refuse food she was placed in a large state hospital where she remained for seven months, after which time she had apparently recovered, and was discharged.

After two years of a marginally successful adjustment, Gertrude began to have a relapse. In church she would have uncontrollable fits of giggling during very solemn parts of the services, disturbing everybody around her. She began to wander away from home and, when remonstrated for this, threatened her mother with personal injury. This led to her rehospitalization at the age of twenty-nine, providing a permanent home for her until her death fifty-eight years later.

Gertrude took very little interest in ward activities, and was usually very reticent with patients and personnel. However, she did, upon occasion, indulge in mischievous pranks, and even could be assaultive at times. Her appearance was neglected to the point that she was actually filthy.

As Gertrude's years in the hospital increased, her behavior became progressively more regressed. She constantly attempted to escape by wandering away from others, but never was successful. Her behavior became more silly and childish, and her pranks increased in frequency. She began to hide food and rags in her clothing, and took to stealing laundry and throwing it from the windows. She developed the delusion that she was married to the hospital superintendent, and began to sign her name as Mrs. X. She became resistive to ward routine, and talked constantly, to the distress of those around her.

As the years progressed Gertrude began to require more and more assistance in dressing and personal hygiene. If she was not dressed, combed, and washed she would be content to appear slovenly. She would tie rags in her hair, carry food in her dress, and wear soiled clothing taken from the laundry bag. She would eat ravenously, grabbing food from everyone, eating with her fingers, and soiling herself in the process. Quiescent, withdrawn states would alternate with mischievous and troublesome periods of constant activity, but the latter began to predominate. After twenty-five years in the hospital the following interview took place:

Doctor: How long have you been in this place?
Gertrude: It is nearly two years now, or over a year.

Doctor: How long have you been in this hospital?
Gertrude: A long time—for thousands and thousands of years, I guess.
Doctor: Why are you here?
Gertrude: I came up with the boys to bring the people back home.
Doctor: Do you know how old you are?
Gertrude: I was 29½ when I came.
Doctor: What year were you born?
Gertrude: 1873 (actually, 1874).
Doctor: What year is it now?
Gertrude: 1831 or 32. I am going home. I must really go home. I am better now. I am child-bearing. I am all better now so I must go home. I must run along and get my teeth fixed at Dr.——'s office when I get home. Will you let me out when you get out. I asked for a clean dress and she didn't give it to me. She is in the storeroom fixing up. I must go home. Colgate Cream. The doctor said if I took this she would let me go home. The nurse took my little box.

On another occasion she said:

No, I never was crazy, a little nervous. Look at my teeth, I came here to have my teeth fixed. We're going to have a strawberry party now. Yesterday I heard voices. They said "I ran to the drugstore and I am going home tomorrow." I heard J. B. Scott's voice and it came from up here in the air. We've got 39 banks on Market Street. We've got lots of property. Say, take me home and I'll give you three laundry bags. I'm 29 and a half, 29 and a half. Now I want you to get me ten apples—ten of your most beautiful apples and two dozen lemons. Now listen, if I get you some pineapple will you preserve it.

Gertrude became more and more destructive as the years passed, destroying shrubbery in the yard, taking pictures from the wall, and rearranging rooms. She would decorate herself with tinsel and paper and run around the ward, creating a disturbance. Much of Gertrude's later years were spent in a camisole in order to restrain her. She died of arteriosclerosis at the age of eighty-seven.

From Zax & Stricker, 1963, pp. 67–69.

Schizophrenia, Catatonic Type

While affective disturbance is marked in catatonic schizophrenics, their most conspicuous symptoms are motoric. In more dramatic manifestations one finds a generalized inhibition resulting in a stuporous, mute state, in which the patient fails to change his position for hours on end and is capable of maintaining grossly uncomfortable positions in which he has been placed by others (*waxy flexibility*). At other times, however (sometimes following emergence from a stuporous phase), the patient becomes frenzied (*catatonic excitement*), and his behavior is entirely unrestrained, indiscriminately destroying anything around him. During these periods he may do considerable harm to himself and others. Two

CASE 6–3:   A CASE OF CATATONIC SCHIZOPHRENIA

Henry E., a thirty-seven-year-old divorced father of three, was committed by his brother for the fourth time to a state institution in the large mid-western city where he had spent his life. He had been living with his parents in the family home before admission.

Henry was the eldest of three boys. His parents were briefly described as being attentive to him, and, with reference to his early experience, he would only say that he related well to his entire family. During World War II he attended a state university while in the Army, and later was graduated from a denominational college near his home. Following the war he married and had three children. The marriage was not successful, according to Henry, primarily because of religion, and he was separated from his wife one year before his readmission. He did not seem able to give any further description of his relationship with his wife or its failure. He worked at various bookkeeping jobs throughout his life, and felt he was fairly successful in his work. He described himself as a happy, well-liked person who was very active in community affairs.

Henry's history for the ten years before his admission is in marked contrast to his own description of his life. Henry began to develop fanatical religious ideas soon after his marriage. He felt that it was his personal responsibility to do penance for the souls of sinners, and his first act of penance was to burn his Christmas gifts as a sacrifice to God. He also resigned as an alumnus in a college fraternity because he no longer believed in secret societies. His new ascetic habits resulted in a severe weight loss, and three prior hospitalizations. His symptoms continued virtually unabated from their onset, but he was able to work between hospitalizations.

During the year previous to his current hospitalization, Henry did not walk, talk, or eat unless he felt he was specifically instructed by God to do so. Occasionally he would become excited and violent, and when these episodes occurred he was indiscriminately destructive. The chaos this caused in the family home led his brother to seek his rehospitalization. When admitted, Henry was in an emaciated state, and refused to eat or talk. He would only lie passively in bed, staring fixedly at the ceiling. His occasional changes of expression suggested the possibility that he might have been actively hallucinating. There was no waxy flexibility, in the strictest sense of the term, but Henry did not seem to be distressed by holding himself in uncomfortable positions for long periods of time. He would obey simple commands, such as "Show your tongue" or "Grasp this pencil," but would not respond to more complex requests, such as "Walk across the room and open the door." Henry made rare spontaneous remarks, but generally experienced long periods of absolute mutism. When first admitted, tube feeding was necessary, because Henry refused to eat by himself, or be fed.

After a few weeks on the ward Henry gradually and spontaneously began to improve, and was able to recall everything that had occurred upon admission. He made a fair adjustment to ward routine, but remained withdrawn and negativistic in his approach to others. He had to be taken to his bath, meals, and other activities, but would in fact respond to these pressures, whereas previously he had been completely unresponsive. Tube feeding was discontinued, but special attention at meals remained necessary. After eating Henry would carefully wipe off his chair so as to prepare it for "the Lord and his disciples." His emotions were usually flattened and apathetic, but occasionally he would be seen smiling, with no apparent cause.

When Henry had achieved a state of remission sufficient to care for himself, he was placed on convalescent care, and returned to his family. While at home he would periodically have "crazy fits" in which he became violent and destructive, and then lapsed into a mute state. At these times he would be returned to the hospital until partial remission again occurred.

From Zax & Stricker, 1963, pp. 77–78.

---

subtypes, *catatonic type, excited,* and *catatonic type, withdrawn,* are distinguished by the predominance of excitement or stupor.

Schizophrenia, Paranoid Type

The primary features of paranoid schizophrenia are the presence of persecutory or grandiose delusions, ideas of reference, and, frequently, hallucinations; considerable religiosity is also common. The thinking of the paranoid patient tends to be autistic and his behavior is consistent with his delusions. A fairly constant hostile, aggressive attitude, however, is commonly present. Delusional systems in such patients may have good or poor organization, depending upon how much touch with reality remains. Generally there is less personality disorganization than is found in hebephrenia or catatonia.

CASE 6–4: A CASE OF PARANOID SCHIZOPHRENIA

George N., a thirty-year-old unmarried taxi driver was voluntarily admitted to a state institution in New England after having been an outpatient at a Veterans' Administration clinic for three months. An only child, he had been living with his elderly mother in a small apartment in the medium-sized city in which he had been reared.

*   *   *

For a year or two before his hospitalization George had been restless and troubled. He had a tendency to leave jobs impulsively without any apparent reason so that his work record was very unstable. About six months prior to his hospital admission he became involved with a widow who aggressively insisted that they marry. Around this time his generally anxious feeling became intensified. He began to claim that he was very ill and in danger of death without showing any overt physical symptomatology. When fellow workers and his few friends noted this intensification of symptoms, he began to avoid them as much as possible. At times he would get into his car and drive aimlessly about for hours at very high speeds. In order to avoid contact with people he would keep his head down when walking in the street and would bolt his food at mealtimes to avoid having to talk to his mother.

When examined in the hospital he freely verbalized concern over his abnormal feelings and particularly his anxiety about homosexuality, but was quite flat emotionally. Although his recent and remote memory were very good and he was well oriented and able to calculate well, the content of his thought was delusional. He spoke of feeling that people were talking about him and looking at him peculiarly. It was for this reason that he attempted to avoid others. He also felt that at times people made remarks about the way he walked or his feminine features. He also revealed that he felt that his body had changed a great deal in that his bones had become smaller and his gestures were becoming effeminate.

George remained in the hospital for three months. During this time his symptoms subsided and it was possible for him to be discharged in the custody of his mother. He suffered a relapse six months later when his mother became ill and it was necessary that he return to the hospital. At that time he was agitated and confused and had begun experiencing auditory hallucinations in which voices whispered that he was a homosexual. He had become dejected, feeling that no one cared for him. He has not been able to leave the hospital to the present date.

From Zax & Stricker, 1963, pp. 82–84.

Acute Schizophrenic Episode

This is not one of the classic forms of the disorder identified by Kraepelin and Bleuler. Indeed, the entity is not used to describe a stable phase of the disorder. Rather, it describes an acute phase that some patients experience at the beginning of a schizophrenic breakdown. Excitement or depression are typically prominent. In addition, there may be a wide variety of symptoms such as confusion, ideas of refer- ence, perplexity, frightening dreams, and dissociation. The acute nature of this disorder reflects an intense inner struggle. Depending on how this struggle is resolved, the patient's symptoms may clear up in a few weeks or he may become worse. If the latter is the case, his symptoms crystallize into one of the basic reaction types, with an appropriate change in diagnostic labeling. Patients experiencing their first schizophrenic episode are often placed in this category.

CASE 6–5:　A CASE OF ACUTE SCHIZOPHRENIA

Irene L., a twenty-four-year-old graduate student of psychology, was voluntarily admitted for the first time to a private mental hospital in the southwest on the referral of the psychiatrist at the university where she was studying. Until the year before her admission she had lived with her family in a medium-sized city in the southwest.

The onset of her disorder occurred three weeks before her hospitalization after a very frank discussion between Irene and a group of fellow graduate students following a lecture concerning Freud's theories of psychosexual development. She expressed personal feelings in this interaction and shortly thereafter she became uneasy and avoided as many of these fellow students as she could. About two weeks before her hospitalization she came home for a week end, during which she was extremely sensitive and overemotional. When it was time to return to school she was profusely grateful to her parents for having provided such a "marvelous" week end of activities. Her anxiety persisted and two days before she entered the hospital she awoke and told her roommate that she could now see both physical objects and concepts much more clearly than ever before. She claimed that she was experiencing a nirvana-like feeling and spent the entire day in the university chapel. That night she told her roommate that she felt as though she had experienced rebirth. When she awoke in the middle of the night and stated her intention to return to the chapel, her roommate became alarmed and phoned the dean of students, who had her taken to the dispensary. The next day she protested that everything was perfect and that she had now been transformed into the Virgin Mary.

When examined in the hospital she was untidy and dressed only in pajamas and a robe. She cried profusely at the outset and remained rigid and tense for much of the interview, manifesting some psychomotor retardation. She was well oriented, had good memory and retention, calculated well, and had a good fund of general information. Her answers to factual questions were clear and precise. When disturbed by the inquiry, she became evasive. At times she manifested an inappropriately disproportionate elation. Her efforts at maintaining a calm, controlled exterior were not always successful and flashes of irritation intruded on her. While her remarks were logical much of the time, she had a tendency to make strange, nearly autistic statements. As an example, she said that she felt sorry for everyone and, when asked why, replied, "Because when I go, you're going to have to remain and mourn for me. That is much harder than dying especially when I know that life is eternal and everlasting." She also expressed resentment toward a childhood friend who had died and thus left her to mourn.

During the early part of her hospital stay she displayed a great deal of inappropriate affect and was noted to be laughing when no one was near her. At times she cried uncontrollably without overt provocation. Her speech also became noticeably disorganized. After a hospital stay of several weeks she responded gradually to the supportive regimen of the hospital so that she could be discharged to the care of a private psychiatrist.

From Zax & Stricker, 1963, pp. 97–99.

Schizophrenia, Latent Type

Patients are classified as latent types when they display mild schizophrenic symptoms without having a history of blatant psychotic episodes. "Latent," "incipient," "prepsychotic," or "pseudoneurotic" reactions are included in this grouping. Often such individuals, like the simple schizophrenic, can maintain a marginal existence outside a mental institution for considerable periods of time.

Schizophrenia, Residual Type

Patients classified here have suffered a psychotic episode but have recovered and are no longer psychotic.

Schizophrenia, Schizo-Affective Type

Schizophrenia, schizo-affective type, is a category developed relatively recently to include patients with mixed schizophrenic and affective symptoms. For example, the mental content may be predominantly schizophrenic but is accompanied by marked elation or depression more typical of the manic-depressive. Conversely, affective symptoms of a manic-depressive nature may predominate but schizophrenic-like thought or behavior may also be present. Two subcategories, *schizo-affective type, excited,* and *schizo-affective type, depressed,* are self-explanatory.

Schizophrenia, Childhood Type

This category is used when schizophrenic symptoms appear prior to puberty. Most obvious is a failure to develop appropriately, manifested by autistic or withdrawn behavior, a failure to acquire a personal identity, or gross immaturity. Individuals suffering this disorder often appear mentally defective.

Schizophrenia, Chronic Undifferentiated Type

Individuals classified here display a mixture of schizophrenic symptoms involving thought, affect, and behavior that does not fit in any of the other categories of schizophrenia.

THEORIES AND TREATMENT APPROACHES

Bleuler's Views of the Causes and Treatment of Schizophrenia

It is apparent from Bleuler's description of schizophrenia that Freud's thinking influ-

---

CASE 6-6:   A CASE OF SCHIZO-AFFECTIVE SCHIZOPHRENIA

Darlene B., a fifty-eight-year-old widow, was committed for the third time to a private sanitarium in the East. She was the mother of three married children and had been living in a large city on the eastern seaboard. She had been trained as a lawyer and had practiced her profession off and on until age forty-six, when she had suffered her first mental breakdown.

*   *   *

While a law student she met and married a very intelligent and capable man who was studying for a degree in medicine. From the beginning, Darlene seemed to reject the role of the passive homemaker and threw herself into her career. As a result there was considerable marital conflict, since her husband preferred that she remain at home more than she cared to. Darlene never gave in to her husband, but did take the time to bear him two sons and one daughter. She left the raising of the children to servants, however, and her home, family, and married life were always treated as a weight that kept her from achieving her real goals in life. When she reached her middle forties, Darlene began to brood over what she felt was her lack of professional success. She felt that she had not been fully accepted in the legal and business community and was upset that she had not managed to make as much money as she would have liked as a material sign of her personal success. At this time she began remaining at home on the pretense of caring for her family, but found that, over the years, they had learned to do without her. As a result she began suffering periods of depression, interrupted by stretches of elation when she would lay plans, in very grandiose fashion, for returning to her law practice and the business world. During one of her particularly intense hyperactive states, when she was forty-eight, it became necessary to hospitalize her for a period of almost six months. A few years later, after the sudden death of her husband, she again required hospitalization for her depressive state.

The symptoms leading to the most recent hospitalization appeared one week prior to admission, following minor gynecological surgery which required a short hospital stay. Immediately after the operation she began inquiring about the seriousness of this disorder and hinted that she suspected the doctors were holding from her the fact that she had cancer. She rejected the reassurances that were offered and became progressively more convinced of the validity of her suspicions. As she did she became increasingly hyperactive, besieging physicians and nurses with questions and complaints whenever she encountered them. She refused to remain in her room and disturbed fellow patients. Darlene was also quick to lash out irritably when her ideas were disputed. As a result it became necessary to move her against her will to the mental hospital where she had previously been confined.

When examined after admission she was well oriented, displayed good retention and memory for recent and remote events, was able to calculate well, and had a good fund of general information. She seemed to be under some pressure regarding her speech and at times words flowed in a torrent of excitement. Much of the content of her thought involved variations on the theme that she was dying of cancer, and had been badly treated. Her tendency to dwell on the injustices she had encountered suggested a paranoid delusion. On the ward her behavior remained hyperactive. Although superficially charming and ingratiating her forcefulness in intruding on the privacy of others resulted in frequent altercations, and on several occasions it was necessary to place her in seclusion. In addition she made it known to fellow patients and ward personnel that her presence in the hospital was at the behest of the President of the United States in the role of an agent on an inspection tour. She also told of earlier, remarkable business exploits which she claimed resulted in her amassing a small fortune which was stolen by a dishonest partner. She also gave people to understand that she was the adviser and friend of important political figures in state and Washington politics.

Darlene was seen in supportive psychotherapy while in the hospital, and her excited and hyperactive behavior subsided. Many of her delusions disappeared as well, although she retained the one pertaining to her being cheated out of a fortune by her business associate. After five months of treatment she was well enough to be discharged. In the subsequent five years she returned to the hospital twice, each time with both affective symptoms and a more elaborately evolved delusional system.

From Zax & Stricker, 1963, pp. 89–92.

CASE 6–7:   A CASE OF CHRONIC UNDIFFERENTIATED SCHIZOPHRENIA

Nancy L., a twenty-one-year-old single woman, was referred to a psychiatric clinic in a large Middle Atlantic city by a private psychiatrist, after a course of treatment with him had proven unsuccessful.

Nancy's father, an improvident man who gambled compulsively, was killed in a fight when she was still an infant. Her mother remarried a man considerably younger than herself when Nancy, an only child, was five years old. The mother, an undemonstrative and weak woman, was dominated throughout her life by her own mother, who lived next door. Nancy's grandmother was a forceful, aggressive person and she and Nancy's mother were in constant competition over the child. In fact, Nancy had spent portions of her life in both her mother's and her grandmother's house, partially because of her great animosity toward her stepfather. He was a weak, dependent, "mama's boy" who aroused the hatred of the child by punishing her when she was about ten years old, a time which coincided with the birth of her stepsister. From that time Nancy did not speak to her stepfather, and refused to eat at the same table or stay in the same room with him. Her relationship with her younger stepsister was marked by a great jealousy on her part and a strong rivalry between them. Nancy was always a quiet, retiring person who was very fastidious about her appearance.

After a successful and enjoyable time in grammar school, Nancy entered high school, and suddenly began to feel awkward because she was slightly overweight and did not feel as attractive as the other girls. Although she had always been a conscientious student, she began to miss school intermittently, but never for a prolonged period. This occurred with increasing frequency. Throughout this period she felt that she was a fat and unattractive child who was inferior and unloved by her family. This led her to restrict even further her already limited circle of friendships. She felt that she could not go out at night or be in crowds because she would be subjected to overwhelming anxieties. Finally, because of her excessive absences, she was expelled from school. Despite this she obtained admission to a small local business school, but her anxiety prevented her from attending. Instead she took a menial clerical job at a large factory, and, even though she thoroughly enjoyed the job, she had a spotty attendance record. She found herself developing a great number of compulsive habits, such as avoiding cracks in sidewalk pavement, touching doorknobs seven times, and replacing lifted objects exactly in their previous place. She also became increasingly preoccupied with somatic ideas, centering on her looks and awkwardness, and including the feeling that her bones creaked audibly when she arose from a chair. This progressive development of symptoms over a four-year period led her to seek psychotherapy on a private basis. When her symptoms continued to increase, and she began to feel that others were watching her, her psychiatrist recommended hospitalization.

On the ward Nancy was seclusive and continued to be preoccupied with her somatic complaints. She passively resisted all hospital programs designed to aid her or draw her out. Electric shock therapy was attempted and she showed a slight improvement, but remained seclusive. Nancy was released on convalescent care to her parents, but the hospital was very guarded in its prognosis for her.

From Zax & Stricker, 1963, pp. 103–105.

---

enced his position. This is particularly noticeable in his emphasis on the wish-fulfilling functions of the accessory symptoms. Bleuler believed that at least the obvious content of schizophrenia could be understood in terms of Freud's theorizing, thereby acknowledging that psychic forces played a part in determining certain features of schizophrenia. On the other hand, Bleuler saw the essence of schizophrenic disorder as the disruption of thought and affect. He considered carefully, but eventually rejected, the possibility that psychic factors could cause this. He concluded that only brain disturbance (either anatomic or chemical) could be at the root of schizophrenia.

Bleuler believed that whatever disturbance was involved, schizophrenia was a chronic process involving phases of acute exacerbation. With brain disorder accounting for fundamental schizophrenic symptoms such as associative defects, the tendency to hallucinate, and states of clouded consciousness, Bleuler reasoned that the remaining symptoms of the disorder arose indirectly from psychic disturbances. He thus emphasized an interaction between constitutional factors predisposing one to schizophrenia and psychological factors that were partly responsible for the form, and even the severity, of the disorder. In fact, he believed that schizophrenia remained latent until either acute constitutional factors emerged or a "psychic shock" intensified the secondary symptomatology.

Although he believed that organic factors played a central role in causing schizophrenia, Bleuler could specify neither what

such factors were nor how they operated. He reviewed many current theories of the day and found none to provide a conclusive answer to these questions. He had, therefore, relatively little to offer in the direct treatment of the organic defect.

Having few ideas about how to attack what he felt were the primary causes of schizophrenia, Bleuler concentrated on preventing exacerbations of the disorder and on ameliorating its acute phases by creating an optimal psychological situation. For example, he advised members of "hereditarily tainted" families not to marry. Presumably, this was designed to protect them against the strains of such a relationship and to prevent their passing on the defect to offspring. Since he believed that the children of alcoholics were vulnerable to schizophrenia, he advised against excessive drinking. He also insisted that the patient's physical health be looked after carefully and emphasized the importance of proper nourishment and sufficient sleep. Since strong feeling exacerbated the schizophrenic process, Bleuler reasoned that patients should be sheltered from situations which might arouse such feeling. Bleuler also thought that idleness caused "the complexes" to dominate the personality; hence, regular work was prescribed for schizophrenic patients (a practice followed today in the Soviet Union). Ambitious plans which could lead to emotional upset if not achieved were discouraged by Bleuler, in favor of lighter, more routine, activity.

Bleuler was also concerned about the effect of the hospital setting on the schizophrenic disorder and strived to maintain the patient in his natural environment as long as possible. He favored release from the hospital as early as possible, provided that a benign environmental setting for the patient's return was available. During the acute phases of the disorder he believed little could be done but, once improvement commenced, the task was to educate the patient to reestablish contact with reality.

Organic Therapies

A number of organic treatment procedures for schizophrenia have been applied in the past forty or fifty years. Seldom have such approaches been guided by clearly articulated theory. More typically, whatever theory has been advanced to explain the effects of such approaches has emerged after the fact.

The Shock Treatments

The isolation of insulin in 1922 led to one of the first organic therapies for treating schizophrenia. Although insulin was used primarily for the treatment of diabetes, it was also used in small doses as a stimulant for the appetite of patients with certain chronic illnesses, including mental disorders. Some physicians noted that these small doses helped to quiet excited patients. Manfred Sakel, who had been treating morphine addicts, found that his patients became overexcited when abstaining from the drug. He used insulin with them in the hope that it would be antagonistic to the overactivity of the adrenal-thyroid system, which he believed to be causing the excitement. He experimented with varying insulin dosages, gradually increasing them. Eventually he gave excited patients high enough dosage levels to induce coma. He also did this work with schizophrenics, and first reported in 1933 that such patients, especially acute ones, benefited from the treatment.

Sakel's work was not greeted enthusiastically for two reasons. First, his rationale for using insulin treatment was vague, and secondly, acute schizophrenics, in the early period of their illness, respond well to a variety of treatment approaches. These criticisms notwithstanding, insulin therapy was used for a period of years in a number of mental hospitals. It was a relatively expensive and dangerous approach: it required many treatments (thirty to fifty comas were thought to be necessary for optimal effect); patients required extensive care from nurses and attendants; and it entailed the risk that a coma might be irreversible or that circulatory and respiratory collapse might ensue.

Theories of how insulin coma benefits the schizophrenic are both varied and unproven. One recent suggestion is that a reduction of blood sugar helps brain enzymes to find a better equilibrium and thus improves the brain's ability to utilize the minerals found in the blood. Another view is that the reduced blood sugar also reduces the amount of oxygen in the blood, impairing the action of the highest brain centers, requiring the most oxygen, with consequent release of inhibition on the lower centers. From this view, insulin prompts psychological regression in the patient who awakes needing to be fed intravenously and otherwise cared for by outsiders. Such periodic regressions on both a physiological and psychological level supposedly lead to a redevelopment of higher patterns of psychological activity in response to attentive, pleasant, and hopeful nurses and attendants.

The high cost of insulin coma therapy, its none too satisfactory results, especially with chronic patients, and the lack of a good theoretical basis contributed to the exploration of other shock therapies in the 1940s. By that time there had been experimentation with other agents that induced nervous-system shock. Meduna, a Hungarian, who theorized that schizophrenia and epilepsy were incompatible disorders, attributed therapeutic effects to epileptic seizures. He used a substance known as metrazol to induce seizures in schizophrenics. Others also experimented with metrazol but found shortcomings in its use. For one thing the unpredictable time interval between injection of the drug and the onset of the seizure was a period during which patients were quite anxious and uncooperative. For another, because the seizures were quite severe, bone fractures were frequent.

In the late 1930s two Italian researchers, Cerletti and Bini, in the course of investigating brain changes in epileptics, began using electricity in order to study the effects of nonchemically induced seizures. This form of shock induction eventually found favor because it produced a milder seizure, its side effects were minimal, and it was relatively inexpensive.

Electroconvulsive therapy (ECT) was widely used with schizophrenics during the 1940s and early 1950s, often several times a week in treatment courses of more than 100 seizures. The most obvious side effect of ECT was the memory loss that it induced. Amnesia often persisted for several weeks but eventually memory functions returned and no other obvious negative effects remained.

Extensive experience with ECT therapy suggests that it is less effective with schizophrenics than with patients suffering from depression. The approach now has its most widespread use with depressives, particularly the involutional melancholics—patients whose depression first appears around the time of menopause or climacteric. With such patients far fewer treatments are currently used than the long series of shocks typically applied to patients in earlier years.

Ideas as to how ECT brings about symptomatic changes are highly speculative. They can be grouped into two classes: those emphasizing psychological or physiological factors. Psychological theories suggest that recovery after ECT may be due to avoidance of a treatment procedure the patient dreads; a satisfied reaction to punishment that he sought unconsciously; or, a positive after-effect of the discharge of much aggressive feeling through the violence of the seizure. None of these explanations is entirely convincing. One could imagine many other procedures that would arouse dread in the patient, are punishing, or provide release for aggressive feelings, which do not result in positive response. Physiological theories, equally speculative and lacking in empirical support, include the views that ECT stimulates the function of the sympathetic nervous system; it stimulates adaptive adrenocortical responses; or it causes a slight amount of brain damage which erases recent painful memories.

Psychosurgery

Psychosurgery was developed by the Portuguese neurologist, Egaz Moniz (1874–1955), who reasoned that many patients are fixated on a relatively few morbid ideas. Moniz believed that if the frontal area of the brain were altered surgically, such unhealthy ideas would be disrupted. The surgical intervention he favored involved severing the connections between the thalamus, a part of the brain that relays sensory impressions, and the prefrontal lobes, the area of the brain that interprets sensory impressions and brings them into consciousness. A report of a study done with monkeys who became tractable and developed a high tolerance for frustration after such a surgical procedure was encouraging. Another report involved a human who lost part of his frontal lobe during an operation for removing a tumor, and who seemed to be a happier and more spontaneous person later. Moniz began to perform prefrontal lobotomies with mental patients in 1935, and this practice was applied extensively in the 1940s and early 1950s with schizophrenics.

A general finding with psychosurgery, a radical procedure producing irreversible damage to the patient's brain, was that although many patients were easier to manage after lobotomies because they were calmer, they became so placid that they lost ambition, tact, interest in life, and imagination—they were reduced to something that approached a vegetative state. While this had the virtue of simplifying the problems of management and activity with intractable patients, it did not represent a a basic cure of the disorder.

The advent of tranquilizing drugs, which diminished anxiety in patients without the irreversible effects of surgery, led to a decline of interest in this approach.

Psychopharmacology

Throughout man's struggle with mental illness there has always been the hope that a drug would be discovered which would cure such disorders. For example, bromides were used to control highly excitable patients during the mid-nineteenth century, and by the 1920s were widely proclaimed as the solution to problems of mental illness. Eventually, it was recognized that patients only maintained improvement as long as they took bromides continuously. The disillusionment that followed did not, however, diminish the hope that a drug that would be a "perfect cure" would eventually be found.

In relatively recent years this search led to the use of a substance derived from the snakelike roots of a small plant found in India, commonly used to treat snakebite. The names given to the plant, "snakeroot plant," "serpentina," reflected its source. It was found to induce tranquility (the calmness and serenity that Epicureans called "ataraxia") without attendant confusion or cloudiness. By the 1950s the tranquilizing property of *Rauwolfia serpentina* was well known in the western world and drugs made up, in part, of alkaloids from its roots were widely used in the treatment of schizophrenia. The best-known ones were Serpacil and Reserpine. This was the first widespread usage in the modern period of tranquilizing or ataractic drugs.

About the same time, another group of tranquilizers related to phenothiazine was found to have tranquilizing effects. One of these, *chlorpromazine*, was first used in France in 1952 to treat psychosis and, later, compounds of this drug—such as Thorazine, Sparine, and Compozine—were widely used in treating psychoses in general and schizophrenia in particular. Somewhat later, another drug, *mephenesin*, which had been used as a muscle relaxant, attracted attention as a potential tranquilizer. Since the effects of this drug were found to be short-lived, a related compound, having longer effects, *meprobamate*, came into more widespread usage with mental patients. This drug has been produced under trade names such as Equanil and Miltown.

The physiological effects of these drugs are varied. The phenothiazines make people less aware of stimuli, so that although one might continue to feel pain while under their influence one would be relatively less attentive to it. Similar reactions occur with psychological stimuli. Rauwolfia derivatives act primarily on the hypothalamus to inhibit sympathetic nervous system function and to stimulate the activity of the parasympathetic system. As a result their action includes side effects such as decreased blood pressure, increased activity of the gastrointestinal tract, and constriction of the pupils. The most serious of these side effects is the induction of depression. Meprobamates slow the transmission of impulses from the thalamus to the cortex and thereby achieve some of the effects of a lobotomy without the negative or irreversible effects of such surgery.

Tranquilizers have been widely used with schizophrenics and, while they are no longer seen as a complete cure, they can provide enough symptom relief in many patients to make the difference between the need for institutional care and the ability to continue functioning outside a hospital. Considerably more experience with such drugs will probably be necessary before their optimal use is well understood and before psychiatrists will know how they best fit into a program aimed at basic and long-lasting therapeutic effects.

The Psychoanalytic View of Schizophrenia

Since Freud was primarily concerned with understanding the neuroses, his comments on schizophrenia were both infrequent and incidental, most of them being comparisons between this disorder and neurosis.

In a paper on narcissism (a state wherein one treats his own body as a sexual object and experiences complete gratification in looking at it, caressing, and fondling it), Freud set forth some ideas about the basic causes of schizophrenia. He described how the organically ill person withdraws libido from the external world, because of his pain and discomfort, and becomes more narcissistic and less capable than when well of loving external objects. Similarly, during sleep there is a narcissistic withdrawal of libido from external reality in service of the pursuit of sleep. Another example of narcissism is found in hypochrondriasis, characterized by a redirection of libido from external objects to one's body.

Freud believed that both the schizophrenic and the neurotic withdrew libido from external objects because of frustrated impulse gratification experienced with such objects. The prime difference between these two groups, however, is that the neurotic redirects the libido onto objects that are held internally, in fantasy, whereas the schizophrenic renounces objects entirely. Eventually, in the neurotic, the libido returns to the ego which effects a relationship with external objects through the use of defense mechanisms that divert id aims and come to represent the symptoms of psychoneurosis. In the schizophrenic, objects are renounced and libido is focused on the self as in an infantile state. The process that leads toward a recovery of contact with objects in schizophrenics, corresponding to the use of defenses against the id impulses in neurotics, involves alteration by the ego of the troublesome external world. Ordinarily, the external world impinges on the ego through stimuli constantly received from outside, or through the collection of memories of earlier perceptions that make up one's "inner world." In the schizophrenic, perceptions stimulated from outside the person are limited and the inner world is altered so that, rather than reflecting what is outside, it conforms primarily to the pattern of the id impulses. Thus, whereas in neurosis the ego remains in contact with the external world while struggling to control id impulses, in schizophrenia the outside world is either renounced or attempts are made to bring it into line with the demands of the id.

In the clinical picture of schizophrenia

one therefore finds three types of phenomena: (1) those reflecting the remnants of a normal or neurotic state that preceded the psychosis; (2) those representing renunciation of objects (detachment of libido from objects, megalomania, and regressive behavior); (3) those attempting to reestablish contact with reality (certain types of delusions, hallucinations, ways of using language, and so on).

Some of the ways in which schizophrenics use language—such as condensation and displacement of ideas, and the use of symbolism—were viewed by Freud as signs of regression, very much as in dreams. Other schizophrenic uses of language were seen as attempts to regain contact with external objects—as when analogies are made between objects that have very little in common. For example, one of Freud's patients equated a pore in the skin to the vagina on the grounds that both are, literally, holes. Here, Freud points out that the idea of the word has been separated from the idea of the thing which it represents. The latter involves a cathexis of memory images of the object, or at least some remote memory trace of it. When such cathexes are withdrawn, all that remains is the idea of the word which is now treated as though it were the thing itself. The word is then cathected as a first, primitive step toward reestablishing contact with objects.

According to Freud, the frustration that leads either to neurosis or psychosis involves the failure to fulfill some insistent impulse of the id. This frustration inevitably derives from the external world, although in some cases it may result from action of the superego, which is, itself, an internal agency representing a part of the outside world. Whether a neurosis or a psychosis results from such frustration depends, according to Freud, upon the state of the ego. If the latter is strong enough to "remain true to its allegiance to the outer world," it masters the id. If not, it is overwhelmed by the id and fails in its task of coping with the demands of reality. Therefore, from the psychoanalytic viewpoint, conditions of early life that make for the development of a weak ego, and biological states responsible for the intensity of the drives that cannot be fulfilled, predispose to schizophrenia.

Because of the fundamental weakness of the ego of the schizophrenic, psychoanalytic treatment of this disorder is very complicated. In the neurotic the ego is relatively strong. Its resistances must first be surmounted in order to render anxiety-creating id impulses conscious so that the ego can develop more adaptive means of handling them. In the schizophrenic the ego is weak and the id forces are very close to the surface. The primary task of therapy is therefore to strengthen the ego so that it can better control the id while maintaining an allegiance to reality. A major problem in shoring up the ego of the schizophrenic is the patient's narcissism, his withdrawal from external objects. Therefore, analysts who have attempted to treat schizophrenics tend to emphasize establishment of a therapeutic relationship with the patient. In such a relationship the patient must trust the therapist enough and find contact with him rewarding enough to embark on the therapeutic venture with him (Fromm-Reichmann, 1950; Arieti, 1961).

"Direct Analysis" of Schizophrenia

A treatment approach to schizophrenics deriving from psychoanalysis has been described by John Rosen (1953, 1962). Rosen sees an essential similarity between the dream and the psychotic state. In the dream forbidden wishes are experienced in disguised form. When the disguise is too transparent and the true nature of the wish begins to be recognized, sleep is interrupted and the person awakens recalling some details from his nightmare but not the forbidden wish. The psychotic state is likened to the dream state, with unacceptable wishes or impulses being continually experienced but in a form well enough disguised so that the psychotic does not awaken. He is caught in an interminable nightmare. Therefore, the job of the therapist is to strip the psychosis of its disguises and jog the patient into renouncing it.

Rosen believes that the therapist must become a "loving, omnipotent protector and provider for the patient," "the idealized mother," in order to help him grow up once again—but properly this time. Material needs such as food and protection can be provided easily, but more importantly, the therapist must respond instinctively in such a way as to help the patient grow. This requires an almost reflexive sensitivity to the patient's deep inner needs. It cannot be guided by conscious effort. When a therapist possesses the proper reflexes he recognizes it by the beneficial effect he has on the patient. Rosen finds that successfully analyzed psychotics always have this kind of sensitivity. Therefore, Rosen uses a number of such individuals as "associate therapists" in his work with schizophrenics.

The most important technique in Rosen's treatment approach is *direct interpretation*. Whereas the neurotic must be prepared for interpretations of his behavior through analysis of his ego resistances, this is unnecessary with the psychotic, who lacks the ego structure of the neurotic. In using direct analysis the therapist assumes that anything the patient does has a latent meaning which should be interpreted to him.

Thus, to the male patient who was preoccupied with developing the most powerful automobile transmission possible by using fluid to gain power, the analyst interpreted, "How can you transmit mother's milk to your mouth?" To a female who was a kleptomaniac before becoming psychotic and who expressed concern for what would happen when her stealing was found out, the therapist replied, "If your mother wouldn't give it to you, you had a perfect right to steal it." These direct interpretations are advocated by Rosen in order to speak directly to the unconscious, forbidden impulses and concerns of the patient.

Rosen feels that this approach in essence awakens the psychotic, helps him to come out of the psychotic state in the same way the dreamer is jogged out of his sleep by a nightmare. Once having cast off the grossly psychotic state, Rosen feels the patient must undergo prolonged psychoanalysis in order to be strengthened against a return to that state.

Sullivan's Views on Schizophrenia

One of the few systematic personality theories derived from experience with schizophrenic patients was that of Harry Stack Sullivan (1892–1949). Sullivan was a Freudian at the beginning of his career. He strunggled to fit his observations into the psychoanalytic frame. Eventually, he found that he could not do so successfully and remain faithful to his clinical experience. He therefore evolved a personality theory of his own. Despite having moved far afield from Freud's thinking in many respects, he never saw himself as being basically opposed to Freud. Many aspects of Freud's theory were simply deemphasized or ignored by Sullivan in favor of other factors that he considered more basic or more significant.

Sullivan emphasized social factors above all others, so much so that his approach is known as "the interpersonal theory of psychiatry." Sullivan's theory traces the development of the human from birth through his assuming mature membership in society. He is interested in both the significant social forces that mold the human at every stage in this process, and in how he reacts to those forces. His approach is phenomenological. He is less concerned with the objective nature of stimuli than he is in how stimuli are received and interpreted by the organism. Such interpretations, he believed, were in part a function of maturation and in part a result of previous experience.

Sullivan (1953, pp. 34–35) identified two important constructs: *absolute euphoria* ("a state of utter well-being"); and *absolute tension* ("the maximum possible deviation from absolute euphoria"). The nearest one comes to euphoria is in the deep sleep of the infant. Absolute tension is approached in the state of terror. When either euphoria or tension is high, the other is low. Euphoria presents no problem for the person. Tension, however, creates profound problems and it, therefore, occupies an important place in Sullivan's theorizing.

Some tensions are related to biological imbalances that occur periodically. The need for food, water, and warmth arises from time to time and since the infant cannot satisfy these himself, some outsider, "a mothering one," must look after him. The gratification of such needs is referred to as *satisfaction*. Signs of tension in the infant arouse tension in the "mothering one." Most needs for satisfaction are present from birth. One very important one, "lust," develops in adolescence as a result of sexual maturation.

Tension in the infant also arises from another important source—anxiety in the mother. This fact and its implications are central to Sullivan's theory. Sullivan firmly believed that when the mothering one is anxious, anxiety is induced in the infant. Although he recognized that the process of transmitting anxiety from mother to child was unclear, he was certain that it occurred. He called this process *empathy*. Even without fully understanding empathy, Sullivan believed its presence could be established through observation of mother-infant relationships.

Tension created by empathy differs in a very significant way from that induced by the need for satisfactions. Since it cannot be related to a specific imbalance, the means of relieving it are unclear. Nothing that the infant can do consistently reduces it. Accordingly, there develops a need for *security*—the need to be free from anxiety—which takes on greater significance in human interactions than the need for satisfactions. Anxiety, induced as it is by another, is not easily managed by the infant himself. Further, the mother who induces anxiety in the infant finds it difficult to relieve since, often without realizing, her own anxiety is causing it. Anxiety also operates in opposition to tenderness in the mothering one so that its presence impedes need satisfaction.

Sullivan identified six developmental epochs that he believed preceded maturity. These stages were distinguished by the different types of interpersonal relationships characterizing them rather than by the dominance of a particular biological instinct, as Freud. Sullivan was concerned with the ways people experienced what occurs around them during each of the developmental epochs, most particularly the earlier ones. He identified three modes of experience, or ways events are dealt with internally: the *prototaxic, parataxic,* and *syntaxic.*

The prototaxic mode is the most primitive. At this level, stimuli are received in large, undifferentiated bundles. With maturation and learning, the infant begins to differentiate segments of global experience, and temporal relationships between events are noted. This is the start of the parataxic mode of experience, in which events are tied together, either because they occur simultaneously or because one follows shortly after the other. In the parataxic period, therefore, simple cause-and-effect notions arise based on the idea "after, therefore because of." Experience in this parataxic mode is preverbal and therefore cannot easily be communicated to others. The third and most mature mode of experience is the syntaxic. It emerges with the development of language—a most important tool in interpersonal relationships. Syntaxic development takes place as one perceives and learns socially agreed-upon symbols for objects or events formerly experienced parataxically. Thus, repeated exposure to an object and its symbol, embedded in different, parataxically experienced situations, leads to ties between the object and its name. In this way, *consensually validated* symbols—symbols whose meaning has been derived from group experiences with the symbol and the object it signifies—are acquired and the child shares a common currency for interacting with others. The child also learns the principles of logic that accompany language. At this level, experience is made up not only of perceptions of events but also of concepts and thoughts that enable the child to compare and to reflect in common with others on what he has perceived.

Several other concepts of Sullivan's theory should be noted before the developmental sequences are described, because

he refers to them in his account of personality development. One such concept is that of the *dynamism*. which Sullivan defines as ". . . the relatively enduring pattern of energy transformations which recurrently characterize the organism in its duration as a living organism" (Sullivan, 1953, p. 103). Since he defines a pattern as an "envelope of insignificant particular differences" (Sullivan, 1953, p. 104), the concept of dynamism seems similar to that of a habit, and Sullivan regards it as the elemental unit in the study of a person's behavior. One important set of dynamisms are those used to avoid, or minimize, anxiety. These are collectively referred to as the *self-dynamism* or the *self-system.*

The self-system begins to emerge when the infant matures enough to recognize situations, involving the mothering one, that increase his anxiety. At this point he becomes sensitive to small signs indicating that an upsetting situation, involving another person, could arise. The behavior he learns to use for avoiding anxiety constitutes the self-system. This system continues to evolve throughout life.

Another important construct in Sullivan's system is *personification.* A personification is a perception of a person developing out of specific experiences with him. As a summary of extended experiences, it is very much like a stereotype. Thus, experiences with mother that heighten euphoria lead to the personification of a "good-mother." Tension producing experiences with mother lead to a personification of a "bad-mother." Development of the syntaxic mode of experience helps the child to recognize mother as a single unit with good and bad qualities. The original duality, however, may be maintained in dreams.

A personification of the self also begins evolving in infancy and it also consists of several distinct personifications. Behavior that brings pleasant attention from mother contributes to an image of a "good-me." Behavior that provokes anxiety-arousing behavior in mother leads to an image of a "bad-me." Another set of experiences, often difficult to verbalize because they involve extreme tension, are grouped under the "not-me" image. Because it is threatening, the "not-me" is avoided but eventually it is assimilated with the "good-me" and the "bad-me" into a personification of self. The separate personifications afterward only find expression in vague images and dreams.

Sullivan's developmental stages each end with some important interpersonal development that is shaped by our Western culture. Presumably in different societies, developmental stages take different forms. Also, boundaries between stages are not abrupt and the ages at which children move from one to another depend on their social situation.

The Developmental Epochs

Infancy

During this stage the infant learns to communicate his needs to the mothering one, and to appreciate her tenderness in caring for him. He also experiences the mother's anxiety and begins to develop his personifications of self and mother. A self-system begins to emerge and the infant begins to acquire language. This stage ends when articulate speech appears.

Childhood

During childhood interpersonal relationships expand and, with maturation, many manual and motor skills appear. Parents begin to apply rewards and punishment to shape the child's behavior in keeping with social requirements. Dynamisms become complex and the self-system grows. During

childhood infantile emotions are moderated. Many of these developments in childhood expand the youngster's capacity for interpersonal relationships. The child learns to do things that will win favorable attention from adults. He also begins to want playmates, a development that marks the end of the childhood era.

The Juvenile Era

This period, corresponding roughly to Freud's latency period, is seen by Sullivan to be anything but the relatively tranquil phase that Freud described. The major feature of this stage is the further expansion of interpersonal relationships. The child goes to school, and broadens his play activities into the homes of other children. This brings him into contact with many authorities who are not his parents. Any peculiarities in his parents' ways of social-

© J. Brian King 1975

Tender and loving care during infancy lays the foundation for development of a healthy personality.

izing him, therefore, become apparent.

A variety of social patterns is acquired during the juvenile era. The child learns to be subordinate to authority and to accommodate to others' needs. He learns to compete, cooperate, and compromise with peers. He also learns what it means to be rejected or ostracized. The end of the juvenile era is marked by the development of a need for an intimate, special friend—in Sullivan's words, a "chum." The close relationship with such a chum is, in Sullivan's view, very important for the future course of life.

The Preadolescent Stage

This relatively brief stage is crucial for later development. Here the youngster becomes intensely interested in one person—a same sex peer. Through this chum relationship, someone outside the family comes, for the first time, to be highly valued. A reciprocity in interpersonal relations is established that is the basis for all later love relationships.

In the chum relationship there is a potential for making basic changes in the self-system and thereby in the personality itself. This happens as the youngster exposes many of his private thoughts to his chum and has a chance to correct any faulty views he has of himself or of important others. Without such a corrective experience the person may continue to misperceive and thereby fail to develop the social skills necessary for close interpersonal relations in the future. The failure to have a chum may also lead to feelings of terrible loneliness. So important are the interpersonal relationships of preadolescence that Sullivan believed that they are significantly related to how successful psychotherapy could be later in life.

The preadolescent stage ends with the appearance of what Sullivan described as the lust need—the "eruption of true genital interests." Its appearance both complicates interpersonal patterns and introduces the problems of the next developmental stage.

Early Adolescence

In contrast to Freud, Sullivan believed that sexual factors first became significant around the time of puberty. During early adolescence, development of sexual behavior with the opposite sex is the primary achievement. Early adolescence ends when a relatively stable pattern for satisfying genital needs has been established.

Late Adolescence

Late adolescence occurs when the person discovers "what he likes in the way of genital behavior and how to fit it into the rest of life" (Sullivan, 1953, p. 297). Typically, late adolescence is characterized by a tremendous growth of experience in the syntaxic mode. A person should at this time learn about other people's attitudes toward life, patterns of interdependence between others, and how others deal with interpersonal problems. Many of these things are learned through trial and error, from human example. How well a person does in acquiring the learning necessary in this stage depends on the breadth of his contacts with others. Social circumstances have a great deal to do with this. The person who lives in a small town and does routine factory work has fewer chances for advanced socialization than the well-educated city dweller with wide cultural interests.

Maturity

Sullivan says relatively little about maturity and it is not one of his developmental stages. Some of his comments, nonetheless, help to clarify his view of the ultimate goal of proper development. The mature person will have successfully mastered the challenges of each of his developmental eras, and his personality will show it. Earlier success in intimate relationships will have prepared him to be close to others, to collaborate with them, and to be sensitive to their needs. His life will be characterized by ever-widening and deepening interests rather than by monotony and boredom. He is free of anxieties and appreciates the complexities of life.

Sullivan's View of Psychopathology

Sullivan believed that disturbed behavior differed in degree rather than in kind from normal behavior. Behavior disorders are seen as inappropriate ways of dealing with others that come about in an effort to control anxiety. To understand behavior disorder, then, you must understand how anxiety arises and the behaviors that are used to control it.

The earliest anxiety is acquired through empathy, from a mother who is anxious. A mother can also provoke anxiety in the child more directly if she is a "malevolent" person. Being ridiculed or ostracized makes the child anxious. Punishment also causes anxiety. In all such cases, it is most difficult for the child when the anxiety-provoking person's inconsistency makes adaptation difficult. Socializers who are poorly informed about child-rearing practices or who have personality problems themselves are inconsistent.

Because it is very distressing, it is almost reflexive for a person to try to avoid anxiety by becoming sensitive to its early signs. To be free of anxiety a person may avoid

situations that arouse it or avoid responses that have caused it in the past. When intense anxiety occurs too often, or when the person is consistently unable to avoid it, or when anxiety is associated wtih responses essential to the gratification of a physiological need, the stage is set for the development of behavior disorder. Behavior disorders involve ineffective avoidant responses. They are ineffective because: (1) even though they reduce anxiety temporarily, they fail to satisfy recurrent physiological needs; or (2) they predispose the person to further anxiety in the long run.

The self-system's avoidant behaviors include shunning anxiety-arousing situations (by staying away from them), changing the subject of upsetting conversations, or, most importantly, controlling the contents of awareness. This is done by being selectively inattentive and screening anxiety-provoking thoughts out of awareness, or by substituting neutral responses for anxiety-producing ones.

Anxiety-controlling tactics have many potentially serious consequences. First, they restrict the range of functioning. This closes

© J. Brian King 1975

Planned activities such as Little League baseball help to encourage intimate pre-adolescent relationships.

many aspects of life up and denies to the person many potential satisfactions. This can have very damaging consequences for development since many experiences necessary to achieve maturity, such as the intimate preadolescent relationship, may be missed. Second, in order to control anxiety the person may be forced to avoid the interpersonal situations necessary for the gratification of physiological needs. Third, a person who struggles constantly to avoid being "put down" is likely to become awkward in interpersonal situations and may become anxious because of his social failures. This further intensifies his need to avoid and leads to a cycle that further alienates him from others. Finally, Sullivan believed that the most serious potential consequence of anxiety-avoidance is the elimination of crucial responses or relationships. This dissociation is predisposing to serious disorder since, when it involves significant needs, it is virtually impossible to maintain. And when it fails, no defenses remain to prevent the extreme anxiety and avoidant measures that typify schizophrenia.

Serious behavior disorders involve exaggerations of avoidance patterns used throughout life. It is this established "style" that determines the type of disorder that results. Thus, a person who has characteristically blamed others for his failures is likely to develop a paranoid disorder. One who has relied heavily on dissociation may be prone to schizophrenia. Since his primary interest was in schizophrenia, Sullivan elaborated especially on how it developed.

He believed that early in life the schizophrenic dissociated anxiety-producing events. When this defense can no longer be maintained and the self-system fails, control is lost over the content of awareness. Then the person begins to experience terrifying feelings that have been part of the not-me and have never been put into words or been part of waking life. The resultant terror, along with the loss of security stemming from the collapse of a major system for maintaining it, causes a sense of intense urgency. This feeling of urgency leads to a frenzy of activity or intense concentration on developing an explanation for something. Tremendous amounts of energy go into this. The purpose of this urgent activity is to stave off a collapse that is sensed even if it cannot be put into words. For Sullivan, this state marks the beginning of a schizophrenic disorder and he believed that, of the classic forms, it most resembled catatonia. He, therefore, regarded catatonic schizophrenia as the "essential schizophrenic picture" out of which the other classic forms evolve.

The stupor that typifies the catatonic schizophrenic was thought by Sullivan to emerge only after he has engaged fruitlessly in much urgent overt or covert activity. Whatever the person attempts under these circumstances "miscarries appallingly" and merely goes to prove further that he is "crazy." It is this realization that results in a stuporous state—a tying up of all skeletal activity.

Sullivan believed that some people develop paranoid symptoms from this essential catatonic state and others become hebephrenic, and that the direction taken in any given case depends upon previous life experiences. The person who used projection of blame successfully in the past is likely to develop a paranoid dynamism; the one who has learned to despair that interpersonal contacts will ever be satisfying will become hebephrenic. Simple schizophrenia was thought by Sullivan to be an organic disorder characterized by a gradual falling apart of the personality.

Laing's View of Schizophrenia

R. D. Laing (1967a; 1967b) holds a viewpoint on schizophrenia that is markedly influenced by Sullivan's theories. Essentially, he sees what is called schizophrenia as a product of a social network within which the family plays a key role, at least at the outset. Laing sees the person who is called a schizophrenic as being labeled at some point and then put in the role of a schizophrenic. The person so labeled does engage in some behavior that prompts the designation, but for Laing (1967b, p. 140) the "endless spiral of social transaction" has not begun or ended at that point.

Once designated schizophrenic a person is treated by family members, physicians, nurses, mental health workers, and others in ways that *cause* many behaviors that are taken as further evidence to substantiate the original diagnosis. Laing argues that the label "schizophrenia" causes behavior that we call schizophrenic. He proposes, therefore, that a very important research study of schizophrenia would compare a group of "normal" subjects treated as though they were schizophrenic to a group of "early schizophrenics" treated as though they were normal. He predicts that the "normals" would display more "symptoms" of schizophrenia than before and that the "early schizophrenics" would show fewer.

In keeping with his view of schizophrenia, Laing is vitally interested in the social events immediately leading up to the occurrence of behavior that is labeled as schizophrenic. His experience leads him to believe that such behavior is always "a special strategy that a person invents in order to live in an unlivable situation" (Laing, 1967a, p. 115). The victim comes to feel that he cannot do anything, or even do nothing at all, without subjecting himself to "contradictory and paradoxical pressures and demands." Unfortunately the people around the victim usually don't perceive his dilemma. They do not realize that he is at the bottom of a heap and that they are crushing him without intending it. This cannot be seen if the victim's behavior is viewed out of context. Laing makes an apt analogy to illustrate the point: "From an ideal vantage point on the ground, a formation of planes may be observed in the air. One plane may be out of formation. But the whole formation may be off course. The plane that is 'out of formation' may be abnormal, bad or 'mad,' from the point of view of the formation. But the formation itself may be bad or mad from the point of view of the ideal observer" (Laing, 1967a, pp. 118–119).

Laing goes on to reflect on why the so-called schizophrenic engages in the strange behavior that causes him to be labeled, what it represents, and why people react to it as they do. He points out that movement characterizes all of life. People may feel high or low, may travel in circles, go forwards or go backwards. Of all these possibilities, going backwards (regressing) is the most tabooed. Laing feels that at certain points in a person's life he or she may need to go backwards to engage in a voyage inward. He sees nothing inherently unnatural in this. The journey within takes the traveler "through one's personal life, in and back and through and beyond into the experience of all mankind, of the primal man, of Adam and perhaps even further into the beings of animals, vegetables and minerals."

While most men and women can accept outer explorations to the deepest of jungles or the highest of Everests, they are threatened by the return to deep inner realms. Yet such a return from Laing's viewpoint is part of a "natural *healing* process" necessary for many who are labeled schizophrenic. The steps taken to "treat" schizophrenia, however, interfere with the process. They often prevent its being carried out to a natural conclusion and doom the victim to a life of suspension in an inner world. Left alone, Laing feels that the so-called schizophrenic would eventually find his way back to life outside himself. Families and hospitals try to prevent the disturbed person from embarking or proceeding on a curative trip. The behavior that signals the beginning of such a journey is often taken as the early sign of a schizophrenic illness, when, in fact, Laing sees it as the "beginning of becoming well."

For Laing the ideal treatment setting is an "anti-hospital." It is a living situation in which no one is labeled "staff" or "patient." In such a setting the person with a problem has the freedom to work it out in his own natural way with interference from no one.

Schizophrenic Behavior as Learned from Societal Reactions

B. F. Skinner (1938, 1953) has theorized that behavior, in man as in animals, is learned as the result of the reinforcements that follow it. A reinforcement is defined as any stimulus that is associated with increased emission of the behavior preceding it. For Skinner all behavior results from *learning*, the creation of a functional relationship between a stimulus and a response.

Skinner identified two learning paradigms: *respondent* or classical Pavlovian conditioning, and *operant* conditioning. In respondent conditioning a stimulus precedes the response and actually elicits it. An example of this is the pairing of an unconditioned stimulus such as food with a neutral stimulus such as the sound of a bell. Since food alone elicits salivation, the pairing of food and bell eventually makes it possible for the bell alone to produce the salivation response. In the operant paradigm the sequence of stimulus and response is reversed. Here the organism makes a response that has certain environmental consequences. If these consequences are reinforcing, the operant behavior will be repeated. Generally, responses associated with the voluntary musculature are learned in the operant paradigm and responses associated with the involuntary musculature involve respondent conditioning.

Responses to most social stimuli are operant responses. They are shaped by the reactions made to them by others. To make a "proper" social response one must be able to attend to and obtain information from a stimulus, make a response to it, and be reinforced for it. Abnormal behavior is seen as behavior that is unexpected. It seems to be in response to cues that most people would regard as idiosyncratic or trivial. As such, abnormal behavior is unpredictable and upsetting. In many cases abnormality is seen to occur because the individual simply lacks the skill to respond as he is expected to.

Ullmann and Krasner (1974) have applied Skinner's theories to the study of schizophrenia. Behaviors characteristically labeled as schizophrenic are seen by Ullmann and Krasner to result from the fact that the patient is attending to a different set of cues from most other people. Attention itself is seen as an operant behavior that will be directed toward one or another set of stimuli depending upon whether it is reinforced. One who manifests schizophrenic behavior is seen not to have been reinforced for attending to the cues most people find significant. Thus the fundamental problem for one who behaves in ways described as schizophrenic is that his attention to the social stimuli to which "normals" generally respond has been extinguished.

On this basis, the affective blandness and emotional withdrawal of the schizophrenic can be seen as a renunciation of people who have failed to reinforce him. The frequent development of somatic complaints in the early stages of a schizophrenic break is explained as a new attempt to win reinforcement, stemming from the recognition that one is not well regarded by others. If ordinary symptomatic complaints fail, more bizarre symptoms may be used. Delusions may be regarded as an attempt to achieve understanding of a situation in hopes that will lead to "normality" and the winning of reinforcements once more. Hallucinations are seen to emerge when attention to usually meaningful external stimuli is extinguished and internal and external stimuli take on equal significance.

Ullmann and Krasner emphasize the role that the hospital plays in maintaining and even extending schizophrenic behavior. As a large, impersonal institution regarding mental illness very much as physical disease, the mental hospital fosters the patient role of a clean, quiet, passive individual. The patient is seen as not responsible for his behavior, a position that absolves him from blame but also holds that he cannot be trusted with matches, belts, shoe laces, and freedom to move about the hospital. As the hospital ratio of patients to professional staff increases, the attendant takes on a greater and greater significance in the life of the patient. Since attendants must organize and control large numbers of patients, they are reinforced when patients are quiet and conforming. Because of his powerful position as one who can influence the patient's position with other patients and doctors, the attendant becomes a most important source of reinforcement: he can provide desirable jobs, more comfortable sleeping arrangements, minor luxuries such as coffee, privacy, and prompt attention to requests for a light or the use of a phone. The attendant's attitude to the patient will be imitated by fellow patients, and it is through the attendant that the psychiatrist gathers much of the information on which to base important administrative decisions about the patient.

Since the attendant is a powerful reinforcer, the behavior he chooses to encourage will be readily learned. Unfortunately, much patient behavior that makes the attendant's job easier is not adaptive to life outside an institution. The individual who helps with routine chores and otherwise is willing to sit unobtrusively in a dull, drab environment where he is denied comfort, privacy, and many potential sources of stimulation is seen as the good patient. Self-assertive responses that might serve well on the outside are extinguished—these are troublesome. Even conspicuous efforts to have contact with a physician who might help with one's problems are usually looked upon as disruptive behaviors. The net effect of this pattern of reinforcements is to encourage withdrawn, passive compliance—behavior that is often looked upon as schizophrenic. Thus, the hospital situation is seen by Ullmann and Krasner as homogenizing the behavior of individuals labeled schizophrenic. They hypothesize that much of the consistency in behavior attributed to schizophrenia is caused by methods used to treat it rather than by anything inherent in the "disease."

Mental Illness as a Refuge

Braginsky, Braginsky, and Ring (1969) have asserted that many people "use" the mental hospital as a refuge from a terribly unhappy daily routine. The wealthy can afford to vacation in places remote from home and work, where they are distracted from their daily cares. The poor cannot manage this. They, therefore, use the hospital as a "resort."

From this view, the behavior associated with serious mental illness, particularly schizophrenia, is learned and engaged in to gain a necessary relief. Braginsky et al. have done several studies to support this view. In one they showed that the new patient's way of life in the hospital is more like his weekend routine than his weekday routine at home. Further, they found that new patients who had expatient friends came into the hospital with attitudes more similar to those of long-term patients than to those of newly admitted patients without such friends. Also, many patients admitted from a particular locale were found to live closer to each other than would be expected by chance.

Braginsky et al. also suspected that patients who had already had a long hospital stay were where they wanted to be, whereas newcomers might look forward more to leaving. To demonstrate this, two groups of patients, one newly admitted and the other having been hospitalized for more than three months (most were hospitalized more than three years), were given a test. Half of each group was told it was a "mental illness" test and that a high score could increase a person's chances of staying in the hospital. The other half was told it was a "self-insight" test and that a high score could increase a person's chances of leaving the hospital. As the authors hypothesized, long-staying patients got significantly higher scores on the "mental illness" test and significantly lower ones on the "self-insight" test than the newcomers.

In another study along similar lines, three groups of patients were asked to speak for 2 minutes in response to the question "How are you feeling?" One group was told the interviewer wanted to know how ready people were for discharge. A second was told they were being evaluated for open-ward privileges. The third was told the interviewer simply wanted to know how they were getting along in the hospital. Psychiatrists then rated recordings of each two-minute response for degree of pathology displayed and amount of hospital control needed, without knowing what instructions the patient had before responding. As hypothesized, Braginsky et al. found that patients who thought they were being evaluated to stay in the hospital, but on an open ward, were judged to be the least disturbed and to require the least control. Patients who thought they were being evaluated for readinesss for discharge were rated as showing the most pathology and needing the greatest amount of control.

The implication of this research is that the kind of behavior that leads to hospitalization, and schizophrenic behavior is prominent in this category, is at least partly an effort on the part of the patient to achieve a desired end. A provocative study by Rosenhan (1973) provides data to support this view. In his experiment, 8 sane people, most of them professionals, gained admission to 12 different mental hospitals by simply complaining in the admission offices that they had been hearing voices. The actual sounds they reported hearing were vague but they were said to resemble the words "empty," "hollow," and "thud." Otherwise, except for using fake names and employment descriptions, the pseudopatients told the truth about themselves and their life histories. While on the hospital ward they behaved as normally as they could.

In all cases, but one, the patients were diagnosed as schizophrenics. When discharged, each was diagnosed as a schizophrenic "in remission." Furthermore, despite their normal behavior, the pseudo-patients averaged 19 days of hospitalization, with a range of from 7 to 52 days. In many cases fellow patients recognized the normality of the pseudopatients and were suspicious of their presence on the ward. Rosenhan speculates that the physicians' failure to detect the sanity of the pseudo-patients is because they have a bias for calling a healthy person sick rather than the reverse. Furthermore, ward personnel of all types (attendants, nurses, and psychiatrists) were found to have very little contact with patients once they were admitted.

Rosenhan's findings indicate that the "impression management" theory of Braginsky et al. may well explain some schizophrenic behavior. Their findings led Braginsky et al. to recommend that communities set up institutions to which its members who cannot afford vacation resorts can go as places of refuge without being stigmatized as mental patients. The availability of such places would, in the opinion of Braginsky et al., eliminate many traditional symptoms of "mental illness."

CONCLUSION

An attempt has been made in this chapter to describe what is the most baffling and at the same time the most fascinating of the mental disorders. Despite the efforts of many theorists, researchers, and clinicians since Bleuler's time, his description of the disorder and his nosology prevail. Sullivan's personality theory has been presented in some detail because it is the most prominent to be developed by a clinician whose primary experience and interest has been in schizophrenia. As such it probably contains more penetrating insights than most other theories. Some of Freud's theories seem to have relevance, but these are not based on actual contact with schizophrenic patients. The organic treatment procedures, which are more widely used with schizophrenics than psychological approaches, offer little basis for understanding the disorder even when they result in some symptom relief. Approaches based on operant principles seem to offer hope and are now being applied widely.

The most that can be said for the material presented in this chapter is that several avenues for studying schizophrenia have been suggested. Which will lead to dead ends and which to important findings is still an open question. The next chapter will summarize many of the research approaches that have been taken in recent years.

SUMMARY

1. Schizophrenia is one of the most highly researched but least understood of all the behavior disorders.
2. Bleuler's conception of schizophrenia's essential character has dominated twentieth-century thinking about the disorder. Bleuler saw schizophrenia as involving, most basically, a disharmony in the thoughts, feelings, and behavior of the victim. Fundamental symptoms were seen to include thought and affective disorder. Accessory symptoms giving the "external stamp" to schizophrenia include hallucinations, illusions, and delusions.

3. Current classification of schizophrenia in DSM–II includes the four classic subtypes (simple, hebephrenic, catatonic, and paranoid) and several other subtypes identifying the phase of the disorder (acute, latent, residual, childhood, and chronic undifferentiated). One relatively new subtype, schizo-affective, combines symptoms of schizophrenia and affective psychosis.

4. Bleuler believed that some sort of organic brain disturbance was at the root of schizophrenia. Psychological factors were seen to interact with the constitutional to determine the disorder's form. Bleuler concentrated on measures to prevent the exacerbation of the disorder.

5. Many organic therapies for treating schizophrenia were introduced in the twentieth century. These include: insulin shock, electric shock, psychosurgery, and the use of various drugs.

6. Although Freud never worked directly with them, his ideas have been applied to schizophrenics. He saw the schizophrenic as having withdrawn libido from external objects and having retreated to a narcissistic state similar to that found in the earliest period of life. This occurs in people with a very weak ego associated with unsatisfactory object relations in the oral stage of development.

7. John Rosen likens the schizophrenic state to the dream state. Unacceptable wishes are continually experienced but in disguised form. Treatment consists of stripping away the disguises and encouraging the patient to renounce the psychotic state.

8. Harry Stack Sullivan theorized that social more than biological forces shape the personality. Developmental stages are determined by changing social factors associated with increasing age. Schizophrenia is seen to involve ineffective dissociative techniques for controlling anxiety.

9. R. D. Laing feels that much behavior that is called schizophrenic is induced by the reactions of people to an individual who has been labeled by them as schizophrenic. The curative process requires deep inner exploration that is so often a threat to outsiders that the schizophrenic commonly becomes frustrated and frozen in a regressed state.

10. Behavior modifiers, stimulated by Skinner's theories, see all behavior as shaped by the pattern of reinforcements received. Schizophrenics are seen to respond to stimuli ordinarily ignored by most individuals because they have not been reinforced for response to the usual cues. Much institutional experience of schizophrenics is seen to reinforce behavior that is called schizophrenic.

11. Braginsky, Braginsky, and Ring view much schizophrenic behavior as purposefully designed to achieve a desired end. They recommend that those needing escape from the cares of daily life be provided with nonstigmatizing refuges by their own communities.

CHAPTER 7

Schizophrenia

Research and Attempts at Understanding

John D. 44-year-old business executive. Brought to clinic by wife. Physically violent toward family. Hostile to fellow workers. Passed over for promotion to department manager after 20 years with company. Feels superiors are trying to force him into leaving job. Believes family members have lost respect for him as a result. Does not seem willing to accept help. Outlook for treatment: not very promising at present.

The doctor who wrote these notes, like many other therapists before and after, will try to analyze the information he has and make a real effort to understand the patient.

Few theorists and researchers, despite their great interest in schizophrenia, have been as systematic as Sullivan in their theories or have attempted to develop a general personality theory. Rather the tendency has been to focus on a significant facet, either psychological or physiological, of the broader problem of schizophrenia, and to seek to understand that element in the hope that it might provide a key to the mystery of this puzzling disorder. In the sections to follow, a representative sampling of recent research and practice in schizophrenia will be presented.

THE PROCESS-REACTIVE DISTINCTION

Garmezy (1968) points out that the process-reactive concept in schizophrenia is based on Kraepelin's historic concern with prognosis. When Kraepelin found exceptions to what he theorized was a lawful relationship between the diagnosis and the outcome of the disorder, he presumed that a diagnostic error had been made. Bleuler disagreed that such diagnostic-outcome lawfulness exists and spoke of a "group of schizophrenias" in which recovery was a possibility. Others, notably Meyer and Sullivan, stressed the influence of psychic factors. This gave a place to life-history experiences as significant forces in the development of schizophrenia.

The process-reactive grouping is a dichotomy set up to distinguish between two types of schizophrenics. Essentially, the *process schizophrenic* is seen to deteriorate progressively with little chance for recovery. The *reactive schizophrenic* is seen to have a favorable prognosis because his premorbid development was sound and his breakdown occurred in the face of much stress. Table 7.1 depicts more fully the distinguishing features of the two schizophrenic types.

To compare process and reactive schizophrenics certain variables from the life history (such as employment history) and the history of the illness (such as the immediate precipitating factors) are examined. In most studies this is done through the use of formal scales, systematically applied to the patient's case history. Scales developed by Wittman (1941), Kantor, Wallner, and Winder (1953), and Phillips (1953) have been widely used to study the process-reactive distinction.

One series of studies has examined the possibility that process schizophrenia is organic and reactive schizophrenia psychogenic in origin. These studies have included measures of autonomic nervous system activity, autonomic reactivity to the injection of mecholyl, and organic signs on the Rorschach test. The results have been inconclusive. Becker (1956) has pointed out that the organic-psychogenic distinction erroneously implies a dichotomy between "pure" process and reactive schizophrenics. There is, however, so much overlap between these two groups on research measures that it is far more likely that process and reactive "types" are merely labels for the extreme points of a continuum, and that a particular patient places somewhere on this continuum as a combined function of many etiological factors. Any simple causative interpretation implied by the process-organic and reactive-psychogenic dichotomies seems unjustified.

Other studies have attempted to delineate psychological differences between process and reactive patients. Rodnick and Garmezy (1957) described a number of such studies done by their students, using the Phillips (1953) scale to differentiate patients with good and poor premorbid histories. This scale involves ratings of: (a) recent sexual adjustment, (b) social aspects of the recent sexual life, (c) past history of personal relations, and (d) the recent adjustment in personal relations. Ratings are also made of the factors that seem to have precipitated the illness. In these studies poor premorbids, as compared to good premorbids, have been found to: (a) show greater reminiscence following censure, (b) manifest more discrimination deficit in viewing a scene of a mother scolding a young boy, (c) have poorer retention on a memory task, (d) see their mothers as more rejecting and have less capacity to evaluate

TABLE 7.1
Items Defining Frame of Reference for Case History Judgments

PROCESS SCHIZOPHRENIA	REACTIVE SCHIZOPHRENIA
Birth to the Fifth Year	
a. Early psychological trauma	a. Good psychological history
b. Physical illness—severe or long	b. Good physical health
c. Odd member of family	c. Normal member of family
Fifth Year to Adolescence	
a. Difficulties at school	a. Well adjusted at school
b. Family troubles paralleled with sudden changes in patient's behavior	b. Domestic troubles unaccompanied by behavior disruptions. Patient "had what it took."
c. Introverted behavior trends and interests	c. Extroverted behavior trends and interests
d. History of breakdown of social, physical, mental functioning	d. History of adequate social, physical, mental functioning
e. Pathological siblings	e. Normal siblings
f. Overprotective or rejecting mother. "Momism"	f. Normally protective, accepting mother
g. Rejecting father	g. Accepting father.
Adolescence to Adulthood	
a. Lack of heterosexuality	a. Heterosexual behavior
b. Insidious, gradual onset of psychosis without pertinent stress	b. Sudden onset of psychosis; stress present and pertinent. Later onset
c. Physical aggression	c. Verbal aggression
d. Poor response to treatment	d. Good response to treatment
e. Lengthy stay in hospital	e. Short course in hospital
Adulthood	
a. Massive paranoia	a. Minor paranoid trends
b. Little capacity for alcohol	b. Much capacity for alcohol
c. No manic-depressive component	c. Presence of manic-depressive component
d. Failure under adversity	d. Success despite adversity
e. Discrepancy between ability and achievement	e. Harmony between ability and achievement
f. Awareness of change in self	f. No sensation of change
g. Somatic delusions	g. Absence of somatic delusions
h. Clash between culture and environment	h. Harmony between culture and environment
i. Loss of decency (nudity, public masturbation, etc.)	i. Retention of decency

From Kantor, R. E. Wallner, J., & Winder, C. L. Process and reactive schizophrenia. Journal of Consulting Psychology, *1953, 17, p. 158.* Copyright 1953 by the American Psychological Association. Reprinted by permission.

them critically, and (e) overestimate the sizes of mother-child pictures in a perceptual task. These authors also reported that poor premorbids saw their mothers as having been dominating, controlling, and powerful, and their fathers as weak. The opposite was found in good premorbids.

More recently, Zigler and Phillips (1960) developed a scale of social competence based on the assumption that normal development is characterized by the achievement of levels of adequacy in six areas of functioning: age reached before initial breakdown, intelligence, education, occupation, employment history, and marital status. For each area three levels of adequacy are defined. The scale is used to rate the social maturity of patients. In an early study Zigler and Phillips (1960) demonstrated that classic schizophrenic symptoms (such as "avoidance of others") were more characteristically found in low-social-competence patients than in highs. A later study (Zigler & Phillips, 1962) demonstrated that within a large schizophrenic sample, those highest in social competence (good premorbids) were characterized by symptoms involving "turning against the self," while those low in social competence (poor premorbids) more often displayed symptoms of "avoidance of others," "self-indulgence," and turning against others." Zigler and Phillips (1961b) also hypothesized that normal development is characterized by a shift from action to thought as the mode of response to one's needs. The very young react to needs immediately and externally while the more mature use symbolic, conceptual, or ideational patterns. They hypothesized that more socially competent patients would be higher in "thought" symptoms (suspiciousness, bizarre ideas, obsessions, depersonalization, and so on) than in "action" symptoms (assault, perversions, compulsions, irresponsible and violent behavior), and that the reverse would be true for those low in social competence. The results of their study confirmed these hypotheses.

Herron (1962), following a careful and extensive review of work on the process-reactive distinction in schizophrenia, pointed out that schizophrenics can be assigned successfully to these two categories and that the distinction helps us to understand the heterogeneity commonly found in their responses when they are not so classified. The process-organic and reactive-psychogenic distinctions, however, are not seen by Herron to be valid, nor is any other distinction predicated on a dichotomy between process and reactive patients. There is more likely to be a continuum of reactions between these theoretical extremes and the present need is for a continued search for criteria that differentiate among patients found at various points on the continuum.

GENETIC THEORIES OF SCHIZOPHRENIA

One type of organic theory of psychosis with a long tradition is the view that heredity or genetic makeup profoundly influences onset and development of mental disorder. This theory has been proposed to explain schizophrenia, and an approach often used in seeking to verify it has involved the demonstration that schizophrenia occurs with greater frequency in children of schizophrenic parents than in children of normal ones. Environmentalists, however, dismiss such data with the argument that they are as well explained by psychological factors as by hereditary ones. That is, if the disorder is a learned one, it is more likely to be learned from parents with such pathology than from nonaffected parents.

A theoretically less vulnerable approach, therefore, has been to study the incidence of schizophrenia in identical and fraternal twins. Although the environmental factors are roughly equivalent, identical twins are characterized by similarity of genetic makeup whereas fraternal twins are no more similar genetically than any other siblings. If concordance rates were higher for identical than for fraternal twins, it would argue for the importance of heredity.

Franz Kallman (1946, 1953) reported

that for a group of 174 identical twin pairs in which one twin was schizophrenic, the second twin was also found to be schizophrenic in 69 percent of the cases. For 517 pairs of fraternal twins with one schizophrenic twin, only 10 percent of the second twins were also found to be schizophrenic. In a second study Kallman (1953) reported an 86 percent concordance among 268 identical twin pairs while for 685 fraternal twin pairs the concordance was only 15 percent. Kallman's use of the categories "separated" and "non-separated" identical twins (Kallman, 1946) indicated that some of the identical twins had been reared apart and achieved high concordance for schizophrenia nonetheless. This further strengthens the argument for the importance of heredity.

The seemingly impressive evidence for the significance of hereditary factors in schizophrenia has not gone unchallenged. Jackson (1960), for example, emphasizes the fact that Kallman's "separated" identical twins actually lived together, on the average, until five years before the onset of the first psychosis at a mean age of 33. Thus, for the most part, these twins had shared a common environment through the formative years and well into adulthood. Despite this, the separated group had lower concordance rates than the non-separated group, a result that favors an environmentalist interpretation. Jackson also pointed out that an extensive literature survey had uncovered only two cases of concordant identical twins reared apart. He asserts that environmental differences between the twins in these two cases had been greatly overemphasized when originally reported, and that in both cases the separated twins were reared in families that were antagonistic to each other but insistent on maintaining contact with each other. Later each pair of twins had contact with each other, and

their relationships mirrored those of the families in which they had been raised.

Careful examination of the schizophrenia twin studies turns up other important bases for criticism. Rosenthal (1962) has done a very thorough analysis of Kallman's surveys, pointing up several prime weaknesses in them that account, at least in part, for the high concordance rates reported. One major weakness implicates Kallman's sampling methods. Examination of consecutive hospital admissions in twin surveys reporting concordance rates lower than Kallman's reveals approximately equal numbers of male and female twin pairs. However, when samples were drawn from large pools of already hospitalized patients, as was the case in Kallman's studies, a significant preponderance of female twin pairs results. Other studies have shown that over long periods of time male and female patients are admitted to and discharged from mental hospitals in approximately equal numbers. However, more males than females *remain* discharged. Among readmitted patients more males are redischarged and more females remain in the hospital. What this suggests is that among hospitalized schizophrenics chronicity of illness is more typical of females than of males. Thus the preponderance of female over male twin pairs in studies such as Kallman's is probably due to the fact that his samples consist largely of chronic schizophrenics. The index case (that is, the twin who determines that the pair will be included in the sample) is thus likely to be chronically ill. Twins with a favorable prognosis are relatively less likely to be included in a study such as Kallman's, and this omission of the more favorable cases has undoubtedly inflated his concordance rates.

Gottesman and Shields (1966) have recently reported a study bearing directly on this point. These investigators sought to relate severity of illness to concordance rates in twins. Their sample consisted of all patients admitted to a hospital between 1948 and 1964, diagnosed as schizophrenic, and members of a same-sex twin pair. This procedure uncovered 57 pairs of identical or fraternal twins. For each hospitalized schizophrenic twin, degree of concordance with the pathological status of the other twin was judged in terms of four grades: (1) close concordance—co-twin also hospitalized with diagnosis of schizophrenia; (2) moderate concordance—co-twin hospitalized for emotional disorder other than schizophrenia; (3) least concordance—co-twin not hospitalized but treated in outpatient clinic for emotional problem, having a neurotic or psychotic MMPI profile, or being manifestly abnormal on interview; (4) no concordance—co-twin apparently normal. The close concordance was 42 percent for identical twins and 9 percent for fraternals. If the moderate and least concordant categories were included in the overall rate figures, the percentages changed to 79 percent and 46 percent respectively.

One aspect of the Gottesman and Shields study seems to test Rosenthal's hypothesis that sampling bias is involved in the separate computation of concordance rates for index cases as a function of the severity of their schizophrenic disorder. Gottesman and Shields defined severity in terms of total length of hospitalization and work status on follow-up, and as more stringent definitions of severity were adopted, thus isolating more chronic cases, concordance rates rose. This would seem to support Rosenthal's hypothesis about the effects of sampling on Kallman's findings.

Another important factor in evaluating twin studies of schizophrenia, pointed out by Rosenthal and highlighted in the study by Gottesman and Shields, is how one arrives at diagnoses. The problem here pertains to judgments made about the co-twin rather than the index case, who reaches the researcher's attention because he has already been diagnosed independently as schizophrenic. Often the co-twin has not previously been hospitalized, and a judgment that he is schizophrenic is made by a researcher who either sees him briefly or who bases his opinion on possibly inadequate hospital records, in cases where he has been hospitalized. Many investigators have failed to specify the criteria they have used for diagnosing schizophrenia or, when they attempt to do so as did Kallman, the criteria are difficult to apply and reliability figures are not offered. Furthermore, as Gottesman and Shields have demonstrated, the magnitude of concordance rates is related to the degree of similarity in the severity of the illness in each member of the twin pair. As Jackson points out, no twin studies to date have utilized "blind" diagnoses of co-twins and, if one is trying to prove that genetic factors are significant, the bias toward finding schizophrenia among co-twins may be great indeed.

That factors such as the nature of the samples studied, methods for arriving at diagnoses, and potential experimenter bias effects potentially affect the findings of co-twin studies of schizophrenia is suggested in a recent review by Kringlen (1968), who summarizes ten major investigations in this area in several countries and spanning forty years. Kallman's figures for monozygotic concordance in schizophrenia (69 percent–86 percent) are among the highest ever reported; other investigators, for example, Tienari in Finland, report monozygous concordances of less than 20 percent.

Kringlen carefully investigated this problem using detailed records submitted (for all people born in Norway during the period 1901–1930) by all psychiatric hospitals to a central psychoses register. Some 519 pairs of twins were located on this register, of whom in 342 pairs one or both twins were hospitalized in Norway for *functional* psychosis. For monozygotic twins, concordance figures for schizophrenia varied from 25 percent to 38 percent depending both on whether hospital records alone were accepted or personal assessment of the patient was added, and breadth or narrowness of the definition of schizophrenia. The comparable concordance figures for dizygotic twins were 4–10 percent. Two conclusions are suggested from Kringlen's work. Even using his most "liberal" definition of concordance, the incidence figures he reports for monozygous twins are less than half Kallman's comparable figures. However, using either liberal or conservative definitions of the disorder, Kringlen does indeed find substantially more concordance among monozygous than among dizygous twins. These findings lead him to the conclusion that both environmental and hereditary factors are etiologically significant in schizophrenia, and that genetic predisposition to this disorder is polygenic (caused by a combination of many different genes).

Those leaning toward more environmentalistic explanations of the etiology of schizophrenia have raised other issues not fully resolved by current genetic studies. For example, if schizophrenia is an hereditary disorder, its mode of transmission is unclear. Much current opinion on this matter suggests that transmission occurs through recessive genes. If so, schizophrenia should appear less often in the children of index cases than in their own siblings. In fact, however, the reverse is usually found. Furthermore it should appear in all of the children of cases where both parents are schizophrenic, and nothing approaching a 100 percent rate for such a group has ever been reported.

Many other factors argue against a strict genetic transmission of schizophrenia. These include: the hypothesized tendency of schizophrenics or those from schizophrenic families to mate selectivity with others from similar backgrounds; higher mortality rates among schizophrenics than in the general population; and the fact that schizophrenics are less likely than normals to marry and have children. The overall effect of these factors would be to reduce the number of offspring of schizophrenic parents and, ultimately, the total percentage of schizophrenics from generation to generation if genetic factors are all-important. That such a reduction in the number of schizophrenics has not occurred argues against a strictly genetic theory.

The data and arguments presented thus far do not permit conclusive choice between essentially genetic or environmentalist explanations of schizophrenic etiology. There is ample basis for recognizing the potential significance of both strands of determinants. This is the conclusion of the geneticist Böök, who stated, "The important conclusion that I think is fully justified is that major gene differences are the basic prerequisite for the initiation of a chain of events which may result in a psychosis. Unless this specific genetical prerequisite exists, the illness will not occur, provided we are not dealing with a supposedly rare nongenetical schizophrenic syndrome" (Böök, 1960, p. 31).

Meehl (1962) takes a similar position. He feels that neural defects predisposing to schizophrenia are inherited. This condition of vulnerability is called *schizotaxia*. The interaction between life experiences and schizotaxia often results in a *schizotype*. The schizotype has many of the qualities seen in "schizophrenic personalities." These include a tendency to think illogically, avoidance of interpersonal relationships, difficulty enjoying pleasurable occasions, and ambivalence. If the schizotaxic's environment is relatively nonstressful, he remains a schizotype. He may behave peculiarly from time to time but does not become schizophrenic. If the environment is stressful for him, however, he will become schizophrenic.

Sameroff and Zax (1973b) agree with Meehl's view that constitutional predisposition is an essential element in the ultimate appearance of schizophrenia. They question, however, whether a simple interaction between vulnerability factors and stress fully explains the emergence of schizophrenia. They add the point that the potential schizophrenic influences his environment as well as being influenced by it. For example, a hyperactive, cranky infant (who may be this way because of constitutional factors) may seriously strain an already disturbed mother who is not secure in her caretaking ability. Such a mother might be at her worst with a difficult child but be altogether adequate with an easy child. Thus, the "transaction" between mother and child in which each affects the behavior of the other helps to produce the stressful environment.

THE DIATHESIS-STRESS HYPOTHESIS

Influenced by notions like those of Meehl, who sees schizophrenia as resulting from a combination of constitutional predisposition (diathesis) and adverse environmental circumstances (stress), several recent studies (Heston & Denney, 1968; Kety et al., 1968; Rosenthal et al., 1968) have been carried out to identify significant diathesis-stress factors in the development of schizophrenia. Efforts are being made to study groups in which either genetic or significant experiential variables are held constant to determine whether and how much each contributes to the problem.

Heston and Denney studied 97 people who had been permanently separated from their mothers within two weeks of birth. The mothers of 47 of these were schizophrenic (the experimental group) while the mothers of the remaining 50 (the control group) showed no history of psychiatric disorder. Experimental and control groups were matched for sex, type of placement (adoptive, institutional, or foster family), and length of time in child-care institutions. Comparison of these two groups was seen as a way to assess the genetic contribution to schizophrenia since the environments in which all subjects were reared were presumably free of the influences of a schizophrenic parent.

The psychological status of all 97 subjects was evaluated, 72 through interviews and 25 through extensive records. The Menninger Clinic's Mental Health Sickness Rating Scale (MHSRS) was used to measure the degree of psychological incapacity. Specific diagnoses were also assigned to all subjects where possible. Psychological disability was found to be significantly greater in experimental subjects than controls, with the difference deriving primarily from the extreme disability found in slightly more than 50 percent (26 out of 47) of the experimental group. A total of 5 schizophrenics were identified in the sample of 97 (all of whom were evaluated without knowledge of which group they belonged to) and all were from the experimental group. This yielded an age-corrected rate of 16.6 percent for schizophrenia, a figure consistent with findings of earlier genetic studies.

In addition to the findings relevant to the incidence of schizophrenia, Heston and Denney found that a preponderance of experimental subjects were diagnosed as

sociopaths (8 males) or as emotionally labile (6 females and 2 males). Only 2 control subjects fell into these categories. It is also interesting to note that the 21 experimentals manifesting no serious psychological impairment were not only successful but seemed also to be more spontaneous and colorful than the controls. They also tended to be in more creative occupations (musicians, teachers) and were more imaginative in their hobbies (antique aircraft, oil painting).

Heston and Denney conclude that their findings support a genetic theory of schizophrenia. The fact that schizophrenia as well as other psychological disabilities predominated in their experimental group suggests that families in which schizophrenia appears are "tainted." This is contradicted, however, by the fact that a significant percentage of their experimentals were among their best adjusted, most creative subjects. Several possible explanations are offered by Heston and Denney for these findings. First, schizophrenia may be caused by a combination of many genes. A subcritical combination of pathogenic genes may, therefore, predispose one to disorders less extreme than schizophrenia and perhaps certain combinations of such genes may make for an especially adaptive, creative personality. Another possibility is that schizophrenia is caused by a single gene whose impact can be modified in various ways by other genes, such as those controlling intelligence or body type. Finally, they

suggest that schizophrenia, as a biological entity, may be much broader than the clinical entity we have delineated. Thus the emotional and behavioral problems identified in the experimental group might more accurately, from a biological viewpoint, be identified as schizophrenia rather than as some other diagnostic entity.

A study similar to that of Heston and Denney has been done by Rosenthal et al. (1968), who have made a preliminary report of their findings. The purpose was to establish the validity of a diathesis-stress theory of schizophrenia and to describe the behavioral and psychological aspects of the diathesis.

Subjects were drawn from a large sample who had been adopted at a very early age (between the years 1924 and 1947) by families unrelated to their own. This study was done in Denmark where, because of the existence of a central psychiatric registry, it was possible to determine who among the approximately 10,000 identifiable biological parents of these 5,500-odd adoptees had at some time been diagnosed schizophrenic. Case records of parents identified as schizophrenic in the psychiatric register were screened by several project psychiatrists. Where a full consensus of psychiatrists and psychologists held that a given case was schizophrenic, the child given up for adoption by that parent became an index case for the study. The children of a few cases in which there was some diagnostic question or in which manic depressive psychosis was found were also included. Several potential control subjects, matched for sex, age, age at adoption, age of transfer, and socio-economic status of adoptive parents but born to parents with no known psychiatric diagnosis, were selected for each index case. Following this identification process, prospective index and control subjects were invited to participate in a two-day examination procedure by professionals unaware of the group to which a given subject belonged.

A total of 69 index cases was identified (31 males and 38 females). In 56 of these cases a parent was seen as clearly being schizophrenic (the ratio of mothers to fathers was about 2.5 to 1). In 8 cases the parent was diagnosed as suffering a manic-depressive psychosis. The remaining 5 cases were schizophrenics or manic-depressives about whom there was some diagnostic question. Only 11 parents (16 percent) out of the 69 parent-child pairs had been admitted to a psychiatric facility before the child was born, in contrast to Heston's sample in which all schizophrenic mothers were actively psychotic when his index cases were born.

Rosenthal et al. were able to examine 39 index cases among the 69 they identified, 14 having refused to participate and the remainder having died or migrated out of the country. Of 86 controls, 47 were examined. In this group 15 refused to participate and the remainder were dead or had left the country. Examinations included standardized psychiatric interviews, self-assessment procedures, conditioning of autonomic responses such as those done by Mednick and Schulsinger (1965), and psychological tests for evaluating cognitive functioning as has been done by Singer and Wynne (1963; 1965a; 1965b). The first report of this work includes only results from the psychiatric interviews and the self-assessment procedures. It was found that in the entire sample of 155 identified subjects (69 index cases and 86 controls) there was only 1 hospitalized schizophrenic and he was an index case. Of the 86 subjects who were examined (39 index cases and 47 controls) 3 were diagnosed as schizophrenic and all were index cases. Seven cases were seen to be borderline schizophrenics and 6 of these were index cases. Ten other cases were diagnosed as schizoids or borderline paranoids and 4 of these were index cases. Thus of 20 cases receiving diagnoses in the "schizophrenic spectrum," 13 were index cases. Since these 13 were diagnosed from a total of 39 index cases whereas only 7 of 47 controls were so diagnosed, the rate for index cases was about twice that for controls. These findings support those of Heston and Denney in suggesting a genetic component in schizophrenia. Contrary to Heston and Denney's findings, Rosenthal et al. did not find a high frequency of sociopathic behavior in nonschizophrenic index cases. This suggests that environmental factors are important determinants of whether an individual with a schizophrenic diathesis who does not develop schizophrenia becomes a sociopath instead.

Results on the two self-assessment instruments that were used were inconclusive. One, the Minnesota Multiphasic Personality Inventory (MMPI), yielded no significant differences between groups. The other, consisting of a series of 52 attributes, each of which was self-rated on a seven-point scale, yielded significant differences between index cases and controls on six attributes. Index cases saw themselves as significantly less shy, having more close friends, and being better talkers than controls. They also expressed a significantly greater feeling of unreality, a stronger feeling that they did not control their own fate, and the feeling that they had less of a sense of humor than controls. While the latter three differences are consistent with expectancies, the first three are not.

A third study exploring the genetics of schizophrenia has been done by Kety, Rosenthal, Wender, and Schulsinger (1968). Its purpose was to compare the prevalance of mental disturbance in the biological and adoptive families (parents, siblings, and half-siblings) of adoptees who had become schizophrenic. If genetic factors contribute most weightily to the disorder of the adoptee, there should be a greater prevalence of mental disturbance in his biological family, whereas mental disturbance should predominate in the adoptive family if environmental factors are particularly important. This study was also done in Denmark with index cases identified from among adoptions granted in Copenhagen between 1924 and 1947, following procedures similar to those used by Rosenthal et al. A group of adoptees who had no history of mental disorder was matched to the index group, as in the study by Rosenthal et al.

Thirty-three index and 33 control cases were mixed together in a single group and all research operations were carried out without knowledge of the group to which a given subject belonged. Searches were made of the various registers in Denmark to identify parents, half-siblings and full siblings, both biological and adoptive, of each of the 66 subjects. For index cases, 98 percent of biological mothers, 92 percent of biological fathers, and 98 percent of adoptive parents could be identified. In all, 463 relatives of the index and control cases were located. The psychiatric registers in Denmark were then searched to ascertain who among these relatives had received psychiatric care over the years: The case records of the 67 relatives so identified were then studied independently and rated on a four-category scale: (1) definitely not schizophrenic; (2) chronic or acute schizophrenic or borderline state; (3) inadequate personality; (4) uncertain.

It was found that 13, or 8.7 percent, of the 150 biological relatives of index cases were classified in category 2 (chronic or acute schizophrenic or borderline state) whereas only 3 (1.9 percent) of the 156 biological relatives of controls were so classified. This is a highly significant difference. Among the adoptive relatives or index cases only 2 of 74 and, among the adoptive relatives of control cases, only 3 of 83 were classified in category 2. Furthermore, when the index and control cases were refined to include only those separated from their biological parents very early (before the age of one month), similar relationships were found. For the 19 index cases in this group 9 of 93 biological relatives were classified in category 2 while none of the 92 relatives of the 20 controls in this group were so classified. Two of 45 and 1 of 51 adoptive relatives of the index and control cases respectively were seen to be schizophrenic or suffering some borderline condition.

The findings of Kety et al. support the hypothesis of a genetic transmission of schizophrenia as did the studies of Heston and Denney, and Rosenthal et al. Kety et al. are careful to point out that their results suggest that some polygenic model rather than a monogenic one best describes the way in which schizophrenia is transmitted Such a view is compatible with the diathesis-stress model that Meehl has proposed.

The well-designed and well-controlled studies described in this section provide some of the best evidence to date on the importance of genetic factors in schizophrenia. They also speak to the importance of establishing longitudinal studies of children who are high risks for becoming schizophrenic, beginning in the very earliest years of life. Only in this way can the nature of the stress that interacts with genetic factors to produce a schizophrenic be specified.

A number of fairly recent studies have suggested that pregnancy and birth complications (PBCs) represent a type of stress which may be related to the emergence of schizophrenia. Several years ago Pasamanick and his coworkers (Pasamanick, Rogers, & Lilienfeld, 1956) demonstrated repeatedly that a relationship existed between PBCs and mental disorder in general. More recently, Pollin and Stabenau (1968) studied 11 sets of identical twins. In each pair one was schizophrenic and one was not. Detailed life histories of each pair revealed that the schizophrenic member had either a lower birth weight than his twin or suffered an illness soon after birth causing him to be looked upon as weaker or more vulnerable than his twin. The authors felt that the disturbed twin's disorder resulted from the fact that what started as a constitutional weakness became converted to a self-image of psychological weakness and vulnerability. The conversion is attributed to differential parental reactions to the pair.

Mednick (1970) reported a follow-up study of 20 children of schizophrenic mothers who suffered serious psychiatric disturbances. He found that this group differed significantly from control subjects with respect to the presence of severe perinatal distress in their history. Mednick's research group (Mednick et al., 1971) pursued this work with an extensive survey of the birth records of 83 children born to either a schizophrenic mother or father. Their data showed that these youngsters tended to have lower birth weights than control children and that their mothers had more difficult pregnancies than normal mothers. At five days of age the children of schizophrenic parents showed more abnormalities than controls and at one year the experimental group was retarded in motor development in comparison to controls.

Sameroff and Zax (1973a) also reported that children born to schizophrenic women suffered more birth complications than normal controls. They found, in addition, that the same was true for the children of depressive mothers. Furthermore, when their schizophrenic and depressive mothers were differentiated with respect to the chronicity of their psychological disorder, Sameroff and Zax found that high chronicity related to number of delivery complications irrespective of diagnosis.

Garmezy (1974, p. 31) sums up much of this recent work by pointing out that PBCs may play a complex role by "the manner in which they may ultimately condition negative transactional elements in the later mother-child relationship." In this respect he echoes the earlier-stated position of Sameroff and Zax (1973b). The significance of the role played by PBCs must ultimately be viewed in terms of their behavioral consequences for the child.

BIOCHEMICAL THEORIES OF SCHIZOPHRENIA

Although biochemical study of schizophrenia has burgeoned recently as a result of growing technical and scientific sophistication, the fundamental idea that severe mental disease stems from the adverse effects of internal substances on brain function is an old one. It has been suggested by numerous theorists, beginning with Hippocrates.

Work in this area has been characterized by the attempt to isolate significantly greater or lesser concentrations of chemical substances in psychotic patients (usually schizophrenic) as compared to normals. Investigators in this area are particularly interested in substances whose presence or absence presumably relates to schizophrenic-like behavioral manifestations. Accordingly, there has been great interest in the hallucinogens and other psychotomimetic drugs such as mescaline and LSD. Many studies have been done on substances normally found in the brain that are similar to LSD and mescaline, in order to detect whether they might account for psychotic symptomatology similar to the reported effects of mescaline and LSD.

Heath (1960) has recently advanced a biochemical theory of schizophrenia. His prime concern is with a substance called *taraxein*, isolated from the blood-serum of schizophrenics, which supposedly causes schizophrenic-like symptoms in nonpsychotic volunteers. Heath reports that intense feelings of pain and pleasure are the most prominent behavioral symptoms resulting from excesses of taraxein. Schizophrenia is characterized by Heath as involving a prime defect in the pain-pleasure mechanism. This defect is seen to be basic to the fundamental symptoms of the disorder described by Bleuler. Heath believes that only those who have a predisposing inherited defect (schizotypes) and who experience additional psychological stresses succumb to schizophrenia.

Because of the inherited defect, which limits the ability to experience pain and pleasure normally, the schizotype is susceptible to specific types of stress: to situations that confuse his identity—who he is and how he fits into the overall scheme of life around him. When life is well regimented by external forces and the schizotype is clearly informed about expectations others have of him, and he is identified with a group in which morale is high he can function effectively even in the face of objectively dangerous situations. Heath thus believes that many schizotypes do well in the military despite the obvious stresses of such a life. The important point is that schizotypes are predisposed to having

identity-difficulties because of the pain-pleasure defect, hence their most serious stresses are those that call identity into question and force them to recognize their essential difference from other people. Heath considers this point to be very significant for psychotherapy since schizotypes are likely to get worse rather than better if they experience therapy procedures that raise identity questions.

Heath believes that the intrafamilial dynamics often thought to be predisposing to schizophrenia are, instead, caused by metabolic defects shared by family members. Thus, the "schizophrenogenic mother" is also a schizophrenogenic wife, neighbor, and friend but she does not cause schizophrenia in others as she seems to in her child because they do not share her genes. Furthermore, just as the schizotypic child may be adversely influenced by the behavior of those around him, his own behavior is also seen to make a basic contribution to the overall family pathology.

In evaluating this theory of schizophrenia Heath has done considerable research on taraxein concentrations in the brains of normals and schizophrenics, and the effects of administration of this substance on behavior, and he has recorded electrical activity in areas of the brain presumably affected by taraxein. An evaluation of this work will be offered later.

Biochemical research on schizophrenia has been done with many substances other than taraxein, including *adrenochrome* and *serotonin*. *Adrenochrome* has attracted interest because it is a metabolite of adrenalin and chemically similar to mescaline. Adrenalin is of course commonly found in the human body and the view has therefore developed that perhaps its metabolite, adrenochrome, might have the same psychologic effects as mescaline. Were this the case, the schizophrenic might in effect be manufacturing his own mescaline and constantly suffering its effects. Research interest in serotonin developed when it was found that LSD blocked its action on smooth muscles. This, coupled with the fact that serotonin is normally found in the brain, suggested that the profound emotional effects of drugs such as LSD might result from a serotonin deficiency.

Kety (1959a, 1959b) has reviewed recent biochemical theories of schizophrenia and weighed the evidence for each. For each substance already mentioned, as well as for others that have been studied, findings are at best equivocal. Typically, evidence both supporting or contradicting a given theory can readily be found. Not infrequently, positive findings from one laboratory are entirely contradicted by negative ones from another. Clearly none of the substances has yet been shown conclusively to be implicated in producing schizophrenia. Kety, in fact, has considered the possibility that the chemical make-up of the schizophrenic's brain might be quite normal but that there may be a genetic defect resulting in inappropriate neural connections or pathways. Were this the case, the physiological psychologist the neurophysiologist or the anatomist might be more likely to reach a conclusive understanding of the disorder before the biochemist.

Before completing consideration of the relation of biochemical factors to schizophrenia, another of Kety's major criticisms of work in this area is pertinent. This pertains to the relatively poor controls that have been used in most biochemical studies of patients. Kety points out that inadequate diet, vitamin deficiency, and chronic infections (especially of the digestive tract), each potentially resulting from unhygienic living conditions, as well as previous exposure to drug therapies, and possibly even to electric shock treatment—all have poten-

tial effects on human biochemistry. Furthermore, emotional stress affects biochemical functioning. Since most biochemical studies have been done with institutionalized patients, it is likely that their contradictory findings are related to the failure to control for such variables. For example, one study may find excessive or deficient amounts of a biochemical substance in schizophrenics whose diet has lacked certain vitamins. Another investigator may study the same substance in schizophrenics whose diets include the relevant vitamins in sufficient quantity and fail to confirm earlier findings. In this instance a relationship between biochemistry and vitamin deficiency may have been demonstrated that has little bearing on schizophrenia.

Another source of error that Kety warns of is the subjective bias of the investigator. The motivation to find the key to such a tragic and pervasive disorder as schizophrenia is high. This can lead to a dangerous experimenter-bias in situations where measurements of change in mental state are highly subjective and where extreme care must be taken to establish optimal experimental control. There is the further subconscious tendency to rationalize away good data that weaken a hypothesis or to accept, uncritically, data that support it.

A salient conclusion deriving from this brief survey of biochemical studies of schizophrenia is that, however logical it may be that this extreme behavior disorder is related to biochemical anomaly, such a relationship has yet to be demonstrated. The failure of many studies to use adequate controls may, in part, account for the sharp disparities in reported results. Accordingly, until research methodology in this area is improved it will be difficult to know how useful this approach is in advancing our understanding of schizophrenia.

STUDIES OF THE FAMILIES OF SCHIZOPHRENICS

In recent years a number of studies have been done of the families of schizophrenics. These have been based on the assumption that the disorder can, at least in part, be understood on the basis of the characteristic interaction patterns among members of the patient's family. The frequent observation that severe psychopathology arises in disturbed family settings has prompted this approach.

The Communication Approach

One group of investigators (Bateson et al., 1956) has focused on communicative patterns within the family of the schizophrenic. They have described a distinctive pattern known as the *"double-bind"* that takes place in two-person interactions (especially between mother and child) and has the following characteristics: (1) the listener feels it is essential to understand a message so that he can make an appropriate response; (2) the communicator delivers a message with contradictory meanings (affective vs. verbal); (3) the listener is unable to discriminate a single, distinctive message to which to respond, nor can he do anything to express his confusion.

The double-bind is possible because people are capable of communicating at many different levels simultaneously. Thus, words are used to convey one meaning while the tone of one's voice, the gestures used, the context, and so on, convey another, sometimes very different, meaning. When meanings are incongruent or contradictory, and one must respond to the message without an opportunity to clarify it by talking about sources of confusion in it, a double-bind

exists. The mother who says to her child, "Come here, dear, and sit on my lap" in a tone of voice that implies "Go away, I am not really interested in you," is making a double-bind communication.

This form of communication is seen when the mother has simultaneous needs to love and to reject the child, perhaps because she is anxious about her role as a mother and hostile at the same time. When no one else in the family recognizes the mother's contradictory feelings and incongruous messages, the child is confronted with them directly. He will thus be led into situations in which he is "damned if he does and damned if he doesn't." If the child responds to the love and not to the rejection, he must distort what he is hearing. If he does this he may find that his mother becomes anxious because her hostility is aroused. Conversely, if the child responds to the negative aspect of his mother's message, she may become anxious because this implies that she is not a good, loving mother. In either case the child is likely to be punished and this, in effect, is the double-bind in which he finds himself.

Haley (1959) has pointed out that in all interactions efforts are made to define relationships through the communication of messages. It is difficult to avoid such definition of relationships since messages often have the dual function of reporting something and of asking that certain responses be made. For example, the message "I feel bad today" both reports something about an internal state and requests that the listener "Do something for me" or, at least, "Think of me as a person who feels bad." Even a failure to communicate verbally defines a relationship. Silence may be a request to another person that he take the lead in defining what is to take place. For Haley, the only way to avoid defining a situation altogether is to communicate so that the specific words used are negated by qualifications attached to them. This mode of communication is used by a person who wishes to avoid defining a situation because of his mixed feelings about it. For example, on being asked to help with the dishes, the reluctant husband who does not wish to anger his wife responds by saying, "I would like to do the dishes, but I can't. I have a headache!" This phrasing allows him to deny that he is defining the situation, despite his refusal.

Avoidance of defining one's relationship to others takes place in a number of ways. Since there are four formal characteristics of interpersonal messages—(1) I (the speaker) (2) am saying something (the content) (3) to you (the object) (4) in this situation (the situation)—the message can be negated through denial of any one of these elements. A person can deny that he is communicating by presumably speaking for an authority, or for someone else, or under the influence of alcohol or a drug. One can deny the content by claiming amnesia, or by qualifying his message so as to negate it. One can deny that he is speaking *to* the other person (the object) by saying he is thinking out loud, that he is addressing the status position of the other, or by speaking of people in general. Finally, one can deny that he is speaking of a current situation by referring to situations involving other times or places. Where one's touch with reality is tenuous, more literal denials of each of these elements are possible.

In a broadened view of the double-bind hypothesis, Haley suggests that the schizophrenic has learned to avoid defining relationships because he was reared in a family in which such avoidance is common. Constantly confronted with incongruent messages at home, the child learns that his safest course is to be equally incongruent. In fact, parents of schizophrenics may actu-

ally reinforce incongruence because they are threatened by congruent messages. When the child has little opportunity to interact with clear communicators he is led to deal with all relationships in a distorted fashion.

Weakland (1960) further expands the double-bind situation by discussing the "three-party interaction" involving both parents and the child. He suggests that all key elements of the two-party situation also exist where three parties are involved. Contradictory messages (because they cannot readily be separated) are sufficiently difficult to confront when they come from a single sender, but the problem is equally difficult when there are two senders and the messages are widely separated by person, time, and phraseology. One parent may negate the message of the other by communicating at a different level of abstraction, or the two parents may communicate as one and present double-bind messages as though they came from a single unit ("We want you to . . . ," or "Your father and I agree . . ."). Thus the significance of the double-bind remains even in complex familial interactions.

Family Conflict and Schizophrenia

Lidz and his coworkers (Lidz et al., 1957; Lidz & Fleck, 1965; Lidz & Lidz, 1949) have also studied the families of schizophrenic patients and have reported a high degree of instability within such families. Large percentages of schizophrenic patients came from homes in which a parent had been lost early in life through death or divorce. In cases when both parents had been in the home the marriage was often marked by serious discord and many of the parents themselves were either psychotic, seriously neurotic, or psychopathic.

Thus in a high percentage of schizophrenic cases the familial history of child-rearing practices was judged to be faulty or frankly bizarre.

The same investigators have more recently reported studies of 17 families of schizophrenics and have described typical interaction patterns within such units. Two notable patterns that they have observed are those of *marital schism* and *marital skew*. The former describes the situation in which each parent is immersed in his own problems and neither is able to create a set of roles for himself that is reciprocal to the roles of the other. Each attempts to induce the other to live up to *his* or *her* expectations and they fail utterly to offer support to each other. Threats of separation and divorce are common and these crises, rather than bringing the spouses closer together in a more harmonious relationship, lead to further emotional separation and postpone solution of common, basic problems.

In marriages characterized by such schism children were subjected to competition in which parents "undercut" each other's worth and appeals were made by each for the child's loyalty. Typically it was the father who lost out in this familial power struggle and became an outsider who occasionally tried to assert dominance through a tyranny that was circumvented by newly formed family alliances. In many marital schism families both parents remained more involved in their parental homes than they were in their own.

Cases of marital skew were characterized by an alliance between one dependent—perhaps even masochistic—partner and the other who was strong and dominant. In such marriages few emotional ties to the parental families were found. The psychopathology of the dominant partner pervaded the home and created an abnormal environment. However, acceptance of this environment by the submissive parent implied to the children that it was not really abnormal.

Experience with disordered family patterns prompted Lidz and Fleck (1965) to conceptualize schizophrenia as a "deficiency disease." They believed that three groups of developmental needs of the child remained essentially unmet in such families and that these deficiencies were predisposing to schizophrenia. First, as a result of unmet nurturance needs, the child fails to grow up to be independent or to feel secure about his personal boundaries. Second, the families fail to help the child direct his drives into conflict-free areas so that he can acquire age- and sex-appropriate social roles needed to facilitate interaction with people outside the family. Finally, these families are deficient in transmitting communicative and other fundamental techniques of the culture to the child. For Lidz and his coworkers, the orthodox psychoanalytic view that oral frustration is the primary cause of schizophrenia is too narrow. That formulation includes only one element in a complex picture and ignores two other deficiencies that Lidz et al. find highly significant.

On the matter of nurturance deficiencies, these investigators point out that the hypothesis that the schizophrenic's mother is basically rejecting of her child is an oversimplification. It is not simply a lack of interest in the child that produces deficiencies in nurturance. Indeed, the mothers they studied were usually quite involved with their children. The more fundamental difficulties were typically those of the mother's own developmental deficiencies leading to profound insecurity in rearing her own child. This problem was exacerbated as the child grew older and became more capable of doing things for himself. The mother's personal sense of inadequacy was then projected onto the child and limitations and controls were applied to alleviate her own considerable anxiety. This resulted in disturbances at all developmental levels, not only the very early oral stage. The net effect of such experiences rendered the child totally incapable either of directing his life or of feeling personally capable in any sphere.

The second major nurturance deficiency stems from the fact that the family, as a social institution, does a poor job. Ideally the family functions to produce members of society capable of assuming certain social roles. In the successful family the child experiences not only the changing age-appropriate roles of a growing child but is also exposed to models of adequate husband and father, wife and mother, man and woman, and boy and girl. The adequate family has two leaders, each primarily responsible for certain essential functions: a mother who provides affection and security, transmits child-rearing traditions, and fosters healthy socialization; a father who, while contributing to the gratification of the emotional and security needs of the child, also provides for the family's material needs and is its leader as far as outsiders are concerned. Under ideal circumstances these roles are reciprocal and mutually supporting. The marital schism and skew characterizing the schizophrenic family cause it to fall far short of ideal fulfillment of essential parental roles. There may be antagonism rather than a coalition between the parents. Instead of respect for each other's roles there is often competition and undercutting, or an abdication of one parent in favor of the other. The parents' eccentricities, in themselves, may foster a distorted view of life in the child. Often in such a setting, the child tries to bring the parents together or failing that, to become a scapegoat who draws the parents' fire in

a manner that hides their differences. He may attempt to meet the needs of both parents or of the one whose support he needs most. Whatever his task, he subordinates his autonomy to the distorted objectives and interactions of the family.

Finally, the schizophrenic family fails to provide the child with adequate tools for communicating meaning. Most of our actions are based on the assumption that words have a predictive and reliable quality. We assume, for example, that we can sit on a "chair." The accuracy of our predictions deriving from the words we use depends upon how specifically words are defined for us by our "teachers"—primarily the members of one's family. In the schizophrenic family word meanings are often vague and idiosyncratic. These disturbances of communicative style in the parents of the schizophrenic result in deficiencies in the child's thinking.

Schizophrenia as a Family Process

Bowen (1960) reported a series of studies of families in which a schizophrenic child was living with his parents. A salient conclusion was that the patient's psychosis is a "symptom of the total family problem." Bowen, however, hypothesized that a process spanning three or more generations was necessary for the schizophrenia to become manifest. The following case history illustrates the three-generation hypothesis.

The father of one schizophrenic patient had mature and respected parents and siblings who were much more mature than he was. The patient's father had been the most dependent child in his own family situation. He reacted against his strong dependency needs when he reached adolescence, and strove for independence and a genuine sense of adequacy. Although these qualities led to a very successful business career, they also resulted in his becoming aloof and distant from his family. Perhaps he was more successful in business than his siblings and colleagues because he needed such success more.

The childhood of the patient's mother was in some respects similar to the father's. She was more attached to her mother than to her siblings. However, when she reached adolescence, unlike her husband she did not detach herself from the home to seek success outside. Rather she became poised and resourceful in the home and increasingly managed affairs there. In both cases a basic dependency and immaturity was sealed over by denial and overcompensation. Neither parent could relate warmly to others and both were lonely. Hence at one level they seemed well suited to each other. They married after a year's acquaintance. Conflict arose almost immediately.

In keeping with the three-generation hypothesis, Bowen reasons that these parents were especially vulnerable to having at least one very immature child who would become schizophrenic in the course of trying to adapt to the demands of growing up. This is offered not as a specific proposition about the etiology of schizophrenia but as a reflection of what has been actually observed in schizophrenic families. Essentially, one child from among several siblings is more immature than the others, and this defect exists in that child who has the most intense early attachment to the mother. Furthermore, the immaturity in the child is roughly equivalent to the combined levels of immaturity in the parents. Incidentally, Bowen offers no clue as to how one might quantify these variables.

Many other features typify the family of the schizophrenic. First, there is considerable emotional distance (in Bowen's terms, "emotional divorce") between parents,

which may be manifested by formality and controlled by maintaining physical distance from each other. Second, the parents have trouble making decisions and whichever takes the lead in so doing becomes the overadequate one who regards the other as a shirker. Third, the parents seem to have been attracted to each other by their facades of overadequacy, in the very process of mate selection, rather than by more basic subsurface characteristics. Finally, conflict between the parents arose shortly after the marriage, and it concerned decisions about routine problems of living together.

The decision to have a child was usually the most difficult of all for these parents to make. The crucial conflict for the mother was that between seeing the child as a source of "womanly fulfillment" and her doubt about being able to have a normal baby. Husbands tended to resist passively the idea of having a child on the grounds that they could not afford it. Typically, when the wife became pregnant, her relationship with her husband suffered and her emotional investment was centered on the unborn child. This intensified after the baby was born as the mother became engrossed in protecting and caring for it.

In one family that followed this pattern, shortly after the baby's arrival the mother felt very adequate with the infant because he was, realistically, helpless. Feeling more secure because of this, the mother was also more stable, and this increased the father's stability as well. A consequence of this change in feeling was that he became more aloof and related to his wife much as he had toward his mother during adolescence.

The child's problem developed out of the ambivalence of a mother who was intensely involved with him. She made overt demands that he grow up to be mature and capable. At the same time, however, she made more forceful, emotional demands that he remain helpless. This was done subtly and in ways not easily dealt with on a conscious level. The driving force in the mother's reaction was her long-standing concern over the child's capacity to be adequate in a variety of ways. Bowen speaks of this as the mother's "projection" of her own inadequacies, much as Lidz and his coworkers do. Thus, if the mother felt helpless and was compelled to deny this feeling, she attributed it to her child and babied him. This made her feel better, particularly so if the family agreed with her perception. What began as the mother's distorted feelings became a reality for the child.

Bowen also points out that this process produces a child who is more concerned about meeting the mother's demands than initiating his own. Thus he tries simultaneously to meet the conflicting demands of remaining his mother's child and maturing and becoming an adult. The weaker the child, the more readily does he comply with the mother's emotional demand that he remain helpless while ignoring her opposite verbal statements. The healthier child resists the mother's emotional demands, in a token way, but is vigorous in disagreeing with her verbal ones. In the latter case the mother becomes anxious herself. In relating to the very sick child she grows less anxious as the child complies and manifests more regression and psychosis. Thus the mother's anxiety is "sensed" by the sick child as a sign that she needs him to help her by becoming infantile. So active is the child's participation in this that he did not seem, according to Bowen, to be a victim of this process. Indeed Bowen considered that many schizophrenics saw the job of helping the mother as their prime mission in life.

In subtle ways the patient uses his helplessness to make demands on the family.

Thus the schizophrenic family is organized around the patient's needs. Both parents and child are victims of a pathological process in which all are equally ensnared.

Fathers in this type of schizophrenic family have only a peripheral relationship to the child. They may be viewed as being in a psychological position comparable to the divorced father who has lost custody of the child to the mother. The mother may choose to relinquish the child periodically to the father but takes him back when she wants him. Basically the father does not have a primary relationship with the child, unless his relationship with the mother, which is in effect an "emotional divorce," is altered.

Normal siblings in such families are involved in the family conflicts from time to time but they are generally able to withdraw and lead lives of their own. The core conflict involving the father-mother-child triad fortunately excludes the normal sibling, thereby providing him an opportunity for less disrupted development. The father and mother achieve some semblance of emotional equilibrium only through the sick child; hence, despite a conscious wish to have the child grow up to be adequate, they share a need to keep him helpless and their actions accomplish this. All the families studied by Bowen had low anxiety tolerance and functioned on the principle of "peace at any price." The child learns to "be for the mother" so as to insure that she will be less anxious and more predictable. That he is "helpless for the mother" and she "strong for the child" place them in a situation that is damaging for both. In the process of "being for the mother" the child cannot "be for himself." In "being strong for the child" the mother loses any opportunity to resolve her basic problems with her husband and her feelings toward herself.

The child's growth is the primary threat

to the symbiotic relationship that develops between mother and child, and it is during periods of rapid growth that anxiety emerges in both. From this standpoint, adolescence is the most difficult stage and it results in heightened anxiety for all members of the triad. The almost instinctive impulse of the parents is to force the adolescent back into a position of helplessness, and the youngster tries to comply with this. Outside pressures, however, heighten the conflict between having a helpless child and having an adequate one, and these pressures cause anxiety in mother, father, and child. As the adolescent begins to grow up, mother becomes acutely anxious and infantilizes him. When, as a result, he becomes helpless, another type of anxiety besets her and she demands that he grow up. Unfortunately, the child is by then poorly equipped to grow up, since after years of helplessness there is preciously little "self" of his own. The core dynamic in the psychosis that develops is the complete helplessness of the patient as a reaction to unsuccessful attempts to become a functioning adult—something he cannot do because of his faulty equipment.

Bowen observes, as does Lidz, that the rejecting mother, who does not use her child as part of her defense system, was not seen in his schizophrenic families. If the mother is regarded as rejecting by her child, it is because she has been so insensitive to the child's needs. At the same time, though, she is often attentive to and involved with the child, more so as her anxiety increases. A striking observation in therapeutic work with such families is that as the parents draw closer together emotionally the patient improves. Regressions in the patient occurred in periods when the parents drifted apart emotionally and one of them became overinvested in him.

Schizophrenia and the Social Organization of the Family

Other investigators who have considered the family of the schizophrenic offer both theoretical comments about the etiology of schizophrenia (Wynne, 1958) and empirical studies of thought-disorder in such families (Singer & Wynne, 1963, 1965a, b; Wild, 1965). This work has particular relevance to patients whose illness appears during late adolescence or early adulthood rather than to "process" schizophrenics. The theory emerging from the work of Wynne and his colleagues rests on two basic assumptions: (1) that the need for relationships with other humans is fundamental in all human existence; and (2) that each individual strives for a sense of personal identity, a means whereby the self can be perceived as distinct from objects.

These two needs—for relationships and identity—may be dealt with in three ways. The first is *mutuality*, in which people come together, each with a well-preserved sense of who he is and a respect for the individuality of the other. In such a relationship they are able to learn something about each other's identity and to appreciate each other's potentialities. A second is *nonmutuality*. This characterizes the myriad of casual contacts one has with people such as sales clerks, in which interaction is minimal and for a specific purpose. In such cases there is no investment in developing a relationship that brings the two parties closer together. The third, *pseudomutuality*, typifies interactions of members of families that produce schizophrenics.

Pseudomutuality is characterized primarily by a strong investment in maintaining

Photograph Copyright 1975 by Arthur Sirdofsky

When two people have a clear sense of each other's identity and a respect for that individuality, they are experiencing a relationship of mutuality.

the *sense* of a relationship. For whatever reason (such as failure in other relations or anxiety over separating from an established relationship) the members engaged in this form of relationship strive, above all, to maintain it. To do so family members may develop the illusion of perfect matches between their behavior and expectations and those of each other family member. There is an absorption in fitting together even at the price of destroying the individual identities of the persons involved in the relationship. Individual assertions of personal identity heighten tension because they threaten to destroy the relationship. Divergence of interest or viewpoint cannot be tolerated in pseudomutuality because the peculiar strength of the relationship lies in the illusion of unity. By contrast, in the mutuality relationship

each individual's strength enables him to tolerate, appreciate, and even learn from the other's divergence. Thus, in pseudomutuality, divergence, a process which potentially leads to growth, so threatens the overwhelming importance of the relationship that the potential for growth must be sacrificed at the altar of holding together.

While pseudomutuality was not seen by Wynne and his coworkers as the exclusive cause of schizophrenia, it was viewed as a major feature of settings in which a reactive schizophrenic develops. In families of potential schizophrenics pseudomutuality had existed for so long and had been so intense that shared family mechanisms had developed to prevent recognition of deviation from prescribed roles within the family. Such mechanisms also prevented individual family members from develop-

© J. Brian King 1975

Political demonstrators often have little in common beyond the specific cause of their gathering. Their relationship is one of non-mutuality.

ing personal identities, either within or outside the family. These mechanisms diffuse, distort, or blur even the early perceptions that lead to an articulated communication reflecting divergence. This, in turn, produces characteristic forms of thinking and communicating, to be discussed more fully later, that support pseudomutuality.

The person who grows up in the pseudomutual setting develops only a blurred image of his identity and even this refers primarily to his place within the family. He is thus handicapped in extrafamilial functions and his family role takes on an all-encompassing significance to him. In a normal family, the person sees himself as a member both of the family group and of a larger social unit, and the parents prepare the growing child for a place in the larger society. The family of the preschizophrenic often seeks to characterize itself as a self-sufficient social unit with its own boundary. This boundary, however, has been described by Wynne et al. as a *rubber fence* because its position is never clear and because it stretches to include things that can be interpreted as complementary to its

structure and contracts to extrude things alien to that structure.

A variety of mechanisms are used to maintain pseudomutuality in the schizophrenic family. One is the myth that a catastrophe might follow open divergence from the family-role structure. Another is the bland approval of all behavior of a family member, whether or not it is compatible with the values of the family. Under such circumstances it requires a truly dramatic event, like a schizophrenic break, to promote an appreciation of differences. Secrecy is another mechanism used to support pseudomutuality. Thus, if the behavior that threatens family unity is not revealed, it cannot be threatening. Often, then, the father's personal characteristics, which are fundamental to his success as a job-holder, are entirely unknown to his family. Another mechanism is communication through an intermediary. This helps to blur direct expectations that one member might have of another. Finally, the schizophrenic illness itself may be seized upon as the reason for disrupted family relationships. Here the patient's unsettling behavior is attributed to illness rather than to an inherent flaw in the family structure.

In the type of family setting described, the reactive schizophrenic internalizes a diffuse identity, fragments his experience, and evidences disturbed ways of perceiving and communicating. The child who must learn to deny the presence of obvious contradictions inevitably comes to distrust his senses and emotions as guides to what is expected of himself and others. Instead of experiencing well-defined affective states, his feelings, ranging from mild disgust to panic, are vague. If he begins to express individuality a flood of anxiety is called forth. His ego development is therefore restricted and he must pick out of the totality that he perceives only those elements which complement pseudomutuality. Schizophrenic breakdown arises when dissociative processes no longer succeed in keeping what is noncomplementary out of awareness.

The defenses that maintain pseudomutuality undergo greatest strain as one grows, loses family figures, or is exposed to new situations outside the family. The most serious crises arise when one is forced into extrafamilial relationships where the diffuse family identity no longer serves. In this sense schizophrenia can be viewed as an identity crisis accompanied by anxiety and guilt over leaving the family structure. More chronic phases of schizophrenia involve reestablishment of pseudomutuality at some psychological distance from family members.

Aspects of this theory, having to do particularly with communication styles and the kinds of feelings that characterize members of a family producing a schizophrenic, have been formalized and applied in a series of interesting predictive studies (Singer & Wynne, 1963, 1965a, 1965b; Wild, 1965). Projective test (Rorschach and TAT) protocols as well as protocols of the reasoning used to categorize disparate objects on the Object Sorting Test were studied. These tests were given to the parents of schizophrenics and to those of other more or less seriously disturbed patients. Applying the principles derived from Wynne's theory to such protocols, Singer reports considerable success in differentiating the parents of reactive schizophrenic children from those with neurotic or autistic children. She has also successfully matched parent records with those of their schizophrenic children.

In a formal scoring manual that has emerged from this work Singer and Wynne (1966) elaborated four basic criteria used in the matching and predictive studies. These criteria are reflected in the following conclusions from Singer and Wynne's study. First, the parents of reactive schizophrenics communicate in a style that reflects disturbance of their basic attention to a stimulus. They thus respond with percepts that are amorphous, blurred, vague, and shifting. Second, they relate with inappropriate distance or closeness to others and to their schizophrenic offspring. At times during testing they are overly aloof and remote; at other times they are excessively personal, awkward, or unsophisticated about what is proper social distance. Third, they produce responses pervaded by a feeling of meaninglessness, emptiness, and lack of purpose. And, finally, responses of family members of reactive schizophrenics indicate that they are enormously threatened by the possible impact of experiences such as separation, loneliness, anger, or lust—each of which is potentially disruptive of pseudomutuality. As a result, they respond in ways that suggest a surface tranquility which forms a thin veneer over turbulent and troublesome feelings.

These predictive studies offer partial validation for the preliminary theory of Wynne et al. Hopefully, their criteria will be further elaborated and formalized. If they can be communicated to and learned by other clinicians they might form a basis for a much more valid approach to personality diagnosis in schizophrenia than has been hitherto available.

Interpersonal Interaction in Schizophrenic Families

Mishler and Waxler (1968) have done an extensive study of interaction among members of a family having a schizophrenic child. They monitored communication patterns between parents and their children as they engaged in a free discussion about a standardized topic. In their study Mishler and Waxler carefully controlled for a number of relevant factors. For example, they included the families of good premorbid schizophrenics, poor premorbid schizophrenics, and families with normal children. In addition, besides monitoring the discussion of parents with the schizophrenic child, they also monitored the discussion of the same parents with another child of theirs fairly close in age to the schizophrenic child but who had no history of serious mental disorder. Thus, they were in a position to compare differences in interaction patterns among two types of schizophrenic families and normal families as well as differences that might exist between the way parents interact with their disturbed child and their normal child. Further, the experimental design included families in which the schizophrenic was a male and in which the schizophrenic was a female. This made it possible to check on whether differences occurred as a function of the child's sex.

Mishler and Waxler were interested in five interaction areas: expressiveness, attention strategies, personal control, speech disruption, and responsiveness. On the expressiveness measure it was found that normal families were more expressive and more positive in the kind of emotion they expressed than were the schizophrenic families. Major differences on this variable were attributable to the pattern found in normal male families and the families of good premorbid males. The good premorbid family tended to express very negative feelings toward the disturbed member.

With respect to differences in attention patterns, it was found that normal families direct their feelings toward many targets other than those immediately present. By contrast, the families of poor premorbids tended to focus closely on the people they were with. Families of good premorbid sons seemed unwilling to risk direct confrontation with the people present. However, this was not the case in the families of good premorbid daughters. Other family studies have noted similarly that families of male schizophrenics showed less manifest conflict than those of female schizophrenics.

On the measure of control strategies, the major differences were found btween the normal and good premorbid families. Parents, and particularly the father in the families of male schizophrenics, have the highest status and are respected by the son who clearly has the lowest family status. There is also a status hierarchy in normal families, but it does not carry with it the authoritarian or coercively controlling quality that is seen in the schizophrenic family. Attempts at influencing other people are more clear in the normal family where even low status children are likely to use control strategies such as interrupting the parents. This occurs far less often among members of a schizophrenic family. Some interesting differences are found between male and female patient families. Schizophrenic sons assume the controlling or high status position in the family along with the mother, and the father tends to have little influence. Schizophrenic daughters, on the other hand, hold very low status positions and are generally ignored in discussions. Neither pattern provides an appropriate identification model for sons or daughters.

Speech disruptions and speech pattern variability were expected to occur most commonly in patient families and to be infrequent in normal families. The reverse was found. Normal families showed the greatest amount of speech disruption and good premorbid families showed the least. Mishler and Waxler feel that this indicates that a certain degree of variability in speech patterns is probably adaptive. Speech variability provides an opportunity to introduce new information, to change the direction of thought, and to allow for the development of ideas. The opposite, nondisruptive speech, has a rigid, ritualistic quality that is not adaptable.

The responsiveness measure is concerned with whether acknowledgment is made of another person's response. This produced sharp and consistent findings. Normals were found to be the most responsive and poor premorbids the least. The families of male normals show the highest degree of speech fragmentation. There is much disruption and interactions that are essentially "noisy." Still, speech is highly responsive to what's happening. Other people's opinions are recognized and respected. By contrast, poor premorbid families tend to focus on the rules of the experimental situation without responding to each other's behavior. Good premorbids fall between these two groups. They are moderately responsive to the behavior of others.

Overall, Mishler and Waxler find that the sharpest differences in parent-child interactions occur because of differences in parents' behavior toward their schizophrenic child and their normal child. The differences do not occur because of the schizophrenic child's behavior. The schizophrenic seems to behave with his parents in ways that are quite similar to the behavior of normal children with their parents. Mishler and Waxler suggest that this indicates that cultural norms regulating the behavior of children with their parents are so strong that they override the effects of pathology. On the other hand, there are differences between the mothers and fathers of schizophrenic children and each differs markedly from the behavior of parents of normal children in many respects. What seems to happen is that some general behavior style is exaggerated, or the variability of behavior is reduced when in the presence of the schizophrenic child. Thus,

many tendencies that are present in the parents of a schizophrenic child when they interact with their own normal child simply become exaggerated and more obvious when they interact with their disturbed child. This finding suggests either that the parent of the schizophrenic expects some kind of strange behavior from the child and is acting in some way that will keep him from displaying it, or it indicates that the disturbed child can behave adequately with his parents but must do so in the face of the added stress of having to deal with parents whose behavior is deviant.

Comments on the Family Studies of Schizophrenics

Studies of the families of schizophrenics have produced interesting descriptions of basic intrafamilial processes and have led to the formulation of potentially worthwhile hypotheses about environmental forces predisposing to schizophrenia. Unfortunately, in many of these studies control groups have not been used, thus making it difficult to know whether the so-called characteristic interaction patterns of families that produce schizophrenics are also present in nonschizophrenic families. The Mishler and Waxler study is an exception and some of its most provocative findings stem from the controls that were used. The tough-minded researcher should always require a normal base against which to compare the observations of schizophrenic families.

Control groups in family studies of schizophrenia are essential on other grounds as well. Fontana (1966) has pointed out that a major assumption underlying family studies is that observed interaction patterns have caused schizophrenia. An equally plausible interpretation is that the occurrence of schizophrenia in a child has caused the particular interaction patterns that are observed. To differentiate between such possibilities schizophrenic families should be compared to families in which there is a severely ill, but not schizophrenic, child.

Another shortcoming of the familial studies with schizophrenics is that observations have not been well formalized, hence certain interaction patterns may have received inordinate attention while others were ignored. Another hazard of unsystematized observational approaches is that it is not hard, using this method, to find evidence to corroborate a theory that one held before observing the data and to ignore contradictory data. In reading the reports of research groups in this area, a similarity in the ideas of different investigators may often be noted. This can either reflect the fact that each group is observing the same phenomenon in such families or that once the phenomenon has been reported by one team, others look for it in their data and incorporate it in their theories if it is at all compatible.

The predictive and matching studies of Singer and Wynne and the interaction studies of Mishler and Waxler represent a good beginning toward formalization and systematization of observations that may lead to even sounder data on this topic. Hopefully, as family studies, which are really in their infancy, are extended greater rigor in control and more systematic, well-defined observations will be introduced.

SCHIZOPHRENIA AS A LEARNED THINKING DISORDER

Mednick (1958) has advanced a theory of schizophrenia based on clinical observation of such patients, their performance in conditioning and learning situations, and general studies of the conditioning and learning process. He believes that the potential schizophrenic has a low threshold for anxiety arousal. Since anxiety, in learning-theory terms, is considered to be a drive state, the schizophrenic may be characterized as a high-drive individual. Starting with this assumption, Mednick cites a series of relevant learning principles from the research literature. Organisms in high drive states condition more readily and their responses are both faster and of higher amplitude than those of individuals in a low drive state. When an individual learns to respond to a given stimulus, he will also respond more readily to similar stimuli—a process known as *generalization*. Since drive intensity relates to response strength, organisms high in drive generalize responses more readily.

The tendency toward greater generalization in the high-drive subject is a handicap to learning in complex situations since responses are made to inappropriate as well as to appropriate stimuli. Mednick cites

Sarnoff Mednick has hypothesized that schizophrenia is a learned thinking disorder.

data showing that high-anxiety subjects have greater difficulty than low-anxiety subjects on complex serial learning tasks, because high drive causes them to learn incorrect as well as correct responses.

With these assumptions, Mednick reasons that the preschizophrenic is, for whatever reason, extremely anxious—high in anxiety drive. Thus many stimuli around him arouse an anxiety response. He also generalizes readily from specific anxiety-arousing stimuli to similar ones, leading to a cycle in which more and more things around him become noxious, and he, in turn, becomes more anxious. If, early in such a process, he is able to restrict his environmental contacts and live a tightly controlled, limited life, he may be able to avoid situations that are potentially anxiety-arousing. People who succeed in doing this are often looked upon as borderline schizophrenics or schizoid personalities. When the circumstances of life make such avoidance impossible the individual is exposed to ever-increasing anxiety.

That the organism's anxiety level does not under the continued pressure of circumstances get pushed to a physiological limit is primarily because the high-anxiety state actively stimulates the thought processes. The resultant thoughts are often "out of contact" or "silly." This further heightens anxiety about one's own "craziness." New thoughts develop, offering "rational" explanations of what is happening on a basis other than that of losing one's mind. Examples of the latter "explanations," typically bizarre to the external observer, might be about mysterious rays, radio transmitters, the FBI, and so on, depending on the individual's past experience. These bizarre explanations serve to reduce the anxiety generated by the thought that one is going crazy, and are thereby reinforced. Essentially what is being learned is a pattern of

psychological avoidance and—for Mednick —this learned avoidance (through the use of deviant rationalizations) is the essence of schizophrenia.

This general formulation can be challenged on the grounds that everyone is highly anxious at some time or other without being caught up in the deadly spiral leading to schizophrenic thinking. Mednick recognizes this problem and cites three characteristics that he believes predispose particular individuals to respond to stress in this extreme way. The first is a low threshold for anxiety. The second is slower recovery from anxiety and the consequent tendency to remain anxious to some degree, after an upset, much longer than do others. The third is the tendency to generalize over-readily. The person who becomes anxious but recovers quickly has less opportunity to generalize and thus to be exposed to still greater anxiety. Instead his anxiety remains specifically tied to the original stimulus.

Mednick considers that schizophrenia becomes chronic when the individual's anxiety-provoking thought responses lead to remote, highly generalized associations which remove the anxiety-provoking thoughts. Thus the remote associations are reinforced and are more likely to recur whenever a cue for an anxiety response is present. At first the repertoire of irrelevancies is limited (and the patient's thinking may seem stereotyped) but gradually it broadens out and provides effective protection against anxiety. This makes it difficult to bring any anxiety-provoking materials to awareness since the individual carries (within himself) the machinery for shutting out the feeling. Eventually much of his time is occupied with irrelevant thoughts and he displays little emotion—he shows, in other words, the typical "flatness" ascribed to the chronic schizophrenic. If, perhaps, certain actions or postures accompany drive-reducing situations, these too are learned and repeated to combat anxiety.

To test some of his basic formulations Mednick set up a longitudinal study of 207 adolescents who were high risks for becoming schizophrenics by virtue of having schizophrenic mothers (Mednick & Schulsinger, 1965). These subjects were carefully matched with 104 controls and all have been tested for autonomic responsiveness, conditionability, stimulus generalization, word association, and intelligence. They have also undergone psychiatric interviews. Their parents or guardians and teachers have also been interviewed regarding the subjects' behavior.

Comparison of the high-risk and normal group on initial testing confirmed certain of Mednick's assumptions. The experimental group responded to conditioning with greater response amplitude, and generalized more readily, than did the controls. However, the assumption that high-risk subjects would show slower recovery from anxiety responses was not confirmed. It should be noted that the high-risk group includes many subjects who will not become schizophrenic (only about 15 percent of such a group is expected to succumb). For this reason the critical test of Mednick's assumptions about predisposing factors in schizophrenia can only be made after he identifies the relatively small subgroup that will ultimately display the disorder.

In a preliminary report of findings Mednick and McNeil (1968) have indicated that 20 members of their high-risk group have suffered serious psychiatric breakdown (not necessarily schizophrenic). These subjects were matched with 20 other high-risk subjects whose psychological adjustment had improved and with 20 low-risk subjects. Comparison of these three groups on various measures taken when all were adolescents reveals that the group that suffered breakdown had more serious birth complications, suffered the loss of their mother from the home at an earlier age, demonstrated more autonomic lability, and showed greater tendency to "drift" away from a stimulus word on a word-association task than the other two groups.

Both Mednick's theory and the longitudinal study devised to test it are most interesting. Although it is one of the few well-controlled studies in this area, time and specific empirical data will be needed for its ultimate evaluation. In the meantime, several criticisms have already been leveled at it (Lang & Buss, 1965) and questions have been raised about the firmness of the base for each of Mednick's assumptions. For example, there is some dispute as to whether schizophrenics do, in fact, condition faster than others, do more poorly in complex learning situations, and overgeneralize; and whether high anxiety leads to overgeneralization. Lang and Buss (1965) have taken Mednick to task for allegedly attempting to account for schizophrenia entirely in terms of anxiety; they cite Mednick's statement that "high drive, slow recovery rate, and the number of fear arousing stimuli are highly correlated factors" as exemplifying such a view.

Objections to Mednick's assumptions rest for the most part on interpretations of a number of studies with schizophrenics in which findings have not been consistent. This is not surprising, since the term "schizophrenia" represents an umbrella under which diverse subject groups may be found (process-reactives, acute-chronics, and so on). Moreover, the affective disorganization of schizophrenic patients is such that test results with them are often unreliable. Hence, the weight of existing research data neither overwhelmingly supports nor contradicts Mednick's assumptions. The charge that anxiety is the sole causative factor in Mednick's formulation seems overstated. Even if Mednick's assertion—that high anxiety, slow recovery rate, and the large number of stimuli which arouse anxiety are correlated—were accurate, unless these correlations approached unity, as they almost certainly do not, there would be room to explain the development of schizophrenia on some basis other than just anxiety. Indeed, Mednick's theory need not depend exclusively on the potential schizophrenic's being highly anxious. What does seem crucial is that he have a nervous system which does not handle anxiety effectively.

Another criticism of Mednick's theory has been advanced by DeMille (1959). He pointed out that if stimulus generalization heightened anxiety by rendering formerly neutral stimuli anxiety-provoking, it is difficult to see how remote associations ever became anxiety-reducing. If they were associated to anxiety because of the spread of generalization, they would be anxiety-provoking rather than anxiety-reducing. In Mednick's (1959) response to this point

he indicated that remote associations were made only when anxiety was high and generalization quite broad, and that the generalization gradient in such instances was not characterized by zero slope. Thus, although remote thoughts are associated with anxiety, far less is involved than is true for more relevant thoughts; hence the overall effect of irrelevancies is reinforcing.

CONCLUSION

This survey of research on schizophrenia touches on only some high points of the monumental volume of work done on this topic. It does, however, provide a hint of the massive effort devoted to understanding and treating this disorder. In spite of the attention schizophrenia has received, one cannot yet be optimistic about our prospects for solving the riddle. Promising beginnings have appeared with respect to a few facets of the problem, but these are only beginnings and it is difficult to say how much time and refinement of research technique will be necessary before major breakthroughs are achieved.

SUMMARY

1. One of the earliest distinctions, based on prognosis, to be made among schizophrenics involved the concepts of *process* and *reactive* schizophrenia. The process type was seen to suffer lifelong adaptation problems and to deteriorate progressively. The reactive type was seen to break down only in the face of severe stress and to have a good prognosis for recovery. Studies have failed to isolate two "pure" types on this dimension.
2. Genetic factors have been studied extensively as possible causes of schizophrenia. Studies in this area indicate that heredity alone cannot account for the disorder, although an inherited constitutional vulnerability may be an important factor.
3. Studies have been done to assess the adequacy of the diathesis-stress hypothesis. These substantiate the role of an inherited vulnerability in

schizophrenia and suggest that subtle nervous damage associated with birth complications may be implicated.

4. Biochemical studies of schizophrenia have been poorly controlled. Therefore, it is difficult to determine whether biochemical differences occasionally found between schizophrenics and nonschizophrenics are caused by the disorder or by its concommitants.

5. Family dynamics which may account for schizophrenia have been studied extensively. Many interactional factors have been suggested as significant, but these studies have not been well controlled so that their results have not contributed greatly to an understanding of schizophrenia.

6. Mednick has hypothesized that schizophrenia is a learned thinking disorder occurring in people who cannot control anxiety efficiently. This hypothesis has been criticized on a number of counts and is undergoing test in a longitudinal study being carried out by Mednick and his colleagues.

CHAPTER 8

Other Psychoses

In Rome around the end of the first century A.D. Arataeus sensed a relationship between mania and melancholia and he considered that both states were manifestations of a single illness. He believed that younger people were more likely to be manic and older ones to suffer melancholia. He speculated that those who were ordinarily "irritable, violent, easily given to joy" (Zilboorg & Henry, 1941, p. 74) tended toward manic attacks, while people who readily became depressed tended to suffer melancholia. Such manifestations were described even earlier in the epics of Homer and in the medical writings of Hippocrates.

For many centuries these ideas were forgotten. In fact, such disorders attracted little attention from theorists and researchers, who were more concerned with schizophrenia and the psychoneuroses. Yet affective, involutional, and paranoid psychoses represent a significant percentage of the patient population.

THE AFFECTIVE PSYCHOSES

The *manic-depressive reactions* described in ancient times are chief among the serious affective disorders (disorders involving mood and emotional control). It was not until the nineteenth century that other observers arrived at conclusions similar to those of Arataeus. In 1851 Falret, a French psychiatrist, described the disorder, stressing its intermittent nature and, somewhat later, Kraepelin included it with dementia praecox as one of the major divisions of the psychoses. He conceived of severe mania and depression as a single syndrome for three reasons: (1) they shared many similar features; (2) they commonly replaced each other in the same patient: and (3) the prognosis for both was similar. Since Kraepelin regarded prognosis as the basis for distinguishing among psychiatric disorders, the last factor was decisive for him. He noted that the manic-depressive patient usually recovered from a psychotic episode despite the fact that other attacks were to be expected, while the dementia praecox patient typically got worse. Having formulated this distinction, Kraepelin had no more to say about the etiology of manic-depressive psychosis than he did about dementia praecox: he spoke vaguely of "defective heredity" as being important in a very high percentage of cases. Nor did his approach provide leads about therapy. His recommendations emphasized alleviation of specific symptoms, once they had arisen, and simple preventive measures such as avoiding excitement by those susceptible to suffering this disorder (Kraepelin, 1923).

Classification of the Major Affective Disorders

DSM-II (1968) specifies that disorders in this category are "characterized by a single disorder of mood, either extreme depression or elation." Thinking is dominated by this mood state and any loss of contact with reality is caused by it. Further, the onset of the abnormal mood seems *unrelated* to external events. In this respect the major affective disorders are distinguishable from *psychotic depressive reaction* and *depressive neurosis* (both of which will be described later). Included among the major affective disorders are *involutional melancholia* and the various types of *manic-depressive illness*. Involutional melancholia will be described in a later section of this chapter along with the *involutional paranoid state*. The subtypes of manic-depressive illness are described in DSM-II (1968, pp. 36–37) thus:

Manic-Depressive Illness, Manic Type

This disorder consists exclusively of manic episodes. The episodes are characterized by excessive elation, irritability,

---

CASE 8–1: A CASE OF MANIC-DEPRESSIVE ILLNESS, MANIC TYPE

Helga D., a forty-two-year-old mother of two sons, was committed for the first time by her family to a state institution near a large city on the eastern seaboard. She had only a grade-school education and at twenty-one, after working for four years at a semi-skilled factory job, married her present husband and kept house. Her husband, who was three years older than she, was a tool and die maker in a large industrial concern. He was a steady worker and the family was of middle-class circumstances.

* * *

The onset of the most recent disorder was precipitated by Helga's concern over the disposition of a piece of property owned jointly by her husband and his brother. She feared that she and her husband were to be cheated in the transaction. About a week before her hospitalization she became so preoccupied with this matter that she could not keep up with her household chores, lost her appetite, and began to have difficulty sleeping. When her husband tried to dispute what he felt were unreasonable fears, she became very disturbed. Though she had previously abstained from alcoholic beverages, she began to drink wine. Her heightened concern over the matter of the property prompted her husband to take her to seek the advice of an attorney. When the man they went to see failed to keep his appointment, Helga became very excited and had to be taken home. That night she awakened at 3:30 A.M. and began shouting that she was about to die. She quieted down after some assurance but remained irrational. Most of the next day she spent praying while completely undressed and insisting that she was to die imminently. She also recalled that a clerk in a store had recently stared at her as if she were God. The family physician was called and a nurse secured to care for her. When she became abusive toward the nurse and began to curse and use vile language, she was placed under sedation and taken to the hospital.

At the mental hospital, Helga was completely out of contact, agitatedly keeping up a stream of associations. Noisy and resistive, she threatened personnel and only occasionally could maintain her attention long enough to offer a relevant response to a question. Her speech was so rapid and under such pressure that she was rarely coherent. Her mental processes seemed to operate more rapidly than her ability to speak. She manifested ideas of persecution and grandiosity with much religious content, and she experienced both auditory and visual hallucinations. In typical fashion, when she was asked what her trouble was, Helga replied, "Would you like to be tied up and lay here? I had an Easter suit to wear. I would like to have a higher priced one. Will you please leave my husband in here and get me out of here—please, deliver me anywhere—I won't give you another word because I want to get out of here. Before twelve o'clock we will be millionaires. You are trying to get my confession and put me in the garbage can and put the cover on—go to hell and stay there. I will cut you all to pieces. I will put a bullet right in you. I won't listen to you because you know more than I do—get out of here, go to hell. I'd rather die than be the way I am."

On the ward she was hyperactive and restless, and interfered with other patients. Unless restrained, she tore her clothes, screamed obscenities, and talked at the top of her voice. She was given frequent sedatives and was often kept in a camisole. After a period of five months she began to show a gradual improvement, so that after fourteen months of hospitalization she was discharged. In about seven months she suffered another attack and was returned screaming, ". . . I feel good, how do you feel? I said when I solved the crime I'd come back and see you, didn't you, it's God's will. I don't know what it is but I can tell why you are writing. I still have blood and new—true, true—who—who." During the next twenty years this symptom pattern continually recurred and Helga was in and out of the hospital on innumerable occasions, never to stay out more than a few months at a time.

From Zax & Stricker, 1963, pp. 33–36.

talkativeness, flight of ideas, and accelerated speech and motor activity. Brief periods of depression sometimes occur, but they are never true depressive episodes.

Manic-Depressive Illness, Depressed Type

This disorder consists exclusively of depressive episodes. These episodes are characterized by severely depressed mood and by mental and motor retardation progressing occasionally to stupor. Uneasiness, apprehension, perplexity, and agitation may also be present. When illusions, hallucinations, and delusions (usually of guilt or of hypochondriacal or paranoid ideas) occur, they are attributable to the dominant mood disorder.

Manic-Depressive Illness, Circular Type

This disorder is distinguished by at least one attack of both a depressive episode and a manic episode. This phenomenon makes clear why manic and depressed types are combined into a single category.

Both mania and depression are often graded in terms of their severity. The mildest form of mania, called *hypomania*, is characterized by boundless energy and a very good mood. Such patients seem clever, witty, confident, and quick. They sometimes appear domineering, aggressive, incapable of following through on a plan, and extravagant. At a more severe level, *acute mania*, the patient is euphoric rather than pleasant

---

CASE 8–2: A CASE OF MANIC-DEPRESSIVE ILLNESS, DEPRESSED TYPE

Lillian H., a sixty-two-year-old spinster, was admitted voluntarily for the third time to a small midwestern private mental institution. Although her formal education had ended at the conclusion of grade school, she had, over the years, held a responsible position as an office manager with a large industrial concern. She had lived alone for several years in a large midwestern city at some distance from the small town in which she had been born and reared.

Lillian was second in a family of four girls and one boy (the youngest) born to Russian immigrant parents who were devoutly religious, orthodox Jews. These parents were described as people who lived by a strict religious code which severely limited the activities of their children. The father, who owned a small grocery, was a very stoical man whose life centered about his religion and who absorbed many slights and indignities without retaliating. The mother instilled in her children a high sense of moral purpose, particularly with respect to anything even remotely resembling sexual contact. In the family setting emphasis was placed on the finer intellectual things of life—good literature, music, and stimulating conversation. When Lillian's mother was forty-seven she suffered a "nervous breakdown," and Lillian had to leave school to care for her. For the remaining twenty-five years of her life the mother was ailing and the primary responsibility for her care fell to Lillian, who was herself described as having always been "a nervous person." In her early twenties she took a stenographic position in her home town and worked steadily at this until her mother died, when Lillian was thirty-one. Shortly after this she experienced intermittent periods of depression and hyperactivity punctuated by impractical schemes which resulted in great expenditures of money for little profit of any sort. After one such disastrous episode involving the remodeling of the family home in order to make apartments which might be rented, her agitation mounted and she was hospitalized for six months. When she was discharged she moved from her home town to the city where she was living at the time of her most recent hospitalization. There she again took up office work and rose to a responsible position before succumbing to a depressive episode, at age forty-eight, which required another brief period in the hospital. Lillian's sisters also suffered depressive disorders which required hospital treatment. Her oldest sister spent several years in an institution after the death of her husband. Only her brother, who rejected the family's strict heritage and was considered a "black sheep," never suffered a serious emotional disorder.

The episode which led to hospitalization began seven months prior to admission when Lillian began to feel that she was not able to work as efficiently as she wanted. It was also suspected that she resented the fact that younger people were advancing at a faster rate than she. As a result she retired and remained alone, living in a single room, having few friends and only her solitary interests in reading and music. After a few months she attempted to go back to work, taking several jobs which she held for only short periods of time. Finally, about one month prior to admission she returned to her home town for a vacation with her younger sister, who, on a visit to her, found her depressed and mildly agitated. Lillian gradually became more and more depressed, eating sparsely, sleeping little, and roaming aimlessly about the house saying "what shall I do—it's too involved." She suffered crying spells, a loss of weight, constipation, and gradually began to feel dejected throughout the day.

When these symptoms became extreme Lillian was admitted to the hospital, where she presented a neat appearance, spoke logically and coherently and displayed a good memory for both recent and remote events. She was also able to calculate well and manifested a good grasp of general information. She sat rigidly in her chair, wringing her hands and continually saying, "It's too involved, too complicated, you can't help me. I don't know what to do." The interview was frequently interrupted by her pacing back and forth, only to sit down again and begin to moan. Although she seemed alert, she responded to questions only after long pauses, if at all, and often said simply, "It's too involved," or "Don't ask me any more questions, I don't talk about that."

During her two-month stay in the hospital she was treated with eight electric shocks. After four of these her behavior improved, her sleep pattern became more regular, and she required less sedation. After eight shocks she slept well, but manifested some confusion, which lifted after one week. Since her depression had by then disappeared and she was sleeping well, she was discharged, and during the next five years she experienced no recurrence of the disorder.

From Zax & Stricker, 1963, pp. 27–29.

CASE 8–3: A CASE OF MANIC DEPRESSIVE ILLNESS, CIRCULAR TYPE

Ellis K., a forty-year-old married man, was voluntarily admitted to a small private mental hospital in New England. He was the only son of a prominent businessman who owned a very large textile mill in the central New England area. A high-school graduate, he had been unsuccessful in his efforts to win a degree from an exclusive midwestern men's school and had taken an accounting course in a business school in his home town. His main employment for several years prior to admission was the management of his mother's estate after the death of his father. Childless, he and his wife lived in his mother's home and were supported by her. His only independent activity involved his employment with an accounting firm for a few years after completing business school. The most recent hospital admission was his third.

Ellis' father was an extremely energetic, driving person who came from poor circumstances and achieved considerable success and rapid advancement in local businesses, culminating in his acquiring control over one of the major industrial concerns in the local community. As a result of his father's immersion in business affairs, Ellis could only speak of him in vague terms and could recall spending time with him only during summers when vacation trips were taken. Despite his great financial success Ellis' father was subject to periods of depression and, while in his mid-forties, during such a spell he was killed in an automobile accident. There was some speculation that this might have been a case of suicide. At that time Ellis was seven. Ellis' mother was overindulgent with him and even during his adult life stood by to get him out of trouble. After his father's death she took charge of the family business and, even though she was in her late sixties at the time of Ellis' hospitalization, still controlled the financial affairs of the family. Ellis himself was a good student until his last year in high school, at which time he failed and found it necessary to attend a prep school before entering college—where he failed in his first year. He suffered his first period of depression at that time and was hospitalized. When he recovered he attended business school. In his early twenties he impulsively married a vivacious woman who enjoyed a life full of travel and activity. They agreed to avoid having children since children would limit their enjoyment of the kind of life they preferred. Between the time of his marriage and the present hospitalization, he suffered one serious depressive episode, accompanied by hyperactivity, after suffering a minor business reversal. This occurred about three years prior to the current hospitalization and required institutional care.

About four months prior to the current hospitalization Ellis invested some money in a business venture with some acquaintances in the hope of turning a quick profit and earning enough to finance a world cruise he and his wife wanted to take. When this venture was unsuccessful and he suffered a loss, he became furious and accused the people of swindling him. When he found that he had no legal redress he became preoccupied with the incident and could talk of nothing else. He began to be overtalkative and arose very early in the day to begin work. He was quarrelsome with anyone who commented on his unusual behavior. He became progressively more restless and talkative, smoked incessantly, walked faster than usual, and his handwriting changed from small neat script to a large scrawl. He himself noted these changes, but despite some conscious effort on his part could do little to control his behavior. When his wife suggested that he return to a hospital where he had been a patient after his second depressive attack, he resisted for a time and then acquiesced.

In the hospital he presented the picture at first of a neat, well-dressed person of athletic build. He was restless and talkative and quickly displayed an amorous interest in young nurses, relating to them his sexual incompatibilities with his wife. He was easily irritated and when disturbed would become sullen and silent for a time. If his silence was met with calm he would begin to talk freely and was soon in high spirits. He would alternate between denying completely that he was ill and admitting that something was wrong but insisting that it was due to his excessive drinking. With time his activity increased so that, for example, he could bowl game after game without displaying fatigue. He began to deluge the nurses with amorous letters and notes. Because Ellis was so disruptive to ward routine he was kept away from other patients as much as possible. His sleep was sporadic and he continued to rise early. On some nights he failed to sleep at all and on such nights would create a commotion that disturbed his fellow patients. During this whole period his appetite was excellent, he was well oriented, showed no memory loss, showed a good fund of information, and calculated rapidly and accurately.

After a visit from his wife, he became depressed, especially in the morning when he was weepy and self-depreciating. This feeling gradually cleared during the day so that by evening he was once more hyperactive, irritable, and amorous. One night he moved his bed into the dining room and when he refused to move it back, he was moved to a different ward. There he became destructive, and was especially so at night. He slammed doors until the plaster would fall off the walls. He bent the legs of steel tables and on one occasion broke a wooden chair into pieces small enough to be carried out in a waste basket. Because of his impatience he began soiling himself, and he also began exposing himself. His morning depressions became more intense, and he began praying beside his bed for long periods of time. His destructiveness culminated in his lighting a fire in his room. After this incident he was given sleep treatment, in which he was kept asleep with medication for nearly two weeks. After this he was calm, quiet, and unspontaneous and, with his elation gone, it was possible to discharge him five weeks after his admission. In the next twenty years he was hospitalized on five more occasions for episodes involving either depression or hyperactivity.

From Zax & Stricker, 1963, pp. 36–38.

---

and witty, boastful and overbearing rather than confident. He is inclined to laugh boisterously, to speak loudly and raucously, and to ignore social proprieties. He passes rapidly from one idea to another ("flight of ideas") and the resultant train of thought is difficult to follow. In such a state the patient is easily provoked to anger and his eupohria can quickly change to violent destructiveness. In *delirious mania* the patient is confused, extremely excited, and frequently violent. His activity is constant and his ideation so rapid that it is impossible for him to talk with others. In delirious mania weight loss may be extreme and debilitating, and death from exhaustion is possible.

The mildest form of depression, *simple depression*, is characterized by a melancholy, discouraged feeling, with some retardation in both physical and mental activity. The person feels drained and too empty to attend to everyday affairs. There may also be feelings of personal worthlessness. In *acute depression* psychomotor retardation is intensified, the patient actively avoids others, and, rather than merely feeling unworthy, blames himself for a variety of events such as natural disasters or economic misfortunes. Suicide is often contemplated and may be attempted. In *depressive stupor*, the most extreme state of depression, the patient is entirely inactive and unresponsive. He must therefore have all of his basic needs looked after by others.

Psychotic Depressive Reaction

Another mood disorder of psychotic proportion is the *psychotic depressive reaction*. It is described in DSM-II (1968, p. 38) as follows: "This psychosis is distinguished by a depressive mood attributable to some experience. Ordinarily the individual has no history of repeated depressions or cyclothymic mood swings. The differentiation between this condition and *depressive neurosis* depends on whether the reaction impairs reality testing or functional adequacy enough to be considered a psychosis." Case 8–4 provides an example of the psychotic depressive reaction.

Theoretical and Research Approaches

Psychoanalytic Theories

The first of the psychoanalysts to have reported his experiences with manic-depressive patients was Karl Abraham. In 1911 he (Abraham, 1966a) reported his experiences with six treated patients. One of his major points is that the person subject to a manic-depressive psychosis resembles the obsessional neurotic in many ways. Like the obsessive he has great difficulty in cathecting objects because of the simultaneous love and hate he feels towards them. His hostile impulses minimize his capacity to love, and a felt need to repress the hatred robs him of energy that might allow normal libido development. This renders him uncertain of his own identity, who his sexual object-choice ought to be, and makes him feel inadequate in situations requiring that he use his judgment or take a resolute stand. As with the obsessive, the patient's illness was seen by Abraham to arise when a conclusive decision had to be made about his future relationship to the world (such as a decision to marry or to enter a particular profession). At such times an inability to feel love was experienced and depression followed.

Abraham felt, however, that there are differences between the obsessive and the depressed patient in the development of overt illness. The obsessive simply substitutes new aims, in the form of various compulsive behaviors, to replace the libidinal ones he is too conflicted to attain. The depressive, on the other hand, projects his own hostile impulses. Where his real attitude may be expressed by the statement "I cannot love people; I have to hate them," projection leads to a perception that "People do not love me," which leads to depression. Failure to repress and to project the hostility com-

CASE 8–4: A CASE OF PSYCHOTIC DEPRESSIVE REACTION

Virginia R., a sixty-one-year-old widowed mother, was placed in a private institution in a large midwestern city by her only daughter.

Virginia was the youngest child in a close-knit family of seven. Her father, who had left a civil service job to become a prosperous businessman, died when she was in her early teens; however, this did not seem to cause any untoward reaction in Virginia, since they had never been close. While her father had been a happy, outgoing man, the mother tended to be reserved and secretive, and taught her children to keep to themselves. Virginia was most sympathetic to her only sister, who was but five years older than she, and the girls remained close friends throughout life. At the age of sixteen Virginia left high school after completing three years because, although she had done well, she wanted a chance for some independence. She went to work as a bookkeeper in a large corporation, and held this job until her early thirties, when she met and married a junior executive in the company. Her only child was born when she was in her late thirties, and it proved to be a very difficult birth. Shortly afterward Virginia's mother died, but Virginia was able to bear this loss quite well.

The family was a close one, and enjoyed doing many things together. They were all devout Catholics, and regular churchgoers. Her husband and daughter enjoyed tennis and golf, and Virginia would go with them when they went to play. Basically a passive and dependent woman throughout her marriage, Virginia devoted much of her energy to her family. She entertained regularly, and she and her husband had many friends. She also derived pleasure from her collection of antiques.

About two years prior to admission, Virginia's husband died suddenly of a cerebral hemorrhage. She had a normal grief reaction, but seemed to respond gracefully to the loss. Her daughter, who had been planning to live at the dormitory on the campus of the nearby college she was attending, decided to continue with her plans, leaving her mother alone in the house. Following her graduation, Virginia's daughter decided to marry a classmate who had been her steady beau and who was about to enter the service. As soon as she could she moved to the west coast to join her husband at his post of duty. Virginia continued to live alone until about ten months prior to admission when Virginia's closest friend came to live with her following the death of her own husband. They were both very happy with the arrangement and enjoyed a warm relationship. Five months before Virginia's admission the friend became ill, necessitating a series of costly operations and close personal care for which Virginia assumed the responsibility, financially and physically. During her friend's convalescence Virginia spent a short vacation with her daughter and son-in-law and disclosed to them that she was reluctant to return home and resume responsibility for the friend's care. One month prior to admission the friend died, and, although there was no striking grief reaction, this seemed to precipitate Virginia's symptomatology.

She was again alone in the large house, and now took to sleeping downstairs on the divan, rather than in her upstairs bedroom, because she was afraid to be there alone. She became seclusive and failed to answer either the phone or doorbell, although she was certainly physically capable of doing so. She stopped writing to her daughter and calling on her friends, and also began to neglect paying her bills.

At the suggestion of concerned relatives, she agreed, five weeks before admission, to attempt to sell her house, although she was skeptical about her ability to do so since she felt nobody would want a "decaying old house." To her surprise the sale was successfully completed within a two-week period. Shortly after the sale she began to claim that the house hadn't been sold, since the real estate man was a fast talker. Because she believed that the buyers had been duped with a false deed, she was afraid to spend any of the money from the sale, and began to complain about her financial state. At this time she had close to $75,000 in the bank and in sound stocks.

With the help of a sister-in-law Virginia reluctantly found an apartment into which she could move. She was becoming more seclusive and would only speak about her imagined depleted finances. She refused to drive her car, claiming that she was a bad driver. After the sale of the house her appetite decreased sharply, she began waking early in the morning, and she became constipated. Finally her sister-in-law called Virginia's daughter, who flew back to see her mother. Virginia told her that her in-laws would break up her marriage because she, Virginia, had done everything wrong. She felt that everything was going "down, down, down" and she was going along with it. She told her daughter: "I let myself go down through carelessness." The day before Virginia was to have moved into her new apartment, her daughter entered her in the local hospital.

Upon admission Virginia appeared depressed and was uncommunicative with the hospital staff. She left sentences unfinished, and did not (or would not) recall the answers to the questions of the interviewer. She frequently would answer "I don't know," or begin sentences only to trail off, leaving them incomplete. Her answers were all retarded, incomplete and inadequate. She frequently interspersed "I've been careless" with the few responses she did make. She was able to say that she felt unreal, as though she were in a fog or in a dream.

Virginia was given a series of six electroconvulsive shock treatments, and this removed the depression, although she remained confused. After a period of two weeks the confusion lifted and she was released for outpatient psychotherapeutic treatment.

From Zax & Stricker, 1963, pp. 46–49.

---

pletely results for the depressive in dreams and behavior such as annoying others or feelings such as the desire for revenge, which reflect the presence of hostile feelings. Such feelings and behavior are related by the patient to his unhappiness about his psychic or physical defects rather than to the inadequately repressed anger at their source. Delusions of guilt frequently follow the suppression of hatred and the desire for

revenge; these may attain enormous proportions.

In his early writings Abraham viewed the manic attack as the reverse, in terms both of external appearances and of intrapsychic dynamics, of the depressed state. He believed, however, that the same conflicts were responsible for both states. The reversal involved only how the conflict was dealt with. Whereas the depressive attempts to repress the threatening impulse, the manic is indifferent to it and his impulses find overt expression. Thus the manic often feels "swept off his feet" by his impulses and both positive and negative ones are consciously expressed. This state is equated, by Abraham, to what is experienced by a young child in whom conflicts between impulses are not foreseen. Mania is thus felt by the patient as a state of being reborn, in contrast to the depressed state in which the negation of life is more like death.

Freud's attempt to explain the etiology of manic-depressive psychosis appeared in a paper published in 1917 (Freud, 1956a), in which he compared the depressive state to that of mourning after the death of a loved one. He pointed out that the distinctive features of depression, such as dejection, loss of interest in the outside world, diminishing capacity to love, inhibition of activity, and a tendency to self-reproach with a perhaps delusional expectation of punishment, are also found in one who is grieving. The sole exception is that the self-reproach is usually not present in the mourner. Thus, Freud believed that by understanding the function of normal mourning and the events that set this process in motion the development of depressive symptomatology could be understood.

Freud believed that normal mourning could be accommodated within the framework of his theory. The process begins with the loss of an object in whom a significant quantity of libido has been invested. Reality-testing indicates that this object no longer exists; hence the libido invested in it must be withdrawn and reinvested in other objects. This reinvestment is not accomplished simply, since people are reluctant to abandon earlier gratifying investments. This reluctance may be reflected in a struggle to deny the loss by hallucinatory or fantasy wish-fulfillment. Gradually, however, the demands of reality prevail and in normal mourning the libido attached to the lost object is, bit by bit reinvested. Presumably this takes place because needs must be met and clinging to memories of the lost object and to fantasies of wish-fulfillment does not accomplish this end.

Freud believed that, as in mourning, the depressed patient suffered an object loss, albeit in this case an *unconscious* loss. His further theorizing about the etiology of depression was based on the assumption that the depressive is generally full of self-reproach but the mourner is not. As Freud put it, "In grief the world becomes poor and empty; in melancholia it is the ego itself." This suggested to Freud that whereas the mourner lost an external object, the depressive or melancholiac lost an internalized object.

The process of internalization of an object thus required explanation. As Freud saw it, the process began with an object in which a person had invested much libido. Some

© J. Brian King 1975

When a person suffers an object loss, the world may seem poor and empty.

real disappointment, frustration, or loss of connection with this object should lead to withdrawal of libido from the object and, in the normal course of events, a transfer of the libido onto another object. The potential depressive did not, however, follow this normal course. Instead of withdrawal of libido and *reinvestment*, libido is withdrawn and *retained* within the ego, where it is used to create an internalized object similar to the one lost. This introjection of the lost object is manifested by the depressive's taking on many of the object's qualities. In support of this view, Abraham (1966a) cited cases in which effort's were made by patients to restore the lost object by identifying with it, by being like it to some extent. As Freud put it, "Thus the shadow of the object fell upon the ego."

Freud reasoned that for such a development to take place, there needed to be considerable investment of libido in the object, but (and this is seemingly contradictory) the object cathexis must have relatively little power to withstand frustration. To explain this paradox one must assume that the individual had related to the object in a highly narcissistic way (that there was little reciprocity in the relationship, with the depressive ego using the object solely to gratify needs). Thus when obstacles arose, it was a relatively short step to regress from a narcissistic object-cathexis to further narcissism in which the person himself becomes the loved object. Thus, the potential for becoming seriously depressed springs from the tendency to make highly narcissistic object choices.

In summary, the onset of symptomatology in the depressive was seen in a real object loss followed by introjection of that object. At this point the ambivalence that is common in love relationships appears and negative feelings toward the object are directed inwardly, toward the aspect of the object that lives within oneself. This permits inward expression of hostility toward the loved one without outward expression. The extreme manifestation of such a process is suicide, which Freud saw as always involving murderous feelings toward others.

Freud also attempted in the same 1917 paper to explain the development of mania. He agreed with Abraham's view that the "complexes" basic to melancholia were also at the root of mania. He believed that the manic state resulted from a situation in which great mental expenditure had initially been necessary to deal with a long-sustained condition and where something happened to make such an expenditure no longer necessary. This process is similar to what the impoverished man feels when he wins a large sum of money and is suddenly relieved of the pressure and anxiety associated with earning a bare subsistence. It is as if an overpowering burden is suddenly thrown off. One feels joyful and ready to engage in a variety of activities, heretofore inhibited. Freud saw mania as precisely this sort of "triumph."

To explain how a person in the depths of depression might become manic, Freud reasoned that the object loss is somehow overcome by the ego and the energy formerly devoted to self-castigation becomes available for seeking new objects. Thus, the now manic individual seems "like a starving man after bread." On the question of how the object loss is overcome, Freud was vague. He speculated that it might result from the resolution of a series of struggles taking place within the unconscious. Whereas in normal grieving detachment of libido from the lost object and its redirection is largely a *conscious* process, in depression the struggle is *unconscious*. In depression the relationship to the loved object is more complicated than it is in mourning because of ambivalence which can be "constitutional" (a term Freud used to describe ambivalence in individuals readily prone to such conflict) and can arise even when an object loss is merely threatened but not actual. Thus depression may result from a wider range of causes than grief, and it consists of a myriad of small conflicts in which love and hate contend for the same object.

With the depressive's struggle taking place in the unconscious, only the outcome is consciously felt. If the attachment for the object cannot be given up, depression is the result. If the negative side of the ambivalence, the hatred, prevails the object is abandoned, and mania results. In a later formulation, written in 1921, Freud (1960) characterized depression as resulting from a conflict between the "ego-ideal," an aspect of the superego, and the ego. Mania was seen to develop when an alliance is formed between the ego and ego-ideal, thereby freeing up the energy that had been devoted to the conflict and making it available for uninhibited pleasurable pursuits.

By 1924, Abraham, as a result of further experience with depressive patients (Abraham, 1966b), postulated a series of factors that he felt were etiologically significant in their illness. While some of these repeated Freud's speculations, others were comparatively new at the time. Abraham proposed five factors, and argued that each needed to be present in a given case if depression were to eventuate. The presence of any one of these might result in some other emotional disorder.

The first was a constitutional one in which the individual inherited overly strong oral needs. Second, Abraham believed that as a result of such a constitutional predisposition the potential depressive derived inordinate pleasure from eating and other oral activities, such as affectionate exchanges. Frustration of these desires is emotionally traumatic. The third factor is the experience of having the need for oral affection repeatedly frustrated. A fourth is that these frustrations occur prior to resolution of the Oedipal conflict, when repression has not yet dampened Oedipal wishes. Such frustration facilitates the introjection of love-objects such as the mother and father. Thus, when disappointments similar to the primary ones are experienced later in life, the stage has been set for a depressive psychosis. Depression in the adult is thus a reenactment of a primal depression arising in the first years of life.

The Study of Manic-Depressives through Intensive Psychotherapy

Many other psychoanalysts have elaborated Freud's and Abraham's views of the etiology of depression and several have made original contributions (Klein, 1950; Spitz, 1946). It was not until the 1950s, however, that a group of psychotherapists studied the manic-depressive psychoses with an eye to understanding better the early life experiences which led to the development of the particular type of oral character that was prone to such a disorder (Cohen et al., 1954; Fromm-Reichman, 1959). This group was strongly influenced in its approach to patients by Harry Stack Sullivan, but it did not share his belief that constitutional factors predominated etiologically in the manic-depressive. On the contrary, these workers set out to determine afresh those psychological factors that seemed to be the most significant etiological precursors of this condition. Because these workers conducted their investigation while practicing psychiatry in and around Washington, D.C., they will be referred to here as the "Washington group."

Each member of the Washington group conducted intensive psychotherapy with several manic-depressive patients. On the basis of the way patients related to the therapist in these psychotherapeutic encounters, inferences were made about the early life experience of the patients. The nature of the transference was assumed to reflect attitudes and feelings formed to significant adults early in life, and these data were used to reconstruct, inferentially, the patient's significant early interpersonal relationships. On the basis of their experience with 12 manic-depressives, the Washington group formed conclusions about the general atmosphere of the family during the patient's early life, the nature of his psychological development, his character as an adult, and the factors that precipitate psychosis.

Family Atmosphere

All 12 patients studied by the Washington group came from families isolated from their milieu because of some distinguishing factor that varied across patients. These isolating factors included minority group membership, adverse economic circumstances, and serious mental illness in the

© J. Brian King 1975

A warm and supportive family atmosphere early in life can do much to prevent the development of psychoses.

family. In each case the social isolation was keenly felt and vigorous efforts were made to increase family acceptability by conforming to the perceived standards of the people around them. Thus, there was great concern for what the neighbors might think. Additional family prestige was also sought through attempts to raise economic levels or to win unusual honors.

The children of such families, therefore, grew up with a strict and highly conventional standard of good behavior deriving from the interpersonal authority, "they" (the family's interpretation of the standards of outsiders). Furthermore, such children were treated as instruments for pulling the family up by the bootstraps. Thus, the patients were typically devalued as children and their financial, academic, or other accomplishments became important only to the extent that they served the need to elevate the family.

Inculcating the need for prestige in the child who was to become manic-depressive was usually carried out by an ambitious mother. Since the status of the family in the American culture is typically measured by the father's accomplishments, the mother's indoctrination of the child necessarily carried with it a devaluation of the father. Furthermore, since it was the mother who emphasized the importance of achievement, she was regarded as the stronger of the parents, and as a moral authority whose approval was necessary although she was not particularly affectionate or loving. The father was often regarded as much warmer although weak. Incidentally, his lack of achievement was not, necessarily, absolute. That is, he might have been considered successful by outsiders but, because he fell short of the exacting standards set within the family, he was regarded as a failure. Generally, the father accepted the idea that he was inadequate in comparision to what he *should* achieve and thereby implied to his children that they should avoid emulating him.

Early Development

The Washington group felt that the earliest experience of the potential manic-depressive was with a mother who responded positively to the complete dependence of her infant. Therefore the early stages of infancy were characterized by considerable comfort and satisfaction. As the baby grew, however, and began to display independence or perhaps even rebelliousness, the mother, a highly conventional person, became uncomfortable. As a result her attitude toward the child shifted rather abruptly; a very dutiful, giving person with her helpless babe, she demanded conformity from the growing child. This shift took place about at the end of the baby's first year. For the child, now anxious and puzzled, the problem was one of integrating two very different images of the mother—one in which she is viewed as a good, giving person, and the other as a controlling, punishing one. While normal children are also confronted with the fact that significant adults are pleasant at times and not pleasant at others, the task of integrating such differences and recognizing the whole person for what he or she is, is easier for the normal than for the potential manic-depressive child, because the contrast between the two images is more extreme for the latter. The experience of sharply differential and irreconcilable perceptions of the mother is thought to be the basis for the later ambivalence of the manic-depressive. His positive feelings about the mother he knew during his first year and the negative ones engendered by the different kind of mother he must later contend with have separate, unintegrated existences.

Development during Childhood

The Washington group believed that in childhood the potential manic-depressive stands out in his family as a particularly talented person—usually the most capable member of the family. He, therefore, has a special position in the family, which places a special burden of responsibility upon him, subjects him to the envy of siblings, and even throws him into competition with a parent. Nevertheless, he jealously guards his special status, maintains a close allegiance to the family, and invests considerable energy in trying to counteract the envy of his siblings. He also tries to live up to the parents' expectation that he will rescue the family by elevating its status. He thus feels responsible for hardships or failures that arise in the family.

In order to maintain his allegiance to the family, the potential manic-depressive goes out of his way to minimize the envy and competition his siblings feel toward him because of his special status and outstanding abilities. He does this by underselling himself and trying to hide his superior ability. A similar pattern is followed with others later in life.

The Pattern in Adulthood

The potential manic-depressive, particularly one who is hypomanic, gives the appearance of considerable interpersonal facility. Although he seems to know many people and to get along well with them, such contacts have little depth. Most of his interpersonal relationships are in fact characterized by a stereotyped social performance involving a fast patter, wit, and a certain amount of aggressiveness. His behavior fails to take account of the other person who, generally, is merely enjoying an entertaining performance. In only one or two relationships does he display deep feeling—typically, profound dependency. This is manifested by extreme demands for affection and attention presumably due him because of his great need and his readiness to sacrifice himself for the other. However, there is only a minimal ability to reciprocate in kind for the other whose needs he cannot readily perceive. At the same time he feels that in his personal underselling and self-devaluation he has contributed greatly to the relationship with the other individual. In this underselling such individuals actually limit their own achievements and may be viewed by others as lacking in ability. This creates additional problems by provoking hostility both toward those who regard them as inferior and toward themselves, because they sense that their own deceptive behavior has resulted in this perception on the part of others.

Apart from his dependency relationships the potential manic-depressive may be fairly well adjusted between attacks. A conventional person, he works hard and is capable of real successes. His extreme conscientiousness can suggest to others that he is obsessional but, unlike the obsessive, he has no need to control others for the sake of holding power nor is his conformity tinged with the rebellion often seen in obsessives. If he seeks to control, it is in the service of his dependency needs, and what he fears most is abandonment.

Relating the foregoing behavioral pattern to early life experience, the Washington group hypothesized that the early failure to develop integrated conceptions of people causes the pre-manic-depressive to view them as objects to be manipulated. He tries desperately to get these people to be consistently good to him. What he fails to comprehend are the interpersonal subtleties that result in certain types of behavior on the part of others. He fails to recognize that people can be unpleasant at one time while retaining the capacity to be entirely pleasant under different circumstances. There is, therefore, an all-or-none quality to the pre-manic-depressive's view of the behavior of others.

The Development of Psychosis

The Washington group believed, as did others, that severe depression was always prompted by some *felt loss* on the part of the patient. At times this loss can be recognized by an outsider but at other times this is not the case. For example, a patient might become depressed after being promoted at work. Although this might be interpreted by an observer as a gain rather than a loss, the important thing is that the patient regarded it as a loss, possibly because it cut him off from a needed dependency relationship or exposed him to the envy of others. The important thing in evaluating such precipitating causes is to understand how the patient feels about an incident; invariably, if depression has resulted, some loss has been felt regardless of external appearances.

Manic attacks also were seen as reactions to situations in which love was lost. Generally such attacks were preceded by at least a transient period of depression. The Washington group regarded manic behavior as a defense utilized to keep underlying depression from awareness. Where it followed depression it was seen as a straightforward escape mechanism. Where mania was followed by depression the mania was simply thought to have failed as a defense. The Washington group believed that hypomania is a continual life style for many people, who use such behavior as a means of self-protection against potential depression. This group could not differentiate between forces prompting manic behavior and those initiating depression, and considered the salient diagnostic question to be, "What circumstances make mania available as a defense for some but not for others?"

Essentially, the pre-manic-depressive gets along by appealing to others for care and affection. As long as such appeals are fairly well controlled and satisfied, he goes along with some stability. Disappointment, however, results in the initiation of great demands which, by their very childishness, are more likely to be rejected. Thus a cycle is set in motion that leads to a descent into deep depression and a feeling of being deserted by those who had formerly been supportive. At this point the depressive seems to try to extort affection through his display of misery. He has little capacity to look at his problems, to understand how they arose, and to do something about them. When the typical depressive pattern for winning affection is abandoned and before any substitute for it has emerged, suicide is a very real possibility. Such a dramatic act is regarded by the Washington group as an extreme, irrational attempt to reestablish the relationship the depressive wants. It is as if the act of committing suicide will finally communicate his sense of helplessness and desperation to others and prompt them to come forward with the supplies he needs. For some depressives the fantasy of needing to die to be reborn and thus to recapture the bliss of the first year of life may also be active.

The Washington group takes an individual position toward the guilt feelings often noted in depressives. They do not regard the potential depressive as having a particularly stern superego, because the early years were marked by overindulgence rather than frustration and control. What passes for a superego in these people is their attempt to be the kind of person they feel authorities expect them to be. This maximizes their chances of getting the responses they seek

from such figures. Guilt, therefore, is unconsciously used as a technique for winning approval. Displays of suffering are resorted to rather than more rational steps to alter interpersonal relationships in order to achieve a position of greater stability.

Comment

Interesting as the studies and conclusions of the Washington group are, several issues must be resolved before their views can be applied to manic-depressives in general. One basic flaw in their work, as in most family studies of schizophrenics, is their failure to use a control group. It is therefore impossible to say that processes considered basic to the families of such patients are in fact unique to them and are active ingredients in the etiology of the illness. Furthermore, in a study based on relatively unsystematized observations, it is difficult to differentiate between conclusions based on empirical evidence and those that derive from a "pet theory" of experimenters who have set out to find data for its verification.

Another serious problem is the danger of generalization from the 12 patients studied to manic-depressives as a group. The group studied was special in that it included only individuals who both were well motivated for intensive psychotherapy and could afford to pay for it. These factors imply upward striving and material success, and conceivably conclusions by the study group regarding the importance of such factors in the background of the manic-depressive may reflect the life style of an unusually successful segment of the population. These so-called differentiating factors may be far less evident in the backgrounds of manic-depressives whose social and professional accomplishments are more modest than those studied by the Washington group.

Because of some of the shortcomings of

this study, Gibson (1958) did a follow-up of it and collected additional relevant data with other patients at the same time. He administered a 15-item questionnaire to the 12 patients studied by the Washington group as well as to 27 manic-depressives and 17 schizophrenics at St. Elizabeth's Hospital in Washington, D.C. The questionnaire focused on the five categories highlighted in the conclusions of the Washington group as basic to the background of the manic-depressive: relation to the community; envy; role of the parents; authority in the home; and conventionality. For each area there were three items designed to ascertain the degree to which certain experiences occurred. Ratings were made by a person familiar with the patient's background.

In this study, 11 of the 12 patients studied by the Washington group were rated by their therapists, and the twelfth was rated by the author after reading the case records. All the St. Elizabeth's patients were rated by the author and a social worker, who combined their individual ratings. Comparisons among the three sets of groups demonstrated that both manic-depressive groups differed significantly from the schizophrenics with respect to the family's relation to the community, the degree of envy to which they were subjected, and the degree of conventionality found in the home. Specifically, the manic-depressive groups were judged, in comparison to schizophrenics, to come from families placing greater emphasis on the need to raise family prestige and with stronger aspirations for the patient to accomplish this. Manic-depressives were exposed to more envy and competitiveness, and they tended to undersell themselves more, as a result. Finally, both manic-depressive groups were characterized by considerably more concern about the approval of others than were the schizophrenics.

A series of studies (Becker, 1960; Becker, Spielberger, & Parker, 1963; Spielberger, Parker, & Becker, 1963) has been made to test the hypotheses deriving from the researches of the Washington group and Gibson concerning achievement and conformity in manic-depressives. Becker (1960) and Spielberger, Parker, and Becker (1963) compared individuals who had once been hospitalized and diagnosed as manic-depressives to subjects who had never suffered a serious psychological disorder on two tests measuring need for achievement and a tendency to value achievement as well as on tests measuring authoritarianism and conformity to family values. In earlier studies those found to have a high need for achievement were people concerned with "living up to an internalized standard of excellence." By contrast, those valuing achievement highly have been found to be responding to parental pressure toward achievement and recognition. According to the Washington group the manic-depressive should value achievement to a greater degree than control subjects but not necessarily show a higher internal need for achievement. They should also display more authoritarian attitudes and greater conformity to family attitudes than controls. This was confirmed in the later studies.

Becker, Spielberger, and Parker (1963) repeated the earlier studies, adding a control group consisting of non-manic-depressive patients (schizophrenics and neurotic depressives). They found that on measures of authoritarian attitudes, the degree to which achievement was valued, and adherence to family values, manic-depressives scored highest and normal controls lowest. The differences between normal controls and manic-depressives were significant for all measures but differences between manic-depressives and other patient controls on these measures were not significant. These findings partially support the contentions of the Washington group but the failure to differentiate between manic-depressives and other patients raises some question about the specificity for manic-depressives of high value achievement, high authoritarianism, and conformity.

Heredity

Kallman, whose work on the hereditary basis of schizophrenia was described in Chapter 6, has attempted to establish an hereditary basis for manic-depressive psychosis. In 1952 Kallman (1952) reported that he had uncovered 23 manic-depressives who were members of identical twin pairs and that 22 of the co-twins were also manic-depressives. Beck (1967), who has reviewed Kallman's work as well as that of a number of others in this area, has challenged Kallman's findings on several grounds. Like those who questioned Kallman's methodology in his work on schizophrenic twin pairs, Beck disputes the reliability of the diagnosis of the nonhospitalized co-twin, and suggests that there was a sampling bias in the twin pairs drawn from a resident patient population, and that Kallman's method of determining whether a twin pair was identical or fraternal was faulty. Beck has also reported on other studies of identical twins suffering affective psychoses in which concordance rates were far lower than those reported by Kallman. In summarizing his review Beck concludes that the great variation found in reports of the frequency of affective disorder within the families of patients suffering affective disorders makes it impossible to be conclusive about the significance of heredity for such disorders.

Biochemical Studies

Beck (1967) has reviewed many studies that attempted to demonstrate biochemical abnormalities that might account for manic-depressive psychosis. His conclusion is that few consistent results have been found and in the few cases where positive findings seem to be confirmed, it is unclear whether the biochemical abnormalities caused the psychosis or are secondary to poor diet, reduced activity, and increased glandular secretion. In many respects Beck's reservations about the results of these biochemical studies of manic-depressives parallel those held by Kety (1959a, 1959b) with respect to biochemical research in schizophrenia (see Chapter 6).

Studies of Endocrine Function

Michael and Gibbons (1963) have done a comprehensive review of the relationship between certain glandular functions and emotional arousal. They point out that normals confronted by a variety of stresses, such as the prospect of having major surgery and anticipation of major exams, show the effects of an increase in adrenocortical activity. Similar increases are found in psychiatric patients displaying anxiety or depression. When depressed patients improve there is a decrease in adrenocortical function. Furthermore, removal of the adrenal glands, with maintenance of the patient by administration of the hormones normally secreted by that gland, results in a more serene, stable emotional life than was experienced prior to the operation. This evidence suggests that adrenocortical functioning plays a central role in the emotional changes characterizing manic-depressive psychosis.

EEG Studies of Sleep in Depressed Patients

A number of studies have been done of the sleep patterns of depressed patients by continuously monitoring their brain waves during the night. Beck reports that the consensus of such studies indicates that depressed patients have more periods of light, restless sleep, and sleep for less time than do normals. Furthermore, their sleep is more readily disrupted by noises.

Psychotherapy

The psychological theories advanced in an effort to understand depression have not necessarily suggested a psychotherapeutic procedure for alleviating it. Descriptions have been offered by those working with depressives of the special types of problems that they present as patients. However, no effective system has emerged for treating such individuals.

Their experience in treating manic-depressives led the Washington group to describe a characteristic transference pattern among such patients. Not surprisingly, one common feature in the transference is their dependency. The depressive seeks to extort gratification from the therapist, neither expecting that it will be forthcoming nor being able to accept it when it is. His demands involve expressions of his misery, of how much he needs the therapist, and of the therapist's responsibility for failing to meet his demands.

Another characteristic of the manic-depressive's transference is his view of the therapist as a carbon copy of parent figures. Accordingly, the therapist is to be manipulated in order to win sympathy and moral reassurance from him. It is expected, however, that the therapist will not really satisfy his demands and will instead be critical and rejecting while giving only occasional token-approval. In taking this viewpoint the patient makes it difficult for himself to see things in a new way through the therapist, and this is one of the most serious stumbling blocks to therapy.

The Washington group believed that it is anxiety-producing for the manic-depressive to see others or himself as unique people in their own right. To recognize this—and that a given person could reasonably display both good and bad traits—would make it difficult to be dependent on such a person and would thrust on the manic-depressive a measure of threatening independence. This entire problem is avoided by denying the complexity of others and retaining the simple way of regarding them developed in the early years of life.

Beck distinguishes between approaches to be used with the patient in the depressed state and in the post-depressed state. When depressed the patient is seen to need reassurance that his disorder is self-limiting and that he will feel better, an opportunity to ventilate feelings about life situations that are troublesome, and direct guidance concerning changes in his routine which will interrupt his self-preoccupation.

Once the acute depression has passed Beck feels the patient may be capable of developing some insight into what specific experiences and feelings bring on his depression. This, hopefully, will insulate him against future relapses. Such insight is arrived at by reconstructing carefully the development of the depression. The object here is to help the patient to see his disorder as a reaction to a specific set of problems he faces in his everyday functioning. For example, one patient could trace the onset of his depression to a morning when his wife, who had been awake most of the night with their new baby, failed to get up to prepare his breakfast. This provoked memories of earlier life experiences in which he felt hurt at not receiving as much attention as he would have liked from teachers, parents, and even close friends. The recognition of his own inordinate need for affection and attention insulated the patient against being overwhelmed in the future by stresses that shake his sense of personal worth.

Drug Therapy

Two drugs, *imipramine* and *iproniazid*, introduced in 1957, are used as antidepressants. Each has been studied by the classic double-blind procedure, where neither the patient taking some substance nor the physician administering it knows whether it is the drug being tested or a placebo. In this way the psychological effects of a physician who expects the drug to have positive effects and/or a patient who expects to be helped can be differentiated from the true effects of the drug. Beck (1967) reports that the research on antidepressants has been inconclusive so that their efficacy remains in doubt.

Schlagenhauf, Tupin, and White (1966) have reported dramatic success in treating a small group of manic patients with *lithium carbonate*, a drug first used in Australia in 1949. These authors have also reviewed 18 separate evaluations of the effects of lithium treatment on manic patients. Collectively, these studies indicate that about 81 percent of patients show behavioral improvement. Further controlled, double-blind studies should probably be undertaken before these results can be accepted as conclusive.

Electro-Shock Therapy (EST)

Paradoxically, a physical method of treatment, electro-shock therapy (EST), for which there is no clear-cut theoretical rationale, has proved quite useful in alleviating at least the acute symptoms of depression and involutional melancholia. The technique involves administering from 70 to 130 volts of electricity for one-tenth to one-half of a second. The current passes through electrodes placed on the patient's temples and stimulates a generalized seizure with immediate loss of consciousness. Shock is typically administered in relatively short series, ranging from 2 to 10 seizures. The most common post-treatment reaction is a loss, varying in degree, of memory for pre-shock events. This memory gradually returns, though a period of amnesia may persist for weeks or even months after treatment is terminated.

EST seems to bring quick relief of acute depressive symptomatology without necessarily affording protection against future relapse or fresh outbreak of symptoms. It has the advantage of bringing the patient quickly to a state wherein psychotherapeutic efforts, aimed at either bolstering the personality against future stresses or helping the individual to learn techniques for avoiding situations that stimulate depressive attacks, can be substituted.

As has been noted, there is no well-accepted theoretical rationale for the positive effects of EST. Alexander and Selesnick (1966) have reviewed a number of relevant psychological and physiological theories and have pointed out that all are highly speculative.

THE INVOLUTIONAL PSYCHOSES

These disorders arise from the stresses typical of the involutional period of life, the time of menopause or climacteric. Symptoms such as worrying excessively, feelings of guilt and anxiety, agitation, and somatic concerns are common. The appearance of a psychosis during the involutional period is not reason enough to label it an involutional psychosis. Often, therefore, it is extremely difficult to differentiate between an involutional psychosis and other psychoses that happen to occur during the involutional period.

Kraepelin was the first to describe the involutional psychoses, particularly the melancholia (depression) seen at this time of life, as separate disease entities. Many of his contemporaries objected to this distinction arguing that such melancholias were simply forms of manic-depressive psychosis. Kraepelin held fast to his position

---

HOSPITAL SHOCKED BY FINDING NO SOCK IN ITS SHOCK MACHINE

By Raymond R. Coffey

LONDON—For two years patients in a mental hospital in the north of England were given electric shock treatments on a machine that—unknown to anyone—did not work.

The problem was discovered only when a new nurse arrived on the staff and noticed that the patients were "not twitching."

The bizarre story is recounted in an article in the current issue of World Medicine, a magazine for doctors published in London every two weeks.

And its author, a doctor involved in the treatment with the nonworking machine suggests that the experience raises a further question about whether electric shock treatment—"electric convulsive therapy," and a controversial treatment anyhow—really does patients any good.

For, he says, the patients seemed to benefit as much from being put to sleep in preparation for the shock treatment—with anesthetics—as other patients do from the shock treatment itself.

The article is signed by "J. Easton Jones," a pseudonym for a general practitioner who was working in the hospital as both anesthetist (putting the patients to sleep) and electroconvulsive therapist (supposedly administering the shock treatment).

The trouble began, he writes, when an old shock treatment machine quit working and was replaced with a new model which was "obviously a great improvement on the previous edition."

This new machine, he says "had dials and lights and switches for different wave forms."

But, although the red light went on and needles moved as they were supposed to, he noticed that the patients were not twitching as they had under the old machine.

He asked if the machine might not be working but was assured by the head nurse that "yes, it is. This sort does not give any reaction in the (patients) . . . It's in the instructions."

The doctor checked the instructions, the nurse seemed to be right and, the doctor says, "We used the apparatus for two years with no complaints from the patients."

Then a new head nurse arrived on the scene and after assisting in only three treatments declared that the machine was "not working."

She was told it was, as patients were not supposed to "twitch" while under treatment from this type of machine.

"Look," she said, "I've just come from a hospital with (a machine) just like this and they twitch all right."

The machine was examined—and the new nurse was right.

"All the patients had been getting for two years," the doctor concludes, "was thiopentone and a shot of scoline (anesthetic to put them asleep)—and not one had noticed."

Reprinted by permission from the *Chicago Daily News*, September 20, 1974.

and more recent workers have retained the involutional category as a separate form of psychosis. Kraepelin's position in this matter is not unassailable, however.

Cameron (1963) pointed out that the old concept of involutional melancholia referred to a state of *agitated* depression seen in women during "change of life." It was originally thought to derive from the glandular changes associated with menopause, and, thus to be organically derived. Recent thinking has emphasized the psychological nature of disorders arising in the involutional period, when certain specific stresses arise. The term *involutional psychotic reaction* is, therefore, viewed as a compromise between the old notion that the disorder is caused by glandular changes and the more recent view that life stresses typical of this period prompt a psychological regression.

Cameron believed that it was difficult to distinguish between involutional psychoses and other psychoses arising during the involutional stage. For Cameron the only practical criterion in establishing the diagnosis is the patient's age at the time of onset of the disorder. However, he recognizes that age is less and less useful as a diagnostic criterion, because in actual diagnostic practice age boundaries (about 45 to 55 in women and about 55 to 65 in men) are stretched. Thus, depression in a female in her late thirties or early forties may be attributed to approaching involution, and depression in a woman in her sixties may

be conceived of as a delayed reaction to menopause.

Cameron concludes, therefore, that the retention of a separate diagnostic category for involutional disorders is unjustified. The process of aging involves difficulties to which different people react in different ways. Some suffer transient adjustment problems, some become neurotic, and others become psychotic. Cameron argues that a distinctive category is not needed to classify one of an array of possible reactions to growing older. Beck (1967) concurs in this opinion.

Classification of Involutional Psychoses

In DSM-II (1968) *involutional psychotic reaction* has been divided into two separate categories: *involutional paranoid state* and *involutional melancholia*. The former is now classed under paranoid states but will be discussed here. *Involutional melancholia* is classed as one of the categories of the *major affective disorders* and is described thus:

> This is a disorder occurring in the involutional period and characterized by worry, anxiety, agitation, and severe insomnia. Feelings of guilt and somatic preoccupations are frequently present and may be of delusional proportions. This disorder is distinguishable from *Manic-depressive illness* by the absence of previous episodes;

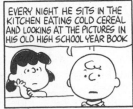

© 1965 United Feature Syndicate, Inc.

it is distinguished from *Schizophrenia* in that impaired reality testing is due to a disorder of mood; and it is distinguished from *Psychotic depressive reaction* in that the depression is not due to some life experience. Opinion is divided as to whether this psychosis can be distinguished from the other affective disorders. It is, therefore, recommended that involutional patients not be given this diagnosis unless all other affective disorders have been ruled out (p. 36).

DSM-II (1968, p. 38) describes the involutional paranoid state as follows: "This paranoid psychosis is characterized by delusion formation with onset in the involutional period. Formerly it was classified as a paranoid variety of involutional psychotic reaction. The absence of conspicuous thought disorders typical of schizophrenia distinguishes it from that group."

The kind of concern Cameron expressed about classifying involutional disorders as distinct entities seems to be reflected in the DSM-II descriptions of involutional melancholia and involutional paranoid state.

Nonetheless, many prefer to retain separate diagnostic classes for involutional disorders. They see the cause of these disorders in a combination of physiological, social, and psychological factors unique to the involutional time of life.

Physiological Factors

The involutional period is the time of life when the activity of the endocrine and reproductive glands diminishes. Menstruation ceases, either abruptly or gradually. Accompanying this change in the menstrual cycle are phenomena paralleling those seen when the ovaries of the adult female are removed: atrophy of the genital apparatus and vasomotor symptoms, such as hot flashes, which vary from very mild to quite distressing. The hormones responsible for the so-called secondary sex characteristics diminish and, in many cases, these characteristics are lessened or altered in the direction of the opposite sex. Generally, sexual desire remains unaffected and may even be heightened for several years afterward.

CASE 8–5: A CASE OF INVOLUTIONAL MELANCHOLIA

Karl T., a fifty-six-year-old druggist, voluntarily entered a private mental institution in a large city in the South. Married, and the father of three teen-age children, he had recently retired to live, in upper-middle-class circumstances, off income from investments.

*   *   *

After high school Karl attended a pharmacy school on the advice of a cousin who pointed out that one could support oneself while attending such a school. After he received his degree he was employed as a druggist in a local store. At the age of thirty-three he married, eventually having three teen-age children. He continued to work for others until the age of forty-two, when he opened his own store and made a great success of the business. His daily routine called for him to work twelve hours a day seven days a week. His only interest other than the store was athletics, and he frequently exercised in the local Y.M.C.A. gymnasium. There he became proficient at squash and was proud of his ability to beat much younger men at this vigorous sport.

Even though Karl was successful in business, and wise in his financial investments, he saw himself as a dependent, insecure person who had always been apprehensive about the future. Perhaps as a result of his insecurity he never felt satisfied if he merely met the requirements of a job, and felt that he must do more than just what was expected of him. He was very reluctant to accept responsibility, and considered it a great accomplishment when he was able to operate his own business so successfully.

About two years before his hospitalization he suffered a fall in which he tore some of the cartilage in his leg, and was then forced to abandon his athletic activities. Eight months before his hospital admission he impulsively sold the pharmacy in order to have more time to relax. Although he still received an adequate income from property investments, Karl found that he was unhappy without his accustomed routine. Symptoms developed five months before admission to the hospital, when he began to brood over having sold the business. This feeling gradually became more intense, and was accompanied by feelings of guilt. In an effort to dispel these he tried working for others, but this only intensified the depression. He began to have difficulty falling asleep and would awaken at four or five in the morning and pace up and down. His interest in his surroundings waned, and having no appetite, he suffered some loss of weight.

Karl was constantly preoccupied with having sold his store, and he began to feel that he had let his family down and "killed his future." He felt guilty over not having spent more time with his family and accused himself of being impulsive and childish. He refused to dine out wtih his wife because he felt too inferior to be seen in public. He gave up the hope that he would ever do anything worthwhile again, and his concern lest something happen to his family grew because he felt that he could no longer care for them. When a well-to-do businessman of his acquaintance committed suicide Karl was quite shaken and feared that he might do the same. At this point he saw his family doctor, who recommended hospitalization.

When interviewed after his admission to the hospital Karl presented the picture of a well-developed, neat man who looked younger than his stated age. He was anxious and restless as he talked and intermittently ran his hands through his hair, walked around, sat down, wrung his hands, and twiddled his thumbs. His mood was clearly depressed, and tears came to his eyes as he discussed his mother's death. He was generally friendly and cooperative and well able to reason logically. Orientation, attention, memory, and his grasp of general information were all good. He admitted to sexual impotence, which upset him a great deal during the previous four months, and caused him to worry that he would never be well again. He regretted not having been more attentive to his parents when they were old and alone and worried about the stigma his emotional illness might place on his family.

Karl was hospitalized for approximately one month, during which time he was treated with five electroconvulsive shocks. After the third he was free of all symptoms, but on discharge he was advised to continue psychiatric treatment in order to consolidate the gains made during hospitalization.

From Zax & Stricker, 1963, pp. 18–20.

CASE 8–6: A CASE OF INVOLUTIONAL PARANOID STATE

Hilda S., a forty-eight-year-old mother of two children, was committed to a mental hospital by her family. She was a person of European birth who came to this country alone when in her mid-twenties to work on the New England farm of distant relatives. After a few months she left the farm with the hope of earning more money by working in a large city. She lived alone at this time and worked as a domestic, the main focus of her life being her work. Her formal schooling in this country consisted of only a few years of night classes, which provided her with a modicum of facility with the English language. After seven years in this country, while in her early thirties, Hilda met her present husband, and after a relatively brief courtship they were married. Her employment as a domestic terminated permanently at the birth of her first child, one year after marriage. Her husband was a lower middle class farmer.

Before the onset of her illness, Hilda was a rather quiet woman whose life centered about her home. Gardening interested her and provided a hobby to occupy her spare time. She always had a tendency to be easily upset, and in such situations chose to confide in her husband, obtaining some comfort in this way. She had a few friends, but preferred to entertain them in her home rather than to visit theirs. She was a regular churchgoer, but never was preoccupied with religious questions or affairs. The onset of the disabling symptoms which eventuated in hospitalization was said to be relatively acute, beginning at the time three months prior to admission when she experienced her last menstruation (prior to that there had been none for several months). She became restless and seemed continually on the verge of losing her emotional control. There were expressions of dissatisfaction with her life on the farm and a demand that the family move to the city. About two weeks prior to admission she began complaining of severe headaches which were unrelieved by sedation. During this time it became obvious that she was becoming forgetful and that her remarks lacked logic. These symptoms were accompanied by a difficulty in sleeping, followed within a few days by talk of seeing spies in her home. Hilda began to respond to auditory hallucinations, and became seclusive, refusing to leave her bed. She engaged in much praying accompanied by frequent episodes in which she would rush around the house kissing holy pictures. Immediately before hospitalization she became quarrelsome toward members of her family because they failed to sympathize with her delusions about spies.

At her admitting interview it was found that although this was Hilda's first hospitalization, she had, for several years, been mildly suspicious of people, and this feeling that others might attempt to harm her was seen as being intensified in the current episode. The interview was marked by behavior and verbalizations which bespoke a severely depressed, agitated mood state. Her facial expression depicted suffering, and almost before the interview began she was complaining of a pain in the lower part of her neck. Her agitation was manifested by frequent moving about in her seat, holding her hand, in turn, to her head, her cheek, and her chin, and continually shifting the position of her body. Her remarks were often punctuated by moans and, at times, groans. She was disoriented for time and place, and both recent memory and attention span were poor.

Hilda's delusions took the form of a fear that both she and her family would be destroyed because of an incident in which she had been involved shortly after she came to this country. When asked why she had come to the hospital she cried, "I heard them say they wanted to put me away on account of the baby. I thought they were going to hang me. They were hanging everybody. They put my children away and I got so scared." Further probing revealed that the baby referred to was the child of a family for whom she had worked over twenty years before. Hilda said that once, during her employment with this family, she had "made the child touch my body." This incident had been a source of guilt ever since.

Shortly after hospitalization Hilda was treated with five electroconvulsive shocks within a period of one month. She responded to treatment very well, and when she was free of delusions she was placed on convalescent care at home. For the next year she was treated with tranquilizers, and except for recurrent but mild depressions she achieved a good recovery.

From Zax & Stricker, 1963, pp. 9–11.

There is some disagreement as to whether the male experiences a stage analogous to the menopause in women. Szalita (1966) believes that the process of aging inevitably brings a man to a point of "gonadal insufficiency with concomitant atrophy of the genital apparatus, disturbances in the neuroendocrine balance, and emotional reactions of varying degree." For the male this period is known as the climacteric, and his psychological reaction to it may be similar to that of the female during menopause. However, the male's sex glands generally continue to function longer than do the female. Furthermore, in men the relationships between testicular insufficiency and sexual functioning are not well understood. For example, castration after puberty may or may not result in changes in secondary sex characteristics or in sexual activity. These facts suggest that there is no simple relationship between testicular secretion and sexual adequacy. This in turn may account for some of the confusion about how men experience the stage in life that is physiologically related to the menopause in women.

Psychological Factors

Inevitably the dramatic physical changes accompanying menopause have important psychological implications. The female often feels that she faces a crisis. It has been suggested that her psychological reaction to puberty is a portent of what she will feel in menopause. However, despite their possibly traumatic impact, the physiological changes of puberty often lead to hopeful anticipation of reaching the full flower of adulthood. During menopause the dominant feeling is, instead, hopelessness. As a result depression, tearfulness, mood swings, and sleep disturbances are common. Women at this time face a combination of regret at no longer being able to conceive (and thus, for many, no longer being a woman) and the despair of approaching old age, debilitation, and ultimately, death.

The fate of man in this respect has perhaps been more gentle. Traditionally less of his self-esteem has been tied up in his manly appearance, therefore the loss of physical attractiveness alone, which the female has learned to bear, has affected him less significantly. Also there is not, for the male, the dramatic loss of the biologically central and symbolically important process of menstruation. He too, however, reaches the point where the inevitability of decline and death looms large and he is then confronted by feelings similar to those that upset the female. That the male's sexual decline (both in terms of fertility and, eventually, potency) is more gradual than the female's is a mixed blessing. On the one hand, it staves off for a time the stress of facing his loss of sexual power. On the other hand, by the time sexual ineffectiveness is imminent he is at a more advanced age and is less intact organically than the female at menopause. Thus he has fewer resources with which to combat the psychic trauma he faces. Despite this, however, involutional psychoses are two or three times more prevalent in females than males and perhaps this differential is partially accounted for by differences in the social forces experienced by the two sexes.

Social Factors

The female has a great emotional investment in her family, where she functions as a very important executive. Not uncommonly, around the time she enters menopause her children have reached a point in life where they are striking out on their own, either to enter college or to marry. The process of dissolution of the family group takes place over a period of several years, but it typically begins to loom large when the female is in her forties. Therefore she has to contend not only with the physiological effects of menopause, but also with a rather drastic social reorganization in her life which takes place at this inopportune

time. In essence, at the very time when she feels she is losing personal value as a female and as an organism, she is also becoming less important as a mother and as a codirector of a family. Women with careers outside the home and women who never marry are perhaps less susceptible to involutional problems.

The male is also subject to similar social stress with advancing age and the onset of climacteric but, again, it is probably experienced more gradually. If a man has maintained occupational stability and the experience he has accrued helps to compensate for loss of youthful vigor, he can function effectively in a most important area of life, despite entering the climacteric. Many men, however, find themselves in situations not dissimilar from what the female faces when her family begins to break up. If a man must compete with younger males in areas where youth is a definite advantage the situation may disrupt central social roles at a time when his general physiological decline is most noticeable.

The Involutional Psychotic Syndrome

It is not surprising that a very common symptom of the involutional period is depression. Often, however, involutional depression takes a characteristic form. Mixed as it is with anxiety and foreboding, instead of the usual picture of psychomotor retardation and quiet withdrawal, involutional patients are often dramatically agitated and hyperactive. Symptoms such as pacing, handwringing, and self-reproach abound. Some writers on this topic have suggested that many involutional patients are exhibitionistic about their symptoms. Such patients feel that disaster is just around the corner and anxiously anticipate it. Their overt self-derogation and apologetic manner are used as an attempt to stave off catastrophe.

At the same time, strongly paranoid trends may either predominate or coexist with the agitated depression and self-reproach. Such patients are capable of hurling self-blame at the listener in such a way that he feels implicated in the blame. When paranoid tendencies predominate, frank persecutory delusions emerge that are fairly well organized but lack the bizarre content of those seen in paranoid schizophrenics. Instead such patients are very bitter and hostile. Another interesting and understandable symptom of involutional reactions is the feeling that organs are deteriorating and parts of the body drying up. There is thus a specific hypochondriacal concern about exaggerated failing of the body functions that mirrors some of the premorbid preoccupations of these patients.

Etiological Theories of Involutional Psychoses

This is a disorder that has received relatively little attention from prominent personality theorists or those concerned with causes of mental illness. Even psychoanalysts, who range quite widely in the application of their theory to behavioral phenomena, have generally overlooked this area. Fenichel (1945), who performed the monumental task of summarizing the bulk of psychoanalytic writings on behavioral disorders, dismissed the involutional melancholias in one short paragraph. He pointed out simply that such disorders are distinguished from the manic-depressive psychosis, and that they occur in rigid compulsive characters whose defense systems fail in the climacterium. This, he suggested, leads to an oral regression "due to physical altera-

tions of the economy of the libido" (p. 406).

In discussing depression Fenichel pointed out that when unstable times deprive the orally ungratified of their "power and prestige and habitual ways of regulating self-esteem" (p. 406), their dependency and narcissistic needs increase. Such losses of the usual sources of self-esteem are reacted to with depression. Although Fenichel did not do so, this point could be extended to the involutional psychotic.

It is commonly noted that the prepsychotic personality picture of the involutional patient is that of a relatively inhibited, compulsive person who has been unobtrusive, intense, honest, frugal, and worrisome. His standards have been exacting and inflexible and he has been rather humorless. He tended to be dominated by the spectre of guilt over nonconformity to rigid superego demands. The need to be approved by others is often inordinately strong in involutionals, and the premorbid picture is typified by an absence of adequate means for handling aggressive or hostile impulses. The latter are sealed over through a lifetime of doing the right thing in a humorless, dogmatic way in the hope that correctness and propriety will bring the recognition and esteem that is felt necessary.

For such a person the stresses of the involutional period, given the profound losses of self-esteem associated with physiological changes and the typical alterations of the family structure, are overwhelming. Furthermore, the frustrations of the period inevitably stimulate hostile feelings that the individual has never been able to handle comfortably. The resultant agitation and depression may thus entail a mixture of grief felt over the loss of love and esteem, anxiety over the potential loss of control over one's own dreaded anger, and fear of the death that human beings inevitably face throughout their lives but which is more real and forcible at a time when physical powers are waning.

Treatment of Involutional Psychoses

As mentioned when depressive reactions were discussed, electro-shock therapy (EST) is commonly used, in relatively short series, to treat the acute symptoms of this disorder. The use of EST brings about a quick remission of the more severe symptomatology. This has resulted in a lowering of the suicide rate among involutional patients, a matter of considerable significance since the danger of suicide is probably higher among acutely agitated involutional psychotics than it is among any other patient group.

It is generally felt that EST should be followed by psychotherapy aimed at supporting the patient through the many stresses of involution. Such therapy also encourages the development of new sources of esteem, and aims at lessening the pressures of a demanding superego.

PARANOID STATES

DSM-II (1968) describes *paranoid states* in general as "psychotic disorders in which a delusion, generally persecutory or grandiose, is the essential abnormality." Disturbances of mood, behavior, or thinking that may be present are seen to derive from the delusion. This is intended to distinguish the paranoid states from schizophrenia and the affective psychoses in which thought and mood disorders are central. Still, DSM-II acknowledges that most authorities question whether the paranoid states are distinct clinical entities rather than variants of other disorders such as schizophrenia at one extreme and paranoid personality, to be discussed in a later chapter, at the other.

Classification of Paranoid States

The two subcategories of the paranoid states are *involutional paranoid state* and *paranoia*. The former was described above along with involutional melancholia. Paranoia is described as follows in DSM-II (1968, p. 38):

> This extremely rare condition is characterized by gradual development of an intricate, complex, and elaborate paranoid system based on and often proceeding logically from misinterpretation of an actual event. Frequently the patient considers himself endowed with unique and superior ability. In spite of a chronic course the condition does not seem to interfere with the rest of the patient's thinking and personality.

Etiological Theories of Paranoid Disorders

Efforts at understanding how paranoid disorders develop have been many and varied. Rather than attempting to survey these exhaustively, examples of three different approaches to this problem will be presented in some detail.

The Psychoanalytic Approach

Freud's theory of paranoia is developed in his discussion in 1911 of the case of Dr. Schreber (Freud 1956b). Dr. Schreber an eminent judge had about six months of treatment in 1884 for what was described as an attack of hypochondria. He became ill again in 1893 shortly after assuming a new post of great responsibility. His earliest symptoms on this second occasion were hypochondriacal but these were soon followed by delusions and Freud regarded him as a paranoiac. Freud never saw Schreber as a

> Doctor Gordon was fitting two metal plates on either side of my head. He buckled them into place with a strap that dented my forehead, and gave me a wire to bite.
>
> . . . I shut my eyes.
> There was a brief silence, like an indrawn breath.
> Then something bent down and took hold of me and shook me like the end of the world. Whee-ee-ee-ee-ee, it shrilled, through an air crackling with blue light, and with each flash a great jolt drubbed me till I thought my bones would break and the sap fly out of me like a split plant. I wondered what terrible thing it was that I had done.
>
>   * * *
>
> . . . Doctor Nolan said. "I'm going over with you. I'll be there the whole time, so everything will happen right, the way I promised. I'll be there when you wake up, and I'll bring you back again."
>
> . . . Miss Huey began to talk in a low, soothing voice, smoothing the salve on my temples and fitting the small electric buttons on either side of my head. "You'll be perfectly all right, you won't feel a thing, just bite down. . . ." And she set something on my tongue and in panic I bit down, and darkness wiped me out like chalk on a blackboard.

These quotations describe two different experiences with electroconvulsive shock. They are from *The Bell Jar* (Harper & Row, 1971), by Sylvia Plath, who underwent electro-shock therapy.

patient but based his analysis on an autobiographical account of his illness which Schreber published in 1903. Freud pointed out that his own practice afforded him little opportunity for direct contact with paranoiacs. As he put it "we cannot accept patients suffering from this complaint, or at all events, we cannot keep them for long, since we cannot offer treatment unless there is some prospect of therapeutic success."

Dr. Schreber's delusional system included the belief that he was inspired by God to embark on a mission to redeem the world. He further believed that this world redemption must be preceded by his own transformation from a man into a woman. Schreber felt that this transformation was not something that he desired but rather was entirely

necessary given "the order of things." He also felt that such a miracle was possible in his case because he was a special man. Schreber believed that his transformation to "femaleness" took place painfully over a period of years during which various bodily organs underwent injuries that no other man could have survived. Having managed to live through this metamorphosis, Schreber felt that he had reached a state of "femaleness," that a multitude of "female nerves" had already become implanted in his body, and that a new race of men would emerge from these nerves, following Schreber's being impregnated by God.

Freud was interested primarily in the stages through which Schreber's thinking passed as he approached the full-blown

CASE 8–7: A CASE OF PARANOIA

Barbara S., a forty-two-year-old married mother of three, was admitted to a private psychiatric clinic on the referral of her psychiatrist. She had been living with her family in a privately owned house in a middle-class residential district of a small middle Atlantic community.

Barbara was the older of two girls born to a middle-class couple. Her father, although a strict disciplinarian, was described as a very happy and affectionate man, and Barbara felt she was always very close to him. Her mother was a blunt, frank woman, who tended to be critical of others and who seemed very vigorous and efficient herself in dealing with problems. Although Barbara was not very close to her mother during her childhood, their relationship increased in warmth as Barbara grew older. Barbara was always jealous of her younger sister, and their relationship was always a very competitive one in which Barbara actually felt inferior. Barbara was a very lively child at home, and tended to be tomboyish in her activities, although she was timid with people she didn't know very well. She was a very good student who was graduated from high school, and then completed training as a technician in a medical laboratory. She married her childhood sweetheart, and they had three children and what was described as a successful marriage. Nevertheless, their sexual adjustment had been difficult. Early in the marriage it was very poor, due to the failure of her husband, but improved after one year. It became a great cause for concern shortly before Barbara's hospitalization.

Four years before her admission Barbara's uncle died. He had lived with her family, and for a short time she was disconsolate. Quite soon after this her husband suggested that they decrease their frequency of sexual intercourse from once a week to once a month, and she perceived this as a rejection. Soon afterward she became pregnant, and her pregnancy and delivery were far more comfortable and uneventful than had been the case with either of her other children. During her pregnancy she had several sexual fantasies about her obstetrician, and shortly after the delivery, while speaking to him on the phone, inadvertently asked him to date her. He expressed great shock, and she was very embarrassed and hurriedly apologized. However, while speaking to him, she heard a voice similar to her own telling her not to apologize. Later this voice told her, "But he was demonstrative," an ambiguous statement with no apparent referent.

Two years prior to her admission, shortly after changing doctors, Barbara began to suffer a gynecological disorder which required hospitalization and minor surgery. The operation was successful, but she told her husband that she was extremely suspicious of the doctor and his assistant, who happened to live in their neighborhood. She had vague feelings that they had harmed her, and thought that while under anesthesia she had been asked personal questions.

One year before hospitalization Barbara suddenly hired a lawyer, and asked him to look into this incident, giving him permission to look into the hospital records. When nothing extraordinary was found she became convinced that the damaging evidence had been destroyed. At this point she was referred to a physician who gave her reassurance and a placebo, and after a period of some improvement, referred her to a psychiatrist. She was advised to take an extended vacation, and did so, returning relaxed and feeling much improved. However, upon her return she began to feel increasingly tense and her suspicions again began to increase. Her husband told her that if she didn't change she would have to go to a mental hospital, and she showed a slight improvement, but then relapsed again. When drug therapy failed to help she was referred to a psychiatric clinic. There she made a good adjustment and, with the aid of drug therapy, was soon released to the care of a private psychiatrist.

One year after this treatment she attempted to reinstate legal proceedings against her first obstetrician and her most recent doctor for harming her, and against the neighbor-assistant for spreading facts about her sexual history. When she began to spend money wildly, in anticipation of the $250,000 she was to collect from the suits, she was rehospitalized. Barbara was again placed on drug therapy, with the result that her symptoms abated and she was once more discharged.

From Zax & Stricker, 1963, pp. 114–116.

---

megalomaniacal delusion described. Freud believed that essentially two ideas predominated in Schreber's system. The first was that he was selected to redeem mankind and the second was that he must be transformed into a woman to accomplish this mission.

In tracing the delusional ideas that preceded the final product, Freud became convinced that the primary delusion was that of feminine transformation. This idea was first experienced as an act of persecution that was not welcomed by Schreber. In fact, he saw himself as having been emasculated by an agent who intended to abuse him sexually. He also heard voices that derided him for this transformation. Even prior to this, however, the germ of the transformation idea occurred in a fantasy that Schreber had while half-asleep, in which he desired to be a woman submitting to a male in the act of copulation. Finally, Freud pointed out that the idea of becoming a woman survived Schreber's recovery. He inferred this from Schreber's admission that, when alone, he enjoyed looking at himself in the mirror with his chest adorned by various feminine articles such as ribbons and necklaces.

Schreber's conceptions of man and God were considered highly significant by Freud. Schreber believed that man possessed a body and a soul and that the latter was composed of *nerves* which were like the finest of threads. God, on the other hand, was made up entirely of nerves. Man had a finite number of immortal nerves but God possessed an infinite number which were far more sensitive than those of man. However, Schreber felt that man's nerves, in an intensely excited state, could exert a powerful attraction on those of God, so that God could not free himself and would risk the danger of his own destruction. This, Schreber felt, was precisely what happened in his own relationship to God.

Another theme that Schreber dwelt on was that God had no understanding of men who were alive, being involved largely with the dead. Because he lacked understanding of the living, God made the mistake of initiating a plot against Schreber, regarding him as a dement, and exposing him to his debilitating ordeals. In essence, therefore, Schreber regarded his illness as a struggle between himself and a far-from-perfect God, in which he, Schreber, prevailed in spite of his weakness because "the natural order of things" was on his side.

To explain the two basic elements of Schreber's delusional system Freud focused on the patient's relationship with his first physician, a psychiatrist named Flechsig. Schreber referred to this man several times in his autobiography, and prefaced the volume with an open letter to Flechsig. In this letter Schreber said that the voices which beset him continued to use Flechsig's name and identified him as the patient's persecutor, even though all contact between the two had long since terminated. It appeared to Freud, therefore, that the idea of God as a persecutor essentially supplanted the idea of Flechsig as a persecutor. This feature of Schreber's case, as well as the study of other cases involving persecutory delusions, led Freud to postulate a characteristic relationship between the paranoiac and his supposed persecutor. This significant figure in the paranoiac's life is usually someone who occupied an important place in his life before the illness developed, or someone who substituted for such a person. Strong feelings had been held toward this individual and these were simply projected outward and qualitatively changed to their opposite. Thus, the person who is hated and feared as a persecutor is one who had once been loved and admired greatly.

Applying this principle to Schreber's case, Freud believed that there was evidence that the patient was indeed warmly grateful to Flechsig after having been treated by him for an earlier illness. Schreber's subsequent dreams and fantasies, involving his physician, also reflected the assumption of a "feminine attitude" toward Flechsig. As further evidence of the latent homosexual element in this case, Freud pointed to the onset of Schreber's disorder. It took place at a time when the patient's wife was away on a brief vacation. During this separation, Schreber recalled having had as many as six emissions in one night. He dated his mental breakdown to that occasion. Freud reasoned that fantasies must have stimulated these emissions and speculated that they were homosexual in nature.

As Schreber found such fantasies unacceptable, Freud believed that both the aim of his impulse and the direction in which it flowed were distorted. Thus the feeling became one of persecution and exploitation rather than love, and these were seen as promulgated by Flechsig toward Schreber rather than the other way around. A distinctive feature of Schreber's case was that Flechsig as persecutor was replaced by the more imposing figure of God. In essence this further distortion took place as a way of making the situation more acceptable to Schreber. While the thought of being a love object of his doctor was threatening to Schreber the notion of consorting with God himself was a more comfortable one. In this way his "feminine" desires found an outlet and his ego went undisgraced.

Turning from the specifics of the Schreber case Freud advanced some general ideas about libidinal development from autoeroticism a narcissistic stage to object-love. Freud believed that the very young organism is entirely autoerotic until sexual interests become unified and he is prepared to take a love-object. Initially he cathects an object outside of himself who has genital equipment similar to his own. Thus an intermediate point between self-love and the love of a heterosexual object is a homosexual stage. Ultimately, a heterosexual object-choice is made. However, if the person retains particularly strong homosexual impulses later in life, the attractions of this intermediary stage remain potent. Also, when a regression in the direction of narcissism takes place, it brings one back through this homosexual stage. Conversely, recovery from a narcissistic retreat also brings one back through this intermediary position.

The observations about Schreber's case, together with Freud's basic theory about sexual development (in which homosexual impulses inevitably play a role in everyone's life), led him to formulate a theory of paranoia based on the view that the core conflict was an unacceptable homosexual impulse. Essentially the problem for the patient is "I (a man) love him (a man)." When such an unacceptable impulse exists, steps must be taken, at an unconscious level, to prevent its admission to consciousness. Freud believed that the limited number of ways in which the simple statement of a love relationship could be contradicted shaped the ways in which a paranoid disorder was expressed.

On this basis, four manifestations of paranoia were delineated. The first involved delusions of persecution in which hate is substituted for love and the conflictual impulse is experienced as "I hate him" instead of "I love him." Hatred is not, however, felt in a pure form by the paranoiac. Since unreasonable hatred is itself unacceptable, it must first be projected, leading to the subjective experience of "he hates me!" Under such circumstances a certain amount of hatred in return on the part of the paranoiac becomes justified.

A second form of paranoia involved what Freud termed "erotomania"—a condition of exaggerated heterosexual fixation. Here it is not the love that is denied but the object of that love. Thus, the initial proposition is "I love her." The paranoiac's propensity for projection leads to a transformation of the statement to "She loves me"—its most typical manifestation. Since the first alteration ("I love her") of the core statement is not necessarily unacceptable, it may also be present in consciousness.

The overt manifestation of the third form of distortion is jealousy. In this case the core conflict is denied by an alteration of the subject, achieved by the assertion "*I* don't love the man, *she* loves the man." In this case projection is unnecessary since the impulse has already been thrown off and attributed to an outsider. This form of distortion implicates one's mate with any individual who stimulates homosexual impulses.

A final form of distortion involves denial of the core-conflict in its entirety. In such a case one feels "I don't love another at all." Since libido is present, however, and it must be applied somewhere, this statement is the psychological equivalent of "I love myself only." Freud described the resultant behavior as megalomania, a condition he termed as "a sexual over-estimation of the ego" (p. 451).

Freud believed that the conflict producing a paranoid disorder is experienced as an internal catastrophe. The projection of the dreaded impulse is equivalent to an ending of the world since it involves a withdrawal of love from it. The delusions that emerge make it possible for a paranoiac to live once more in the world. To be sure, it is now a distorted one, but at least it is one in which he can comfortably exist. In this sense delusions, which are the most dramatic feature of paranoia, are an attempt at recovery—at reconstituting a relationship that had become unbearable.

Cameron's Theory of Paranoid Disorders

Cameron regarded the paranoid disorders as, essentially, behavior disorders stemming from "individualistic, unique and deviant symbolization" (Cameron & Magaret, 1951, p. 373). He pointed out that in daily living people were inevitably required to act in a variety of situations without being as fully informed as they would like. Therefore inference comes to play an important part in the lives of all of us. Instead of getting all pertinent facts before taking action, we make inferences and then proceed.

Experience with many different situations provides a basis for making inferences, or interpretations based on minimal cues, which are reasonably accurate. Inevitably though, mistakes are made and at such times the well-adjusted person can correct easily and speedily. Such corrections involve comparison of one's own interpretations with those of others and adjusting in terms of consensus.

The need to act in the absence of complete certainty pervades interpersonal and social functioning. When someone extends his hand he may be offering to shake hands or he may be attempting to push another person. The context should help us to anticipate which action is intended, but when the context itself is ambiguous, highly personal needs or fears become the primary basis for deciding. A similar situation exists with respect to more complex social roles. To get along well socially, we must understand our own roles well, but we also need to know those of others. Only in that way can we accurately anticipate what others are likely to do, and to understand what they have done after they have acted.

For Cameron, the uncertainty that is always a part of a situation in which we must act and react makes possible the development of certain pathological behavioral and thought processes. This is because man's need to structure the unclear is almost irresistible. If the data necessary for accurate inference are absent, judgments are based on imagination, inner needs, and so on. Cameron identified three mechanisms (which play a part in the development of delusional systems) to which people resort in striving to interpret the unclear. These are *compensation, rationalization,* and *projection.*

Compensation is the tendency to substitute "some other need-satisfaction sequence for a frustrated or an anxiety-inducing one" (Cameron & Magaret, 1951, p. 376). Examples of this process are the child who is angry at a playmate, but instead of striking him, pounds nails into a board; or the woman who "attacks" her housecleaning when she feels irritable and angry toward her children. This mechanism is similar to what the analysts called displacement. Cameron pointed out that the substitutions used in this mechanism may be indirect ones; hence the relationship between the original target and its replacement can become complicated. Among the important varieties of compensation Cameron cited *reaction-formation* (substituting a reaction which is opposite to an anxiety-arousing one) and *sublimation* (substitute of a socially sanctioned reaction for one less acceptable). Most significant, however, for the development of paranoid thinking, Cameron felt, was the substitution of fantasy for an unacceptable reaction.

This is a common practice for seeking to attain things beyond one's reach, because of financial limitations or social strictures. Through dreams, a passing thought, or an honest-to-goodness daydream one can have the rich foods he covets, the wealth he yearns for, and the forbidden fruit he has not had the courage to seek. The potential dangers of such compensatory activity are, however, exemplified in the delusions of the paranoid person.

Cameron defined *rationalization* as "the technique of inventing and accepting interpretation of behavior which an impartial

D. Doty

When a child experiences rejection in one aspect of his life, he may learn to compensate in another. This child could become a splendid musician.

analysis would not substantiate" (Cameron & Magaret, 1951, p. 379). Examples of this process include the implausible excuses people fall back on to explain personal failings or inadequacies. As such, rationalization is a mechanism that depends entirely upon symbolic processes. Finding excuses and inferring explanatory motives are, inevitably, based in language and thought. Common to all rationalization is the attempt to come up with an explanation of an occurrence that will make it consistent with a long-cherished view. Thus, if one sees oneself as a great runner, losing to another person must be explained away on the basis of something other than skill at foot-racing. "Explanatory" notions such as poor physical condition on the day of the race, a track to which one was unaccustomed and, even, cheating by the other person, are advanced.

Cameron considered that, since all men like to believe that they understand what goes on around them, rationalization was a commonly used mechanism even for normals. Not uncommonly rationalizations are challenged by the beliefs of the consensus and in such cases they are abandoned by the reasonably well adjusted person. When the need to retain a belief not shared by others is strong, and the rationalization cannot be abandoned, it is defended against assault by further rationalizations. This is an integral part of the process leading toward the development of delusions.

Projection is the ascription of "our own attributes to other persons, groups, objects and symbols" (Cameron & Magaret, 1951, p. 381). Cameron argues that there are two types of projection. One, *assimilative projection*, refers simply to anthropomorphizing, wherein the person assumes that other people, animals, or objects feel the same way as he does about things. Assimilative projection is commonly seen in the young child who imputes his own motives and feelings to his toys, the animals and trees around him, and his peers. When assimilative projection is directed to other people it can enormously simplify relationships with them. Often others *do* feel as we do about situations and, by projecting, one is saved the trouble of investigating thoroughly each attitude and reaction of others. However, if a person is chronically angry with others and attributes the same feeling to them, he will find himself in a self-made environment of hostility. He can check his accuracy about such feelings if he remains in close enough touch with others, but if he lacks the necessary social skills for this validation procedure, defense against his own projections will occur. This, Cameron believed, is what happens when delusions of persecution develop.

The second form of projection described by Cameron is *disowning projection*. Here the individual projects his own repressed feelings, which are not acknowledged as personal attributes. This mechanism affords the advantage of permitting expression of the repressed feeling in retaliation for the projected impulse. Thus, a person can justifiably seek vengeance against an imagined oppressor who is presumably doing his best to harm him. Cameron believed that this mechanism is prominent, along with compensation, rationalization, and assimilative projection, in the emergence of a structure that he called a *pseudocommunity*.

Cameron defined a pseudocommunity as "a behavioral organization, structured in terms of the observed or inferred activities of actual and imagined persons, which makes an individual mistakenly seem to himself a focus, or a significant part, of some concerted action" (Cameron & Magaret, 1951, p. 387). This behavioral organization arises when inferences the indi-

vidual must make about the attitudes and motives of others go uncorrected. Three circumstances predispose the development of a pseudocommunity: (1) chronic anxiety and marked frustration; (2) lower cerebral competence (usually involving a reduction of biological efficiency); and (3) interference with, or failure in development of, the ability to take the role of others.

Cameron believes that a relationship exists between chronic anxiety and the failure to acquire skill in social role-taking. He reasoned that the very anxious, guilty child needed more security than others but that he faced greater obstacles to achieving it, primarily because identification, through which social skills are learned, was limited. Other circumstances also interfere with the learning of skills that foster communication between individuals, such as growing up in a family where suspicion and distrust toward outsiders prevail. Such feelings are acquired directly by children, and the ensuing behaviors place barriers between the child and others that may never be overcome. Being reared in isolation or moving frequently from place to place are other circumstances that make it difficult for one to acquire skill in social role-taking and interfere with the development of a capacity to communicate easily with others.

Cameron stressed that the person who is deficient in role-taking skills, for whatever reason, gets along adequately only to the extent that his environment does not make special demands on him and he is relatively free of anxiety. When his anxiety level is raised or he feels pressure from the environment, the person is prone to developing delusions that can assume the organization seen in the paranoid disorder.

Cameron's definition of delusion is "a conviction based upon misinterpretations, unwarranted inferences, or unjustified conclusions" (Cameron & Magaret, 1951, p.

392). He considers delusions to be pathological when they result in distortions that interfere with interpersonal relationships. Delusions are central to paranoid disorders, which Cameron characterized as "behavior dominated by more or less systematized delusional reactions in which disorganization, sadness and elation, if present, are incidental" (Cameron & Magaret, 1951, p. 405).

Cameron's position stresses an ambiguity inherent in all human interrelationships that forces people to overinterpret and thereby allows for misunderstanding regarding the motives and attitudes of others. Mechanisms such as compensation, rationalization, and projection, while often serving a useful purpose, have within them the potential for further misunderstanding. Once a misunderstanding is established, its tenacity determines whether it is best described as evidence of pseudocommunity or delusion; it is the latter mechanism that typifies paranoid disorders.

In a more recent statement on paranoid disorders Cameron (1959) has pointed out that paranoid symptomatology rarely occurs in the absence of other symptoms such as depression, schizophrenic thinking, and elation. It is therefore difficult, diagnostically, to distinguish paranoid disorders from schizophrenia or manic-depressive psychosis. Many current thinkers, therefore, no longer grant it status as a separate diagnostic entity. On the other hand, in his discussion of etiology Cameron continued to stress the fundamental importance of weakness in social role-taking skill to the development of paranoid symptoms. His review also led to several additional conclusions not stressed in his earlier writing.

The first of these is the view that people who become paranoid have often, as children, experienced extreme sadism which reappears in the paranoid delusion. It is sometimes difficult for therapists working with paranoid patients to distinguish between fantasies and actual experiences of abuse and bad handling. There is however sufficient evidence of overtly cruel treatment in the clinical studies of paranoids for many observers to agree that this is a central etiological factor. In none of his theories does Cameron mention homosexuality as a causal factor in paranoid disorders, and he has written (1959) that there is general disagreement with Freud's position regarding the centrality of homosexual impulses to the development of paranoid disorders.

Sullivan's View of Paranoid Disorders

Sullivan (1956a) has discussed the "paranoid dynamism," a complex of habits designed to defend the individual against anxiety. The special characteristic of this dynamism is that it is designed to protect against the conclusion that one is inferior. The ordinary person's self-system is ill-equipped to protect against the awareness that others fail to respect him. It is designed to afford security with respect to many potential sources of anxiety, but the reactions of others reflecting disrespect for the total personality cannot be coped with and promote a feeling of inferiority. When this feeling is sufficiently pervasive, it injects an element of insecurity into all interpersonal relationships and makes life difficult.

Such a weakness in the self-system elicits efforts to correct the troublesome situation. These efforts take place on the level of "refined cognitive operations" (1956, p. 146), and the full-blown paranoid dynamism appears as a "sudden inspiration." It is welcomed because it offers an hypothesis that relieves the troublesome feeling that one is inferior and transfers blame onto something or someone outside of oneself. It asserts "It is not that I am wrong but that someone is conspiring against me and making me look that way." Thus, for Sullivan, the essence of the paranoid delusion is the *transfer of blame.*

Sullivan drew a distinction between the paranoid-like delusions of the schizophrenic and truly paranoid delusions on this basis. A schizophrenic's delusions involve the identification of an external person or force as the cause of his difficulties in living, but this generally comes about either because of his failure to differentiate boundaries between his own and others' personality or in a desperate attempt to understand what is happening to him. Transfer of blame is usually far from his mind, not because of unwillingness to do so but rather because he has experienced a lifetime of "playing the goat" for others and lacks the sophistication required to turn the tables. He does not understand people and how to deal with them well enough to make them responsible for his failings and unhappiness.

For Sullivan the early emergence of a paranoid dynamism is not sufficient to explain the paranoid psychoses. As he put it, such a dynamism in its early stages is not "bomb-proof" (1956a, p. 147). When others encounter it, it fails to win consensual validation partly because it develops in reaction to early events that occurred when the individual could not really know who properly to blame for his discomfort. Here Sullivan was referring to the empathic period in infancy when the anxiety of significant figures was taken on by the infant. Thus, although the mere intellectual or cognitive process of transferring blame may provide the person with a paranoid slant on life, this is an unstable pattern because the adequacy of such interpretations can be challenged, in any given instance, and their weaknesses easily demonstrated. What is missing in this state is the feeling of absolute certainty that the correct answer has been found. Without this

feeling the person with the beginnings of a paranoid dynamism is vulnerable to anyone who is inquiring and applies his reason to the propositions used to shift blame.

To develop a fully articulated paranoid dynamism Sullivan believes it necessary that the individual do more than merely transfer blame. He must also arrive at an explanation for why others are making life difficult for him. When this happens he has both transferred blame and substantiated its basis through an imagined conspiracy, the evidence for which derives from various misinterpretations. The search for evidence to substantiate the conspiracy is a comforting activity since it promises to help the person to understand the plot that has been woven to induce insecurity and unhappiness in him. Therefore, when situations arise that prompt feelings of insecurity, additional energy is invested in paranoid activity, and the gradual accretion of evidence to support the paranoid ideas is reassuring.

Sullivan took issue with Freud regarding the etiological significance of homosexuality in paranoid disorders. He felt that paranoid disorders arose because of failure in personality development during either the preadolescent or the adolescent stage. For Sullivan the fundamental problem of the preparanoid person is a profound feeling of inadequacy in interpersonal relations that becomes particularly troublesome at a time in life when he feels intense needs for interpersonal closeness. Sullivan believed that there are few sources of anxiety in the developmental stages preceding preadolescence which are so devastating that paranoid symptoms would result. In preadolescence, however, the need for intimacy is sharply felt, and the person is driven to make human contacts. If early experience has handicapped the person in his efforts to acquire the human relationships he needs, he is left with feelings of worthlessness or inferiority that prompt the development of paranoid mechanisms.

The need to cope with sexual impulses follows hard on the heels of the need for intimacy. Feelings of inferiority generated by a failure to develop interpersonal intimacy add to the normal burden of developing an adequate dynamism. This being the case, sexual inadequacies are commonly seen in paranoid disorders. However, Sullivan believed that the latter are antedated by the inferiority deriving from interpersonal failures when such relationships are needed desperately. Although sexual failure is often the last straw provoking the development of a paranoid disorder, it is not the basic cause.

For Sullivan, a disorder in which the fundamental problem is homosexuality is one in which intimacy *was* achieved in preadolescence. In that case, the need for intimacy centered on a person of the same sex, and if lustful stirrings become attached to a same-sexed intimate, homosexual activity follows. Should the individual be unable to move beyond this preadolescent stage, the sexual disorder will remain paramount. To view the paranoid in such terms is, for Sullivan, inaccurate.

Sullivan emphasized the danger of the viewpoint that homosexuality was the basic cause of paranoia because of its detrimental implications for attempts to work therapeutically with the paranoid. The term homosexual is culturally laden with derogatory overtones. A major problem is that the therapist may clearly recognize the paranoid patient's failure to establish intimacy with members of his own sex, but he may also feel that such intimacy is all that the patient is really after in life. This, in effect, is a way of telling the patient that there is a "revolting difference between him and good people" (Sullivan, 1956a, p. 164) which may have no meaning to the patient in terms of

what he has actually experienced. If that is the case, the therapist is cast in the role of a person who sees the patient as inferior and all chance for the development of the necessary therapeutic intimacy is lost.

Cameron, as noted above, pointed out that much current opinion fails to distinguish between paranoid disorders and depression or schizophrenia. To some extent Sullivan's views about the etiology of paranoid disorders support this position. Sullivan believed that all patients manifesting a well-formed paranoid dynamism must have been schizophrenic, if only for a short time, just before the paranoia began to emerge. He held that this had to be true even if study of the patient's history failed to produce substantiating evidence for the idea. He reasoned that a major personality system such as a paranoid dynamism dedicated to affording security could emerge only if the self-dynamism failed to maintain security. When such a failure in the self-dynamism occurred, Sullivan reasoned that the paranoid must have manifested symptoms typifying the early stages of schizophrenia. As the new paranoid dynamism developed, the individual would have become more comfortable and schizophrenic symptoms would have receded, being replaced by those of paranoia.

Finally, Sullivan spoke of the conditions of growth that prompted the later development of a paranoid disorder rather than the symptoms of another psychosis. He believed that certain experiences encouraged the later development of paranoid symptoms while others discouraged them. Thus the ultimate development of a paranoid dynamism in response to insecurity rested, for Sullivan, in having experienced situations that promoted this mechanism and having failed to experience others which undermined its development.

Situations that encourage the use of

blame-shifting include observed instances in the home of the ready transfer of blame and responsibility. Sullivan believed that blame-transfer was well accepted in our culture, but in order for it to have real impact on the growing child he needed to see it in operation at the hands of a significant figure close to him. A second experience that encourages the use of paranoid devices is having success in their application outside the home. Here the empirics of the case are paramount. If a person finds that transferring blame in his everyday functioning fosters greater security than not doing so, this behavior will be supported.

Factors that discourage the use of transference of blame include having in the home a significant figure who pointedly questions the validity of absolving oneself of responsibility by shifting it onto someone else. Sullivan believed that the child was apt to be impressed by the person who raised such objections since this approach was a simple and direct one, involving less complex symbolic operations than those involved in the paranoid delusion. It is simpler, though perhaps more painful, for a person to admit personal responsibility for what happens to him than to go through the complex reasoning required to shift this responsibility. Sullivan believed that "it is biological" (1956a, p. 343) to prefer simple symbolic operations to complex ones.

Another factor that Sullivan identified as discouraging paranoid mechanisms in the growing child was the painful experience of actually using them outside the home and having them fail. This experience prompts caution in the use of blame-shifting devices. One might then apply them only with certain people and situations, where presumably they had a greater chance of being successful. To achieve such discrimination establishes in the personality a critical stance in the use of blame-shifting and pre-

vents such action from becoming a free-wheeling device.

A third factor that interferes with the development of a paranoid propensity is the presence in the family of an older sibling who transfers blame readily. Sullivan believed that an older sibling, especially one who is only a few years older, is a much less complicated personality to observe and understand than is a parent. Consequently, behavior in such a sibling is more open to question and criticism than it is in a parent. An individual exposed to an example of paranoid blame-shifting in such a person would be better able to evaluate it for what it is and to develop a contempt for it, thus rendering the behavior less available as a defense in the future.

Psychotherapeutic Approaches to Paranoid Disorders

The psychotherapeutic approaches proposed by Cameron (1959) and Sullivan (1956a) for treating patients suffering from paranoid disorders differ markedly. This difference is related to the fact that their goals diverge; indeed Sullivan's remarks about therapy seem more directed to paranoid schizophrenia than to paranoid disorders. A description of the approaches of these two theorist-clinicians will portray the variability in current thought about therapy with paranoid disorders.

Cameron and Sullivan agree that paranoid symptoms are instituted in order to deal with anxiety. Cameron believes that to eliminate paranoid thinking and to pave the way for therapist-patient communication that undercuts interpretation based on a pseudocommunity, the first order of business is to lower anxiety. He proposed doing this through a combination of environmental manipulation and the development of a particular type of therapeutic relationship.

The environment is dealt with in order to reduce external sources of anxiety, as for example, separating the patient from family or friends who, for whatever reason, stimulate anxiety in him. Efforts to reduce anxiety may also involve moving from a particular neighborhood or changing jobs. Finally, hospitalization may be needed to bring some measure of tranquility to the patient. Cameron believed that when anxiety subsided, the patient could begin to communicate about what was frightening him, making him angry, or humiliating him. When this occurs, the therapeutic relationship becomes important.

The proper attitude of the therapist, Cameron believed, was that of a relaxed, interested but somewhat detached listener who was not making judgments of the patient. Emphasis was placed on detachment because of the paranoid's fearfulness of overly friendly, intrusive strangers. Suspension of judgment was considered essential since it is difficult, with such patients, to know whether a given statement is fact or fantasy. Cameron argues that the paranoid patient particularly needs someone with whom he can begin to communicate. Thus the therapist should come across as a "safe confidant." This is best achieved by the therapist's being sufficiently comfortable with himself to be able to accept the patient's feelings as they are presented without having to minimize them, argue about them, or be too reassuring. To the extent that the conflicts and fantasies of the paranoid upset the therapist, tension seeps into the therapeutic relationship and raises the patient's anxiety level. This obstructs movement toward the goal of genuine communication, which is a fundamental aim of this type of therapy.

If the patient trusts the therapist and real communication is achieved, he can begin to view the world from another's vantage point. New interpretations of events are then possible ranging beyond the limits of the psychotic fantasy that held sway earlier. It is through this process that a shared, social community can replace what had been a highly personal pseudocommunity.

Finally Cameron believed that the prognosis for successful treatment of paranoid disorders was inevitably guarded. Many such patients become schizophrenic and a few develop a rigid and classic paranoia. He believed that the severity of the psychosis and the length of time during which the delusional system was evolving were related to the probability of successful treatment. Insidious delusional development and deep regression were both thought to be more impervious to change than a sudden emergence of delusions and a relatively mild psychotic state.

In his remarks on treating paranoid patients, Sullivan spoke largely of schizophrenics, presumably patients whom Cameron would regard as having the poorest prognosis in therapy. Perhaps it is for this reason that Sullivan's approach sounds extreme. Though Sullivan acknowledges, as does Cameron, that anxiety is the root symptom of the paranoid, his proposed treatment is virtually the opposite of Cameron's.

Sullivan believed that recovery for a paranoid schizophrenic could only be achieved through the destruction of the paranoid defenses that the patient had erected against anxiety, in other words, the reestablishment of the "unhappy boundless sort of cosmic existence which makes up severe schizophrenic stress" (1956a, p. 350). Rather than attempting to challenge the idea that the patient is perfectly blameless, which is the essence of the paranoid process, Sullivan chose to question the plausibility of the delusions as a means of undermining their usefulness as protectors against anxiety. Success in this therapeutic strategem made the patient vulnerable once more to the feelings underlying the development of the paranoid dynamism, thus providing the therapist an opportunity to help him deal with these feelings more adaptively.

Sullivan was as cautious about the prognosis for the success of such a maneuver as Cameron. He reasoned that the therapist's attack on the patient's delusions precipitated anxiety leading to what he called "the prognostic event." This event involved either the development of the kind of schizophrenic vagueness and upset that he felt must have preceded the paranoid symptoms or an increase in the paranoid symptomatology. If the former occurred, Sullivan believed that there was some limited hope of successful treatment, since the therapist could then deal with a very serious problem in a very handicapped personality. If the latter took place, it was interpreted as evidence of intensification of the paranoid schizophrenic stance and that such a condition was likely to persist.

CONCLUSION

This chapter has considered several psychotic disorders that were recognized early in the history of man's concern with abnormal behavior. Despite the fact that the group of disorders listed under the *major affective disorders* includes a significant proportion of the population of the mentally ill, relatively little research and study have been devoted to them. Perhaps this can be explained on the basis that such patients have generally enjoyed a better prognosis than other diagnostic groups such as schizophrenics. Many affective disorders have a cyclic quality resulting in periodic symptom remissions. Also, recent years have seen the introduction of a treatment procedure, electroconvulsive therapy, which effectively eliminates the acute symptoms of some affective disorders. It may therefore be that these disorders have not attracted the research attention they merit simply because the course of the disorder is not as severe as in many cases of schizophrenia and because superficial symptom change can be achieved relatively simply.

One prominent feature of the patient suffering an affective or involutional disorder but not the paranoid disorder, which is both dramatic and distressing, is the tendency toward suicide. Although successful self-destruction occurs relatively infrequently, considerable interest has been generated in this aspect of affective and involutional disorders in recent years (Farberow & Shneidman, 1961). Research devoted to understanding psychological characteristics of the potential suicide is underway. In addition, "crisis" centers are being established in many metropolitan areas with the goal of offering immediate help to individuals whose despondency has driven them to contemplate suicide.

SUMMARY

1. The affective, involutional and paranoid psychoses have not received the attention of researchers and theorists that schizophrenia has. Nonetheless, they are easily as important in terms of the proportion of the patient population suffering from these disorders.
2. The affective disorders were described relatively early in man's history.

3. Current classifications include various forms of *manic-depressive illness* and *involutional melancholia* as the major affective psychoses.

4. Psychoanalytic theories hold that depression is set off by the loss of an important object. The depressive is not able to reinvest libido onto a new object. Instead he internalizes the lost object, turns libido inward, and then experiences the ambivalence toward himself that characterized his relationship with the loved object.

5. A study of 12-manic-depressives undergoing psychotherapy by Cohen et al. (1954) found the patients: to have come from families in which the mother urged them to strive for prestige; to have had a mother who cared for them dutifully up to the time they began to display independence and who then shifted abruptly to demanding independence; to have been notably talented as children; and to have seemed interpersonally facile as adults without being able to establish deep relationships. Severe depression always seemed prompted by felt loss.

6. The study of Cohen et al. (1954) suffered from a lack of a control group and a bias in the subject sample. A follow-up study by Gibson (1958) confirmed the finding that the families of manic-depressives were more concerned with prestige than were the families of schizophrenics.

7. Other studies have demonstrated that manic-depressives hold more authoritarian attitudes, value achievement more, and adhere more closely to family values than do nonpatients but not more than other patient groups.

8. Findings in studies of hereditary and biochemical factors in manic-depressive psychosis are inconclusive.

9. Studies of endocrine function indicate that increased adrenocortical activity plays a central role in the emotional changes characterizing manic-depressive psychosis.

10. EEG sleep studies seem to indicate that depressives sleep more lightly and for less time than normals.

11. Experience with manic-depressives in psychotherapy indicates that they are very dependent people who use depression to extort affection from the therapist who is viewed as a carbon copy of the parents. Acute depression is best treated by support and reassurance while attempts to instill insight are reserved for the time when depression has passed.

12. While the effectiveness of antidepressant drugs is uncertain, *lithium carbonate* has been successful in creating behavorial improvement in manic patients.

13. Most useful in alleviating the symptoms of acute depression is electroshock therapy (EST).

14. Involutional disorders are associated with the stresses of climacteric and menopause. Some question whether the involutional disorders should be classified separately into *involutional melancholia* and *involutional paranoid state* rather than including them among the affective and paranoid disorders.

15. A combination of psychological and social factors make the involutional period a particularly trying one for women and only somewhat less so for men.
16. Depression and paranoid feelings are common symptoms in the involutional state. At this time of life agitated depression is particularly common.
17. Loss of self-esteem seems to be a particularly crucial feature in the etiology of involutional disorders.
18. Electro-shock therapy (EST) is commonly used to treat the acute symptoms of the involutional disorders.
19. Paranoid states involve relatively circumscribed delusions, either persecutory or grandiose in nature. Thought disorder is not present as in schizophrenia.
20. The psychoanalytic theory of the etiology of paranoid disorders implicates latent homosexual leanings.
21. Cameron feels that people prone to paranoid disorders are particularly inept at assuming the role of another.
22. Sullivan sees the example for a paranoid adjustment to stem from the need to shift onto someone else the responsibility for one's own behavior as well as the example of paranoid parental figures.
23. In his treatment approach for paranoid patients Cameron stresses lowering anxiety. Sullivan, on the other hand, heightens anxiety by challenging paranoid defenses and attempts to promote a schizophrenic adjustment which he feels is more easily treated.

CHAPTER 9

Psychoneurosis

Classification and Treatment

Intro.

The one feature common to all forms of psychoneurosis is the presence of anxiety. In some cases anxiety is the most prominent overt symptom. In other cases it is present in less prominent form, along with other symptomatic behavior. At times it is not overtly present at all. But it is regarded as the constant force behind the development of psychoneurotic symptoms of all types. Some symptoms are successful in diminishing the anxiety to a great extent, or even completely, but at a serious price with respect to overall efficiency and comfort. Therefore, the psychoneurotic generally experiences his illness as an unhappy, burdensome affair and he very much wants to be rid of it.

In comparison to psychotic disorders the psychoneurosis involves a lesser degree of personality disturbance. In the psychoses social functioning is seriously disrupted whereas the psychoneurotic manages to get along fairly well with others despite his symptoms. The psychotic distorts reality considerably because it is unmanageable or unbearable without the distortion. The psychoneurotic maintains good contact with reality and, while he may try to deny troublesome aspects of what is around him, he also tries to conform to environmental demands.

As was seen in the previous chapter, psychoanalytic theory holds that the anxiety with which the psychoneurotic contends is the result of conflict between an unacceptable impulse and a counterforce applied by the ego. In the second half of this chapter alternative conceptions will be presented. Before discussing etiological theories, however, the classification of psychoneurosis will be described.

255

CLASSIFICATION

In DSM-II (1968) eight psychoneurotic subtypes are described. These are: *anxiety neurosis; hysterical neurosis; phobic neurosis; obsessive-compulsive neurosis; depressive neurosis; neurasthenic neurosis; depersonalization neurosis*; and *hypochondriacal neurosis*.

Anxiety Neurosis

This disorder is described in DSM-II (1968) as follows:

> This neurosis is characterized by anxious over-concern extending to panic and frequently associated with somatic symptoms. Unlike Phobic neurosis, anxiety may occur under any circumstances and is not restricted to specific situations or objects. This disorder must be distinguished from normal apprehension or fear, which occurs in realistically dangerous situations (p. 39).

In some respects the anxiety neurosis is the simplest of all the neurotic disorders. Whatever its cause, the anxiety is directly felt in this disorder. None of the defense mechanisms that are prominent in other types of neuroses is utilized to control the anxiety, which is felt diffusely so that the anxiety neurotic exists in a state of constant upset. From a psychoanalytic viewpoint repression is the primary defense mechanism in anxiety neurosis, and its failure results in the presenting symptoms.

Those beset by chronic anxiety are seen by others as tense, timid, apprehensive people who are extremely sensitive to what others think. Many anxiety neurotics also feel inferior and have considerable difficulty making decisions. They set very high standards for themselves and work conscientiously and scrupulously to live up to them.

In most cases only moderate distress is felt so that tension is not intolerable. Those who experience more intense anxiety suffer depression, paralyzing indecision, irritability, a tendency to cry copiously, and strong feelings of inadequacy accompanied at times by paranoid suspicions. In such a state one feels chronically fatigued and, not uncommonly, the fear that one is "losing his mind" is expressed.

In addition to the chronic tension experienced by the anxiety neurotic, such individuals are also subject to acute panic-like states lasting from a few moments to an hour. These are termed *anxiety attacks*. During these exacerbations of anxiety, the heartbeat becomes rapid, there is nausea, diarrhea, and a need to urinate, and breathing is difficult. The pupils of the victim dilate, his face becomes flushed, he perspires freely, he feels dizzy or faint, is tremulous and, often, feels that death is near at hand. Kolb (1968) feels that the anxiety attack is generally caused by hyperventilation, a change in the rhythm of breathing which results in taking in more than the usual amounts of air. The prolongation of such a respiratory disturbance is thought to cause changes in the composition of the blood which in turn alter a number of physiological systems. It is true that many of the symptoms of the anxiety attack are similar to what is seen in hyperventilation: light-headedness, feeling of faintness, profuse perspiration, unsteady gait, and shortness of breath.

Hysterical Neurosis

In DSM-II (1968) this disorder is described as follows:

CASE 9-1: A CASE OF ANXIETY NEUROSIS

Leo R. was the youngest of three children and the only son born to a woman who was a drug addict and whose promiscuous behavior made it impossible to determine who the child's father was. The mother was a childish person, unburdened by any sense of morality, and rather than have her social life restricted, neglected her children. When this was discovered by the welfare authorities, Leo was placed, at the age of eight months, in a foster home. During his childhood he was frequently shifted from one such home to another, spending occasional week ends with his mother, and had very little opportunity to establish any lasting relationships. School provided little in the way of peer companions, both because he shifted so frequently and because he always had to rush home to help with chores. Although he may have been a potentially good student his studies were constantly disrupted, and he finally quit high school in order to find work, which provided a source of income and thus relieved some tension between his foster parents and himself. He received training as a telegraph operator, but was "too nervous" for this work and became a gas station attendant instead.

At nineteen, Leo met his prospective wife and married her after a brief courtship. She was a waitress who was seven years older than he. The couple went to live with her aunt and uncle who had reared her. Her aunt was a domineering woman who ruled the house, and Leo immediately had difficulty with her, bitterly resenting her overbearing attitude. Prior to the birth of their first child less than a year after marriage, this home situation became intolerable, and the two had to move into an apartment of their own. This aunt remained closely involved with them and was highly critical of Leo, who received little support from his wife. She was described as a quiet, withdrawn woman who tended to be secretive, and was quite anxious in company or crowds. This was particularly difficult for Leo, who was an anxious, uncertain person who had little insight into his problems, and a great dependency on his undemonstrative wife.

Leo's symptoms seemed to date from the birth of their first child, just eleven months after his marriage. He began to feel dizzy, and had palpitations of the heart and a throbbing in his head. He originally had a great fear of harming his wife's aunt, but succeeded in talking himself out of this. He worried over transient suicidal ideas, but felt that he would never give in to them. However, they did make him feel irritable and depressed. He joined a Baptist church in an attempt to find some source of support, but his symptoms merely intensified. He became faint and jittery when he had to talk to people, and this kept him from working regularly.

When he was virtually confined to his house by his symptoms he finally was induced by his minister to seek psychiatric help. A psychologist in a large county clinic saw him for almost a year in a series of supportive interviews, during which time Leo's symptoms disappeared.

Leo terminated treatment when he became free of symptoms and continued to be symptom-free until his wife, at her aunt's instigation, began urging him to get a better job. He then began to reexperience a pounding sensation in his head and a tenseness in his neck. He again became fearful when talking to people, especially at work. He began to experience waves of nausea and dizziness and would break out in a cold sweat. He began to fear that he would become insane, and he returned to the clinic to renew his contacts there. He was seen by his old therapist for almost six months of supportive therapy, again achieving some symptomatic relief, but no insight into the genesis of his problems.

Over the years Leo has maintained a continuous pattern of brief sessions of supportive therapy followed by equally brief periods of symptom relief, with recurrences at almost yearly intervals following various family crises. He never achieved any degree of insight, but was able to maintain himself without hospitalization.

From Zax & Stricker, 1963, pp. 140–142.

This neurosis is characterized by a psychogenic loss or disorder of function. Symptoms characteristically begin and end suddenly in emotionally charged situations and are symbolic of the underlying conflicts. Often they can be modified by suggestion alone. This is a new diagnosis that encompasses the former diagnosis "Conversion reaction" and "Dissociative reaction" in DSM-I. This distinction between conversion and dissociative reactions should be preserved by using one of the following diagnoses whenever possible.

Hysterical Neurosis, Conversion Type

In the conversion type, the special senses or voluntary nervous system are affected, causing such symptoms as blindness, deafness, anosmia, anaesthesias, paraesthesias, paralyses, ataxias, akinesias, and dyskinesias. Often the patient shows an inappropriate lack of concern or *belle indifférence* about these symptoms, which may actually provide secondary gains by winning him sympathy or relieving him of unpleasant responsibilities. This type of hysterical neurosis must be distinguished from psychophysiologic disorders, which are mediated by the autonomic nervous system; from malingering, which is done consciously; and from neurological lesions, which cause anatomically circumscribed symptoms.

Hysterical Neurosis, Dissociative Type

In the dissociative type, alterations may occur in the patient's state of consciousness or in his identity to produce such symptoms as amnesia, somnambulism, fugue, and multiple personality (pp. 39–40).

The person subject to a hysterical neurosis as well as the *hysterical personality* (to be described later with other personality disorders) is characterized by a typical mode of expression and way of experiencing feeling (Lorenz, 1955; Shapiro, 1965). The cognition of the hysteric is global and diffuse and this is reflected in a language style that is impressionistic rather than factual. Hysterical communication is full of feeling tone but relatively devoid of facts. Shapiro describes a patient who, when asked to discuss her father, could only respond, "My father? He was wham-bang! That's all—just wham-bang!" (Shapiro, 1965, p. 111).

Subjectively the world of the hysteric is romantic and sentimental rather than objective and factual. Reality is denied in favor of a glossy, Hollywood view of the course and outcome of situations. Memories are devoid of facts, idealized and full of nostalgia. The hysteric responds most readily to whatever arouses strong feeling,

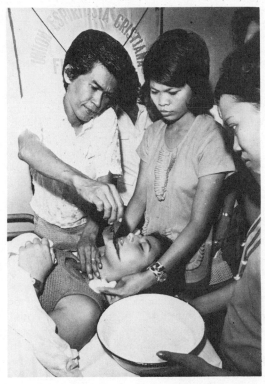

United Press International Photo

People experiencing conversion type of hysterical neurosis are sometimes exploited by "faith healers" who claim painless cures.

seems to be the attitude that nothing he feels or does really has significance. Shapiro likens the hysteric to a child who is playing a game "for fun" rather than "for keeps." Therefore, when predictable adverse consequences follow a piece of behavior, the hysteric is genuinely incredulous. This attitude that the game is just being played "for fun" even makes it possible for the hysteric to be indifferent to his own conversion symptoms (*la belle indifférence*).

In the conversion type of hysterical neurosis, anxiety is not consciously felt but instead is "converted" into a physical symptom in an organ or body part innervated by the sensory-motor nervous system. Besides protecting against anxiety the symptom usually provides some "secondary gain," any benefit that accrues from having a symptom. Conversion symptoms are many and varied in nature, including motor and sensory disturbances and pain in various parts of the body. Many conversion symptoms have been described in previous chapters and will not be elaborated again.

Dissociative symptoms are precipitated by strong negative feelings such as the terror one might feel in war, or extreme shame or guilt. Not infrequently the period of dissociation is preceded by a somewhat confused state characterized by dramatic behavior and verbosity in which speech makes relatively little sense but contains references to intense affective experiences. The commonest dissociative symptom is amnesia. More than simple forgetting of an isolated fact or incident, the amnesia seen in dissociative neurosis involves the blotting out from awareness of a variety of negative experiences and feelings. Most such amnesias are short-lived but they can erase from consciousness significant portions of a person's life, at times the entire life experience preceding the episode. In some cases, it is the present life that is

either positive or negative. He is thus buffeted through life by what is emotionally stimulating without any sensitivity to the less obvious details such as contradictions, weight and measurements, and so on. This insensitivity extends to the hysteric's way of relating to others in a histrionic, play-acting way. He is theatrically emotional with others but in an overdone way which is unconvincing. Yet he has little insight into his own seeming insincerity and simply does not feel it.

Beneath the theatricality of the hysteric, and in spite of his conviction that he is sincere in what he tries to convey to others,

CASE 9–2: A CASE OF HYSTERICAL NEUROSIS, CONVERSION TYPE

Minerva E., a twenty-year-old married woman, was self-referred to a private psychiatrist in a large eastern city. She and her husband had recently been divorced, and she was living alone in their small apartment.

Minerva was the youngest of two children born to a middle-class family. Her father was a former athlete and a very likable person; he seemed to prefer Minerva to his older son. She reciprocated his affection, but disliked her mother, whom she considered an overly sentimental and weak person. Minerva was a tomboy as a child, and was very close to her brother. She was very successful in school, being an above-average student, active on the school paper and in athletics, and was very popular. After high school she decided not to attend college because she felt that she was not a serious student and did not belong there. Instead she obtained employment as a salesgirl in a local store.

Her dating had been confined to one boy throughout high school, but she and this young man drifted apart, and Minerva married a close friend of his whom she had known for quite a while. Her family objected strenuously to this marriage, since they disliked her prospective husband's apparent total lack of ambition. Immediately after the marriage there was a great deal of difficulty because her husband proved to be impotent, and because he could not hold a steady job. He only enjoyed working as a hairdresser, and continually attempted to find such employment, which paid relatively little in that area. A year before Minerva sought help she decided to separate from him and return to her parents' home, but shortly after she left she discovered that she was pregnant, and returned to her husband. Her pregnancy was abruptly terminated a few months later when she fell down some stairs and miscarried. Following this Minerva left her husband and instituted divorce proceedings.

Minerva's symptoms seem to have begun while she was still in high school. Once, while on a hayride with her boyfriend, she felt a tightness in her throat, as though it were closing over and she could not get her breath. Upon interview she referred to this as "globus hysterious." These attacks continued over a period of a few months, seriously handicapping her in school and particularly in social activities. Approximately coincident with medical corrective treatment the symptoms lapsed temporarily. They recurred when she decided to marry her husband and met with considerable family opposition. They returned during the most serious stages of marital discord, abated when Minerva discovered that she was pregnant, and again returned with increased duration and severity after her miscarriage and her divorce. This was what encouraged her to seek treatment.

During the initial interview she spoke intelligently and constructively about her symptoms, but showed little affect in discussing them. She also spoke about her marital problems in this same matter-of-fact, controlled manner. Minerva appeared dressed in a starkly plain, unornamented dress, and had a masculine abruptness in her manner. She seemed most interested in treatment and was accepted for a regime of weekly interviews. At this time Minerva told the psychiatrist that she had not decided whether she was going to stay in that area or move to a large city where she had relatives, and that she would get in touch with him just as soon as she had decided. She never did so, and it is not certain whether she decided to move from the city or lost interest in treatment after enjoying symptomatic relief.

From Zax & Stricker, 1963, pp. 164–165.

---

obliterated and there is a reversion to an earlier period of life with amnesia for all that followed it.

At times the dissociative neurosis takes the form of a *fugue state*, a condition in which one seems to live out cherished but forbidden fantasies. Complicated activities are carried out while in a fugue state, and the individual appears normal to an out-sider. Since behavior manifested in the fugue is in conflict with the conscience or standards of the persons involved, extra protection against being guilty is sought by assuming a false name. These episodes may be of short (less than an hour) or long (several days) duration and are followed by complete amnesia for the period of dissociation.

CASE 9–3: A CASE OF HYSTERICAL NEUROSIS, DISSOCIATIVE TYPE

Marvin K., a thirty-two-year-old father of one child, was born the only child of a woman who was to die in an accident suddenly, while he was still an infant. His father was a minister whose extensive community work kept him very busy, so that he never developed a very close relationship with his son. Marvin was raised by a maiden aunt, who was a kind, quiet person, but who was too old to share much with a young boy. He was closest to another aunt who lived nearby, and to two cousins whom he considered almost as siblings. He was an extremely able student who graduated from a state college with a degree in chemistry. However, he had little interest in entering this field, because while in college his energy was principally devoted to a new interest—dramatics—where he was quite successful. After graduation he ignored his professional training and chose to continue with his dramatics, organizing a small group of touring players that visited small resort hotels during vacation seasons. He ultimately married the lead actress of this troupe, and a stormy matrimony ensued. Their sexual adjustment was very poor, and when Marvin decided to attempt to lead a more responsible life and took a job as a chemist, his wife, disappointed at the lack of excitement in this more staid existence, began to have numerous affairs. Not to be outdone, Marvin also began to be unfaithful, and, after numerous separations, the two were finally divorced. In the meanwhile Marvin had held a succession of well-paying jobs, but had been unable to stay with any of them for any length of time. He continued to date frequently, and became involved in numerous affairs, but never had any serious emotional involvement. He was described as being a temperamental person, given to tantrums when he did not have his way, and prone to making homicidal and suicidal threats. With this, however, he was considered to be a cold and ambitious person who was bent on success at any cost.

About four years before his hospitalization Marvin became very depressed, felt that he was wasting his life, and wanted to settle down. He met his second wife shortly thereafter at a cocktail party, and married her after a ten-day engagement. However, he was preoccupied with his many job commitments and did not pay much attention to her, so she had an affair with a close friend of his. Although this particular incident was resolved, the marriage continued to be beset by quarrels and incompatibility. Finally, two weeks before his hospitalization, his wife left him and returned to her parents' home in a nearby community. Marvin was very upset by this, and a few days later he drove to their house in order to attempt a reconciliation. He and his wife decided to drive to a nearby resort area, where their daughter was staying with some old friends, and vacation there. After a two-day stay they began to quarrel over a trivial matter, and his wife then began drinking and said she would not return with him, although up till then the vacation had been an apparently successful one. He pleaded with her, and then became angry, whereupon he struck her and knocked her down. He began to apologize profusely, but as soon as the friends in whose home they were staying entered the room, he passed out. He came to briefly only to lose consciousness again. After passing out the second time Marvin had an "image" of an automobile accident which happened when they returned from the vacation; his wife and daughter were killed, and he was blinded and deafened.

On the following morning he complained of being amnesic concerning the past three years, deafness to his wife's voice, and obsessive thoughts about the "accident." He was amazed at the size of his daughter, whom he remembered as a one-year-old. The following day, when the amnesia persisted, his friends brought their young son into his room, but Marvin didn't recognize him (he had been born in the past three years). When taken to a restaurant which he had frequented years before, he recognized an old friend in the proprietor and told him that he was confused, and that something had happened to him recently. When amnesia persisted he was brought to the local hospital, where he recovered spontaneously within a week, and then insisted upon leaving without any further treatment.

From Zax & Stricker, 1963, pp. 156–157.

Phobic Neurosis

The phobic neurosis is described thus in DSM-II (1968):

This condition is characterized by intense fear of an object or situation which the patient consciously recognizes as no real danger to him. His apprehension may be experienced as faintness, fatigue, palpitations, perspiration, nausea, tremor, and even panic. Phobias are generally attributed to fears displaced to the phobic object or situation from some other ob-

ject of which the patient is unaware. A wide range of phobias has been described (p. 40).

Kolb (1968) asserts that although phobia is one of the commonest symptoms among individuals suffering emotional disorders, the diagnosis of phobic neurosis is relatively rare. This is because phobias are commonly associated with other neurotic symptoms. The chronically anxious, apprehensive person, for example, frequently suffers from phobias as well.

Characteristically the phobic individual recognizes the groundlessness of his concern about the phobic object but nonetheless cannot control his fear. When the fear-evoking situation is experienced, a typical anxiety attack ensues.

A primary problem in phobia is that the fear may not remain attached to a specific object or situation, but may generalize to other objects or situations bearing some similarity to the one that is feared. Such generalization can make ever-widening aspects of the environment dangerous for the phobic and thereby greatly limit the sphere within which he can function comfortably.

▷ Obsessive-Compulsive Neurosis

DSM-II (1968) describes the obsessive-compulsive neurosis as follows:

This disorder is characterized by the persistent intrusion of unwanted thoughts, urges, or actions that the patient is un-able to stop. The thoughts may consist of single words or ideas, ruminations, or trains of thought often perceived by the patient as nonsensical. The actions vary from simple movements to complex rituals such as repeated handwashing. Anxiety and distress are often present either if the patient is prevented from completing his compulsive ritual or if he is concerned about being unable to control it himself (p. 40).

The thought and language processes of the obsessive-compulsive are particularly noteworthy. Lorenz (1955) sees the obsessive as using language which is "flat and colorless" and as dwelling upon detail. Rather than offering a panoramic impression of a situation as an hysteric might, the obsessive particularizes, describes limits, contrasts. Expressions of feeling are avoided and instead statements like "I suppose," or "I would say" preface remarks as a means of placing distance between the

---

CASE 9–4: A CASE OF PHOBIC NEUROSIS

Irene W., a forty-three-year-old married woman, applied for psychiatric outpatient care in a city on the eastern seaboard. The mother of one young child, she lived in a rural community where her husband operated a feed and grain business. Three years before she had suffered a period of deep depression requiring hospitalization, after having given birth to a long-wanted child.

Irene was the oldest child in a family which included three sons and three daughters. Her childhood was marked by cheerless hard work helping to raise younger siblings; this she accepted without resentment. Because her mother was needed to assist in the management of the small rural grocery owned by her father, many of the household responsibilities fell to Irene. Thus she had the experience of caring for children and managing a home almost before reaching her teens. Irene's mother was described as a neat, efficient person who had a gentle side which permitted considerable emotional closeness. Her father, on the other hand, the son of southern European immigrants, ruled his home autocratically. He was thirty-five when he married, and Irene's mother was only sixteen. In many ways he treated his wife as a daughter throughout their marriage. A quiet person, he displayed no warmth or affection toward anyone and in many ways he was looked upon by his children as a stranger who had to be obeyed instantly and unquestioningly. Rather than expressing resentment at the heavy burdens she shouldered as a youngster, Irene said she was grateful for the experience it gave her and felt that it helped to give her a good relationship with her siblings, to whom she was almost a second mother.

When she was twenty-two Irene married her husband, a man of about her age whom she had known for many years in the small rural community in which both were brought up. From the beginning their marriage was marred by her extreme fear of sexual relations; hence, their adjustment was quite poor. It was only after about ten years of marriage that she would permit intercourse with a frequency greater than about once a month, and she never looked upon it as a source of pleasure. Another source of disappointment for both was their failure to have children for many years. However, when Irene finally gave birth to a son when nearly forty, she required hospitalization for the aforementioned *post partum* depression.

The disorder which brought Irene to a psychiatrist had its onset about two years previously, immediately after she had a hysterectomy. At that time she read a newspaper article about a woman who had developed undulant fever from drinking impure milk. Irene then began worrying that this might happen to her and imagined that the cold chills she was beginning to experience were major symptoms of that disorder. She refused to have milk in her home, and gradually began to fear that other dairy products might contaminate her. Eventually this fear was extended to meat and subsequently to her husband, since his work brought him into contact with farmers who dealt with farm animals.

When she was interviewed she was talkative, but seemed tense and anxious. She was well oriented, coherent, reasoned logically, and displayed good judgment. She seemed depressed, however, and described considerable disability as the result of her symptoms. Tranquilizers were prescribed to diminish her anxiety and arrangements were made for her to come in for weekly interviews.

From Zax & Stricker, 1963, 148–150.

---

speaker and what he says. Further qualifications such as "possibly," "perhaps," "apparently" serve to increase this distance.

Sullivan (1956a) has characterized the obsessive as one who often uses language not so much as a means to communicate but as a defense against anxiety. The obsessive has learned that language can be used in a magical way to protect against the adverse consequences of unacceptable thoughts or behavior. The very young child who finds that punishable acts will be excused if he says "I'm sorry" or " I didn't mean it" begins to learn the magical potential in words. At a more sophisticated stage rationalizations are used to explain away much that could be disquieting, and language is used to obscure rather than reveal feelings.

Shapiro (1965) points out that the obsessive's tendency to focus intensely on certain details is a good illustration of how a great deal of reality is obscured by his thinking and speaking style. By this obsessive concentration his attention is drastically limited and many aspects of experience, often the essence of a situation, which require broader perspective are simply not recognized. Thus, the obsessive rarely has a hunch or is surprised by anything. On the other hand, the overconcern with detail which causes the obsessive to seem rigid and unaware of general meaning can be an asset in a context requiring great concentration and attention to technical detail.

Obsessive-compulsive behavior takes a number of forms, many of which reflect the thinking style just described. Cameron (1963) has identified several varieties of the obsessive-compulsive disorder. In the first type anxiety is controlled by displacing the problem from one situation onto another. An example of this is the young mother beset by an impulse to injure her first child, a daughter, and was found actually to be struggling with her anger toward and envy of a younger sister who had produced two sons. The obsessive-compulsive may also resort—as did this patient— to isolation, in which the intellectual and affective components of an impulse are split, with the former being expressed while the latter is repressed. Thus, this patient could experience the thought of injuring her child without the emotion that might have caused her to carry out the act.

Another type of obsessive-compulsive pattern involves the use of countermeasures to ward off vexing impulses. The patient will, for example, keep his mind busy developing an elaborate philosophy or conceiving of a complicated invention in order to avoid disquieting erotic fantasies. In this case threatening thoughts have been warded off simply by occupying the mind with other content, which may be entirely trivial.

Another pattern involves thought or behavior which the analysts would regard as exemplifying *reaction-formation* and *undoing*. In such cases the obsessive thought or compulsive act has considerable significance. In reaction-formation one thinks or does the opposite of what the unacceptable impulse would urge. Undoing involves saying or doing something to "make right" some wrong for which we have been responsible. A patient described by Cameron (1963) manifested both mechanisms. As a child she was outspoken in her hatred for a newborn brother but shifted with time to being very protective and demonstratively loving of him (reaction-formation). Later in life she became guilty and resentful, as well as frustrated, when sensually aroused by her fiancé. This feeling led occasionally to a violent temperamental outburst followed by a compulsion to cleanse herself by changing her clothes and scrubbing her hands and forearms (undoing). A classic literary example of undoing is the compulsive handwashing of Lady Macbeth aimed at cleansing herself after an evil act. A basic problem underlying the mechanism of undoing is frequently ambivalence, wanting and not wanting at the same time to do something.

Another symptom pattern seen in the obsessive-compulsive is also related to ambivalence. In this case the opposing forces are so nearly equal that no action can be taken and the symptoms seen are indecision, doubt, and rumination. An example of this is the college student who went into a phone booth to call an attractive girl he had just met. Because of his anxiety and indecision he spent an hour without being able either to put the coin in the slot or to give up and leave. Some ruminative patients turn from an indecisive struggle over specifics to irrelevant speculation about highly abstract matters— *What meaning is there in life? Is there a God? What is justice?*

Depressive Neurosis

The description of depressive neurosis in DSM-II (1968) is as follows:

CASE 9–5: A CASE OF OBSESSIVE-COMPULSIVE NEUROSIS

Helene L., a fifteen-year-old high-school student, was brought by her parents to a private psychiatrist at the insistence of a school psychologist, because she had been in constant difficulty in school, and was a marked under-achiever. The family was living in a middle-class neighborhood of a medium-sized city in the Pacific northwest.

Helene was the oldest of two children born to a moderately religious Mormon family. Her parents were cold, rejecting people who never did much more than tend to Helene's physical needs, and certainly were never able to provide her with any understanding, or even with much attention. Her mother had many compulsive symptoms similar to Helene's, but this only seemed to alienate her further from the child. Helene had always been difficult to handle, and her eccentricities both accentuated her parents' rejection and made it difficult for her to get along with classmates. While still at preschool age, when she first learned to count, she felt compelled to count as high as she could, which often reached astronomical numbers. When she entered school this fascination with numbers continued, and she sometimes refused to use words, but would speak in a numerical code. The other students immediately recognized her as odd, and responded by ostracizing and tormenting her. Her only apparent interests were art and chess, and she was quite adept at both. Her artistic products, in a variety of media, won her the only semblance of recognition she ever obtained. Her interest in chess led her to a deep involvement with the history of the game and its great players of the past. However, she shied away from playing the game very much because she feared competitiveness. Since both of these accomplishments were isolated activities, they did not aid her in relating to other students, but only drew her further from them. Considerably more orthodox than her family, she attended church frequently, and seemed to delight in Mormon ritual.

As Helene grew, she increased her repertory of compulsive symptoms. One of the earliest to develop was a feeling that she must count the number of steps she was taking whenever she walked anywhere. Later she began to feel the need to look over her shoulder as she was walking, although she could not express what it was that she was looking for or at. She also began to wash her hands repeatedly, interrupting whatever she was doing to cleanse herself. She felt the necessity to look repetitiously at objects or parts of her body, such as her elbow, at as often as five-minute intervals, although here too she could not express any reason for doing so. She also began repeating various innocuous phrases, such as, "That is a nice home," over and over again. While she could offer no plausible reason for any of these activities, failure to perform them always led to great anxiety, which was relieved only by performance of the compulsive act.

Although Helene appeared to be a bright child she never did very well in school, either academically or socially. Perhaps one reason for her academic deficiency was her preoccupation with ritualistic concerns, which prevented her giving full attention to her work. For example, in the classroom, she might have been struck by the thought that she fully understood a point that was made. Rather than trust her judgment, she sought confirmation by setting a variety of proofs for herself so that she might reason, "If I really do understand, the next thing the teacher says will contain less than five words," or, "If she writes something on the blackboard in the next minute, then I surely am right." She would set up a sequence of these wearisome "proofs," and if her original idea was not "confirmed," or if she attempted not to persist at setting tasks, she became very anxious.

The psychiatrist who saw her agreed that Helene was in great need of psychotherapeutic help, and accepted her to treatment. To date she is still being seen in an intensive treatment program, but there has been a good deal of difficulty in establishing a meaningful relationship.

From Zax & Stricker, 1963, pp. 172–173.

(Depressive)

This disorder is manifested by an excessive reaction of depression due to an internal conflict or to an identifiable event such as the loss of a love object or cherished possession. It is to be distinguished from Involutional melancholia (q.v.) and Manic-depressive illness (q.v.). Reactive depressions or Depressive reactions are to be classified here (p. 40).

The symptoms of the depressive neurosis commonly include a feeling of sadness and anxiety as well as guilt and shame. Hypochondriacal complaints aimed at winning support and affection are also seen. Many neurotic depressives also complain of weakness and fatigue, difficulty in working, and troubled sleep. They are self-pitying and self-deprecating, minimizing their past accomplishments and despairing of the future. Still they continue to work and fail to display the anorexia, constipation, weight loss, and psychomotor retardation usually found in the psychotic depressive.

Onset of the neurotic depression usually follows a distressing event such as the death of a loved one or a financial reverse. For the depressive mourning is prolonged and pathological grief is displayed. Occasionally neurotic depression appears after an important accomplishment. In such cases the new-found success is thought to expose one to more responsibility than he

can be comfortable with or to an overpowering fear that others will be envious and angry over his success.

F. Neurasthenic Neurosis

In DSM-II (1968) neurasthenic neurosis is described thus:

> This condition is characterized by complaints of chronic weakness, easy fatigability, and sometimes exhaustion. Unlike hysterical neurosis the patient's complaints are genuinely distressing to him and there is no evidence of secondary gain. It differs from Anxiety neurosis and from the Psychophysiologic disorders in the nature of the predominant complaint. It differs from Depressive neurosis in the moderateness of the depression and in the chronicity of its course. (In DSM-I this condition was called "Psychophysiologic nervous system reaction.") (pp. 40–41)

While chronic weakness, general fatigue, and a feeling of "nervousness" predominate in neurasthenia, many additional symptoms are also found. There is considerable concern over body functioning, and inordinate sensitivity to noise, bright light, or extremes of cold. Some patients manifest vasomotor instability resulting in flushing and sweating or chills. In the latter case patients

CASE 9–6: A CASE OF DEPRESSIVE NEUROSIS

Hannah M. a fifty-year-old mother of two children, consulted a psychiatrist in private practice seeking help for feelings of depression which she could not overcome. A divorcée, she was living with her son and his wife in their comfortable home in the suburbs of a large eastern city.

In discussing her background, Hannah tended to emphasize her general unhappiness, rather than to focus on relations with specific individuals. She was the youngest of seven children born to parents advanced in years, and was six years younger than the sibling closest to her in age. She always felt keenly that she was not wanted either by her parents or her siblings—especially her three sisters, who were expected to play a major role in caring for her as when she was a young child. Instead of being given a bedroom with the others in the family, Hannah was relegated to a cot in her father's small study in the rear of the house. Eventually she was given the room abandoned by a brother who married, but when an older sister decided that she preferred Hannah's new room to her own, Hannah was forced to trade, thus giving up what had been a symbol of her acceptance by the family. This incident seemed to Hannah to typify the lightness with which her feelings were regarded by her parents and siblings. She recalled also that her clothes were always the castoffs of her older sisters and that she was frequently told that she was ugly and stupid by members of the family.

Hannah completed high school and just a few years later, after a year in secretarial school and two years in office work, married a man she didn't know very well in an effort to establish a home of her own. Her husband proved to be an improvident person who couldn't hold a job for any length of time, and who soon began to be unfaithful. Hannah had two sons in rapid succession, and the combination of the responsibility of caring for them, the austere life she had to lead, and her husband's infidelity, caused her to become very anxious and angry and to withdraw from interaction with friends and family. When this condition failed to clear up in a short time, her family doctor insisted that she take a vacation away from her family. She therefore went on a three-month visit to her favorite aunt who lived in a distant city. While away, Hannah's children were left in the care of a sister and, during this time, her youngest, a two-year-old boy, sustained a head injury when struck by an automobile—an accident which Hannah felt resulted in his later severe mental retardation. When she returned home, Hannah's husband left her and filed for a divorce, which she did not contest. She then went to work as a secretary to support her family and managed to provide enough to permit her oldest son to have a good education. Eventually her son became successful in the insurance business and, after he married, he insisted that his mother and younger brother, who needed much care, come and live with him and his wife.

Hannah's current complaint had its onset about a year after her retarded child died. He suffered a lingering illness and was cared for devotedly by Hannah to the last. She was overcome by fear and depression when he died and felt guilty for having to leave him years before when she was away for a rest. Hannah also began worrying that she was too much of a burden on others and went out of her way to avoid being an imposition or an expense to her older son. Her obsessive fear that she might harm someone made it impossible for Hannah to work and she slept poorly. Just before coming to the psychiatrist she began to think about committing suicide.

In an interview Hannah appeared to be in acute distress. She cried and wrung her hands. A constant theme she expressed involved her not wanting to cause concern or to be a burden on her children. She was accepted for treatment and was seen in a series of sixteen supportive interviews. During this time she developed some insight into her problems and her depression subsided. Hannah was then able to plan more realistically and shortly afterward was able to return to work.

From Zax & Stricker, 1963, pp. 178–180.

---

bundle themselves up in warm clothing and are in constant fear of catching cold. Males may suffer impaired potency and women often suffer dysmenorrhea.

The sleep of the neurasthenic is disturbed by dreams and frequent awakening so that he feels exhausted in the morning, with this feeling gradually dissipating during the day. There are complaints of poor memory which are probably related more to preoccupation with feelings of bodily weakness and minor physical complaints than to any primary memory defect. The general shyness, awkwardness, low self-confidence, and indecisiveness of the neurasthenic suggest chronic moderate depression. Kolb (1968) asserts that many neurasthenics have been reared in families in which somatic complaints have won considerable attention that was not granted for more socially constructive behavior. This view of neurasthenia contrasts with older conceptions of this disorder as a state of physical exhaustion resulting from the strain of controlling inhibited impulses. Freud classed neurasthenia as one of the "actual neuroses" and saw it as a state in which the nervous system was drained of energy by the struggle to contain the sexual instincts.

CASE 9–7: A CASE OF NEURASTHENIC NEUROSIS

A gifted and ambitious engineer complained of continuous fatigue and pressure in the head. He excelled in his work, but felt seriously handicapped because he became easily exhausted. At times he needed eleven hours of sleep, but he slept badly. He complained of frequency of urination, frequent constipation, and impaired potency. His complaints started during puberty, with intense guilt reactions to sexual impulses and masturbation, for which he was brutally punished and threatened.

The patient's father was strict and at times brutal, particularly in his sexual discipline. He was frequently away from home when the patient was a child, and during such periods the mother was very close to him; however, she always had the father discipline the lad on his return. The boy was disappointed in both parents; he felt betrayed, particularly by his mother, and he feared severe corporal punishment from his father. The patient was completely relieved during three years of psychoanalytic treatment, during which the etiology and dynamic meanings of his symptoms were made clear to him.

From p. 445 from *Principles of Abnormal Psychology: The Dynamics of Psychic Illness,* revised edition by A. H. Maslow and Bela Mittelmann. Copyright 1951 by Harper & Row, Publishers, Inc. Reprinted by permission of the publisher.

G. Depersonalization Neurosis

The depersonalization neurosis is described as follows in DSM-II (1968):

> This syndrome is dominated by a feeling of unreality and of estrangement from the self, body, or surroundings. This diagnosis should not be used if the condition *maybe* is part of some other mental disorder, such as an acute situational reaction. A brief experience of depersonalization is not necessarily a symptom of illness (p. 41).

Kolb (1968) has identified two types of unreality symptoms in depersonalization: a feeling that one's own personality has changed; and a feeling that the world around one has become unreal. Often the patient feels that he is in some transitional stage in which he is no longer the person he was but not yet someone different. As a result the emotions that were formerly felt are absent and experience seems disquietingly strange and unreal. Sometimes patients feel as though they are living in a dream or a prolonged trance.

Symptoms of depersonalization may be found in a variety of disorders, particularly the early stages of schizophrenia. Apparently it represents a form of withdrawal from a troubled life situation, which may have either a sudden or a gradual onset depending upon the type of emotional stress that is experienced.

H. Hypochondriacal Neurosis

DSM-II (1968) describes the hypochondriacal neurosis as follows:

> This condition is dominated by preoccupation with the body and with fear of presumed diseases of various organs. Though the fears are not of delusional quality as in psychotic depressions, they persist despite reassurance. The condition differs from hysterical neurosis in that there are no actual losses or distortions of function (p. 41).

The physical complaints of the hypochondriacal neurotic are many and varied. He is exquisitely aware of sensations that normals would ignore, magnifies normal sensations of fatigue, and frequently suspects that he suffers some incurable disease.

II. NONANALYTIC THEORETICAL VIEWS

Freud's work, directly or indirectly, prompted many people to think about the general problem of how psychological forces affect normal development and ab-

Brad Hess Photo

CASE 9–8: A CASE OF HYPOCHONDRIACAL NEUROSIS

A college student complained of extensive gastric disturbances, indigestion, "weak" stomach, belching, aches, and many other symptoms. Questioning showed that he had made a full-time job of studying his eating, his digestion, and his eliminative processes. For instance, he had menus made up for a month in advance in which everything was weighed to the ounce. He always cooked his own meals, because he would not entrust this important task to his mother.

He spent several hours each day using muscle exercisers, breathing according to a special system, and reading medical books.

The problem that brought him to the psychologist was his relation to his fiancée. Questioning revealed that she loved him intensely but had angered him by disparaging his symptoms. He apparently did not love her at all, but intended to marry her because "everybody gets married." He had broken off with her without any feeling of loss, even with relief. He now wanted to know if marriage was necessary to health.

It took some time to convince him that he needed psychological treatment, and this was possible only after a very detailed examination by a medical specialist showed negative results. He never really made contact with the therapist, and no results were being obtained by interviews; therefore he was sent to another therapist, with whom he got along a bit better. However, when he was instructed to give up his pills and laxatives, he never returned.

From Maslow & Mittelmann, 1951, pp. 444.

---

normal behavior. Few such people have developed their ideas by working as exclusively with neurotic problems as did Freud, but many have worked primarily with out-patients, including psychoneurotics. So many workers have by now contributed ideas about the causes and treatment of neuroses that space constraints rule out an exhaustive review. Therefore, only the viewpoints of two prominent workers, Carl Rogers and Joseph Wolpe, will be presented in detail. The thinking of each of these men is as different from that of Freud as it is from each other. Each has had major impact on general thought about neurotic disorders. In addition, two other approaches associated with the efforts of many different workers, the "sociopsychological" and the "humanistic," will also be described.

Carl Rogers: The "Client-Centered" Approach

Like Freud, Rogers developed a personality theory primarily based on clinical experience with patients. Also like Freud, Rogers's theory has grown and changed over the years of his therapeutic practice. In Rogers's case, change has also been promoted as he and his students engaged in research on the process and outcome of psychotherapy. Fortunately for textbook writers, Rogers has made a fairly recent summary statement of his theories (Rogers, 1959); thus the account that follows can be considered as reasonably current.

Rogers is an American psychologist who took his Ph.D. at Columbia in the early 1930s and promptly became involved in clinical work at a child guidance clinic in

Rochester, New York. During this period he was exposed to the thinking of Otto Rank (formerly Freud's personal secretary), who had broken away from orthodox psychoanalytic theory, come to the United States, and had developed a theory and therapeutic approach of his own. From Rank's approach Rogers drew the kernel of several basic ideas that became influential in his own theorizing. This base was elaborated on and shaped by his later experiences in counseling and psychotherapy with college students and through research on psychotherapy with his students during the 1940s and most of the 1950s. During this latter period he was on the faculties of Ohio State University and the University of Chicago. In 1957 he joined the faculty of the University of Wisconsin Medical School, thus gaining access to psychotic patients and providing a base for extending this theorizing.

Rogers has been dedicated to achieving an "inward ordering of significant experience." For him research involves bringing order to what one experiences subjectively. As a therapist he was not content to accumulate experiences that remain little more than a conglomeration of disconnected events. He has made research a basic part of his work and has attracted a number of students whose studies have contributed to the development and evaluation of theories. He views his most recent theoretical statements as the best approximations of the "truth" at which one can arrive, given current knowledge, and warns against a dogmatic "freezing" of the theory that would make it incapable of assimilating new evidence and experience as it accumulates.

In the following summary of his theory, attention will first be focused on his fundamental assumptions about people and how they may best be understood. Next his theory of personality will be taken up,

followed by a presentation of his theory of how pathology arises. Finally his views of how pathology is best treated will be considered. Rogers feels that his theory of therapy and his statements about the nature of the human organism are the best substantiated parts of his work since they are based most closely on his direct observations. Since his ideas about personality development are derived inferentially from his work with patients, he regards them as more likely to contain errors. One more point should be made before discussing the theory itself. Like many theorists Rogers uses some terms in a special way and even invents some others. In the following discussion, terms that have somewhat unique meaning in his theory will be italicized and defined in parentheses the first time they are used.

1. Some Basic Rogerian Themes

Rogers's viewpoint is phenomenological: he insists that people are to be understood only in terms of how they see themselves consciously and how *they* interpret their *experience* ("all that is going on within the envelope of the organism at any given moment which is potentially available to awareness"). Some of these events may not actually be part of awareness at a given moment (such as the feeling of hunger when one is distracted by some activity), but they are potentially available to awareness. Situational events are, therefore, important only insofar as they impinge on the individual. Hence, the internal *perception* ("a hypothesis or prognosis for action which comes into being in awareness when stimuli impinge on the organism") of an event, rather than its objective or external properties, is what is important in guiding behavior. The more aware one is of what he is doing and experiencing in a given situation, the better position he is in to respond in ways that will bring desired results, and this maximal awareness is psychological health.

b. A second cornerstone of Rogers's thinking is his conception of what motivates man. Here he speaks of an *actualizing tendency* ("the inherent tendency of the organism to develop all its capacities in ways which serve to maintain or enhance the organism"). This is regarded as the master motive in life for all people; rather than being "pushed" along as the result of various kinds of experiences of early life, as Freud's theory suggests, Rogers sees man as being "pulled" along. He is drawn by the need to grow and develop his capabilities, to become a more effective organism and to move toward autonomy, a state wherein his own internal forces guide him, and away from heteronomy, in which external forces control him.

Associated with this emphasis on actualization is the conviction that man's nature is innately good and that if he succeeds in following his normal developmental course, he will become a friendly, well-socialized human being. It is the interference with this natural process that causes the individual to learn negative, self-centered, and ineffective behaviors.

c. Finally, Rogers asserts that effective therapy involves promoting conditions that free the patient to become more aware of his experience and to choose the course of behavior that is most compatible with his own actualizing needs. In this sense, the therapist does not change the patient. The patient changes himself once he is given the opportunity to do so.

2. Rogers's Theory of Personality Development

The infant comes into the world with a capacity for awareness. The only reality he knows is the one he experiences. He has an inherent need to actualize and his interactions with the world of reality are solely in terms of this need. Thus, those experiences perceived to enhance the actualizing tendency are valued, and those that inhibit it are rejected. Emphasis is placed on the fact that the infant responds (as do individuals of all ages) to his interpretation of reality, not to its objective properties. He may perceive the attentions of a well-meaning, friendly adult to be upsetting and frightening. Continuing experience with such a person may alter the initial perception but what influences behavior at any given time is reality as it is perceived.

As growth takes place there is a tendency toward differentiation within the personality, which is part of the actualizing tendency. One aspect of differentiation is becoming aware of one's own being and functioning. This is termed *self-experience* ("any event or entity in the phenomenal field discriminated by the individual which is also discriminated as 'self,' 'me,' 'I,' or related thereto"). This self-experience becomes increasingly differentiated through interaction with significant people in one's surroundings and results in a *concept of self* ("the organized, consistent conceptual gestalt composed of perceptions of the characteristics of the 'I' or 'me' and the perceptions of the relationships of the 'I' or 'me' to others and to various aspects of life"). This concept is *available* to awareness at any time (though not always immediately present) and it undergoes constant change in keeping with the nature of new experiences that accrue.

As the self-concept develops there develops also a *need for positive regard* (simply a need to be loved). The satisfaction of this need depends in good measure on the inferences a person makes about other people's reactions to him. There is an important element of reciprocity to this need in that one often experiences positive

© J. Brian King 1975

Development of positive self-regard often depends on the actions of other people.

regard after having satisfied the need for positive regard in another. According to Rogers this need is so potent that the individual may find it more important to be regarded positively at a given moment than to engage in experiences that are useful for *actualizing*.

Gradually, the pattern of satisfactions and frustrations one experiences in seeking to fulfill the need for positive regard results in the development of *self-regard* (an attitude which one holds about his own self). Thus, a person learns to feel positive or negative self-regard even in the absence of association with others and, in a sense, becomes his own reinforcer, or "significant social other."

There are experiences that are judged by others to be worthy either of positive or of negative regard. This is an important determinant of how the self selects and avoids experiences that enhance or diminish positive self-regard. When such selection occurs the individual is described as having acquired a *condition of worth* (in which the positive regard of others is conditional). If one always experienced

unconditional positive regard (circumstances whereby "no self-experience can be discriminated as more or less worthy of positive regard than any other"), conditions of worth would not develop at all and there would never be conflict between actualizing needs and needs for positive regard. This would represent perfect psychological adjustment, an ideal which, though hypothetically possible, is never actually achieved.

Because the individual strives to maintain positive self-regard, he is selective about his experiences, consistent with the particular conditions of worth that he perceives. Thus, experiences corresponding to one's established conditions of worth are perceived accurately and admitted to awareness. Contrary ones are either perceived in a selective or *distorted* fashion to bring them in line with the conditions of worth or they are *denied* to awareness. Distortion or denial comes about when an experience is first dimly perceived (*subceived*) as a potential threat to the concept of self because it is not congruent with it. Distortion and denial are the two defensive processes available to the organism against this threat. In distortion the true significance or meaning of the experience is altered in order to make it congruent with the self-concept. In denial there is a failure to acknowledge the existence of the experience itself. In using denial a person may respond in this way to a statement: "I can hear the words you say, and I know I should understand them, but I just can't make them convey any meaning to me." In distortion a person whose self-concept is that he is a poor student may, for example, react to a good grade by feeling that it was a stroke of good fortune or that the professor is not too bright himself.

These defensive processes limit the individual's range of experience. He fails to recognize some experiences that have relevance for him; others may be assimilated but only in a distorted form. This incongruence between the self and experience is the foundation of psychological maladjustment and vulnerability (that is, incongruence between self and experience that leaves one open to anxiety and disorganization since new experiences which clearly demonstrate the discrepancy always threaten to force their way into consciousness).

Inconsistencies between the self-concept and experience promote behavioral incongruencies. Some behavior is accurately presented in awareness because it is consonant with the self-concept, while other behavior goes unrecognized or it is distorted because it fails to conform. The subception of experiences that are incongruent with the self-structure is reacted to as threatening both because, if they were admitted to awareness, the self-concept would lose consistency and the conditions of worth would be violated. The presence of incongruencies, however, prompts *anxiety* ("a state of uneasiness or tension whose cause is unknown") and calls forth selective perception, or distortion, and/or denial of experience. The result is *intensionality* (tending "to see experience in absolute and unconditional terms, to overgeneralize, to be dominated by concept or belief, to fail to anchor his reactions in space and time, to confuse fact and evaluation, to rely upon abstractions rather than upon reality-testing").

The processes described up to this point characterize most people as they grow. They happen to a greater or lesser degree in different people and at different times but they basically typify normal development. Under certain specifiable conditions, however, actual personality breakdown and disorganization may arise.

3. Rogers's Theory of Psychopathology

When a basic condition of incongruence between the self-concept and experience exists and new experiences that underline this incongruence occur obviously or suddenly, ordinary defensive processes may fail. The individual will then experience anxiety in amounts commensurate with the initial subception of incongruence and with the extent to which the self-structure is threatened. As defenses fail, incongruent experiences impinge on awareness and the gestalt of the self-structure, heretofore protected, is broken, resulting in disorganization. In the disorganized state, the individual's behavior may vacillate between conformity to realities hitherto defended against and conformity to the self-concept.

Rogers sees acutely psychotic behavior as often being more consistent with the formerly denied or distorted aspects of experience than with the established self. Thus, a sexually overcontrolled person may, in the psychotic state, become openly expressive sexually. Once such behavior has been displayed, the organism tries to reestablish defenses and, Rogers suggests, the new experiences may be regnant and

DIAGRAM OF ROGERS' THEORY OF PSYCHOPATHOLOGY

the old self rejected. In other cases parts of the old self are retained but its patterning is altered to accommodate the new experiences. Part of the self-concept may include the notion that one is "crazy," "unreliable," or has impulses that one is too weak to control.

If reintegration is to take place, a process must be instituted to reduce the incongruity between the self-concept and experience. This requires special conditions, presumably comparable to those Rogers regards as necessary for an optimal therapeutic atmosphere.

4. Some Perspectives on Rogerian Theory

While acknowledging the importance to behavior of many psychological forces (as did Freud), Rogers bases his approach on different behavioral phenomena than Freud had done. He has had little interest in the host of instincts that so impressed Freud or in ways in which one learns to adapt to their demands, the demands of the real world, and those of the internalized superego. Instead he sees man as drawn through life in pursuit of one overriding goal, actualization. This has led to a more optimistic theory than Freud's, one which emphasizes what man can become rather than the animal nature from which he has sprung. One cannot help but feel that Rogers has, indeed, pointed out a specific aspect of behavior that Freud neglected. At the same time, however, Rogers generalizes no less about the significance of *this* aspect of behavior than Freud had about the significance of the instincts.

It is tempting, as we have done for Freud, to speculate about the relation between the form of Rogers's theory and the clinical experience from which it grew. It is difficult to pinpoint all problems Rogers dealt with in his early child-guidance work, since such settings are characterized by a great breadth of clinical problems. On the other hand, college students in a university clinic are often preoccupied with problems pertaining to future goals, fears about taking one's place successfully in society, desires to select one's own goals independently of the preference of parents, and so on. In other words, such individuals are as likely to dwell on their needs to actualize as the hysterical female in nineteenth-century Vienna was to talk about her sexual problems. To seize, therefore, on actualization as the universally essential motive may be to overgeneralize.

It also seems excessive to do so from the viewpoint of the behavior that Rogers himself has observed—and which determined the form of the theory. Despite his feeling that man's primary motive in life is to actualize, Rogers speaks of another life force—the need for positive regard—to account for the development of pathology. While actualization leads to expression of individuality and autonomy, the need for positive regard is related to the need for others, for being part of a group. As Rogers treats these two needs actualization is the more important. It is this one that always seeks and finds expression if not impeded and that is referred to at times as the *only* motive in life. On the other hand, the need for positive regard is also a potent force since not uncommonly, it is able to subvert the actualizing tendency. In fact, since true actualization is an ideal that is never entirely achieved, it must be diverted to some extent by the need for positive regard in even the healthiest personalities. Furthermore, one of the necessary conditions for successful psychotherapy is the unconditional gratification of the need for positive regard.

This suggests that the need for positive

regard (even as Rogers describes it) may, at times, assume a status equal to that of the actualizing need in a given individual, and that elevation of one of these motives over the other is unjustified. In other words, happiness for some may inhere primarily in the feeling of being loved by their fellows rather than in the feeling that their unique individuality is finding optimal expression. That actualization is the highest good toward which all men naturally strive is an article of Roger's faith which may not always be consonant with the facts. If one concedes that the need for positive regard may be as strong as the need to actualize, as Rogers's formulations could suggest to the student lacking his faith, then psychotherapy is more complicated than as currently seen by the client-centered practitioner. Diagnosis may be more necessary than Rogerians indicate, and intensive study of the patient's early experiences would be in order. One could certainly argue that before-the-fact efforts to understand what needs are prepotent for a particular individual might minimize the danger of focusing on actualization when the patient may simply need to be "loved."

Finally, Rogers has (quite laudably) emphasized research and has attempted to modify the development of his theory in the light of his own research findings and those of his students. This emphasis has produced a number of interesting studies of therapeutic process and outcome (for example, Rogers, 1959; Rogers & Dymond, 1954). Unfortunately many of these studies rely either on the patients' evaluations or the ratings of a therapist who is sympathetic to Rogers's approach. As Zax and Klein (1960) have pointed out, patients' evaluations of their treatment are likely to depend greatly upon who asks for them and the circumstances under which they are solicited. It is thus difficult to place great faith in such evaluations when no extratherapeutic criteria exist to corroborate them. These authors also indicate that in much client-centered therapy research therapist ratings are doubtless based on the very therapeutic processes whose validity is being tested. To find significant relationships between such "outcome" ratings and the processes hypothesized by the theory is less a test of validity than it is of reliability.

To summarize, Rogers has made important contributions to our understanding of behavior pathology by emphasizing a key force that undoubtedly plays an important part in shaping the behavior of many people. Ineed, it is similar to a force noted by several psychoanalytic theorists as early as the 1930s—Hartmann and Erikson, for example—and more will be heard of it when character disorders and ego psychology are discussed. Rogers has also offered an example of how research can be incorporated into a therapeutic program to the mutual betterment of the research and the therapy. Each of these is a significant contribution to man's thinking about behavior disorder.

B. Wolpe's Reciprocal Inhibition Theory

Joseph Wolpe, a South African psychiatrist, has developed a theory of neurotic behavior and a system of psychotherapy for such disorders (Wolpe, 1958) that is quite different, both in its form and in the soil from which it grew, from those of Freud and Rogers. In developing this theory, Wolpe was most stimulated by his study of Pavlov's conditioning process, Clark Hull's theories deriving from studies of the learning process in animals, and by many studies of the establishment of experimental "neuroses" in animals through conditioning procedures. Thus he did not follow Freud's and Rogers's course of basing theory on material elicited in clinical practice. Instead, Wolpe's theoretical views derive from laboratory studies of the learning process and have been adapted for use in the clinical setting.

Wolpe is specifically interested in treating neurotic symptoms. With others (Dollard & Miller, 1950; Shoben, 1949) he regards such problems as arising from the learning process and, therefore, as treatable through established principles for altering learned responses. Psychoses are thought by Wolpe to be organically based and hence receive little attention from him.

Unlike Freud and Rogers, Wolpe does not offer either a theory of normal behavior or one of development. His interest is entirely in the neurotic symptom that the patient brings to him. This symptom is seen as having been learned in a particular way in a specific situation and is treated by creating circumstances appropriate for its extinction. Wolpe does not believe in an unconscious reservoir of impulses to which such symptoms are tied, and argues that probing for the deep roots of neurotic symptoms is entirely fruitless. Indeed such roots simply do not exist for him. Instead he emphasizes an ongoing process of conditioning in which noxious stimuli come to be associated with previously neutral ones, resulting in an upsetting "neurotic" response to the originally innocuous stimulus.

Understanding Wolpe's theory depends on some knowledge of several elementary principles of conditioning and learning. In Pavlov's typical paradigm a neutral stimulus, the sound of a bell, was paired with a response-producing one, the introduction of meat powder in the mouth of the dog. The meat powder alone induced salivation. Eventually the contiguous association of bell and meat powder made it unnecessary for the latter to be used to elicit salivation. The bell alone produced this response. Moreover, the salivation response, once well-established, could be eliminated through repeated presentation of the bell without following it with meat powder. This latter process is known as extinction.

Wolpe believes that extinction, a term he uses synonymously with *unlearning*, occurs for two reasons. First, there is an accumulation of fatigue related to sheer repetition of a response whether it is reinforced or not (Wolpe essentially equates reinforcement with drive reduction, although he acknowledges that it can also result from response arousal). Fatigue, which has a temporarily inhibiting effect on response, is the basis of *reactive inhibition*, one of two elements accounting for extinction. The condition of fatigue, implying as it does organismic disequilibrium, assumes the status of a drive that is reduced when the activity which produced it ceases. Thus, cessation of the response is contiguous with the reduction of this drive and is associated with internal or external stimuli that are present when the response occurs. Such stimuli will, therefore, be *conditioned to an inhibition* of the response to which they may have been joined previously, the second element accounting for

Diagram of Extinction Process

Conditioned Response ⟶ 1. Fatigue or Reactive Inhibition ⟶ Extinction
without Reinforcement   2. Conditioned Inhibition
                 because of Fatigue

extinction. Thus, dissipation of reactive inhibition after a rest interval will not lead to a recurrence of the extinguished response in its full strength because some of the internal stimuli, formerly associated with making the response, are now tied to its inhibition.

Reciprocal inhibition is treated by Wolpe as a special form of conditioned inhibition. Conditioned inhibition arises in the usual extinction procedure because conditioned stimuli that elicit a given response are related to reactive inhibition. Therefore, if inhibition were to occur for some reason other than fatigue, conditioned inhibition could also be expected to occur. Reciprocal inhibition, then, involves the inhibiting effect of a response that is antagonistic to the conditioned response. Thus extinction of response A occurs when response B, which is incompatible with A, is evoked in association with the stimuli that ordinarily produce response A. For example, if a particular stimulus evokes anxiety and one can elicit a response that is incompatible with anxiety in the presence of that stimulus, the tie between the anxiety response and the original stimulus will automatically be weakened.

Although Wolpe deals with other concepts such as need and drive (considered by him to be innate mechanisms), his view of neurosis and his method for dealing with it can be comprehended merely by using the few principles of learning and extinction already described plus his concept of anxiety, which he feels plays a central role in the development of neurosis. Wolpe views anxiety as an autonomic reaction that ordinarily makes up part of one's response to noxious stimuli. A stimulus is noxious if it provokes avoidance responses and causes "tissue disturbances." Also, anxiety responses are associated with sympathetic nervous system discharges, an important point for Wolpe's theory. Other types of emotional responses are relatively unimportant for the theory unless they are potentially antagonistic to or incompatible with anxiety, in which case they become useful in extinction.

For learning to occur, a stimulus must arise that elicits a response that is promptly followed by the reduction of some neural excitation. It is unnecessary for the response to be actually instrumental in causing this reduction. Learning of the response occurs as long as it is associated with reduction of excitation (which is equated to a drive). There are many factors that relate to *how much* learning takes place. For example, as the time intervals within the cycles of stimulus, response, and drive-reduction increase, learning is weakened. Another important factor is the number of times this sequence of associations occurs. Thus, if the cycle occurs several times, learning will be stronger than if it occurs only once. The time intervals between occurrence of repeated sequences is another factor; more learning results when the sequences have an intervening time interval as opposed to following closely on each other. In general, the foregoing have all been, or can be, worked out in laboratory studies of learning.

Diagram of Reciprocal Inhibition Process

Stimulus for Response A ⟶ Response B which Is Incompatible with Response A ⟶ Reciprocal Inhibition

For Wolpe a relevant stimulus may either be an internal state or an external event so long as it is capable of arousing excitation in the central nervous system that can be reduced by a response. Learning is considered to have taken place if a stimulus elicits a response that it did not previously arouse or if it results in a stronger response than before. A habit is defined merely as a "recurring manner of response to a given stimulus situation."

Wolpe's View of Neurotic Behavior

Wolpe feels that neuroses are simple learned behaviors involving the response of anxiety, that is, essentially "conditioned anxiety reactions." They originate in specific learning situations, and he disagrees with Freud's contention that they can necessarily be traced back to core conflicts which give unity to the entire personality. Some people are more predisposed than others to the development of neuroses because they are subject to more intense anxiety. Such differences in capacity for feeling anxious are related either to constitutional factors or to early learning. Some individuals grow up under circumstances that often arouse anxiety and are laden with many inappropriate anxiety responses. For these reasons they are more susceptible to neurotic disorder. Factors such as fatigue, drugs, and hormones also increase the possibility of intense anxiety responses. Anxiety responses persist because the stimuli that elicit them are rarely paired with nonanxiety responses; hence there is little opportunity for extinction. In addition to this general statement about the development of neurotic symptoms, Wolpe discusses how specific neuroses might develop.

Pervasive Anxiety

Wolpe regards the patient who experiences pervasive ("free-floating") anxiety, as in the "anxiety neurosis," as having a conditioned anxiety response to some omnipresent or regularly recurrent, subtle aspect of the environment. Light, contrasts in shading, shadowy figures, and amorphous noise exemplify such stimuli. Anxiety in these cases is not really "free-floating." Instead, it is tied to a definite stimulus just as any other anxiety response, the difference being that, in this case, the stimulus is both more pervasive than usual and more difficult to identify. Wolpe asserts that careful questioning of patients with this symptom often reveals that some aspects of the environment are more closely related to anxiety than are others.

Two possible factors determine whether a patient's neurosis will include pervasive anxiety. One is the intensity of the anxiety level at the time the neurosis is induced. Wolpe believes that under more intense anxiety, the totality of stimuli in the immediate environment is more likely to take on some degree of anxiety conditioning. This hypothesis is supported by the fact that patients with pervasive anxiety react more intensely than others to specific stimuli. The second explanation for the development of pervasive anxiety is the presence, during the brief period when the neurosis is induced, of only indistinct stimuli. An example provided by Wolpe is the patient whose neurosis originated while he was having sexual intercourse, in a darkened room, with a woman toward whom he felt revulsion and sexual attraction. The experience produced much anxiety related not only to sexual objects but also to dark heavy objects.

Hysterical Reactions

Wolpe regards hysterical reactions as neurotic disorders that are expressed through sensory or motor systems or through functional units concerned with imagery or consciousness, rather than through the autonomic nervous system. Occasionally, both the autonomic and another system may be involved, with distinct symptoms related to both. Wolpe believes that hysteria involves conditioning, in situations of great stress, of sensory, motor, or other physical symptoms rather than of an anxiety response, although both may occur simultaneously. Since this differs from more common instances of neurosis in which an anxiety response is conditioned, Wolpe attempts to explain how such specific learning takes place.

Two possible explanations are advanced. The first is that such nonautonomic reactions are conditioned in anyone when they occur in association with anxiety. The other is that the nonautonomic reactions are unique to individuals with special factors that predispose them to learn non-anxiety responses. Wolpe believes the second explanation to be more probable in that circumstances giving rise to neurosis generally implicate all response systems; thus were the first explanation accurate, hysterical disorders would be more prevalent than they are. Furthermore, the hysteroid personality has long been thought to have distinct personality features—for example, to be extroverted in character. In comparison to introverts, he is thought to be more subjective than objective in outlook, more given to action than to cerebral behavior, and more likely to lack than to have self-control. Extroverts have also been shown to learn efficiently and to generate reactive inhibition more readily than do introverts.

Wolpe also believes that extroverts respond with lower levels of anxiety than introverts in anxiety-arousing situations and that they condition more readily to responses other than anxiety when exposed to stimuli that arouse such responses. He points out that the apparent lack of anxiety in hysterics has long been noted in the description of their classic state of *la belle indifférence*. Also his own pencil-and-paper tests of anxiety indicate that significantly more hysterics than patients in other categories have low scores, indicating lower anxiety levels.

Obsessional Behavior

In the obsessional neuroses complex patterns of behavior, involving well-defined and often complicated patterns of thought or overt behavior, are thought to become conditioned in addition to the anxiety responses. These thought patterns, which may involve insistent impulses that are rarely acted on, or elaborate behavior sequences, are experienced by the patient as intrusive. For Wolpe, their strength and frequency are directly related to the patient's anxiety level. But not just any source of anxiety is relevant here. Obsessional behavior arises only when anxiety is in response to the specific stimuli to which it has become associated through learning.

Wolpe distinguishes two different types of obsessional behavior, one that elevates anxiety and one that reduces it. Anxiety-elevating obsessions are thought to have been learned at the same time the anxiety response was learned. That is, a given stimulus was followed in combination by both the obsessional behavior and the anxiety. Thus, the later appearance of obses-

Lady Macbeth, trying to wash out the blood spot, is a classic case of obsessional behavior.

sional behavior is regularly accompanied by anxiety. Wolpe cites the example of a soldier who felt he was being unjustly arrested. In a helpless rage, he struggled with his captors and was taken by force. Later he struck a policeman who tried to compel him to do some work. The implication of this act disturbed him even more. This sequence doubtless involved many thoughts of striking out at his captors, along with anxiety over his precarious situation. Later in life when he experienced a similar feeling of injustice and the impulse to strike out, he felt intense anxiety along with it.

Obsessional behavior that diminishes anxiety is rapidly learned precisely because it has such an effect. Such behavior is essentially a reaction to anxiety that involves any of a variety of behaviors such as keeping things neat, clean, and orderly, rituals such as avoiding cracks in pavement, or special types of ideation. In the histories of these types of obsessionals Wolpe reasons that anxiety-arousing situations have been alleviated consistently by a particular type of behavior. When similar anxiety subsequently arises, the same behavior will be engaged in to bring the desired relief. The response is maintained as long as it serves to reduce anxiety and this course is favored when there are no other responses available to compete with it in relieving distress.

Amnesia and "Repression"

Wolpe distinguishes two classes of amnesias in the neuroses, according to the significance of the material that fails to register on the patient's mind. The first such instance involves people who are chronically anxious and who may therefore fail to notice trivial occurrences because they are so distracted by their feelings that little attention remains available for the minor stimuli which are present.

The second class of amnesia involves the forgetting of material with great emotional impact—the process Freud felt was at the core of all neurotic disorder. Wolpe believes that such forgetting is quite rare, far more so than Freud implied, and that when it does occur it is simply a response which is learned because it successfully relieves anxiety. Furthermore, he does not believe that the act of forgetting itself plays a part in maintaining the neurosis. In fact, he asserts that recovery is possible without the patient's ever recalling what was forgotten. All that is necessary is that the anxiety response that prompted the amnesia be unlearned.

Secondary Neurotic Responses

There are many active steps that a neurotic may take to relieve anxiety. Wolpe classifies these as secondary neurotic responses. What is overt in such responses is the avoidance behavior. Often, the fact that the behavior is motivated by a need to relieve anxiety is not clearly recognized.

One very direct way of avoiding anxiety-producing stimuli is to keep away from them physically, as in phobias. Mere physical removal from the anxiety-arousing circumstances prevents the occurrence of distress. This is an unlikely tactic when anxiety is too pervasive. Also, there are often social circumstances that prevent its use.

Another way of avoiding anxiety-arousing stimuli is by distracting oneself so that they are not noticed. This is a psychological avoidance rather than a physical avoidance and it may be achieved by concentrating on stimuli that do not elicit anxiety responses. People, for example, may "lose themselves" in their work, in social activities, in athletics, and so on.

Finally, Wolpe believes that some people seek to alleviate anxiety by taking drugs such as alcohol and narcotics. The popularity of tranquilizers is attributed to the fact that taking such drugs is a learned response that combats neurosis. If physiological addictions do not develop, the drug-taking response can be eliminated by dealing directly with the anxiety response and eliminating it.

2. Determinants of Change in Neurotic Symptomatology

Variations in neurotic symptomatology are thought to occur as the result of any one of three conditions: (1) there may be an increase or decrease in the range of anxiety-arousing stimuli; (2) there may be an increase or decrease in the strength of the response to a stimulus; and (3) the anxiety response may change as it gains or loses components or as the "relative strength is altered."

The range of anxiety-provoking stimuli may become enlarged since every new exposure includes new stimuli that are potentially capable of becoming associated with the anxiety responses. Such an enlargement can take place readily when the new stimulus has some feature in common with the original one. For example, a woman who was intensely frightened by an anesthetic mask because she felt that she was suffocating as the anesthetic was being administered, later became anxious in an over-crowded elevator in which she felt hot and stuffy, and still later in situations that were *psychologically* rather than physically confining. New anxiety stimuli are also acquired simply through the contiguous association of any new stimulus that happens to be present when the anxiety stimulus occurs.

Anxiety responses may increase in strength through their contiguous association with stimuli that provoke even stronger anxiety. They may also increase through frequent repetition of the sequence of anxiety stimulus followed by anxiety response.

Wolpe explains the seemingly spontaneous decrease in strength of anxiety responses on the grounds that they can also potentially elicit antagonistic responses in the presence of the anxiety stimulus. Therefore, when anxiety responses are weak to begin with, favorable circumstances for their extinction can arise in the normal course of life. For example, a mildly claustrophobic man may have his anxiety extinguished through sitting in a crowded theater enjoying a film. The pleasure experienced from the film is incompatible with the anxiety so that the latter response fails to occur even though he is confined in the theater. Similarly, anxiety related to a sexual situation may be overcome by the strong positive feelings associated with an attractive member of the opposite sex. Esthetic experiences may, in a similar way, alleviate anxiety.

Finally the nature of the anxiety response may undergo change. This occurs because in repeated experiences with anxiety stimuli, other stimuli are inevitably also present to which one reacts. Therefore, these new reactions become associated with the original anxiety stimulus and become themselves capable of provoking an anxiety response. As an example of this, Wolpe cites the case of a young woman, fearful in social situations, who originally responded to a cluster of social stimuli with anxiety and blushing. Subsequently, whenever she blushed she also became anxious.

3. Perspectives on Wolpe's Approach

Wolpe's approach to neuroses is appealing in that it is based on well-established laboratory principles and involves procedures that seem to be clearly specified and systematically applied. This contrasts with much of the vagueness that surrounds other therapeutic techniques. The latter often provide only the most general principles as guidelines, often resulting in highly individual approaches to therapy by different practitioners. Also, with Wolpe's emphasis on symptom-changes, evaluation is an easier task than it is in many other approaches. Assessment of adjustment from a Freudian viewpoint or of self-actualization from a Rogerian viewpoint is much more difficult than is the judgment that a specific symptom has been alleviated. Another asset of Wolpe's approach is that it requires far less treatment time than other psychotherapeutic approaches.

With respect to evaluation, the basic test of any therapeutic approach, no matter how good it looks on paper, is its effectiveness in achieving its goals. Wolpe recognizes this and has done his own evaluation of therapeutic change in the patients he has treated. He reports that in 210 cases 90 percent have been found to be apparently cured or much improved. In order to rule out the possibility that improvement in his patients is only temporary (a criticism that psychoanalysts, who feel his approach is far too superficial, have made), he followed up 45 cases which were in his *cured* or *much improved* groups, from two to seven years after treatment. Only one of these failed to maintain the original improvement. These findings are impressive, indeed, in light of surveys (Eysenck, 1952) reporting that more traditional approaches, such as psychoanalysis, have only a 45–66 percent success rate. This figure, incidentally, is no better than the percentage of neurotics who improve with only medical care or the passage of time alone.

Further support for Wolpe's claims has been provided by Lang and Lazovik (Lang, 1964; Lang & Lazovik, 1963). They used *systematic desensitization*, one of Wolpe's favored treatment techniques (see Chapter 13), to treat snake phobias in college students. Their experimental subjects showed significantly more behavior change (measured by closeness of approach to a live snake) and feeling change (less fear) than did untreated subjects with similar snake phobias. Further, Lang and Lazovik demonstrated that no other symptoms were substituted for the snake phobias. Indeed, some evidence suggested a drop in substitute symptoms. It is a distinct asset that Wolpe's approach both lends itself to such objective behavioral evaluation and that its component elements can be investigated systematically. Technique changes can thus be based on empirical findings.

Paul (1966) has done a study comparing the effects of insight therapy, desensitization, and two control conditions in treatment of a fear of speaking in public. He found that all of the patients treated with desensitization improved according to objective criteria, whereas fewer than half of those treated with insight therapy showed such improvement. In the insight group the percentage showing improvement was the same as that found in a control group which received some attention and the direct suggestion that a placebo they were given would bring about symptom relief. Follow-up after two years (Paul, 1967) also found greatest improvement in the systematic desensitization group, followed by the insight and attention-suggestion groups.

Perhaps the major shortcoming of Wolpe's early reported work was its limited applicability. He focused on the circumscribed phobic-like problem. Psychosis was dismissed as a constitutional problem and therefore beyond the scope of psychotherapy. Recent observers (Klein et al., 1969) report that Wolpe's techniques are now being applied to a range of patients that goes "well beyond simple phobias or social anxieties." Patients suffering a broad range of neurotic and characterological problems as well as borderline psychotics

are now being treated with behavior therapy.

Interestingly the subjective report of Klein et al. indicates that as Wolpe and his colleagues engage the more complex behavioral problems, many of the unique strengths of behavior therapy are dissipated. Diagnosis becomes increasingly difficult; subjective choices must be made in distinguishing between primary and secondary symptoms. A broader spectrum of Wolpe's therapeutic techniques is applied in the complex case than in the simple one. As such, much of the specificity of the approach, which was seen as an asset, is lost. A good deal of clinical judgment becomes essential to the use of the technique. This lessens the difference between behavior therapy and other therapeutic approaches.

Other characteristics of behavior therapy applied to complex behavioral problems diminish its uniqueness. For example, in behavior therapy the therapist must monitor the progress of the patient carefully in order to know how to proceed. Judgments of the patient's improvement are based on the patient's own evaluations. In many cases, such evaluations may be biased to please, to frustrate, or to manipulate the therapist. A process such as transference (as conceptualized by the psychoanalysts) may therefore begin to play a crucial role in behavior therapy. The therapist's judgments of how to proceed must depend upon his clinical judgment of the patient's progress, a factor which again reduces the distinction between behavior therapy and other approaches.

The advantages that seemed to inhere in behavior therapy with respect to the evaluation of treatment outcome disappear when complex behavioral problems are treated. When a single phobic symptom is being treated, evaluation of improvement is a relatively simple matter even though it hinges on the patient's report. The change that is expected is a fairly objective one and it relates to a circumscribed class of behaviors. When many symptoms are present, one may be convinced that some show change and still be uncertain whether overall improvement has taken place. Thus the outcome problem in such cases becomes as complicated for the behavior therapist as for the Rogerian or the Freudian.

Finally, there are objections to Wolpe's technique because it is neither directed toward man's "higher aspirations" nor does it regard him as a totality. Indeed his position that psychological problems arise in independent response systems runs counter to the traditional view that man functions as an organized whole. This break with a long-standing way of regarding man's behavior is difficult for many to accept. It will gain general acceptance only after considerable additional research to verify Wolpe's viewpoint.

C. The Sociopsychological Approach

In Chapter 6 we described Skinner's view that behavior is learned through reinforcement. In that chapter the application of this approach to understanding schizophrenic behavior was taken up. Ullmann and Krasner (1974) have made similar applications to neurotic behavior. Basic to their formulations is the idea that all forms of neurotic behavior are maintained because they are reinforced. The sociopsychological approach does explain particular neurotic subtypes on slightly different bases.

1. Hysteria and Dissociative Reactions

The basic problem in hysteria is the existence of motor or sensory dysfunction in the absence of an underlying physiological disorder. Ullmann and Krasner feel that the hysteric is behaving in a way that conforms to his concept of a person who suffers a disease affecting his motor or sensory abilities. This way of looking at hysterical behavior raises two questions. First, can people engage in such behavior, and if so, under what conditions are they likely to do so?

To answer the first question Ullmann and Krasner refer to placebo studies demonstrating that subjects will display behavior similar to that of a stooge after taking a placebo without either consciously faking or being unconsciously motivated to conform. Clinical observations of placebo effects are also used to support the idea that many people can and do play expected roles. For example, many patients given a placebo after a surgical operation report that their pain has been relieved and are neither seen to be faking or to be unconsciously motivated. Instead, Ullmann and Krasner see them as being under strong social pressure to produce a certain kind of response and drawing on their past experience of having had relief from pain after receiving medication. To indicate to his doctor that his pain has not been relieved would raise a question about the physician's skill and would thereby be personally threatening. Under such conditions a large percentage of patients having pain after an operation respond favorably to placebos. Admittedly, not all do so, just as not all display hysterical behavior. For Ullmann and Krasner, therefore, the answer to the first question is yes. Some people can indeed behave in ways which match up with their conception of how it is to lose motor or sensory ability.

In response to the question about the conditions under which hysterical behavior is likely to occur, Ullmann and Krasner point out that some "hysterical" behaviors are quite common. For example, the person concentrating intensely on his work or on his studying can "tune out" surrounding noises. In addition, however, in order to assume a role like that played by a hysteric one must "know the lines." That is, most hysterics have either had physical problems like those they are manifesting or have seen such problems in others. Finally, there must be a payoff for behaving hysterically. That is, this particular type of "sick" behavior must be reinforced by the people around the hysteric.

Once hysterical behavior arises, it is not easy to shift from this role back to the prior role. This is because playing the new role has some benefits such as the opportunity to avoid unpleasant situations. Also, the behavior must be maintained because to change it might suggest that the whole business was a "put-on." It is for this reason that placebos may be particularly effective with hysterics. They provide an "out" by avoiding many of the negative consequences of renouncing "sick" behavior.

The sociopsychological theory of dissociative behavior is similar to that of hysteria. A close analogy is drawn between hypnotic behavior and dissociative behavior. Hypnosis is explained as a case of role playing on the part of the subject in keeping with the hypnotist's suggestions. The only alternative to such an explanation of dissociation is to imply that some sort of complex physiological problem exists resulting in such a massive brain disruption that the subject cannot remember his name but is still able to behave in very socially complicated ways. Obviously such a paradox cannot be explained on a physiological basis.

Ullmann and Krasner point out that because attention span is limited, people habitually limit the number of cues to which they respond. Thus, to some extent anyone who is normal is dissociated. Typical behavior involves attending to certain cues and ignoring others. What is appropriate behavior in a classroom is quite different from what is appropriate at a dance, a football game, or on the job. Each situation calls for different clothing, attention to different cues, and the emission of different behaviors. In the dissociative state Ullmann and Krasner feel that certain stimuli lose their meaning and are simply ignored, just as we are oblivious to the number of steps in a staircase that we travel over frequently, while other stimuli which are ordinarily ignored take on new meaning. The reason for the shift is that attention to the new cues brings positive reinforcement.

J. Phobic Behavior

The avoidance behavior of the phobia is seen by Ullmann and Krasner as having at least two possible sources. In the simplest case the person simply avoids a situation in which he cannot perform adequately. If for some reason he cannot respond appropriately to a given situation, it will be very unpleasant to be in and he will avoid it. A second source of phobias involves a classical conditioning situation in which a stimulus to which an individual was able to respond normally becomes associated with a very upsetting stimulus. For example, in one classic case a young child who responded normally to small furry animals became tense and screamed whenever such animals were present after the presence of a rat was paired a number of times with a sudden, loud noise. The child apparently saw the upsetting noise as an element of the animal.

Ullmann and Krasner point out further that while a person's behavior has an effect on himself, it also has an effect on others.

Phobias, therefore, will become well-established as others respond to them with acceptance and sympathy. Reinforcement consolidates phobic behavior just as it does hysterical behavior.

3 . Obsessive-Compulsive Behavior

Ullmann and Krasner assert that repetitious and sometimes nonfunctional behavior occurs which is not regarded as obsessive-compulsive. This is because such behavior, for example, a student's dwelling on studying for an upcoming exam, is considered to be appropriate. When repetitious behavior or thoughts are inappropriate, they are regarded as obsessive-compulsive symptoms. From the sociopsychological point of view obsessions and compulsions may be understood in much the same way as phobias. Both disorders involve learned responses to reinforcing situations. The reinforcement for obsessive-compulsive behavior is often simply the fact that by engaging in it a person avoids other kinds of behavior that might be noxious.

Some compulsions are simply viewed as superstitious behavior. In these cases the compulsion has been associated contiguously with some desired consequence, so it is repeated. In fact, not repeating it leads to discomfort. The unreasonably high standards sometimes found among obsessive-compulsives are seen to be useful excuses to avoid certain activities. The man whose standards with respect to women are very high may on that account be able to avoid dating. Thus, in the case of both phobia and obsessive-compulsiveness avoidance is the prime purpose. For the phobic the avoidant behavior is more directly related to the threatening object. In the obsessive-compulsive the threat is slightly less obvious and the behavior serves the purpose of achieving avoidance

without clarifying just what you are threatened by.

4 . Depressive Reaction

Depressive behavior is characterized by underactivity and the feeling that little seems worthwhile or interesting. Ullmann and Krasner see this behavior as caused by the fact that reinforcements are no longer being received for the person's typical behavior. He must, therefore, learn new behaviors that will be reinforcing. This takes time. Some trial and error is necessary along with the unlearning of responses that were appropriate earlier but are not so any longer. In addition, it is culturally appropriate to be depressed under certain circumstances. Thus, role playing plays a part in symptom formation. Finally, Ullmann and Krasner emphasize that the depressed person receives sympathy, attention, and affection from others because of his symptoms and these reinforcements help to maintain the disorder.

5 . Anxiety Reaction

The anxiety reaction is a disorder in which anxiety is diffusely present. It does not seem to be tied to specific situations or objects as in a phobia. From the sociopsychologist's viewpoint such a conception is impossible. He sees the anxiety reaction simply as a complex phobic reaction, one in which the person is phobic about many widely pervasive stimuli. In addition, as in all other disorders, the fearful responses which typify the anxiety reaction are reinforced by the behaviors of those who sympathize with the suffering individual.

6 . Perspectives on the Sociopsychological Approach

The sociopsychological approach has many of the same assets and liabilities as Wolpe's approach. Laboratory-based learning principles are fundamental to the theory and its applications. Problems are conceptualized operationally so that they lend themselves readily to specific therapeutic tactics. By focusing on symptom change the assessment of treatment effectiveness is greatly simplified. And research on the approach is relatively easy to do.

The difficulty with the sociopsychological approach is that patients do not commonly present complaints that are tied up in the neat, discrete packages that are best handled by the approach. Most often a mixture of vaguely stated symptoms are present. To apply the sociopsychological approach, choices must be made about which symptoms to focus on and when to work on them. This takes something away from the clean-cut objectivity of the approach.

Another aspect of sociopsychology that distresses many is that it ignores man's inner being and deals only with behavior. Some find this to be degrading in its "depersonalization" of the human.

On balance, despite the disadvantages cited, the sociopsychological approach seems to offer many valuable ideas for understanding behavior problems and some very useful techniques for solving them. The complexities of human problems may dim the promise that sociopsychology can turn the treatment arts into a precise science. Nonetheless, it is an approach that well merits application under the right circumstances and further effort to develop ways of defining problems that make applications feasible.

The Humanistic Approach to Neuroses

The humanistic movement is partly a reaction to behavioristic approaches and partly a protest against what many regard as the impersonality of modern society. The humanists lay particular stress on each man's uniqueness and on his inner qualities. They are especially concerned about feelings, love, self-fulfillment, and creative potential.

Many different theorists are associated with the humanistic approach. Not surprisingly, then, many different emphases are found. Still, the humanists as a group tend to agree that a certain limited number of factors are very important. Carl Rogers's client-centered approach which has already been described in this chapter is in many ways a good representative of humanistic theory. Some of Rogers's general themes characterize all of humanistic psychology. For example, Rogers's emphasis on self-actualization has its counterpart in many different humanistic theories. His belief that man's innate nature is good and that his goodness is diverted by the demands of a stifling society is another common theme. Finally, most humanists see man's problems, psychoneurotic and otherwise, as being rooted in a storing up of emotion which has not been allowed an outlet. This storehouse of unexpressed feeling is thought to lead to a variety of adverse behavioral consequences. Most humanistic therapies, therefore, encourage the release of unexpressed affect.

Few humanists devote much effort to describing personality development or even the emergence of pathology. Instead, most seem to stress therapy. Still, a few exceptions may be found who try to explain pathology along with the methods for treating it. These include Wilhelm Reich, Fritz Perls, and Arthur Janov. Reich trained as an orthodox psychoanalyst and made many contributions to the development of psychoanalytic technique (see Chapter 12). Late in his career he developed a theory and a treatment approach which is very much in keeping with modern humanists (Reich, 1949, 1960). Through his experience in psychoanalysis Reich became more impressed with the *way* in which his patients said and did things than he was with *what* they expressed. He came to feel first that anxiety is controlled by a "character armor," a psychological force that protected the individual from exposure to painful emotions.

Eventually Reich began to feel that an actual physical armoring seemed to build up to hold in check feelings that might make one uncomfortable. For example, he felt that a person could control emotion not only by avoiding talking about certain things but also through his voice tone and posture. Reich came to feel that the muscles could become constantly rigid or tense, at first to hold off anxiety and ultimately to control emotions in general. Thus, psychological forces prompt the development of physical armoring. Neurotic as well as other types of symptoms are, therefore, used to avoid expression of feelings.

Perls (1969), the founder of Gestalt therapy, is considered one of the leaders of the modern humanistic movement. He emphasizes phenomenology and the notion of "organismic self-regulation." From this viewpoint, once a need or feeling has been satisfied it disappears. This process is likened to the completion of a "gestalt" or arriving at a sense of closure. The discharge produced by yawning and sighing are examples of organismic self-regulation. Blockage of this process results in anxiety. To relieve anxiety, then, emotional discharge must take place. The most common deterrent to the regular discharge of emotions is socially required self-control. The need for self-control results in repression and a devitalization of the personality, and, in the extreme case, it produces neurosis.

The idea that socially or culturally induced demands for self-control lead to a repression of emotion and then to pathological consequences such as neuroses is repeated in the thinking of many other humanists. Lowen (1958) sees the etiology of neuroses as lying in trauma and deprivation leading to repressed emotions. Jackins (1965) feels that socialization interferes with the discharge of negative feelings associated with distressing events. Thus, a great deal of rational energy must be invested in maintaining control over undischarged feelings, so that ultimately the individual begins to deal nonrationally with many situations.

Janov (1970) also argues that the blocking of painful emotions leads to psychopathology. For Janov the frustration of the very young child's needs for basic necessities such as affection and stimulation leads to "primal pain." Repression allows a temporary escape from awareness of these needs and a variety of tension-reducing techniques (smoking, drinking, drug use, escapism) are adopted. These are in effect symptoms of neurosis. Such symptoms fail to bring real satisfaction but they must be retained until the repressed affect finds expression.

Perspectives on Humanistic Approaches

The humanistic approaches highlight a side of human life that has obvious significance. One cannot question the importance to the quality of life of human values, feelings, self-actualization, and creativity. In fact, such factors have played an important role in other theories about human behavior and treatment that are not classed as humanistic. Certainly the basic importance of feelings in human adjustment has been emphasized in many theories. Thus, we are ready to be sympathetic to an approach that seems to reach toward inner forces with which we are all so familiar. Clearly, this approach has more surface appeal than behavioristic ones that seem to ignore totally the inner man and to think of people as helpless automatons in the grip of uncontrollable forces.

On close examination, however, most humanistic theories prove disappointing. The theories of neurosis, or psychopathology in general, that they advance tend to be extraordinarily simplistic. They ignore the vast complexities of human behavior. They make no attempt to explain why one symptom arises rather than another, and, thus, fail to differentiate treatment approaches as a function of the specific problem. Many humanistic theories with their single-minded emphasis on the adverse effect of stored-up emotion cast people in a mold that does as much violence to man's uniqueness as many of the theories the humanists are reacting against.

Furthermore, most humanists seem to ask that a great deal be taken on faith alone. They conceive of man as a bottomless reservoir of emotions which once aroused and not fully expressed lie simmering and creating problems. Such a conception seems to make sense until one reflects a bit. Unexpressed feelings clearly are central in many of man's behavior problems, but have they been around for years and years or are they of more recent vintage? Most neurotics seem to do well up to a given point in life when their symptoms appear. If the storehouse of old affect has caused the disorder to emerge, why did it take so long, and why did the symptoms break out when they did? Such questions are not trivial since they bear heavily on treatment issues.

When the articles of faith of a given approach do not seem to "square" well with our experience, we need hard-headed research evidence to be convinced. Unfortunately, the humanists are lacking in this area too. Few, if any, have attempted to establish their basic principles through systematic research. Instances of attempts to evaluate humanistic therapy procedures are also very rare.

The humanists have provided a valuable counterpoint to other, more intellectually and more behaviorally oriented, approaches. Their theoretical views may even be very useful for understanding and guiding the treatment of specific disorders such as the extremely upsetting traumas we are all subject to through bereavement and natural catastrophes. However, it is doubtful that humanistic psychology will stand the test of time as an all-purpose theory for all neuroses much less all nonorganic problems, as many specific humanists would like to provide.

III. EXPERIMENTAL PSYCHONEUROSIS

There is a vast research literature on such topics as anxiety and repression that has indirect relevance for understanding psychoneurosis, but it is beyond the scope of this book to review this work. However, research has been done on experimental neuroses and on conflict behavior that has a more direct tie to psychoneurosis as it is seen clinically, and some of this material will be reviewed here.

The first example of an experimental neurosis was described by Pavlov (Maher, 1966). One of Pavlov's assistants conditioned a dog to salivate when viewing a circle and not to salivate when viewing an ellipse. This was done simply by pairing the presence of the circle with meat powder in the mouth and by withholding reinforcement in the presence of the ellipse. Once this discrimination was learned, the ellipse was gradually made more circular until the dog could no longer make a discrimination between the ellipse and the circle. At this point the dog manifested a "neurotic" breakdown in behavior, struggling, howling, and tearing at the experimental apparatus with his teeth.

A number of other investigators, fascinated by Pavlov's finding, have followed up his work. Liddell (1944, 1952a, 1952b) has described induction of experimental neurosis using a metronome as a conditioned stimulus. In this case a metronome rate of 120 beats per minute was always followed by a shock, whereas lower rates were not. Liddell found that when the lower (no shock) rate was increased to 92 beats per minute, the discrimination between shock and no-shock rates was too difficult for the subject of his experiment, a sheep, to make, and "agitated, neurotic" behavior followed.

In other studies Liddell found that neurosis could be induced in a situation not requiring a difficult perceptual discrimination. He placed a goat in a restraining apparatus and after clicking a telegraph key for 10 seconds administered an electric shock to the goat's foreleg unless the leg was lifted off the platform on which it rested. Foreleg flexion in response to the clicking of the telegraph key was readily learned, but many repetitions of the sounding of the key (at regular intervals) eventually produced "neurotic behavior." The nature of this behavior was a function of the length of the interval between presentations of the conditioned stimulus. Using two-minute intervals the goat's reaction was characterized by marked rigidity, with the foreleg extended from the shoulder instead of being flexed freely. This response is described by Liddell as resembling a frozen startle pattern. If intervals of five or six minutes were used between presentations of the conditioned stimulus, the goat is described as being diffusely nervous, breathing irregularly, and making ticlike movements with the conditioned foreleg.

Masserman (1946) has described still another technique for inducing "neurotic behavior" in animals. Working with both cats and dogs, Masserman trained his animals to depress a switch that produced a flash of light or a sound from a bell. The animal was trained to open a box in response to these stimuli, where he found a food pellet. Animals learn these responses readily and continue to make them long after their hunger is apparently satiated. If, however, on irregular occasions the animal is given an electric shock or a blast of air as he reaches for the food pellet, his behavior undergoes a dramatic change that Masserman describes as "neurotic." He is described as trembling, crouching, having dilated pupils, and breathing rapidly and irregularly. His pulse races and blood pressure rises. These signs of anxiety are more intense when the animal is placed near the food box or even when offered by hand food pellets like those he received in the food box. Even when placed in its home cage, the animal becomes startled by sudden sounds or lights.

Maher (1966) attributes much of the "neurotic" behavior seen in the experimental situations just described as resulting from the fact that the animals involved are restrained. Actual escape possibilities would, therefore, presumably diminish the likelihood of developing a neurosis, and some of the deviant behavior occurring in the restrained animal is thought to resemble attempts at escape.

Liddell (1952a, 1952b) explains the "experimental neurosis" on other grounds. He sees the conditioning situation as one that mobilizes watchfulness in an animal periodically confronted by an emergency. When the "stimulus load" represented by these emergencies becomes too great, a breaking point is reached beyond which the animal can no longer deal as effectively with emergencies as he once could and "neurotic" behavior is manifested. Thus, for Liddell, it is less the unavailability of physical escape routes and more the overburdening of the sympathetic nervous system that accounts for experimental neurosis.

Mowrer (1948) offers still another explanation of "neurotic" behavior induced in animals based on learning theory. He advanced his theory to explain a different form of behavior than those seen in experiments already described. Mowrer was concerned with behavior that he called "paradoxical," which involved establishment of a vicious circle from which the animal did not seem able to escape.

The "neurotic paradox" was exemplified for Mowrer by a study in which a rat was placed in the left end of a four-foot alley having high sides and ends and a metal grill door. After the rat was permitted to explore the alley for ten seconds the entire grill floor was electrified. Some frantic scurrying about ensued until the rat discovered a small opening at the right-hand end of the alley which led to a compartment where no shock was received. After only a few introductions to the left side of this alley, the rat learned to run immediately to the right end and safety before the grill was electrified. For a few subsequent trials there might be a slowing down of the running response, but after the 10-second grace period had been exceeded once or twice and shock reexperienced consistently, prompt escape behavior was established. After this the left half of the grill, where the animal was always placed in the alley, was never electrified and the right side was always electrified. Thus, to reach the safety compartment, the rat had always to pass through a section of alley where he would be shocked. However, rather than remaining in the unelectrified left side of the alley where he was placed, the animal in this situation invariably ran to the safety chamber and endured repeated shocks in the process. Literally hundreds of trials were run without resulting in any change in this "paradoxical" behavior.

Mowrer's explanation for the perpetuation of this vicious cycle was that essentially two different types of learning had taken place in the rat. As a result of his early trial-and-error at finding an escape from shock, the rat had discovered the safety compartment and the response of running to it was strongly reinforced by drive reduction (in this case the drive was fear). In addition, the emotional response of being afraid had been learned as the result of a conditioning procedure in which an aversive stimulus (electric shock) was experienced in the presence of a number of previously neutral stimuli such as the grill floor, the particular shape and color of the alley walls, and so on. Thus, he was conditioned to be fearful, and through trial-and-error he learned to reduce that drive. When the circumstances of the study were altered to make the left side of the alley "safe," he remained fearful of the cues that were associated earlier with shock. He therefore continued to engage in the behavior which alleviated that fear even though he could only accomplish it at considerable cost. The implication of Mowrer's position is that alteration of this paradoxical behavior requires efforts to extinguish both the emotional and the behavioral responses to this situation.

CONCLUSION

Acceptance of the psychoneuroses as problems in human behavior worthy of the concern of the helping professions has been a revolutionary development. When that notion finally impressed itself in the minds of professionals a variety of theories were advanced to explain the development of neuroses and, incidentally, to suggest what normal development is like. These theories for the first time placed the sick person on a continuum with the normal and paved the way for the development of theories about behavioral disorders other than neuroses and even for ideas about how to optimize development in the growing child. The significance of this momentous development should become clearer in later chapters.

SUMMARY

1. Common to all psychoneurosis is anxiety, either overtly present or prominent in promoting behavioral symptoms. In neurosis contact with reality is disturbed to a lesser degree than in psychosis.
2. DSM–II describes eight psychoneurotic subtypes: anxiety neurosis; hysterical neurosis; phobic neurosis; obsessive-compulsive neurosis; depressive neurosis; neurasthenic neurosis; depersonalization neurosis; and hypochondriachal neurosis.
3. Carl Rogers's theory stresses the importance of *self-actualization* in man's behavior. He attributes pathology, such as neurosis, to cultural demands which impede or distort man's natural aims.
4. The universality of the need to actualize was questioned and the need for positive regard which often opposes actualization was considered to be equally or more powerful in some.
5. Joseph Wolpe bases his theory of neurotic behavior on the findings of laboratory studies of learning in animals. The contiguous association of anxiety and previously neutral stimuli is seen to account for much neurotic behavior. He rejects Freud's emphasis on "core conflicts" and instead attributes neuroses to specific learning situations.
6. Wolpe's approach seems well supported by the research literature. It

is best applied, however, to relatively specific, circumscribed disorders rather than to the more usual "mixed neuroses."

7. The sociopsychological approach to neuroses is also based on learning principles. It emphasizes the reinforcing effects of the reactions made by others to pathological behavior using Skinner's operant conditioning paradigm.

8. The sociopsychological approach is attractive because it is based on laboratory tested principles. It deals best, however, with discrete, well-defined problems and less well with mixtures of vaguely defined symptoms.

9. The humanists are reacting against the mechanistic nature of the behavioristic approaches and the impersonality of modern society. As such they stress man's uniqueness and his inner nature, his feelings, and his need to create and actualize.

10. Humanistic theories tend to be too simplistic to account for the complexities of man's behavior. Also, they are based more on faith than on empirically established principles.

11. Experimental neuroses have been induced in animals through classical conditioning and other techniques. Maher attributes the "neurotic" behavior to the fact that experimental animals in these studies were restrained. Liddell feels that such neuroses result from too great a "stimulus load." Mowrer describes the paradoxical nature of neurotic behavior as resulting from the fact that two types of learning are involved. One type produces an emotional response while the other produces a motor response.

CHAPTER 10

Psychosomatic Disorders

The work of Sigmund Freud had revolutionary impact, not because of his success in solving long-standing problems of the psychologist or psychiatrist, but rather because his work held promise of alleviating another type of behavioral pathology. This pathology, neurosis, had been virtually ignored by the mental health specialist and was of interest to general practitioners, at best, and to quacks and charlatans at worst. Freud's work thus had the effect of broadening the definition of the scope of the mental health field. In a very real sense, the development of what came to be known as "psychosomatic medicine" was another broadening redefinition of the mental health field.

MIND AND BODY: HISTORICAL APPROACHES

It has long been known that emotions affect physiological functions. When we are frightened the pulse quickens, when disgusted the stomach seems to churn, and when we are sufficiently sad, tears flow. As far back as Cicero's day it was suggested that actual physical illness could result from emotional factors (Alexander & Selesnick, 1966). However, many hundreds of years passed before significant developments took place in the study of psychosomatic disorder, because the view of the human body as an organismic unity, which is basic to thinking in this area, has only relatively recently been widely accepted. Alexander and Selesnick (1966,

p. 389) point out that psychosomatic phenomena are processes "in which the first links in a chain of events are perceived *subjectively* as emotions and the subsequent links are *objectively* observed as changes in body functions." This partially subjective, partially objective quality of psychosomatic phenomena supports the old notion of a dichotomy between mind and body and led to attempts to advance understanding in each realm separately. This separation remained unbridged for several centuries.

The controversy over whether man could best be understood as being made up of two distinct aspects, mind and body, or as being characterized by an organismic unity has existed as a philosophical and practical issue for literally thousands of years. Those who pointed to spiritual or demoniac possession as an explanation of behavioral disorder were affirming a belief that, in addition to man's material side (his physical being), he possessed a nonphysical aspect which was susceptible to corrupting influence.

In classical Greece the mind-body problem was recognized. In his emphatic insistence on the natural causes of all illness, physical or behavioral, Hippocrates espoused a view of man as a unitary being. This position represented the earliest prominent rejection of the duality implied by spiritism. Plato, however, although an admirer of Hippocrates, expressed a philosophical view that reasserted the duality of the human being. Platonic philosophy held that mind and matter had separate existences, with the former being the true reality, a reality that exists even before a person is born. Anything one seems to learn is actually remembered from the myriad of things that are preexistent. Matter is an inferior element that acquires an imperfect impression of mind. Mental illness is attributed to conflict within the mind between the rational soul residing in the brain which governs intellectual activities, and the irrational soul which contains the affects located in various body parts. Aristotle, Plato's pupil, accepted the notion of a rational and irrational soul but saw them as part of a totality that included the body. Like Hippocrates, Aristotle attributed all illness to organic defect.

The seventeenth-century influence of the Renaissance and the Reformation saw many advances in scientific thought and, along with them, new speculations about the mind and the body. René Descartes (1596–1650), one of the towering scientific figures of his day and the father of physiological psychology, accepted the mind-body dualism. Matter consisted of extended substance which operates according to purely mechanistic principles. The soul, on the other hand, is unextended substance and is, therefore, entirely free in its mode of operation. By such a formulation Descartes could pursue his scientific study of certain aspects of human psychology

D. Smith Collection, Columbia University

René Descartes, the father of physiological psychology, believed that mind and body interacted with each other.

without compromising his religious faith. The two kinds of substance were seen to interact with each other through the pineal gland, so that mind can affect body and body can affect the mind.

G. W. Leibnitz (1646–1716), another important figure in the early history of psychology, also accepted the mind-body duality. Leibnitz theorized about such basic psychological phenomena as consciousness and postulated that the elemental substance in all being is the *monad*. As an element, the monad cannot be created, changed, or destroyed. Yet, within itself, it undergoes a process of development in keeping with its own structure. Leibnitz conceived the monad as very much like a perfectly constructed watch which, once wound and set in motion, will run its course forever. Any two such watches will be seen to agree but not because they are in any way related to each other. This analogy is the one Leibnitz used to explain the relationship between mind and body. Each was seen to follow its own separate course, so that although the mind and the body in no way impinge directly on each other, they agree because their courses are parallel.

One effect of creating a mind-body duality was to advance our understanding of each of these realms separately. In the nineteenth century a great deal was learned about the function of physiological systems, and Freud's work greatly advanced our understanding of the functioning of the mind. However, there was an inherent invalidity to the mind-body distinction which became obvious to physicians attempting, with little success, to treat certain physical disorders. Stainbrook (1952) has reviewed medical practice and thinking with respect to this problem in the nineteenth century.

While specific research studies and books stand as landmarks in the development of psychosomatic medicine, Stainbrook portrays a climate of thought in nineteenth-century medicine that led, inexorably, to a more organismic view of physiological functions. Many teachers of medicine noted the effects of strong and sustained emotions on physiological systems. One, for example, characterized two-thirds of diseases as fevers and the remaining third as "hysterical passions" and asserted that he could self-induce an attack of gout by concentrating thought on his big toe for a half hour. Another observer implicated fear in disorders such as enuresis, diarrhea, and seminal discharges. Anger was recognized as augmenting, grief as slowing, circulation. Breast cancer was thought by one observer to be caused by grief, inhibiting secretions leading to irritative fever and eventually to a cirrhous tubercle. For most of the century hysteria was thought to be caused by a constitutionally based hyperirritability that produced symptoms in the face of emotional stress. Late in the nineteenth century relationships between emotions and blood pressure and volume were experimentally demonstrated.

Major nineteenth-century landmarks in the emergence of psychosomatic medicine were the publication of books such as Falconer's *A Dissertation on the Influence of the Passions upon Disorders of the Body* (1796), Tuke's *Illustrations of the Influence of the Mind on the Body* (1872), and Creighton's *Illustrations of Unconscious Memory in Disease, Including a Theory of Alternatives* (1886). In addition, many disorders involving specific physiological systems began to be tied closely to emotional factors.

With respect to the gastrointestinal system, the work of William Beaumont stands out. A patient of his had suffered an injury that exposed a portion of his gastric mucosa. It was thus possible for Beaumont to make observations, over an eleven-year period, of the effect of a variety of stimuli, including emotions, on the lining of the gastrointestinal tract. He observed, for example, that fear or anger limited secretions, causing the coating of the gut to become red and dry, with a rough, unhealthy appearance. This work was repeated by other physicians with patients similarly afflicted.

An increasing variety of physical disorders came to be linked to emotional causes. Angina, for example, was thought to result from a damaged heart muscle that was overworked because of an emotional state. Amenorrhea was attributed to anxiety and depression or even to a dread of pregnancy. Skin diseases were viewed as arising from perspiration-inhibiting fear, with resultant congestion. One writer of the time linked mental strain to tooth decay. Migraine was regarded as a "vasomotor neurosis," and emotional factors were commonly seen to be one of its determinants. Finally, a relationship between emotional factors and asthma was described as early the first half of the nineteenth century.

The increasing popularity of the idea of a link between emotions and physical illness and the further work that was done from this point of view during the twentieth century had several major consequences. Its broadening effect on the scope of the mental health field was only one side of the coin. It also led to a broadening of the viewpoint of physicians, who had heretofore focused more on diseases in physiological systems than on people. The danger of this specialization was that, while much could be learned about specific functions of organs and systems, diseases that arose from the organismic interplay of systems might be entirely misunderstood. Psychosomatic medicine emerged because the weaknesses of the specialized approach became more apparent in the practice of medicine.

Another result of the developing interest in relationships between emotions and physiological functions was a change in the status of psychiatry as a medical specialty. For many years it had been a stepsister among medical specialties. The striking advances that characterized most medical subfields in the nineteenth century were not shared by psychiatry. The struggle, particularly by the German school, to ally psychiatry closely to the neurology and physiology of the day led to a fuller understanding of nervous system function and malfunction. However, even when such triumphs were won, it was the cause of neurology rather than psychiatry that was advanced. A dominant view was that if all mental disorder could be understood on the basis of physiology, there would be little excuse for the specialty of psychiatry. This situation was changed by the rise of psychosomatic medicine. For the first time, the psychiatrist, a specialist in disordered behavior based on emotional upset, had something unique to contribute to the function of the internist. As theories of personality developed, beginning with Freud's, these contributions became more specific and were regarded as more essential. Today virtually all medical practitioners feel constrained to acquire at least a smattering of information about psychological functioning. The rise to prominence of the psychosomatic approach required more than the hunches and speculations of nineteenth-century physicians. It came about largely as a result of the sophisticated efforts of physiologists and psychiatrists of the twentieth century.

DEVELOPMENT OF THE PSYCHOSOMATIC APPROACH

Interestingly, some of the early ideas relevant to psychosomatic illness arose as the result of work with conversion hysteria, a disorder not considered to be psychosomatically based according to the criteria generally used to define such disorders. As an example, there is Freud's finding that chronic emotional stress can result in physical symptoms, as observed in hysteria. In this instance Freud theorized that the symptoms of the hysteric were symbolic expressions of an internal conflict, a compromise between a compelling emotion and the ego's efforts to curb it. The hysterical symptoms always involved physiological processes under so-called voluntary control, such as the neuromuscular and sensory systems. However, the force that impelled the symptom was seen as being unconscious.

Taking a cue from what had been learned about hysteria, psychoanalytic writers tried to extend this knowledge to an understanding of physical disorders arising in other parts of the body and involving other physiological systems. As an example of this viewpoint, a physical symptom such as a peptic ulcer might be viewed as a product of conflict between an unacceptable impulse and defenses against it. The problem inherent in this position is that a peptic ulcer arises in the viscera, an organ controlled by the autonomic nervous system and not thought to be subject to volition. We cannot will to have our stomach acids secrete or to have our blood pressure rise. This does not mean that emotions cannot be related in some way to vegetative functions, but rather that they are probably not related in the same way that the feelings and ideas of the hysteric are related to symptoms he develops.

A basic distinction, therefore, can be made between hysteria and psychosomatic illnesses. In hysteria the symptom is an attempt at discharging an emotion, albeit in an indirect way, through the voluntary neuromuscular system or through sense-perceptions. Psychosomatic disorders are not attempts at emotional discharge but rather responses to a persistent emotion in a particular physiological system, not under voluntary control. High blood pressure is not an attempt at relieving one's feeling of rage but the body's way of preparing to express this feeling. Relief comes only through some overt expression. Persistence of the feeling in the absence of any fulfillment simply results in a persistence of the physiological symptom.

While the mental health professionals of Freud's time were preoccupied with conversion hysteria, specialists in internal medicine noted the detrimental effect that persistent emotions had on the functioning of various physiological systems such as the gastrointestinal and cardiovascular. What

United Press International Photo

Hysteria is sometimes relieved through emotional expression at mass religious meetings.

they observed was not discernible change in bodily issue but an alteration of the coordination or intensity with which an organ functioned. These relatively mild changes were known as "functional disturbances" and at first were considered to be best treated by psychotherapy. Accordingly the province of the therapist expanded from hysteria, involving physical symptoms with no physical defect, to the functional psychosomatic disorder in which no structural changes had arisen, but in which there were disruptions in proper organ functioning.

This change led, naturally, to a still broader role for the therapist in dealing with psychosomatic illness. Since he was already involved in treatment of a functional disturbance acknowledged to be set in motion by emotional factors, it was also understandable that he should treat the structural disorder thought to be caused by further persistence of these emotional problems. Very simply, emotional factors were seen to lead to chronic functional disturbances, which eventually caused tissue changes and organic disease. While treatment had to be instituted for the organic symptoms, the therapist's efforts were also necessary to cope with the forces that had created the problem. Ignored, the latter would continue to cause systemic malfunction almost regardless of the physical treatment.

In addition to developments in clinical practice designed to establish a firmer base for the field of psychosomatic medicine, basic physiological studies were also making important contributions to this area. One of the earliest and most prominent of these was carried out by Walter B. Cannon (1920), whose classic work was concerned with alterations in physiological systems accompanying the "major emotions."

Based on his research on the physiological effects of pain, fear, hunger, and rage, Cannon identified three divisions of the autonomic nervous system. These were the cranial and sacral divisions and a third division, the sympathetic, that innervated many of the same organs as the first two, and therefore seemed to separate them. Cannon believed that in organs having nerve ends from both the cranial and sympathetic or the sacral and sympathetic divisions, the two types of nerves operated antagonistically.

The sympathetic system was devoted to those functions necessary for preserving life in the face of emergencies. When activated it released the body's stored energy reserves, increased the flow of blood to nerves and muscles that were most deeply involved in a struggle, and prompted a rapid heartbeat to speed blood circulation. In a sense Cannon saw the body preparing for conflict, like a nation at war, by increasing the functions that must bear the brunt of struggle. Also like a nation at war, such preparation by the body precludes other activities that might predominate in peacetime. The normal activities of the cranial autonomic system, such as the accumulation of energy reserves through such activities as eating, drinking, and the complicated process of digestion, are interrupted. Activity of the sympathetic system also suppresses sexual functions and disrupts normal eliminative functions that depend upon the innervations of the sacral autonomic system.

The significance of Cannon's work was that he further elucidated ways in which emotions operated to affect various physiological processes. On the basis of his work, it became possible to understand how interrelationships among people, and the impact of situations on people, could result in psychosomatic disorder. To the extent that such relationships arouse persistent

Bachrach Portrait

Walter B. Cannon helped to shed light on how our emotions operate to affect our physiological processes.

strong feelings, a variety of functional and, eventually, structural disturbances may take place.

III. THEORIES ABOUT PSYCHOSOMATIC DISORDERS

Following Cannon's lead, many theories of psychosomatic disorders have been developed over the years. These deal primarily with two questions: (1) Why does one develop a psychosomatic disorder rather than another form of psychological dis-

turbance? and (2) When one does have a psychosomatic disorder, what determines the location and nature of the specific symptom?

A. The Conversion Theory

The conversion theory, already mentioned, is probably the most venerable of all those offered. It is simply an extension of the psychoanalytic theory of hysteria and was advanced by early psychoanalysts such as Georg Groddeck and Felix Deutsch (Alexander, Eisenstein, & Grotjahn, 1966). The essence of the theory is that a psychosomatic symptom, like an hysterical symptom, is the symbolic resultant of a neurotic conflict. Objections to the theory have already been noted: (1) hysterical symptoms virtually always appear in organs under conscious control while psychosomatic symptoms generally arise in organs which are not under such control; and (2) hysterical symptoms may be looked upon as the compromise expression of a combination of impulses, whereas the psychosomatic symptom almost always appears *not* to be a form of impulse expression, but merely the *preparation* that the body makes for its expression

B. The Personality Profile Theory

The conversion theory was challenged by Flanders Dunbar who, in the mid-1930s, surveyed the evidence for the psychogenic bases of a variety of physical disorders (Dunbar, 1935). Dunbar was convinced that there was good reason to implicate psychic causes in many organic disorders. Later (Dunbar, 1943), she asserted that there was a relation between specific personality types and the emergence of certain organic disorders, and she attempted to describe the personality types that were subject to disorders such as peptic ulcer, migraine, and coronary occlusion. Others have extended this theory by hypothesizing a relationship between the personality profile of the mother and the psychosomatic symptomatology in her child, particularly for disorders such as asthma.

Psychosomatic Illness as Specific Response to a Conflict

This approach has been identified primarily with Franz Alexander (1950) who rejected Dunbar's notion that a relation existed between personality types and the emergence of certain psychosomatic conditions. He regarded this as a long-held position that had been supported primarily by anecdotes until Dunbar attempted to develop systematic psychodynamic descriptions characterizing patients with certain illnesses. Alexander acknowledged that, to some extent, a given personality might predispose one to a life style which made certain physical occurrences more likely than others. For example, the undisciplined, impulsive person might be prone to accidents. A more complex example is the high frequency of coronary disease among individuals in positions of greater responsibility, such as professionals and executives. In the latter instances Alexander reasoned that a way of life which makes for a certain kind of accomplishment may also bring about a somatic state which is predisposing to vascular changes ultimately leading to coronary disease. In these examples, Alexander argued, there was no direct relationship between personality type and somatic disorder. Rather, any relation that existed between the two resulted from the fact that both were mediated by a third factor—the life style of the individual.

For Alexander it was essential to find relationships not merely between personality factors and a somatic symptom but rather between the symptom and a specific emotional state. He believed that this molecular approach held greater promise for establishing direct relationships between psychosomatic symptoms and their causes than did the attempt to tie general personality characteristics to symptoms. He also argued that the same symptoms are frequently found among different personality types. These individuals do, however, share similar needs. Thus, while peptic ulcer patients are often driving personalities who repress their needs for love, some ulcer patients fail to show this personality pattern at all. Instead, some are openly and childishly demanding of help and affection. Both types, however, share an inordinate need for love which prompts the stomach to anticipate actively the receipt of food, a symbol of the needed love.

Alexander stressed the importance of understanding psychosomatic symptoms as the body's response to specific, persistent emotional states set in motion and maintained by specific needs or conflicts between needs. This position was a natural heir to Cannon's basic assumption that specific emotional expressions called forth specific physiological responses. From this view, chronically angry people, regardless of what prompts their anger and regardless of their personality structure, will have chronically elevated blood pressure, and this will lead to a specific psychosomatic disorder. Similarly, other insistent emotions such as feelings of dependency or fear of separation from the mother will have their characteristic somatic consequences notwithstanding diversity in the types of personality displaying such feelings.

D. The Somatic-Weakness Hypothesis

At the same time that he developed his theory of a specific relationship between emotions and somatic symptoms, Alexander acknowledged that there were circumstances under which purely somatic factors led to the development of bodily disease (Alexander, 1950; Alexander & Szasz, 1952). Recognizing that the same emotional factors typically found in people suffering from a specific disorder such as peptic ulcer, also existed in others who did not have the disorder, he suggested that "local or general somatic factors, as yet ill-defined, must be assumed, and only the co-existence of both kinds of factors, emotional and somatic, can account for ulcer formation" (Alexander, 1950, p. 51). Essentially this introduces the idea that specific organs or physiological systems may be especially vulnerable to disease in given individuals. For Alexander the development of a psychosomatic symptom depended upon an interplay between emotional conflict modifying normal activity of a specific organ or system and its special vulnerability in that individual.

A variant of the organ-weakness or "Achilles' heel" theory was suggested by Wolff (1950). Rather than considering that specific weakness in a given system or organ accounts for symptom development, he believed that each individual has a characteristic, hereditarily determined, somatic response to generalized stress. This predisposition governs particular féeling states, bodily adjustments, and behavior all occurring at roughly the same time. This aspect of Wolff's view contradicts Alexander's view of the situation as involving a chain reaction in which the person's emotional arousal is followed by unusual or emer-gency activity in some organ and ultimately by some kind of behavior. Essentially, Wolff's theory is that a given individual and his family deal with stress in a similar way and differently from the way used by members of other family groups. As long as a person remains free from prolonged stress his personal pattern of adaptation is unrecognized. When prolonged stress elicits the appearance of his congenital response pattern, its nature will become obvious by virtue of the disorders arising in specific organs. Thus, the stomach responder will manifest a gastrointestinal disorder, the heart responder coronary or vascular symptoms, and the nose responder nasorespiratory symptoms.

Wolff believes that when specific symptoms occur, characteristic emotional reactions accompany them. He, therefore, decribes ulcerative types, migraine types, asthma types, and so on. This aspect of Wolff's theory closely resembles Dunbar's position. The difference between the two lies in Dunbar's suggestion that the personality style causes symptoms, whereas Wolff sees such styles as *resulting from* the appearance of symptoms.

Three central aspects of Wolff's theory are: (1) a given person reacts to many different kinds of stress in the same way; (2) the individual's reaction to stress is typically one that is characteristic of his family; and (3) different people, in whom similar bodily changes occur as the result of stress, have similar emotional reactions to such stress. These views are susceptible to empirical test and attempts should be made to verify or reject them.

E. The Regression Hypothesis

Michaels (1944) introduced the view that psychosomatic symptoms develop because the victim retreats to a mode of behavior and bodily functioning typical of earlier periods of life. This position has won many adherents in recent years. The physical expression of a psychological problem is viewed as a regression from an adult to a more infantile way of functioning physiologically. Margolin (1953) characterizes infancy as a time when disturbances of homeostasis are wide and balance is achieved, not by a central regulating agency within the organism but from the actions of those around one. He believes that in psychosomatic disorders biological regression takes place such that the functional properties of cells are altered. As a result, central control is lost and there is greater reactivity to physical stimuli. Margolin believes that both psychological and physiological regression typify the individual beset by psychosomatic symptoms and psychosis.

Szasz (1952) characterizes psychosomatic phenomena as resulting from "regressive innervation." Pointing out that the parasympathetic nervous system antedates the sympathetic physiologically, Szasz holds that hyperactivity in one part of the nervous system is a regression or retreat for the purpose of adapting to stress. In keeping with his position he characterizes the majority of syndromes seen in clinical medicine as instances of chronic, localized excitation of the parasympathetic system. Szasz believes that Cannon's emphasis on the sympathetic nervous system's role was misleading in that it turned attention away from the parasympathetic.

In evaluating regression theories of psychosomatic disorders Mendelson, Hirsch, and Webber (1956) raise some important objections. Chief among these is the failure of this view to explain some important empirical data regarding psychosomatic disorders. For example, it is Szasz's assumption that disorders such as ulcerative colitis, peptic ulcer, and asthma are regressive, and are caused by excessive parasympathetic excitation. Engel's research on ulcerative colitis (Engel, 1954a), however, indicates that this disorder may begin at any age from infancy onward and that abnormal bowel symptoms such as constipation may be present for many years prior to the development of symptoms. Both facts argue against a relatively sudden physiological regression. In a direct evaluation of Szasz's theory, Engel (1954b) casts further doubt on it by pointing out that sharp distinctions cannot readily be made between sympathetic and parasympathetic functions in the nervous system. Along similar lines, there is only weak support for the idea that the basic physiological rhythm of the gastrointestinal tract reflects parasympathetic dominance.

The implication that may be drawn from Engel's work is that ulcerative colitis, a disorder of the vascular system of the mucosa and submucosa of the bowel, has no counterpart in the normal physiology of the infant. In fact, when the infant's bowel is subjected to the same somatic process that causes ulcerative colitis in adults, it too develops the disease.

Mirsky (1953) found that the rate of gastric secretion for patients with duodenal ulcer, another so-called regressive disorder, is approximately double that of individuals without the disorder and that this elevated rate of secretion continues after all lesions are healed. His studies of an "apparently healthy population" indicated that 11 percent had gastric secretion rates exceeding the average for a group of patients with duodenal ulcers. He followed 2 percent of a group whose secretion rate was more than one standard deviation above the average rate of ulcer patients, and found

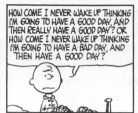

that one member of the sample developed an ulcer in a year and another manifested ulcer symptoms after two years. In neither case was the appearance of a lesion precipitated by further elevation of secretion rate. Rather, the symptoms appeared when something occurred that "was very obviously responsible for a mobilization of fears of loss of love and security" (Mirsky, 1953, p. 162). In sum, there is much evidence to support the view that psychosomatic symptoms are not necessarily precipitated by regression in physiological function. In fact, both for duodenal ulcer and ulcerative colitis the relevant organ has functioned poorly for some time prior to the appearance of symptoms and this by itself has not been a sufficient cause for the disorder.

Some have argued that psychosis frequently supplants psychosomatic symptoms and used this as evidence that psychosomatic states are regressive. Reviews of the literature pertinent to this postulated relationship fail to support it. While psychoses do alternate with psychosomatic illnesses in some individuals, this pattern is hardly a predominant one; furthermore it is not uncommon to find both psychosis and a disorder like peptic ulcer in the same individual, simultaneously.

F. Conclusions Regarding Theories about Psychosomatic Disorders

Of the theories described, only the first, holding that psychosomatic symptoms, like those seen in hysteria, are symbolic expressions of conflict, has been rejected by most workers. Each of the others still has its adherents. To an extent they complement each other and simply emphasize one or the other feature. Perhaps more time and experience will help us to assess the relative value of each and weave them into a single theory. One must agree with Mendelson et al. (1956) that the ultimate solution to psychosomatic problems awaits "painstaking empirical observations" that can be used to support or reject theories.

IV. CURRENT CLASSIFICATION OF PSYCHOSOMATIC DISORDERS

DSM-II (1968) labels psychosomatic ailments as *psychophysiologic disorders*. In these disorders there is an emotionally caused physical symptom involving a single organ system usually innervated by the autonomic nervous system. The physiological changes found in these disorders are the same as those associated with certain emotional states except that they are more intense and longer lasting. Not uncommonly the sufferer is not consciously aware of his emotional state. A listing of the various systems, along with examples classified under each, illustrates the variety of disorders suspected of having psychophysiologic origins.

1. *Psychophysiologic Skin Reaction*

Included here are neurodermatoses, pruritis, atopic dermatitis, and hyperhydrosis.

2. *Psychophysiologic Musculoskeletal Reaction*

Such disorders as backache, muscle cramps, myalgias, and "psychogenic rheumatism" are included in this category. It is one in which distinctions from conversion reactions are difficult to make.

3. *Psychophysiologic Respiratory Reaction*

Such disorders as hiccoughs, bronchial spasm, sighing respirations, asthma, and some hyperventilation syndromes are included in this category.

4. *Psychophysiologic Cardiovascular Reaction*

The most common disorders found in this classification are hypertension, migraine, paroxysmal tachycardia, and vascular spasms.

5. *Psychophysiologic Hemic and Lymphatic Reaction*

This category is used for disturbances in the blood and lymph systems in which emotional factors are implicated.

6. *Psychophysiologic Gastrointestinal Reaction*

A number of fairly common disorders are found here, including peptic ulcer, chronic gastritis, ulcerative or mucous colitis, constipation, hyperacidity, pylorspasm, "heartburn," and "irritable colon."

7. *Psychophysiologic Genitourinary Reaction*

Menstrual disturbances, dysuria, and polyurea are included in this category.

8. *Psychophysiologic Endocrine Reaction*

This category is used to classify endocrine disorders (such as diabetes mellitus) in which emotional factors are thought to play a causative role.

9. *Psychophysiologic Reaction of Organs of Special Sense*

Disorders, excluding conversion reactions, in which emotional factors disrupt the function of special sense organs, are included here.

PSYCHOSOMATIC FACTORS IN SPECIFIC DISORDERS

Several specific disorders in which psychic factors have been implicated as important causal agents have already been mentioned. The section to follow takes up a group of such disorders that have received wide attention and reviews specific hypotheses and studies pertinent to these conditions.

Λ. Essential Hypertension

Among the cardiovascular disorders, one of the most common is *essential hypertension*. It is characterized by chronically elevated blood pressure in the absence of obvious organic cause. Typically, in the early phase of this disorder blood pressure is labile, displaying marked elevations from time to time along with reductions in pressure. Eventually a chronic phase is reached in which the blood pressure remains consistently high. This condition, in turn, may cause organic changes in the heart and blood vessels.

Organically, the elevation in blood pressure is caused by a constriction of blood vessels and the malfunction of a set of nerves, called baroreceptors, that ordinarily depress blood pressure when a critical level is reached. Efforts to discover a morphological basis for vasoconstriction have not been successful, nor is it clear how the function of the baroreceptors is disrupted. Our lack of understanding of the physiological bases of essential hypertension has led to attempts to relate psychological factors to this condition.

Cannon found that fear and rage cause blood pressure elevations in experimental animals. Furthermore the physiological reactions of the animal overcome with rage include an increase in arterial tension and, hence, a constriction of the blood vessels. This leads, readily, to the hypothesis that chronic feelings of hostility are implicated in essential hypertension. In his review of psychiatric studies of essential hypertension, Alexander (1950) concluded "inhibited hostile tendencies play an important role in this phenomenon" (p. 147). His own psychoanalytic studies of patients with essential hypertension led him to conclude that, despite many personality differences, they were all unable to express aggression freely, even though, superficially, they seemed well adjusted, mature, and compliant.

Maher (1966) has reviewed both empirical and anecdotal studies of essential hypertension and has summarized their findings. Empirical studies demonstrate that increase in blood pressure is a common response to stress and that susceptibility to such increase varies from individual to individual. Chronically tense individuals, often ones who would be described as neurotic, are most susceptible to prolonged blood pressure elevations. Clinical and empirical studies focusing on the relationship between aggression and hypertension show that the two phenomena are related. Furthermore, since prolonged high blood pressure causes permanent tissue change, hypertensive symptoms can persist long after their psychological impetus has been removed. Less clear from the clinical studies is whether the hypertensive individual shows blood pressure changes in response to stresses other than those involving frustrated aggressive feelings.

6. Migraine Headaches

Headaches can arise from so many different causes that they are regarded as symptoms rather than as separate disease entities. While the immediate causative factors in head pain vary, it is generally agreed that distension of the blood vessels in the head and increases in the fluid content of the cranial cavity, with consequent changes in intracranial pressure, are basic factors.

Among the variety of forms headaches take, migraine attacks are well enough defined, in terms of symptoms and physiological mechanisms, to constitute a discrete clinical entity. For this reason attempts have been made to relate migraine to a variety of factors, including the emotional. Such prospective linkages are not possible for headaches in general.

In the typical migraine patient there are periodic attacks and a set of prodromal symptoms, such as visual disturbances involving the development of a blind spot (scotoma), speech difficulties, and abnormal sensations (paresthesias). The pain is almost always focused on one side of the head, and the attack itself is accompanied by nausea, vomiting, and photophobia. Many patients enjoy a feeling of well-being for a while after the attack. It is widely believed that the cause of pain in migraine is the stretching of the arteries supplying blood to the brain. A link between this physiological phenomenon and emotional factors has been suggested by many who have treated migraine patients.

Alexander's review (Alexander & Szasz, 1952) of a number of studies and case reports with migraine patients identified a number of attributes commonly characterizing such individuals. These include intelligent, ambitious, hostile and envious, compulsive, and perfectionistic. The clinical picture of the personality constellation of the migraine patient is that of an ambitious, striving, but highly conventional person who has been required to conform to strict patterns of behavior that stifle direct expressions of aggression. When rage is aroused, his attachment to the family is threatened and the associated conflict and anxiety is thought to lead to vascular changes causing the headache. Alexander, in support of such a formulation, has pointed out that psychoanalysts have had numerous opportunities, during interviews with patients, to observe the onset of a migraine attack and often report that the arousal of a state of repressed rage seems to trigger it. Furthermore, the attack seems to subside strikingly when the anger is expressed directly. This evidence prompted Alexander to distinguish among several disorders in which hostility is implicated as a causal factor.

He theorized that specific physical symptoms are a function of the stage at which inhibition of hostility takes place. If inhibition occurs early, even before psychological preparation for being aggressive can take place, migraine is likely to result. If the hostility builds and inhibition starts after some vegetative preparation for an attack, hypertension results. Finally, if inhibition emerges at a later stage when actual motor activity is imminent, the result is arthritis.

It would be misleading to imply that this "stage of inhibition" hypothesis is well supported. With respect, for example, to the specific development of migraine symp-

---

CASE 10–1: A CASE OF MIGRAINE HEADACHE

Sarah A., a forty-eight-year-old mother of two grown daughters applied to a New York neurologist for treatment. She was referred by her family doctor, who had been treating her for severe recurrent headaches for several years. Sarah lived with her husband in a small apartment—their children having married—and she worked part-time as a clerk in one of the small neighborhood stores.

Sarah, the youngest of two children, lost her mother in an accident when she was only four. For the next four years until her father remarried she moved about quite a bit, staying with different relatives in various towns in western Massachusetts. When she was eight she moved back with her father and new stepmother. The latter was a rather self-centered person who resented the presence of her husband's children in the home and did little to disguise this feeling. Sarah reacted by conforming as best she could and going out of her way to avoid upsetting her stepmother. Deprived of warmth and understanding at home she became absorbed in her schoolwork and was an excellent student. After being graduated from high school, however, it was necessary that she once more put aside personal satisfactions in the form of further education, since her father was ailing and what she could earn working was needed in the family. Her social life was also restricted because of the need to attend to her father. At twenty-three she met her husband. He ran a small grain business which failed soon after their marriage. They then moved to New York, where he eventually acquired a civil service job with the city.

Sarah's primary symptom, headache, dated back to her early years as a schoolgirl. These headaches were described as beginning at a point over the left eye and gradually radiating over the head and down into the neck. Occasionally the tension and aching descended to the shoulders. Despite this recurrent symptom, her appetite had been good and she managed to sleep well. As the frequency and intensity of her complaint increased, Sarah became markedly incapacitated. Changes in the pattern of her symptoms seemed to accompany various situational difficulties she was experiencing. These involved such incidents as leaving a part-time job where she was being grossly underpaid and overworked, while other workers with less responsibility asked for and received salary readjustments, and having to work very hard arranging a women's club affair because her fellow committee members failed to do work assigned to them. She was also distressed over her relations with a new neighbor who was extremely outspoken and prying. In all such situations Sarah was unable to express her feelings, and was only dimly aware that she was angry. She would restrain herself, and shortly thereafter would come to feel an ache flowing down from the top of her head into her neck and shoulders, but could only vaguely if at all associate the restraint with the ensuing headache. This symptom was so debilitating when it occurred that it caused her to withdraw from activities which would force her to leave her home, for fear she would be taken by a headache. This led to an increased feeling of depression and helplessness.

When she was first interviewed she appeared to be angry but insistently denied that this was so. Her anger seemed to mount at the suggestion that emotional causes might lie at the root of her disorder. For much of the session she vented strong feelings of resentment without giving the interviewer an opportunity to structure or direct the trend of her discussion.

Sarah was referred to a psychiatrist for a short series of therapy interviews which tended to follow the same pattern set in the diagnostic interview described. Much anger poured forth and all efforts to explore its source were resisted. She tended to respond best to reassurance and a directive approach aimed at environmental readjustments. When she was able to accomplish these with the support of her therapist, her headaches subsided and, although they had not ceased entirely, treatment was terminated.

From Zax & Stricker, 1963, pp. 126–128.

toms, Alexander's own uncertainty about the view is reflected in his willingness to acknowledge both the familial nature of migraine and the possible operation of constitutional factors in the form of unspecified "peculiarities of cerebral circulation" in the emergence of this condition.

Peptic Ulcers

Peptic ulcers are areas of inflammation, or lesions, that form in the stomach lining and are sometimes accompanied by bleeding. These lesions are caused by the chronic excess of digestive acids in the stomach. Normally, when the stomach contains food, acids are secreted into it and when food that requires digestion is no longer present these secretions cease. Prolonged retention or excessive secretion of stomach acids produces a state conducive to development of irritations in the mucous lining of the stomach. Patients suffering from ulcers are typically "oversecretors" of acid, often during periods when the stomach is relatively empty, thus raising the question of why such oversecretion occurs.

Alexander (1950) has proposed an answer based largely on emotional determinants. He notes that adults must often suppress primitive yearnings for love and affection since these are not "grown-up." Among ulcer patients, a need for love persists despite efforts to suppress its overt expression and to find pathways to its gratification that do not involve other people. Some of these are regressive, as for example when the desire for love is converted to its primitive predecessor, the wish to be fed. In this case the stomach reacts incessantly as though it were about to receive food, and according to this view the stronger the need for affection and the less its direct gratification, the more serious will the gastric disturbance be.

Mirsky's work (1953), mentioned above,

CASE 10–2: A CASE OF PEPTIC ULCER

Carmen B., a thirty-eight-year-old widow, was admitted to a general hospital in a medium-sized New England city by her family physician. There she was seen by a psychiatric consultant in connection with a stomach disorder and an extended grief reaction that she had been experiencing since her husband's death about eighteen months before.

Carmen was the second of six children born to a lower middle class family in the city where she still lived. Her father worked for years as a foreman in a local shoe factory. He was described as an upright, God-fearing man who insisted that the family attend church regularly and was consciously concerned about instilling a good family feeling in his children. Despite his occasional rigidity in certain matters, he was warmer and often more lenient than Carmen's mother. The latter was described as a hardworking person who maintained a smooth-running household. She did so by imposing a great deal of regimentation on the children, and this made it difficult for them to turn to her for affection. Nonetheless, Carmen defended this trait of her mother, insisting that it was the only proper course to follow under the circumstances. She was critical of modern mothers who fail to impose limits and responsibilities on their children. In further discussing her childhood Carmen was able to offer many facts, but could tell little of the way she felt about her early life and the people around her. She did point out with pride that she was always encouraged to be independent, work hard, and to follow a strict moral code.

Carmen's schooling, at which she did an adequate job, ended in her second year of high school, when she was sixteen. At that time she felt compelled to take a job as a factory worker to help improve the financial state of the family. She remained employed in assembly-type work until her hospitalization. When she was twenty-four, Carmen married a young man she had known since childhood. His work as a long-distance mover resulted in frequent separations for them but she nonetheless, characterized their life together as a very happy one. Her relatives indicated that the couple never had children because Carmen feared pregnancy. Furthermore, they described Carmen's husband as a man who was thoroughly devoted to her and who tried to gratify her every whim. She, for her part, did her best to make a comfortable home for him and was regarded as a good cook and housekeeper. They had few friends or interests apart from occasional activities shared with other members of their respective families.

This placid existence was disrupted for Carmen when her husband was killed in a highway accident while working. Carmen's grief reaction to this tragedy was at first delayed until she found it necessary to resume the threads of her earlier existence. It was then that she found it impossible to return to her own apartment and her old job. She became so despondent at this time that she accepted a younger sister's invitation to move in with her family and lived with them for nearly a year before her hospitalization.

During this period Carmen was able to work, but remained mildly depressed and, in addition, developed a stomach disorder. She began feeling ravenously hungry between meals and especially at night. Later she found that when she would begin to eat she quickly felt satiated and could not complete a full meal. This condition was diagnosed as peptic ulcer and treatment procedures were instituted. When her family physician found that her symptoms were only mildly relieved by medication and diet and that her depression was not diminishing, he recommended a period of hospitalization for a rest and psychiatric observation.

When she was examined at the hospital, Carmen was described as "thin and birdlike." Her face was flushed and she trembled noticeably. She talked quite freely but on many points she seemed evasive. It was the feeling of the examiner that her tendency to gloss over details which had great significance emotionally represented a lifelong pattern of hers. Carmen minimized her depression and focused primarily on her physical symptoms. She seemed to feel that it was primarily due to them that she had undergone hospitalization.

During her hospital stay of two weeks Carmen responded well to nursing care. Within a few days her ulcer symptoms seemed to subside and her spirits brightened noticeably. When she was discharged, she was advised to seek psychiatric care for the time that it would take her to readjust to a new way of life. There is no evidence that she ever accepted this suggestion. She remained in the care of her family doctor, who continued to treat her for her physical complaints, most notably the peptic ulcer.

From Zax & Stricker, 1963, pp. 131–133.

suggests an interaction between constitutional and emotional factors in the etiology of ulcers. He found ulcer victims to have been oversecretors of stomach acids long before actual tissue change was experienced. Mirsky's belief is that ulcers develop when an "oversecretor" becomes fearful that he will lose love and security. Alexander's tacit acknowledgement of the importance of constitutional factors in the etiology of most psychosomatic disorders is not incompatible with Mirsky's view.

Maher's review (1966) of research in this areas suggests that Alexander's hypothesis is not entirely supported by empirical studies. Studies with animals, and a few with humans, indicate that ulcers arise when a specific combination of circumstances occurs. These conditions include gastrointestinal hyperactivity and prolonged stress. Gastric hyperactivity may be a chronic condition, as reported by Ader, Beels, and Tatum (1960). They found that only rats with high gastric activity levels developed ulcers following 20 hours of starvation and restraint, a procedure that induces ulcers in rats. Brady (1958) found that a stressful situation, in which electric shock had to be avoided, was most effective in producing ulcers when the stress coincided with the peak point in the animals' natural cycle of gastric activity. Such findings, while not contradicting Alexander's theory, indicate that a combination of general stress and a specific constitutional disposition can produce ulcers. This is a broader view than Alexander's. It suggests that, while loss of love might be sufficiently stressful to produce ulcers in constitutionally predisposed people, other types of stress also could eventuate in a similar outcome. Personality factors are thus important primarily in helping to determine what constitutes a significant stress for a given individual.

Bronchial Asthma

Bronchial asthma is a disorder of the respiratory apparatus. Its symptoms include difficulty in breathing, wheezing, gasping for air, and the sensation of imminent suffocation. Physiologically, it is caused by spasms of the bronchioles that decrease the diameter of the bronchia—a set of tubes through which air passes on its way to the lungs.

Alexander's observations of this disorder

CASE 10–3: A CASE OF ASTHMA

Salvatore L., a twenty-eight-year-old father of six children was referred to a community clinic by a welfare agency social worker as potentially dangerous. Although he had previously worked steadily for six years as a florist, he was currently unemployed, and his family was receiving public assistance. He had never before been treated psychiatrically.

The behavior in question, which had its beginning about two years prior, was an explosive tendency to lose self-control and shout and scream, usually while at home. In addition he had on occasion struck his children and his wife after only minor provocation. The onset of this violent demeanor had been accompanied by another—and to Salvatore, at least—equally disturbing symptom, a feeling of pressure in the chest and a difficulty in breathing, particularly in damp weather and at night. A clinic internist had diagnosed this as an asthmatic condition and prescribed medication for it. Nevertheless, Salvatore was forced to give up his trade as a florist, since it was suspected that allergic reactions to some flowers worsened his condition. Following this he attempted other jobs which involved considerable physical effort and, when his symptoms intensified, he was forced to leave those. During the year preceding his psychiatric referral, he had not worked at all and on two occasions had to be hospitalized because of asthmatic attacks.

Salvatore was the youngest in a family of six children born to lower-class immigrant parents. He was able to recall that as a youngster he held a favored position in the family, being doted on by both his mother and his two oldest sisters, upon whom he looked as surrogate mothers. His father was pictured as a hard-working, silent man who was employed as a laborer much of his life. He had little to do with his own children and seemed emotionally close only to Salvatore's mother. Salvatore recalled his past as having been quite happy up to the time of his mother's death, when he was in his third year in high school. By that time his older sisters were married and he felt very much alone. He completed high school, and soon after he went to work as a florist he met the woman he was to marry. She was three years older than he and after an engagement of about one year they were married. He was twenty at the time. It was not a very happy union, particularly for the few years prior to his application for treatment. Salvatore was most troubled by the fact that they had as many children as they did. Although a Catholic, he preferred to limit the size of his family, however, his wife would not accept any birth-control measures which were unsanctioned by the Church.

Salvatore dated the onset of his symptoms to about the time his fourth child was born. There followed a marked intensification of the asthmatic condition after the birth of the fifth child. When he was interviewed, Salvatore seemed tense and anxious. He described some difficulty, involving primarily much trouble getting to sleep; although his appetite was described as poor, he had suffered no weight loss. He seemed to feel that his problems might be solved simply if his wife could be convinced to cooperate in practicing birth control. Since he manifested little interest at the time in accepting personal psychotherapy, he was advised of the services offered by the clinic and invited to return should he decide he himself needed help. Subsequent contacts with his wife revealed that they ultimately underwent a period of separation climaxed by a suicidal gesture on Salvatore's part. This act was seen as a transparent attempt to enlist his wife's sympathy and to force a reconciliation on his own terms.

From Zax & Stricker, 1963, pp. 124–126.

---

underlie his view that both constitutional factors in the form of specific allergies and emotional factors combine to produce asthma. His position, stemming from psychoanalytic case studies of asthma patients, is that the asthmatic attack, which superficially resembles an attempt to restrain crying or sobbing, is actually a suppressed cry for the mother. Spontaneous reports of asthmatics that they have difficulty crying, as well as observations that asthmatic attacks terminate when feelings are relieved through crying, support this contention. Thus, for Alexander, the crucial conflict for the asthma patient is strong dependency on the mother, or another person, which cannot be accepted or expressed directly.

Studies with asthmatic patients have uncovered distinctive personality characteristics. Barendregt (1957) found, on the basis of Rorschach responses, that asthmatics are more constricted, hostile, and impulsive than ulcer patients. Miller and Baruch (1950) reported that asthmatic children had greater difficulty in the outward expression of hostility and a greater tendency to turn hostile feeling inward than did controls. Knapp and Nemetz (1957) studied 40 asthmatics and found a variety of personality types represented. A direct relationship between severity of somatic symptoms and the severity of general personality disturbance was found.

None of the studies, however, directly supports or contradicts Alexander's position. The reported difficulty of asthma patients in dealing with hostility could well be a concomitant of their strong dependency needs. Indeed, the variety of personality types found among asthmatics is in keeping with Alexander's assumptions. He insists that it is the specific conflict, rather than the personality type, that is the emotional "key" to the psychosomatic disorder.

Other observations support the view that psychological factors play a role in asthma. These are, however, of a different order from the ones identified by Alexander. Noyes and Kolb (1963) report, for example, that there are many instances of asthmatic attacks in the absence of a specific antigen. They describe one situation in which a patient suffered asthma attacks not only when she came in contact with roses, but also when she was exposed to a papier-mâché rose. Other examples include patients who experienced attacks at a specific hour each day or when they heard a particular song or story. These examples

suggest that while asthma attacks may be induced partly by contact with certain substances to which the person is allergic, they also become psychologically conditioned to cues associated with allergy-induced attacks. In fact, a study by Dekker, Pelser, and Groen (1957) demonstrated this. These authors induced asthma attacks in two patients by having them inhale oxygen mixed with the pollen to which they were allergic. In time, attacks were induced simply by having the subjects inhale pure oxygen through the experimental apparatus. One of the subjects eventually was stimulated to attack merely by taking a piece of the glass tubing, associated with the apparatus, in her mouth. As is the case with other psychosomatic syndromes that have been discussed, further empirical work to understand the determinants of asthma is necesary.

Psychological theories thus far offered have not found conclusive support. Indeed, the physiology of these disorders is not yet well understood. While there are hints that emotional or psychological factors do play an etiological role, their specific nature and precise contributions are not as yet clarified.

CURRENT TRENDS IN PSYCHOSOMATIC THEORY

Theories about etiological factors in psychosomatic illness have moved from an emphasis on the importance of broad personality variables toward considering specific life experiences as the most significant causal determinant. Theories of early psychoanalysts, who likened psychosomatic symptoms to conversion symptoms, as well as that of Dunbar, emphasized that broad personality styles are centrally related to the development of psychosomatic symptomatology. Alexander rejected the causal importance of overall personality style in symptom development and, instead, emphasized the specific core conflict that generated adverse physiological reaction. The "Achilles'-heel" theory focused on the physiological predisposition of a poorly functioning organ and implicated general stress as the trigger-mechanism for symptom development. More recent theories discussed below have looked to still more specific causes of psychosomatic disorders.

A·

Object Loss
and Somatic Illness

One approach involving a specification of the experience-symptom relationship has recently been proposed by Engel (1962). He has described the feeling of "giving up" which results from situations involving object loss, real or threatened, or other types of overwhelming psychic stress. The physiological concomitants of such states are admittedly not well understood. These include: a reduction of general motor activity and muscle tone; slumped posture; and a general failure of the person to be involved with his environment. The motor and secretory activity of the gastrointestinal tract is diminished and the mucosa of the stomach and colon become pale. Food does not go through normal metabolic processes and loss of weight may occur even with an adequate diet. Physiological reactions to stress may actually be diminished.

Engel cites a variety of data, much of it anecdotal, to suggest that the state of giving-up is pathogenic. For example, there are reported instances of sudden death in people and animals who have been confronted by overwhelming and inescapable stress. Soldiers have died without being injured when confronted by combat stress, and wild animals have succumbed suddenly when trapped and restrained. Among

primitives who believe firmly in the powers of "voodoo," a spell cast over one may be sufficient to lead to death. At times apparently healthy people seem literally to die of grief. Thus, a serious loss may lead to collapse and physical decline terminating in death.

One study by Richter (1957) bearing on this phenomenon found that rats forced to swim under a jet of water, a stress they could not evade, suddenly died. Death occurred long before a state of physical exhaustion was reached, but at a time when the animals reached a point of "giving up" and could struggle no further. Rats subjected to the same stress, but removed before reaching the point of helpless surrender, could be exposed repeatedly to the stress without disastrous consequences. The periodic removal from stress was seen to sustain the hope that respite was possible, thus building up resistance to giving up.

These dramatic, albeit anecdotal, examples of the potent effects of the feeling of hopelessness on susceptibility to physical decline lead Engel and others to reason that such feelings also predispose people to a variety of physical disorders, short of death itself. The effect of hopelessness is conceptualized as disruptive of the natural capacity for resisting disease, thus making the person vulnerable to a variety of stresses, some already present and others to be encountered while in a susceptible state.

Schmale's study (1958) sought to verify this hypothesis. He interviewed 42 medical patients and at least one relative of most of these patients. His purpose was to obtain a detailed developmental history of the illness as well as an account of the patient's interpersonal activities prior to the onset of illness. Schmale reported that object loss, either actual or symbolic, or the threat that such loss might occur, was found to immediately precede physical symptoms in 30 of his 42 patients, despite the fact that the form of illness varied widely. This study, which suffers methodologically from lack of a control group, exemplifies the research needed to evaluate Engel's hypotheses.

B .

Psychosomatic Effects as a Function of Learning

Miller (1969) has summarized a series of studies demonstrating that a variety of visceral reactions may be learned directly. An essential requirement is that the response occur and be reinforced in an instrumental learning or operant conditioning situation. All of the studies he described were with rats, but collectively they provide impressive testimony to the relationship between specific learning situations and specific physiological responses.

In one of the studies reviewed, two groups of rats were exposed to electric shock under circumstances where one group was able to respond to avoid shock while the other could do nothing to avoid it. Both groups received equal amounts of shock since the animals who could avoid the shock did so both for themselves and for their nonavoidant partners. Rats who were not allowed the avoidance response were found to weigh less and were more prone to developing stomach lesions (ulcers), when placed in a partial restraint situation, in comparison to avoidant animals.

Other studies reported by Miller relate to the specific learning of visceral responses involved in psychosomatic symptoms such as fluctuation of heart rate, intestinal contractions, and kidney activity. Traditionally, such responses have been regarded as conditionable only by the classic Pavlovian paradigm in which an unconditioned stimulus capable of producing the response initially elicits it. Subsequently, the response becomes attached to a new stimulus presented in close temporal association with the original one, and is, so to speak, learned. Miller and his students have set out to demonstrate that similar learning takes place when spontaneous occurrences of these somatic responses are reinforced. Thus he would argue that animals can be taught to salivate or not to salivate spontaneously by judicious use of reinforcement. Similarly, Miller has reported that by consistently rewarding small changes in heart rate, rats could be taught to increase or decrease heart rate by as much as 20 percent. Miller has also reported that intestinal contractions can be increased or decreased independently of heart rate and vice versa, suggesting considerable specificity to this type of learning. The degree to which specificity is possible was demonstrated by teaching rats to make responses in peripheral blood vessels without changing general heart or blood pressure. Moreover, it has been demonstrated that increase in urine formation can be taught.

In most of the studies reported by Miller, reinforcement consisted of direct electrical stimulation to a part of the brain that produced a pleasurable sensation. Conceivably there was something unique about such a reinforcement; clearly it is one that is unlikely to occur in most real-life situations. Therefore, Miller and his students did additional studies to demonstrate that responses such as increases or decreases in heart rate or in intestinal function could be taught when the reinforcement was escape from, or avoidance of, a noxious stimulus such as electric shock. This lends a generality to the studies that increases their relevance for understanding and perhaps controlling psychosomatic illness.

The classic formulation of psychosomatic symptom-development holds that an affective state, such as chronic anger, acts as an unconditioned stimulus for a physiological reaction, such as elevated blood pressure, thus producing structural change. The implication of Miller's work is that psychosomatic symptoms can also arise when a physiological response occurring spontaneously is followed by any one of a variety of reinforcements. He suggests that those rewards often described as secondary gains provide such reinforcement. He thus views some psychosomatic disorders as similar to conversion symptoms, which may be learned on the same basis.

Miller's viewpoint suggests a number of new possibilities for treating psychosomatic symptoms. For example, there may be utility in a behavior-therapy approach in which reinforcement contingencies are set up to change undesirable visceral responses to more desirable ones. Through use of behavior-modification techniques, treatment of a variety of abnormal physiological responses, well beyond those ordinarily thought to be implicated in psychosomatic illnesses, might profitably be explored.

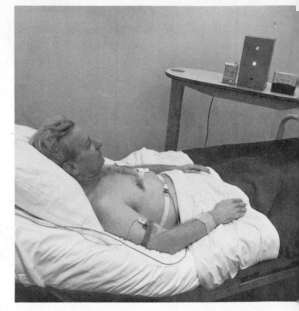

Baltimore City Hospital

The devices attached to this man allow him to "see" his brain waves and his breathing.

Biofeedback

The visceral conditioning studies described above have focused on the animal subject. By now a number of studies have been done with humans on the control of autonomic functions (Engel & Shapiro, 1971). Most of these studies rely on *biofeedback* for helping the subject to institute control over physiological functions formerly thought to be totally involuntary. The term biofeedback refers simply to the technique, actually many different techniques, used to present information to the subject about the ongoing workings of one of his physiological systems.

By using instruments that measure and amplify the operation of internal systems a person can "see" physiological responses that he seems incapable of sensing otherwise. If the added information a person gets about his "innards" allows him to control his physiological responses, such change can easily be explained as an example of operant conditioning. In this case the mere recognition that you can control a physiological response you were formerly unaware of can be very reinforcing.

The use of biofeedback to control physiological responses has obvious relevance for psychosomatic disorders. As Engel and Shapiro point out, many people develop symptoms in reaction to psychological stress. One researcher has reasoned that many with psychosomatic symptoms have learned to react to stress with definite expenditures of energy that have remained undetected. Though undetected, this energy has a significant effect on the endocrine and autonomic nervous systems. For example, holding the body rigidly and on guard makes a person vigilant and perhaps fearful. But it may also disturb smooth muscle function with adverse consequences for digestion. Ultimately this can result in disorders such as ulcers and colitis.

Engel and Shapiro (1971) report cases in which patients suffering backache, headaches, and even severe depression have been successfully treated with biofeedback. Organized programs are being directed toward teaching people to reduce their respiratory resistance (as an aid to overcoming asthma), and to control heart rate and blood pressure. Preliminary findings indicate that some subjects can learn these responses while others cannot. Paradoxically, subjects who do learn successfully cannot articulate clearly what they have learned to do to achieve the desired control. One subject, when asked to explain, simply shrugged and said, "How do I move my arm?"

Obviously a good deal more remains to be done in this area. The use of biofeedback does, however, promise some exciting possibilities for understanding better the etiology of many psychosomatic disorders, as well as for developing more effective treatment procedures.

Early Experience, Stress, and Somatic Disease

A number of workers have been interested recently in greatly broadening the concept of psychosomatic disorder. Rather than attempting to uncover the etiology of specific somatic conditions in which psychic factors play a key role, they have focused on relationships between aspects of the organism's early life experiences, including stress, and the development of illness in general. They have assumed that any disease process requires the presence of an infectious organism in a disposed host (Friedman & Glasgow, 1966). The interest of this group is precisely in those characteristics of the host that cause him to react to bacteria, and to various forms of stress, by becoming ill. Such work is in its infancy and has been done primarily with animals. With no pretense at exhaustiveness, examples are cited that illustrate variables that have been implicated in determining susceptibility to illness.

A number of studies have demonstrated that body weight in young rats is affected by various stresses. For example, Brady, Thornton, and Fisher (1962) demonstrated that young rats exposed to periodic electric shocks lost significant amounts of weight. Weight-loss was most marked when shocks were signaled beforehand. This study was extended by Friedman and Ader (1965), who were interested in the differential effects on body weight of various temporal relationships between the warning signal and delivery of shock to the animal. Their design included a group of rats housed in small groups in their home cages and a group moved to individual cages before undergoing the experimental conditions. Significantly less weight-gain was found in the latter group, indicating that simply living for a time in what was a novel environment for the subjects of the study had an adverse effect on somatic processes. In addition their findings confirmed those of Brady et al. (1962) that electric shock has particularly deleterious effects when it is preceded by a warning signal.

Ader (1967) has made an important

review of a number of investigations of the relationship of aspects of early experience and subsequent susceptibility to a variety of diseases. The early experience variables considered include the nature of the animals' housing, manipulation of mother-litter interactions, handling early in life, and a combination of handling and type of housing. Studies on the effects of housing, such as those cited above, have compared animals caged in groups to those raised in individual cages with respect to susceptibility to a variety of illnesses. Results have varied depending upon the nature of the illness being considered. For example, group-housed animals have been found less susceptible to spontaneous mammary tumors, spontaneous leukemia, human adenocarcinoma, rumenal ulcers, spontaneous convulsions, encephalomyocarditis virus, and isoproterenol toxicity. Individually housed animals, on the other hand, have been found less susceptible to trichinosis, alloxan diabetes, gastric erosions, anaphylactic shock, hypertension, x-irradiation, and amphetamine toxicity. Though early housing arrangements may thus relate to later susceptibility, the relation is a complex and as yet poorly understood one, in which specific antecedents may have either positive or negative consequences.

Studies that manipulate mother-litter relationships have compared groups of animals raised normally in their own litters to those separated from their mothers before the time of natural weaning. Here, again, susceptibility findings have varied but in this case more as a function of sex than of the specific disorder. Animals separated early from their mothers succumbed earlier (females only), were more prone to develop asthma-like symptoms when frustrated, and were more susceptible to rumenal ulcers (males only). Early separation has also been related to a sig-

nificantly faster death rate after receiving tumor transplants.

Studies on the effects of early life experiences typically use two forms of stimulation. One, "handling," varies from gently stroking the animal for several minutes to merely picking it up, placing it briefly in a container, and returning it to its home cage. The other form of commonly used stimulation consists of brief periods of electric shock. One study, on susceptibility to disease, demonstrated that handled animals survive longer than nonhandled animals following transplant of carcinosarcoma cells, in the absence of differences between groups in size or incidence of tumors. In a more complex study the effects on tumor growth of handling or electric shock during the first, second, or third week of life, and during the entire preweaning period, were compared. Growth of tumors was found to be significantly retarded in animals handled for longer periods of time during the preweaning period. However, a higher percentage of rats handled or shocked during infancy displayed tonic-clonic seizures in response to electroconvulsive shock than did unmanipulated controls (Ader & Friedman, 1965).

Ader (1965) compared the effects of handling and electric shock under varying conditions of housing on susceptibility to gastric erosions in the rat. One group of his experimental animals was handled for three minutes daily throughout the preweaning period while another received three minutes of electric shock daily during the same period. In addition, an unmanipulated control group was used. After weaning, half of each group was housed individually and half with like sexed age mates. Eventually all animals were completely immobilized for 18 hours, a procedure that frequently produces gastric erosions, but no significant differences were found between the shock and control groups. Among the group-housed animals the shocked ones were the least resistant, the handled animals were the most resistant, and the control animals fell between these two groups. This study demonstrates that susceptibility to illness is related to early life experiences, but the specific effects are modified by environmental factors.

A summary of the findings in this area suggests that while important demonstrations of the effects of early experience on disease susceptibility in animals have been reported, considerable further work is necessary. One area requiring additional investigation involves the specifics of relationships between early experience and susceptibility to particular diseases. As Ader (1967) says: "It is clear that early experiences, at least those types of stimulation that have been used, do not influence the organism's response to all forms of pathogenic stimuli. Moreover, in those instances where experiential factors do influence susceptibility, the direction in which manipulated and unmanipulated animals differ is not always the same" (p. 233). Ideally, we should establish what physiological changes accompany different types of early experiences and how such changes relate to various susceptibilities. Perhaps this goal is too visionary for the near future.

Susceptibility to Disease and Biological Rhythms

Another interesting line of research which bears on the field of psychosomatic disorder is that concerned with the relationship between the body's reaction to potential threats (for example, drugs and toxic substances such as bacteria) and biological rhythms. Rhythms, or cyclic processes, exist at all levels of biological functioning. Reinberg (1967), who has reviewed the litera-

ture in this area, points out that, within limits, the period, amplitude, and timing of circadian rhythms are related to environmental cycles such as night-day alternation, hours of work and rest, hot and cold, and noise and silence. A person's environment is thus a kind of clock to which biological rhythms are tied. Given the conditions of most people's lives (most activity during the light hours and most rest during darkness), man's circadian (or cyclic) rhythms tend also to be on a 24-hour cycle.

Animal studies have shown that the injection of a fixed amount of poisonous substances may or may not result in death depending upon the phase of the organism's circadian rhythms. Mice living under a certain light-dark regimen were found most likely to succumb to the drug *ouabain* if injected at eight o'clock in the morning or evening. Perhaps shifts in the animals' lighting schedule might have altered the times of maximal and minimal susceptibility. Reinberg reports that mice have also been found to be differentially susceptible to audiogenic convulsions at different times. Periods of differential resistence of mice to chemicals or physical agents such as Librium, Ethanol, ACTH, chemical carcinogens, and x-rays are also well documented by Reinberg.

The same author reported efforts to extend to humans the finding that physiological responsiveness changes as a function of time of day. Asthma patients have more frequent and more serious attacks at night. Studies have been undertaken on the assumption that this might, in part, be related to circadian rhythms. Since asthmatic attacks can be suppressed by cortisone, it is reasonable to speculate that the cortisone-producing adrenal gland is implicated in this disorder. Total urinary excretion of adrenal steroids, over a 24-hour period, has not been found to be significantly greater in asthmatics than in other allergy patients, but the latter have been found to excrete minimal amounts of urinary steroids at night and maximal amounts in the morning. Moreover, in the asthmatics studied, attacks occurred when adrenal secretions were low. While these findings do not identify the cause of asthma, they do suggest conditions of biological rhythms under which attacks, perhaps stimulated by other factors, occur.

Similar work was described on allergic reactions to house-dust. Patients who developed positive skin reactions to injections of a house-dust extract were found to follow a circadian rhythm in their skin reactions.

Related research with allergic patients has been directed to the effectiveness of drugs as a function of time of their administration. The antihistaminic effect of Periactine has been found to last 15–17 hours when administered at 7:00 A.M. but only 6–8 hours when administered at 7:00 P.M.

The relevance of these findings to psychosomatic problems is more to treatment procedures than to an understanding of etiology. As Reinberg (1967) indicates, work on circadian rhythms suggests the need for an entirely new research domain concerned with temporal pharmacology, temporal toxicology, and temporal therapeutics. Future research may establish that factors such as biological rhythms are essential contributors to psychosomatic disorders. To the extent that such rhythms are environmentally influenced, psychological study remains as an essential approach to their understanding and treatment.

CONCLUSION

In addition to emphasizing the incomplete state of knowledge about psychological components of physical illness, this cursory review underscores ways in which the concept of psychosomatics is being broadened. From a concern about understanding relatively few disorders in which psychological factors were thought to be implicated, interest in psychosomatics is rapidly expanding to include psychological influence in many conditions heretofore regarded as purely somatic. Also, whereas interest was once largely limited to gross physiological effects of strong persistent emotions, it has now expanded to include the relatively subtle effects of many of life's circumstances heretofore simply taken as a matter of course. As has already been emphasized, this progression typifies the broadening field of abnormal psychology.

SUMMARY

1. The development of "psychosomatic medicine" represented a broadening of the mental health field.
2. The concept of psychosomatic disorder pointed up the fallacy of the mind-body duality that has guided thought about man's psychology for many years and emphasized man's unitary nature. This came about because many physical disorders could not be understood and treated successfully as disturbances exclusive to some physiological system.
3. Some of the early theories of psychosomatic illness involved applications of psychoanalytic theories about conversion hysteria. Psycho-

somatic disorders are distinguished from hysterical disorders in that in hysteria the symptom seems to reflect an attempt to discharge an emotion while the psychosomatic symptom seems to derive from physiological preparations to discharge a persistent emotion.

4. Several theories have been offered to explain why a person develops a psychosomatic disorder at all, and why a particular symptom appears. The conversion theory holds that the symptom is the symbol of a conflict. The personality profile theory asserts that specific personality types are prone to certain organic disorders. Another theory holds that the nature of the psychosomatic illness that emerges is a function of the type of conflict involved. The somatic-weakness theory assumes that most people have an especially vulnerable physiological system (an "Achilles heel") in which symptoms will arise when stress mounts. Finally, the regression hypothesis holds that the psychosomatic symptom represents a retreat to a primitive mode of bodily functioning.

5. Current DSM–II classification of psychosomatic disturbances calls them *psychophysiologic disorders* and differentiates among them in terms of the physiological organ systems involved.

6. Essential hypertension, a common cardiovascular disorder, seems to occur in chronically tense people.

7. Migraine headaches are thought by some to occur in people who must stifle direct expressions of anger.

8. Peptic ulcers seem to occur in people who suffer both chronic gastric hyperactivity and psychological stress.

9. Bronchial asthma seems to be induced by substances to which people are allergic but also by psychological factors including conditioned responses.

10. Several recent lines of thinking and research have implications for the etiology and treatment of psychosomatic illness. One holds that object loss creates vulnerability to physical illness. Another has established that animals can learn through operant conditioning to control internal functions not previously thought to be under voluntary control. Studies using biofeedback have established similar results with humans. Vulnerability to physical illness has been related to a combination of early life experience and the experience of stress. Finally, biological rhythms are thought to be a factor in disease susceptibility.

11. The concept of psychosomatic illness has undergone considerable broadening over the years.

CHAPTER 11

Personality Disorder:

Development of
the Concept and
Psychopathic Behavior

33

All are corrupt; there's nothing to be seen
In court or town but aggravates my spleen.
I fall into deep gloom and melancholy
When I survey the scene of human folly,
Finding on every hand base flattery,
Injustice, fraud, self-interest, treachery . . .
Ah, it's too much; mankind has grown so base,
I mean to break with the whole human race.*

Moliere's *The Misanthrope* expressed these loathsome views in 1666. The character was viewed as an object of amusement then and continues to entertain audiences today. Since the seventeenth century (and probably long before) such persons have existed in reality, although they have not always met with such pleasant reaction. A gradually developing recognition of *personality disorders* (earlier known as *character disorders*) by mental health professionals resulted in a redefinition of what previously had been regarded as mental illness. This resulted in the inclusion as illness of both very subtle behavior disorders and more dramatic ones that formerly had been primarily the concern of the legal authorities.

This broadening redefinition of mental illness has brought the professional's attention to the problems of vast numbers of individuals who might

---

* Translated by Richard Wilbur. Copyright 1954, © 1955, by Richard Wilbur. Reprinted by permission of Harcourt Brace Jovanovich, Inc.

formerly have been seen as experiencing the minor perturbations of the normal personality. Thus, a much larger segment of society than ever before is now seen as falling within the scope of the discipline. It should become clear in what follows that conceptualizations about personality disorders are being extended so that an even more dramatic broadening of the scope of abnormal psychology is underway, relating to recent developments in what has been generally termed community psychology.

THE CONCEPT OF CHARACTER

While the concept of character or personality disorder has had a relatively short history in abnormal psychology, the concept of character itself in areas such as general personality theory, education, and theology is venerable. At times the term "character" has meant very much the same thing as "personality." In other contexts it has referred only to a certain aspect of personality, most notably volition. In this sense it takes on moral overtones. People are seen as "having character" because they are stable, dependable, able to work sustainedly toward remote goals, and, in the process, to inhibit impulses favoring more immediate ends. Allport (1937) reasons that in so using the term, "character is personality evaluated, and personality is character devaluated." He felt that students of personality whose proper stance is to shun evaluation of the phenomena they study could dispense with the term "character." While not all psychologists have, as Allport, abandoned the term, it has most commonly been used to refer to the deeply rooted, stable, personality traits that typify the individual. For many, such a view encompasses virtually all that would be implied by the term "personality." The

same has been true in certain psychiatric circles (Michaels, 1959).

Taking a historical view of the concept, Roback (1952) stresses that the study of character is virtually as old as humankind itself. Literary characterizations of "universal" personality types are to be found in the Old Testament, the dialogues of Plato, and the Nicomachean Ethics of Aristotle. Aristotle's pupil Theophrastus was a "pioneer" in the area of characterology, who described thirty human types. In more recent times a number of other literary figures have engaged in the description of character—Chaucer, Ben Jonson, Addison and Steele, Samuel Johnson, George Eliot, and so forth, as well as more psychologically oriented thinkers, such as La Bruyère. In all this work MacKinnon (1944) identified two implicit theories about personality structure: (1) some single trait dominates the personality and is a directive force that lends stability and consistency to it; and (2) it is a unique life style that gives particular coloring to all of a person's traits.

The legacy of the literary characterologists seems to have fallen in recent times to theorists who describe a relatively small segment of personality that they believe has important bearing on the whole. These are the typological psychologists who have attempted to identify significant personality types based on one or another theory. Empedocles' humoral theory was an early precursor of these personality typologies. This theory postulated that there were four basic bodily humors (black bile, blood, yellow bile, and phlegm) which corresponded to the four basic elements (earth, air, fire, and water). Empedocles assumed that improper proportions of the humors resulted in disease. Furthermore, this theory, as later elaborated by Aristotle, held that there were four temperamental types (melancholic, sanguine, choleric, and phlegmatic) corresponding to the humors and that, depending on the nature of humoral imbalance, one or the other temperamental disposition would predominate in the personality.

More recent typologies, such as Kretschmer's (1936), have assumed a relationship between physique and temperament. Kretschmer assumed that schizophrenics and manic-depressives represented extreme cases of two distinct temperamental types. These he termed the schizoid and the cycloid types respectively. Kretschmer's personality studies of schizophrenic and manic-depressive patients resulted in the identification of characteristics that he believed typified all schizoid and cycloid types. The schizoid was said in most cases to be "unsociable, quiet, reserved, serious (humorless), eccentric" (p. 155). The cycloid, on the other hand, was most frequently seen as "sociable, good-natured, friendly, genial" (p. 128). Although some individuals in both groups were occasionally found to manifest other personality characteristics, this was considered to be relatively rare.

Kretschmer's investigations of physical types led him to identify three distinct forms found more clearly among men than among women: these were *asthenic*, *athletic*, and *pyknic* types. The typical asthenic person was described as a thin, narrowly built man who appears taller than he is, with lean arms and legs, underdeveloped muscles, a long flat chest, delicately boned hands, a thin stomach, and skin that seemed poor in secretion and blood supply. The athletic person was portrayed as well-muscled, displaying broad shoulders, a powerful chest, a tapering trunk, and solid legs which are in proportion to the upper half of the body. The pyknic type was described as a person of average height, with a rounded contour, a soft, broad face, a short thick neck, a fat paunch. The limbs of the pyknic are soft and rounded rather than muscular, and the shoulders are rounded and high instead of broad as they are in the athletic type.

Although Kretschmer initially established

TABLE 11.1
Kretschmer's Body Typology

	ASTHENIC	ATHLETIC	PYKNIC
Physical Characteristics	Thin, narrow; lean arms, legs, and stomach; muscularly underdeveloped; skin poor in blood supply.	Broad shoulders; powerful chest; well-muscled, solid legs.	Rounded contour; short, thick neck; fat paunch; rounded shoulders.
Temperament Type	Schizoid	Schizoid	Cycloid
Personality Characteristics	Unsociable, quiet, reserved, serious, eccentric.	Unsociable, quiet, reserved, serious, eccentric.	Sociable, good-natured, friendly, genial.

physical and temperamental types through the study of psychotics, his primary interest was in the normal personality. The psychotic was viewed essentially as a caricature of the normal. Therefore, Kretschmer preferred to speak of *schizothymes* and *cyclothymes* rather than schizoid and cycloid personality types. His studies of normal personalities led him to conclude that pyknics were cyclothymic in temperament while athletics and asthenics were temperamentally schizothymic. Kretschmer wrote brief literary descriptions exemplifying the varieties of these two basic temperamental types.

Many other personality typologies have been advanced. Carl Jung classed people as introverted or extroverted, E. R. Jaensch described a B-type and a T-type, William Sheldon (1944) pursued a line of study similar to Kretschmer's and attempted to relate bodily types to temperament. The basic assumption of all such approaches was that personality consists of recognizable elements which are more or less enduring.

Freud's developmental personality theory, which was discussed in Chapter 4, is also the basis for a characterology. Events in each of his early stages of development —the oral, anal, and phallic—can become the basis of a character type that will endure through life in addition to laying a foundation for psychopathology. Examples of such characterological traits were described earlier and will be reiterated here only briefly.

Experiences in the oral stage, if pleasant, are seen to result in a warm, outgoing, optimistic personality. If they are not satisfying, they can result in an insecure, dependent, distrustful, anxious person. Optimal adjustment during the anal stage is seen to result in a responsible, productive person; a poor adjustment to the demands of the anal stage is regarded as the founda-

tion for later miserliness, self-doubt, destructiveness, and so on. If all goes well during the phallic stage the child is thought to adopt parental attitudes which will guide his behavior throughout life; if things fail to go well in the phallic stage the child will presumably be left with an uncertainty about what he stands for and a constant need to prove himself.

In relatively recent years characterologies have been developed by Erich Fromm and David Riesman which, unlike Freud's, are based less on biological development and more on social and cultural forces (Rosenhan & London, 1968). Fromm sees his character types as based on the way a person relates to his world, and he identifies two basic orientations, a *productive* and a *nonproductive* orientation. Four nonproductive types of orientation are identified: the *receptive, exploitative, hoarding*, and *marketing* types. The person with a receptive orientation sees the source of all things as outside himself and is primarily concerned with being loved, being accepted, not being rebuffed. The exploitative character also feels that all good is externally derived but, not expecting that it will be given freely, he feels he must steal or grab for it. The person who hoards is more concerned with having goods than he is with their source and jealousy guards what he accumulates. The "marketer" is one who sees himself as a commodity and feels that it is insufficient to be competent, useful, skillful, and that one must be capable, in addition, of putting oneself across, selling onself. This orientation is seen by Fromm to be a product of modern capitalism.

Fromm sees the person with a productive orientation, a positive approach from the point of view of society as well as the individual, as being primarily concerned with *doing* and *being productive*. He is relatively indifferent to receiving, hoarding, marketing, or exploiting. The latter types are basically concerned only about themselves whereas the productive person achieves his goals by being concerned with those outside himself.

Riesman has developed a tripartite typology related to the stages of development of a given society. Old societies that are quite stable in population size tend to produce *tradition-directed* types. Among such societies individual choices are restricted and conformity, dictated by centuries-old traditions applicable to age, sex, caste, clan groups, and so on, is required. Societies undergoing rapid population growth experience sweeping transitions in social structure, and traditional behavioral boundaries are found to be too confining. Such societies tend to push out frontiers to accommodate expansion and require individuals who are *inner-directed*. The inner-directed person works toward general goals instilled in him early in life but is less a conformist regarding specific behaviors than is the tradition-directed person. When a society ceases to expand its population, has the resources to satisfy the needs of its members, and begins to experience a decline, the focus shifts from developing natural resources and material goods to a cultivation of people. This produces an *other-directed* personality concerned less with producing than he is with getting along well with others and being liked. Thus, the individual becomes sensitive to the wishes and needs of others and his behavior is determined by these (very much like Fromm's marketing type).

EARLY PSYCHOANALYTIC CONTRIBUTIONS

In focusing on the enduring elements of personality most type theorists were interested in understanding the normal personality. They were far more concerned with explaining the predominance of different clusters of traits in different individuals than in any quest for the discovery of subtle behavioral abnormalities. The recognition of personality disorders as an entity is rather attributable to another group of professionals—psychoanalysts—who were working intensively with neurotic patients. Among the most significant early contributions to this area was *Character Analysis*, written in the mid-1920s by Wilhelm Reich (1949).

Reich's book was concerned with the technique of psychoanalysis. In it he alluded to many problems he and other therapists were encountering as they attempted to apply the approaches dictated by psychoanalytic theory. He believed that these problems stemmed from basic, widely prevalent characteristics of human beings which had received little notice up to his time.

Specifically, one problem that Reich encountered was that in attempting to apply the Freudian dictum that troublesome unconscious forces must be uncovered, interpreted, and thereby brought under conscious control, he found serious obstacles in the form of resistances on the part of the patient which impeded therapeutic advance. Although a fundamental rule of psychoanalysis was that free association would provide clues to significant unconscious elements, most patients were simply not able, at first, to free associate. Reich thus found that a major portion of the therapeutic work involved overcoming resistances against exposing the unconscious. His book was devoted primarily to the problems encountered in that phase of therapy.

Reich asserted that there were two kinds of neuroses: "symptom neuroses" and "character neuroses." In the former, classic neurotic symptoms predominate while in the latter the most notable features are the neurotic character traits. Reich further argued that the neurotic character must be presumed to exist even in cases where classic neurotic symptoms predominate. Thus, he reasoned that the resistances of the character structure were forces to contend with in all cases. He allowed that in some instances these resistances were more prominent than in others but believed that they were always a factor in emotional illness. From this viewpoint the distinction between chronic neuroses, which develop early, and acute neuroses, which develop later in life, is immaterial since both forms of disorder stem from a neurotic character structure, itself formed in the early years of life.

In describing the neurotic character, Reich contrasted the patient in whom such symptoms predominate with the classic neurotic, and isolated two distinguishing criteria: insight into illness and rationalization. The character neurotic tends to be without insight into his own condition whereas the symptom neurotic experiences his symptoms as an acutely uncomfortable, alien condition, imposed on him from without. The lack of insight on the part of the neurotic character stems from the fact that his symptoms have long been part of his personality and have been accepted as a given. Although the shy person may be "unhappy" about his shyness, he hardly regards himself as ill because of it. Should this symptom become exaggerated to the point that he begins to blush readily and to be made uncomfortable by it, he might be more likely to accept the idea that he is ill.

The second distinction between the symptom neurotic and the character neurotic, related to the first, is that character traits are rationalized more readily than are neurotic symptoms, that is, reasons for explaining away symptoms are more read-

ily and plausibly offered for character traits than for neurotic symptoms. A person's shyness can be lightly dismissed on the grounds that "he is just that kind of person," implying that in the natural order of events some people are just born this way. Neurotic symptoms, however, because they are often dramatic in nature, cannot readily be ignored or dismissed as a quirk of fate.

Reich pointed out that occasionally behavior resembling a neurotic symptom may turn out to be a character trait. For example, compulsive habits such as inordinate neatness and orderliness may become incorporated into the personality as general qualities and, as long as these behaviors do not become extreme, they are regarded as "peculiarities" rather than signs of illness. This suggests that neurotic symptoms are fluid to the extent that they can be incorporated in the character structure. In turn, the character trait may become exaggerated to the degree that it takes on the quality of a neurotic symptom.

Reich pointed out that character traits are of primary significance in psychotherapy. It is relatively simple for a therapist to deal with neurotic symptoms because patients are usually so upset and inconvenienced that they want to do all they can to eliminate them. Character traits, however, have been developed to protect one against both inner urges and stimuli from without. Their function is to establish some psychic equilibrium in order to minimize anxiety. A psychotherapeutic process that attempts to disrupt a stable, self-protective, but only partially effective organization is seen as a threat and is defended against. Thus, Reich referred to character traits as a kind of "armor" that one wore to protect against psychic injury. As a result of Reich's theorizing the terms *character armor* and *defense mechanisms* came to be more widely used and discussed.

One important effect of Reich's approach

was to focus the attention of psychoanalysts on *ego functions*, since character armor and defense mechanisms were manifestations of this aspect of personality. Whereas early analysts emphasized the significance of the id in mental functioning, and the need to master the potent forces it unleashed, Reich's work led to a much heavier emphasis on the significance of ego functions. Accordingly clinicians became as much concerned with *how* the patient communicated and related as they were with *what* he revealed.

Anna Freud's classic work, *The Ego and the Mechanisms of Defense* (1946), appeared in the mid-1930s and drew even more attention to the significance of the ego. Like Reich, she asserted that while the major interest of the early analysts was in the functioning of the id, current practicing analysts inevitably became deeply involved with the vicissitudes of the ego. In the early phases of treatment ego defenses had to be contended with as obstacles to the exposure of unconscious forces, and at its end a restoration of ego-integrity was necessary.

Anna Freud went beyond Reich's position in her emphasis on the significance of the ego. Contrary to the earlier held notion that the ego consists merely of perceptual consciousness, she posited that a large portion of the ego, like the id, is unconscious. It followed from this view that any analysis which stressed uncovering of the id to the neglect of the ego would be one-sided. Though such an analysis might reveal a great deal about the content of the patient's instinctual life, the transformations through which such instincts have gone in their ultimate expression, or lack thereof, would remain unknown. In like manner an analysis that emphasized ego functions and ignored the id would also be one-sided in revealing much about how the patient defended himself but very little about what he was defending against.

Anna Freud believed that the goal of analysis should be to make conscious what is unconscious, whether it was id- or ego-related. In pursuing this purpose the analyst is regarded as a "liberator" by the id forces. The latter seek expression in themselves and the analyst reinforces tendencies toward their exposure. On the other hand the ego, or that aspect of it that Reich termed "character armor," regards the exposure of id forces as a threat. Therefore, it throws up a variety of resistances, in the form of defenses, against allowing the instincts to emerge. Much of Anna Freud's consideration of this topic consists of a discussion of the forms taken by the ego's defensive mechanisms.

Without having spoken specifically of character disorder, Anna Freud's work on the ego reinforced the distinction between dramatic neurotic problems, supposedly engendered by competing instinctual impulses, and a more subtle, but more pervasive class of problems. Virtually everyone finds it necessary to defend against id impulses. As compromises, such defenses exact some toll from the overall efficiency and sense of satisfaction of the personality, and in this sense become problems.

FORMAL RECOGNITION OF CHARACTER DISORDERS

The foregoing observations of psychoanalysts led, eventually, to the formal recognition of character disorders—later called personality disorders. This recognition, however, lagged considerably behind psychoanalytic thinking and writing of the 1920s and 1930s. Most standard psychiatric textbooks published in the late 1930s and early 1940s (Henderson & Gillespie, 1944;

Noyes, 1939; Strecker & Ebaugh, 1940) make no mention of personality disorders. Each devotes a chapter to the dramatic and socially troublesome psychopathic disorders that have subsequently been included with the personality disorders, but no mention is made of the subtler character problems alluded to by the psychoanalysts. In his text, Henry (1938) included a chapter on "Psychopathology of the Normal" in which he spoke of many personality characteristics such as feelings of inferiority, compensatory strivings, hypomanic, depressive, or paranoid temperaments, as well as some sexual perversions, all of which were later subsumed under the rubric of character disorder. Henry, however, regarded these as quirks within the normal personality, rather than as disorders in their own right.

This same inattention to problems of character typifies the major textbooks of abnormal psychology in the 1930s and 1940s (Dorcus & Shaffer, 1934, 1950; White, 1948). No mention is made of the subtle behavioral aberrations later subsumed under the character disorders. The 1951 edition of the text by Maslow and Mittelmann (1951) includes a chapter entitled "Character Disorders" that takes general cognizance of psychoanalytic thinking about character neurosis but offers no systematic organization of the varieties of such disorders.

EARLIEST CLASSIFICATION OF CHARACTER OR PERSONALITY DISORDERS

It was not until the appearance of DSM-I (1952) that personality disorders were granted formal and widespread recognition by the mental health professions. In the 1942 version of the manual such disorders as drug addiction, alcoholism, and psychopathic personality were listed among a group labeled "Without psychosis." In the revision these same disorders were listed within one of three subsections of the personality disorders. The other two subsection listed various personality types experiencing subtle problems described in diverse writings earlier.

CLASSIFICATION OF PERSONALITY DISORDERS

DSM-II (1968) characterizes the personality disorders as involving "deeply ingrained" behavior patterns that, while maladaptive, are qualitatively different from neuroses and psychoses. These patterns are generally established early in life and are discernable by the time the person reaches adolescence. The several different types of personality disorders are described as follows:

Paranoid Personality

This behavioral pattern is characterized by hypersensitivity, rigidity, unwarranted suspicion, jealousy, envy, excessive self-importance, and a tendency to blame others and ascribe evil motives to them. These characteristics often interfere with the patient's ability to maintain satisfactory interpersonal relations. Of course, the presence of suspicion itself does not justify this diagnosis, since the suspicion may be warranted in some instances.

Cyclothymic Personality

This behavior pattern is manifested by recurring and alternating periods of depression and elation. Periods of elation

CASE 11-1: A CASE OF PARANOID PERSONALITY

James Z., a twenty-five-year-old married man, applied to a psychological clinic in a west-coast university which was open to the general public. He had many complaints about his marriage—his second—which brought him to treatment. He worked as a designer of women's clothes, but because of his erratic temper, had held several different jobs during the past few years. He and his wife, a clothes buyer in a small department store, lived in a middle-class neighborhood in a suburb of a large California city.

James was the only child in his family. His father was a moderately successful accountant who was completely devoted to his work. A neat, perfectionistic man, he spent long hours in his office. When he was home, he was a rather formal, serious person with whom a growing child could find little ground on which to relate. James's mother was likewise a neat, compulsive person, but the boy was able to establish a warmer relationship with her. She suffered many physical complaints which incapacitated her periodically, and at these times James would have to help around the house. At school James felt disinterested and did poorly. Nevertheless, he completed high school, his parents desiring that he do so.

The work history that followed was a very inconsistent one. He tried a variety of different jobs, most of which he left impulsively. Part of the reason for this seems to have been his unrealistic feeling that he really couldn't perform well at any of these jobs because he wasn't very capable. He felt that others knew that he was incapable, and were quick to take advantage of him. Eventually he began an apprenticeship in designing women's fashions and remained with that type of work, though he still changed firms frequently. Even in this work James was unhappy, feeling that he was underpaid and that he might not amount to much in the future.

James indicated that he had come to the clinic because of the fear that he had over the very likely failure of his second marriage. In this he felt that his impulsiveness and his recurring thoughts about his wife and her former husband might undermine their relationship. Although he suspected his fears might be unwarranted, he constantly worried that his wife might become enamored of another man, particularly because her job brought her in contact with many successful businessmen. Because the thought of his wife's relationship with her first husband was so painful to him James destroyed every vestige of the furniture and household goods they had shared. This, however, was not enough, since, when they visited his wife's sister in a distant city, James began wondering if he and his wife were sleeping in the same bed she once shared with her former husband, and he had many fantasies about their sexual activities. James also felt that his wife's old friends compared him unfavorably with her former husband. He was able to reason that one of the causes for these concerns was the fact that he had met his present wife while she was still married; he therefore feared that someone might be able to entice her away from him, just as he had stolen her from her first husband.

In his initial interview at the clinic James expressed many extreme and somewhat unusual views. In discussing veterans (James was not one) he said, "Most of them are jerks unless they saw action." Other examples were

"I don't believe in our legal system. If people kill they should be killed. All communists should be exterminated. In fact I think all gangsters who rape children should be killed." James seemed to recognize that his ideas differed from those of others and showed concern over this. He also worried about his impulsiveness. Despite these seemingly genuine concerns about himself, toward the end of the interview he admitted that a major reason for coming to the clinic was because he felt his wife was less likely to leave him if it appeared that he was concerned over his emotional state. He also insisted that he was in no financial position to become involved in an extended series of therapeutic interviews, no matter how low the cost. This obvious lack of motivation made it pointless to consider any psychotherapeutic approach, and James was invited to return to the clinic should an emergency arise.

From Zax & Stricker, 1963, pp. 204–206.

---

may be marked by ambition, warmth, enthusiasm, optimism, and high energy. Periods of depression may be marked by worry, pessimism, low energy, and a sense of futility. These mood variations are not readily attributable to external circumstances.

CASE 11–2: A CASE OF CYCLOTHYMIC PERSONALITY

Max E., a sixty-seven-year-old father of three children, was referred to a private psychiatrist in connection with acute symptoms of dejection that he had been experiencing for about four months. He lives with his wife in a fashionable suburb of a large city on the eastern seaboard and, when he was well, took a part in the management of a large automobile agency that he owned.

Max had been born the eldest in a family of four children in a small Russian village where his father worked as a shoemaker. Max's father was remembered as a deeply religious, hard-working, silent man who had few friends or interests beyond his work and his synagogue, and offered none of the children a chance for a close relationship. He imposed cheerless work on Max as soon as he was old enough to manage it, and the young child faced a bleak, burden-filled future. Max's mother was a happier person who was much more talkative than his father and infinitely more approachable. As a result he felt that he adopted many of her traits in later life. Because of the press of duties and responsibilities Max never developed a warm relationship with his younger siblings, two brothers and a sister.

When he reached the age of seventeen, Max decided to flee the difficult and austere life he was living and the empty future he faced by following the lead of some older cousins who had migrated to the United States. Despite his inability to speak English and his impoverished circumstances, he settled with one of his cousins in the city where he eventually developed a prosperous business and a prominent social standing. He started his career by collecting scrap metal, paper, and rags and selling them to dealers. Eventually, by dint of extremely hard work he became a scrap-metal dealer himself and later specialized in dismantling used cars and selling parts. His shrewdness as a businessman, enormous capacity for work, and natural gregariousness were factors which made him a wealthy man.

At the age of twenty-five Max married a woman who, herself, had been a Russian immigrant and who, throughout the marriage, remained subservient to his every wish. She bore him three sons who were thirty-nine, thirty-seven, and thirty respectively at the time Max applied for treatment. They had all been well educated and entered into the family business, where they began engaging in a subtle conflict with their father for its control. Max readily admitted that throughout his life he had been a poor family man and father, but attributed his failings to the urgent press of his business affairs. Such business affairs were viewed broadly by Max, who felt that they extended well beyond the demands of the work day. He had always been obsessed with the feeling that his ultimate success rested not only on what he had to sell but also on how he stood in the community. Thus he was constantly engaged in social affairs, organizational functions, fund drives, and charities, none of which included his wife and children. Such activities kept him away from home until the early hours of morning, and when these did not demand his time he engaged in less formal social contacts with "friends," nearly always people who might be "useful" in regard to his business. Max's vacations were rare, and when he embarked on one it excluded his family. This constant round of activity was interrupted only occasionally by brief periods of dejection.

About eight years before his appeal for treatment and about the time his youngest son entered the family business Max began to experience more prolonged bouts of depression. These were characterized by a loss of interest in his work, including the social activities he once considered such an essential part of it. He would remain in bed throughout the day, despite the fact that he ordinarily subsisted on a minimum of sleep, and spoke to no one. These states seemed to clear spontaneously after a week or two until he experienced a similar episode about four months before he applied for treatment. At that time, in addition to the usual symptoms, Max began to despair over his business, began sleeping poorly and eating sparsely, so that he lost twenty pounds. When he started to entertain suicidal thoughts, his family doctor referred him to a psychiatrist.

When he was examined, Max was well oriented, completely coherent, logical, and quite spontaneous. The content of his thought was pessimistic and self-deprecatory, however. He saw himself as no longer capable of competing with younger people, not well enough educated or intelligent enough to maintain his business, and worst of all, an "old man."

Max was advised to undergo hospitalization for a brief period (about three weeks). He responded well to routine care and after his discharge was seen infrequently in a superficial, supportive regimen.

From Zax & Stricker, 1963, pp. 200–202.

Schizoid Personality

This behavior pattern manifests shyness, over-sensitivity, seclusiveness, avoidance of close or competitive relationships, and often eccentricity. Autistic thinking without loss of capacity to recognize reality is common, as is daydreaming and the inability to express hostility and ordinary aggressive feelings. These patients react to disturbing experiences and conflicts with apparent detachment.

Explosive Personality

This behavior pattern is characterized by gross outbursts of rage or of verbal or physical aggressiveness. These outbursts are strikingly different from the patient's usual behavior, and he may be regretful and repentant for them. These patients are generally considered excitable, aggressive and over-responsive to environmental pressures. It is the intensity of the outbursts and the individual's inability to control them which distinguishes this group.

Obsessive-Compulsive Personality

This behavior pattern is characterized by excessive concern with conformity and

---

CASE 11–3: A CASE OF SCHIZOID PERSONALITY

Raymond A., a twenty-two-year-old unmarried man was admitted the first time to the psychiatric unit of a county hospital after having been arrested for disturbing the peace. Unemployed, he was living in the suburban middle-class home of his parents when he was arrested.

Raymond was the only child of a couple whose marriage was generally marked by an undercurrent of dissatisfaction. His father was a retiring, passive, almost withdrawn person who took pride in the fact that he had no close friends and did not feel the need for any. This aloofness characterized his manner with his wife and son as much as it did his relations with outsiders. He was a man content to do his daily work as a bookkeeper for a large hardware business and then return home to the life of a recluse. He assiduously avoided the job of disciplining his son and seemed to assume that matters would take care of themselves if ignored long enough. This general attitude toward life was one which upset Raymond's mother, an active, more gregarious person who would have liked to have a wider circle of friends and a husband who could be more of a companion. To meet some of these needs she had chosen to work throughout her marriage as a receptionist for a physician and to leave the rearing of Raymond to sundry relatives, baby sitters, and nursery schools.

Raymond's early years were uneventful, except that it was noted that he never displayed much emotion, even when it seemed evident to outsiders that he must be heartbroken. He made a good school adjustment, becoming an early favorite of teachers because of his quick mind. Socially, however, he chose to remain a lone wolf. An early interest in and talent for playing the trumpet earned him a place in the high-school band, but he failed to capitalize on this activity to make friends with fellow band members or with young people who came to the various functions at which the band performed. Despite his apparent disinterest in other people, he went through a stage in early adolescence in which he was unusually meticulous about the way his hair was combed and would literally spend hours arranging and rearranging his hair. He never displayed any interest in the opposite sex and once confided in his mother that he feared that females might be sexually aggressive if he dated them.

After being graduated from high school, Raymond decided to enroll at a small school of music in a large eastern city. He attended this school for only one term before becoming discouraged, feeling that he lacked the talent to succeed as a musician. Upon his return home he attempted to find work with which he would be happy but seemed to drift aimlessly from one job to another. Eventually he began seeing himself as a nonconformist and began identifying with the existentialist movement.

About three months before his hospital admission Raymond gave up any attempt to find work and began saying that anyone who had to work to earn his own living was a failure in life. He became personally untidy and unkempt. The same clothes were worn for days on end, and most of his time was spent alone in his room, where he practiced his trumpet-playing and wrote long essays to express his philosophy of life. He refused to alter these habits and resented any attempt by his mother to clean his room or to persuade him to change his clothes and be neater. He spoke of wanting to remain by himself forever in his own room and began refusing his mother admittance.

On Christmas Eve Raymond was repeatedly invited to participate in the family celebration that was taking place in his house, but he refused. Finally, harried by his mother's persistence, he slipped out his bedroom window and was later arrested by police on the complaint of neighbors that he was parading down the middle of the street playing his trumpet. Raymond's mother convinced the police that he should be placed in a hospital where he might be observed for a psychiatric disorder.

During the thirty days that he was hospitalized Raymond was as indecisive about the course his life should take as ever. He offered various unrealistic plans which would take him out of his home town, the state, and even the country. Although he felt he should spend much of his time writing, he eschewed the idea of attempting to sell what he wrote and seemed to have no idea how he could support himself—nor was he greatly concerned. After a thirty-day period of observation he was released from the hospital on the grounds that he did not display a severe enough disorder to warrant his remaining.

From Zax & Stricker, 1963, pp. 192–194.

---

adherence to standards of conscience. Consequently, individuals in this group may be rigid, over-inhibited, over-conscientious, over-dutiful, and unable to relax easily.

Hysterical Personality

These behavior patterns are characterized by excitability, emotional instability, over-reactivity, and self-dramatization. This self-dramatization is always attention-seeking and often seductive, whether

or not the patient is aware of its purpose. These personalities are also immature, self-centered, often vain, and usually dependent on others.

Asthenic Personality

This behavior pattern is characterized by easy fatigability, low energy level, lack of enthusiasm, marked incapacity for enjoyment, and oversensitivity to physical and emotional stress.

CASE 11–4: A CASE OF OBSESSIVE COMPULSIVE PERSONALITY

Sally June R., a thirty-year-old mother of one son, was referred to the psychological clinic of a large state university in the South. She was married to a commercial artist and resided in the middle-sized university city in which she was reared.

Sally June was the second of three daughters born to a rather wealthy family. Her father, a crude, uneducated man, had built a small family grocery business into a chain of self-service markets which covered a wide area of the section of the state in which they lived. He was a harsh, demanding person who dominated everyone in the family. Proud of his own ability and material accomplishments, he expected a great deal of everyone else and was none too gentle about letting them know whenever he felt they didn't measure up to his standards, which was quite often. As a youngster Sally June did her best to please her father and seemed always on edge in her relationships with him. This seemed partly owing to her own sensitivity and partly because, in his uniquely heavy-handed manner, he might at any time scold and curse at one of the members of the family. Sally June's mother, a quiet, dependent woman, was not exempt from his attacks and rarely provided a source of refuge for her intimidated children.

Sally June completed high school with an undistinguished record but chose to attend the local state university because she felt her father expected this of her. There she majored in home economics, managed to compile an average record, and be graduated. While in college she met her future husband, an art student at the same institution, and they began a courtship that was to last almost ten years.

Once her education was completed Sally June took a job in her father's business office. She did secretarial work there and was generally uncomfortable for fear that she would do something to displease her father. She was described by fellow workers as an extraordinarily conscientious, careful worker who was quite humorless. To those in whom she could confide, she often spoke of her doubts about the adequacy and correctness of things she might have done.

When she was twenty-seven, Sally June married her fiancé. He had been struggling to develop a career in the field of commercial art so that he could afford marriage. He worked for a local newspaper and throughout their marriage the couple struggled to make ends meet. Sally's ever-present uncertainty about how well she was doing her job as a wife and homemaker drove her into many activities. She almost methodically became active in church affairs and the "right" community organizations. In those activities she never developed any close friends, but many people respected her thoroughness and the care with which she undertook any task, and soon responsibilities were heaped on her. These compounded her concerns over her personal adequacy, and, when her son was born about a year and a half before she appealed for treatment, Sally June became even more impaired. She began to be immobilized by her doubts and found it difficult to decide what to cook for dinner, whether to take the baby out for a walk, when to visit friends, and so forth.

Gradually she found it difficult even to do the shopping for groceries, being full of doubt that she was buying the right things. After making purchases she regretted her choice and feared that she had overpaid for articles. Things reached a point that she could not bring herself to buy clothing for herself, because the task of making a choice was such an overwhelming one for her. When her condition came to the attention of her younger sister, who was herself in treatment at the clinic to which Sally June eventually went, she was urged to seek help.

When first seen, she was obviously tense and anxious. Despite efforts at maintaining tight controls, she became tearful several times. She had difficulty talking at first, but once she had warmed up to the situation she talked constantly and rapidly in a monotonous, dry tone of voice. Her verbalizations were interrupted occasionally by a forced, mechanical smile. Although her verbalizations were never inappropriate, the rapidity of her recital and its disconnected quality made it difficult to get a clear picture of her background.

Sally June was accepted for weekly sessions in psychotherapy and was seen for a period of about ten months. During this time she achieved some symptom relief and was less immobilized by her fears.

From Zax & Stricker, 1963, pp. 230–232.

Antisocial Personality

This term is reserved for individuals who are basically unsocialized and whose behavior pattern brings them repeatedly into conflict with society. They are incapable of significant loyalty to individuals, groups, or social values. They are grossly selfish, callous, irresponsible, impulsive, and unable to feel guilt or to learn from experience and punishment. Frustration tolerance is low. They tend to blame others or offer plausible rationalizations for their behavior. A mere history of repeated legal or social offenses is not sufficient to justify this diagnosis.

CASE 11–5: A CASE OF ANTISOCIAL PERSONALITY

Thomas L., a sixteen-year-old high-school student, was admitted to a northeastern metropolitan hospital on the order of the juvenile court, following a conviction for juvenile delinquency. He had been charged with illegal possession of a pistol, resulting in the fatal shooting of a neighbor's child. He lived in a lower middle class neighborhood with his adoptive parents.

According to the court record, Thomas was an illegitimate child who was abandoned by his mother at birth and brought up in a large orphanage until he was seven. Due to the number of children in the orphanage, and the extreme personnel shortage, his care was of the most routine and remedial sort, and there was no opportunity for any individual attention to him. He had been placed for adoption twice before his legal adoption by his most recent parents; however, he had previously been returned because of difficulties in adjusting to siblings and neighborhood children or because he was disliked by his foster parents. Both of his adoptive parents always worked, so that Thomas frequently was left at the homes of relatives and neighbors. Since his parents also moved frequently, it took Thomas a long time before he came to believe he belonged to them. He always was made to feel that his life must be regulated so as to fit into their schedule.

As might be imagined, with this checkered history Thomas attended many different schools, and got into difficulty over his behavior in each. He was extremely disrespectful to teachers, restless and overactive in the classroom, frequently involved in fights, and truanted frequently. Fighting and generally destructive behavior were also characteristic of him outside of school, although whenever he broke and otherwise marred articles at home he attempted to conceal his responsibility by lying and blaming others. He often stole small articles from stores and, if apprehended, lied about how he happened to have the objects in his possession. He rarely referred to those incidents after they were settled, and never seemed at all penitent about them.

Thomas had always been fascinated by guns, and had often asked, to no avail, for a gun of his own. Shortly before his current difficulty began, when staying with a neighbor while his parents were at work, he rummaged through their closets and happened upon an old German Luger and a box of bullets. He took these and went to the school playground in order to show off his new acquisition. The first person he met was a neighbor's daughter who was much younger than he, and who didn't believe the gun was real. In order to prove it Thomas loaded the gun. His stories as to what ensued were variable. According to one version of the story there was a noise which startled both children, and in turning rapidly the gun was discharged, hitting the child in the temple and killing her instantaneously. However, Thomas told other versions in which he claimed that he didn't realize the gun was loaded. In any case, when the girl fell to the ground Thomas became very frightened, and immediately rode away on his bicycle. He abandoned the pistol and bullets in a deserted lot and then rode back to the playground to see if he could help the injured girl. There were no witnesses to the accident, but after the shot a number of people saw Thomas riding away, and they called the police. Thus, when Thomas returned, the police were already on the scene and looking for him. He first told them that another boy had done the shooting, fully described this imaginary boy, and claimed he had just arrived for the first time. He appeared very calm and composed and continued to alibi, frequently changing the story in repetition. When his parents arrived on the scene he broke down and admitted he had done the shooting, but insisted that it was accidental. He took the police to the abandoned weapon and explained that he had been too frightened to tell the truth earlier. His mother said, "Tommy never tells the truth even when it's easier." He was convicted by the juvenile court and referred to a psychiatric clinic for observation.

Thomas was a very attractive and affable boy who was almost defiantly polite. He spoke of the incident which led to his hospitalization in a nonchalant, unfeeling way, and was very suave and unnaturally composed in explaining why he was on the ward. He said, "I was showing her the gun. I didn't know it was loaded. She turned her head and it got her in the temple. I told the police that I was very sorry. You're to find out if there is anything mentally wrong with me. I thought I'd have to go to reform school. This is the better of the two stories." For the first few days Thomas was very engaging, undemanding, and cooperative. He became progressively more demanding, did not seem overly pleased when his demands were granted, but pouted and/or became hostile when they were denied. Since his demands were usually excessive, often they were not granted, so that his ward adjustment rapidly deteriorated. He was discharged after two weeks for assignment to a psychiatric school.

From Zax & Stricker, 1963, pp. 238–240.

Passive-Aggressive Personality

This behavior pattern is characterized by both passivity and aggressiveness. The aggressiveness may be expressed passively, for example, by obstructionism, pouting, procrastination, intentional inefficiency, or stubborness. This behavior commonly reflects hostility which the individual feels he dare not express openly. Often the behavior is one expression of the patient's resentment at failing to find gratification in a relationship with an individual or institution upon which he is over-dependent.

CASE 11–6: A CASE OF PASSIVE-AGGRESSIVE PERSONALITY

Myron C., a twenty-nine-year-old married man, applied for treatment as a self-referral to a community-supported outpatient clinic in a large southern city, where he had recently moved to operate a business. He had become acquainted with the services offered by the clinic through a cousin who had once been a patient there.

Myron was born in a large metropolis in the north. His parents operated a real estate agency and were always quite comfortable financially. Myron's father was described as a somewhat ineffectual person whose financial success was attributable largely to the efforts of his wife. His father often found it difficult to get to work on time and frequently ignored important details—which irritated clients and was damaging to the success of the concern. As a result Myron's mother gradually took over the more active role of seeing clients and managing the work of the agents they employed, relegating her husband to the role of office manager and bookkeeper. Despite his own apparent lack of drive, Myron's father, along with his mother, always cherished the idea that his only son would achieve considerable success in one of the professions. The two older children in the family were females and less was expected from them.

At school Myron was something of a disappointment to his parents. He was obviously bright enough to do well, but failed to develop any serious interests, and never exerted enough energy to do more than a mediocre job. After leaving high school he attempted college work by taking evening courses in a large university in the city. His father quite willingly supported him at this time without requiring that he work at anything but his studies. Nevertheless, Myron developed the pattern of sleeping much of the day, so that he failed to keep up with assignments; and when he would fall far behind, he would simply stop attending classes. Despite an investment of two years in evening school, Myron finally decided to quit and readily accepted his parents' offer to teach him the family business. In this new function he was no more successful than he had been at school and for the same reasons. He lacked the drive to do well as a seller of real estate and his general passivity and lack of responsibility made his efforts in the office fruitless. Although he remained nominally an employee of his parents until he was twenty-four, he never contributed materially to the success of the business and his salary represented little more than an allowance.

At the outbreak of the Korean conflict Myron was in imminent danger of being drafted; it had also become abundantly clear that he was of no use to the family business, so he enlisted in the Army. In retrospect he admitted that he knew he could not continue living as he had been, and this seemed the easiest way out. While in the Army he experienced much difficulty with service routine and, although he had a good job as an assistant in the supply room, was in frequent "hot water" because of his lackadaisical attitude.

When he was discharged at the age of twenty-eight, Myron married the daughter of some old friends of the family and resolved to mend his ways and make something of his life. Soon after his marriage an unparalleled opportunity turned up for fulfilling this resolution. His father's brother, having reached retirement age, invited Myron to move to the southern city where he lived, and to take over the management of a very successful pawnbroker's business that he owned. His uncle promised that the business would eventually revert entirely to Myron provided he could demonstrate ability to help it flourish.

With high hopes Myron and his wife moved to the South, where he took charge of the pawnshop. Myron managed to do an adequate job as long as his uncle was with him in the shop teaching him the routine. As soon as he was left to his own devices, the business began to deteriorate. Many mornings he was not able to rouse himself in time to open the shop on time. He also decided he needed to hire an assistant; once he had done so, he began spending much time away from the business on extended lunch hours and in afternoon movies. As a result of his neglect and his belated discovery of his assistant's dishonesty, profits took a sharp nose dive, and his uncle began to express grave concern. It was at this time that Myron began questioning his adequacy as a person and considered psychiatric assistance.

When he was examined, Myron was described as a stocky, passive man, quite verbose but circumstantial. He seemed to be trying very hard to be pleasant, cooperative, and agreeable, but despite this managed to spend a great deal of time evading fundamentals. To a great extent he seemed to control the interview and block its progress in spite of his superficial conformity.

Despite grave doubts that he would make a genuine investment in psychotherapy, Myron was offered the opportunity for weekly meetings which would be directed toward helping him deal with the practical problems he faced. After appearing for three such sessions, Myron failed to return or offer any explanation for his withdrawal.

From Zax & Stricker, 1963, pp. 223–225.

Inadequate Personality

This behavior pattern is characterized by ineffectual responses to emotional, social, intellectual and physical demands. While the patient seems neither physically nor mentally deficient, he does manifest inadaptability, ineptness, poor judgment, social instability, and lack of physical and emotional stamina.

CASE 11–7: A CASE OF INADEQUATE PERSONALITY

Philip L., a twenty-eight-year-old married man, was referred to a community psychiatric clinic by a welfare agency social worker. His work record throughout life had been very inconsistent, and from time to time he and his wife had to rely on public assistance as a sole source of support.

Born in a small town in New Jersey, Philip was the fourth in a family of eight children born in close succession to immigrant parents. He recalled having relatively little contact with his mother as a very young child because she always seemed occupied with an even younger child. When Philip was only eight and she in her late thirties, his mother died of a kidney ailment. His father, a tailor, did his best to hold his family together after his wife's death by assuming much of the work she used to do. He also expected a great deal of his children, and Philip recalled frequent beatings which resulted whenever his actions in any way diverged from his father's expectations. This and the memory of the family's poor financial situation, which required them to go on welfare periodically, are among Philip's most vivid memories of his early life.

One of the few other things he could call to mind from that time was the constant difficulty he had in rousing himself early enough to get to school. During his school years one of their neighbors took a motherly interest in him and took steps to insure that he would get to school regularly. She went so far as to come to his home in the morning, help him dress and take him to his own room at the school. Although Philip did well as a student, he did not enjoy his school years. He had few friends and was shy about talking to other children because he felt very self-conscious. He completed only grade school and at sixteen decided to leave home by joining the Merchant Marine. He didn't care for life aboard ship and, after making a few sea voyages, resigned. He returned home and held various jobs, generally as an unskilled laborer, and was either fired or impulsively quit each. When he was nineteen World War II had broken out, and he was drafted for Army service. His adjustment in the Army was poor and after committing several infractions of the rules, he was examined psychiatrically and subsequently discharged for emotional instability.

Shortly after his return from the Army, when he was twenty-one, Philip met and impulsively married a waitress who was twelve years his senior. In relating this he stressed what for him were the "practical" advantages in this alliance, such as her regular income. He had no illusions about loving his wife, particularly so since he found sex to be "repulsive" and a trivial part of life. Throughout his marriage Philip's work history was checkered. He managed to get a variety of jobs as an unskilled worker, but could hold none of them. He would generally get into conflict with bosses or fellow workers and then quit or was fired. As a result his wife had to work as often as she could, despite the fact that she was a sickly person.

At the clinic Philip was vague about the problems which he felt needed treatment. He did acknowledge that he had a poor attitude toward life and accomplished little because he could not stick to activities once begun. He was also subject to much impulsive behavior, which did not help matters. In general he complained of a lack of will power. He also pointed out that he did not have very strong feelings about other people, and he recognized that he was different from others in this respect. Admittedly, however, this did not bother him much.

In his initial interview, Philip seemed like a pleasant person and made a good superficial impression. He tended to be aggressive whenever he was made anxious and it was the interviewer's impression that his frequent conflicts with others were in reaction to dependent needs which were denied. There was also some doubt in the interviewer's mind about the amount of genuine concern Philip had over his problems. This doubt was confirmed when Philip refused to accept psychiatric treatment on the grounds that he couldn't see the value of simply talking to another person. He went on to admit that his coming to the clinic in the first place was mostly a maneuver to please the welfare agency worker.

From Zax & Stricker, 1963, pp. 188–190.

Related to the personality disorders are other nonpsychotic behavior disturbances such as addictions and sexual deviations. Addictions will be taken up in some detail in Chapter 13. Sexual deviation is described in the next chapter.

RECENT DIAGNOSTIC DEVELOPMENTS

A particularly interesting change in DSM-II is the development of a new major grouping, "conditions without manifest psychiatric disorder, and non-specific conditions." This new major grouping includes "individuals who are psychiatrically normal but who nevertheless have severe enough problems to warrant examination by a psychiatrist." Subcategories under this major heading are: *marital maladjustment, social maladjustment, occupational maladjustment,* and *dyssocial behavior.* This new diagnostic grouping ushers in formal recognition of yet another new and broad set of behavior problems—problems being addressed by those in the community psychology movement.

Much as psychiatric texts of the 1940s described personality disorders as minor dysfunctions of essentially normal personalities, current nomenclature acknowledges the existence of pervasive but subtle behavior problems that are coming to the attention of mental health professionals who are still somewhat reluctant to label them formally as psychiatric or psychological problems. It is doubtless recognized that there is a substantial percentage of serious emotional disorders among individuals experiencing various kinds of social and occupational maladjustments. While this awareness has attracted increasing attention to such precipitants of more traditional behavioral aberrations, the framers of the current nomenclature have not yet formally recognized the precipitants themselves as conditions requiring the attention of mental health professionals.

PSYCHOPATHY

One of the personality disorders, *the antisocial personality*, has received a great deal of attention over the years because the behavior characterizing it has such serious social implications. Much of the literature has referred to the behavior displayed by the antisocial personality as psychopathic, or reflecting psychopathy. Because of its prominence the remainder of this chapter will be devoted to the concept of psychopathy.

History of the Concept

The concept of psychopathy is generally conceded to have originated with Pinel in the early 1800s. He described an unusual patient who, in spite of having grown up in a good family setting where he was indulged, never felt that his desires were satisfied. Small obstacles aroused fury in him and, ultimately, in an enraged state, he threw a woman who had offended him into a well.

Individuals who behaved in this way had long been recognized by psychiatrists, but it was not until Pinel conceptualized the disorder and named it *manie sans délire* that it was studied systematically. Pinel's categorization included several disorders in addition to what is currently called psychopathic behavior—paranoia, some hysterical symptoms, and paroxysmal behavior thought to typify the epileptic personality. This mixture, which prevailed for many years, has impeded understanding of many important features of psychopathy.

In 1835, a British psychiatrist, J. C.

Pritchard, introduced the term *moral insanity* to describe those in whom "the moral and active principles of the mind are strongly perverted or depraved; the power of self-government is found to be incapable, not of talking or reasoning upon any subject proposed to him, but of conducting himself with decency and propriety in the business of life" (McCord & McCord, 1964, p. 24). In this description of moral insanity Pritchard came close to characterizing the current entity of psychopathy; however, he also included in this category several psychoses involving behavior similar to that seen in psychopathy. The problem Pritchard, and many who followed him, faced was that few mental disorders were clearly delineated on any basis in his time. Accordingly, any definitions of new disorder typically collected, under the same umbrella, conditions that shared outstanding symptoms with it. It was not until subtle facets of the new disorder were identified that fine differentiations could be made.

Through the nineteenth century the idea that man's moral sense could become diseased gained currency among medical practitioners since it seemed to explain the behavior of many aggressive patients. The same view, however, horrified legal and religious authorities. Lawyers anticipated, and rightly so, that a concept such as moral insanity would greatly complicate the question of criminal responsibility. Theologians believed that the concept challenged the notion of free will that was basic to most religions. This controversy was highlighted by the trial of Charles Guiteau, the assassin of President James Garfield, in 1881.

Defense lawyers in the Guiteau trial contended that their client was morally insane and, therefore, not responsible for his acts. The prosecution countered with the testimony of psychiatrists who asserted that

The Bettmann Archive

Charles Guiteau, assassin of President Garfield. His trial raised the question of moral insanity.

Guiteau could distinguish between right and wrong. Although the verdict went against Guiteau, the controversy over how courts should deal with crimes committed by the emotionally disturbed remained very much alive. The current status of that controversy will be discussed below.

Much of the nineteenth-century work on psychopathy was devoted to semiphilosophical questions such as: "Can one's moral sense be diseased while the intellect remains intact?" Much thought was also directed to the question of whether moral insanity was best viewed as a separate diagnostic entity or a stage in other forms of mental illness. By contrast, few papers were devoted to the etiology or psychology of the disorder.

The turn of the twentieth century witnessed a decline in the speculative-philosophical approach to psychopathy together with increased effort at being more scientific about its study. As part of a new look at this disorder, new terminology was introduced. The concept of moral insanity, by then considered to have too many negative connotations, was replaced in Europe by the term *psychopathic inferiority* (first introduced in 1888). The word "inferiority" in this new term encompassed any defect preventing the individual from adjusting satisfactorily to his environment. In the United States, Adolph Meyer introduced the term *psychic-constitutional inferiority* to avoid confusion deriving from the fact that, up to that time, the term "psychopathic" was synonymous with insanity. Eventually, a combination of the German and American names, *constitutional psychopathic inferior*, was introduced and gained widespread acceptance. Ultimately, however, the term "psychopathic" lost its general reference to insanity and came to be restricted in meaning to the syndrome under discussion.

Quite beyond the establishment of a new name for psychopathy, the twentieth century saw the initiation of empirical studies of the disorder. McCord and McCord (1964), in their extensive review, cite the investigations of Bernard Glueck in 1918, and John Visher in 1922, as prominent examples of such work. Glueck studied 608 convicts at Sing Sing prison, of whom 115 (about 19 percent) were classified as psychopaths. He found that psychopaths, in contrast to other criminals in this group, began their antisocial behavior earlier, consisted of higher proportions of alcoholics and drug addicts, and displayed greater recidivism. Visher studied 50 psychopaths intensively and found them to be impulse-ridden characters with little guilt over their behavior. In addition, he found them markedly egotistic, with little capacity to concentrate and strong tendencies to project.

In the 1930s psychopathy was studied

from two new viewpoints: the organic and the psychoanalytic. The organic approach originated with the observation that encephalitis can produce behavioral symptoms resembling those seen in psychopathy, thus suggesting that brain dysfunction might account for the disorder. A spate of research, some described below, ensued. Psychoanalysts, particularly Franz Alexander, sought to extend analytic theory to an understanding of the psychopath. Alexander described "neurotic characters" as those whose attempts to solve inner conflicts take the form of living-out their impulses and attempting to alter the environment in order to allow for release of inner tension. Alexander believed that such individuals were regressed, self-destructive, and characterized by an underdeveloped ego and a dominant hatred of their fathers.

Despite the considerable thought directed to psychopathy, it remained, as late as the 1930s, a puzzling, poorly specified diagnostic entity. An extremely heterogeneous array of psychic dysfunctions including hysterics, compulsives, sex deviants, and borderline psychotics were being lumped under the rubric "psychopathic personality." The confusion engendered by this diagnostic morass prompted some students of the disorder to reject the entire concept as a wastebasket to which the poorly classified were relegated. Others, however, believed that psychopathy was a distinct disorder worth retaining and set themselves the task of clarifying and redefining the concept. Prominent among the latter were Benjamin Karpman and Hervey Cleckley.

In his classic work, *The Mask of Sanity*, Cleckley (1941) presented a series of case studies of psychopathic patients, and distilled from these a profile that typified such individuals. Like many writers before him he recognized the extreme egocentricity, guiltlessness, emotional shallowness, and impulsivity of the psychopath. In addition, he described the superficial charm behind which many psychopathic personalities hide their asocial nature. He further observed that the psychopath rarely learns from his experiences and often appears to seek external control or even punishment for his behavior. While recognizing that the psychopath's legal transgressions often resulted in incarceration, Cleckley asserted that many could be found outside of prisons—indeed, even in society's most respected positions.

Karpman (1946) did psychotherapy with a number of individuals manifesting psychopathic behavior. His experience led him to conclude that the majority of such individuals are actually neurotic or psychotic and that their psychopathic behavior obscures the basic dynamics. This group he labeled *symptomatic psychopaths*. Karpman reported, however, that there was a small group in which he could find no dynamic features that satisfactorily explained their extreme behavior. He diagnosed this group as *primary* or *idiopathic psychopaths*—another diagnostic term he used for this group was *anethopaths*.

Karpman believed that the major utility of his diagnostic distinction was that it allowed one to differentiate a group which was amenable to psychotherapy (the symptomatic psychopath) from one which was not (the primary psychopath or anethopath). He considered the primary psychopath to be virtually incurable and believed that he required indefinite institutionalization. Karpman likened such patients to the typhoid carrier who could not be released from quarantine until he was completely free of the germ.

Karpman's designations aroused considerable uneasiness in many students of psychopathy. In essence his argument was that there existed a group of psychopaths that *he* had been able to understand and work with psychotherapeutically; therefore they were presumed to be hidden neurotics or psychotics. A second group that Karpman was unable to understand or to work with on his own terms, was, by default, relegated to the class of incurables experiencing a behavioral disorder of mysterious origin. Many who were interested in psychopathy found Karpman's conception of an idiopathic form of the disorder objectionable since it was based primarily on the failure to find basic conflict or a dynamic pattern that could explain the behavior.

Effort directed to the identification of a pure diagnostic entity that we call psychopathy has considerable significance. The behavior that typifies this disorder is so dramatic and vexing that, when it has appeared, it has quickly been labeled with little regard to its underlying dynamics. When similar behavior can be elicited by vastly different dynamic patterns, as apparently happens in what has been called psychopathy, attempts to develop causal understanding of the behavior are bound to result in confusion. Such a state of affairs is apparent with respect to research devoted to the causes of psychopathy. McCord and McCord (1964) have reviewed such research extensively, and the materials to follow draw heavily on that source.

Causes of Psychopathy

Heredity

In trying to understand the causes of psychopathy a variety of emphases can be identified, including hereditary, neurological, environmental, and sociocultural. Several investigators leaning toward hereditary explanations of psychopathy have traced the lineage of people they diagnosed as psychopaths and have reported a high incidence of a variety of disorders such a psychopathy, epilepsy, alcoholism, and "maladjustment" in their ancestors. Unfortunately, in these studies psychopathy was typically defined vaguely, and control groups, in which the ancestors of normals were also studied, were not utilized. Indeed, a study on the family background of normal individuals revealed as high a percentage of "neurotic taint" as was found in the families of psychopaths (Mental Deficiency Committee of Royal Medico-Psychological Association, 1937). Further, most of these studies failed to isolate the relative contributions of heredity and environment to the disorder. Even if it were established that a psychopath has many psychopathic relatives, the finding might speak as eloquently for environmental as for hereditary causation.

Franz Kallman, who has been the main proponent of a genetic explanation of schizophrenia (see Chapter 6), found that a higher percentage of children of psychopaths than siblings of psychopaths were themselves psychopathic, indicating that the disorder does not follow the closest blood lines. One admissible explanation for his finding is that children whose psychopathic parents are institutionalized experience a decline in family status and are thereby more likely to behave psychopathically. This explanation emphasizes environmental factors.

In an effort to determine the relative contributions of nature and nurture to psychopathy, twin studies have been undertaken. If heredity is the determinant of prime significance, the concordance of psychopathy in identical twins, whose genetic structure is identical, should be higher than in fraternal twins, whose genetic structure is no more similar than that of ordinary siblings. One study by Lange (1930) found 6.4 times as much concordance for prison record in identical twins as in fraternal twins; another by Rosanoff (1943), however, reported a concordance of only 1.4 times as often in identical twins as fraternal twins. Both studies have been criticized on the grounds that poor criteria were used for establishing the nature of the twinship and that the criterion information on subjects was unreliable. Furthermore, the "identical" twins in Rosanoff's sample who had been reared apart were less concordant for criminality than those reared together.

It is probably a fair summary of the work described, as well as of other studies related to a genetic explanation of psychopathy, that a conclusive hereditary basis has not been established for this disorder. In general these studies are done poorly, and their results have been contradictory. The specific finding that psychopathy does not follow closest blood lines is especially discouraging to the genetic position. Cleckley's survey of this area led him to conclude that ". . . any consistent or even any suggestive history of familial inferiority is notably lacking in the present series" (Cleckley, 1941, p. 254).

Brain Damage

A second potential explanatory basis for psychopathy that has attracted the attention of researchers is brain defect. It has long been observed that brain damage, through accident or surgery, can result in dramatic behavior change. In many cases such change includes the appearance of psychopathic-like behavior. Certain brain diseases, particularly meningitis and encephalitis, have been reported to result in aggressive behavior, disinhibition, or loss of control, in the absence of guilt or anxiety. Observations of the effects of brain damage or disease led to the belief that such dysfunction may lie at the root of psychopathy.

A methodology for testing this hypothesis became available when electroencephalography was developed. The electroencephalogram (EEG) measures electrical impulses emanating from the brain. An early encephalographic observation was that damaged areas of the brain give out abnormal patterns of waves, either unusually sharp spikes or particularly slow waves.

A spate of EEG studies was done seeking to identify neurological defect in psychopaths. McCord and McCord (1964) report that several investigations in the early 1940s indicated that 60–75 percent of psychopaths showed "abnormal" EEG patterns, thus supporting the belief that psychopathy could be understood as a brain disorder. However, later studies did not confirm these high rates of EEG abnormality in psychopaths. Two of these later investigations (Greenblatt, 1950; Simmons & Diethelm, 1946) found that only about 30 percent of their psychopathic subjects had abnormal EEG patterns, and a third (Simon, O'Leary, & Ryan, 1946) reported no differences in rate between a group of psychopaths and a group of normals. McCord and McCord explain these contradictory findings as resulting from the vague standards used in selecting the psychopaths who were subjects of these studies.

Despite the confusion from the disparate results of early EEG studies, McCord and McCord concluded that a greater proportion of abnormal tracings were found in psychopaths than normals. The same, however, can be said for studies relating EEG abnormality to *other* behavioral disorders. EEG findings are, thus, at best suggestive, and fail to provide a sound basis for differentiating psychopathy from a variety of other disorders.

Other approaches have been used in an effort to establish a neurological basis of psychopathy. These include comparative studies of the reflexes, tics, or tremors of psychopaths in comparison to other groups; studies of their galvanic skin reflex (GSR); and examination of early history of psychopaths with special concern for the presence of cerebral trauma. Indeed, the findings in many of these studies are "positive." Psychopaths have, for example, been reported to : (1) show more signs of neurological disorder (abnormal reflexes and tics, and so on) than other response groups; (2) be more likely than normals to suffer early brain damage; and (3) be more physiologically responsive to stimuli. Yet for each of these positive findings, directly contradictory ones have been reported. Doubtless, McCord and McCord's criticism of EEG studies also applies to this cluster of neurologically oriented investigations. Failure to carefully define the psychopathic group in specific studies and variations in definition from study to study have doubtless led to inconsistent findings. In addition, many of the variables researchers have attempted to relate to psychopathy are sufficiently subjective to be susceptible to the critique of experimenter bias. For example, the "abnormality" of many neurological reflexes is often less than clear-cut and for the experimenter with a stake (conscious or otherwise) in a given experimental outcome it might be difficult to avoid a biased judgment. To avoid such judgmental bias a very careful experimental procedure is required, in which examiners are aware neither of the hypothesis of the study nor of the status of the subjects being examined. Such niceties of design were infrequently attended to in the period when the foregoing studies were carried out.

An overall impression from the results of studies exploring neurological bases of psychopathy is that, while a fair number argue for some such bases, they are in the main equivocal. The neurological approach has not yet resulted in significant breakthroughs that help either to understand psychopathic behavior better or to provide a sounder basis for its treatment.

Environmental Factors

From an environmentalist viewpoint the most commonly proposed cause of psychopathy is parental rejection. Several studies of the life histories of psychopaths offer evidence of a high incidence of parental neglect or rejection. Support for this finding is also drawn from several indirect sources. For example, one study is cited in which children who spent their early years in institutions, where presumably they experienced less love than in a sound family setting, were found to have fewer inhibitions and to display "incomprehensible cruelty" to both humans and animals in comparison to noninstitutional children. Other studies of young children reported a high relationship between parental rejection and hostile behavior in the child, with the more severely rejected displaying the poorest controls. Since the aggressive behavior and poor self-control seen in the rejected child are *somewhat similar* to what is seen in the adult psychopath, it is inferred that parental rejection plays a key role in the development of psychopathy.

Despite the evidence mustered to support the significance of parental rejection as a background factor in the etiology of psychopathy, the validity of this contention has not been universally accepted. Cleckley, for example, reviewed a variety of etiologic theories of psychopathy and concluded that "I have not regularly encountered any specific type of error in parent-child relations in the early history

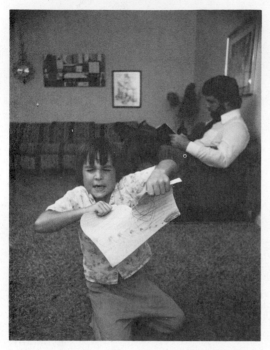

© Chris Rollins

When a child is ignored, he often becomes aggressive.

of my cases" (Cleckley, 1959, p. 584). Furthermore, with respect to studies bearing on early life experiences that could account for psychopathy, Cleckley warned, "I am increasingly impressed with the difficulty in obtaining objective and reliable evidence of what was felt twenty or thirty years ago between a child of one year (or of three) and his parents. Assumptions about infantile, and even intrauterine, experience are sometimes made solely on the basis of analogy and symbolism. These methods can be used with such elasticity that it is not difficult to 'discover' in the unconscious virtually anything the investigator chooses to seek" (Cleckley, 1959, p. 584).

Cleckley's points are well taken. It should also be noted that studies of "re-jection" are beset with definitional problems. Many forms of parental behavior can be labeled as rejecting, ranging, for example, from instances in which physical and psychological contact is absolutely minimal to those of intense psychological and/or physical involvement. In the latter case, a parent's intense concern and involvement may be based entirely on his or her own need system and thereby be quite rejecting of the child with needs different from those of the parent. Yet another aspect of this same argument is that there are many who emphasize the *underlying* rejective components of the syndrome of parental over-protection which on the surface is a polar opposite of outright rejection.

With such a wide spectrum of parental behavior that can be interpreted as rejection, the researcher who expects to find a high incidence of rejection in the back-grounds of psychopaths can scarcely fail to do so unless he carefully and operationally delineates how he is using the term. And if he succeeds in defining how rejection is specifically manifested, he still faces the thorny problem of getting a sufficiently detailed and reliable description of the life circumstances of the family unit dating back to a period of some fifteen to twenty years earlier.

Thus, evidence for an environmental explanation of the causes of psychopathy is once again at best suggestive. There is clear need, in this area, for better definition of the concept and operations of rejection and for experimental designs that are relatively free of the criticism of experimenter bias. There would also be merit in identifying for study youthful delinquents who seem inclined toward adult psychopathy. Since this is a group which is relatively closer to environmental roots that might be etiologically significant, it would be easier to study such roots in them.

Sociocultural Factors

McCord and McCord (1964) attempted to relate four classes of sociocultural forces to psychopathy: social crisis, social class, the complexity of the society, and culturally determined child-rearing practices. None of the studies referred to in any of these areas was concerned directly with psychopathy. Instead they described behavior which could be related to what we know of as psychopathy. In most cases such relationships were so remote as to be virtually meaningless. The most convincing evidence was offered for the relationship between social crisis and psychopathy.

The most common prolonged social crises arise during wartime. Wars cause separations within families, disrupt normal family relations, and direct energies into many extrafamilial activities. To the extent that emotional deprivation predisposes one to

Environment, combined with sociocultural forces, often can lead to psychopathic actions. Urban street gangs act to reinforce such behavior. (From *The Vice Lords*, by R. Lincoln Keiser, Holt, Rinehart and Winston, 1969.)

psychopathy, the social crisis represented by war may be a causal factor. Several studies of the effects of war stress on children have uncovered considerable antisocial behavior, a lack of conscience, aggression, impulsivity, and low tolerance for frustration (Bowlby, 1952; Freud & Burlingham, 1944; Pritchard & Rosenzweig, 1942).

Whether the reported effects of wartime stress actually result in high rates of psychopathy has not been studied directly. It must therefore, be concluded that, even in this area, considerable work needs to be done to establish ties between sociocultural factors and psychopathy.

Treatment of Psychopathy

The results of efforts to treat or change the behavior of the psychopath are generally gloomy. Society's most common response to crimes committed by psychopaths has been incarceration. Many studies of the effects of this procedure indicate that it does little to reform the psychopath. While in prison psychopaths are guilty of greater numbers of offenses than other prisoners and spend more time in solitary confinement. One study reports that, on the average, the psychopathic convict has had twice as many convictions as the ordinary criminal. Punishment alone, therefore, has little corrective impact on the behavior of psychopaths.

In several prison settings, group therapy programs have been instituted for psychopaths. Although proponents of such programs have issued optimistic reports of their effects, they have generally failed to do systematic evaluation studies, much less follow-up studies to determine long-range effects. While occasional reports of remarkable changes in single cases have appeared, these provide little basis for a general approach to the treatment of the psychopath.

Reports have been made of the successful treatment of isolated cases through psychoanalysis or hypnoanalysis (the most celebrated example being Lindner's *Rebel without a Cause*). However, a substantial number of studies have reported the failure of psychoanalysis or psychotherapy to effect fundamental change in the psychopath's way of life. Since there is a lesser likelihood that reports of therapeutic failures will find their way into the literature than successes, it seems safe to conclude, with Cleckley (1959), that psychotherapeutic attempts to treat psychopathy have been disappointing.

Psychopaths have been treated with a variety of drugs (dilantin, sodium, phenobarbital, benzedrine sulphate, amphetamine sulphate, and so on). Reports of the effectiveness of such procedures are qualitatively similar to reports of the effectiveness of psychotherapy. Occasional success is claimed but many failures are also reported. Even where the psychopath is judged to have benefited from a drug, follow-up studies are lacking as are reports of what ensued when the drug was discontinued.

McCord and McCord's (1964) review of attempts to treat the adult psychopath ends on a pessimistic note. They believe that the psychopath's lack of anxiety and guilt, along with his apparent difficulty in identifying with others, makes him a poor prospect for psychotherapy. Cleckley (1959) was likewise negative in his evaluation of attempts to treat the psychopath. He argued, however, that a more realistic view of the psychopath, on the part of society and the courts, was needed. He believed that judgments about the psychopath's legal competency should be made on the basis of his actual conduct rather than his abstract reasoning powers. If the psychopath's behavior can be used to declare him incompetent, even if his reasoning is intact, society can obtain considerable control over him. Cleckley thus believed that institutions should be set up and organized specifically to deal with psychopaths on a long-range basis because they are not fit for unrestricted freedom in society. Although such institutions might seek to identify cures for psychopathy, even if they failed in this society would benefit from the fact that the psychopath's destructive, antisocial propensities would be checked and his constructive potentials might be utilized.

McCord and McCord, too, believe that control of psychopathy lies in institutional programs. They favor a special focus on the child with psychopathic potential in an almost preventive sense. Reform school settings emphasizing discipline have failed, however, to produce more encouraging results with children than similar restrictive approaches with adult psychopaths. McCord and McCord believe, however, that treatment programs for delinquent children emphasizing affection and permissiveness show promise. Prominent among such approaches was the program developed in Austria by August Aichhorn, a Viennese psychoanalyst (Aichhorn, 1935). Aichhorn established a home for delinquent children in which they were treated permissively even in the face of aggressive attacks. Absence of punishment was a new experience for these youngsters, as was the affection they received from the staff. These techniques led to the establishment of rapport with the institution and its personnel, following which demands could more readily be made on the children and social controls could be imposed. Aichhorn believed that once the delinquent acquired an affectional bond to someone, this bond could be used to bring him a sense of social responsibility which had been lacking.

Aichhorn reported remarkable success with his delinquent children, and other institutions attempted to copy his methods. Unfortunately, few of these experiments have been evaluated objectively. One exception is the work done at the Wiltwyck School for Boys in New York, which was studied by the McCords (1964) in 1953. The program at Wiltwyck stressed a loving, initially permissive environment in which permissiveness is gradually replaced by efforts to teach social control and responsibility (much the same emphasis as Aichhorn's). Comparing 35 Wiltwyck children to a control group of 35 boys at a typical public reformatory, on a battery of personality tests, the McCords found several differences. Over a period of time, Wiltwyck youths decreased significantly in anxiety, authoritarian tendencies, and prejudice, whereas reformatory subjects showed no change or an increase in these variables. Wiltwyck boys were also different from reformatory boys in many other significant ways. They came to be more satisfied with themselves over time, more tended to view the world as good than evil, had a more loving ideal of parents, had more interest in constructive activities, selected student-leaders who were themselves constructive, and related more closely to staff, each in contrast to the controls. Neither group decreased significantly in aggressiveness.

Encouraged by this comparison of the effects of the atmosphere at Wiltwyck with those of a typical reformatory, the McCords (McCord & McCord, 1964) undertook a more detailed study of the response of different types of children to the Wiltwyck program. Among the 107 children at the school between June 1954 and February 1955, 15 were identified as being truly psychopathic personalities. Others were diagnosed as neurotics (23), borderline psychotics (6), and behavior disorders (63), who were delinquents but, in addition, displayed many neurotic traits. All youngsters underwent a series of interviews and tests and were observed in standard behavioral situations. All subjects were tested in 1954 and a sample of boys, who were newly arrived at the time of the first test, were retested in 1955 to provide a measure of the effects of the treatment program. The data indicated that the behavior disorders and psychopaths responded most positively to treatment. They showed an increase in internalized guilt, became less fearful of authorities, and behaved less aggressively. Neurotic and prepsychotic children, on the other hand, showed less improvement.

The study undertaken at Wiltwyck provides no estimate of the permanence of changes that took place, as was true of Aichhorn's observations earlier, but it stands out for the McCords as one of the very few encouraging approaches for dealing with psychopathy. Unfortunately, equating delinquency with psychopathy risks creating the same definitional problems seen in the early work on psychopathy. Care needs to be taken in future studies of such programs to assess their effects on clearly identified psychopathic groups, not mixtures of several disorders.

Psychopathy and the Law

Often texts in abnormal psychology discuss the legal position on behavior induced by mental illness in the section on psychopathy. While psychopaths are more likely than other diagnostic groups to commit crimes and to become involved in court proceedings, they are by no means the only group to do so. Therefore, what is said about the current stance of the courts with respect to criminal responsibility does not apply exclusively to psychopaths.

We have noted that as the mental health professions redefined their scope and became involved with broader and subtler behavioral problems they impinged on areas formerly of prime concern to the church and the courts. For example, Bernheim's theorizing on the significance of suggestion in causing criminal behavior as well as Freud's heavily deterministic emphasis did much to complicate thinking about criminality. Before these views took hold man was seen to have an entirely free will which could steer him toward good or bad behavior. Courts were set up to judge and fix punishment for those who "willfully" misbehaved. Occasionally, and only in extreme cases, a lawbreaker was perceived to be so deranged mentally that he had no conception of the significance of his behavior. Such criminal acts were therefore excused and the person involved was committed to a mental institution rather than a prison.

Gradual acceptance of a deterministic view of man's behavior complicated matters for the courts. Strict determinism, as Maher (1966) put it, implies that "no man is free to do other than what he does do in response to any specified situation." This principle tends to be accepted by courts primarily in extreme cases, particularly those involving unlikely sets of circumstances that have little chance of being repeated, as when one kills to defend his own life or when one commits an illegal act because he has been forced at gunpoint to do so. The behavioral scientist, however, views all behavior as determined by forces which, though less dramatic than those in the examples given, are equally compelling. The conflict generated for the courts by this deterministic position is reflected in recent changes in the criteria for deciding whether a person is responsible for a criminal act.

The notion that a person might not be responsible for a criminal act was first introduced in an English court in 1724. There it was held that a man could not be held accountable for a crime if "he doth not know what he is doing, no more than . . . a wild beast" (McCord & McCord, 1964, p. 174). In the 1840s a group of English judges was commissioned to establish criteria for determining legal insanity following the trial of Daniel McNaghten who killed a man under the "instruction of God." This commission ruled that to establish a defense on the grounds of insanity it must be demonstrated that: (1) the defendant suffered from such defective reasoning that he was unaware of the quality of his act; or (2) if he was aware of the quality of his act, he was unable to distinguish between right and wrong. This came to be known as "the McNaghten Rule"— the dominant legal criterion for a defense based on insanity until recent years.

Precedent established in a trial in Ohio in 1834 set forth still another guideline for evaluating responsibility in criminal cases. Here insanity was ruled as established if a person was judged to have been driven to act by an impulse that was irresistible. Thus, if insanity could not be established under the McNaghten Rule, it could be done if the accused was judged to lack freedom of choice because he was driven by an irresistible impulse. The additional criterion is still followed in many states in the USA.

The McNaghten Rule has been criticized as being based on a simplistic theory of faculty psychology, under which the brain is viewed as highly compartmentalized, with certain units responsible for specific ideas or actions. One such unit was thought to subserve the "moral sense." Defects in the functioning of that area of the brain were considered to result in failure to control irrational impulses. The criterion of irresistible impulse is also vulnerable to serious criticism. If a given impulse can be defined as irresistible, why should others be defined differently? The determinist argument on this point is that all manifest behavior must be regarded as the only thing the individual can do under a given circumstance. The criterion of irresistible impulse implies that this is so in some cases but not in others, without specifying how to differentiate between the two.

Current views of mental functioning and human behavior emphasize a complicated interplay of a variety of forces: biological, social, psychological, and so on. Some of these forces are conscious, others are unconscious; some rational, others irrational. Accordingly, the criteria of the McNaghten Rule and the doctrine of irresistible impulse are both difficult to apply. This dilemma has led both to confusion in legal proceedings and to the rejection, by psychologists and psychiatrists, of such criteria.

In 1954, the United States Court of Appeals handed down a ruling which many believed might help to clear up the difficulties encountered in establishing legal responsibility for a crime. This case involved a defendant named Durham with a history of serious mental disorder and crime (automobile theft and forgery). After having served a prison sentence and having been hospitalized for a mental disorder, he was released, and subsequently he was rearrested for breaking into a home. He was returned to a mental hospital and, after 16 months of treatment, faced trial once more. In testimony before the court a hospital psychiatrist held that, while Durham was definitely of "unsound mind," he could not certify that the defendant was legally insane. He further stated that although, by most standards, Durham was mentally ill, he could distinguish between right and wrong. The trial judge found Durham guilty, and the case was taken to the court of appeals. Judge Bazelon reversed the ruling of the lower court and set forth a new criterion for criminal responsibility: ". . . an accused is not criminally responsible if his unlawful act was the product of mental disease or mental defect" (McCord & McCord, 1964, p. 180). This rule is broader than any used before and eliminates the necessity of speculating about the defendant's cognitive state at a particular time in the past. It permits the psychologist or psychiatrist to evaluate the general psychological condition of the individual and to arrive at a diagnostic judgment much as he does in his everyday clinical role.

Although many have welcomed the Durham decision as a necessary liberalization and simplification of the criminal responsibility test, the new rule has not been universally implemented. Courts in various jurisdictions have been slow to adopt it, and lawyers have found fault with the rule. Many of the latter reason that although the Durham Rule eliminates the need to establish the state of the defendant's mind and his "moral knowledge" at the time of the crime, it requires that the presence of mental illness be established as well as the fact that such illness *caused* the defendant to commit the crime. This problem is comparable in complexity to that posed by the McNaghten Rule.

For the psychopath, the McNaghten Rule and the principle of irresistible impulse offer little protection from prosecution. The psychopath does not manifest the cognitive disruption or drive-quality required to sustain a defense on the grounds of insanity. Whether the Durham Rule offers him any protection depends upon how the term "mental disease or mental defect" is defined. If such definition is limited to the traditional psychoses, it fails to protect the psychopath from prosecution. Typically, psychopathy has not been classed as a mental disorder in the courts even though most psychologists and psychiatrists believe that the psychopath's crimes are a product of his personality defect. The basic conflict between the principle of free will and the deterministic view that the individual is a helpless pawn in a myriad of forces is not resolved by a single legal decision. Rulings set forth by courts must be viewed in terms of how one stands on the more basic and philosophical issues. Until society takes a definitive stand on these, the confusion about determining criminal responsibility is likely to remain.

CONCLUSION

Introduction of the concept of character disorder is very recent and represents a new broadening of the scope of the mental health field. Besides bringing the attention of the mental health professional to many subtle behavioral problems, the inclusion of psychopathy within this concept has brought the mental health worker into what had been the traditional domain of the legal authorities.

SUMMARY

1. The concept of character or personality disorder greatly broadened the scope of abnormal psychology.
2. Historically, the concept of character is venerable. For some it meant much the same as "personality." Literary characterology attempted to describe "universal" personality types. Many early personality theories as well as a few recent ones were typologies that focused on some small segment of personality thought to have significant bearing on the whole.
3. Wilhelm Reich was a psychoanalyst who described ego defenses as "character armor" against exposure of id impulses. Many behavior problems were thought to be rooted in this defensive structure. He contrasted character neuroses and psychoneuroses.
4. Formal recognition of personality disorders as diagnostic entities was not accorded until the appearance of DSM-I in 1952.
5. DSM–II (1968) distinguishes ten different types of personality disorder as follows: paranoid; cyclothymic; schizoid; explosive; obsessive-compulsive; hysterical; asthenic; antisocial; passive-aggressive; and inadequate.
6. DSM–II (1968) includes a new major category entitled "conditions without manifest psychiatric disorder, and non-specific conditions." This includes such problems as marital, social, and occupational maladjustment, problems that are coming to the attention of psychiatrists with great frequency. Like the personality disorders in earlier diagnostic schemes, they are now regarded as problems occurring in the normal personality.
7. Psychopathy has received much attention because the behavior involved

in it has seriously adverse social consequences. The term is applied to impulse driven people who, despite adequate intelligence and a seemingly proper upbringing, readily transgress against society's laws and fail to learn by their experience.

8. Psychopaths were once seen to suffer "moral insanity." Later they were thought to be constitutionally inferior. Research on psychopathy indicates that the behavior leading to the diagnosis can result from any of a variety of dynamic patterns. Thus, the failure to describe pure diagnostic entities has impeded understanding of the causes of the disorder.

9. Heredity has been looked to as one possible cause of psychopathy but research has not established this conclusively.

10. Some defect in brain functioning is another potential cause. Findings in this area are equivocal and have not helped with understanding or treating the disorder.

11. Parental rejection is emphasized by some as a crucial factor in psychopathy. Studies in this area are difficult to carry out and this causal theory can only be regarded as suggestive.

12. Some implicate sociocultural factors as causes of psychopathy. This idea still needs to be tested through research.

13. While reports occasionally appear claiming psychotherapeutic success in treating psychopathy in individual cases, the overall track record of psychotherapy with this group is poor. The same may be said of drug-treatment programs. Some feel that only long-range institutional programs can succeed with psychopaths.

14. Because he so often encounters legal difficulties, the position taken by the courts with respect to criminal responsibility and the law is important for the psychopath.

15. The earliest legal criterion to absolve a defendant from legal responsibility, the McNaghten Rule, required that he be so deranged that he was either unaware of the quality of his act or that he could not distinguish right from wrong. A more recent rule, set forth in the Durham decision, holds merely that a defendant is not responsible for a crime if it was a "product of mental disease or mental defect."

16. The psychopath can find no legal shelter for his crimes in the McNaghten Rule. Whether or not the Durham Rule protects him depends upon how a particular court chooses to define "mental disease or mental defect."

Sexual Disorders

Respectable Victorian women believed that good husbands would never dream of making certain sexual demands of their wives. And their contemporaries generally did not even acknowledge the existence of homosexuals. For many years, sexual disorders were thought to result from deeply-lying personality problems. Society's firm position about what was right and proper in sexual matters strongly influenced psychoanalytic views.

Today it is no longer so easy to talk or write about sexual disorders with the confidence that the general public view is being reflected. Modern society has become aware through the work of Kinsey (Kinsey, Pomeroy, & Martin, 1948; Kinsey et al. 1953) and others that many sexual practices formerly thought to reflect disorder are widely prevalent, even in polite society. Thus, standards for what is right or wrong, good or bad, healthy or unhealthy have become muddied. What we are left with is the realization that whatever practices are satisfying to those engaging in them are okay. It is only when the sexual practices of one person are harmful to another or are unsatisfying to himself that we are justified in speaking of "sexual disorders."

Within the broad class of sexual disorders some widespread problems are generally referred to as complications or inadequacies rather than serious deviations (McCary, 1973). The major sexual disorders are often referred to diagnostically as sexual deviations. Most so-called deviations involve some variance in the way of functioning or the quality of the sex urge or variance in the choice of sex partner.

358

© Chris Rollins

Although prostitution is still considered wrong by most of society, many people today are questioning the justness of this classification.

I. SEXUAL COMPLICATIONS OR INADEQUACIES

In men the most common sexual complications are *impotence* and *ejaculatory dysfunction*. Their counterpart in women are *frigidity* and *dyspareunia* (painful coitus).

A. Impotence

Impotence is defined as "a man's inability to attain or maintain an erection of sufficient strength to enable him to perform the act of intercourse" (McCary, 1973, p. 333). The condition can arise from three causes. In *organic impotence*, a rare disorder, a defect in the reproductive or nervous system is the cause. In *functional impotence* the problem can result from any of several conditions that can interfere with the func-

tioning of the sex organs. These include overuse of alcohol or drugs, circulation problems, aging, physical exhaustion, or hormonal deficiencies. By far the most common form of impotence is *psychogenic impotence*. Emotional factors play a central role in this disorder.

Masters and Johnson (1970) classify psychogenic impotence into two types: primary and secondary. The person suffering *primary impotence* has never been able to maintain an erection sufficiently to have successful coitus. From their experience treating 32 males suffering primary impotence, Masters and Johnson conclude that the problem preventing effective sexual functioning in these cases originated "almost entirely in derogatory influences of family background." Because of these influences the individual faced intolerable levels of anxiety either just prior to or during the initial phases of his attempts to have sexual relations. This anxiety resulted from a variety of factors including the influences of the mother, the inhibitions instilled by religious orthodoxy, earlier involvement in homosexual relationships, or terribly adverse experiences with prostitutes.

The thread common to these various types of experiences seems to be the arousal of very intense feelings that conflict with the relaxation and sense of assurance necessary for entering into a sexual act and enjoying it. Several of Masters and Johnson's patients had seductive mothers who insisted that they sleep with them and who manipulated their genitals when they were well into their teen years. The patients who came from a very orthodox religious background were instilled with a sense of guilt about the sexual act itself and for the most part had wives from a similar background having similar feelings. Those who had had homosexual experiences had apparrently never voluntarily given up the idea of homosexual alliances but were abandoned by their partners. Those who attempted to have relations with prostitutes had very dehumanizing and physically repulsive experiences with women who made fun of their anxious, virginal efforts.

Secondary impotence is defined by Masters and Johnson as occurring in men who have had successful coitus at least once but then lost the ability to maintain an erection sufficiently to carry out the act. In the usual case the man's sexual performance has been successful "with the first 50, 100, or even 1000 or more coital encounters." One failure at successful coitus is not regarded as evidence of secondary impotence. Fatigue or distraction may account for an occasional failure in many men. Masters and Johnson do not speak of secondary impotence unless there is failure in one of every four attempts at coitus.

The potential causes of secondary impotence are seen to be quite varied. Any time a man has the opportunity for sex and finds that he cannot achieve or maintain an erection long enough to carry out the act successfully, he is seen to suffer from the shadow of doubt which may make him anxious about his future capabilities, despite a long history of successful coitus. A quite common background factor in the man suffering secondary impotence is an earlier problem with premature ejaculation. A second most common precursor to instances of secondary impotence is a specific incident in which a great deal of alcohol was used before the sex act was attempted. In both cases Masters and Johnson feel that the man has a great deal of anxiety about his potential performance. The premature ejaculator has probably had such concerns over a long period of years whereas in the case of the alcoholic the performance fears are seen to develop rapidly. Other factors found by Masters and Johnson to be associated with secondary impotence include domination by the

Scott F. Johnson

William Masters and Virginia Johnson, pioneers in the treatment of human sexual inadequacies. (Courtesy Little, Brown and Company.)

mother or father during childhood, religious orthodoxy, homosexual conflict, and inadequate sexual counseling.

In their treatment approach to impotence Masters and Johnson emphasize three goals. The first is to reduce the male's fears concerning his sexual performance. The second is to change his behavior so that he becomes an active participant in the sex act rather than the spectator he has customarily been. And, finally, Masters and Johnson try to reduce the female's concern about her partner's sexual performance. A very great stress is placed on keeping sex within its natural context. Masters and Johnson feel that when a man begins to evaluate a sexual performance of his own or that of his partner during an encounter, he is removing it from its natural context. In keeping with these views and their stated goals, Masters and Johnson assiduously avoid a direct approach to the symptoms of impotence. In fact they avoid attempting to treat symptoms at all, for this would require trying to educate or train the male to attain a satisfactory erection. If the therapist were to do this, he would be in precisely the same position as the impotent male who is trying to get an erection through sheer will. The important thing for Masters and Johnson is to produce a state in the impotent male that will allow the natural process to take over.

Masters and Johnson describe the natural cycle of sexual response as involving input from two sources. Sexual excitement results from the arousal that the man senses in the female as he approaches and stimulates her. The signs of her own physical arousal such as increased muscle tone, rapid breathing, flushed face, and vaginal lubrication are usually sufficient to stimulate an erection in the male even without any physical approach from the female. The second source of stimulation for the male

arises from the female's approach to him and her direct physical contact with him. Whatever form it takes, the female's approach to his body in general and the pelvic area specifically is generally exciting enough to produce an erection. The combination of stimuli from both sources of excitation as found in mutual sex play causes a rapid arousal of sexual tension and a full, demanding erection.

The female's role in aiding the male in overcoming his sexual difficulties is essential. Treatment, therefore, always involves a couple. The treatment process entails a series of sessions in which the couple is instructed simply to learn that through giving pleasure to each other they receive pleasure in return. They are instructed to engage in mutual sex play through fondling and caressing of arousing areas. They are never given the specific goal of bringing the male to an erection. The couple is simply encouraged to relax and do what is enjoyable. It is expected that in time an erection will spontaneously occur because neither member of the pair feels compelled to produce it. Once this happens the couple is encouraged to allow the penis to become flaccid and then to restimulate it over and over again. This is done to allow the male to learn that if he has an erection and loses it, he will be able to have another. Actual coitus is not attempted until the couple have been stimulating each other for about ten days. At this time the wife is encouraged to initiate an attempt at coitus.

Ejaculatory Dysfunction

Two kinds of dysfunction are associated with the male's ejaculatory mechanism. The one that is best known is *premature ejaculation.* The other dysfunction is called *ejaculatory incompetence* by Masters and Johnson.

Premature ejaculation is difficult to define. Many attempt to define it on the basis of time. Thus, a man may be labeled a premature ejaculator if he cannot control the ejaculation process for at least 30 or 60 seconds after penetrating the vagina. On the other hand, there are couples who manage quite happily with 30 to 60 seconds of intravaginal penetration. Some women if sufficiently excited before coitus are quite ready to have an orgasm after only a few thrusts of the penis. Masters and Johnson have attempted to resolve this definitional problem by considering a man a premature ejaculator if he cannot control his ejaculation long enough to satisfy his partner in at least half of their coital contacts. Of course, if the female is non-orgasmic for reasons other than the rapidity of the male's ejaculation, this definition does not hold.

In their experience with this problem Masters and Johnson find that concern over premature ejaculation tends to be the greatest among the best educated. The poorly educated rarely ask for help with this kind of problem. Masters and Johnson speculate that among the poorly educated and the low socioeconomic classes the man's satisfaction is of primary concern in the sexual union. For the woman who does not expect equality between the sexes with respect to sexual satisfaction, the sex act may be looked upon as a duty and rapid ejaculation may be seen as a benefit. Generally, the one who complains about the rapidity of ejaculation is the female. If she feels that her own sexual fulfillment is just as important as that of her husband, she will be left unsatisfied when he ejaculates after a few thrusts and will feel considerable frustration.

Masters and Johnson feel that all men who suffer from premature ejaculation show a similar history. The common historical theme involves early sexual experiences in which rapid ejaculation seemed desirable or necessary. In the over-40 age group early sexual experiences have often involved prostitutes. In the old-fashioned house of prostitution every effort seems to have been made to satisfy the male's sexual tensions as quickly as possible because the more customers who could be serviced the better the financial return. Thus, 25 to 55 years ago the young man who set out to "prove his manhood" was subjected to the prostitute's insistence that he finish the sex act as quickly as possible. Masters and Johnson feel that only a few such experiences are enough to establish a pattern in the young man of "self centered expression of sexual need with its resultant physical pattern of rapid intromission and quick ejaculation."

Younger men who suffer this problem or men who have not frequented prostitutes often have a history of having their first sexual experiences in the back seats of cars, at drive-in movies, or in quick visits to motels renting rooms by the hour. Performing the sex act in situations that were semi-private at best or in which there were many pressures concerning the possibility of being observed or surprised in the act encouraged its rapid completion. The male was primarily interested in achieving his own orgasm and took little time to be concerned about his partner's sexual release. Again, only a few such encounters are thought by Masters and Johnson to establish a sexual cycle that is repeated for many, many years.

The practice of withdrawal as a form of contraception is another pattern cited by Masters and Johnson that predisposes the male to quick release and to disregard his partner's needs. Indeed, under these circumstances the female is generally so anxious about the fact that the male may not withdraw in time that she has little opportunity to think about her own sexual release. Thus, the male's withdrawal and ejaculation outside the vagina is looked upon as a relief, and he is encouraged to complete the act as quickly as possible.

In treating premature ejaculation Masters and Johnson first have a discussion with the couple to assure them that the problem can be successfully reversed. This is done to ensure that the couple is not so upset by their prior failures that they are unwilling to try to be sexual partners again. It is stressed that if they can cooperate fully the chances of reversing the pattern of premature ejaculation are very high.

Once cooperation seems assured, the female is encouraged to have a session in which she stimulates the male manually until he achieves an erection. As soon as he attains a full erection, the "squeeze technique" is employed. In this technique the female applies strong pressure to the head of the penis, as a result of which the male immediately loses his urge to ejaculate. In the process he may also lose his erection to some extent. After an interval of 15 to 30 seconds following the release of pressure, the penis is again stimulated to full erection and the squeeze technique is again applied. Alternation of periods of stimulation and pressure ultimately results in the possibility of 15 to 20 minutes of sex play without an ejaculation.

After two or three days of this practice at establishing ejaculatory control, the couple is encouraged to engage in a form of coitus. The male is instructed to lie flat on his back with the female mounting from above. Initially she concentrates on holding the penis within the vagina without the added stimulation of motion. This gives the male the sensation of being contained by the vagina without the threat of a rapid ejaculation. If the male's excitement

mounts to the point that he feels that he is losing control, he is instructed to tell the female. She can then disengage and apply the squeeze technique in the same manner that was practiced earlier. After three or four seconds she can reinsert the penis and again envelop him without adding the stimulus of her own thrusting. This position is practiced in subsequent days with the male being instructed to do just enough thrusting to maintain his erection. Eventually full control can be established through this practice. Masters and Johnson are quite optimistic about the chances of treating this problem successfully.

A second type of ejaculatory dysfunction is *ejaculatory incompetence*. The problem in this case is that while the man can attain and maintain an erection, he cannot ejaculate while the penis is within the vagina. This problem often but not always arises in the first attempt at coitus and continues through all subsequent encounters. In some cases men suffering ejaculatory incompetence can have normal coitus outside of their marriage but not with their wives. The disorder is relatively rare. Masters and Johnson report seeing only 17 such cases in an 11-year span.

Three causes seem to predominate in producing this problem in the cases seen by Masters and Johnson. One is a very traumatic incident, often during the first coitus. Examples include the young husband who, on his wedding night, was told by his wife that as a teenager she had been raped by two men, and the case of a very religious man of puritanical background who was horrified to find on his wedding night that his bride was not a virgin. A second cause offered by some men was simply the fact that they disliked, rejected, or were openly angry at their wives. A third cause involved a fear of causing pregnancy.

Although in some respects ejaculatory incompetence is quite the opposite of premature ejaculation as a problem, the basic treatment approach advocated by Masters and Johnson is similar. The couple is counselled together to establish that they are interested in trying as a unit to overcome the problem. Once cooperation seems assured, they are encouraged to engage in sex play in which the female stimulates the penis manually. Of course, the squeeze technique which is advocated for use with the premature ejaculator is avoided. Instead, the female is encouraged to manipulate the penis "demandingly" and to seek the male's directions concerning how she should stimulate him and what is particularly pleasing. The first milestone in treatment is the female's production of an ejaculation in the male manually. This may take several sessions, but the couple is advised that they need not be concerned about how much time it takes. The production of ejaculation through the female's stimulation is considered a vital step in the necessary direction. It is felt that once he finds that his partner has been able to please him sexually, the male will have less of a tendency to withdraw psychologically from contact with her.

Once the male can have an ejaculation through his wife's masturbatory efforts, the next step is taken to encourage ejaculation within the vagina. This is done by stimulating the male manually until he is close to the point of ejaculation and then rapidly inserting the penis into the vagina with the wife in the female-superior position. Such efforts accompanied by vigorous thrusting on the part of the female are generally sufficient to result in an ejaculation within the vagina. If not, more manual stimulation can be applied. Masters and Johnson stress that the first ejaculatory episode within the vagina is extremely important psychologically both for the male and the female. Once the couple has had a series of successful coital episodes using this technique, precoital play to arouse the male becomes less and less necessary and normal sexual relations are possible.

Masters and Johnson report that 14 of the 17 cases they have seen suffering from ejaculatory incompetence were treated successfully. Two of the failures involved men who were traumatized by some incident either in the premarital or early marital years which seemed to account for their incompetence. The third case involved a male who simply felt no regard for or interest in his marital partner. In retrospect Masters and Johnson feel that such a case should not have been accepted for treatment.

C. Orgasmic Dysfunction

Orgasmic dysfunction is a term used by Masters and Johnson in place of the word *fridigity* that had commonly been attached to the female who seems lacking in sex drive. As McCary (1973) points out, frigidity is a very confusing term because it may mean different things to different people. For example, the husband who would like to have coitus every day of the week may see his wife as frigid if she is only interested three or four times per week. A different man who needs coitus only twice per week might find the same woman's sex drive quite normal or even on the high side. Masters and Johnson, therefore, consider a woman as having an orgasmic dysfunction when her sexual response consistently fails to reach orgasmic climax. They also distinguish two major categories of orgasmic dysfunction. In the case of the first, *primary orgasmic dysfunction*, the woman has never been able to have an orgasm in her entire life through any type of sexual stimulation whether it be heterosexual, homosexual, or masturbatory. The second type is *situational orgasmic dysfunction*. The woman in this category has been able to achieve orgasm at some point in her life by some sexual means but is no longer able to do so.

McCary lists three classes of factors which seems to cause orgasmic dysfunction: organic, relational, and psychological factors. Organic factors include injuries to the sexual apparatus or constitutional deficiencies in them, hormonal imbalances, nervous system disorders, excessive use of alcohol or drugs, and aging. Relational factors include problems with the mate's sexual approach which "turn her off." This can involve overeagerness and self-interest which destroys any romantic mood and produces instead resentment and possibly revulsion. In addition, a woman may find her mate unattractive sexually because she lacks respect for him as a provider or as an adequate male.

The most common cause of orgasmic dysfunction is psychological. Here, the feelings of shame, guilt, and fear are particularly important. Our culture tends to instill in females, sometimes directly, sometimes indirectly, that they must not be open about their sexual feelings and, indeed, that there may be something wrong in having any such positive feelings. Thus, Masters and Johnson find that a high percentage of their cases of orgasmic dysfunction came from a very rigid religious background in which negative sexual attitudes were firmly instilled. From this point of view, the female sees her sexual function as simply providing a receptacle for the male who is thought to have a more powerful sex drive than her own and who must have the "beast" in him satisfied. Her own role is seen to be a passive one from which she does not expect pleasure. In addition, many females associate coitus with physical pain so that for them the sex act is actually to be dreaded. Other causes of orgasmic dysfunction in some women include prior homosexual experiences, and an overconcern about having orgasm. When the female is grimly determined to achieve orgasm, she tends to be quite self-defeating in her efforts.

In treating orgasmic dysfunction in females, Masters and Johnson stress the importance of understanding the female's sexual value system. Society has burdened the female far more than the male with the feeling that she needs permission to express and enjoy her sexuality. Thus, treatment begins with a round-table discussion involving both sexual partners in which the therapists attempt to clarify what pleases the female sexually and what does not. It is then stressed that her response to sexual stimulation must be made within her own framework of attitudes and desires.

Following this the couple is advised to engage in a series of "sensate focus" sessions extending over a period of a couple of weeks. In these sessions they are told to find a private setting that is very comfortable for both of them. They are instructed to remove all their clothing and the male is told to sit on the bed with his back against the headboard and his legs spread. His mate sits between his legs with her

There was a young lady named Wilde
Who kept herself quite undefiled
By thinking of Jesus
And social diseases
And the fear of having a child.

back to him resting against his chest, her legs over his. In this position the male's hands are free to play over the female's body and can easily be guided by her to indicate which sensations are particularly pleasing.

In successive sessions the couple is instructed to direct stimulation toward the inner thighs, the lips of the vagina, and the area around the clitoris. They are cautioned to avoid direct stimulation of the clitoris because of its great sensitivity and the possibility that this would be painful or unpleasant. Also, the female who is struggling to overcome her resistance to expressing her sexuality may feel threatened by sexual feelings that are too intense. It is expected that the couple will move from one level of pleasure to a higher one with each successive session. They are discouraged at first from attempting to achieve orgasm. Instead they are instructed merely to seek sexual pleasure and sustain it.

As the couple begins to approach the higher delights of sex, the next major step in treatment is to have the female mount the male in what is the most comfortable, pleasing position for her. Once the penis is inserted, the male remains motionless and it is the female who is expected to move in ways that are particularly pleasurable for her. She is expected to increase the pace of her movements and to direct her husband's movements in keeping with her own feelings of pleasure. Ultimately, orgasm will be achieved if the exercise is comfortable and unhurried, unimpeded by the feeling of necessity to produce it.

Masters and Johnson report impressive success rates using this treatment technique. They have successfully treated 83 percent of their cases of primary orgasmic dysfunction and 77 percent of their situational cases.

Dyspareunia or painful coitus is another type of orgasmic dysfunction. Although most common in women, it can occur in men too. Among men it involves pain associated with orgasm and results from physical causes. In women dyspareunia also rises from a variety of physical causes which must be treated by physical means, but psychological factors such as anxiety and tension also play an important role. This is particularly the case when the cause is inadequate vaginal lubrication.

Masters and Johnson psychologically equate vaginal lubrication in the female to the male's attainment of an erection. The most common cause of inadequate lubrication is disinterest in sex because of the setting, negative feelings toward the sex partner, concerns over the adequacy of sex performance, pregnancy fears, or fear of pain from deep penetration. Women who prefer lesbian relationships also often tend to lubricate poorly in heterosexual relationships.

Masters and Johnson feel that their therapeutic techniques for treating orgasmic dysfunctions are successful in most cases involving inadequate vaginal lubrication. Two categories of women, however, are particularly unresponsive to treatment. These include those preferring homosexual relationships and those who have little respect or affection for their mates.

Another type of orgasmic dysfunction involves the symptom of *vaginismus*. In this disorder there is a powerful, and often painful, contraction of the muscles around the vagina. These contractions may make penetration by the penis difficult or even impossible. Spasms seem to arise in anticipation of pain associated with penetration or feelings of guilt about having sexual intercourse. Strangely, Masters and Johnson find that the disorder is rarely seen in low socioeconomic or poorly educated groups and, indeed, is seen almost exclusively in the well-educated. One prominent apparent cause outlined by Masters and Johnson is repeated failure at sexual intercourse with an impotent male. Other causes include traumas such as rape, guilt over homosexual leanings, and physical abnormalities that make intercourse painful.

Part of Masters and Johnson's treatment approach to vaginismus involves the use of dilators of increasing size that are inserted into the vagina to stretch the muscles in that area. When the female can insert and hold the largest dilator without discomfort, she is instructed to keep it in place for many hours or perhaps for a whole night. A three- to five-day regimen with the dilators usually suffices to relieve involuntary muscular spasms. However, because the problem also has a significant psychological component, the psychotherapeutic approach advocated for orgasmic dysfunctions may also be applied. Masters and Johnson report success in treating 26 of 29 patients suffering from vaginismus.

SEXUAL DEVIATIONS

DSM-II (1968, p. 44) describes sexual deviations thus:

> This category is for individuals whose sexual interests are directed primarily toward objects other than people of the opposite sex, toward sexual acts not usually associated with coitus, or toward coitus performed under bizarre circumstances as in necrophilia, pedophilia, sexual sadism, and fetishism. Even though many find their practices distasteful, they remain unable to substitute normal sexual behavior for them. This diagnosis is not appropriate for individuals who perform deviant sexual acts because normal sexual objects are not available to them.

The more common sexual deviations include homosexuality, fetishism, pedophilia, transvestism, exhibitionism, voyeurism, sadism, and masochism. Within this group, however, changing times and standards have raised questions about whether several of these sexual preferences should properly be termed deviations. Clearly, it was always the case that when these so-called deviant sex practices were engaged in discretely among consenting partners, there was little likelihood that they would come to the attention of a mental health professional who might label them as deviant. Now, particularly with respect to homosexuality, psychiatrists themselves are wavering about the propriety of applying the term deviancy.

Homosexuality

The homosexual prefers a person of his or her own sex as a sexual object. In some cultures such as ancient Greece and Rome homosexuality was practiced quite widely. Intellectually, homosexuals can be quite superior and well-educated as well as highly successful in their chosen fields. Some have risen to world-wide prominence. For example, Michelangelo, Alexander the Great, Oscar Wilde, and Tschaikovsky are all thought to have been homosexuals.

Kinsey's research led him to conceive of a continuum ranging from complete homosexuality to complete heterosexuality. The anchor point at one end of this continuum is defined by exclusive heterosexuality classifying those who have never had homosexual contacts. The other end is defined by complete homosexuality, a category for those who have exclusively homosexual contacts. Various mixtures of the two types of sexual approaches are found in the intermediate points. The continuum's midpoint is applied to those who have about equal numbers of heterosexual and homosexual contacts. McCary's summary (1973) of studies of the reported incidence of homosexuality indicate that 60 percent of males and 33 percent of females have experienced at least one instance of homosexual play by the age of 15. Thirty-seven percent of male and 13 percent of females were found to have reached orgasm at least one time in their lives through homosexual contacts. Of the men surveyed, 8 percent had been exclusively homosexual for at least three years and 4 percent for their entire lives. Authorities generally agree that there are two or three times as many male homosexuals as females. The average male homosexual seems to have had his first homosexual experience before age 14. The average lesbian tends to have her first homosexual experience at about 19 or 20.

Some attempts have been made to classify the type of homosexual expression as either active (assuming the male role), passive (assuming the female role), or mixed (active at one time and passive at another). Clearly the mixed role seems to be the most common one for most homosexuals. The sexual practices engaged in by homosexuals include mutual masturbation, anal intercourse, oral-genital coitus, and interfemoral (between the thighs) coitus. McCary reports that homosexual practices vary from culture to culture. Some studies indicate that homosexuals in the United States and England prefer oral intercourse to anal coitus. Mexican male homosexuals on the other hand seem by far to prefer anal intercourse.

McCary classifies causal theories of homosexuality as stressing heredity, environment, or sex hormonal imbalances. The more convincing causal theories for McCary, however, are those that emphasize environmental factors such as the pattern of family life that has been experienced. One common pattern in the male homosexual's background finds the mother to be unhappy with her marriage and turning to her son for a relationship that is at least tinged with romance and seductiveness. This makes the son uncomfortable and guilty because of the desires that are aroused for his mother. As a result he eventually comes to avoid women in general since involvement with another female would either reflect disloyalty to the mother or is somehow equated with incest. Commonly in this family the father has a preference for his daughters. As a means of seeking approval from the father and avoiding incestuous impulses the boy may turn away from the masculine role and try to be like a daughter.

Other family patterns may play an important role in impelling a boy toward homosexuality. One involves the presence of a very weak, distant father who plays such an insignificant role in the family that the boy develops an overly strong attachment to the more dominant mother. Still another pattern that can result in homosexuality is the presence of an overwhelmingly powerful father who is so strong and so far beyond what the boy can aspire to that he can never achieve a close relationship with him. The father may try to turn the boy into a "he-man" but the vast emotional gulf between them makes this effort likely to end in failure. Such efforts frighten the boy even more about his capacity to function as a male.

Still other environmental factors which may predispose a male toward homosexuality are very negative experiences with females that become so upsetting that the boy turns away from the opposite sex and looks for companionship in those of his own sex. The same kind of pattern may be found in the female who finds boys rejecting and unfeeling, and no longer wishes to risk hurt. She turns, therefore, to other women for warmth and acceptance.

The attitude of the American culture toward homosexuality varies as a function of whether it involves males or females. In most other cultures there tends to be greater acceptance of male homosexuality than female homosexuality, while in America the reverse is the case. The threat of male homosexuality is apparently much more intense for Americans than is that of female homosexuality. McCary summarizes several studies which indicate that homosexuals in our culture display no more personality problems than one would expect to find in the normal population. Heterosexuals cannot be distinguished from homosexuals on a variety of psychological tests or life history assessments in any way other than with respect to their sexual preferences.

United Press International Photo

Organized homosexual groups have been influential in the decision of the American Psychiatric Association to remove homosexuality from their list of psychiatric disorders.

Perhaps partly in response to studies that fail to discern adjustment differences between homosexuals and heterosexuals, and partly in response to pressure exerted by organized homosexual groups, the American Psychiatric Association has in recent years approved a change in its manual of psychiatric disorders to indicate that homosexuality as such should not be considered a psychiatric disorder ("The A. P. A. Ruling on Homosexuality," 1973). This position has aroused considerable debate and controversy. Standards in our society concerning sexual behavior are shifting, and this shift is apparently being reflected in the altered position of the American Psychiatric Association. Part of the difficulty with such changes is the question of why they come about. If sexual standards were better rooted in well-established theories of mental health or of scientific notions of physical fitness, there might be less controversy over such shifts. Instead they seem to be tied to public opinion, and many are terribly uncomfortable with the idea that psychiatric diagnoses should be influenced by a standard emerging out of the feelings of the lay public.

B. Fetishism

The fetishist is sexually aroused by some object or body part that serves in place of a whole person. Articles of clothing such as shoes or gloves are examples of common fetishistic objects. The hair, the thighs, the buttocks, the ears, or the eyes often serve as arousing body parts for the fetishist. McCary points out that virtually all fetishists are men and that many will steal the objects that excite them.

Fetishism may be seen as an intensification of tendencies that are found in many normal males. Not uncommonly a man finds particular female bodily parts to be especially exciting. Thus, one man may be referred to as a "breast man" and another a "leg man." Fetishists seem, therefore, only to be a bit more extreme in this respect. Typically, the fetishist is an aggressive person who may break the law readily and be troubled by fears of impotence. The sexual attraction to a particular love object usually results from a conditioning process taking place in childhood. An object or part of the body was apparently associated with particularly intense sexual excitement or with the feeling of being loved and accepted by a mother figure. The combination of receiving considerable pleasure from specific objects and not having satisfying current relationships with people seems to be the most frequent cause of fetishism.

Associated with fetishism is compulsive stealing (kleptomania) and compulsive firesetting (pyromania). The kleptomaniac often steals objects that are of no great material value but that have important sexual symbolism for him. Female undergarments would be one such example. The pyromaniac is aroused sexually by setting fires. He enjoys the excitement and tension release of setting a fire and watching it burn. He may even achieve orgasm in the process. Once this occurs he feels guilty and often will help to extinguish the fire.

C. Pedophilia

The pedophile receives erotic pleasure from having some form of sexual relationship with children. This may involve merely exposing the genitals but can involve manipulation or even penetration of the child. Most pedophiles are men and they constitute about 30 percent of the total population of sex offenders. Although pedophiles are not as aggressive or forceful as rapists, their behavior arouses intense public outrage. They are typically referred to as "sex fiends," "perverts," or "sex maniacs." Men who molest children are generally dull intellectually, psychologically disturbed, or alcoholic. Most of them range in age from 30 to 40.

The stereotype of the pedophile is of a person who hides in alleys and shadows waiting to seize innocent, helpless children. Actually, this is not the typical case. Most studies demonstrate that from 50 to 80 percent of child-molesting is carried out by family friends, relatives, or acquaintances. While the children who are the victims find the experience upsetting and even terrifying, McCary points out that it is probably no more frightening than many other traumatic experiences they may have such as accidents or being attacked by a dog. Any lingering effects that occur seem to be brought about by the hysterical reactions of parents to what has happened.

As a group pedophiles tend to be rigid and puritanical about sex. For them, women are either good, virginal, and pure or they are bad and nonvirginal. Religion is very important for many pedophiles, but, despite their devotion to religious ritual such as regular Bible reading and daily prayers for their sinful nature, they are preoccupied with sex. Their sexual urges are viewed as a weakness against which they must constantly struggle.

The pedophile's desire for sexual relationships with children is seen as an effort to cope with his concerns over his own failure in normal adult heterosexual relationsips. He is afraid that he will not manage sex with other adults well, so he turns to children.

Apparently child-molesting is far more common than is recognized. In Kinsey's sample 20 to 25 percent of middle-class females reported that between the ages of 4 and 13 they had been approached sexually by adult males. College students report that 30 percent of men and 35 percent of women had exposure to adult sexual deviants when they were children. Among the women in this sample, half of these experiences were with exhibitionists, whereas for the boys, about 85 percent of these experiences were homosexual approaches.

D. Exhibitionism

The exhibitionist receives sexual gratification from exposing his genitals to people who don't expect it and who usually are upset by it. Of those arrested for sexual violations, McCary reports that about 35 percent are exhibitionists. The vast majority of these are men, but it is difficult to determine whether exhibitionism as a sexual disorder is actually more common among men or women. Our society is far more tolerant of the exposure of the female body than of the male body. Many female fashions such as the miniskirt and hot pants are accepted by society and may well serve the exhibitionistic needs of some women.

The male exhibitionist is generally found, according to McCary, to be a relatively nonaggressive, timid person who is very unsure about his own adequacy. His background is typically characterized by relatively puritanical attitudes about sex, and he tends to have been dominated by a strong mother. Most exhibitionists are married, but their relationships with their wives are generally poor. The exhibitionist tends to be a person who has considerable doubt about his masculine adequacy, a feeling that is confirmed by the fact that he has relatively infrequent coitus and, not uncommonly, suffers from impotence.

The apparent motive behind exhibitionistic behavior is to win attention from others. The exhibitionist seems to need to prove to himself or herself that the basic genital equipment is there and that it makes an impression on other people. As a result,

United Press International Photo

The streaking craze that hit college campuses in the 1970s is not considered a sexual disorder but merely harmless, youthful fun.

the way people respond to exhibitionistic behavior is an important element in preserving it. The victim who becomes excited or upset at the exhibitionist's display reinforces the behavior.

E. Transvestism

The transvestite is sexually aroused and gratified by dressing in the clothes of the opposite sex. Most transvestites are commonly thought to be homosexuals. This seems decidedly not to be the case! McCary reports that in one survey of 272 male transvestites, 74 percent were married, 69 percent were fathers, and only 25 percent reported ever having any homosexual experiences at all. Since Kinsey found that 37 percent of all men he surveyed had at least a single homosexual contact, if anything, transvestites have less homosexual contacts than do normal males. It is very difficult to estimate how prevalent transvestism is, since it is an activity that can be engaged in secretly. McCary estimates that less than one percent of the population engages in the practice. Transvestites vary with respect to the pattern of opposite sex dress that they adopt. One pattern may involve the wearing of the clothing of the opposite sex only occasionally. Another may involve regular wear of the underclothing of the opposite sex. Typically the transvestite reports feeling pleasure and relaxation when he or she is dressed in the clothing of the opposite sex.

Transvestism generally begins in childhood and seems to be related to a feeling of being rejected by a parent because of one's sex. Thus, the ungainly little girl who does not seem very feminine may take to dressing up in boy's clothing. Another possibility might find a mother who, disappointed in the fact that her male child is not a girl, may attempt to deal with this by dressing him up as a girl and allowing his hair to be long and curled for an extended period of years before he goes to school. Since he gets so much approval from others for looking like a girl, the boy can easily be conditioned to find gratification in female clothing.

F. Voyeurism

The voyeur receives particular sensual pleasure and erotic gratification from seeing nude bodies and genitalia or from actually observing the sexual act. While the enjoyment of observing the naked body of one's sexual partner is quite normal, pleasure in viewing is regarded as an abnormality only when it is preferred to actually engaging in sexual intercourse. Many voyeurs prefer to do their viewing surreptitiously. For this reason they are often referred to as "Peeping Toms." Such individuals will peek through bedroom windows, or through keyholes or small openings in the walls of toilets or dressing rooms. Men outnumber women in arrests for voyeurism by about nine to one (McCary, 1973).

As is the case with many other examples of sexual deviancy, voyeurism is thought to arise in a person who is very threatened about his own adequacy. The act of viewing the sexual organs in detail or observing coitus gives great pleasure without risking any personal failure in the act. In addition the fact of being an outsider who is watching people in a very private activity gives some sense of superiority.

G. Sadism

The sadist receives his sexual gratification, or at least a heightening of sexual pleasure, when he causes his partner physical or psychological pain. Physical pain is typically caused by whipping, slapping, pinching, or biting. On a psychological level pain is inflicted through sarcasm, teasing, threatening, or humiliating the sexual partner. Men are more commonly sadists than are women.

There are probably several potential causes of sadism. In some cases the person finds the sexual act to be a shameful, disgusting affair and in his cruelty he is punishing his partner for engaging in something so evil. Another possibility is that by being cruel a person is reassured of his power over his partner. Any person who needs such reassurance, of course, has serious doubts about his capacity in the sexual relationship and finds the situation terribly threatening. Still another possibility is that in being cruel the sadist is merely expressing a great deal of pent-up hostility that has been repressed.

Masochism

Masochism is just the opposite of sadism. In this disorder primary sexual pleasure is derived from being hurt either physically or psychologically by the sexual partner. The masochist may enjoy fantasies of being mistreated or he may actually seek out physical punishment such as being chained or beaten. On a psychological level he may enjoy being abused verbally.

As is the case in sadism, masochism is often thought to result from feelings of shame and disgust concerning sexual relationships. By being punished or mistreated the masochist is thought to be relieved of the guilt he experiences because of his participation in the sexual act. At times the masochist may feel that his ability to endure pain and suffering make him superior to the partner who is inflicting it. In still other cases the sexual partner is identified with a domineering parent who may

have aroused sexual excitement in the child by beating him. Another possible dynamic underlying masochism might be an intense wish on the part of the masochist to show his partner that he is willing to endure all sorts of mistreatment because he fears rejection. By accepting punishment he is trying to win from the partner acceptance and affection.

Necrophilia

Necrophilia is a very rare disorder but one that most experts regard as the most aberrant of all sexual deviations. In necrophilia sexual gratification is received either from observing a corpse or actually having intercourse with it. At times the necrophiliac will mutilate the corpse and even go so far as to cannibalize it. Obviously, this disorder nearly always involves a psychotically disturbed person.

Bestiality

In bestiality sexual pleasure is obtained by having sexual relations with animals. Among people raised on farms, Kinsey has found that approximately 17 percent have achieved orgasm through some kind of sexual relations with animals. Thus, bestiality may simply be an alternative to masturbation as a form of sexual release in some rural societies. On the other hand, if this form of sexual behavior becomes well established, it may indicate a pattern that is used to avoid the chance of failing with the opposite sex.

CONCLUSION

Sexual disorders have long been thought to have deep roots in the personality structure. As such they were thought to be difficult to treat. The recent work of

Masters and Johnson indicates that for many who suffer disorders successful treatment need not be an extended, complicated task. On the other hand, Masters and Johnson are obviously treating a select sample of those who suffer from sexual disorders. Their clients are well-motivated for change, willing to talk openly and in great detail about their problem, and prepared to cooperate in the procedures recommended by Masters and Johnson. Undoubtedly many others suffering from sexual disorders are far from ready to engage in such a direct approach to their sexual problems. Indeed many patients have a hard time acknowledging after much treatment that they even have such problems. Such people may need considerable preparation and treatment before they can participate in sexual therapy.

SUMMARY

1. Sexual disorders were thought to have deep-lying roots in the personality structure.
2. Sexual disorders are not easily defined in a society where standards are undergoing change. Most current experts hold that there are no fixed absolutes in the sexual realm. Only when a sexual practice is harmful to another or unsatisfying to oneself should the term sexual disorder be applied.
3. Mild but possibly widespread sexual problems are referred to as "complications" or "inadequacies."
4. *Impotence* is a common complication in males. It involves the inability to attain or maintain an erection long enough to carry out the sex act. Masters and Johnson have worked out procedures for treating this problem successfully in a high percentage of cases.
5. Another common sexual complication in males is *ejaculatory dysfunction*. This can involve either premature ejaculation or ejaculatory incompetence. Masters and Johnson's studies have shed light on the origins of both such problems and suggested specific treatment techniques.
6. A common sexual complication among women is *orgasmic dysfunction*, a term many experts prefer to *frigidity*. This refers to an inability to achieve orgasm. Masters and Johnson have treated this disorder with much success.
7. *Dyspareunia* (painful coitus) is a type of orgasmic dysfunction that is common in women but can affect men as well. In many cases both physical and psychological causes produce this disorder. This disorder too has been treated with considerable success.
8. *Vaginismus* (powerful contractions of the muscles around the vagina) is still another type of orgasmic dysfunction. Its largely physical treatment has met with much success in recent years.
9. Sexual deviations involve having primary sexual interest in other than the opposite sex, receiving primary gratification from acts other than coitus, or engaging in coitus under bizarre circumstances.

10. The most common sexual deviations are *homosexuality, fetishism, pedophilia, transvestism, exhibitionism, voyeurism, sadism, and masochism.* Changing social standards have raised questions, however, about whether even these disorders, particularly homosexuality, can properly be termed deviations.

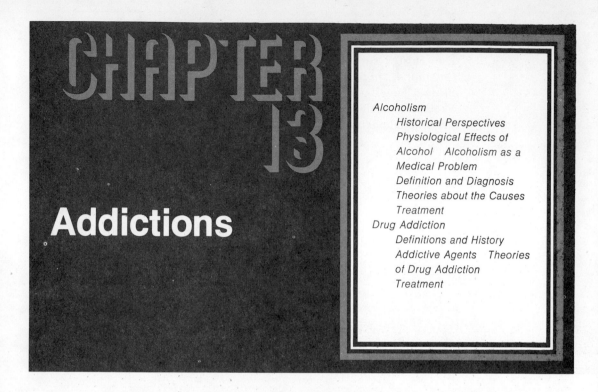

CHAPTER 13

Addictions

29

"It's been a trying morning, so I deserve to have a martini for lunch," the harried advertising executive rationalizes as he takes the first of his many daily drinks. And the ghetto youth says she's going to kick the habit and find a job tomorrow, but she needs a little something to help get her through the night.

The immediate gratification provided by alcohol and drugs indicates that addictions are based on long-standing personality traits. As a result of this and other factors, addictions are a very serious social problem and are extremely difficult to treat.

People can become addicted to a variety of substances. Two major addictive substances are alcohol and drugs of various sorts. Alcoholism has been the most prevalent of the addictions for a number of years. In recent years drug addiction has begun to rival alcoholism as a major social problem.

I. ALCOHOLISM

A. Historical Perspectives

The materials for making alcohol (water, sugar, and yeast) have been available for at least two hundred million years. Doubtless alcohol was first discovered in the form of fermented fruit juice, grain, or honey. Etymologists who have traced the origin of the word "mead" (fermented honey) found that its root in both Sanskrit and Greek is a word that has a range of meanings including "honey," "sweet," "intoxicating drink," and "drunkenness." The association of honey, rather than fruit or grain, with intoxication suggests that this was a major early source of alcohol.

Practically everywhere that man has lived, alcohol has been present in some form. Early European explorers found local wines and beers in the deepest corners of Africa, and even among the least advanced Indian tribes of North and South America. Of the many Stone Age cultures surviving to modern times only three seem not to have used alcohol: those living in polar regions, Australian aborigines, and primitives living in Tierra del Fuego. This presence of alcohol in nearly all existing Neolithic cultures testifies to its significance as a force in man's life.

The oldest examples of cuneiform writing in Mesopotamia, dating back about 5000 years, indicate that alcohol was used at that time for pleasure. Later writings reveal that as early as 2300 B.C. there were taverns in Mesopotamia. This civilization also produced the earliest recorded clinical description of intoxication, as well as the first of many proposed remedies for a hangover: "If a man has taken strong wine, his head is affected and he forgets his words and his speech becomes confused, his mind wanders and his eyes have a set expression; to cure him, take licorice, beans, oleander (and eight other unidentified substances), to be compounded with oil and wine before the approach of the goddess Gula [or sunset], and in the morning before sunrise and before anyone has kissed him, let him take it, and he will recover" (Roueche, 1960, pp. 15–16). The ancient writings of the Egyptians, Hebrews, and Greeks allude to drinking and drunkenness. Genghis Khan cautioned his soldiers to limit themselves to one drunken bout per week; the Greek lyric poet Alcaeus warned that "One that hath

The use of alcohol in ancient times is documented by artifacts such as this fifth-century B.C. Greek vase painting which shows Dionysos banqueting with wine. (The Metropolitan Museum of Art. Gift of Samuel G. Ward, 1875).

wine as a chain about his wits, such a one lives no life at all" (Roueche, 1960, p. 20); and Pliny the Elder reviewing the drinking preferences of the peoples of Egypt, Spain, and Gaul, concluded, "Indeed, in no part of the world is drunkenness ever at a loss" (Roueche, 1960, p. 20).

Physiological Effects of Alcohol

To understand how alcohol affects people psychologically, it is necessary to consider the way in which it is metabolized in the body. Alcohol is released from the body primarily by a process known as oxidation, wherein the alcohol fuses with oxygen and its basic elements leave the body as carbon dioxide and water. A small fraction (2–10 percent) passes out in unaltered form through the lungs, kidneys, and skin.

Of the various types of alcohol, ethyl alcohol oxidizes most readily, which makes it suitable as a beverage. Methyl (wood) alcohol is virtually incombustible and cannot be chemically broken down and eliminated from the body without great physiological effort. It therefore accumulates in the blood, and ingestion even of small amounts leads to high concentrations. The effects of methyl alcohol are prolonged and dangerous both because of the amount of time required to discharge it from the system and because one of the by-products of its oxidation is formic acid, a substance that can destroy the optic nerve.

Unlike most foods, which are absorbed into the body from the small intestine, alcohol can be absorbed directly from the stomach, through the rectum (enema), or through the lungs (by inhalation). As long as alcohol is confined to the gastrointestinal tract, its psychological effects, apart from the purely suggestive, are controlled. Upon absorption into the blood stream a train of physiological events begins that predisposes to a cluster of behaviors known as drunkenness. Several factors influence the amount of alcohol absorbed by the stomach and small intestine. Among these are the speed with which it is consumed and the presence of other food in the stomach. Proteins, chemically the most complex foods, require the most time to digest, and they therefore maximally retard absorption of alcohol.

Once alcohol passes into the blood stream it circulates and its effects persist until it is completely oxidized. Unlike other foods that are oxidized at an irregular rate, depending upon the body's needs, and that may even be stored away as fat, alcohol, once introduced into the blood stream, must be completely eliminated. The prime site

for oxidation of alcohol is the liver, hence the speed of this process is a function of the liver's size and condition. The average-sized liver, in healthy condition, can break down about one-half ounce of alcohol per hour (one ounce of 100-proof whiskey). Although a variety of factors can retard this process, none is yet known that can speed it up.

Since oxidation of alcohol is slow, a large percentage of the alcohol that enters the blood stream at any one time circulates through the body. A small amount is eliminated directly when it passes through the lungs and is exhaled. Since a consistent proportion of the alcohol in the blood stream (about 1 part to 1200) passes out through the lungs, the amount of alcohol in the breath is used as a measure of its concentration in the blood.

As it circulates in the blood, alcohol has its most profound effect on the functions of the brain in ways that are not yet well understood. Some investigators believe that alcohol disrupts brain function by impeding the transmission of nerve impulses across synapses. Depression of nerve function is experienced first in the most complicated, most recently evolved part of the brain, the cerebral cortex. As a result, complicated functions, such as judgment, are disrupted, and there is a release of inhibitions on emotions and impulses normally held in check. This is why alcohol is readily mistaken for a stimulant.

While brain centers that are structurally lower and more primitive than the cerebral cortex are less affected by the presence of alcohol in the bloodstream, they are susceptible to very heavy concentrations. Alcohol-induced cerebellar dysfunction leads to disturbance in balance and in a variety of fine motor skills; thalamic and hypothalamic disruption may induce a comatose state; and depression of the functions of the medulla oblongata can result in a disruption, or even cessation, of breathing and other vital functions. The last result is unusual, because typically unconsciousness intervenes before the person can take in sufficient alcohol to impair the medullar functions. The relatively few occurrences of this condition are attributable to rapid ingestion of very large doses.

Alcoholism as a Medical Problem

The notion that alcoholism is a medical problem probably goes back as far as the third century in Rome, where certain legal commentaries held that repeated drunkenness was a medical rather than a legal problem. In the thirteenth century James I of Aragon issued an edict specifying that the chronic drinker should be hospitalized. Despite these and other occasional assertions that excessive drinking was better classed as a disease than as an illegal act, it was not until the early nineteenth century that a disease-concept of alcoholism was explicitly formulated.

Thomas Trotter, a Scottish physician, argued at that time that "In medical language, I consider drunkenness, strictly speaking, to be a disease, produced by a remote cause, and giving birth to actions and movements in the living body that disorder the functions of health . . . The habit of drunkenness is a disease of the mind. The soul itself hath received impressions that are incompatible with its reasoning powers" (Roueche, 1960, p. 105). Trotter's assertions were vigorously disputed when they appeared in print, particularly by the clergy. The church objected to this view of alcoholism on the ground that it denied the basic tenet of free will and thereby destroyed the role that clergymen had assumed in redeeming the chronic drunkard. Church opposition to the disease concept of alcohlism was an obstacle to the development of treatment centers for alcoholics throughout the nineteenth century.

By the early twentieth century, the opposition to viewing alcoholism as a disease wavered first in Europe and later in the United States. It was not, however, until 1946 that the Presbyterian Church became the first religious organization of some size to withdraw formally its opposition to the disease view of alcoholism. At a general assembly in Atlanta, the Presbyterians accepted the idea that "once drinking has passed a certain point, alcoholism is a disease; that is, the drinking cannot be stopped by a mere resolution on the part of the drinker" (Roueche, 1960, p. 108).

Definition and Diagnosis of Alcoholism

Although many different definitions of alcoholism have been offered, identification of this syndrome is considerably less complicated than is the case with psychopathy. Definitions based on causes of alcoholism are as diverse as notions about its etiology. Those that are based on its behavioral attributes, however, have much in common. The American Medical Association offers this definition: "Alcoholism is a disease which is characterized by a compulsive drinking of alcohol in some form. It is an addiction to alcohol. The drinking of alcohol produces continuing or repeated problems in the patient's life" (Chafetz & Demone, 1962, p. 34). The Cooperative Commission on the Study of Alcoholism (Plaut, 1967, p. 39) has defined alcoholism as a "condition in which an individual has lost control over his alcohol intake in the sense that he is consistently unable to refrain from drinking or to stop drinking before getting intoxicated." Chafetz and Demone (1962, pp. 38–39) described alcoholism as "a chronic behavioral disorder manifested by undue preoccupation with alcohol to the detriment of physical and mental health, by a loss of control when drinking has begun although it may not be carried to the point of intoxication; and by a self-destructive attitude in dealing with relationships and life situations." Each of these examples shares the idea of loss of control over drinking behavior.

Despite the fact that there is considerable agreement about what alcoholic behavior is, diagnosis of the disorder is complicated. This is so because in making a diagnosis a great deal of other behavior in addition to drinking must be considered. Since diagnosis often imputes certain causal factors, the issue may be as complex for alcoholism as for any other disorder. For example, one excessive drinker also displays severe neurotic symptoms and the drinking may be a derivative of the psychic pain caused by the neurosis. Another heavy drinker may be an inordinately passive-dependent person whose drinking occurs when he must stand on his own two feet as a responsible adult. A third man may drink a great deal as a manifestation of early signs of a psychotic break, so that drinking may be the final defense against psychic disintegration.

The diagnosis of alcohol addiction, listed among the personality disorders, is theoretically used when no other underlying disorder seems to be present. The term "addiction," however, implies a physiological addiction induced in a very short time (two to four weeks) by minute amounts of certain narcotics in most people who use them. Addiction to alcohol, by contrast, occurs in only a small percentage of users (no more than 1 percent), and requires large amounts and a long period of use (three to twenty years). It is unclear whether dependence on alcohol is psychologically or physiologically based (as in narcotic addiction). The characteristics of drug addiction include building tolerance for the drug, development of

a physiological state that requires continuous drug consumption to stave off severe withdrawal symptoms, and emotional dependence upon the effects of the drug. While emotional dependence is commonly seen in alcoholism, increased tolerance is is not. In fact, Jellinek (1952) has pointed out that chronic alcoholism is characterized by a *decrease* in tolerance. Also, the need to maintain heavy drinking, to avoid the physiological effects of withdrawal (shakes, DTs, and so on), is relatively unimportant in the history of many alcoholics. Therefore, the straightforward signs that identify narcotic addiction do not exist in alcoholism, and their absence complicates the diagnosis of alcohol addiction. The guidelines in DSM-II (1968) for diagnosing alcohol addiction, in cases where no other underlying disorder can be identified, are also not too helpful. Whether one recognizes an "underlying" cause is not unrelated to whether one expects to find it and how hard one looks for it.

Theories about the Causes of Alcoholism

Physiological Theories

As with many other behavior problems there are both physiological and psychological theories of the etiology of alcoholism. Physiological explanations have related alcoholism to food addiction, defect in the ductless glands, and nutritional abnormality, among other factors. All such theories share the assumption that physiological predisposition toward alcoholism is congenital.

The food-addiction theory (Chafetz & Demone, 1962; Roueche, 1960) holds that some people become sensitized to certain foods that produce an immediate, though temporary, decrease in unpleasant feelings. Because relief is for only the short term, the person soon feels let down, and further consumption is necessary for further relief from unpleasant feelings. Many grains that are prime sources for alcoholic beverages (wheat, corn, rye) are said to be prominent producers of such reactions. Little objective evidence is offered in support of this theory.

Smith (1949) argued that alcoholism is a by-product of metabolic dysfunction resulting from insufficiency in the functioning of the adrenal cortex. Presumed behavioral and clinical similarities between *delirium tremens* and Addisonian crises, prompted

Delirium Tremens (From *A Psychiatrist's Anthology*, by Louis J. Karnosh, published in 1942 by the Occupational Therapy Press, Cleveland City Hospital. Reprinted with permission of the author.)

by hypofunction of the adrenal cortex, led to the development of this theory. Unfortunately, most of Smith's evidence to substantiate this position was based on subjective impression and logic rather than empirical data.

The position that alcoholism stems from a nutritional deficiency has been summarized by Williams (1959), who offered a threefold hypothesis. He suggested that the need to drink is an inner urge mediated by certain "regulatory nervous structures," that the function of these regulatory structures may be disrupted by alcohol poisoning or malnutrition, and that each individual has a unique body chemistry which renders his regulatory nervous structures more or less vulnerable. The particularly vulnerable person may suffer disruption of his regulatory nervous structures as a result of several factors including, particularly, poor nutrition and consequent vitamin deficiency.

This theory was based on the findings that vitamin-deficient rats preferred an alcohol solution to plain water, and that alcohol consumption could be sharply reduced by introduction of a proper diet. Lester and Greenberg (1952) also studied the effects of nutrition on alcohol preference in rats, but in addition to allowing rats a choice between water and an alcohol solution, they provided a sucrose solution. These authors reasoned that nutritionally deprived rats might prefer to drink any caloric solution rather than plain water and thus when alcohol was their *only* alternative, they drank it. Given another alternative, taste preferences might determine what they ingested. The authors found that when sucrose was available to the nutritionally deprived rats, alcohol consumption was greatly reduced even when vitamins were entirely eliminated from the diet. They concluded that regarding nutritional deficiency as the cause of alcoholism was too simplistic.

2. Psychological Theories

It would be helpful to any attempt to understand alcoholism as a psychological disorder if a typical "alcoholic personality" could first be identified. Were this possible, one could concentrate on determining the constitutional make-up and life experiences that produce such a personality. Unfortunately, most students of alcoholism now agree that alcoholics cannot be characterized by a particular personality constellation. Excessive alcohol intake is found in a variety of personality types, presumably in response to a variety of personal problems.

Zwerling and Rosenbaum (1959), however, have pointed out that even though a wide range of clinical diagnoses is found among alcoholics, they may still share *some* common personality characteristics. Intrinsic to this viewpoint is the belief that alcoholism is a defensive maneuver that can be utilized by a variety of people in response to many different conflicts. A review of some psychological theories of the etiology of alcoholism provides a picture of the nature and range of early conflicts thought to be predispositional to alcoholism.

Rado (1933) emphasized that it was the *need* to use a toxic agent rather than the direct effects of the agent that made a person an addict. He, thus saw little distinction between narcotic and alcohol addiction and spoke of each as a manifestation of the same disease, *pharmacothymia*. Rado emphasized that drugs have two important effects: they alleviate pain and they produce euphoria. How pleasurable the effects of a drug will be depends on how prepared one is to experience pleasurable effects. Addicts are people with intense needs for pleasure despite the fact that their addiction causes them considerable suffering in the long run.

For Rado, the person who deeply needs the immediate pleasure afforded by drugs responds to life's inevitable frustrations with "tense depression." Such people have low tolerance for discomfort and unhappiness and, for them, relief is an urgent necessity. With such readiness to enjoy drug effects, the first pharmacologic pleasure is experienced as one of life's most impressive events. The elation deriving from one's first, or at least from an early drug contact, must be intense if the person is to fall prey to addiction. The magical effect of the drug returns one to an early narcissistic state in which interest in reality is lost and unsatisfied instincts find expression.

The "morning after" is marked by the initial depression and the return of reality, but now the ego is even less strong than it was before. In addition, guilt is associated with having suspended concern for reality and there may be still more pressure from outsiders. This process makes further use of the drug necessary until ultimately the ego devotes all of its attention to a single problem, depression, and uses a single solution, drugs.

Knight (1937), like Rado, viewed alcoholism as a symptom in people attempting to resolve their emotional conflict by denial and flight from reality. Although he did not accept the position that there were common features in the personalities of all alcoholics, Knight attempted to describe characteristics of those who drank excessively. Particularly, he implicated an excessively indulgent, early mother-child relationship. Knight argued that most of the baby's early tensions are relieved by nursing and that feelings of comfort and security follow taking something into the mouth. Most mothers avoid building a strong association between such positive feelings and ingesting food by feeding on schedule, tapering off nursing, and gradual weaning. Knight believed that the alcoholic's mother encourages her child to seek oral pacification, and builds a very strong habit in the child. When attempts are made, thereafter, to wean the child, he responds with rage. He can again be pacified through oral means but, ultimately, weaning is necessary and the child feels betrayed. His subsequent life is dominated by attempts to recapture the state of indulgence he experienced as a baby. Knight believed that fathers of alcoholics were typically remote, severe, undemonstrative persons, and poor identification figures who could only give grudgingly as a response to the mother's mediation. As a result the future alcoholic tends to identify with his mother in ways that may create obstacles to a comfortable adjustment later in life.

Knight reasoned that as the potential alcoholic grows up he develops a superficially attractive personality that wrests from others the attention that he needs. Still, life is inevitably frustrating for him and the consequent anger is felt as inner resentment and uncomfortable turmoil. As children and as adolescents prealcoholics are in one scrape after another. Ultimately, drinking begins as a reaction to a frustrated need for indulgence and because it is viewed as a masculine activity. Thus, drinking gratifies the primary need to gain security by oral satisfaction, and alleviates doubts about masculinity inevitably created by early problems of the alcoholic in identifying with his father. When drinking begins in the alcoholic it must typically be increased gradually in order to maintain a sense of well-being. Eventually, the drinking behavior is extreme enough to incur the condemnation of others; guilt then becomes prominent and new distresses are added to old ones to prompt still more drinking.

Menninger (1938) emphasized the self-destructive aspect to alcoholism. He viewed excessive drinking as a form of intended self-cure to relieve the pain of facing reality. He identified factors that he considered predisposing to such a personality and described many adult characteristics of the alcoholic and his parents. The pain that may push the alcoholic to extremes is irrational and unconscious. It derives from intense frustration, consequent rage, and the fear and guilt attending such strong feeling. The alcoholic child is characterized as having experienced profound and unforgiven disappointment from parents who led him to expect more than they could provide. Such early life experiences cause the alcoholic to remain a lifelong oral character with a deeply hidden wish to consume the world orally and to destroy it. Drinking thus serves, at least partly, as a form of revenge.

Menninger believed that the adult alcoholic cannot express his anger directly both because this would entail threatened loss of the loved object and constitute self-threat due to the intensity of his own hostility. Superficially, the alcoholic, seeking popularity, may present a picture of gaiety and charm. Neither the alcoholic nor his parents are very sensitive to his weaknesses. If superficial popularity is achieved, all is thought to be well. Failures resulting from heavy drinking, often after the apparent achievement of considerable success, come as a complete surprise. For this reason he is unwilling to seek help. When he eventually does seek help, it is because of external pressures from a variety of sources. Because the alcoholic feels profound hopelessness and because treatment threatens to rob him of his only form of relief from unbearable suffering, his efforts to get help are often insincere. Both the alcoholic and his parents shy away from getting at the real causes of the disorder. More typically they display a "pathological optimism," even after very superficial treatment procedures, that the problem will simply disappear and all will be well. Menninger believed that the threat of confronting the origin of the psychic pain is for the alcoholic more terrifying than the "suicidal flight" inherent in the addiction.

Schilder's (1941) formulations about alcoholism, while in some ways unique, basically resemble those of Menninger. Schilder began his analysis by examining the effects of intoxication. He noted the profoundly depressing effects of heavy drinking on complex cognitive functions such as judgment, but focused particularly on the mood changes brought about by intoxication. He considered the latter to be most significant and characterized such changes as moving from euphoria and self-confidence to a feeling of self-importance and love for oneself as the state of intoxication deepens. When a person can love himself, he feels loved by others and previously inhibited impulses, including sexual ones, are released.

Given these assumptions about the significant effects of intoxication, Schilder reasoned that the self-deprecating person, who feels undeserving of love, is particularly drawn to overdrinking. The self-assured person may enjoy drinking to some extent but feels no real need for it. The depressed, who must struggle constantly against their impulses and who have deeply repressed sexual urges, find welcome release in drinking.

Bergler (1946) views the alcoholic's drinking as a form of self-destruction. Unlike Menninger, however, he reasons that this form of self-injury is an attempt to destroy a bad mother, with whom the alcoholic has identified, rather than as sheer escape from unendurable suffering. Bergler believes that the adult life of the alcoholic is characterized by a "refusal" to live up to a variety of responsibilities. Alcoholics, for example, refuse to provide stability and security for their wives and children, and

their marriages are inevitably unhappy. The alcoholic often chooses a shrewish wife and, if she is not so either naturally or sufficiently, she is provoked to be malicious. Presumably this recreates his prior experience with an evil mother, with whom the alcoholic has identified despite his hatred for her. The maternal identification generates considerable self-hatred and leads to the characteristic alcoholic drinking cycle.

The sequence of moods that reflects the alcoholic's inner conflicts proceeds as follows: "jocose-morose-bellicose-comatose." Since the alcoholic's drinking is an effort to

© J. Brian King 1975

The jocose mood of an alcoholic leads some people to assume falsely that winos are happy.

poison the bad mother, he feels initially jocose at winning some revenge. This feeling soon disappears and, in its stead, there is a return to the depression and moroseness that prompted the drinking in the first place. Moroseness stimulates a more desperate struggle, which leads to bellicosity manifested by destructiveness, fighting, and sexual acting out. Eventually, sleep sets in followed by a guilt-laden hangover.

Lolli (1956), together with the theorists just reviewed, considers that the alcoholic's problems stem from a poor relationship with his mother. Lolli, however, believes that the primary problem is that he has not had sufficient love early in life and, to some extent consciously, he continues to need experiences associated with being a loved baby such as coddling, pleasurable skin sensations, and warm feelings in the stomach. Along with these he experiences yearnings for security, self-respect, independence, and even omnipotence. The infantile nature of these needs makes frustration inevitable. This, combined with a constitutionally low tolerance for stress (either physical or psychological), encourages a reliance on alcohol designed to help the patient to deny noxious elements of the real world and to sustain the reality of his unconscious. Thus, alcohol substitutes for the mother's milk which is associated with desperately needed love, warmth, and security. Lolli relates the alcoholic's constitutionally low tolerance for stress to internal inconstancy that makes adjustment to external inconsistency difficult. Lolli asserts that the alcoholic is characterized by considerable lability in biological functions such as blood pressure, blood sugar level, and emptying time of the stomach, and that these instabilities are responsible for low stress tolerance.

The descriptions of alcoholics and their problems so far presented agree about some characteristics but not about others. Virtually all view excessive drinking as an attempt to escape a painful life situation. Some emphasize denial of reality as the prime motivation while others emphasize self-destruction. All, however, with the possible exception of Bergler, agree that the alcoholic's prime motivation is the avoidance of unendurable pain. Rado and Lolli allude to a constitutionally low tolerance for stress, which generates heavy reliance on a substance that facilitates psychological escape. Others stress the alcoholic's depressive tendencies and their derivative psychic pain.

Several authors refer to developmental disorders in the oral stage. However, specific formulations regarding the precise nature of the oral problems vary. It is clear that formulations about faulty oral development, since they are based on retrospective review of events that preceded symptom development by many years, are highly speculative. By contrast, flight from painful reality and the struggle against depressive tendencies are currently observable; accordingly, greater agreement on such features is not surprising.

Animal research dealing with effects of alcohol on emotional trauma supports the view that alcohol relieves anxiety. In a classic study, Masserman, Yum, Nicholson, and Lee (1944) created an "experimental neurosis" in cats by administering a blast of air or mild shock at the moment they began eating. The blast aroused somatic manifestations of anxiety and inhibited eating. This "neurotic" behavior disappeared after the cats were given enough alcohol to produce intoxication. The "neurosis" returned as the intoxicating effects of the alcohol wore off. Before induction of conflict most cats preferred plain milk to milk "spiked" with alcohol, but after exposure they preferred the alcohol and milk cocktail. Once the "neurosis" was cured, the cats returned to their original preference for plain milk.

The study by Masserman et al. confronted the cats with an approach-avoidance conflict that interfered with an instrumental response. Conger (1951) sought to establish whether alcohol resolved the conflict by increasing the approach gradient (making the goal more desirable) for food or by decreasing the avoidance gradient (reducing the anxiety associated with approaching the goal). His study demonstrated that alcohol reduced the noxious element in the conflict. This finding led Conger to hypothesize that alcohol acts as a potent reinforcer in humans by reducing fear and, in so doing, makes it possible for drives inhibited by fear to be gratified. He explained the variable effects of alcohol on different individuals in terms of the fact that fear inhibits *different* responses in *different* people (or even in the same person at different times). Thus, reduction of fear can result in the emergence of many different kinds of behavior.

Dollard and Miller (1950) share Conger's view that alcohol reduces the strength of fear and proposed that alcoholic symptoms are learned in accordance with reinforcement principles. The effects of alcohol intake are considered to be particularly reinforcing because they are so immediate. Since alcoholism provides prompt relief from many types of anxiety, the person can build a strong drinking habit relatively easily if there is considerable anxiety to defend against. Dollard and Miller note that one serious drawback to reducing anxiety with alcohol is the fact that it reduces desirable, as well as undesirable, fears. Alcohol may, therefore, reduce the stress of cocktail-party socializing while making the drive home afterward hazardous.

Further support for the view that alcohol's anxiety-reducing effect is a major factor in alcoholism is found in cross-cultural research on the subject. Horton (1943) found a significant correlation, for different cultural groups, between degree of reported insobriety and subsistence hazards that should be related to the amount of anxiety experienced. Bales (1946) studied a number of cultures with various rates of compulsive drinking. He concluded that an important cause is the degree to which the cultural structure creates inner tensions in its members. He also noted that cultural attitudes toward drinking and the degree to which the culture provides tension-reducing alternatives to drinking also affect alcoholism rates. Bales thus argued that alcoholism rates were highest in cultures which aroused considerable tension, in which the attitude toward drinking was convivial, and where few alternative tension-reducing means were available. Cultures that aroused much tension but insisted on complete abstinence from alcohol and provided other means of dissipating tension should have low rates of alcoholism.

McCord, McCord, and Gudeman (1959) attempted to evaluate several of the foregoing theories of alcoholism in an intensive study of 29 alcoholics. All had been part of a project that yielded extensive physiological and psychological data about their home environment prior to adolescence. Unfortunately, the sample was small, particularly since, in many analyses, it was necessary to divide the group into several subgroups. Accordingly, the findings, while suggestive, cannot be regarded as definitive. McCord et al. found no support for etiological theories relating alcoholism to nutritional deficiencies, hereditary factors, self-destructive tendencies, orality, parental pampering, restriction of activities as a child, or parental attitudes toward drinking. They found, however, that ethnic background was related to alcoholism. Significantly more native American, western and eastern Europeans, and Irish in their sample were alcoholic than were Italians and other Latin groups, or British West Indians. They also found that a higher percentage of alcoholics came from homes characterized by considerable overt conflict. A higher percentage of alcoholics came from homes in which both parents were alcoholics than homes in which parents were either moderate drinkers or abstained completely. Finally, there were more middle-class alcoholics than lower-class ones. There were no upper-class subjects in the study.

On the basis of data pointing up the anxiety-reducing effects of alcohol, Ullman (1952) advanced the view that alcoholism is a symptom of a need to reduce tension deriving from the ordinary problems of living. Ullman did not consider it important to know why a particular personality was predisposed to experience considerable tension in the face of life's common demands as the basis for dealing effectively with alcoholism. He believed that treatment approaches with alcoholics which attempted to ferret out basic causes were not successful. Rather he favored approaches that deal with the day-to-day difficulties of the alcoholic and emphasize alternative forms of tension-reduction.

Considerable observation and data support Ullman's viewpoint. That alcohol is tension-reducing has been widely noted by theoreticians and clinicians, and this generalization is well supported by empirical research. Hartocollis (1964) has emphasized that the basic problem in the treatment of alcoholics is that heavy drinking results in "more gain than pain." Therapies that focus on the question "why" about a given form of behavior inevitably draw the person closer to sources of psychic pain. If the alcoholic is peculiarly intolerant of such pain (as many have noted), attempts to provide him with insight may serve primarily to generate further reliance on alcohol for surcease.

Perhaps the most fruitful approach to understanding alcoholism is one that conceptualizes it as a form of self-therapy for unbearable tension. The patient's recourse to such "self-treatment" is probably a function of both constitutional and psychological factors. Constitutionally, the alcoholic may have less tolerance than others for psychic pain and frustration. Psychologically, he is a person who attempts to deal with life's rough spots by avoidance. Many clinical descriptions of the alcoholic in a sober state emphasize his denial, unrealistic optimism, and inability to confront the psychological conflicts that beset him. Not only does the alcoholic lack insight, an attribute he shares with other types of patients, but he is usually also so sketchy and vague about his experiences and feelings that a therapist finds it difficult to develop rich insights about his problems. The alcoholic's denial and vagueness are mechanisms for blurring

© J. Brian King 1975

The ready availability of alcohol in modern society may seem to make things easier for a person who deals with life's stresses by avoidance. But although drink may be comforting, it won't solve his problems.

reality and thus minimizing its painfulness. When such defenses fail, alcohol is used to augment them because it both lowers anxiety directly and disrupts cognitive functioning.

People whose psychological defenses require clear cognition would be threatened by loss of intellectual control resulting from excessive drinking. If a person deals with conflicts through mechanisms such as intellectualization, rationalization, or obsessive thinking, he needs to have full use of his powers of reason, memory, imagination, and so on in order to feel secure. Thus, alcohol has threatening rather than comforting effects for him.

The treatment implications of this view of alcoholism (in contrast, for example, to the treatment of obsessive-compulsive neurosis), are similar to the view developed by Ullman. Efforts to impart insight, often a prime goal with other patients, are contraindicated. The first order of business is treating the symptom and working at developing more adaptive tension-reducing techniques. Also, efforts must be made to help the alcoholic to reorganize his immediate life situation in order to minimize its pressures. Not uncommonly this requires examination of current interpersonal relationships with the family that encourage excessive drinking, unwittingly, at the same time that complaints are being voiced about its effects.

Treatment of Alcoholism

Alcoholics Anonymous

Alcoholics Anonymous (AA) is a self-help organization founded in 1935 by a physician, Dr. Bob, and a stockbroker, Bill W., both of whom were alcoholics. Both had previous contact with the Oxford Group Movement, which was dedicated to the redemption of mankind by striving for absolute goods such as purity, love, unselfishness,

and honesty. AA's founders could not expect the alcoholic, struggling with his weakness and the practical problems it created, to adopt the broad, religious aims of the Oxford Movement but, as Chafetz and Demone (1962) point out, the spiritual, even mystical, nature of the Oxford movement was transferred to the new organization.

The AA program is based on 12 steps and 12 traditions, which are intended to guide the lives of members. Most of these 12 steps have to do either directly or indirectly with God, underscoring the basic religious nature of the approach. Bill W., one of AA's founders, attached particular importance to these 12 steps and believed that unless an AA member followed each as well as he could he signed his own death warrant. The first step of the 12 requires the admission that one is helpless in the face of alcohol and that life is unmanageable as the result of it. The remaining steps depend on step one. If step one is not fully accepted, if the alcoholic does not feel that he "hit bottom," he is not regarded as sufficiently motivated for the AA program.

The remaining 11 steps, as cited in Chafetz and Demone (1962, pp. 149–154), are as follows:

STEP TWO: "Came to believe that a Power greater than ourselves could restore us to sanity."
STEP THREE: "Made a decision to turn our will and our lives over to the care of God as we understood Him."
STEP FOUR: "Made a searching and fearless moral inventory of ourselves."
STEP FIVE: "Admitted to God, to ourselves, and to another human being, the exact nature of our wrongs."
STEP SIX: "Were entirely ready to have God remove all these defects of character."
STEP SEVEN: "Humbly asked Him to remove our shortcomings."

STEP EIGHT: "Made a list of all persons we have harmed, and became willing to make amends to them all."

STEP NINE: "Made direct amends, to such people whenever possible, except when to do so would injure them or others."

STEP TEN: "Continued to take personal inventory and when we were wrong promptly admitted it."

STEP ELEVEN: "Sought through prayer and meditation to improve our conscious contact with God as we understood Him, praying only for knowledge of His will for us and the power to carry that out."

STEP TWELVE: "Having had a spiritual awakening as the result of these steps, we tried to carry this message to alcoholics, and to practice these principles in all our affairs."

Acceptance of the 12 steps commits one to turning to God, to attempting to right all wrongs personally inflicted on others, and to helping others, particularly other alcoholics, by spreading the gospel. Once the individual has achieved continuing sobriety by moving through the 12 steps, the 12 traditions must be adopted as a means of providing continuity to the AA organization. The 12 traditions commit each member to the unity and independent existence of the organization free of professional influences, to helping other alcoholics by spreading the message of AA, to accepting any member who wishes to stop drinking, to standing aloof from controversy regarding public causes in general, to supporting the autonomy of individual groups, and to remaining anonymous with respect to the organization. Anonymity is stressed as a means of submerging individual identity for the sake of the larger principles of the group.

AA groups have frequent meetings at which speakers tell of their trials with alcohol and new members are welcomed. Each new member is placed under the tutelage of a sponsor. As the convert begins to achieve sobriety he is given greater responsibility in AA and eventually becomes a sponsor. Continued involvement in the group can bring him to a leadership role.

The growth of AA was slow at first but by 1952 the organization estimated that it had brought sobriety to 150,000 alcoholics, and to 200,000 by 1960. It is difficult to evaluate the accuracy of these estimates because they are not based on scientific studies. However, there is a general impression that the AA program is an effective one for at least some alcoholics.

Observers have speculated extensively about the bases for AA's success. It has been suggested (Chafetz & Demone, 1962) that AA offers a better self-concept to its more outgoing and sociable members, who are more likely to be attracted to and remain within the program. Considering that the alcoholic is seen as a moral weakling and shunned both by society and professional groups, perhaps membership in a large organization that welcomes rather than looks down on him is a major attraction for him. Chafetz and Demone cite other features of the AA program that may account for its effectiveness. First the program focuses on symptoms rather than psychodynamics, which well fits the preference of most alcoholics. Second, alcohol, which "lubricates social intercourse," is replaced by a common cause that binds AA members together in camaraderie. Third, AA removes the alcoholic from a self-destructive path and directs him back to a middle-class life. He places himself in God's hands and finds forgiveness.

2. Conditioned Reflex Theory

This approach involves building a simple association between alcohol intake and a noxious response, vomiting. It is accomplished by having the alcoholic drink a mixture of liquor and some noxious drugs such as Emetine or apomorphine. Conditioning sessions require from one-half to one hour and generally are given in a series of four to six, one every other day. It is routine to repeat such treatment series after six months and one year.

Surveys of the effectiveness of this approach (Chafetz & Demone, 1962) indicate that the greatest success is achieved with alcoholics who are depressed, and from the relatively higher socio-economic levels. The "skid row" alcoholic, for example, tends not to respond to this approach.

Another form of aversive conditioning that has been suggested for alcoholics is called "covert sensitization" (Cautela, 1966). In this approach the patient must imagine many highly aversive situations associated with drinking both in sessions with a therapist and at home. Hopefully the association between the undesirable situation and the desired drinking response will make the latter unpalatable. An example of the type of aversive image that can be used is as follows:

You are walking into a bar. You decide to have a glass of beer. You are now walking toward the bar. As you are approaching the bar you have a funny feeling in the pit of your stomach. Your stomach feels all queasy and nauseous. Some liquid comes up your throat and it is very sour. You try to swallow it back down, but as you do this, food particles start coming up your throat to your mouth. You are now reaching the bar and you order a beer. As the bartender is pouring the beer, puke comes up into your mouth. You try to keep your mouth closed and swallow it down. You reach for the glass of beer to wash it down. As soon as your hand touches the glass, you can't hold it down any longer. You have to open your mouth and you

puke. It goes all over your hand, all over the glass and the beer. You can see it floating around in the beer. Snots and mucus come out of your nose. Your shirt and pants are full of vomit. The bartender has some on his shirt. You notice people looking at you. You get sick again and you vomit some more and more. You turn away from the beer and immediately you start to feel better. As you run out of the bar room, you start to feel better and better. When you get out into clean fresh air you feel wonderful. You go home and clean yourself up. [Cautela, 1966, p. 37]

3. Antabuse Treatment

In Denmark in 1948 it was discovered that small amounts of a drug called disulfiram (manufactured under the trade name of Antabuse) produced a marked intolerance for alcohol. It was tested in the USA in 1949 (Fox, 1967) and has come to be widely used in the treatment of alcoholics.

The alcoholic is instructed to take Antabuse daily, on a regular basis. By itself it has few side effects. However, if alcohol is ingested while Antabuse is in the system, within from five to ten minutes the individual's face becomes very red, his throat constricts and gets irritated, and he begins to cough. These symptoms become more intense in about thirty minutes. If a large amount of alcohol has been taken, the victim, in from thirty to sixty minutes after the onset of symptoms, may become nauseated, pale, suffer a drop in blood pressure, vomit, and feel very uncomfortable. Dizziness, head pressure, blurred vision, breathing difficulty, and numbness of the hands and feet have also been reported. Since Antabuse is discharged from the body very slowly (four to five days), it effectively discourages impulsive drinking by its users.

As a treatment approach Antabuse is directed only at alcoholic symptoms. It does not reach for underlying causes and is effective only as long as the alcoholic takes the drug regularly. It does deter impulsive drinking bouts. Many alcoholics are threatened by this treatment approach, recognizing that they will not be able to turn to alcohol whenever they feel a need for it. Some also express concern that they might accidentally drink a beverage which, unknown to them, contains alcohol. It is generally felt in treatment agencies that Antabuse is useful in helping some alcoholics achieve control over a drinking habit but that it should be administered in conjunction with other therapeutic efforts.

LSD Therapy

In recent years attempts have been made to use LSD, either alone or in conjunction with group therapy, as a means of treating alcoholism. Ditman (1967), who reviewed results of the LSD therapies with alcoholics, reports that the particular therapist's orientation determined the way in which the drug was used and the dosages that were administered. Those therapists who consider the major value of LSD to be its ability to induce a transcendental experience that reveals unconscious motives and conflicts to the patient administered large doses. Other therapists who believe the primary values of LSD to be that it enhances recall, makes one less defensive and more aware of the present, prescribed the drug in small doses as an adjunct to insight therapy.

There are numerous reports of LSD therapy with alcoholics, many indicating that high percentages (50–75 percent) of alcoholics who were unresponsive to approaches like AA improved under this regimen. Unfortunately none of these studies was done under double-blind conditions in which neither therapist nor patient knew whether LSD or a placebo was being used. Thus, it is impossible to determine how much of a role the therapist's own enthusiasm about the treatment played in determining the drug's effects or in shaping the obtained results. Until more definitive studies are done with LSD as a treatment agent or adjunct, its utility cannot be well assessed.

DRUG ADDICTION

Definitions and History

The World Health Organization has defined drug addiction as "a state of periodic or chronic intoxication, detrimental to the individual and to society, produced by the repeated consumption of a drug (natural or synthetic)" (Kolb, 1968, p. 516). Three characteristics of drug addiction are identified: (1) the addict feels overpoweringly compelled to obtain the drug by any necessary means in order to continue taking it; (2) higher and higher dosages are required to maintain the feeling the drug provides, a phenomenon called *tolerance*; and (3) both a psychological and a physical dependence on the drug effects can develop. A psychological dependence can emerge because of the tension-reducing effect of a drug. Physical dependence can emerge because repeated ingestion of the drug alters the normal physiological state so that attempts to abstain from its use results in an illness called the *withdrawal syndrome*. The symptoms of this syndrome vary with the drug which has been used.

As is the case with alcohol, man has used various narcotics throughout recorded history. Opium, made from the opium poppy, was in use as far back as the Sumerian civilization, which named it "the plant of joy." Hemp, from which a variety of narcotics is derived, has an equally long history. It was

The Bettmann Archive

This opium den in New York City was frequented by young working women in the
1880s.

nesses, having undesired side effects, being
toxic, and being available in a pure enough
and appropriately potent state for use with
patients. The legal status of drugs varies
considerably, depending upon social use.
Alcohol and tobacco have been so widely
used for so long that controls on them are
limited. Peyote, which has been controlled
more strictly, is made legally available to
certain North American Indian groups for
use in religious rituals that have long been
practiced.

In a recent book on drug use in colleges,
Nowlis (1969) has detailed the complexity
of settling on a meaning for the term "drug"
and has adopted the very broad pharmacological definition cited above. In these days
of the proliferation of synthetic drugs and
the widespread use of many common substances (banana skins, glue) for their potential psychological effects, such a broad
definition seems appropriate. The remainder
of this section will be devoted to a sampling
of currently prominent addictive agents, a
discussion of the psychodynamics of addiction, and a presentation of some recent
treatment approaches.

used very early in India as a part of certain
religious rites. The chewing of coca leaves
has been a custom among South American
Indians since at least the eleventh century,
although cocaine did not find its way to
Europe until the mid-eighteenth century.

Before proceeding to a discussion of drug
addiction, some effort should be made to
define the term "drug," which can have a
variety of meanings. Definitions of the term
can be based on many factors. Pharmacological definitions are broad and objective:
"any substance that by its chemical nature
alters structure or function in the living
organism . . ." (Nowlis, 1969, p. 5). A more
popular definition might be "any chemical
substance that alters mood, perception or
consciousness and is misused, to the apparent detriment of society" (Nowlis, 1969, p.
5). Physicians think of drugs in terms of
their potential for treating or diagnosing ill-

B Addictive Agents

1. Opium: Its Derivatives and Synthetic Equivalents

As indicated above, the use of opium can
be traced back thousands of years. Until
1903 it was used in its crude form, either
being smoked or, as a tincture called laud-
anum, taken orally. Early in the nineteenth
century an active constituent of opium
known as morphine was isolated and within the next thirty years several alkaloids
deriving from opium (such as codeine) were
discovered. Heroin, another substance isolated from opium, was discovered in 1898
and was welcomed at the time because it
was thought to be nonaddictive and there-

fore a good substitute for morphine as a painkiller. It took fifteen years of widespread medical use before its addictive properties were recognized. Currently heroin addiction is seen by some as one of the most difficult to cure. Demerol and methadone are synthetic equivalents of the opiates, which were hailed, like heroin, as nonaddictive, until it was discovered after a short period of use that they did cause addiction. Nyswander (1959) has classified the various opiates and their synthetic forms for addictive potential: in decreasing danger they are morphine, heroin, Demerol, methadone, and codeine.

For a number of years the drug used most widely by addicts has been heroin. Two sufficient reasons are its potency and its availability. The amount taken varies widely and changes for a given individual as tolerance increases. If the drug is withdrawn, after undergoing the withdrawal syndrome, tolerance for such opiates decreases and the dosage level used before withdrawal can be fatal.

Use of the opiates typically brings a feeling of relief and exhilaration along with an increase in efficiency. The positive aspects of this feeling are so pleasant that as they wear off the desire for more of the drug to maintain the effect is irresistible. With further use the original dosage is sufficient to ward off the withdrawal syndrome but not enough to bring the exhilaration that had formerly been felt. Therefore, an increased dosage becomes necessary. Eventually, when these drugs are used in high doses, there is a complete contentment with the drug-produced, pleasurable effects and a consequent loss of ambition. Usually, opiate addiction is associated with a loss of moral and ethical values. This is not attributable to any direct drug effects but rather to the social consequences of being addicted to a drug that is illegal and expensive and that saps one's motivation for steady work. The opiates are not thought to have any direct detrimental physical effects.

The withdrawal syndrome associated with opium addiction is severe. The early symptoms of yawning, sneezing, perspiration, and tearfulness appear if a dose of the drug has not been repeated within 12 to 14 hours. Further passage of time leads to an intensification of these symptoms (loss of appetite, tremors, dilated pupils) until, after about 36 hours, muscle twitching becomes uncontrollable and leg, stomach, and back cramps develop. At this time there is considerable restlessness, inability to sleep, a rise in blood pressure and pulse rate, and, frequently, vomiting and diarrhea. These acute symptoms reach a peak at about 48 hours of abstinence and persist at this level for another 72 hours. They diminish gradually thereafter over a five- to ten-day period. The intensity of the abstinence syndrome is positively related to the dosage level of the drug that was being taken. The only means of limiting the intensity of the abstinence syndrome is the administration of small quantities of the drug. In medical settings withdrawal is accomplished gradually because abrupt withdrawal is regarded both as inhumane and unsafe.

Cocaine

Addiction to cocaine is rarer than to the opiates. This may be due in some measure to that fact that the drug is less available and partly because continued use of cocaine leads commonly to terrifying visual and auditory hallucinations. Early in their experience with cocaine, addicts are stimulated by the drug. It produces a sense of exhilaration and self-confidence that may actually enhance capacity for work, along with a flow of ideas and pressure toward speech and activity.

The withdrawal symptoms associated with cocaine are feelings of weakness, depression, and irritability. In addition there may be digestive difficulties, tremors, spots before the eyes, confusion, and impotence. These are, in general, far less severe than the symptoms associated with withdrawal from the opiate drugs.

3. Barbiturates

In 1903 the first sleep-inducing barbiturate was synthesized. Since that time about fifty derivatives have been developed. These may be classified in terms of their duration of action: among the long-acting barbiturates phenobarbital is the best known; those of intermediate duration include amobarbital (Amytal), pentobarbital (Nembutal), and secobarbital (Seconal); the very short acting types include hexobarbital (Evipal) and thiopental (Pentothal).

Barbiturates act primarily as depressants affecting a broad spectrum of functions, such as the nerves, skeletal muscle, smooth muscle, and coronary muscle. Depending on dosage level, the central nervous system reaction may range from mild sedation to coma. Like alcohol, which is also a depressant, moderate doses of barbiturates can lead to euphoria related to disinhibition. An overdose of barbiturates results in poisoning that may lead to convulsions, coma, and even death. The amount of barbiturates representing an overdose varies from person to person and even within a given individual from one time to another. One factor related to whether a given dose is excessive is the presence of large amounts of alcohol in the system. Normally harmless amounts of barbiturates can lead to severe reactions in one who has been drinking heavily.

The tolerance phenomenon is found in habitual users of barbiturates even when dosage levels have been low, and physiolog-ical dependence on the drug can develop. In the latter case abrupt withdrawal can lead to extreme sequelae such as convulsions, coma, stupor, and death.

4. Amphetamines

The amphetamines produce effects resembling those experienced when the sympathetic nervous system is stimulated, hence they are classed as "sympathomimetics." The general effects include reduced appetite, heightened wakefulness, inhibition of intestinal function, increases in heart function and certain metabolic actions, and stimulation of blood vessels supplying the skin and mucuous membranes. Different sympathomimetic drugs induce different degrees of each of the above actions. Amphetamine (Benzedrine), the more potent dextroamphetamine (Dexedrine), and metamphetamine (Methadrine) are potent stimulators of the central nervous system in addition to possessing all the general characteristics of sympathomimetics.

Amphetamines are generally taken orally, but there are increasing reports of its administration (particularly Methedrine) intravenously. Many who "shoot" amphetamine, or take it by injection, for "kicks," take excessive doses over a short period of time and run the risk of severe toxic reactions. As in the barbiturates, what amounts to a toxic dose varies among individuals. Toxic reactions include a variety of central nervous system, cardiovascular, and gastrointestinal effects such as restlessness, irritability, tenseness, panic states, dizziness, headache, nausea, and vomiting, chest pain, and stomach cramps. Fatal doses result in convulsions, coma, and cerebral hemorrhage.

Unlike most other central nervous system stimulants, amphetamines lead to tolerance that has selective effects on various aspects of the system. Thus, more of the drug might be required to maintain a feeling of well-being, but this increase may lead to restlessness and insomnia. As a result amphetamines are frequently used alternately with barbiturates.

Withdrawal from amphetamines does not lead to the dramatic symptoms found in the case of other drugs, so that it is questionable whether a true physical dependence develops. Nowlis (1969) cites some investigations in which abstinence has been seen to result in considerable drowsiness and long periods of sleep followed by a ravenous hunger for food which are taken as indications of physical dependence. There seems to be little question of a psychological dependence on amphetamines in many individuals who need the drug to maintain an energetic, self-confident state.

5. Marihuana

Strictly speaking the term *marihuana* refers only to certain forms of *cannabis*, a substance obtained from the hemp plant, and, contrary to popular usage, is not synonymous with cannabis. Cannabis is derived from a residue found primarily in the top of the female hemp plant but also present in lesser concentrations in the plant's leaves and shoots.

A number of factors relate to the potency of cannabis: the climate and soil in which the plant grows; the time when it is harvested, as well as the method used; and the part of the plant from which it is obtained. The most potent form of cannabis is used in the form of cakes in India where it is called *charas* and in a white powder in the Middle East and Northern Africa where it is known as *hashish*. A less potent form of cannabis taken from the dried leaves and shoots of the hemp plant is called *bhang*. The marihuana commonly used in the United States is made from the dried, chopped-up stems and flowering tops of the plant and is less potent than bhang. Marihuana from hemp plants grown in North America is less potent than that made from plants grown in more suitable climates. Thus, a wide range of potency exists among the many forms of cannabis. Nowlis asserts that North American marihuana "may have a potency relationship to the 'best' charas like that of beer to 190 proof alcohol" (1969, p. 93).

The effects of marihuana vary widely as a function of how it is administered (usually it is smoked), the dosage, the personality of the user, and the circumstances surrounding its use. The lower the dosage level the more highly related are its effects to the user's personality and expectations. Within a given individual effects vary from occasion to occasion. Most marihuana users find that low dosage levels produce pleasurable effects such as contentment, exhilaration, a ready flow of ideas and imagination, and a feeling of floating beyond reality with time expanded and objects seeming further away than they are. High dosage levels can have unpleasant effects such as vivid hallucinations.

Toxic reactions to cannabis are reported only among those using high doses of the substance. Such reactions are manifested by acute psychosis. The toxic physiological states seen in the excessive use of amphetamines, barbiturates, alcohol, and other drugs are rarely found with cannabis.

It is currently agreed, according to Nowlis (1969), that only a slight tolerance develops for marihuana and that regular use of the less potent forms of cannabis rarely leads to a physical dependence on it. In parts of the world where the more potent forms of cannabis have been used over extended periods of time there have been reports of the development of a psychological dependence on the drug. Nowlis cites one study of nine

Indian soldiers with severe withdrawal symptoms after being transferred from India, where the drug was available to them, to another country.

In recent years research studies have suggested that the use of marihuana causes a variety of adverse effects. These include irreversible brain damage, a lowering of the body's resistance to infectious diseases, an increase in the likelihood of birth defects, lung damage, and sterility or impotence or both. A recent review (Brecher, 1975) of a mass of research on marihuana and its effects indicates that few, if any, of the findings of marihuana's adverse effects are reliable. Whenever a particular research result could be checked through a replicated experiment or a better one, the allegation that marihuana had adverse effects did not hold up. The conclusion drawn in this review was that marihuana, while not especially harmful, is probably not safe or harmless to everyone who uses it at whatever dosage levels and conditions of use are applied.

Lysergic Acid Diethylamide (LSD)

LSD is one of the most potent of a group of drugs characterized as "psychotomimetic" (imitating psychosis), "hallucinogenic" (producing hallucinations), or "psychedelic" (mind-manifesting), depending upon one's attitude toward them. Some of LSD's effects, such as increased blood pressure, stepped up pulse and heart rate, dilation of the pupils, tremors, flushing, chills, nausea, irregular breathing, and anorexia, indicate stimulation of the sympathetic nervous system. In addition, however, these drugs (psilocybin and mescaline in addition to LSD) have profound psychological effects.

LSD is an alkaloid synthesized from lysergic acid, a component of some alkaloids of ergot, a fungus that grows on rye and wheat. Compounds containing lysergic acid

are also found in certain varieties of the morning glory plant. LSD was first synthesized by Stoll and Hoffman in Switzerland in 1938, but its potent psychological effects were not noted until 1943 when it was found to produce dizziness and restlessness along with marked perceptual and cognitive effects that were likened to a temporary psychosis.

LSD is such an exceedingly potent drug that a normal dose is only 100–250 micrograms (an amount equivalent to two aspirin tablets would provide 6,500 100-microgram doses). It is taken orally and disburses widely throughout the body. There are no well-established theories of how LSD acts physiologically. It is thought to have some direct effects on a variety of cells, tissues, and body organs in addition to interfering with the synaptic transmission of nerve impulses. It may conceivably even change a biochemical system the functioning of which is essential to proper central nervous system function.

Despite the fact that psychological effects of LSD, like any other drug, are a function of a host of factors like dosage level, the personality and physiological state of the user, his expectations, the setting, and so on, dramatic perceptual alterations are experienced most commonly. Vision is generally affected most profoundly. The objective properties of objects take on a new intensity. Colors are more vivid than usual, patterns stand out and may become wavy, and formerly unnoticed textural qualities are emphasized. Emotional meaning is attributed to colors. Senses, other than visual, become more acute so that music, for example, may sound far richer than ever before. Visual experiences in the absence of appropriate cues do occur, but these are usually recognized as being caused by the drug and are not reacted to as true hallucinations. At times, though, these experiences relate to one's earlier life situation and may be very unpleasant and upsetting.

Toxic reactions or "bad trips" do occur, but it is impossible to estimate their frequency. The most common form of such reactions involves a feeling of panic, severe physical complaints, and unmanageable behavior. Depression is the most common prolonged effect, but there are numerous reports of psychotic disorders and suicide attempts. Most recently, conflicting reports have been made of toxic effects of LSD on certain body cells. Broken chromosomes have been found in blood samples of individuals taking LSD. The implications of these findings are not yet clear.

Like marihuana, LSD has been used for too short a time to form many definitive impressions of its long-range effects. Nowlis' conclusion (1969), however, seems well taken: "It is certainly reasonable to hypothesize that any substance which closely resembles endogenous substances, which affects many systems, which is potent in infinitesimal amounts, which has its main effects long after it seems to have been eliminated from the central nervous system has important effects throughout the body" (p. 107).

η. Caffeine

Caffeine stimulates the functions of the central nervous system and the heart. It is, of course, found in a variety of popular beverages such as coffee, tea, cocoa and cola drinks. Those who use these beverages to a high degree tend to develop tolerance as well as a physical dependence and craving for them when they try to give them up.

Caffeine's desirable effects are not dissimilar to those resulting from the use of cocaine and the amphetamines. It stimulates cerebral cortical functioning so that the user thinks more clearly and feels less drowsy than normally. As a result the user can sustain intellectual effort and has a keen appreciation for sensory stimuli. Reaction time steps up and motor activity tends to be increased. Thus, the typist, for example, can type faster and make fewer errors with caffeine. In addition to cerebral cortical effects, caffeine affects the heart rate and rhythm, the diameter of blood vessels, blood circulation and pressure, urination, and many other physiological functions. Further, it stimulates gastric secretions. This can be a problem for those suffering from peptic ulcers. Caffeine also increases the basic metabolism rate. The excessive use of caffeine can have some very adverse effects. Restlessness and disturbed sleep, irregularities in heartbeat and rhythm, and a rapid heart rate are examples. Irritation to the gastrointestinal tract and diarrhea are other common symptoms.

Obviously many of caffeine's seriously adverse effects only result from the intake of extraordinarily high doses of the drug. Then why can so many caffeine-containing substances be used quite commonly without causing considerably more damage than they do? The answer is that caffeine is generally taken in such dilute forms that it would be difficult to consume a dangerous amount in one sitting. In addition substances in common use that contain caffeine have been domesticated. Coffee is usually taken with cream. Most caffeine drinks are used along with a meal or even after a meal. All this affords protection for the stomach lining.

8. Nicotine

Nicotine is a drug found in tobacco. As such it is used by anyone who smokes cigarettes, cigars, or a pipe to a great extent or by those who chew tobacco or use snuff. Its effects vary. For some people at certain times it can be a stimulant. For others or at other times it can be a depressant or a tranquilizer. Physiologically tobacco is one of the most damaging substances that man uses. The smoke associated with various uses of tobacco is a prime cause of lung cancer. The use of cigars and pipes as well as chewing tobacco increases the risk of cancer to the oral cavity. Nicotine itself has adverse effects on heart function and is a cause of various heart and circulatory diseases.

The addicting properties of nicotine are hard to deny. The sailors of Columbus and other early explorers learned the smoking habit from their contact with American Indians. Once taught to use tobacco they could not give it up easily and the habit as well as the tobacco leaves and seeds were carried back to Europe where its use spread widely. Over the years despite its high cost the use of tobacco spread even to the poor. By the middle of the seventeenth century tobacco use had spread throughout central Europe and one report of the time pointed out that even those who could barely afford their daily bread were finding the money for tobacco. Various attempts to prohibit its use by church leaders as well as heads of state failed. One recent report of tobacco use points out that no country that has ever taken up the use of tobacco has been able to give it up. Furthermore, its use has not been replaced by other drugs. Tobacco smokers who learn to smoke opium or marihuana continue to smoke tobacco along with them. This indicates that there is something in the tobacco itself that is basic to the addiction rather than simply the act of smoking. Many studies indicate that the nicotine in tobacco clearly causes a craving.

On a number of grounds people have tried to deny that smoking is addictive. It has been argued that giving up smoking does not result in withdrawal symptoms. Studies in this area, however, indicate that when smokers do give up nicotine they report feeling drowsy, suffer headaches, digestive disturbances, as well as other symptoms. Furthermore, the craving that people have for a smoke may be seen as an aspect of physiological withdrawal. A second argument used against the idea that one can become addicted to nicotine is that a tolerance does not develop for it. This argument too seems fallacious. Most people start out with no more than a puff or two on a cigarette and eventually build up to a point where they use 10, 15, or far more cigarettes per day. Finally, it is argued that cigarette use is unlike the use of other addictive drugs in that it does not result in antisocial behavior. This would seem to imply that there is something inherent in a drug like heroin that causes antisocial behavior. Actually it is the fact that the drug is unavailable legally that results in its surreptitious distribution and exorbitantly high cost. This factor leads to antisocial behavior. But the same situation arises when cigarettes are in short supply. In war-torn countries where cigarettes were scarce, black markets quickly developed in which tobacco was one of the main commodities. This was the common experience of GIs in occupied Germany and Japan after World War II. In this black market operation much illegal behavior was engaged in by both those who sold cigarettes and those who had to do what they could to get the money to buy them.

Brecher (1972) has made a number of suggestions for minimizing the dangers of tobacco use. Since smoke inhalation is a major cause of lung cancer, he suggests developing short cigarettes that are very high in nicotine content so that the smoker can take in a maximum of nicotine with a minimum of smoke. Other suggestions include converting cigarette smokers to cigars and pipes, the smoke of which is not usually inhaled, and developing smoke-free ways of bringing nicotine to the lungs. These would, of course, only be partial solutions since the use of cigars, pipes, and chewing tobacco still entails the risk of mouth cancer. Furthermore, nicotine itself causes heart and circulatory diseases. Thus, a further necessary direction in conquering this addiction is to find a substitute for nicotine that does not damage vital organs.

Theories of Drug Addiction

As is the case with alcoholism, theories of drug addiction emphasize either physical or psychological factors, although fewer theories of any kind seem to be offered to explain drug addiction than alcoholism.

Physical Theories

The physical dependence that develops for many drugs is regarded by some workers as an important etiological factor in drug addiction. Certainly in the treatment of addiction, the initial problem that demands attention is physical withdrawal from the drug. Tolerance and abstinence phenomena are other dramatic aspects of experience with many drugs and the belief is plausible that many people, through accident, curiosity, or a variety of other possibilities, become ensnared by a drug whose tenacious grip they are unable to break.

Ausubel (1961) minimizes the role of physical dependence in the development and maintenance of an addiction. He asserts that the withdrawal syndrome is no more severe than a bad case of influenza and that it never lasts longer than 10 days. It is inconceivable to Ausubel that people remain addicted, with all of the risks and disadvantages entailed, simply to avoid a 10-day illness. Furthermore, he points out that addicts do not take the minimal amount suffi-

cient to forestall abstinence symptoms but rather that which will produce a more positive drug effect. Many addicts also become readdicted after undergoing withdrawal— Hunt and Odoroff (1962) found that 90 percent of 1881 addicts were readdicted within six months of hospital discharge. For these reasons Ausubel rejects physical dependence as a significant factor in drug addiction and stresses psychological causes.

Wikler (1968) is less ready than Ausubel to reject physical dependence as a major contributor to addiction. He has argued that after the addict has undergone the dramatic symptoms of withdrawal and is presumably no longer physically dependent on a drug, he may still suffer a subtle "derangement of homeostasis" predisposing him to relapse. In addition, Wikler reasons that abstinence symptoms become conditioned to many environmental stimuli so that even after withdrawal is achieved, the cured addict can reexperience abstinence symptoms through contact with aspects of the old environment to which these symptoms have been conditioned. This factor, too, would predispose the addict to relapse. The problems presented by the homeostatic disruption and conditioning are thought by Wikler to have gone entirely unnoticed while playing a major role in the intractibility of addiction.

Psychological Theories

Most theorists who discuss the psychological factors fundamental to drug addiction tend to emphasize the importance of the immediate effects of the drug rather than the individual dynamics that may have prompted one to become involved with drugs. Rado (1933), whose theory of alcoholism was described earlier, emphasizes the significance of the earliest drug experience in an emerging addiction. Wikler (1952, 1953) stresses the effectiveness of

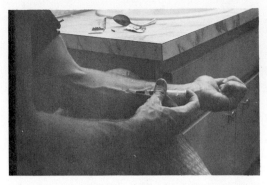

© Chris Rollins

An intravenous injection of heroin produces an almost instantaneous euphoria for addicts.

morphine in relieving anxiety and reducing fear of pain, hunger, or sexual impulses. Fort (1954) describes the sensations experienced by addicts in his study thus: ". . . within seconds after the intravenous injection of heroin or heroin and cocaine, they were 'hit' by a warm, glowing sensation, vaguely localized in the intestinal region, which gradually spread over the body and could be compared only to a sexual orgasm —a comparison volunteered by a number of addicts."

Ausubel (1961) also emphasizes the important "euphoric" qualities of drugs in causing addiction but he recognizes other factors as well. He believes that both external and internal forces play a role in the development of addiction. External forces involve such matters as the availability of a drug and social pressures for using it. By internal forces Ausubel means the state of personality development. When the major impetus to the use of a drug derives from transitory external forces such as adolescent rebellion and the pressure of the peer group, the chances an addiction will develop are low. On the other hand, when personal im-

maturity is marked the chance that one will develop a serious addiction is high.

The position taken by Chein, Gerard, Lee, and Rosenfeld (1964) is similar to Ausubel's. These authors studied male adolescent heroin addicts and found symptom relief to be one of the most striking effects of drug use. Chein et al. feel that opiates can be used to break the ice in an uncomfortable situation just as a person might use the "social drink" at a cocktail party. If, once into a situation, the person displays adequacy, the danger of addiction is minimized. However, if the drug-taker does not achieve successfully, further anxiety is generated, more of the drug is needed to maintain a comfortable feeling, and the risk of addiction is high.

Chein et al. characterize the "high" that is experienced on drugs as far from a euphoric state. Instead it is more like what is meant by "nirvana," a tensionless state. The addict may experience this as a "high" only relative to his characteristic discomfort. Drugs give him a feeling of comfort, disengagement from the world and even from his own fantasies, with a sense of having all of his needs satisfied.

From a dynamic point of view, Chein et al. see the male addict as having a weak ego and superego, inadequate identification as a male, an unrealistic future outlook, and a distrust of social institutions. These personality characteristics are seen to stem from a defective family life. Most notably the father in the male addict's family is found to be a shadowy figure at best and entirely absent in a high percentage of cases. If at home, he is emotionally distant or overtly hostile. He also tends to display the example of immoral, unethical, or criminal behavior. Relations between the parents are frequently disturbed. Divorce and separation are very common in the addict's family.

Mothers of male addicts are not, as a group, distinguishable from mothers of nonaddicts.

Male addicts studied by Fort (1954) are also described as lacking adequate identification as males. Many of Fort's subjects were found to come from broken families and to have had fathers who were distant or entirely absent from the home. Fort stresses that the addict's mother tends to be a controlling person, bitter about men, who derogates them in the presence of her children. As the addict grows older he feels the need to conceal his own dependency as well as his guilt over being a man. Much of his anger is directed toward society as a cover for aggressive feelings toward parents, and this prevents his being comfortable with personal success. Fort feels the addict's attitude toward drugs is an ambivalent one in which he recognizes that the drug is the source of many of his problems, but it is also seen as his only pleasure. The good side of the addict's feeling toward drugs is reflected in one of the names he uses for them, "G.O.M." or "God's Own Medicine"; the bad side is represented by other names such as "junk" or "crap."

As mentioned before, the psychological theories on drug addiction agree largely about the relief-giving impact of drugs. There is the feeling that some individuals have particularly intense needs for such relief, which are related to the inadequacy of personality development. Few studies have been done, however, on the factors which might account for defective development. The features which have thus far been identified as prominent in the background of the addict—such as a weak, distant father and a controlling mother in a tempestuous marital relationship—are virtually identical with those seen in the backgrounds of other pathological groups such as schizophrenics and manic-depressives.

Treatment of Drug Addiction

Withdrawal

At one time virtually the only treatment for drug addiction was physical withdrawal from dependence on the drug. This provided very disappointing results. As pointed out earlier, one study (Hunt & Odoroff, 1962) found that 90 percent of 1881 patients withdrawn from drugs at the U.S. Public Health Service Hospital at Lexington, Kentucky were readdicted within six months of discharge. A five-year follow-up of 453 of these patients (Duvall, Locke, & Brill, 1963) showed that 97 percent became readdicted sometime during the follow-up period. By the end of the five-year period, however, only 46 percent remained addicted and 49 percent were abstinent. Within the follow-up period 41 percent returned to the hospital to be withdrawn once more. Also noteworthy is the fact that 70 percent had one or more arrests in five years and 41 percent had no jobs.

Methadone Maintenance

Dole and Nyswander (1968) introduced a method of treating drug addiction that was aimed at ending the addict's criminal activity. They wanted to find a medication that would reduce the addict's need for drugs so that he could live a normal, productive life without engaging in the criminal behavior that is usually necessary to support a drug habit. They reasoned that anyone who uses an opiate over an extended period of time develops a prolonged physical craving that prompts the person to continue to use opiates. Thus, they sought a drug that would relieve this craving without disrupting ordinary functioning so that the person could work and lead a normal community life.

Methadone, a synthetic opiate, proved to be such a drug. It relieved the craving for opiates without making the patient apathetic or putting him in a heavily sedated state. Dole and Nyswander also discovered that when used in sufficiently high doses methadone blocks the effect of heroin. It prevents heroin from producing the "high" that it ordinarily does. By relieving the craving for drugs like heroin, methadone programs make it possible to attempt to rehabilitate the addict.

An article written in 1972 (Langrod et al., 1972) estimated that more than 50,000 former heroin addicts were being treated in methadone maintenance programs throughout the country. Criteria for entering a methadone treatment program are fairly liberal. In most programs the lower age limit is 18 and the patient is required to have a two-year history of heroin addiction. Many patients have a history of having abused a variety of drugs, some have records of mental illness and complicating medical conditions, and many have arrest and prison records.

A methadone program is generally applied in three phases. The first phase, lasting from three to six weeks, involves giving the patient the medication for the first time, working out dosage levels, and assigning him to a counselor. The counselor's job is to serve as a role model and to help the patient with his social adjustment and future plans. The counselor must also often deal with the patient's anxiety about the physical side of the treatment program. In phase two, which lasts about one year, patients report to the clinic about six times per week at first for medication and counseling. During this time it is expected that the patient will be taking steps toward establishing a normal life. He should get a job or go into an education or training program, form new friendships, and seek whatever services he may need in addition to those provided by the program. As the patient shows progress, the number of times he must report each week is gradually reduced. From a high of six times per week it may be dropped to about twice a week after six months. In the program's final phase the patient should be doing well enough so that he can be trusted to come to the clinic only once per week for his supply of medication. By this time he should be free of other drug use, have a job, and should be functioning normally in society.

Studies evaluating the effectiveness of methadone maintenance programs provide very positive results (Langrod et al., 1972). For example, one study indicates that about 80 percent admitted to programs over a six-year period have remained in treatment. Another study of 1800 patients indicates that 70 percent were either employed, in school, or functioning as homemakers after being in treatment for three months. Still another study of 723 male methadone patients admitted to a program over a 42-month period showed that nearly two-thirds of those remaining in the program were working or were students after three months of treatment. Prior to admission only 15 percent of this group had worked consistently and 85 percent were being taken care of by someone, or supported themselves through criminal activities. The most impressive finding in studies of the effects of methadone treatment is the sudden and very dramatic drop in criminal behavior. This indicates that the criminally involved addict is doing what he must to maintain his heroin habit. All in all, methadone maintenance programs seem to provide a most promising approach to the rehabilitation of the drug addict on an ambulatory basis.

3. Therapeutic Communities for Drug Addicts

The first therapeutic community for treating drug addiction is the program developed by an organization called Synanon (Volkmann & Cressey, 1963; Yablonsky, 1967). Founded in May 1958, by Charles Dederich, an ex-alcoholic, Synanon (the name was coined by an addict who was mispronouncing the word "seminar") evolved from a discussion-group spin-off from Alcoholics Anonymous to an organization in which a group of addicts live together.

The main criterion for admission to Synanon is a willingness to join a group that hates drug addiction, a group that refers to its members as former "dope fiends." Synanon is structured as an autocratic family designed to allow the recovering addict to buy time but encouraging ultimate self-reliance. Every member is assigned an appropriate job within the institution that brings him into daily contact with other members. At the same time he is encouraged to read the classics, and efforts are made through seminars to impart spiritual concepts and values thought to encourage self-reliance. There is strong group pressure toward "staying clean"—not using drugs.

A central part of the program is the "synanon," a form of group therapy. Groups meet three times a week, with the group membership varying from meeting to meeting. Ideally, the synanon consists of three males, three females, and one Synanist who has for some time been abstinent from drugs. The sessions are spirited. Members are expected to "dump their emotional garbage." Self-deception is regarded as a particular danger for the addict, so the synanon is used to relieve the everyday emotional pressures that might lead to a flight through

turning to drugs. The Synanist's job is to moderate and, as a former addict, to sense attempts by group members at evading the truth. To do his job the Synanist relies on his insight and may ridicule or attack members frontally if it seems necessary.

In the day-to-day program functioning members are encouraged to complain and rebel verbally against institutional authority, but they are required to *perform* as ordered. Another Synanon mechanism that is used to release feelings and promote emotional security is called the "haircut." The "haircut" is a session attended by relatively new patients and four or five of the Synanon members who play a prominent role in the institution's family structure. The performance of each new member is analyzed with blunt frankness. He may be praised for positive efforts or brutally attacked verbally for his failings. Despite the apparent threat in such confrontations, new members are said to welcome these sessions.

Volkmann and Cressey (1963) have done a study of the background and reactions to Synanon of 52 early Synanon residents. They found that of the 38 males and 14 females in this group fewer than 50 percent completed high school, 81 percent had unstable work records, and that males averaged 5.5 previous institutional confinements and females 3.9. After living for a time in the Synanon program, 4 of the 52 were living in the community and abstaining totally from drugs. Twenty-three more (44 percent) were not using drugs and were still living at Synanon. The remaining 25 (48 percent) had left the program against the advice of other members.

Most Synanon drop-outs (90 percent) leave within three months of admission. Of the 143 members remaining at Synanon for at least three months, 95 (66 percent) were still abstinent at the time of the Volkmann and Cressey survey. Of the 87 who remained as long as seven months, 75 (86 percent) continued to be abstinent. These figures indicate that an encouragingly high percentage of those addicts who can stick with the Synanon program over an extended period of time can leave it without resort to drugs.

Although Synanon is the best known of the therapeutic communities for drug addicts, many others have been developed (Rosenthal, 1973). These include Daytop Village on Staten Island, the Addiction Research Center in Puerto Rico, and the Phoenix House Program in New York City. Most of these communities vary only slightly from the model and aims of Synanon. Unlike Synanon, for example, the Puerto Rican program used professionally trained therapists and made a greater effort to return its residents to society than did Synanon. Phoenix House offers a formal program of education and job training pointing toward the addict's ultimate departure from the program and need to have marketable skills. In addition, Phoenix House trains a large number of paraprofessionals to work as addiction specialists in therapeutic community programs.

Evaluations of the Phoenix House Program (Rosenthal, 1973) produce results similar to those found with Synanon. About half of those enrolling at Phoenix House drop out before completing the program. Those who do remain stay off drugs and seem to make good social recoveries.

CONCLUSION

Addictions to both alcohol and drugs are seen to be related to the relief giving properties of those substances as well as their physiological effects. As such they are difficult disorders to treat. In treatment the addict is called upon to give up the immediate benefits of the addictive substance and endure periods of considerable physical and psychological discomfort in favor of some uncertain future benefits. This asks a great deal. In addition, those who become addicted generally must adopt life styles that place them outside the realm of ordinary society. Therefore, part of recovery requires finding a way back to an orthodox social life.

Despite these problems effective methods are being developed to treat some alcohol and drug addicts. By and large, they are not traditional psychotherapeutic approaches. Some are physically based. Most of those that are psychologically based rely on group pressures and supports. Hopefully, such efforts will be greatly expanded and still other approaches can be developed to reach those who are not able to benefit from existing services.

SUMMARY

1. Addictions are found to alcohol and a variety of drugs, broadly defined.
2. Alcohol has been used in virtually all civilizations back to the beginnings of recorded history.
3. Physiologically, alcohol is metabolized at a slow, fixed rate and, while present in the system, it circulates in the blood and has a persistent effect on brain function.
4. Definitions of alcoholism based on direct behaviorial observation are

easily arrived at. When the clinician attempts to incorporate causal factors in his thinking about alcoholism, diagnosis becomes very complicated.

5. Several physiological and psychological theories have been advanced to explain the development of alcoholism.

6. The earliest, most widespread, and perhaps the most successful approach to treating alcoholism, is Alcoholics Anonymous. Recently other treatment approaches such as conditioned reflex therapy and the use of *Antabuse* have been introduced.

7. Many different meanings may be applied to the term drug, as used in drug addiction. In these days when so many different substances are being used by addicts, a very broad pharmacological definition seems most sensible.

8. One of the earliest used addictive agents was *opium*. Its derivatives, such as *morphine* and *heroin*, and its recent synthetic equivalents (*demerol, methadone*) are the most widely used addictive drugs.

9. Other addictive agents include *cocaine, barbiturates*, and *amphetamines*.

10. *Marihuana* is obtained from hemp and is widely used. Many studies claim to demonstrate that it has seriously adverse effects. These claims are not well substantiated.

11. *LSD* is the most potent of a group of hallucinogenic drugs. Definitive research on its long-range effects has not yet been done, but its potency and widespread effects on physiological systems counsels considerable caution in its use.

12. Caffeine and nicotine are addictive drugs contained in very popularly used substances. Their overuse can cause some seriously disabling and damaging effects.

13. Many physical and psychological theories of the cause of drug addiction has been advanced.

14. Treatment methods for drug addiction include physical withdrawal, methadone maintenance, and therapeutic communities such as Synanon and Phoenix House. The latter two approaches seem to show particularly promising results.

CHAPTER 14

Individual Psychotherapy

Schizophrenia, psychoses, psychoneuroses, psychosomatic disorders, personality disorders—now that we have explained these syndromes, what can we do for their victims? Actually, there can be many links between how we understand psychological problems and how we go about treating them. In some cases the treatment theory followed logically from a theory of personality and pathology (for example, behavior modification). In other cases (for example, psychoanalysis) the treatment theory seemed to precede the theory of pathology.

Classifying psychotherapy approaches is not easy. Despite many vigorous differences in theoretical leanings and disagreements about fine points in technique, there is often a good deal of overlap on many relevant dimensions between presumably very different therapeutic schools. Therefore, we will simply identify three dimensions that we regard as significant in virtually all psychotherapies and present examples of approaches that seem to stress each. The three dimensions are intellectual insight and understanding, emotional expression or catharsis, and behavioral change.

I. INSIGHT-ORIENTED THERAPIES

A. Psychoanalysis

The best known of the insight therapies is psychoanalysis. Chapter 5 describes well the early form of the approach that was to grow into psychoanalysis. Freud stressed emotional catharsis in his earliest therapeutic efforts. Eventually he came to believe that cure came from disclosing the source of the patient's defensive maneuvers—particularly his repressions. Anxiety-creating ideas were thought to come from primitive unconscious wishes. Psychoanalysis then became a process for making the patient consciously aware of unconscious instincts that prompt symptom development. Thus, the ego could assume control over the instincts. The dictum, "Where id is, ego shall be," sums up the objective of psychoanalysis very well.

Freud first used the free association method to attain this objective, when access to the unconscious was believed to be direct and the psychoanalytic process concentrated on dealing with instinctual forces. Experience with many patients (and, no doubt, with many failures in treatment) led to the recognition of complex forces that resisted cure, and treatment grew correspondingly complex.

These resistances were essentially twofold. First, there were the *defense mechanisms*. Those maneuvers the ego had learned to use earlier in life to divert or to inhibit instinctual urges now resisted the analyst, whose efforts threatened, as did the instincts themselves, to result in unpleasantness and anxiety. In this way the patient's cure was made more difficult by his employment of his earlier choices of adaptive behavior. The analytic process thus often had to be directed toward the ego forces that closed off access to the instincts.

The second form of resistance was known as *transference*. This was described by Freud as the unique pattern that each individual develops in "the exercise of his capacity to love"—the conditions that must pertain if he is to love, the impulses that are satisfied by loving, and the aims of loving. Throughout life, when circumstances per-

mit, this pattern will be repeated. It is therefore likely that those who have not had full resolution of their transference needs will direct them toward the analyst and will exhibit toward him the stereotyped pattern they have developed in relationships with figures from early life. This idea essentially explains the reactions of Breuer's patient, Anna O., to her doctor.

Although to some extent this stereotyped pattern is conscious, its unacceptable components are unconscious. The conscious, positive manifestations of transference (usually called simply *positive transference*) include such feelings as sympathy, trust, friendship, and love; these often assist the process of psychoanalysis. Negative aspects of this process are likely to be repressed. As such feelings become accessible to consciousness, through the process of analysis, they become attached to the analyst; it is this *negative transference* that is the basis for much resistance in treatment. It is manifested by negative *feeling* toward the analyst stemming not from the interaction of analyst and patient but from the latter's unhappy experiences with potential love objects much earlier in life.

A basic aspect of the analyst's job, then, is to analyze the various forms of resistance that arise in treatment in order to neutralize them. As this occurs in therapy, and behavior is modified, the effect is generalized to behavior outside therapy. Permanent changes in the patient's defensive patterns are thus made possible, and this facilitates dealing more directly with the unconscious instinctual forces lying at the roots of neurosis. The analysis ends when the patient's symptoms have diminished, when he feels free of former anxieties and inhibitions, and when the analyst feels that sufficient personality change has occurred to make further significant changes as a result of additional treatment unlikely.

Psychoneuroses are a function of both constitutional factors—which determine the intensity of the instincts that must be controlled—and adverse experiential factors. The ideal patient, therefore, is the one whose difficulties derive primarily from his experiences, since analysis cannot alter constitutional factors. Furthermore, since the analytic process allies itself with the patient's ego, the ego should have some strength and resources if successful treatment is to take place. This, for Freud, ruled out the use of the analytic approach with psychotics. Other desirable patient attributes were thought to be a good education, verbal facility, a good character, and youth. For example, once the patient reached age 50 he was regarded as being too difficult to teach; moreover it was felt that older people had such a mass of material to deal with that analysis might well go on indefinitely. Finally, where it was necessary to deal quickly with a "dangerous" symptom, Freud felt psychoanalysis was contraindicated.

Freud's original theory stimulated a number of other theories dealing with the etiology of behavioral disorder. It also served as a point of departure for several members of his original inner circle, who felt his emphasis on biological factors and the sexual instincts was exaggerated. Adler, Jung, and Rank selected other forces within and around man as being of primary significance in his development. Others, like Franz Alexander, have suggested modifications of the practice of psychoanalytic psychotherapy.

Perhaps the major modification of Freud's theory to have gained widespread acceptance within the orthodox psychoanalytic family is the reevaluation of Freud's views about ego development. Two assumptions in particular have been called into question: (1) that all psychic energy resides with the id; and (2) that ego functions depend entirely upon the diversion of such energy for use by a psychic system that emerges only to assist the id in its adaptation to the demands of the external environment.

Sullivan's Treatment Approach

Harry Stack Sullivan's therapeutic approach relates to his theories of personality development and pathology that were described in Chapter 6. It is an approach that stresses intellectual understanding (Ford & Urban, 1963). A primary objective for Sullivan was to "elucidate" what the patient did in key interpersonal situations, of which the therapy interaction itself is one example. *Elucidation* involves learning to see accurately how one is behaving and evaluating it candidly. Once this occurs behavior change is expected to follow. Like psychoanalysis it stresses insight. Unlike psychoanalysis it is more present- than past-oriented.

Sullivan's conviction that disorders, as well as behavior in general, arise from interpersonal relationships profoundly influenced his treatment method. It was his view that in order to understand a patient's problem, knowledge of its context was essential. He was therefore not satisfied with general descriptions of patients that characterized them, for example, as hostile, dependent, or emotionally immature. Rather, he wanted to know about the circumstances that elicited the special behavior. He further argued that since psychotherapy was fundamentally an interpersonal situation, the therapist, he felt, was inevitably both a stimulus and a potential reinforcer to the patient. Accordingly, Sullivan insisted that any evaluation of patient behavior in the therapeutic interview must take into account the part played by the therapist in establishing the context within which the patient responds. The therapist's role as a *participant observer* is advantageous to him provided he can recognize his own stimulus value to the patient. If he can do this, he can obtain first-hand information on how the patient reacts in a specific context.

For Sullivan, behavior change is brought about by uncovering sources of anxiety, discovering the types of avoidance patterns used to control anxiety, and attempting to modify these patterns. Put another way, the patient needs to be able to see his own behavior for what it is, conceptualize it symbolically, and then deal with it honestly. Although not completely explicit about the principles of learning underlying behavior change, Sullivan subscribed to the theory that people were drawn to behavior that diminished anxiety and tension and avoided behavior which increased such feelings.

Sullivan regarded the therapist as an expert in human behavior who contracted with a patient, having a specifiable problem, to attempt to deal with that problem. As such, he worked in a methodical way toward defining, both for therapist and patient, exactly what the problem was and what the therapist could and could not reasonably be expected to achieve. He also sought to establish both short- and long-range goals with the patient and periodic evaluations of progress, hopefully to avoid a confused, aimless series of interactions. He also believed that it was necessary to show progress to the patient in order to maintain the latter's motivation.

Sullivan's recognition that a variety of problems could emerge from an infinitude of interpersonal contexts militated against his creation of a model into which all patients would be forced. Instead he tailored therapeutic technique to the patient. In some of his writings he has discussed problems that are common to many patients, at least in certain phases of therapy. For example, early in treatment many patients feel that they should not need to be helped with behavior problems, that they should be able to control themselves better, that their own logic should be sufficient to carry them through, and so on. Sullivan offered specific examples of how he dealt with such frequently encountered responses. Basically, however, he argued that each treatment procedure must be looked upon as unique and must be carried out in connection with specific problem areas, mutually delineated by therapist and patient.

Rogers's Client-Centered Therapy

Carl Rogers's approach poses a classification problem, even within the broad framework outlined here. The client-centered therapist is greatly concerned with helping the client to uncover and clarify his feelings. But, at the same time, his purpose is "to free the patient of his faulty learnings so that he can be what he was innately built to be" as Ford and Urban (1963, p. 422) put it. The client-centered therapist also has the primary purpose of helping the client change his way of attending to, thinking about, and evaluating himself and his world. Behavior

Carl Rogers, proponent of client-centered therapy.

change is expected to follow from these largely cognitive changes. For this reason, client-centered therapy will be classed as an insight rather than a cathartic therapy. The following description of client-centered therapy draws heavily on the discussion in Chapter 9 of Rogers's theory of personality and psychopathology.

From Rogers's view, to reverse pathological processes there must first be a decrease in conditions of worth. That is, the person must get over the idea that some of his behavior is less worthy than other behavior. At the same time he must increase his unconditional self-regard. This occurs when he perceives the unconditional positive regard of some significant person. To communicate unconditional positive regard that other person must show an *empathic* understanding (the ability to perceive the "internal frame of reference of another as if one were the other person but without ever losing the 'as if' condition").

Perception of such circumstances by the organism leads to an increase in unconditional positive self-regard. This, in turn, results in a reduction of perceived threat and in a reversal of the defensive process. The person is then able to perceive threatening experiences more accurately and to integrate them in the self-concept. Success in so doing diminishes the likelihood of experiencing threat in the future; it also means that defenses will be reduced. There will also be an increase in self-regard, positive regard for others, and hence, psychological adjustment. Increasingly, actualization motives are restored as the prime basis for behavior.

In order to reverse the disorganizational process it is not necessary, according to Rogers, to know the specific etiology of the patient's problem. Indeed diagnoses are regarded as undesirable from an ethical viewpoint since they implicitly convey the notion of the control of behavior, thus violating the client's right to self-determination. Furthermore, diagnosis is felt to stand in the way of the objectives of therapy (freeing of the subject to guide his own behavior) through the preconceptions it instills. Finally, purely pragmatically, Rogers questions the potential accuracy of diagnoses since the client's problem involves situations that only he can view directly.

Rogers places greater emphasis on the personal attributes of the therapist than he does on therapeutic technique. In valuing sensitivity, objectivity, empathy, respect for the individual, and the ability to accept feelings, behavior, and so on, Rogers's primary concern is with the therapist's personality and attitudinal quality. Thus, for example, being "genuine" is more important than any specific therapeutic implementations.

Emphasis in the therapy situation is placed on creating an atmosphere in which the patient feels comfortable, and in which exposure to criticism or other potentially threatening experiences is minimized. In other words, the optimal therapy situation is one in which the patient is able to examine himself, openly and freely, devoid of psychological threat. Negative, threatening stimuli have promoted the development of the emotional problem in the first place, and their reduction is necessary if the pathological process is to be reversed. In addition to providing a relatively nonthreatening therapeutic atmosphere, a second major function of the therapist is to help the patient to focus attention on troublesome aspects of his life situation. Thus, of the many things the patient speaks about, the therapist responds primarily to those which evaluate oneself, others, or events or situations relevant to self and important others. The responses of the therapist are less attempts to change such feelings than they are efforts to summarize and reflect them as accurately as possible. It is expected that in the nonthreatening therapeutic atmosphere the patient can attend to significant feelings and deal with them in his own way, which is presumed to be the *best* way.

Since this approach is considered suitable for *all* patients, no attempts are made to select patients particularly "suited" to the method. In a summary of his treatment approach, Rogers (1959) acknowledges that current research will doubtless result in further tailoring of therapeutic technique to the particular problem. For example, it has been found that patients who blame others for their problems are more likely to be therapeutic failures than those who more willingly accept responsibility for problems. Such findings leave open the possibility that other patient characteristics may be related to more or less successful treatment outcomes.

Rational-Emotive Psychotherapy

The approach that goes the farthest in relying on logic, insight, and understanding is the rational-emotive psychotherapy of Albert Ellis (Patterson, 1966). Originally a marriage counselor who gave direct advice to his counselees, Ellis turned first to orthodox psychoanalysis to help his clients with their emotional problems. Dissatisfied with this approach, he gradually moved toward a more and more directive approach. He reasoned that since he knew what was troubling his clients, there was no point in sitting around waiting for them to develop their own awareness of what the problem was. Ultimately, Ellis came to feel that he could teach his clients to change their way of thinking so that they could use a rational approach to their problems.

Philosophically, the rational-emotive therapist makes certain assumptions about man's nature and what makes him unhappy or disturbed. First, man is seen as being capable of behaving rationally or irrationally. When he is rational, he's effective and competent, and he feels happy. What we call emotional disturbance is the result of irrational, illogical thinking. Furthermore, thoughts and emotions are seen to be tied together. Emotion accompanies thinking and, in effect, is actually biased, irrational thinking. We have irrational thoughts because we learned illogical things from our parents and culture. The disturbed person perpetuates his illogical behavior by continually verbalizing his irrational ideas internally. Because of this self-stimulation, disordered behavior and disturbed emotions are never extinguished. It is also for this reason that acquiring an understanding of the origins of disturbance is not enough to change behavior. Persistent emotional disturbances are not caused by external circumstances. They arise because we perceive and feel negatively about external events and then incorporate these illogical attitudes into internalized sentences that we make about them.

The goals of rational-emotive therapy are to reorganize perceptions and thinking so that logic is introduced and the irrational can become rational. The therapist tries to show the client how his self-verbalizations have caused his emotional disturbance, how they are illogical, and how to straighten out his thinking to make it more logical and thus not associate it with negative emotions. Ellis identifies a number of irrational cultural values in Western society that inevitably lead to behavior disorder. For example, he feels that most people see it as essential that they be loved and approved of by practically everyone around them. Another example is the notion that in order to be worthwhile a person must be perfectly competent. Still other examples in-

clude the ideas that some people are in- E.
herently bad and should be punished, that
if things are not the way we want them to
be it is a serious catastrophe, and that every
problem has a perfect solution.

Rational-emotive therapy proceeds
through four steps. In the first step the
client is shown that he is illogical and efforts are made to show him how he got
that way. In addition, the relationship between his irrational ideas and emotional
unhappiness is pointed out. In the second
step the rational-emotive therapist shows
the client that his disturbance persists not
because of anything that happened to him
earlier in life, but because currently he is
continuing to think illogically. The third
step in treatment involves helping the client to get rid of his illogical thinking.
Finally, the therapist goes beyond his concern for the client's specific illogical ideas
and takes up the general irrational ideas
that characterize society. The therapist expresses a rational philosophy of life so that
the client can be inoculated against falling
victim later on to more irrational thinking.

The therapeutic technique in rational-
emotive treatment is a very active one very
much like teaching. After completion of the
first stage of treatment the counselor attempts, quite overtly, to reeducate the client. He shows the client how illogical his
disturbance is, how he fell victim in the
past to illogical thinking, and how he is
causing his problems to persist by continuing to think illogically. The therapist
overtly serves as a counter-force against
the client's self-defeating thoughts. He contradicts the client and challenges what are
seen to be illogical, superstitious notions.
In addition, he encourages and even urges
the client to engage in certain activities
which can lead to contradictions of the
illogical thoughts that caused the client's
problems.

The Existential Approach to Psychotherapy

Existential psychotherapy developed
through the experience of many psychotherapists (prominent among these are
Ludwig Binswanger, Victor Frankl, and
Rollo May) who found that people coming
to them for help were not the typical neurotics that Freud described. Instead, their
complaints centered around feelings of
loneliness, alienation, and an emptiness in
their lives (Ford & Urban, 1963). For these
therapists existing theories of personality
and treatment did not seem to provide an
adequate basis for helping such patients.
Furthermore, many who were to become
existential analysts were unhappy at trying
to apply scientific procedures to analyzing
and explaining man as the psychoanalysts
and behaviorists did. The existentialists feel
that man's uniqueness lies in his self-awareness and his ability to strive toward certain
goals. They feel that existential philosophy
provides a better foundation than existing
psychological theories for understanding
man from this viewpoint. For their study of
man they turn to phenomenology, an approach that acknowledges every man's
uniqueness and insists that a person must
be understood on the basis of how he experiences his life situation, not on how an
observer perceives it.

From the existential point of view the
psychologically healthy person has a broad
awareness of himself, the situation around
him, his behavior, and the stimuli to which
he responds. Furthermore, he makes choices
actively about how to deal with situations
rather than being driven helplessly by immediate pressures. He analyzes situations,
decides on proper goals, forms plans to
reach his goals, and then carries out the
plans. Such assumptions about what consti-

tutes psychological health in a very real sense define the goals of existential therapy. The patient should be helped to become aware of the range of choices open to him so that he can direct his life responsibly. In essence he must be put in touch with significant factors that will enter into the making of proper choices. These include his own values, sensations, and beliefs, as well as the many possibilities open to him in his environment.

The existentialists' basic assumptions about man's inherent nature have bearing on their therapeutic approach. The existentialists assume that behavior goes on continuously and changes as a result of interaction with surrounding events. Man is aware of this fact and this awareness provides him with a personal identity, a sense of "being." Because of this awareness man can make choices about what he will respond to and how he will respond. The choices that are made reflect man's innate behavioral repertoire and in some ways he shapes the environment to fit himself and shapes himself to fit the environment. He responds simultaneously to the natural world around him, other people, and himself continuously. In having self-awareness he recognizes the possibility of losing his identity by losing his relationship to the environment. This can lead to a sense of "nothingness." "Nothingness" causes anxiety that restricts behavior, and, in turn, results in guilt. The "being" person can make decisions, interact with the environment, get things done, and enjoy life. The "nothingness" person cannot make choices, fails to act, limits his behavior, and suffers anxiety and guilt.

The existentialists are unspecific about therapy technique. This may be because they feel it is damaging to treat a patient as an object, and talking about therapy technique tends to do just that. Nonetheless, Ford and Urban have distilled some commonalities in the approach used by most existentialists from a variety of published material. One common feature involves the therapist's attitude toward the patient. Existentialists approach the patient with the conviction that he is a person of worth who has the responsibility and capability of making his own choices in life. The only way to understand and help him is by trying to see the world through his eyes, to appreciate his feelings and values, and to comprehend his way of communicating about them. Since the therapist must inevitably use his own thinking style to try to see with the patient, he must be very much aware of his own thought patterns and work constantly at minimizing their influence.

Whereas the typical therapy situation tends to involve one person who is seen as superior (the therapist) and another who is seen as being in some ways inferior or subordinate (the patient), the existential therapist tries to structure the therapy relationship in such a way that the patient remains responsible for himself. The therapist avoids allowing the patient to wait passively for someone else to deal with his problems. Instead, the therapy relationship is approached as a kind of partnership in which the therapist shares his own experience with the patient as a way of encouraging him. Therapy is seen to be a model of a variety of other human interactions. In therapy the patient's typical way of dealing with situations can find expression, be understood and changed.

Communication modes are very important to the existential therapist. People use words differently so that for two different people the same words may refer to two different kinds of events. To really understand a given patient, the therapist must be certain of the events to which the patient's verbalizations refer. The patient's statements must be taken in the context of other behavior such as how he talks, the gestures he uses, and the tone in his voice. In therapy attention is concentrated on present events, things that are actually going on in the therapy interaction. The past and the future are important only as they are reflected in the ongoing therapy situation. Since the primary goal is to help the patient to enlarge his capacity to choose from the many options open to him in life, the therapist is particularly sensitive to situations arising in therapy in which the patient must make choices. He is concerned with the way the patient goes about handling these situations and the consequences of his style. The therapist's job is to help the patient relearn to use his freedom of choice most effectively.

CATHARTIC APPROACHES TO PSYCHOTHERAPY

Therapy approaches that stress emotional expression or catharsis are associated with the *humanistic* movement in psychology. This movement appeared as a reaction to a society that is so computerized and impersonal that it seems to have lost touch with individual values. Like the existentialists, the humanists find that many patients are lonely people who feel alienated from others. They feel that their lives lack purpose and direction. Also like the existentialists, the humanists see man as capable of taking part in his own treatment and as being the best judge of what is good for him. However, whereas the existentialists stress the need to increase the patient's understanding and awareness as a means of opening up greater possibilities for individual choice, the humanists emphasize man's need to relieve himself of troublesome feelings. Pent-up emotion is presumed to prevent

Fred Weiss

Humanist psychotherapists encourage patients to relieve themselves of pent-up emotion before attempting to deal with their problems.

perceiving the world realistically and dealing with it effectively.

The relationship between intense emotional expression and relief of psychological symptoms has been obvious for many many years. Primitive religious rituals often stimulate emotional outpourings that seem to make people feel better. The spontaneous bursts of feelings associated with traumatic experiences such as bereavement often bring considerable relief psychologically. Breuer and Freud's work in the late nineteenth century, one of the earliest systematic attempts at psychotherapy, emphasized catharsis, as was described in Chapter 5. In this forerunner of psychoanalysis the patient was encouraged simply to talk out the problems of the day accompanied by all of the affect that had been aroused. In recent years, many therapists have come back to the idea that the process of "spilling one's guts" is the potent element in psychotherapy

Though humanistic theories which emphasize the significance of emotional expression vary with respect to certain details, they share many common assumptions. One of these is that in the course of development man is forced to inhibit many strong feelings. Such feelings do not dissipate. Instead they accumulate within the psyche. As they build up they become more and more difficult to control so that defenses must be set up to prevent their expression. These defenses constitute the symptoms that patients want to have treated. Of course, the source of these inhibitions is a society that encourages people to feel that strong emotional expressions are not acceptable. Even as youngsters we are taught not to cry because it is childish and not to be overly aggressive because it is not nice. Very few people are free of a burden of emotional inhibitions. One humanist (Janov, 1970) asserts that no one is truly free of neurosis unless he has gone through a therapeutic process that purges him of the pent-up feelings that have led to defensive maneuvers.

From this point of view, the goal of therapy is straightforward. The patient must simply be helped to let out the feelings that have caused him to become defensive. Once this occurs he is expected to be able to perceive the people around him and his own life situation objectively, and his functioning will become more effective. This basic theme characterizes most humanistic approaches. For the most part variations among approaches are based on the means by which catharsis is brought about.

Reichian Therapy

Modern psychotherapy schools that emphasize emotional expression can look to the work of Wilhelm Reich (1960) as a direct ancestor. Reich began his career as an orthodox psychoanalyst and made important contributions to psychoanalytic theory. In his work with patients Reich became especially impressed by the difficulty patients have in uncovering old memories associated with negative feelings. In time his interest focused on the way patients go about resisting emotional expression rather than the content of what they were actually revealing. He delved first into the psychological and later the physical ways that people used to suppress emotional expression. Eventually he concluded that patients invested a great deal of energy in a struggle to hold back feelings and to control sexual impulses. Cure, therefore, required the release of suppressed feelings and sexual impulses so that the energy tied up in defenses could be liberated.

In his earliest concern with defensive behavior, Reich concentrated on psychological forms of defense. As his work progressed, however, he shifted to an emphasis on physical forms. He decided that chronic muscular rigidity developed to protect against anxiety and later to control feelings in general. Thus, a kind of psychological armoring or defensiveness eventually is turned into a physical or muscular armoring. Muscle groups are actually thought to develop a chronic rigidity from psychological causes. The goals of orgone therapy are to bring about a relaxation of muscle groups, to encourage direct expression of emotions, and to analyze or provide insight into situations that arouse anxiety and prevent affect expression. In addition, the Reichian therapist attempts to help the patient accept sexual impulses as natural ones that should not be suppressed.

The Reichian therapeutic technique involves a direct attack on muscular armor. At the beginning of treatment the patient is examined physically to determine the degree and type of muscular rigidity that he suffers. In the treatment session the patient wears only underwear or a bathing suit. Clothing is seen to reflect defensiveness so that a lack of clothing is thought to help overcome this. In addition the patient's scanty attire provides the therapist with a chance to observe the patient's muscle state.

The Reichian therapist sees the body as being divided up into seven vertical segments with each segment controlled by certain muscles. Therapy involves the systematic breaking down of the rigidity or armor segment by segment. The seven segments are the ocular, the oral, the cervical, the thoracic, the diaphragmatic, the abdominal, and the pelvic. The attack on the armor of each sector is carried out by urging the patient to express his feeling through the muscles of each segment. For example, to attack the resistance of the ocular muscles the patient is told to hold his eyes wide open as though frightened, and to express as much emotion as possible through the use of the muscles that control the eyes. Muscles of the oral segment are loosened up by having the patient move his mouth and jaw vigorously, by having him change his voice, or, at times, by encouraging him to cry. The systematic attack on the various muscle segments is expected eventually to result in a release of much of the emotion that has been bottled up and that is responsible for defensiveness and armoring. This process is expected to permit the patient to live a natural, nondefensive life in which he feels comfortable with his impulses. The ultimate criterion for the success of treatment in Reich's system is the ability to have a fully potent and satisfying orgasm.

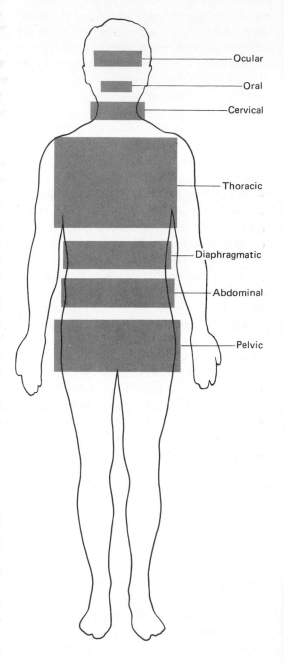

REICH'S SEVEN VERTICAL SEGMENTS

Ocular
Oral
Cervical
Thoracic
Diaphragmatic
Abdominal
Pelvic

B.

Gestalt Therapy

One of the best known and most popular recent therapeutic approaches is Gestalt therapy, largely the creation of a single person, Frederick S. Perls (1969). A physician, Perls studied psychoanalysis, was a student of Wilhelm Reich, and later fell under the influence of Gestalt psychology. This latter contact impressed him with the importance of immediate experience and led him to emphasize phenomenology. Gestalt psychology led Perls to apply the idea of "organismic self-regulation" to the realm of emotional experience. He postulated that once feelings were expressed or discharged they disappeared. This process is similar to the perceptual process of perceiving good, complete gestalten or forms. When the feeling that accompanies an experience finds appropriate expression, the experience is completed and the gestalt is good. Certain reflexive behavior is pointed to as a built-in means of self-regulation. Yawning or sighing are examples of this. Blocking psychologically self-regulating mechanisms prevents completion of the gestalt and results in anxiety. The only way to get rid of this anxiety is to find a way for emotional discharge to take place.

Achieving a state of balanced self-regulation with respect to emotions is difficult because many powerful forces resist the expression of feelings. Gestalt therapy involves the application of a set of techniques that attempt to restore the patient to a state in which spontaneous emotional discharge becomes possible. In common with Reich and other humanists, Perls locates the origins of resistance to affective expression in a set of cultural procriptions that prevents it.

In the extreme case the devitalizing effect of repressions that are prompted by society leads to neurosis. Therapy attempts to liberate emotions. What stands in the way of this liberating process is the fact that people avoid the feelings that are the basis of their neurosis. Perls feels that we undergo a conditioning process to withhold the expression of feeling. For example, the sad person stands dejectedly, holds his mouth in a drawn position, and has an expressionless face. To hold back the feeling of sadness he tries to smile and thereby to destroy the pattern associated with sadness. This keeps him from being aware of the feeling and discharging the emotion associated with it. In this manner various types of feelings and impulses are interfered with by a chronic muscular state. The job in therapy is to remove the barriers to affective expression.

In Gestalt therapy catharsis is encouraged. But it is catharsis related to the *immediate* moment by moment experience of the patient in the therapy situation. It is thus different from many other therapy approaches that stress the importance of the "here and now." Perls is not concerned with the patient's current life situation or even what is happening over a relatively short period of time in the therapy situation. Instead he is concerned with the patient's immediate instant by instant experiences as the session progresses. His focus is on the ways the patient is restraining expressions of the immediate feelings aroused by the therapy interaction. In this sense therapy is an arena for learning about one's own repressive processes and overcoming them.

One example of this process involved an inhibited man in group therapy. As a female patient in this group spoke, the man sat tapping his finger on a table. When asked to reflect on what the other patient had said, he responded with only mild concern or involvement but continued to tap. The therapist then urged him to intensify his tapping, to make it louder and more vigorous. As the patient did so he began to feel more fully the emotion that had been aroused by the woman and, before long, was pounding on the table and disagreeing violently with her. The experience gave the patient an opportunity to see how he exerts control over very strong impulses. In addition he was able to liken the woman's remarks to some annoying ones that his wife often makes. This provided some historical perspective on what made him so angry in the first place.

Naranjo (1970) points out that since there are relatively few immediate external provocations to account for the strong feelings that are poured forth in therapy, such feelings very likely relate to long-standing, deep-seated concerns. The embarrassed patient, for example, may learn that it is not the little things that happen in therapy that cause him embarrassment but rather a deep sense of personal shame that he has carried with him for some time.

Despite its central role in Gestalt therapy, Perls recognizes some limits on the use of catharsis. Obviously since full expression of long withhheld, intense emotion is required for the patient to benefit, the therapist must be prepared to allow such expression to take place. If he is afraid or inept about permitting feelings to follow their course, the patient will not benefit. Another problem is that the patient may be encouraged to uncover long hidden feelings and not be properly supported during their expression, a time when he is enormously vulnerable.

Perls also points out that the discharge of feelings does not end one's affective problems. New emotions are always being stimulated by our interactions with the world. Another important job of therapy, then, is to help the patient learn to deal effectively with his feelings outside of therapy. Catharsis cannot be engaged in freely in the real world. Intense anger can be spilled out in therapy but it can create serious problems in the real world. Emoting freely cannot be a way of life in most cultures that we know of. Thus, the patient must learn to achieve a balance between repression and an unchecked flow of feelings. The ideal result in Gestalt therapy is for the patient to be able to deal with the real world in such a way that emotions are discharged in small quantities as they are stimulated without storing them up to such a degree that large amounts of energy are needed to control them.

Primal Therapy

Primal therapy, the creation of Arthur Janov (1970), is one example of a group of therapeutic approaches within the humanistic school which, while differing from each other in some details, share essentially similar theories of psychopathology and have virtually identical treatment goals (Casriel, 1972; Jackins, 1962, 1965). Janov's theory of psychopathology is very simple. We become emotionally disturbed because we store up many feelings that were not allowed expression. Cure consists of reexperiencing these painful emotions.

As he grows the child is helpless and dependent on the parents for the satisfaction of many needs. Included is a need for affection along with basic psychological needs. Frustration of affectional needs leads to "primal pain." The child can escape from this pain by finding symbolic gratifications and repressing awareness of his frustrated needs. For example, the youngster who wants his parents' love but who instead only receives an occasional compliment for his achievements may repress his needs for love and strive only for achievement. Even if he becomes successful, however, he will never be satisfied because he gets only symbolic gratification and his basic needs for affection are never met. Unmet suppressed needs arouse tension or anxiety and the person works very hard to avoid the experience of this feeling. Neurotic symptoms from Janov's point of view are simply the techniques used to reduce the tension caused by repressed pain. Tension releasing mechanisms, however, never drain the primal pain itself, so that neurosis is perpetuated until the person becomes aware of these basic needs and allows himself to experience the feelings associated with them.

Janov's treatment approach is devoted to uncovering the pain of childhood and allowing the emotional component of that pain to find full expression. The techniques used to bring this about include catharsis and regression. Janov's unique therapy format involves individual psychotherapy sessions every day for three weeks. Then the patient is assigned to weekly group sessions in which he participates with 40 to 50 other patients and a number of psychotherapists for a period of several months. The goals of the individual sessions are to bring the patient to a state whereby he can relatively easily reach back deep into his past and expose the feelings that have long been buried.

This reexperiencing of the past must take place as realistically as possible and the episode that characterizes this process is called the "primal." It is toward helping the patient achieve primals readily that the three-week session is devoted. In the primal the patient relives childhood frustrations so vividly that he experiences all of the agonizing pain associated with them, reverts to childlike babbling, and screams with the anguish and intensity of an infant. It is this scream that Janov regards as the curative factor. The scream is a dramatically painful moment not uncommonly accompanied by agonized writhing in pain.

To provoke the deep emotional reaction that he feels is necessary for cure, Janov, though vague about many of his techniques, seems to attack defenses directly. The new patient is instructed to remain awake for 24 hours before his first session and to avoid all tension-lessening outlets. This means that he must isolate himself in a hotel room, is not permitted to smoke, read, watch television, or engage in anything distracting. Likewise during therapy any behavior that Janov regards as tension reducing is tabu. This includes smoking, nervous habits like foot-tapping, or being overly polite. The therapist insists that emotions be experienced directly and not side-stepped.

The intensive daily sessions of the first three weeks presumably prepare the patient sufficiently so that he can continue the process of uncovering deeply hidden feelings in group sessions. In the primal therapy group there is very little interaction between members. Instead, each has his own agenda which is to retrieve deeply painful emotions and to experience them. The fact of being in a room full of people all dedicated to the same process and reacting in various stages of emotional release probably serves as a potent stimulus to catharsis.

BEHAVIORALLY ORIENTED THERAPIES

Several varieties of behaviorally oriented psychotherapies have appeared in the past 25 years. They share a common focus on changing extratherapy behavior. In some cases cognitive or affective variables are manipulated but the goal always is to change behavior in some desired direction. Usually the patient decides what he would like to have changed but at times the therapist determines for him what behaviors should be added, altered, or eliminated.

Another feature common to all behavior therapies is that they are based on learning principles established in laboratory studies with animal subjects. Since experimental learning studies have emphasized different principles and resulted in a variety of learning theories, it is not surprising that behavior therapies vary in form quite a bit. The particular form of a treatment approach is, of course, determined by the learning theory on which it is based. A sampling of the prominent behavior therapies follows.

A.

Wolpe's Approach to Psychotherapy

In treating the neurotic, Wolpe attempts to construct situations in which anxiety responses are actually manifested in the therapy situation so that he can create the conditions for extinguishing them. To accomplish this Wolpe conceives of therapy in two distinct phases.

1. The Diagnostic Phase

In the diagnostic phase the therapist tries to find out as much about the symptoms and their origins as he can. He seeks particularly to identify conditions under which symptoms first appeared and circumstances that aggravate or ameliorate them. If the patient has difficulty identifying such circumstances, Wolpe simply inquires into as many details as possible concerning the range of stimuli that currently elicit anxiety responses.

Wolpe also inquires into the patient's developmental history and seeks to reach an understanding of his habitual mode of reaction in certain major situational contexts. These include his dealings with members of his family and other people, his accomplishments in school and at work, his sexual and marital relationships, his religious training, and finally, any other situations which arouse fear or distress that had not been covered. Patients' statements are neither questioned nor criticized and the therapist tries to convey the feeling that he is entirely on the patient's side. In essence, the therapist tries to free the patient from additional anxiety.

The formal history-taking typically requires between one and twelve 45-minute sessions. When the history is completed the patient fills out the Bernreuter Self-Sufficiency Questionnaire, which Wolpe feels provides cues as to how long treatment will take. Low scores suggest that the patient will have difficulty in later assignments essential to the conduct of therapy. The patient is next asked to complete the Willoughby Personality Schedule, which inquires about anxiety responses to common social situations.

Once the diagnostic phase is completed, Wolpe informs the patient of his theory of the etiology of the neurosis. He distinguishes between appropriate and inappropriate fears and explains, nontechnically,

Townsend Wentz, Jr.

Joseph Wolpe helps his patients to learn new and appropriate responses to anxiety.

how the latter develop through conditioning. He uses material from the patient's history to explain straightforwardly how past experiences have led to the patient's present distress. Wolpe then indicates the steps he will take to diminish the patient's inappropriate anxiety responses.

2. The Therapeutic Phase

Wolpe believes that therapeutic change is brought about through the use of eight types of responses: (1) assertive responses; (2) sexual responses; (3) relaxation responses; (4) respiratory responses; (5) "anxiety-relief" responses; (6) competitively conditioned motor responses; (7) "pleasant" responses in the life situation (with drug enhancement); (8) interview-induced emotional responses, or abreaction. Since the specific form of the therapy interaction varies, depending upon which response is being used, they will be discussed individually.

a. Assertive Responses

Wolpe does not use the term "assertive" synonymously with "aggressive." He believes that friendly or affectionate responses, openly expressed, can compete with anxiety. In practice, however, he often works with aggressive responses. This form of treatment is applied in cases where inappropriate anxiety responses are experienced in interpersonal situations. In such instances Wolpe explains to the patient that his problem stems from maladaptive anxiety in specific interpersonal situations. Together, therapist and patient discuss other, more adaptive responses that the patient might make that are incompatible with the anxiety response. The therapist applies as much pressure as is necessary to encourage the patient to engage in the behavior that they had agreed was appropriate. The patient is as-

sured that he will feel better if he can try the behavior in question, and attempts are made to justify this behavior on the basis of its appropriateness. Illustratively, if hostility is encouraged in a given situation, the injustices that the patient has experienced in such a situation are pointed out, and expression of anger is portrayed as an entirely reasonable response.

Assertive behavior is advised primarily in instances where the patient's anxiety is inappropriate, and conversely where assertiveness would be entirely appropriate. If, for example, he were advised to express open resentment at his boss's attitude, he could be fired and would react to this punishment with further anxiety, thus reinforcing the initial anxiety response. On the other hand, it is often possible to encourage indirect expressions of aggression that run little risk of drawing a punishing reaction from others. The "ploys" described in books on "one-upmanship" illustrate such behaviors, and Wolpe does not hesitate to assign such reading to patients.

Ultimately the success of this form of therapy depends upon the patient's making the requisite responses in a real-life situation. He is prepared for this and encouraged by the therapist, but his anxiety is not thought to be affected until he can make a response incompatible with anxiety to the anxiety-producing stimulus.

b. Sexual Responses

When anxiety responses have been conditioned to stimuli arising in the sexual situation, attempts are made to use sexual responses against the anxiety. When the anxiety is so intense that it inhibits sexual responses entirely, other techniques are necessary. However, there are many instances of patients whose problems relate only to some identifiable part of a complex situation or else to easily definable, sex-relevant situations. In such cases, the patient is told that his or her problem stems from inappropriate fears that are associated with the sex act. He or she is encouraged to become involved in sexual situations but to participate in them only to the extent that they are predominantly pleasurable. If an act arouses anxiety, it should, for the moment, be terminated. The patient is advised to "let himself go" as far as he or she can with pleasure, but not to strive for more than can be tolerated comfortably at any particular time. If this is done, Wolpe asserts that sexual responsiveness will gradually replace earlier, characteristic anxiety responses. Eventually the range of situations in which pleasurable sexuality occurs is extended and the anxiety responses grow weaker.

Wolpe encourages the patient to confide in his sex partner about his specific problem and to enlist cooperation in helping him to extinguish anxiety responses. He asks for patience during this process and a willingness to engage in intimate sexuality without expecting sexual intercourse at first, and without being critical. The patient is encouraged first simply to lie in bed, nude, with his partner and to be as relaxed and comfortable as possible. He is told to do only what he is comfortable doing at any time and *no more*. He should feel unencumbered by a need to achieve a particular criterion on a given occasion. Wolpe reports that with each such encounter anxiety responses diminish and the patient feels more excited, both sexually and in his ability to come closer to satisfactorily completing the sexual act.

Relaxation Responses

Wolpe's best known, most frequently used, technique is relaxation, which is thought to be automatically antagonistic to anxiety responses. Relaxation is used mainly in a procedure known as *systematic desensitization.*

To use relaxation responses effectively, Wolpe first trains the patient in how to relax, and encourages him to relax muscles that are not in use at all times. The technique used for relaxation training begins by teaching the patient how it feels to be relaxed. This is done by encouraging him to tense certain muscle groups especially hard and then to relax them. Wolpe then directs the patient's conscious effort toward progressive relaxation of specific muscle groups. Patients are given the assignment of practicing relaxation for a short period each day. Generally, no more than seven relaxation-training sessions are required.

Once relaxation training has been completed Wolpe uses the relaxation response to extinguish anxiety responses to specific stimuli. This is the essence of systematic densensitization. A hierarchy of anxiety-producing situations, ranging from minimal to maximal, is worked out with the patient (for example, seeing a picture of a snake, stepping on a dead snake, and touching a live one). To extinguish anxiety associated with each of these specific situations, they must be engaged under circumstances that elicit other than an anxiety response. This can, of course, only be done "symbolically" in the therapy situation, and this is precisely the procedure that Wolpe follows.

Specifically, Wolpe relaxes the patient, and asks him to imagine, as vividly as possible, an anxiety-producing experience—initially one that is very low in the hierarchy. The patient is instructed to raise his hand as a signal as soon as he begins to feel anxiety. He is then told to stop thinking about that situation. As many scenes as possible (usually no more than three) are introduced during each session, and when a given scene no longer elicits anxiety it is omitted. By proceeding in this way from the less intense to more intense anxiety-provoking scenes, all scenes in the hierarchy are eventually experienced without anxiety. As long as the patient can learn to relax and can vividly imagine anxiety-producing scenes even if he is not hypnotizable, he is thought to be capable of benefiting from this approach.

At times during treatment it is necessary to reorganize or reconstitute part of the anxiety hierarchy—if, for example, a scene supposedly involving the weakest anxiety response arouses so much anxiety that it cannot be inhibited by relaxation. In addition, if the initial hierarchy suggested by the patient is in error, it must be revised. New hierarchies also have to be constructed as unrecognized sensitivities are uncovered. This is particularly the case when two adjacent steps in the initial hierarchy prove to be "too far apart." It is assumed that the anxiety experienced through imagery approximates that felt in real-life situations and, further, that when the anxiety is extinguished in therapy the real-life situation will cease to call forth anxiety.

Respiratory Responses

Respiratory responses are manipulated by having the patient inhale a gas mixture of 70 percent carbon dioxide and 30 percent oxygen. This results in a short period (for from 5 to 15 seconds) of heavy breathing which gradually subsides, followed by tingling sensations in the extremities and genital organs, visual experiences of light flashes, colors, or blackness and, occasionally, a brief loss of consciousness. Such inhalations may be administered as many as four times during a single session and their long-range effect is to induce complete muscle relaxation, for a day or more.

This technique is used primarily with patients whose anxiety responses are "free floating" or pervasive. The artificially induced feeling of relaxation is carried into the many former anxiety-producing situations and the relaxation response is antagonistic to the anxious feeling. As a result the anxiety response is extinguished and the state of relaxation substituted for it. The patient can thus remain relaxed even without the artificial induction of the gas mixture. Wolpe believes that relatively few inhalation sessions can produce profound amelioration of anxiety

Anxiety-Relief Responses

This is a technique that Wolpe has used only rarely. It is based on the assumption that responses which follow termination of an uncomfortable electric shock have anxiety-inhibiting effects. In the use of this technique Wolpe applies shock to the patient's forearm and instructs him to tolerate it as long as possible and to say the word "calm" when he wants it terminated. During any given session there are 10 to 20 repetitions of shock, in each case terminated following the use of the word "calm." For many patients, after two or three such sessions, the word "calm" evokes the relief experienced when the shock is terminated. When that has happened the word itself is available as a response to compete with the anxiety response in other situations. Wolpe believes that this approach works best with patients who experience much *emotional* upset (as distinguished from mere sensory discomfort) from electric shock.

Competitively Conditioned Motor Responses

Wolpe considers it necessary at times to extinguish a response other than anxiety (for example, the motor responses in obsessiveness or hysteria). In such cases Wolpe again uses the principle of opposing the undesirable response with an antagonistic one. One way of doing this is to have the patient imagine the object or situation that prompts obsessive behavior. When he indicates that he has a clear image of this situation a severe electrical shock is delivered to his forearm. This procedure may be repeated from 5 to 20 times per session.

Wolpe treated hysterical arm paralysis in one case by hypnotizing the patient and having him imagine, in as much detail as possible, the events that occurred at the time his symptoms developed. A series of these sessions resulted in a complete recovery of function in the arm. Presumably the relaxation induced during hypnosis successfully competed with the responses to the precipitating event, which had led to the feelings of pain, stiffness, and weakness that characterized the hysterical symptom.

g ·

"Pleasant" Responses in the Life Situation (with Drug Enhancement)

Wolpe devotes very little space to describing the use of "pleasant" responses. One of his case reports is about a patient with a severe tic who was treated with a drug, Atarax, on Wolpe's advice, even before she was seen by him. By the time he did see her, she was much improved and required only one further session with him. Presumably, the symptom was part of an anxiety response that was eliminated by the drug.

h ·
Interview-Induced Emotional Responses or Abreaction

Wolpe points out that all psychotherapeutic procedures have in common the interview format. Since therapeutic schools can claim roughly equivalent success rates, this may be due to the common elements of the therapeutic interview relationship, regardless of the therapist's theoretical persuasion. Therefore, Wolpe speculates that emotional responses of many kinds are called forth in the therapy interview, and among these are many that are antagonistic to anxiety. If this is the case, and if such responses are strong enough, they will reciprocally inhibit anxiety responses that are certainly elicited by some of the interview content. If there is too little emotional response in the interview or too much anxiety, extinction will not occur; in fact in the latter case the patient may get worse.

Abreaction (the release of strong feeling) in which emotionality is intense, is seen as a special case of interview-induced responding. If, in the presence of strong feeling, the therapist's sympathetic acceptance is felt by the patient, it prompts responses antagonistic to the anxiety that inevitably appears, and the net effect of the abreaction is beneficial.

B ·

Implosive Therapy

Based on learning theory, implosive therapy was developed during the 1950s by Thomas Stampfl (Stampfl & Levis, 1967). Implosive therapy provides an interesting contrast to Wolpe's therapeutic approach. Both see psychopathology as developing in similar ways and their therapeutic procedures share many common features, but certain aspects of the treatment technique are widely divergent. Stampfl feels that a person's specific life experiences involving punishment and pain in the presence of previously neutral stimuli produce anxiety responses. Once this has happened the memory or visual image of the upsetting experience arouses anxiety. Thus, imagery and many other stimuli associated with the painful experience must be avoided. Any behaviors that are useful in preventing the recurrence of previously painful stimuli will be learned quickly and they are maintained because they reduce anxiety. These mechanisms for avoiding anxiety are the symptoms of neurosis and psychosis as well as various personality disorders such as homosexuality, alcoholism, and speech disturbances. The task for the therapist is to find a way to reduce the anxiety arousing potential of stimuli and thereby to make avoidance unnecessary.

Stampfl uses a laboratory learning paradigm to explain the acquisition of anxiety responses. Similarly, he applies principles developed in the laboratory for extinguishing learned behavior to psychotherapy. Stampfl points out that Pavlov's original technique extinguishes learned responses very reliably. In this paradigm the conditioned stimulus is presented repeatedly in the absence of the unconditioned stimulus until the learned response no longer occurs. Carrying this procedure over to the psychotherapy situation it seems necessary that the cues that originally produced anxiety be represented as realistically as possible, that the anxiety response be made as intensely as possible, and that the response *not* be reinforced. If this happens often enough the learned anxiety response will be extinguished.

Carrying out this procedure with patients is a far more complicated process than extinguishing a learned response in the laboratory. The precise circumstances of the original learning situation are generally not known in the case of the human patient. The therapist must rely entirely on the patient's verbal reports about his past experiences. Also some time is required for the therapist to gather the information he needs to be able to reconstruct the original cue situation that was

responsible for the learning. Still, Stampfl feels that the therapist can, after only a few diagnostic interviews, make some shrewd guesses about the circumstances under which a patient's symptoms developed. Clearly the therapist will only come up with an approximation of the original learning situation, but even at that he will doubtless identify some of its important components. Furthermore, where the traditional therapist feels the need to wait until the patient is ready to accept an interpretation before sharing his suspicions about what caused a problem, the implosive therapist is not bound in this way. He is untroubled by the need to have the patient "understand" or "accept" the significance of certain cues. All that is important for him is that he, the therapist, understand them so that he can use them in implosive therapy.

The therapy procedure itself involves presenting the important cues to the patient as vividly and as realistically as possible, encouraging him to develop a visual image and even a tactual sense of what was happening to arouse great anxiety. If the cues that are presented to the patient arouse anxiety the therapist knows that he is on the right track and that the anxiety response was conditioned to them earlier. The greater the amount of anxiety aroused, the more reason there is to pursue the presentation of these particular stimuli. The patient's anxiety can be recognized either through the use of psychophysiological measures or, more commonly, by simply observing his behavior (for example, sweating, reddening of the face, fidgeting). If the cues presented by the therapist do not result in anxiety, he knows he is on the wrong track and must develop a new hypothesis about what has upset the patient.

Usually the implosive therapist does

two or three diagnostic interviews to gather the information he needs to proceed. He assumes that the basic problems result from the patient's avoidance of certain cues. The therapist is, therefore, constantly concerned with identifying the conditioned stimuli the patient is avoiding. It is expected that there are many such stimuli and that they can be ordered hierarchically in terms of how threatening they are. Thus, some cues have relatively low anxiety loadings, while others have very high loadings because they were associated with terribly traumatic situations. Once some notion of this hierarchy is developed, the implosive therapist encourages the patient to visualize a scene associated with a low-level anxiety response, as Wolpe does in systematic desensitization. A person who is suffering a driving phobia, for example, is encouraged to think about driving a car. The therapist encourages the patient to visualize these scenes as realistically as possible and also to imagine that he cannot engage in the avoidance behavior that characterizes his symptom. To do this well the therapist must become very involved and very dramatic. In his systematic desensitization process Wolpe stresses relaxation and the avoidance of anxiety. The implosive therapist on the other hand tries to stir up as much anxiety as he possibly can. The process is repeated again and again with the expectation that the anxiety response will gradually diminish and eventually disappear. At that point the patient and therapist proceed to another situation higher up on the patient's anxiety hierarchy.

Stampfl reports that as the anxiety around a given situation is reduced the patient is often able to describe still other situations that are anxiety arousing for him. These provide the cues for new situations to be placed in the hierarchy. Essentially,

Stampfl feels that there are ten areas within which anxiety hierarchies must be developed, and for most patients efforts are made to work in each of these areas. The ten areas include fears of aggression, punishment, rejection, bodily injury, guilt, loss of control, one's own autonomic functioning, and concerns related to oral, anal, and sexual impulses.

Operant Approaches to Behavior Therapy

Chapters 6 and 9 have described the sociopsychological approach to understanding schizophrenic and psychoneurotic disorders. This approach was stimulated by Skinner's theory of operant learning. In this section we will deal with the psychotherapeutic

B. F. Skinner, originator of the theory of operant learning.

Leonard P. Ullmann

Leonard Krasner

Advocates of applying the operant approach to specific deviant behaviors.

approach that follows from operant theory. From the viewpoint of operant theory behavior is maintained by its consequences. Changing behavior requires understanding the consequences that have been maintaining it and making changes in the environment to assure the reinforcement of desired behavior and the failure to reinforce undesirable behavior.

Krasner (1971) points out that *abnormal*, or, preferably, *deviant* behavior is learned in a social context and it is in this context that it must be changed through manipulation of its consequences. Thus behavior is the direct focus of the treatment process and "real" changes in the person are expected to be part and parcel of changes in his behavior. The therapist, then, is a trainer or a social reinforcer to the patient and anything that increases his reinforcement value is important to his role. This includes personality characteristics such as the therapist's age and apparent experience, his prestige, his socioeconomic background, and how confident he seems to be about what he is doing. What will be reinforcing to the patient

must be determined pragmatically. Anything that succeeds in changing behavior is useful as a reinforcer. What will reinforce one person may not be effective with another. Thus, the therapist must determine for each patient what will be reinforcing for him and, conceivably, certain reinforcers may be effective for only limited periods of time.

In order to apply the operant approach in therapy what is thought of as mental disorder or mental disease must be broken down into the component deviant behaviors that characterize it. The goal of therapy then is to change these specific behaviors by manipulating their consequences. For example, schizophrenia may be thought of as being some combination of disorganized thinking, apathy, social withdrawal, and bizarre verbalizations (Ullmann & Krasner, 1974). To treat the schizophrenic, efforts must be made to change each of these component behaviors. Krasner (1971) summarizes a number of studies demonstrating that each of these behaviors can, in fact, be changed through the direct manipulation of their consequences. Patients can, through appropriate reinforcement, learn to interpret proverbs abstractly, to increase their use of emotionally toned words, to become more involved with their surroundings, and to talk more with other people.

Delinquents have been treated by defining desirable behavior in a measurable way, and reinforcing the emission of such behavior. Severely disturbed children have likewise been treated through operant approaches involving an analysis of the component behaviors that cause them to be regarded as disturbed and introducing a set of environmental manipulations for changing these behaviors. Krasner (1971) describes the application of operant principles to the treatment of still other problems such as stammering and adjustment to physical disability. The social and vocational skills of ex-mental patients have been enhanced by operant methods and, within mental hospitals, token economy programs have promoted adaptive behavior in patients. Still further applications of operant technology to more and more behavioral problems are currently being carried out.

Modeling

Modeling is another behaviorally focused psychotherapeutic approach (Bandura, 1971). Modeling differs from most interview approaches in that the content of the therapeutic interaction, the locus, and the treatment agents are different. In modeling the content is the actual behavior that needs to be modified rather than a discussion of the behavior. The locus of modeling approaches is, wherever possible, the natural setting in which the problem has arisen, rather than an office. Finally, treatment is carried out under professional supervision by people who ordinarily have a great deal of contact with the client in his natural environment.

In the modeling approach an example is provided for the client of a set of experiences or behaviors that he can imitate in order to bring about necessary behavioral changes. Modeling is thought to have three potential effects. First, it can help the client develop new forms of behavior that were not present in his behavioral repertoire earlier. Secondly, modeling can be used to strengthen or weaken the client's inhibitions. Finally, modeling can help to facilitate responses that are already available to the client. In this case he does not learn to do things he could not do before but simply to engage more readily in behaviors that he was already capable of performing.

Modeling procedures have been used in a variety of ways (Bandura, 1971). Autistic children have been taught self-care skills, appropriate sex-role behaviors, and intellectual skills. Delinquents have been treated with modeling to develop social and other skills necessary for vocational success. Nonassertive patients have been trained to become more assertive. Preschool children have been taught to increase their dramatic play with peers.

RESEARCH IN PSYCHOTHERAPY

Research has been carried out on many different aspects of psychotherapy: patient variables; therapist variables; process studies; and outcome studies. Some psychotherapeutic schools have lent themselves readily to research, or in some cases adherents of these schools have been particularly devoted to research. Some schools have stimulated practically none. In the late 1940s and early 1950s a good deal of research was done by those interested in the client-centered approach. Since that time by far the greatest amount of research seems to have been stimulated by the behavioral approaches to psychotherapy (Bergin & Suinn, 1975). We can hardly attempt a thorough review of research in psychotherapy and will therefore focus in this section on outcome studies, since these seem most relevant to our purposes. Some mention will also be made of the "placebo effect," a factor that has probably been least adequately controlled in therapy research.

Outcome Studies of Psychotherapy

In earlier sections of this book reference has been made to the writings of Eysenck (1952, 1965) which summarized a number of outcome studies of psychotherapy and drew conclusions about the effectiveness of the process. Eysenck compared results reported in such studies to the results of studies that purport to reflect "spontaneous recovery" from psychoneurotic problems. Bergin (1971) has examined the studies on the basis of which Eysenck drew his conclusions. His reading of these studies indicates that Eysenck chose to interpret their findings in the most pessimistic light whereas a more balanced or more conservative interpretation would have resulted in more favorable outcome rates than those reported by Eysenck. Overall, Bergin contends that the evidence, though modest, indicates that psychotherapy "works." A later review by Bergin and Suinn (1975) reaffirms this position. This indicates that a high percentage of patients entering into psychotherapy benefit from it.

Even if high percentages of people who undergo psychotherapy benefit from it, how do we know that psychotherapy is more beneficial than some other treatment form, or possibly even no treatment at all? This question touches on one of Eysenck's most telling criticisms of the therapy studies he reviewed. They simply failed to use nontreated control groups. As a means of constructing such nontherapy control groups, Eysenck described two studies that seemed to indicate that the percentage of untreated patients experiencing "spontaneous recovery" is just as high as the improvement rate in treated patients. In one of these studies the discharge rate of hospitalized neurotics in New York State was found to be 72 percent (Landis, 1937). In another such study 72 percent of untreated life insurance disability claimants (for psychoneurosis) were found to have improved (Denker, 1946). Bergin (1971) counters that there are many other studies on the basis of which one can assess the rate of spontaneous recovery. For example, one reports the condition of psychoneurotic patients who were treated in medical clinics. Another involved patients who had suffered from peptic ulcers for from 4 to 15 years without any change in the status of their symptoms. Still another followed the course of a neurotic population for from 13 to 20 years and found only modest improvement rates. On the basis of these and other such studies Bergin concludes that the median improvement rate seems to be around 30 percent rather than the 72 percent figure that Eysenck used in his reports.

Furthermore, Bergin questions the value of the concept of spontaneous recovery. It is a label for an unknown process that implies that some events occur for no reason at all. This notion Bergin quite rightly feels is contrary to the most basic scientific principles. He argues that when seemingly spontaneous positive personality changes occur some therapeutic process has taken place in the natural environment.

Whatever it is that happened occurred outside of some therapist's office and may involve forces that are ignored or not well understood by therapists. Some studies indicate, for example, that most people who have psychological disturbances do not go to mental health professionals for help. A study cited in Chapter 1 by Gurin, Veroff, and Feld (1960) indicates that clergymen and physicians are considerably more likely to be appealed to for help with emotional problems than are mental health professionals. Conceivably, many people who are counseled by their clergyman or family doctor are helped and that may explain their "spontaneous recovery" in the absence of formal psychotherapy.

In a general criticism of outcome research in psychotherapy, Bergin points to the inadequacy of gross studies, the type most commonly found. We can only hope to get a clear idea of psychotherapy results by studying the component parts of psychotherapy. We need to get answers to questions like, "What kinds of patients benefit from treatment?", "How do we define benefits?", "What kinds of therapists are most effective?", and the like. Thus, the samples studied should be roughly homogeneous. The therapists involved should be of equivalent skill and experience. The outcome must be defined in terms of precise criteria. Control groups must be well defined. Only when such conditions prevail can the results of therapy studies be clear. Furthermore, therapy outcome studies should specify the kind of patient change that is expected to take place and should use measures relevant to such change.

The overall impact of these reviews of psychotherapeutic effectiveness indicates that considerably more research remains to be done and that to be optimally useful it must be much finer grained than it has

been. We need to learn about what patients improve best under what kinds of treatment provided by what kinds of therapists according to what kinds of criteria. The wide-ranging shotgun approach that typified most research in the past has simply failed to make this kind of detailed analysis. It is naive to expect that a study or series of studies can be done to indicate the general utility of psychotherapy. This would be tantamount to claiming that aspirin cures physical symptoms. Though very useful in some respects, aspirin may be entirely useless with respect to a variety of symptoms. Happily, Bergin and Suinn (1975) report in a recent review that current outcome studies are beginning to assess the components of psychotherapy and their individual effects.

B.

The Placebo Effect

A major problem in assessing the effectiveness of any treatment approach, physical or psychological, is the *placebo effect* (Shapiro, 1971). A *placebo* is any form of therapy or component of therapy that is purposely used because, while it is presumed to have a specific effect, unknown to the patient and/or therapist, it is actually ineffective for the condition being treated. The term placebo effect refers to the "nonspecific, psychologic, or psychophysiologic effect produced by placebos." Any form of therapy may be used as a placebo. In the case of a drug, the placebo effect is largely psychological, and it may be favorable or unfavorable, but it is unrelated to the objective properties of the drug itself.

Shapiro points out that the history of prescientific medicine is replete with instances of the use of various organic and inorganic substances as treatment agents that were either useless or dangerous. For example, baldness was treated by the use of bear fat. Falling sickness was treated with mistletoe because it grows on an oak tree which cannot fall. Consumptives were administered the lung of the fox, a long-winded animal. Despite their seeming senselessness physicians used these treatments for literally thousands of years. Shapiro reasons that this must have occurred because many patients were actually helped by them. He concludes that whatever help was provided by such medication was due to the psychological factors associated with the placebo effect. In fact, Shapiro feels that virtually all medicines used up until fairly modern times were placebos.

The role that the placebo effect plays in psychotherapy is obviously quite significant. After an extensive review of a series of studies bearing on this issue, Shapiro concludes that the psychotherapist's interest in the patient and the treatment approach that he is applying has direct bearing on how successful he is in treating patients. The more interested a practitioner is in his theory of therapy, especially if he has developed it himself, the more effective his work tends to be. Patients seem to share in their therapist's confidence about what they are doing and respond positively toward it.

In psychotherapy the issue of how to deal with the placebo effect is much more complicated than it is in medicine. After all, the disease-afflicted medical patient who enjoys a placebo effect-related psychological benefit from a drug, a faith healer, or a religious ritual may avoid other forms of treatment and eventually die of the disease. In psychotherapy, though, the name of the game is psychological benefit. It is what all therapies obviously strive for.

Thus, those factors that enhance the placebo effect to promote a positive response to treatment need to be well understood and used for the patient's benefit.

In evaluating treatment, or particularly when comparing different treatment approaches, the placebo effect complicates matters considerably. For example, when a therapeutic approach is being enthusiastically applied by its innovator and a group of recent converts, patients are apt to respond to it much more positively than they will once it has become an established approach. Furthermore, it is very difficult to know, without a better understanding of how the placebo effect works or careful research that controls for it, how much the results one gets in therapy have anything to do with the specific nature of the treatment being applied. It is probably for this reason that so many different approaches to psychotherapy are possible. Perhaps largely as the result of the placebo effect many innovative approaches have early successes and manage to become established. In such cases the techniques applied may be as worthless as eating bear fat to cure baldness. Still, treatment successes related to the placebo effect can be claimed, and that keeps interest up in the approach and attracts converts. Once an approach has been around long enough to lose its enthusiastic originators, its successes may well diminish because it is required to stand on its merits alone with little assistance from the placebo effect. But this process takes much time so that approaches to psychotherapy proliferate faster these days than they are discarded.

What seems badly needed is considerably more research into the placebo effect itself. Its various dimensions need to be better understood. We need to know what kind of people respond favorably to what kinds of factors under what types of circumstances. Until we have such data future psychotherapy researchers must pay more attention than they have in the past to the possible placebo effects that can account for the results of a given therapeutic approach.

CONCLUSION

Psychotherapy takes many and wonderful forms. The diversity reflected in this chapter's review needs to be considered within the perspective of the diversity of human problems that therapists try to deal with. It is too much to expect that a single way of doing psychotherapy would suffice for every kind of human problem that comes to the attention of the counselor or therapist. On the other hand, some of the field's diversity also results no doubt from the fact that specific psychotherapeutic approaches are so difficult to evaluate. Criteria for judging the worth of a given approach are hard to set up. The methodology for establishing good experimental tests of psychotherapy are just becoming better understood. And, finally, the busy practitioner would generally prefer to use his time trying to treat the many people who come to him with problems in preference to conducting research.

Still, research evidence is gradually building up in a form that may not yet provide answers to many crucial questions but at least begins to frame better questions than have been asked in the past. For example, it is becoming quite clear that we can no longer expect studies to evaluate the effectiveness of psychotherapy in some global way. It is clear now that therapy studies need to ask narrower questions such as "What kinds of therapy work best with what kinds of problems under what kinds of circumstances?" Hopefully, as such evidence accumulates we will be in a better position to sort out from among the diverse approaches to psychotherapy those that are most effective. Ultimately we need to be able to say what there is about a given treatment approach that is useful and with whom it can best be used.

To arrive at such a point we must become considerably more concerned than we have been in the past with the placebo effect. Most therapists have some sense that such an effect operates and recognize that factors such as the appearance of the therapist, his office, his manner, and the like have bearing on the patient's response to treatment. Obviously, the good clinician capitalizes on such factors and creates an optimal setting for treatment success. In addition, however, schools of psychotherapy seem to grow up around the enthusiasm that a charismatic leader conveys, a factor that is also found to exercise a potent placebo effect. The problem with this is that, while carried along on this wave of enthusiasm, many patients may receive considerable benefit, but it is the enthusiasm rather than the specifics of the treatment approach that may be the only potent factor in the interaction. This may not be a severe problem for patients as long as there are enthusiastic, charismatic practitioners to represent the school. However, most therapists, like most people, lack charisma. Thus, ineffective treatment approaches may persist for many years on the basis of a track record that was made in its early beginnings. Only through research efforts that identify factors associated with the placebo effect can we arrive at early and relatively definitive evaluations of new approaches.

SUMMARY

1. Psychotherapy approaches may be categorized in terms of whether they stress intellectual insight and understanding, emotional expression, or behavior change.
2. Psychoanalysis is the best known example of an insight approach. Other examples include Sullivanian therapy, the client-centered approach, rational-emotive therapy, and existential analysis.
3. The emotionally expressive or cathartic emphasis characterizes the various humanistic approaches to psychotherapy.
4. Behaviorally oriented therapies place little emphasis on the patient's need to understand the source of his problems. Neither do they necessarily strive for intense emotional expression unless it is a by-product of their efforts to change behavior directly. The best known behavioral approaches have been developed in relatively recent times by Wolpe and followers of Skinner's work on operant conditioning.
5. Evaluative studies of psychotherapy have aroused much controversy. Some interpretors of this work conclude that the effectiveness of psychotherapy has not been demonstrated. More recent views dispute this interpretation without claiming that the work in therapy evaluation is yet definitive.
6. A major need for future evaluation research is to explore the significance of many of the components of therapy. Ultimately we need to find out what kinds of therapies, applied by what kinds of therapists, work best with what kinds of patients under what circumstances.
7. The *placebo effect*, the psychological benefit derived from aspects of the treatment situation that are not essential to the approach being applied and that are unintentional, was cited as requiring considerable further study. It is a factor in all psychotherapy outcome studies and may account for much of the temporary success of new treatment approaches that contain few other potent therapeutic elements.

CHAPTER 15

Group Psychotherapy

Not too long ago when people spoke of psychotherapy it was always individual psychotherapy, the preceding chapter's topic, that they had in mind. The past 20 years or so have seen a dramatic growth of interest in group approaches. Most of these developing group efforts are frankly regarded as forms of psychotherapy. Some, however, are seen to be opportunities for broadening self-awareness in essentially untroubled people who simply want to get more out of life. All will be discussed in this chapter.

Historically, precursors to group therapy are very old indeed. As Frank (1961) points out, mass conversion techniques and certain religious healing procedures such as those used at Lourdes very likely depend for their impact upon powerful group forces. For example, the afflicted one is accompanied to Lourdes by his priest and members of his family. Those seeking to receive the miracle cures at Lourdes are the ones who firmly believe they will be helped and are strongly supported by their entourage. Such phenomena go back literally hundreds of years in man's history. Even the more formal group psychotherapy approaches which involve bringing together the same group of people over an extended period of time have their roots in the early twentieth century. Gazda (1968) has described the group meetings held by Dr. Joseph H. Pratt as early as 1905 in which he brought tubercular patients together for the purpose of instructing them on hygienic practices. Although Pratt initiated this practice simply to save time, he eventually came to appreciate the impact that various group members had upon one another, in this seemingly purely didactic approach.

Trigant Burrow, a psychoanalyst, spoke out in the mid-1920s (Burrow, 1927) for the need for group psychotherapy in order to take into account the social forces which affected man's behavior. Burrow was reacting to the psychoanalytic practice of treating the individual as though he were a unit wholly isolated from his fellows. Another very influential contributor to the early development of group therapy was J. L. Moreno, whose practice with groups and patients began in the early 1920s. After emigrating to the United States in 1925, Moreno introduced psychodrama and actually coined the term "group psychotherapy." Since the 1930s, and particularly in recent years, the use of group treatment approaches has expanded considerably.

Frank (1961) has described some properties of group experience that are significant for psychotherapy. He pointed out, for example, that the individual's psychological growth is a product of the interactions that he has had with other people. Man's earliest influences are his parents and the other older people in his immediate family group. Eventually as he grows older he becomes aware of differences between his generation and the older generation and falls under the influence of his own age mates. Most individuals, therefore, identify with peer groups, use them to validate their own feelings, and seem to require a feeling of belongingness to a group in order to maintain a sense of self-identification. Ostracism is dreaded, and to belong to an accepting group produces strong positive feelings. Group treatment approaches harness these powerful group properties to assist patients with psychological difficulties.

Group therapy differs in significant ways both from individual therapy and from the everyday social group interaction. Being in a therapy group rather than in individual therapy puts the patient in a context of individuals who are, more or less, like people he deals with daily. In essence, he is in a miniature society when in group therapy. There are some important differences, however, between therapy and social groups. First, the therapy group encourages, even demands, free expression of feelings and attitudes. Any topic can be discussed and group pressures encourage open expression. A second difference between therapy and social groups is that in the former efforts are made to suspend value judgments. Group members are not necessarily encouraged to succeed. Admission to the group in the first p'ace comes about because the individual has experienced some failure in living. His status with the group depends far less on ability to demonstrate achievement and success and more on ability to deal honestly with his feelings.

The combination of meeting with other troubled individuals, being encouraged to explore personal feelings openly, and the lack of concern about one's individual success in the usual sense has several important consequences. Therapy group members for example often report, as one of the most significant aspects of group participation, the discovery that there are other people who have problems not too different from their own. This diminishes the sense of inadequacy that they have lived with for so long. Exposing personal weaknesses and finding them accepted by the group make it easier for one to accept those weaknesses himself. Another significant consequence of the therapy group format is that patients have the opportunity to help each other. This can greatly enhance the self-esteem of someone who has long dwelt on his own inadequacy. Another advantage of the group approach is that the changes that take place are more likely to endure and to generalize to outside situations than are those that occur in individual therapy. This is partly because of the tendency to internalize the standards of the group with which one has identified. In addition, the therapy group forces one to deal with the real world. In individual psychotherapy the patient can dwell on his own private world and still retain the serious attention of his therapist. When he speaks up in the therapy group, however, he uses time that could be used by others who may have little patience with his dreams or fantasies. Thus he is forced to deal with realities which have meaning for all group members.

Along with the advantages described above, certain disadvantages are found in group therapy. For example, it may be more difficult for a person to be entirely candid about highly charged material in a room full of strangers than when talking privately with a respected professional. Also group members can be destructive toward one another in damaging ways that are hard to control.

Classifying group therapy and other group phenomena is no simpler than classifying individual psychotherapy. Broadly speaking the same three emphases found in individual psychotherapy, the insight or understanding focus, the stress on catharsis, and the emphasis on behavior change, can be identified. Several examples of group approaches will be described, therefore, as falling into one or another of these camps.

I. INSIGHT-ORIENTED APPROACHES

A. Psychoanalytic Group Psychotherapy

Perhaps the best-known exponent of analytic group psychotherapy is S. R. Slavson (1969). For Slavson the goal of group psy-chotherapy is to bring about a permanent intrapsychic change in the patient as the result of imparting insight. He makes a distinction, however, between insight and understanding. For him understanding comes from information giving. By insight Slavson seems to refer to a developing awareness of one's own internal emotional state dating back to the trauma of very early life. Thus, insight for him combines an intellectual and an emotional process.

In analytic group psychotherapy efforts are made to achieve insight by working with a group of patients no larger than eight or smaller than five. Care is taken that, diagnostically, each member is suitable for the process that is to be engaged in. This process involves free association by each member just as would be the case in individual psychoanalysis. The group therapist interprets individual resistances and transferences, and tries to impart insight to each of the members individually. Successful treatment is thought to depend upon the working through of the sexual and aggressive conflicts of each member.

To achieve the necessary working through each patient must relive the traumatic events of his early life along with all of the feelings experienced at the time and with all of the accompanying distortions and fantasies. The group setting is, of course, free of the threat that characterized the patient's early life experience. The reliving takes place in the presence of mature attitudes provided by the therapist and the other patients. An essential requirement in analytic group psychotherapy is that all patients participate freely and spontaneously. As one patient unburdens himself and stirs up ideas or feelings in fellow patients, everyone must feel free to express himself. This freedom ultimately brings each patient to the point where he can touch on the repressed memories that lie at the core of his problems. Once this occurs, insight into his ways of defending and reacting becomes possible.

Transactional Analysis (TA)

Transactional analysis (TA) was originated by Eric Berne (1964) and popularized through a book, *I'M OK—YOU'RE OK*, by Harris (1967). TA emphasizes the different aspects of each individual's personality and examines what is thought to be a person's characteristic life position. This is done through observation of the *transaction*, the basic unit of social intercourse. When any two people are together, sooner or later they communicate either through words or some other way. In TA the therapy process involves examining the transaction in which one person does something to another and the other person does something in return. In addition, TA couches the information received from an analysis of the transaction in a language that has meaning to everyone involved in treatment.

Berne became aware in his work with people that each of us seems to be made up psychologically of many different people. These differences are apparent in changes that take place in a given person even during the course of a single conversation. Gestures change, facial expression and voice tone vary. Even the choice of language and the posture change as a function of what is being talked about, to whom one is talking, and the like. From such observations Berne concluded that people are made up of three different psychological realities: a Parent; a Child; and an Adult.

The Parent inside each of us consists primarily of the warnings and rules that are handed down to a child by his parents

Eric Berne, the originator of transactional analysis. (Courtesy Grove Press.)

either verbally, or in the way they looked when they spoke, or through the sound of their voices. Some of the Parent includes the prohibitions and expressions of displeasure and shame that parents direct to the child. Another part of the Parent includes the obvious pleasure and pride that parents conveyed when they felt the child was behaving well. Confusion and unhappiness arises for the youngster whose parents convey inconsistent messages. This can happen because one of the parents is inconsistent himself so that he says one thing and does another. But at times it is because the parents do not agree with each other. Inconsistent communication is difficult to understand and creates unhappiness. In the grownup, Parent-type communication is reflected in information-giving about how to do things and in many gestural cues. These may include furrowing the brow, showing a look of horror, or tapping the foot. Certain verbalizations also typify the Parent. Examples include such phrases as "I am going to put a stop to this once and for all," and "I can't for the life of me." Evaluations of behavior are also felt to come from the Parent.

At the same time that the youngster's experience with his parents is helping to create a conception of the Parent in him, a conception of the Child is also developing. This stems from the child's feelings about what is happening to him. Since much of this occurs within the first five years of life, language is either absent or relatively limited. Thus, most of what is recorded in the Child is on a feeling level. Because the youngster is small, dependent on others, and limited in his understanding of what is happening around him, most of what gets recorded in the Child is negative. He keeps feeling that he cannot do things or that he does them badly, that he is weak, that things are his fault, and the like. On the positive side, the Child has creativity and curiosity. He has the impulse to learn about his surroundings and enjoys making new discoveries. When grown up, the manifest signs of the Child are usually seen in some sort of physical expression. Whining, pouting, delighted squeals, giggling, and squirming are all representative of the Child. On a verbal level any use of baby talk or special phrases such as "I want" and an excessive use of superlatives reflects the Child.

At about the age of 10 months, when the child is showing some independence and can direct himself, the third psychological reality begins to emerge. This is called the Adult. This reality takes shape as the child begins to learn for himself what is real in the world around him and how it differs both from what he was taught in his Parent and what he feels in his Child. Obviously since the youngster is limited in how much exploring he can do during his first year and parents' directions may prevent some exploration, the Adult tends to be of limited significance in the first year. Still, people continue to mature and continue to accumulate first-hand experiences of reality. The Adult is that part of every person that combines what he has learned from parents, what he has felt in his Child, and what he himself has experienced in life. The Adult's most significant function is to be critical about these three sources of information and to reject what the Parent has taught and what the Child in him feels if it does not fit with what he can see with his own eyes. The Adult's existence within the individual is to be recognized in the way he listens. His facial expression indicates that he is taking things in. His language is typified by questions such as "What?," "Why?," and "Where?," and in words such as "True," "False," and the like.

In TA each individual is seen to assume one of four "life positions" based on the kinds of life experiences he has had. These four positions are: (1) I'M NOT OK—YOU'RE OK; (2) I'M NOT OK—YOU'RE NOT OK; (3) I'M OK—YOU'RE NOT OK; and (4) I'M OK—YOU'RE OK. No matter how happy one's childhood might have been, a baby is essentially helpless and weak and his first year's experience inevitably conveys to him the feeling I'M NOT OK. He is taken care of by adults who are inevitably seen as strong and capable. This prompts him to feel YOU'RE OK. By the end of the first year of life everyone has adopted the position I'M NOT OK—YOU'RE OK. Many people never alter this position throughout their lives. Feeling I'M NOT OK—YOU'RE OK can influence a person's behavior in two ways. One way is that he may try to live a role that confirms the NOT OK. In this approach he withdraws, seeks his pleasure through fantasy, or perhaps behaves badly to prove over and over again that he's NOT OK. Perhaps a more common way of living out this position is to assume that I may be NOT OK but I can be OK *if*. Such a person tries continually to win the approval of those around him who are thought to be important.

The other three life positions described in TA are variations that sometimes develop after the first year of life on the original I'M NOT OK—YOU'RE OK stance. The I'M NOT OK—YOU'RE NOT OK position arises in people whose parents look after them dutifully only up to the point where they begin to show some independence. At this point such parents become cold and distant. They show little affection, refuse to baby the child, and punish him more frequently and more severely than before. This makes the child resentful of them and the feeling I'M NOT OK—YOU'RE NOT OK grows. Such a person is seen to withdraw, feeling that life is a hopeless state that you have to try to endure. A person in this position may well live out his life in a mental institution.

The I'M OK—YOU'RE NOT OK position develops in a situation where the parents have been very harsh and unrewarding. The parents in such cases are so brutal that the child can only conclude that they are NOT OK. The I'M OK feeling arises because the child's only source of comfort is from within himself. Being left alone gives him rare pleasure and he comes to feel that he will be OK if others just do not bother him. One outcome of this position is seen to be criminal psychopathic behavior.

The most hopeful of the four life positions is I'M OK—YOU'RE OK. One way this position differs from the other three is that it is arrived at consciously and is based on much thought and self-understanding. The other three positions are lived out largely at a feeling level. Each was learned when the person was very young and there was little language available to change, understand, or moderate these positions. They, therefore, exercised an unconscious influence over the person's life. TA's goal is to help a person acquire the I'M OK—YOU'RE OK position. To manage this a person needs to learn how his childhood experiences caused him to assume one of the other three positions and how his current behavior is influenced by these positions.

Basic to the TA approach is the faith that a person can *choose* to change. The transactional analyst feels that we can only speak of determinism in the case of the inanimate. The concept of determinism cannot, however, explain human behavior. Because man can anticipate his future he is not entirely a pawn to what happened to him in the past. What he chooses to hope for in the future then becomes a guiding force in his life.

In the transactional analyst's first hour with the patient, about half the time is spent having the patient talk about his problem. In the remaining half the therapist describes the concepts of Parent, Child, and Adult. During this first interview a "contract" is formed. The therapist agrees to try to teach something that the patient will try to learn during treatment. In the TA session the therapist identifies for each patient those aspects of himself that are Parent, Child, and Adult as they engage in interactions with each other. Ultimately each patient is expected to become an expert at analyzing his own transactions. Symptoms are dealt with through analysis of the patient's daily transactions. Improvement will result when the person's Adult becomes sufficiently free to permit new behavioral options and the exercise of greater creativity.

TA is a process that can be carried out on a one-to-one basis, but Harris feels that it works best in groups. Being in a group allows patients to confront each other concerning the ways in which they rely on their Parent and Child rather than on the realities. Furthermore, people have to live with other people outside of treatment so that the group setting seems to be a realistic one in which to begin to resolve problems.

The Training Group (T-Group)

The T-Group is one of many types of group procedures that has been developed in recent years which are not, strictly speaking, intended as therapies in the usual sense of the term. It grew out of research conducted by the Massachusetts Institute of Technology Research Center for Group Dynamics during the 1940s (Benne, 1964). Benne traces the origin of fundamental T-Group principles to a workshop held in New Britain, Connecticut, in 1946. This workshop was set up to develop local leaders who could facilitate understanding of and compliance with the Fair Employment Practices Act. Participants, therefore, consisted of a mixture of teachers, social workers, businessmen, and interested citizens.

For this workshop three small groups were formed, each having ten members and a leader, and they focused on practical problems that group members faced at home. Group discussion was brought to bear on these problems; role playing was utilized both in order to diagnose certain aspects of the problems that were presented and to practice approaches that might help to solve them. There was no intention to analyze the here-and-now in-

teraction that was occurring within the group.

Research observers attached to each group coded observed behavioral interactions with no intention of taking them up with participants. Rather, staff members and research observers planned to get together in the evenings to pool their process observations for each group. When some participants heard of this plan, they asked to attend the research meetings and, after some discussion among staff, were allowed to do so. The innocent staff decision to permit participants to sit in on these discussions did not anticipate what was to come.

It became apparent that these post-mortem "research" discussions of the group's behavior had an unanticipated and "an electric effect both on participants and on the training leaders" (Benne, 1964, p. 82). Group participants who were expected to remain relatively passive in these conferences, which were, after all, devoted more to research issues than anything else, became very actively involved with trainers and staff. One person, for example, might deny the accuracy of an observer's comments only to have it stoutly defended by another. Participants soon joined the observers and training leaders in attempting to analyze and interpret what had gone on in the group. Before long, all group participants were attending the evening sessions which lasted as long as three hours. Participants reported that they were deriving a very important understanding of themselves and of the behavior of the group in which they were participating through those sessions. The training staff also recognized the powerful impact of the evening meetings and was struck by the reeducative potential of confronting group members with more or less objective data about their own behavior and its effects on the group.

Thus, what started out strictly as a research group became the forerunner of the modern T-group. In this early period no thought was given to the possibility of eliminating that part of the initial group procedure which focused on substantive problems back home. Instead it was felt that this aspect of the group interaction could be supplemented by a "here and now" analysis of what was going on in the behavior of individual group members.

The staff involved in the New Britain workshop in 1946 planned a second workshop for the summer of 1947 to be held in Bethel, Maine. A basic feature of this workshop was a small continuing group called the Basic Skills Training (BST) Group. The BST group was conceived to have several functions: helping members to internalize certain systematic concepts regarding group phenomena; learning about planning for change and the skills required by the change agent; conveying knowledge of group variables to help members recognize indices and criteria for group development. Role playing was used to provide BST group members with practice in diagnostic and action skills as change agents. It was hoped that participants would, through this program, develop a deep understanding of democratic values.

The BST experience convinced staff members that overloading the group with so many functions reduced opportunities to examine and analyze ongoing behavioral events. Many training functions posed for the group required that the trainer engage in didactic interventions which interfered with his role as a group collaborator in helping participants to develop and to test what they could learn about themselves and the ongoing life of the group. Furthermore, it was felt that members resisted looking at themselves and their group behavior in addition to analyzing and interpreting the behavior of other group members. Thus, by including a variety of tasks that were obstacles to self and group analysis, such resistance was heightened. Therefore, the third stage in T-group evolution was to move toward an exclusive emphasis on the here-and-now situation—its current characteristic stamp. It became a mechanism for understanding how a person functions within a group, how he is looked upon by others, and the effect of his actions on overall group functioning.

Since its primitive beginnings in the 1940s, the T-group movement has enjoyed considerable acceptance and popularity. The National Education Association established the National Training Laboratory in Group Development and has sponsored workshops at Bethel, Maine, each year. The National Training Laboratory has sponsored workshops for very diverse groups including, for example, Red Cross workers, industrial managers, religious workers, Puerto Rican government workers, public school teachers and administrators, college students and faculty members, and leaders in community development. In addition, a number of regional laboratories have been set up in various parts of the country sharply extending the T-group movement. These regional laboratories, usually based at university centers, have experimented with changes in the original T-group procedures to adapt them better to local problems and conditions. Thus, many innovations on the traditional T-group have been introduced.

The T-group procedure has been directed largely to the "normal" person. While it may attract many individuals with emotional problems, this is incidental to the primary purpose of the development. The thrust of T-groups is toward improving the functioning of an already adequate individual. In that sense this procedure may be seen as an early move toward prevention, often aimed at enhancing the functioning of key individuals in important positions within the community.

II CATHARTIC APPROACHES IN GROUP PSYCHOTHERAPY

A Humanistic Therapies

The previous chapter described a number of humanistic approaches to psychotherapy, all of which share an emphasis on emotional catharsis. Some of these approaches such as Gestalt therapy are at times conducted in a group format. Others such as Janov's primal therapy include a group component. The goals of these humanistic therapies, of course, are the encouragement of emotional release whether they are done individually or in groups. A few humanistic approaches such as Casriel's new identity therapy (Casriel, 1972) are applied exclusively in groups.

B Psychodrama

One of the oldest forms of group therapy was originated by Moreno (1969) in the late 1920s. He first used psychodrama with children and in 1936 established a sanitarium in Beacon, New York, with the Therapeutic Theatre, the first psychodrama theatre. Psychodrama is seen by Moreno as a technique for encouraging the subject to release his or her fantasy and spontaneity by taking part in a dramatic production. Man's creativity and spontaneity are seen to have become bridled by a set of perceptions and images that he or she has had to carry around concerning his or her parents, spouse, and children, as well as certain self-images that he or she feels must be lived up to. By living out these images in the drama, and by reversing roles of

parent figures or employers, he has a chance to learn things about them that he cannot learn in ordinary life. The subject can let himself be the kind of person he would like to be and thereby throw off the limitations placed on him by others. His true self can be exposed, be reorganized, and be put together again in a way that takes into account who he really is. The kind of reality the subject experiences through psychodrama is fuller and broader than any he or she has been able to find in real life. Thus, Moreno sees psychodrama as involving a "catharsis of integration."

In psychodrama five "instruments" are used to carry out the technique. These include the stage, the subject, the director, a staff of therapeutic aides, and an audience. The stage provides the subject with a maximally flexible living space. He can turn it into anything he wants, unlike the usually confining living space of reality. In the psychodrama theatre the stage is made in circular form with several levels denoting a vertical dimension to allow for considerable mobility and flexibility in action. The actor in the drama is encouraged to play out his own inner world. He must be himself rather than an actor and must expose his very private being in connection with whatever role is set forth by the director. Roles can involving acting out a scene from the past, a current problem, or a problem that might be faced in the future.

The director has three functions: producer, counselor, and analyst. As producer he must pick up on the clues that the subject offers and turn them into part of the dramatic action. This requires sticking to what is relevant for the subject while at the same time keeping the audience involved in what is happening. In his counseling role he may attack or shock the subject, or perhaps laugh and joke with him. He may become so passive on some occasions that the session seems to be under the subject's direction. In his role as analyst the director makes interpretations about what is happening on stage using at times responses that are being made by members of the audience.

The therapeutic aides, sometimes known as auxiliary egos, have two roles. As extensions of the director they explore and help to guide the drama. As extensions of the subject they assume the roles of the people that the subject includes in his drama.

Finally, the audience has two purposes. The audience participates in the drama by expressing its opinion through spontaneous responses and comments made as the subject is acting. These responses may vary from laughter to protest. In this way the audience may help the subject. Its other purpose though is to be helped itself by the subject. This happens when the drama that is portrayed relates to the problems of the audience members and they benefit from seeing it played out.

Encounter Groups

The term "encounter group" has been introduced relatively recently. It is sometimes used synonymously with the term T-group, but whether used that way or more broadly, the encounter group development is basically a direct outgrowth of T-groups. Burton (1969) uses the term "encounter group" to describe a variety of approaches aimed at developing sensitivity, enhancing awareness, and expanding one's consciousness. This definition, plus the examples offered by encounter-group practitioners such as Schutz (1967), suggests some fundamental differences between the encounter group and the traditional T-group. Where the T-group's goal is to develop better understanding of oneself

and one's impact on his fellows, encounter groups encourage even deeper understanding of one's own internal processes, both psychological and physical.

Burton describes traditional psychotherapy as an intellectual exercise, divorced from life. Its goal of providing insight is limited since an important part of one's total reality is what he *feels* empathically, intuitively, phenomenologically. Encounter groups focus on this latter aspect of reality, and a variety of techniques have been developed to help group members to achieve this goal.

The diverse techniques of encounter groups have nowhere been classified, and different practitioners describe different approaches to the achievement of their aims. Rogers (1969) deals primarily in verbal interaction in his encounter groups. Schutz (1967) describes a variety of techniques, many physical, that he uses to promote his goals. An example of a procedure used by Schutz to facilitate interaction among group members is as follows: group members are gathered closely together, either sitting on the floor or on chairs, and are first encouraged to close their eyes and to feel the space around them. During the five minutes that such an exercise requires, members develop different feelings about intruding into the space of individuals around them or of being intruded on by others. An ensuing discussion helps to clarify such feelings. Having thus approached the conflict between keeping to oneself and being together, a further, nonverbal step is taken to explore more deeply the nature of one's attitude toward others. This calls for group members to close their eyes, stand up, and mill around the room. As people make contact, they "explore," in whatever way and for however long they desire. Sometimes music accompanies the exercise to intensify the experience.

Another example from Schutz's work describes a method used when words used by group members in conflict obscure an issue rather than encourage confrontation. In such a case the two members in conflict stand silently at opposite ends of the room, look into each other's eyes, and then very slowly walk toward each other. They are told to act completely spontaneously as they approach each other and to do whatever they feel impelled to do at the moment. The participants are encouraged to persist in this activity for as long as they wish. When the activity ends, the two participating members are encouraged to talk about what they felt; other group members contribute their own observations on the encounter.

For the group member who has particular problems both in giving and receiving affection, Schutz describes another nonverbal exercise. The individual in question is asked to stand in the center of a circle made up by other group participants. He closes his eyes while the others approach him and express their positive feelings nonverbally—by hugging, stroking, massaging, lifting, or whatever the particular group members feel. This is described as a moving experience both for the member who is the focus of the exercise and for the other participants. Different people react differently to the massive expression of affection. Some, limited in the degree to which they feel affection, are very disturbed by this exercise. Others feel very deeply and may be moved to tears as a result of it. For all, such an exercise is seen to provide an opportunity for further exploration of their internal mechanisms, although frequently groups feel that to discuss the whole experience dilutes it and they do not take it up verbally.

The examples that have been offered provide a view of the deep dimensions of human experience plumbed by the encounter group as compared to the traditional T-group.

Marathon Groups

Marathon groups, initiated by Stoller and Bach (Stoller, 1968), involve relatively brief but very intensive interaction between group members. The idea behind the marathon group, the purposes of which are the same as for encounter groups, emerged from Stoller's experience with T-groups. He came to feel that the involvement of group members could be markedly enhanced if they worked together for a period of days. This would lead to a more powerful impact than was characteristically derived from T-groups and encounter groups. Stoller and Bach have experimented with a variety of marathon approaches, most taking place over weekends. A number of principles have evolved from this experience for arranging and conducting such sessions.

Although group marathons have been conducted in many settings, the private residence is seen to be the most preferable. This is because it is important that an atmosphere be created in which group members are encouraged to be as open and straightforward as possible. The austerity of the typical office is seen to be an obstacle to the development of such a tone. Stoller, for example, holds marathons in his own home with his wife as a participant so that he, as leader, can be as open about himself as group members are expected to be.

The time schedule for the marathon group is always specified beforehand. An arrangement preferred by Stoller is to begin the marathon session at 8:00 P.M. on Friday evening and to terminate at 6:00

P.M. on Sunday with only two eight-hour breaks between 2:00 A.M. and 10:00 A.M. Saturday and Sunday mornings. Groups remain together even during meals so that the session continues during all waking hours. Some marathon group leaders prefer to have their groups continue for 24-hour periods without a sleep break.

The major ground rule for the marathon group is that members remain with the group throughout the entire session. Group members may walk around or exercise or take short breaks to go to the bathroom, but they are expected to commit themselves to sticking out the entire group period. Breaches of this fundamental rule are treated as indications of the individual's characteristic way of dealing with crisis. Another marathon ground rule is that members be as open and honest as possible in their expression of personal reactions to other group members. A variety of techniques that might structure the group, such as psychodrama or role playing, are discouraged, since they are presumed to dilute the authenticity of the interaction among group members.

The marathon group leader is responsible for laying out the ground rules, acting as time keeper, and stating the goals for the session. Beyond these leadership functions, however, the group leader is free to participate by expressing his own feelings and reactions as a group member. Frequently the leader specifies that a follow-up session will be included as part of a marathon group. He decides how and when such sessions will take place and specifies such arrangements at the outset when the group is first organized. Stoller prefers to have one follow-up session, consisting of a single evening meeting, about six weeks after the marathon weekend.

One variation on the marathon group, nude interaction, has recently been de-scribed by Bindrim (1969). Bindrim observes that in the typical marathon a process of moving from mistrust to trust, from "playing games" to honest communication, ensues. As phony roles are discarded and the authentic self emerges, an intimacy develops among group members which, not uncommonly, prompts a spontaneous tendency to put aside clothing. Maslow suggested that the process of achieving intimacy might be speeded up if group participants removed their clothing at the outset. Thus, there has been, by now, considerable experimentation with nude marathon groups.

The group session described by Bindrim (1969) took place in a nudist camp, with a swimming pool and a Jacuzzi bath that could accommodate the entire group. Ten men and ten women, most of whom were single, participated. The ground rules for the session specified that all group members would remain together and participate in all scheduled activities throughout the marathon, that participants were free to remove their clothes or not, that first names only would be used, that no alcohol or drugs would be taken, that overt sexual expression would be prohibited (hugging and kissing were allowed), and that no photographs would be taken. The marathon ran from 9:00 P.M. Friday until 3:00 P.M. on Sunday with two six-hour periods for sleep each night.

At the outset group members met clothed and discussed their feelings about being nude together. After an hour the group repaired to a communal bath where members were given the option of bathing nude or not. Everyone chose to bathe. This session was followed by a final period for the day in which group members were invited to stand in the front of a room where a projector played colored lights over their bodies.

The next day group members discussed their impressions of the day before, their feelings about their own bodies, seeing others unclothed, and the impulses aroused by the whole experience. The group engaged in more bathing and were led by a dance therapist for a one-hour period of "movement and sensory awareness." An hour of "meditation with sensory saturation" was held on Sunday morning which many participants found to be the most moving experience of the weekend. During this exercise participants paired off in opposite sexed couples and sat close facing each other. All closed their eyes as the prelude to Wagner's *Tristan und Isolde* was played. Group members were then instructed to touch, taste, and smell objects (for example, one member touched velvet, ate chocolate, and smelled a rose) each had brought beforehand in anticipation of this experience. This exercise produced a peak state (akin to a drug high), during which members were asked to fantasize their freest, most joyous moments in life. This done, group members were instructed to touch fingertips with their partners and to "gaze quietly" into each other's eyes. Twenty minutes of "eye-centered meditation" was followed by a group session in which members discussed their experiences.

Bindrim believes that the nude marathon has beneficial results. He reasons that the adult needs warm, tactile contact almost as much as the infant. The polite world of society may so stultify a person that even his mate cannot satisfy his need for contact with others. Bindrim thus sees the nude marathon, offering, as it does, a "tenderly sensual" experience under conditions prohibiting purely sexual gratification, as a means of experiencing genuine warmth and acceptance from one's fellows. Self-acceptance, the ultimate goal, is seen to follow naturally from a feeling of acceptance from others.

BEHAVIORALLY ORIENTED GROUP APPROACHES

Systematic Desensitization

There have been a few reports of the application of systematic desensitization in groups. In the earliest of these Lazarus (1961) treated phobics through systematic desensitization in a group format. He brought together patients who had similar phobias and worked out hierarchies applicable to all of the patients in the group. Instruction in relaxation was given to the group as a whole and scenes from the anxiety hierarchy were presented to the whole group of patients at one time. The pace at which the group moved along the hierarchy was determined by the rate of the slowest group member. Follow-up studies of Lazarus's patients indicated that 13 out of 18 recovered after an average of 20 therapy sessions. Only three relapses were found in a nine-month follow-up.

Paul and Shannon (1966) used systematic desensitization to treat anxiety over speaking in public. As in Lazarus's procedure patients were instructed in muscle relaxation as a group, worked out an anxiety hierarchy as a group, and underwent systematic desensitization as a group. Several symptomatic improvements were found by these authors.

Lazarus (1968) has also reported treating a group of impotent males and a group of sexually frigid females. The process in this case involved instruction on the part of the therapist concerning sexual functions and the various ways sexual pleasure can be attained short of actual coitus. In addition, desensitization was applied to the group as a whole concerning specific sexual fears.

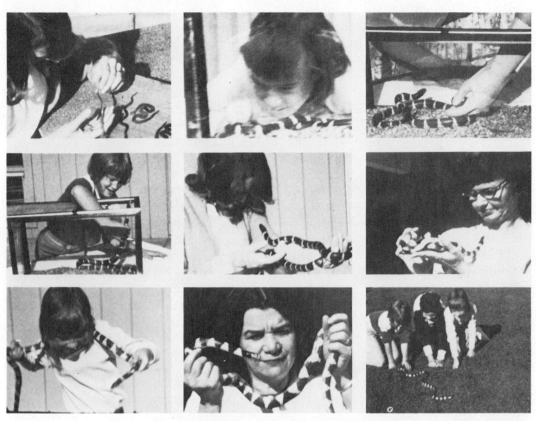

This series of pictures shows systematic desensitization being used therapeutically for snake phobia. (From Relative efficacy of desensitization and modeling approaches for inducing behavioral, affective, attitudinal changes, *Journal of Personality and Social Psychology*, 13, 1969, pp. 173–199, by A. Bandura, E. B. Blanchard, & B. Ritter. Copyright 1969 by the American Psychological Association. Reprinted by permission.)

The Application of Operant Principles to Groups

Behaviorally oriented therapies based on Skinner's operant principles are not applied in the typical group psychotherapy format where a therapist meets a group of patients in a specified place for some specified period of time. Instead, behavioral principles are applied to shape behavior in the actual setting where the patient functions. The therapy becomes part of a way of life that may be planned and directed by a highly skilled professional, but actual contact with the patient is usually made by people of lesser training. Typically, the institution is the best place in which to attempt behavior modification of this sort, since the approach requires a high degree of control over the patient's life. A good example of the behavioral focus in a group approach is the "token economy" of Ayllon and Azrin (1968).

Many researchers (Ayllon, 1963; Ayllon & Michael, 1959; Isaacs, Thomas, & Goldiamond, 1960; King, Armitage, & Tilton,

1960) demonstrated that the symptoms of severely disturbed patients could be modified using Skinner's operant learning principles. These studies, however, are characterized by attention to relatively isolated responses using few reinforcing stimuli applied in short, infrequent sessions. Also, the behavior change was carried out by highly trained psychologists. The transfer of such a program to the average institution would clearly be impractical. Therefore Ayllon and Azrin attempted to develop a program that would be useful in the average hospital setting. They did so by first developing a plan for what responses would be modified, defining the reinforcer for desired behavior, and setting up a series of experiments to test the effectiveness of their program.

The responses chosen for modification were those deemed by the experimenters to be "necessary or useful to the patient." Obviously, considerable latitude in response selection is possible in any given program. Ayllon and Azrin focused on responses such as serving meals, cleaning floors, and sorting laundry. An effort was made to select responses whose performance could be objectively measured. Since many responses may be made continuously during the day, thereby demanding prolonged monitoring of patient behavior, the environment was so arranged that certain responses could only be made at particular times. For example, floor mopping was possible only when a mop was made available.

Selection of reinforcers for desired behavior had been a difficult aspect of earlier behavior-modification studies since it seemed necessary to observe patient behavior over a period of time to determine what stimuli acted as reinforcers for each individual. Clearly, any program requiring different reinforcers for different patients would be too unwieldy to apply in a hospital setting. To surmount this problem Ayllon and Azrin observed the behavior of a group of patients over a period of time, reasoning that whatever behaviors occurred with a high frequency in the group would be generally useful as reinforcers, and could be utilized as such by permitting patients to engage in them at specified times. Six classes were defined: privacy, opportunity to leave the ward, social interaction with the staff, attendance at religious services, recreational opportunities, and opportunity to purchase items at the commissary.

The reinforcers described can obviously be regarded as primary ones that can only be delivered at specified times, since, for example, the staff cannot always be available for interaction with all who desire such contact, and the patient's behavior cannot be periodically disrupted to engage in reinforcing activities. For this reason, and because the immediate reinforcement of desirable behavior is deemed very important, Ayllon and Azrin used a conditioned reinforcer as a bridge between the desired response and the primary reinforcement. The conditioned reinforcer consisted of metal tokens that could be spent for whatever primary reinforcers the patient desired. This has prompted the labeling of such a program as a "token economy."

In a series of experiments on a single hospital ward Ayllon and Azrin were able to demonstrate that: (1) the reinforcement procedures they used were more significant in determining patients' choice of jobs than any reinforcement intrinsic to the job itself; (2) when primary reinforcers become freely available with no work requirement, very little work is done; and (3) job preference is more closely related to the amount of token reinforcement associated with it than to patient's liking for the task. This study is a powerful demonstration of how significant patient behavior can be elicited through the systematic use of reinforcement. It also contributes toward validating the learning principles described by Ullmann and Krasner.

Stimulated by the work of Ayllon and Azrin, Atthowe and Krasner (1968) set up a token economy on an 86-bed open ward of a Veterans Administrtaion hospital housing chronic psychiatric cases. The behavior these authors attempted to manipulate included self-care, attending available activities, interacting with others, and demonstrating a sense of responsibility. Atthowe and Krasner modeled their program after that of Ayllon and Azrin, reinforcing desired behavior with tokens later exchangeable for individual reinforcers such as cigarettes, money, television watching, passes, and even opportunity to feed a kitten.

After one year of a token economy, Atthowe and Krasner reported dramatic changes in approximately 90 percent of the patients on the ward. Prior to the institution of the program, few patients ever left the ward and many slept away the daytime hours. Ward activities and parties drew little interest and the ward housekeeping chores were done by patients from other wards who were considered healthier. During the token economy program these routine duties were taken over by the patients on the experimental ward, most of whom remained on the ward only long enough to earn tokens that could be used to acquire primary reinforcers. Only about 10 percent of the patients failed to work for tokens at all, and these had been "catatonically" withdrawn. The experimenters speculated that such patients might have been better reached by more individualized reinforcement programs. Atthowe and Krasner concluded as a result

of their work that "a contingent reinforcement program represented by a token economy has been successful in combating institutionalism, increasing initiative, responsibility, and social interaction, and in putting the control of patient behavior in the hands of the patient" (Atthowe and Krasner, 1968, p. 42).

Atthowe and Krasner's program extended the token economy from a closed ward setting (the locus of the Ayllon and Azrin experiment) to an open ward where the innovative scheme was competing with the outside money economy. As residents of an open ward, patients were presumably free to do odd jobs off the ward or to use their own accumulating pension funds to acquire reinforcements. Despite this the token economy produced salutary changes.

Ayllon and Azrin (1968) have pointed out that one significant feature of the token economy is that it provides a motivating environment within which the disculturation (deterioration of behavior that is important for outside life) that typifies many mental patients is forestalled. They assert that many patients who have been hospitalized for some behavior disorder are not fit for discharge when the behavior disorder clears up because disculturation has taken place. For this reason families lose interest in patients and are reluctant to receive them at home. As Ayllon and Azrin point out, some of the impetus for the "community psychiatry" movement is recognition of this problem. It might be added that, as we have mentioned, Bleuler recognized the significance of hospitalization as a force promoting disculturation. Ayllon and Azrin add that what is now needed is the adaptation and application of the token economy in a variety of settings. Such extension of the program is currently taking place and may well come to play a significant role in the understanding and treatment of schizophrenia.

EVALUATIVE RESEARCH IN GROUP PSYCHOTHERAPY

Bednar and Lawlis (1971) have reviewed a number of studies that evaluated the effectiveness of group psychotherapy with a variety of different patient types. They observe that while many studies make claim for the effectiveness of group psychotherapy, relatively few of these have been replicated. There is also some evidence to suggest that on follow-up positive treatment effects seem to be short-lived. On the other hand, they point out that many different researchers studying similar group-therapy variables are finding similar results. As the number of these independent evidences of support for group therapy's effectiveness increases, confidence in the durability of these findings goes up.

Bednar and Lawlis have identified three types of outcome criteria used in many of these studies: (1) self-adjustment; (2) environmental adjustment; and (3) mental functioning. With respect to self-adjustment, their overall summary of the findings of many studies using a variety of different criteria bearing on this issue indicates that group therapy relieves mood disorders, anxiety states, and somatic complaints. Other data suggest that group therapy makes some patients more comfortable with and accepting of themselves. On the other hand, serious thought disorders and severe withdrawal do not appear to be affected significantly by group therapy.

Environmental adjustment measures in studies of group psychotherapy generally involve improvement in patient behavior on hospital wards. For the most part these studies have been concerned with overt behavior rather than inferences about behavior. A close look at many of the measures used indicates that group psychotherapy helps patients acquire control over disruptive behavior patterns. Specific measures used to arrive at this judgment include behavior rating scales, staff judgment, movement to less disturbed wards, and test measures of social adjustment. Three studies have found that the intellectual functioning of patients improves after group psychotherapy. Bednar and Lawlis feel that such findings probably result from a reduction of the patient's anxiety level.

In recent years investigators have not only been asking whether psychotherapy helps but also whether it hurts. In their review Bednar and Lawlis have attempted to assess this possibility for group psychotherapy. Their conclusions are that some of the forces operating in group psychotherapy, perhaps the therapist himself being a major factor, do cause deterioration in the adjustment of some patients. Thus, group therapy must be looked upon as a two-edged sword that may help some and harm others. This being the case, more research into issues relevant to the deterioration question is needed. We need to learn about what kinds of therapists do poorly with what kinds of patients and what kinds of patients are unsuitable to group therapy at all. Furthermore, programs are needed to support the terminated group-therapy patient during the first six months or so after he leaves treatment to forestall the dissipation of therapy effects and to prevent relapse.

The potential harmful effects of the group experience is a very prominent issue in connection with encounter groups in which affective expression is a major goal and which are directed primarily toward the "normal" personality. Partly because encounter groups set out to be very powerful emotional experiences and partly because most encounter group leaders deny responsibility for what happens to group participants (Back, 1972) their potential dangers are a very serious concern for many critics of the encounter-group movement. Some studies have been done to assess both the positive and negative effects of encounter groups. Reddy (1972), for example, surveyed many of these studies and reports very low rates of serious negative outcomes. Unfortunately, most of the studies Reddy surveyed did not include systematic follow-ups and considered only very serious and dramatic negative consequences such as psychotic episodes and suicide.

Bebout and Gordon (1972) attempted to survey the outcomes of 150 encounter groups involving about 1100 members. They found that participants tended to report that they had changed by becoming more self-reliant and self-aware. The encounter groups did not seem to have an effect on the practical problems its members might be having in school or at work. A follow-up uncovered only four serious disturbances in group participants, but only about one-third responded to the follow-up. It is difficult, therefore, to know what these data mean.

By far the most systematic and best controlled study of encounter groups has been done by Lieberman, Yalom, and Miles (1972, 1973). They studied 210 subjects each of whom participated in one of 18 groups representing 10 different approaches. In addition, they used a control group of subjects matched to the group participants who did not take part in the groups. Change was measured by pencil and paper tests given when the encounter groups were concluded and again at a six-month follow-up. These instruments allowed group participants to describe both their general attitudes toward the encounter experience and their current functioning.

Group leaders used rating scales to describe changes that had taken place in their group members. Finally, each person who took part in the encounter groups was asked to name several friends who would be willing to make ratings of the individual's behavior. This provided an outside assessment of change.

The study's findings indicate that immediately after the group experience 57 percent of the participants saw it as having been positive, 29 percent saw it as neutral, and 14 percent found it negative. At the six-month follow-up there was a small drop in the positive evaluations: 46 percent were positive, 32 percent were neutral, and 21 percent were negative. At the group's conclusion about 61 percent felt that any changes that had occurred would be lasting. At the six-month follow-up only 55 percent felt that way. Group leaders rating their subjects at the end of the encounter experience felt that 73 percent showed some changes and that about 33 percent received substantial benefit. At the six-month follow-up the friends of both the encounter group and control subjects rated them for behavior change during the period following the encounter experience. This measure indicated that there was no difference in the amount of change found in group participants and controls.

Lieberman, Yalom, and Miles (1973) made a very careful attempt to identify subjects who suffered negative effects from the encounter groups. On the basis of fairly broad criteria a number of casualty suspects were identified (104 subjects). Each of these was then interviewed either in person or by phone. The ultimate definition of a casualty was relatively severe. The authors required that the person give evidence of having decompensated psychologically in some way that persisted and that this seem directly related to the group experience. Lieberman et al. conclude that the casualty rate in the groups they studied was 10 percent. This is a high rate, particularly considering that those who took part in the encounter experience were not psychiatric patients. Furthermore, Lieberman et al. stress that their figures may err on the conservative side and that the true casualty rate is probably somewhat higher.

© J. Brian King 1975

CONCLUSION

Group therapy, as well as other group experiences designed to enrich the lives of "normals," has reached a crest of popularity. This is probably true only partly because such approaches reach more people with less manpower than does individual psychotherapy. Inherent in the group experience are a great many forces similar to those in the patient's or subject's natural environment with which he must contend every day. The group then is a slice of life in miniature and improvements in function as a group member may be expected to transfer easily to the participant's social world.

Just as in the case of individual psychotherapy, however, group psychotherapy can take many forms. Particular stress can be laid on providing insight, on eliciting emotional expression, or on attempting to shape behavior directly. The effects that these varied approaches have on different kinds of group members are not understood. While in group therapy many of the same therapist-client issues as arise in individual psychotherapy need study, the group experience is even more complicated by the fact that each client is part of a small society. The effects of group composition on each individual member needs considerable study. It probably seems commonplace for the reader to hear repeated over and over again "We have so much more to learn" in almost any area of psychology that we look into. Nonetheless, we can only conclude this chapter on the same note. Much more research needs to be done to understand the group-therapy process and to sharpen it to its greatest point of effectiveness.

SUMMARY

1. Group psychotherapy and group experiences for the "normal" personality have become prominent in recent years.
2. The group pressures and support found in mass conversion and faith-healing situations are historical precursors of group therapy. The roots of modern group psychotherapy go back to the 1920s.
3. Group therapy capitalizes on man's need to identify with peers, to validate his feelings through them, and to win support and acceptance. While the group is itself a miniature society, it differs from ordinary

society in that open expression is encouraged, efforts are made to suspend value judgments, and no one is under pressure to be a success.

4. Advantages of group therapy include: (1) it gives people a chance to find that they share similar problems; (2) people can gain self-esteem through helping each other; (3) changes occurring in group therapy may be more durable in comparison to individual therapy since group standards are likely to be internalized; and (4) patients are forced to deal with the real world in the group.

5. The disadvantages of group therapy are: (1) it may be hard to speak openly about sensitive personal matters in a room full of strangers; and (2) group members may be destructive toward each other in ways that are hard to control.

6. Like individual psychotherapy, group psychotherapy may focus particularly on providing insight or understanding, encouraging emotional expression, or changing behavior.

7. Insight-oriented approaches include the psychoanalytic orientation, transactional analysis (TA), and the early T-group.

8. In the psychoanalytic approach group members free associate and the therapist interprets resistances and transference for each individual.

9. TA stresses teaching a scheme that characterizes three psychological facets of man and a particular life position that is purported to be basic to the actions of each individual.

10. T-groups focus on teaching participants how they affect and are seen by other group participants.

11. Cathartic approaches to group therapy include the various humanistic therapies that are applied in groups, psychodrama, encounter groups, and marathon groups.

12. Many humanistic approaches to therapy may be applied in groups or may have a group component.

13. Psychodrama encourages the person to express feelings and fantasies through a dramatic production unfettered by reality's limits.

14. Encounter groups are outgrowths of T-groups in which expression of deep-lying feelings is encouraged as a means to personal growth.

15. Marathon groups reach for powerful emotional expression through brief but very intensive group interaction.

16. Among behaviorally oriented approaches, systematic desensitization has been applied in groups. Operant principles have been applied to groups of people in their natural environment as a means of shaping behavior. The "token economy" is an example of such an application.

17. Evaluative research in group psychotherapy suggests that it is beneficial to patients with mood disturbances, anxiety, and somatic complaints. It is not successful with those suffering thought disorder.

18. Because they involve relatively unselected subjects in an emotionally challenging format, encounter groups have raised special concern. A recent well-controlled study of encounter group effects indicates that the percentage of casualties is alarmingly high.

PART TWO

THE PRESENT AND THE FUTURE

FOREWORD

At several points in this volume a warning was sounded about some of its potentially schismatic qualities. The reason for this may not yet have become obvious. Our concern stems from the fact that we are attempting to straddle two disparate worlds: the traditional world of abnormal psychology and a new brand of the discipline now evolving. To do this is very hard. Enough of the past must be retained to permit the reader to know that it *is* indeed the field of abnormal psychology that is being considered, while presenting enough of today's ferment and problems to understand the new directions being taken. If our assumptions about ongoing change are at all correct, future abnormal psychology texts will increasingly reflect the shifting emphasis strongly suggested in this volume.

Our treatment of the past has gone considerably beyond mere cataloguing and description. Rather, past theories and practices have been set in historical contexts that clarify how abnormal psychology evolved as it has. Abnormal psychology's past also well describes many of its current, established modes. However limited these ways are, however pessimistic one is about their future usefulness, they nevertheless mirror an establishment that exists and will continue to exist, in many significant ways, for a long time to come. It cannot simply be ignored.

The major "discontinuity" of this volume will be found in the contrast between the preceeding 15 chapters and the 5 to follow. Whereas prior sections were primarily devoted to the past and its influence on the present, the remainder is present- and future-oriented, often directly challenging basic aspects of the earlier framework. We shall be reexamining critically a number of controversial issues, some previously touched upon with no more than a hint of concern. In other words, in our prior effort to present a cohesive account of what abnormal psychology has been, we were momentarily willing to accept or simply to "let pass" issues that must be revisited in the interest of more effective future planning.

CHAPTER 16

A Field in Transition

Supply and Demand
Effectiveness of Mental Health
    Services
    Unreached Disorders
    Psychotherapy
Imbalances of Needs and
    Allocation

Early man had little concern with his own or anyone else's behavior until it went seriously awry. So, it is perfectly logical that highly deviant, florid departures from reality should have been the first pathologies to attract attention. Even today, such extreme behavior is the first, if not the only, deviance recognized in primitive societies and in many of modern society's subcultures. Extreme deviance does not follow traditional rules. In not being understandable, it is frightening and threatening. Its very nature is so compelling as to make it impossible to ignore. There have been many explanations for profound dysfunction ranging from supernatural, demonaic, spiritistic views to later rational ones—both biological and environmental. Still the mysteries of cause and cure of extreme psychic dysfunction remain among mental health's most perplexing challenges (Joint Commission on Mental Illness and Health, 1961; Paul, 1969).

Views of psychic dysfunction broadened very slowly over many centuries. These changes came about, in part, because of society's technological evolution and the resolution of many heretofore more pressing problems of physical survival and comfort. Eventually, students of pathology began to recognize less striking criteria of abnormality than extreme bizarreness, for example, waste of human talent, ineffective functioning, damaged interpersonal relations, human misery, internal suffering, and unhappiness. Today, conditions such as symptom and character neuroses, antisocial personalities, and psychosomatic states are part and parcel of the study of abnormal behavior. Indeed, clinicians are now called on to treat even more abstract conditions such as the so-called philosophical or existential neuroses that involve man's concerns about the nature and meaning of life and his place in the cosmos.

The gradual inclusion of such disorders as relevant has vastly expanded abnormal psychology's scope. Broadening concepts of disorder also increase many-fold the number of potential patients. This same broadening process has significantly expanded the search for causes of dysfunction to include the impact of influential people in an individual's life and the social institutions that shape his development and has prompted a search for new treatments for more subtle disturbances.

The verbal dialog we call psychotherapy is one important expansion of our treatment approaches. This expansion first created hope and, later, disappointment. Psychotherapy is not an exact procedure. Even with nonextreme disorders it is far from 100 percent successful. With florid, entrenched pathologies, it works far less well. In fact, a general rule in treating all psychological problems is that the more aggravated and rooted the condition, the more difficult it is to cure (Paul, 1969). As this principle becomes clearer both from clinical and research experience the need grows to develop conceptual alternatives for dealing with disordered behavior.

Many current social forces push toward further important redefinition and expansion of our concepts of dysfunction. The rapid technological growth of Western civilization is one such force. This has led to improved living standards and significant shifts in work to leisure time ratios. Whereas our grandparents worked a 50–60 hour week, today a 35-hour week is typical. Increased leisure time means more interaction with other people and more time for thinking about oneself. Writing on this topic, Rieff (1959) suggests that man has

Brown Brothers

In the early part of this century, people spent most of their time working to meet requirements for survival. There was very little time to think about psychic needs.

passed through stages of "character ideals":
first, the political man, then the religious
man, and finally the economic man. He
considers current forces that are causing
further change including technology which
is "invading and conquering the last
enemy—man's inner life, the psyche itself"
(p. 356). He believes that this development favors the emergence of the psychological man who: "lives by the ideal of
insight . . . leading to the mastery of his
own personality" (p. 356).

Thus, as physical and survival needs
are better met, as living conditions improve,
and as we have more leisure time, we
become more concerned with psychological man—his happiness, security, and effectiveness. In the past these concerns would
have been seen as luxuries which could
not be indulged because survival and
gratification of more primitive needs were
still in question.

The present era is also marked by a
social philosophy that recognizes man's
right to have his higher order needs met.
Recent debate, concern, and action at high
government levels have advanced the view
that everyone has a right to a "square
deal" in life. Specifically, programs to improve housing, overcome poverty, improve
schooling, provide better and more pleasant
jobs, and guarantee basic civil rgihts, have
evolved. Though such programs develop
slowly in a society that has long had fixed
ways of doing things, we are, at least,
committed to trying to cope with such
social problems.

In step with society's rapid technological
growth and the evolution of a new social
philosophy, the mental health field has
been more willing to consider new situations and problems as relevant to its scope.
The dominant view of the last 50 years,
that the sources of man's emotional problems are within himself, has been seriously

© Chris Rollins

Now that work is only part of one's life,
many people get away from their 9-to-5
environment on weekends in the pursuit of
happiness.

challenged. We now entertain the possibility that environmental factors also contribute importantly to dysfunction.

How has this changing view been expressed concretely? In many ways! For
example, social institutions which have
other than mental health functions have,
increasingly, sought direct mental health
service and consultation. Schools, welfare
systems, legal systems, industrial organizations, antipoverty groups, health agencies, and the military all illustrate this
trend. All are coming more and more to
recognize that the mental health fields can
contribute to their mandated functions and
everyday activities. A by-product of this
development is that the mental health
manpower needed to meet rapidly growing

demands for service and consultation cannot always be provided.

As mental health professionals are exposed to new settings they identify new issues and questions. This has helped to redefine long-standing problems and to develop new, innovative approaches for solving them. Some are so impressed with the nature and magnitude of this still unfolding change in orientation that they call it a mental health "revolution" (Hobbs, 1964). Only time will tell whether such a strong term is warranted. What is clear right now is that the development is triggered by presently disappointing answers to a highly relevant series of questions about the current status of mental health. The following are examples: "How *effective* are today's mental health services?"; "Is this 'effectiveness' *evenly* spread across the different social sectors?"; "If we are socially or clinically *ineffective*, what conceptual alternatives could improve things?"

Different experts answer these questions differently. But concern among responsible professionals and community planners surely grows about mental health's limited effectiveness and about its failure, for whatever reasons, to bring effective services to major segments of the population that need help. These realizations force us to consider conceptual alternatives and innovative manpower uses, and to explore new types of mental health interventions.

The mental hospital, the mental health clinic, the private practitioner—collectively the backbone of society's helping efforts—are, together, not enough. They deal with evident, entrenched problems. Such problems outnumber existing resources and those we can, even optimistically, hope to produce in the coming decades. So all we really do now is to try to repair damage! In the long run that is a costlier, less effective, and less sensible strategy than preventing troubles in the first place. Abnormal psychology's first and most important goal should be to put itself out of business. If this is to be more than a pipe-dream, we must do more to foster sound human development and build for psychological health. The psychological first-aid approach that has long epitomized the work-a-day operations of the helping professions is just not doing the job.

SUPPLY AND DEMAND

Several times we have mentioned that the mental health fields face many problems that create pressures for new solutions. The sections to follow describe some of these problems, starting with manpower, in greater detail.

How does one go about counting mental health manpower and resources? It sounds like an easy job, but it is not. One's conceptual stance, which most people concede shapes the nature of mental health programs, also influences how we count manpower. Based on the medical model, we count only certain recognized, degreed professionals. But other approaches use other help agents, and, so, must count differently.

Up to now, the helping professions have, predominantly, seen their job as resolving people's problems. The whys and wherefores of this view were considered in Chapter 3. The important point is that that orientation strongly colors how we assess mental health demand and need and how we report its resources.

One result of abnormal psychology's expanding scope is the increased pressure to help with more problems of more people in more settings. Consequently, even though there are many more trained professionals today than 30 years ago, professional manpower shortages in some settings (for example, state hospitals) are greater than they were then (Arnhoff, Rubenstein, & Speisman, 1969). The problem is that demand has grown more rapidly than resources. For example, recognizing that some problems that used to "belong exclusively" to mental health professionals are closely linked to other complex problems of modern living has created a growing interest in diverse "newcomer" groups (such as, schools, industry) in getting involved with them, and more frequent requests for help from mental health professionals. Expressed demand for help with personal difficulties of living, suffering, and ineffectiveness has simply grown more rapidly than resources for dealing with such problems. Two symptoms of this fact are: (1) many mental health positions stay unfilled for long time periods and (2) when new facilities or personnel become available they are often quickly inundated by service demands.

But, by-passing conceptual qualifiers, for the moment we can describe professional manpower problems using classical medical model assumptions about what dysfunction is and the services and personnel needed to deal with it. First, however, a distinction must be made between demand and need for mental health services. Schofield (1964) uses the terms "countable thousands" and "hidden millions" to highlight this distinction. In so doing, he suggests that demand is a more conservative term than need, and easier to pinpoint. Demand estimates are reasonably operational. They are based on such statistics as the number of mental hospital beds occupied and how many people are getting help from clinics, agencies, community mental health centers, or private practitioners. Such figures are somewhat misleading because we do not have fully accurate censuses for all these types of data. Even so, one investigator (Nichols, 1963) estimated that each year about 3,000,000 people "demand some sort of psychological services."

Demand statistics err in the direction of underestimation. Because they are restricted to reports from known, recognized sources of psychological help, they do not reflect the fact that many people take their emotional problems to other than mental professionals. Gurin, Veroff, and Feld (1960), for example, reported that 42 percent of the sample they studied took their psychological problems to clergymen. Another 29 percent sought help from family physicians. Still another indication of the conservative nature of demand statistics is found in the observation (Sanua, 1966; Schofield, 1964) that as new mental health facilities open, demand accelerates sharply. Also, heavily populated urban centers with dense concentrations of health-care facilities report greater demand than do isolated, rural settings. These indications of the conservativeness of demand estimates hint that need is both greater and more difficult to establish. Demand can be assessed if the following conditions are met: (1) awareness of some psychological difficulty by the individual or someone close to him; (2) being in a position, motivationally and financially, to seek help; and (3) availability of settings and personnel to deal with his problem. If all these conditions are met, the person is counted in demand statistics.

Many people, for many reasons, do not, however, meet all these conditions. For example, the very concept of emotional dysfunction is still alien or threatening to many, such as those who, overtly or covertly, see professionals as "shrinks." Anyone who feels that way is likely to deny his troubles or to take them elsewhere. Perhaps this is, in part, the basis for Schofield's (1964) observation that much of the general medical practitioner's time is taken up by patients' psychological problems, with or without physical ramifications, rather than by physical illness. Schofield estimates that psychological problems take up more than 50 percent of the general practitioner's time.

Another concern is that many people, particularly among the urban disadvantaged, do not see their difficulties in psychological terms, do not have the resources to get help, or find existing facilities and personnel so alien to their way of life and values, that they will not use them. And, for people in rural settings, the sheer lack of facilities or the logistic difficulty of reaching them, often make it impossible for them to get help. So Schofield's concept of the "hidden millions"—including the unhappy, the lonely, the ineffective, the unfulfilled—is very real.

The discussion, so far, presumes that we all agree about what psychological problems are, and about accepted ways for identifying them. If that were really true, it probably would not be too hard to establish the *need* for psychological help. But it is not true! So-called experts vary tremendously in how they define psychological problems and the evidence they must have to establish their presence. While "black vs. white" cases of disordered behavior are clear, most maladjustment is "gray." This point can be highlighted with two different examples. Not even schizophrenia, which has always been seen as the most extreme psychological dysfunction, is universally conceptualized as a mental disorder (for example, Braginsky, Braginsky, & Ring, 1969; Szasz, 1961). And at a different part of the spectrum, two major epidemiological surveys, one in an urban megalopolis (Srole et al., 1962) and the other in a sparsely populated semiurban and rural region

(Leighton, 1956), suggest that no more than 15–20 percent of the population is free of emotional dysfunction.

Several important points evolve from the preceding discussion. The game of estimating the need for mental health services is hazardous! The guidelines used for defining emotional problems markedly influence one's estimates. So, it is not surprising that actual need estimates vary a good deal. In fact, probably the most important determinant of the results of a needs survey is how stringently psychological problems are defined. As abnormal psychology's scope broadens and as interconnections between psychological dysfunction and other problems of living are established, we may be able to develop more realistic estimates of service needs.

Thus, any estimate of mental health need is tenuous! One comprehensive epidemiological study by the Commission of Chronic Illnesses in Baltimore, Maryland (Nichols, 1963) reports a 10 percent need figure, doubtlessly a conservative estimate. A report on the incidence of emotional dysfunction among young schoolchildren (Glidewell & Swallow, 1969) was submitted by a Task Force for the Joint Commission on Mental Health of Children (1969). This study was based on detailed review of many school maladjustment incidence surveys done in various parts of the country. About 30 percent of all American schoolchildren were found to have some school adjustment problems and about 10 percent were so maladjusted that they needed immediate professional help. The 30 percent school maladjustment estimate is close to the figure reported by another group (Cowen et al., 1963; Cowen et al., 1966). These investigators found that one-third of all primary graders either already had school adjustment problems or seemed subject to such problems in the foreseeable future. Such early school adjustment problems often herald later more serious difficulties (Cowen et al., 1973; Robins, 1966). But even using relatively similar judgmental standards, incidence data vary across settings. The 30 percent overall school maladjustment figure cited above, for example, jumps to 70 percent in a big-city ghetto area (Kellam et al., 1972; Kellam et al., 1975).

The data cited strongly suggest that need for mental health services exceeds demand by a factor of at least several hundred percent. This point provides a useful perspective for discussing mental health's resources (that is, settings and personnel) for coping with maladaptive behavior. Before starting that discussion, however, we must again emphasize that it, too, rests on the shaky assumption that mental health's present conceptual frame for identifying and treating disorder is the proper one to use for assessing demand, need, and resources. While this stance can be justified because it helps to bridge from "old to new," the reader is warned beforehand that the discussion will again, necessarily, force reconsideration of classic assumptions about the nature of mental health problems and how to deal with them.

As part of the original Joint Commission Report (1961), Albee (1959) surveyed professional mental health manpower. His findings were shocking and discouraging. Although the extent of shortages varied across professions, Albee found average understaffing figures to range from 25 to 75 percent, using *adequate* rather than *ideal* patient-care standards as the criterion. His report provided several striking examples. For example, at the time, the country needed 50,000 additional social workers; yet social work schools were producing only 2000 social workers per year, scarcely enough to replace annual losses in the field, much less to fill huge, unmet social needs. Similar manpower gaps were found in the other mental health professions. For example, whereas general hospitals had one nurse for each three beds, psychiatric hospitals had only one per 53 beds. Albee points out other aspects of the professional manpower problem in later writings (1963, 1967, 1969b), as, for example, the facts that: (a) academic institutions, alone, could absorb all psychologists produced between now and 2000 A.D., and (b) less than one-third of the approximately 2000 "psychiatric clinics" in America had as many as *one* full-time psychiatrist on their staff (Albee, 1969b).

Unquestionably, professional mental health manpower has increased dramatically in recent years. Using 1950 and 1966 as contrast points, investigators (Arnhoff et al., 1969) report increases in psychiatrists (350 percent), psychologists (500 percent), social workers (400 percent), and psychiatric nurses (250 percent). But even so, we still have severe shortages, positions remain unfilled, and many people who need services do not get them (Ryan, 1969). Many factors contribute to these discrepancies. One is population growth. Albee (1969) estimates that our country's population will reach about 350 million in 2000 A.D. Also, since the once young mental health professions are "aging," many newly trained professionals are simply replacing those who are retiring (Albee, 1969). Most importantly, continued expansion of the mental health field's scope multiplies demand for helping services both from individuals and settings. As Arnhoff et al. (1969) observe, "Our society has changed drastically in the last two decades; the increased demand and expectation for services in all segments of health, education and welfare have been phenomenal and the competition for educated and trained persons grows more acute" (p. 3).

A specific case in point bears citation—the community mental health center de-

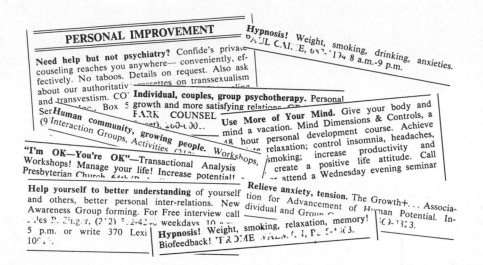

velopment, for which Congress enacted supporting legislation in 1963. The country's long-range blue-print called for one center for each 50,000 in population. This represented a demand for an additional 12,000 psychiatrists, clinical psychologists, and social workers at a time when need was already unmet and gross manpower shortages were widespread. Though many community mental health centers have been successfully rooted, they are often staffed at the expense of other, already understaffed, mental health settings. Even so, professional manpower shortages limit the long-range evolution of community mental health centers. Moreover, the manpower shortages of clinical service settings are not isolated examples. Academic institutions, public and private educational facilities, legal and welfare agencies, industry, the military, medicare, labor clinics, have all added to the growing demand for mental health personnel. Thus Albee's original conclusion still stands, that is, we do not have enough professional personnel to care for mental health problems; nor are future prospects in this area good.

Manpower is not the only supply-demand imbalance in mental health. Such shortages can also be seen at the level of facilities such as hospitals, clinics, outpatient centers, and many other care-giving agencies that offer mental health services. A review of the availability of such facilities (Nichols, 1963) again reveals glaring shortages. Once more, the net result is that help is not available to many people who need it. Despite valiant social efforts since World War II to build an adequate mental health professional manpower pool, we are not gaining in this area. Thus Albee (1966) observed: "The rules of the illness game are such that there can never—and I am really serious about this—there can never be enough professional people available. As long as the illness model occupies the center of the stage, all of the planning, all of the action, is going to deal with treatment and beds..." (p. 19).

So the mental health fields are confronted with a profoundly unbalanced equation. Expressed demand and, certainly, latent need for helping services far exceed resources—particularly professional manpower. So far mental health's main tactic in trying to right this imbalance has been the attempt to increase professional manpower and resources. That this tactic has failed again points to the need for identifying alternatives that might rectify the imbalance. There are such alternatives and the weight of our resource dilemmas demands that they be seriously considered (Cowen, Gardner, & Zax, 1967).

At a simple level we might hope that research could lead to better understanding, and cure of, dysfunction, thus reducing the need for service. Research has always been part of mental health's effort; it is more extensively so today than ever before. But genuine breakthroughs have been few and far between and, possibly as a result of our greater knowledge and expanding concepts, there may be more unresolved problems today than 50–100 years ago. Another alternative is to define and use mental health manpower differently. Without challenging the basic assumptions of past mental health models, necessity has forced reexamination of the question of whether M.D., Ph.D., or M.S.W. degrees are needed to help people in distress. Currently, much experimentation is going on in this area using different nonprofessional groups as help-agents with people experiencing varied adjustment problems (Cowen, 1967; Ewalt, 1967; Guerney, 1969). Many early reports (Gartner, 1971; Sobey, 1970) speak of the effectiveness of such programs. Still, the movement is young and we cannot yet say that it will solve all problems created by professional manpower shortages. Realistically, we are just beginning to study the attributes of different types of help-agents and the ranges of situations in which they can help.

The most important place at which to engage the crisis in mental health professional manpower is the conceptual level.

Manpower problems, as suggested above, arise in part because of the assumptions that govern mental health practice. The model, described in Chapter 3 as the medical, disease, or illness model, has long determined mental health professionals' behaviors and interventions. That model focuses on dysfunction and repair, in the same way that physical medicine approaches influenza, measles, syphilis, or other physical ailments. Albee (1969) recently pointed out a strong link between this model's assumptions and current manpower problems: "Unless we develop a viable alternative to the illness model as an explanation of mental disorder, we must face the next several decades with the realistic understanding that the mental health manpower picture is going to worsen because we cannot train enough professionals to meet the manpower needs of the institutions this model demands" (p. 109).

Albee urges adopting an environmental, social-learning theory model in which mental health and illness are seen as continuous rather than discontinuous. Such a view deemphasizes traditionally defined mental health manpower. Instead, it highlights the prospective contributions that community and educational settings, and personnel, can make to human development and to building psychological health in people. Otherwise stated, preventing dysfunction may offer a theoretically attractive route for resolving our present professional manpower dilemmas. If we can cut down the flow of disorder we can balance the presently imbalanced supply-demand equation.

Similarly, Arnhoff, Rubenstein, and Speisman (1969) argue that the global aim of "improved mental health" is nebulous. They urge that it be "disaggregated" (that is, broken down) into more specific subgoals, as, for example, building resources in people and maximizing growth through effective education. Mental health professionals do not bring special expertise to the latter objectives. To meet them may require new settings, approaches, and personnel. As such developments unfold, the mental health professional's role may increasingly merge with that of educators, clergymen, and the like. Eventually, the contributions of many people not previously counted within the mental health establishment must be recognized as significant. In the words of Arnhoff & Speisman (1969, p. 197): "By starting at the point of specifying services to be delivered and functions to be performed one might free himself from preconceptions as to how they can be accomplished and by whom. Hopefully this offers access to other kinds of manpower supplies that are now lost or neglected."

In summary, demand for mental health services, especially for professional manpower, far outstrips resources. Need for such services is even greater. Future extrapolations suggest that these imbalances will increase if we stay on our present course. Alternative approaches and innovative use of new sources of manpower are needed.

EFFECTIVENESS OF MENTAL HEALTH SERVICES

Progress in the mental health fields depends on realistic appraisal of past achievements and current unresolved problems. This can be done following several guidelines: "How have we done in coping with the major behavior disorders?", "How effective are mental health's current methods and what are their limits?" and, "How are helping services distributed and do these allocations meet social need?"

Unreached Disorders

The Joint Commission Report (1961) stated that: "major mental illness is the core problem and unfinished business of the mental health movement" (p. xiv). If "unfinished business" means understanding the sources of disorder and developing effective methods for dealing with it, the same statement could have been made for many centuries. Hence, we cannot quarrel with the quote's descriptive accuracy. Schizophrenia is the prime case in point; it has long been the most baffling and challenging of all psychological aberrations (Romano, 1967).

The Joint Commission's further statement that "intensive treatment of patients with critical and prolonged mental breakdown should have first call on fully trained members of the mental health professions" (p. xiv) is, however, more debatable. The weakness of this position lies in its passive acceptance of the fact of major breakdown. The resulting call to concentrate resources in *post hoc* combat with such conditions would only intensify an approach that history has shown to be directionally unsatisfactory. As with Tennyson's brave 600, it calls for another march into a valley of doom.

Scheff's (1966) volume on mental illness reports that more than 5000 research studies have been done on schizophrenia in the past five decades. All this effort, he says, has resulted in little progress either in understanding or treating this profound disorder. Kety's (1967) more limited review of biochemical research in schizophrenia also suggests, from another perspective, that a confirmed causative agent still has not been found. Scheff believes that similar pessimistic statements apply to many functional mental disorders—not just to schizophrenia. Others (Braginsky et al., 1969) share his view.

Realistically, we have made little progress with the functional disorders. Mental health's record in that field is not proud. Although research in this area has been disappointing, we are not proposing that it be abandoned. Indeed, Paul (1969) suggests that there have been several promising recent leads with chronic patients, particularly in the use of behavior modification (Ayllon, 1963; Davison, 1969) and milieu therapy (Ellsworth, 1968; Fairweather, 1964; M. Jones, 1953; Sanders, Smith, & Weinman, 1967). Only time will separate the wheat from the chaff! While research should continue on many fronts, we need also to consider conceptual alternatives. Before-the-fact prevention is one such legitimate alternative. Particularly for those who hold an environmental, learning-oriented, rather than organic, view of cause (for example, Albee, 1969a), preventing mental illness is not only an acceptable concept, it is essential!

Psychotherapy

We can evaluate mental health's specific techniques and approaches, as well as its success in treating particular disorders. At this second level, it is important to focus on psychotherapy's effectiveness, because mental health professionals have used that approach so extensively as a helping method. A century ago, psychotherapy did not exist as a formal entity. People have certainly taken their troubles to their fellows from time immemorial. But such interactions were not systematic, planned "talking-cures" with a therapist following certain procedures and rules, and a prior agreement between two people on the general nature of what is to happen.

Freud's pioneering, still influential work developing psychoanalysis for treating emotional dysfunction was a major mental health breakthrough. For the first time in man's history, there was potential for dealing in theoretically grounded, systematic, effective ways with major psychological disorder. There was, to be sure, considerable early resistance to this development, but it centered more on the threatening aspects of Freud's theoretical formulation than on the structural concept of therapy. As experience indicated that the procedure worked, psychotherapy was more warmly accepted. Fairly soon it moved to a preeminent place in the mental health professional's tool-kit.

Originally psychoanalysis was all of psychotherapy. That is no longer so. Offshoots from early analytic "orthodoxy" sprang up rapidly, and as these derivatives gained acceptance, entirely new psychotherapy approaches started to root. Today, for example, we recognize nondirective (client-centered), implosive, rational, existential, gestalt, and behavior-modification schools of therapy (Ford & Urban, 1963), to mention a few prominent examples. These approaches vary in their closeness to psychoanalysis; all, however, pivot around some

Robert de Villeneuve

Unfortunately mental health workers cannot reach everybody who needs help.

variant of the talking-cure and, as such, owe an historical debt to analysis.

Psychotherapy's rise has been vital to the twentieth century's search for cures for human psychological disorders. Some people now see and value it as the *only* true pathway to cure. They regard other approaches as second-class expedients. Many professionals, professionals-in-training, and informed laity hold this view. Indeed, for some, just being in therapy is a mark of special distinction.

The reasons behind psychotherapy's rapid growth and acceptance are complex. For one thing, many clinicians and consumers have found it helpful. Behavior sometimes becomes more adaptive and people are happier and more effective as a result of therapy. Such changes are not to be minimized. When they occur, few are inclined to look the gift horse in the mouth by asking about the whys and wherefores of change. The mere fact of relief from nagging personal distress is enough to justify the process. Other reasons for psychotherapy's rise are less often publicly discussed. For example, it brings economic benefit, social prestige, power, and control to its practitioners. These are powerful human needs—sufficiently powerful to inhibit rigorous, impartial evaluation of the method's effectiveness.

Psychotherapy became more and more accepted by professionals and the lay public during each decade of the current century—at least through the 1950s. The prime factors that limited its spread were the lack of enough qualified therapists and power struggles among the mental health disciplines about who should control, and engage in, such practice. During all this period, psychotherapy developed in more of a clinical, than a scientific-research, tradition.

Starting in the 1950s, and increasingly since, some of psychotherapy's early momentum has dissipated. At least, more people have raised more and bolder questions about its scope and effectiveness. We can only speculate about why this has happened. Because the first psychotherapy departed radically from earlier treatment approaches, it was resisted. So, much early effort went into establishing it as a respectable family member among treatment procedures. Only after that battle had been won and the psychotherapist transformed from an interloper to an esteemed member of the treatment fraternity did some therapists become secure enough to examine objectively therapy's assumptions, practices, and outcomes. The early research findings in this area indeed raised challenges for those who were previously sold on the approach. Another growing awareness of the era was the realization that however effective therapy was, it could not, by itself, resolve all of societies mental health problems. These considerations fueled the growth of psychotherapy research and a new willingness to consider conceptual alternatives—trends that first appeared in the 1950s and have since gained momentum.

Much impetus for evaluating psychotherapy's effectiveness came from Eysenck's (1952) "devil's-advocate" paper. Eysenck reported that few psychotherapy outcome studies had included control groups. He argued that many interpersonal dysfunctions, particularly the neuroses, are cyclic —that is, their symptoms come and go over time. He therefore contended that, lacking control groups, changes following psychotherapy could be seen as "spontaneous remission" rather than as a product of the intervention. To test this possibility Eysenck accepted as arbitrary control groups for psychotherapy-outcome studies the findings of two surveys—one with state hospital neurotics and the other with in-surance company beneficiaries. These surveys showed that the spontaneous remission rate for neurotic symptoms was, roughly, 70 percent over a two-year period. He then compared the cure rates reported in several dozen therapy studies involving many thousands of patients to the cure rates reported for the two "control" groups.

Eysenck found that improvement after therapy was no greater than the spontaneous remission of neurotic symptoms in the arbitrary control groups. If anything, untreated neurotics did better than therapy clients. Worse yet, he found that patients seen intensively, for long time periods, as in orthodox psychoanalysis, had significantly *poorer* improvement rates than the "controls." More recent updating surveys (Eysenck, 1961) have not basically changed this position. In addition, similar surveys of child psychotherapy outcomes (Levitt, 1971) produced similar pessimistic conclusions.

It is not hard to criticize Eysenck's work. Were the patient groups included in the many studies he reviewed comparable? Might not a psychotherapy-like process have taken place in his control groups? Were the outcome criteria used in the various therapy studies and the control studies equivalent? The literature, in fact, is filled with many such attacks and Eysenck's counterattacks. The core issue (that is, psychotherapy's effectiveness) was considered by Schofield (1964). He concluded that we still lack proof of the general value of psychotherapy in its effectiveness in treating specific neurotic disorders. A recent, highly scholarly review of this same topic (Bergin, 1971) concluded that psychotherapy is, at best, a moderately effective procedure.

The preceding conclusion can be strengthened by other considerations. Peo-ple who seek psychotherapy, that is those included in studies of its effectiveness—are not unselected. Psychotherapy's clientele comes from the richer, better-educated, more intact, more personable, more verbal sectors of society. Schofield (1964) speaking to this point uses the acronym YAVIS (Young-Attractive-Verbal-Intelligent-Successful) to identify the people that clinicians chose to work with in therapy. So, Eysenck's findings are all the more serious because psychotherapy samples include those, among the distressed, with relatively more favorable prognoses.

These facts should give pause to those who, unquestioningly, hail psychotherapy's clinical effectiveness. Much remains to be demonstrated in this regard, even under conditions that favor positive outcomes. Another aspect of psychotherapy's limited effectiveness is that it is hard to apply to the functional psychoses. And, of course, no limitations list is complete without including psychotherapy's restricted scope and social *in*effectiveness. This complex topic is more fully developed in Chapter 19. Here, we need only note that large segments of the population that need help are not reached because traditional psychotherapies are either not offered to them or are found to be inappropriate or unpalatable.

Despite these heavy constraints, most mental health professionals still see psychotherapy as their prime helping tool. This is so for many reasons. The method sprang up in the current century with great promise as a breakthrough in the struggle against emotional dysfunction. Most of today's mental health professionals have been both weaned, and sold, on the approach; it is what they know best and feel most comfortable doing. Truthfully, we have had few viable alternatives for dealing with the problems that psychotherapy addresses. Evolving alternatives are still not yet well formulated; moreover, they lack hard supporting data. Beyond the personal and motivational supports for therapy's persistence, the positive outcomes that clinicians and patients alike have witnessed have been powerful reinforcers.

We do not wish to discredit psychotherapy. Rather, we hope to spotlight some factors that clarify its clinical and social limitations. Our position is, simply, that it would be a mistake to emphasize psychotherapy's further development to the exclusion of alternatives. Eisenberg (1962a), speaking to this point, argued that when initially liberating concepts are institutionalized, they can become rigidifying and stultifying. There *is* reason to believe that psychotherapy has advanced the mental health fields, that it may lead to additional future gain, and that newly emerging approaches may well build on some of its bedrock. But the approach should not be viewed as a total, or even prime, solution to modern society's complex mental health problems. It simply lags, in power and scope, behind the weight of today's mental health problems.

Like our prior review of schizophrenia's unsolved riddles, this discussion of psychotherapy also ends on a questioning note. We need to know how current therapy approaches can be enriched and how new, more effective ones can be developed. As noted in Chapter 3 there is much current effort in this direction, particularly with learning theory-based, behavior-modification approaches. But beyond that, we must reexamine the situations that therapy addresses to try to identify parsimonious and effective alternatives. That effort should be sufficiently broad to include mental health problems that have so far eluded psychotherapy's reach. The logical direction of this search is toward preventing

dysfunction. So, the notion of trying to cut down the flow of disorder again comes up as a conceptually attractive way for approaching mental health's heaviest problems.

In summary, mental health's past approaches to major classes of disorder, especially schizophrenia and the functional psychoses, have been less than successful. The clinical and social effectiveness of some of mental health's most basic techniques, such as psychotherapy, have been limited. Innovative alternatives must be explored!

IMBALANCES OF NEEDS AND ALLOCATION

Nearly four decades ago Faris and Dunham (1939) reported a classic sociological study of the incidence of major mental breakdown, as reflected in mental hospital admissions in Chicago and Providence. They found that disorder increased going from the outskirts to the center of a city, just as for other socioeconomic, "marker" variables, such as general or infant mortality, delinquency and crime rates, unemployment, and poverty. Whereas some of Faris and Dunham's findings have held up, others, perhaps reflecting the changing ecology of population centers, have not (Levy & Rowitz, 1973). But there certainly have been many studies of this basic topic and its variants since Faris and Dunham's original work.

One such influential study is the comprehensive ten-year investigation by Hollingshead and Redlich (1958) who report findings on social class affiliation, mental illness, and treatment. Their work was based on interviews with a five percent sample of households in greater New Haven—a metropolitan area of a quarter of a million people. Two key questions guided their study: (1) Is there a relationship between social class and mental illness?; and (2) Does social class status affect treatments that people receive for psychological problems? Answers to both questions were resoundingly positive. Low-income people had the highest judged rates of mental disorder, and both the types of disorders treated by mental health specialists (psychiatrists) and the treatment provided varied with socioeconomic status. A second small-sample study in the New Haven series (Myers & Roberts, 1959) showed that the definition, manifestation, and development of mental disorders also differed across social classes.

While the New Haven studies have been criticized (Kleiner & Parker, 1967; Miller & Mishler, 1964) both for their methodology and substance, the main sense of their findings is not seriously contested. Mishler and Scotch (1963), for example, reviewed nine studies of relationships between social class and hospitalization for psychosis and report that, in all but one, lower socioeconomic status (SES) groups had higher hospitalization rates. The Midtown-Manhattan study (Srole et al., 1962), another ambitious project in this area based on a large-scale investigation of an untreated general population in one area of New York City, also found a negative relationship between mental illness and social class level. The Midtown investigators concluded that emotional dysfunction "may germinate at points of encysted sociocultural dysfunction" (p. 367). Two other workers (Dohrenwend & Dohrenwend, 1969), who reviewed 44 studies in this area, found consistent inverse relations between social status and reported rates of psychological disorder. Their main goal was to try to disentangle the complex methodological snares involved in separating genetic from social environment determinants.

The relation between low social status and emotional dysfunction is not restricted to urban areas. It was also found by Leighton (1964) in Stirling County, Nova Scotia, a region with one small city and its predominantly rural surround. Some key findings from the Midtown and Stirling studies corresponded closely. In Midtown, for example, 47 percent of the low-income interviewees were rated as significantly impaired emotionally and 10 percent as completely incapacitated. About 50 percent of the people from the more depressed areas of Stirling County were judged to have psychiatric disorders resulting in significant impairment. Thus, rural, geographically isolated groups, just as the poor, lack adequate mental health services, though for different reasons. Huessy (1966), Spielberger (1967), and Kiesler (1969) have discussed this question and have given examples of innovative rural mental health programs.

Although poor people have disproportionately higher confinement rates to mental hospitals and are judged by professional experts to have more severe emotional problems than middle class people, it would be premature to conclude that they are "sicker." Many factors restrict such a sweeping generalization (Levy & Rowitz, 1973; Sanua, 1969). First, the very concepts of health and illness are value judgments reflecting the predominant middle-class ethic. The sanctity of these judgments has been challenged by many (for example, Szasz, 1961). Standards and norms, tolerance for certain behaviors, and, in a very real sense, functional definitions of health and pathology, vary with SES (Reiff, 1966). Using middle-class values in situations where their appropriateness is questionable, biases reported findings. Statistics showing higher pathology rates among low-income groups may only reflect the fact that the poor have limited access to certain services because of geographic or financial constraints, or lack of information. Thus, if a public, tax-supported institution is the only place that low-income people in distress can go, it is circular to cite their disproportionately high use of such facilities as evidence that the group is less healthy.

Finally, the task of judging dysfunction is carried out by middle-class professionals. Diagnosis in mental health is, as we have seen, less than clean-cut. At times, the process itself is a huge projective technique. That being so, there is much room for experimenter-bias (Rosenthal, 1966) to operate. If the clinician knows that the person in question is poor and if he knows the scientific-clinical lore about relationships between social class and pathology, his supposedly objective, dispassionate judgment can easily become biased.

There are strong suggestions that this actually happens (Hollingshead & Redlich, 1958; Lorion, 1973; Pasamanick et al., 1964). For example, McDermott, Harrison, Schrager, and Wilson (1965) found that children of blue collar workers received less favorable diagnoses and more pessimistic prognoses than children of white collar workers. Riessman and Miller (1964) argue that projective test responses of low-income subjects, supposedly personality-determined, are confounded by such extraneous variables as strange test settings, the clinician's unfamiliar language and jargon, and his disinterest. Such factors encourage test responses and behaviors that can easily be misinterpreted by middle-class examiners to reflect personality problems.

Haase's (1964) study provides a good illustration of potential examiner bias in the clinical evaluation of low-income peo-ple. He used Rorschach judgments of trained psychologists as his criterion. Identical test records were presented to the judges, varying only the preliminary socio-economic background and descriptive data provided about the patient. Two "dummy" histories were prepared. One described a middle-class background (that is, father is a Cornell graduate, working as a CPA, earning $10,000/year, and the family lives in an expensive home in Forest Hills, L.I.). The other depicted a low-income background (that is, father quit high school after several years, now earns $45 week as a vegetable dealer, and the family lives in a small apartment on the fourth floor of a Brooklyn walk-up tenement). Thus, though two judges each viewed exactly the same Rorschach record, in one case it was preceded by a middle-class case history and in the other, by a low-income personal history. Sixteen measures were used to compare the two sets of diagnostic judgments. On 15 of these, significantly more favorable diagnoses were made for the records preceded by a bogus middle-class history. Since all test records were identical, the author concludes that the clinical judgmental process was biased—an "irrational and unfortunate consequence of our insufficiently explored social, economic and professional experiences" (Haase, 1964, p. 245).

Although, for the reasons cited above, we do not really know how social classes differ in adjustment, by most recognized criteria greater pathology is attributed to low-income groups. Hence, it is important to ask how society distributes its mental health services to the various SES groups. It is estimated that less than 10 percent of the people in this country can afford private care for psychological problems (Alt, 1959). Dysfunction and distress are, of course, not limited to that 10 percent.

Available professional mental health hours, however, are heavily overassigned to those who can afford private treatment. For example, there is virtually *no* psychiatric time in more than one-third of the public tax-supported mental hospitals (Albee, 1969b). Most psychiatric time goes into private work for a disproportionately small percentage of the wealthy who can afford it. Income and social status thus vitally influence where one can take his problems, whom he will see, for how long, and the nature of his treatment.

These generalizations have been documented repeatedly in many areas. The early New Haven studies (Hollingshead & Redlich, 1958; Schaffer & Myers, 1954) showed that low SES patients were not likely to be accepted for services by a clinic or a private practitioner, a finding supported by Brill and Storrow (1964). Hollingshead and Redlich (1958) also found that low-income individuals, as compared to high SES patients, initially accepted for service by agencies, received less treatment and were assigned to staff members with less status, training, and experience.

Upper-class neurotics in the New Haven study were likely to receive long-term, intensive, insight-oriented therapies. Low-income patients, however, got short-term treatment for neuroses and somatic treatment or simple custodial care for more serious psychotic problems. The Midtown-Manhattan studies found much the same thing. Among those judged to be significantly impaired psychologically, about 20 percent of the upper-class subjects were out-patients and another 33 percent had previously had such treatment. By contrast, only 1 percent of the diagnostically comparable low-income subjects had received any treatment. Such findings prompt the following strong conclusion by Hollingshead and Redlich: "treatment for mental illness depends not only on medical and psychological considerations but also on powerful social variables to which psychiatrists have so far given little attention" (p. 300).

Because psychotherapy is so important in mental health's current helping structure it is useful, following Sanua (1966), to consider social-class data in relation to therapy services. Sanua concluded after a detailed survey of many studies in this area that low-income people are unlikely to seek out therapy or to be accepted if they apply. If accepted, they are more likely than upper-class people to be seen by inexperienced therapists and to receive supportive or somatic treatments. Their treatment is also briefer and has less successful outcomes. The dilemma posed by these data is captured in the oft-quoted statement that help is least available and least effective where it is most needed. This paradox cannot easily be ignored.

Most of the discussion thus far has been a numbers-game analysis of imbalances between need and resources in mental health for the disadvantaged. The matter, however, is more complex than that. Several other factors must be considered to reach a realistic view of the situation's seriousness. Observers (Reiff, 1966; Reiff & Riessman, 1965) have noted that despite the overabundance of social problems among the poor (school dropout, addiction, joblessness, delinquency, and antisocial acting out, not to mention misery and suffering) as a group they have not raised persistent, vocal demands for mental health services. This seeming paradox can be understood in terms of two related factors: how low-income people define and perceive their problems and the long-standing history of alienation they have felt toward traditional mental health services.

The poor do not share the middle-class

© J. Brian King 1975

Poor people often suffer because they believe that mental health services are only for the real "crazies."

professional's views of health and pathology. The only "open and shut" case of emotional disorder for many poor persons is the florid, wall-climbing assaultive or hallucinatory behavior of the psychotic. Such behavioral departures are seen as "nuts" or "crazy"; lesser deviation or subtle signs of upset or ineffectiveness are thought of in other ways (for example, as moral or physical weakness). Reiff (1966) portrays this ideology vividly:

> To him there is physical illness and mental illness. . . . Sometimes people get upset over physical illness, death, stressful situations; but to him this is not mental illness. It is either a normal reaction to a stressful problem of living or a sign of physical or moral weakness. It follows then that the professional point of view, that failure to meet the problems of living is an emotional disturbance, a milder form of mental illness, to be treated by the same kind of doctor that treats the more seriously mentally ill, only alienates him. To the worker, emotional disability or impairment is either related to a physical illness, and should be treated as such by the doctor, or it is a result of undue distresses or strains in the environment; or it is related to a moral weakness and should be treated by a minister or priest or conquered by oneself or accepted and lived with. If one attempts to treat what is considered to be a moral weakness, the worker, with his present view, considers it a tremendous invasion of his privacy [p. 541].

Cowen (1967) cites other reasons for the low-income person's alienation from mental health services. Poor people tend to see problems in immediate, physical, concrete, crisis-related and practical ways. Middle-class clientele and practitioners define problems in more abstract, dynamic, futuristic terms, emphasizing such concepts as achievement and actualization. Language and communication barriers also exist between low-income people and professionals. Each group has a different concept of where meetings should be held, how they should proceed, and for how long. This often means that the commodity that mental health professionals are "selling" is not meaningful, appealing, or useful to low-income people. The mismatch between how needs are experienced and what services are available is an irritant for many low-income people—a discrepancy that increases felt alienation. Whereas professionals traditionally emphasize the subtleties of human dysfunction, intrapsychic processes, and complex psychodynamic formulations, the poor are inclined to define their needs in the visible, palpable terms of everyday living problems (such as, housing, jobs, food).

Because the poor do not always define their problems articulately or use pigeon-holes that do not correspond well to the professional's training, experience, and biases, the latter's response is often: "They don't understand!" or "I can't help such a person!" This may clarify why the poor are so under-represented in statistical reports of certain types of clinical services, and may also help to explain the alienation that they feel for mental health services. Thus, until recently, the helping professions have simply not been able to accept the problems of the poor as they are put.

Bredemeier's (1964) penetrating analysis offers several hypotheses to explain why the poor under-utilize mental health services and find them ineffective. These include: the failure of the poor person, because of his belief system, to perceive a problem as psychological; lack of knowledge about agency structures, interrelationships and services; objections to the fact that agencies are oriented to sickness rather than to health; lack of trust or confidence that the agency can help; and concern that contact with agencies will result in loss of status, or degradation. On the other side of the coin, Bredemeier observes that agencies are slow to accept the poor as clientele because: they are difficult to work with, have poorer prognoses, and need more time and effort; they often require innovative approaches which the professional cannot provide; the agency's self-image and internal reward system may be tied up with the client's status; the price of failure with the poor may be public censure; and, sometimes, agency personnel just do not like or respect the poor. Bredemeier thus adds a dimension of complexity to the analysis by pointing out two separate components of the situation.

Both the ways in which the poor define mental health problems and their history of alienation from traditional sources of professional help suggest that we need to change direction in our helping efforts. Reiff (1966) believes the core problem in this area to be that of *converting* need into effective demand for services. He states:

> The greatest social need for mental health services today comes from the low-income groups and the poor. Meeting this need is not primarily a problem of manpower, but a problem of ideology. The task is to develop concepts, methods, programs and services that are appropriate, effective, and related to the life styles of low-income people and to their needs, in a way which will create effective demand for them. This will require significant institutional change. [Reiff, 1966, p. 548]

The last sentence, indicating the need for "significant institutional change," should be underscored. To try to improve man's psychological well-being without regard to the behaviorally predisposing attributes of social institutions and environments would, at best, be incomplete, and at worst ostrich-like. Thus, the mental health problems of the poor cannot be discussed meaningfully without considering gut issues of family structure and dynamics, educational systems, housing and living conditions, and job or life opportunities. Each of the preceding areas is of great importance for preventively oriented mental health programs, a point more fully developed in Chapter 19.

In summary, mental health services are inequitably distributed across various social groupings. Present-day approaches have limited effectiveness and meaningfulness for major segments of society needing help the most.

CONCLUSION

The historical trend toward an ever-broadening redefinition of abnormal psychology's scope has accelerated rapidly in this century. Problems not previously considered psychological are now so viewed by increasing numbers of individuals. This, along with a changing social philosophy that places greater value on human dignity and the rights of all individuals to a full life, has led to growing pressures on the mental health professions for services. These pressures come both from people who see themselves as having problems and from social institutions that are witness to distressed, ineffective, human behaviors. Solutions for such problems, many of which have had long-standing histories, have not, however, kept pace with the growing need for them.

This chapter has reviewed some of mental health's more pressing current problems. These include: (1) imbalances between both demand and need for mental health services and supply; (2) acute shortages of professional manpower in all of the core mental health professions; (3) the stubborn unwillingness of major classes of disorder, for example, schizophrenia and the functional psychoses, to bend significantly to any of the many approaches thus far developed to deal with them; (4) the limited clinical and social effectiveness of major techniques (such as psychotherapy) in the mental health professional's tool-kit; (5) the ineffectiveness, limited reach, and questionable appropriateness of traditional helping approaches for large segments of the population, which results in help being least available where it is most needed.

These vexing problems have prompted growing dissatisfaction with mental health's past approaches and a greater willingness to reexamine long-standing assumptions and practices to determine whether they can best meet tomorrow's needs. The restlessness, ferment, and receptivity to conceptual alternatives that are apparent in mental health today serve as the basis for titling this chapter, "A Field in Transition." Some have argued that transition is already sufficiently well-crystallized to suggest that another important mental health "revolution" is in process.

The chapters to follow describe alternative models that the mental health fields can follow in their effort to cope with disorder. They identify some compelling directions for needed change and describe emergent, innovative programs that hold special promise for a more informed "abnormal psychology" of tomorrow.

SUMMARY

1. Changes taking place in the mental health field with respect to its broadening scope have reached "revolutionary" proportions.
2. Some of this foment also comes from a changing social philosophy and dissatisfactions with the old order.
3. One current serious problem is the shortage of professional manpower to meet society's mental health needs. Demand seriously strains supply. Need estimates indicate that far more people could benefit from mental

health services than are now receiving them. Prospects are poor for training enough professional personnel to meet these needs.

4. The most promising solutions to these problems involve changing approaches to the kinds of service offered and redefining who can be a helper. This requires a fundamental change in prevailing conceptual models.

5. Many questions are being raised about the effectiveness of traditional mental health practices. Serious mental disorders have not been conquered. Psychotherapy's effectiveness has not been established.

6. There are major inequities in the allocation of scarce professional services. Socioeconomic status relates both to diagnostic and prognostic evaluations and to the allocation of services; the poor are seen as sicker than the rich, are given graver prognoses, and receive less professional care.

7. Traditional treatments were designed by middle-class professionals to serve middle-class patients. The poor see their problems differently than do middle-class people and feel alienated from established mental health agencies.

8. Alternatives to traditional approaches must be developed if society's needs are to be met adequately.

CHAPTER 17

The Prevention of Disordered Behavior

It may be recollected that the cure of Madness, as well as of all other distempers, consists in 1. Removing or correcting its causes: 2. Removing or correcting its symptoms: 3. Preventing, removing, or correcting its ill effects.

William Battie, M.D.
A Treatise on Madness, 1758

WHAT IS PREVENTION?

For many years people have used the term "prevention" to describe activities and programs that have little relation to each other or to a common set of objectives. Often (Caplan, 1964; Cowen & Zax, 1967; Sanford, 1965) the broad concept has been divided into three components—primary, secondary, and tertiary prevention. This chapter begins with a review of such past usage, both to minimize sources of confusion and to focus on what we consider to be the key features of prevention.

Primary Prevention

Primary prevention can be thought of in several closely related ways (Kessler & Albee, 1975). First (Sanford, 1965), it involves preventing the *development* of disorders, that is, reducing the rate of occurrence of new

478

instances of disorder in the population-at-large. To do that, requires dealing effectively with obstacles to healthy development, whatever these are, before they cause dysfunction. Primary prevention promotes psychological well-being and health (Joint Commission Report, 1961). Primary prevention is aimed at whole groups and communities. Once individual distress is the target, the approach, by definition, is no longer primary. Primary prevention deals with individuals only in terms of what they can carry back to their communities. It focuses either on populations-at-large or on subgroups at high-risk (for example, in the urban ghetto, children from broken homes or with psychotic parents).

Because we understand so little about the complex causes of emotional disorder, it is not easy to spell out the steps of primary prevention. In one sense virtually anything done to improve man's life can be called primary health prevention. This broad view stresses that the knowledge and expertise of many people, not just mental health professionals, are needed to overcome problems of psychological dysfunction. If our question is: "What factors in society contribute to human dysfunction?" significant primary preventive roles must be played by political scientists, educators, economists, physicians, architects, physical scientists, sociologists, and urban planners.

Primary prevention's most important features are that its scope is very broad and that it involves key institutions at the root of our social system—things that change slowly, and with difficulty. Since its activities are costly, time-consuming, varied, and difficult to mount, they require many different kinds of expertise. Furthermore, program effects are not soon seen, and even if they do show up, relationships between programs and outcomes may be fuzzy.

The fact that we all want a psychologi-

© J. Brian King 1975

Children who grow up in an urban environment may well be at a disadvantage in the development of psychological well-being.

cally healthy society does not mean that only mental health specialists can bring it about. Certainly they have not succeeded in doing so thus far, either because they have not tried or because they lack the savvy to do it effectively. We wish less to criticize the mental health fields by that statement and more to reflect the intrinsic complexity of primary prevention. In truth, very few people from *any* field have made noteworthy advances in it. None of this is to suggest there is *no* role for mental health in primary prevention. To the contrary! Because the mental health professional is society's expert on human development and adjustment, he should have much to offer in framing primary prevention questions and in seeking answers to them. The questions he can ask, however, will be quite different from those that have concerned him in the past. Also he will have to work with specialists from fields other than those with whom he has worked in the past.

The mental health professions have not really started to engage some of their most exciting potential challenges. Lemkau (1969) makes this point in a delightful and informative essay. He had the rare opportunity to be a mental health consultant in planning an entirely new city. Lemkau frankly confesses his initial reluctance to participate in the project and his concern about whether he could contribute to such an uncharted field. But, he did. And so, he can portray the important decisions that are made in planning a new city and describe how such decisions can significantly affect the emotional well-being of its future inhabitants. Although we do not often build new cities from scratch, such situations as well as projects of lesser scope harbor important opportunities for prevention in mental health.

Primary prevention is poorly charted terrain. Caplan's (1964) analogy is instructive. He likens primary prevention to a driver's road map of a region that does not provide fine detail. This contrasts with a pedestrian's very specific street map of a city that Caplan compares to the microscopic view that clinicians have when they do individual diagnosis and treatment. In the abstract people can agree pretty well about the definition and aims of primary prevention. But when it comes to the basic question of what you do, there is less agreement. Caplan's (1964) conceptual model for primary prevention assumes that sound psychological development requires that adequate physical, psychosocial, and sociocultural "supplies" be provided continually. He believes that a person who lacks such supplies is vulnerable to maladjustment. Physical supplies include food, shelter, ade-

quate stimulation, and protection from trauma. The term "psychosocial supplies" refers to meeting the person's cognitive, affective, and social needs. Normally, such gratifications come from interactions with people who are close to the individual and from the significant social institutions that mould him. Providing psychosocial supplies means satisfying key psychological needs. The individual gets his sociocultural supplies from society's values and customs. Different role-prescriptions and opportunities are available to those born wealthy versus those born poor. These can facilitate or hinder psychological development.

Caplan believes that primary prevention's first goal is to ensure adequate physical, psychosocial, and sociocultural supplies for everyone—a tall order. He sees social and interpersonal action as the main ways of furthering these aims. *Social action* means bringing about community-wide change in political and social policy, and legislation, in such areas as health, education, and welfare to ensure that everyone will have the three main classes of human supplies. The mental health specialist can help this process through consultation with key administrators, legislators, and influential citizens in the social power structure. Also he can change community attitudes and behavior through helping to achieve better communication, education, and use of the mass media.

Caplan uses the term *interpersonal interaction* to describe face-to-face contacts between mental health specialists and individuals or small groups. This approach is not justified on the basis of the changes it produces in the people who are contacted, but rather by its beneficial effects on community problems in general. Interpersonal action is aimed at those who have extensive contacts with these problems. For example, community *caregivers* such as clergymen, physicians, and school personnel receive many requests for interpersonal help. Strengthening their hand supports the community's base for prevention.

Mental health professionals have had relatively little experience in either social or interpersonal action, but their background and training is better suited to interpersonal, rather than to social action. Formulating comprehensive, effective social plans and carrying out such programs requires the help of experts from other than the mental health fields.

Secondary Prevention

The main goal of secondary prevention according to Sanford (1965) is to stop mild disorders from becoming acute or prolonged. Secondary prevention also attempts to shorten the duration and lessen the impact and negative after-effects of disorder (Cowen & Zax, 1967). Caplan (1964) emphasizes that this approach seeks to lower the rate and prevalence of known instances of disorder. All agree that secondary prevention's main tools are early detection and early, effective treatment of dysfunction.

Although Caplan (1964) is very sympathetic to early detection, he still feels that the approach has limitations. For example, most diagnostic tools, as noted in Chapter 3, are time-consuming and have limited accuracy. Moreover, in many situations disorders are not detected until after signs of disturbance are vivid. So we need rapid, objective, accurate screening procedures that are sensitive to minimal cues of dysfunction, and we must shorten the time between identifying disorders and giving help. These goals can be facilitated by effective consultation and mass education. Routine population screenings for emotional status, such as those used by public health specialists in other areas, have much to offer. But such approaches will be useful only if manpower is available to provide help after problems have been detected.

To be effective, early detection programs must provide prompt evaluation. This has not always happened. The best early detection programs are located in communal structures that house large numbers of people, under unified organizational control. They contain well-defined facilities that are accepted as part of established ways of doing things. The facilities are well known and conveniently located. Settings that meet these specifications, which have made progress in early screening include: schools, the military, industrial establishments, labor union clinics, and student health services in colleges and universities. Currently, many community mental health centers are also trying to do early detection. A common element that binds some of the above settings is that they have well-defined work, achievement, or behavioral objectives. A person's failure to meet such objectives becomes failure in the system, and thus a source of motivation to change. A specific failure may be just one part of a broader failure pattern, but that can be determined through the early detection procedure itself.

Ideally, early detection should lead to prompt intervention. This aim is at the heart of the community mental health center approach, but the ideal is not always achieved. The thing that most restricts early identification programs is the lack of effective follow-up intervention. This observation recalls our earlier discussion of demand/supply imbalances in mental health, shortages in professional manpower, and the questionable effectiveness of existing methods. It stresses that we must develop alternative conceptual solutions to chronic social problems.

One important feature of secondary prevention is often overlooked. The goal of identifying mild disorder and preventing it from becoming acute can be seen in two ways. It can mean trying, as community mental health centers do, to identify and deal promptly with current episodes of dysfunction. For example, if warning signs of an acute schizophrenic reaction can be detected in its first few days, perhaps a full-blown episode can be averted. But secondary prevention also has a longitudinal connotation. If we can detect dysfunction early in the person's life before it becomes chronic, opportunities for effective intervention improve. Also, because young people are relatively malleable, they may be helped effectively in less time than older people.

Although these two types of secondary prevention are not mutually exclusive, they differ in philosophy and in how you carry them out (Cowen, 1967). A longitudinal emphasis puts the young child front and center, something that others (Smith & Hobbs, 1966) have urged for a long time. Early secondary prevention necessarily calls attention to the young child and his everyday environment (for example, his school experience). It forces us to think about primary interventions. The two types of secondary prevention described above are indeed different, and, in our view, the longitudinal, child-oriented approach holds greater promise for advancing mental health's long-term objectives.

Tertiary Prevention

Tertiary prevention seeks to reduce the consequences and residual effects of dysfunction. It is directed at the seriously disturbed. Its main goals are to restore the person at least to a minimal interpersonal and job effectiveness. Most of mental health's activities have been and still are in tertiary prevention (Williams, 1962), but tertiary prevention is prevention in name only. Because its aims and approaches are largely unrelated to those of primary prevention, it would be useful (that is, reducing confusion) to discard the term completely. Sanford's (1965) chapter on preventing mental illness well reflects this view. He devotes one 11-word sentence to defining tertiary prevention and then ignores it completely. Doubtlessly someone once assumed a hypothetical continuum anchored by primary prevention at one end and by tertiary prevention at the other. Such continua are superficially appealing because they provide an orderly shorthand for those who value simplicity. But in terms of aims or procedures, it poses a severe challenge to find meaningful communality between primary and tertiary prevention.

Obviously, the aims and activities historically included under tertiary prevention should not be abandoned. They are simply not prevention. Their ultimate justification must come from the need to reduce manifest human discomfort and to maximize opportunities for all people to live effectively. That ethic is unimpeachable. If we lived in a world of endless resources it would create no problem to pursue tertiary preventive to the utmost, but mental health resources, are of course, limited.

Limits in resources necessarily force choices among alternatives. As noted elsewhere (Cowen & Zax, 1967), the influential Joint Commission Report (1961) did not pay enough attention to this point. By arguing that major mental illness (the functional psychoses) was mental health's core problem and that intensive treatment of major, prolonged illness should have first call on existing and future resources, the

Joint Commission placed its bets on late secondary and tertiary prevention.

Because the Joint Commission was so strongly influential as a master planning group, its recommendation was a *de facto* recommendation against primary types of prevention. Few can dispute the view that the Joint Commission's recommendation supports an absolute good, but the critical challenge in mental health today is the "*relative* ordering of many values, *each* of which may be good in the absolute sense" (Cowen & Zax, 1967, p. 22). If the cost of developing tertiary prevention programs is to exclude primary ones, the price is too high. Nor can we accept, uncritically, the argument that tertiary prevention is justified by the democratic-humanitarian ethic. For if choice is indeed antichoice, achieving one set of humanitarian goals may block others with even greater humanitarian value. Minimizing chronic dysfunction for the few by using all of our scarce resources would be hard to justify on humanitarian grounds if, in so doing, we failed to prevent dysfunction in far greater numbers. Perhaps the major reason for tertiary prevention is the fact that mental illness is considered a blot on society's "ideal image." But "what price glory?" if all that is achieved is to guarantee that the same blot will be there 100 years from now?

Orientation of Present Volume to Prevention

Our review and critique of the past use of the term "prevention" in mental health underscores several points. The most obvious is that it is a nonunitary concept. Many programs that have flown under a preventive flag are different enough from each other to be mutually antagonistic (Trickett,

Kelly, & Todd, 1971). This is particularly so for primary versus tertiary prevention programs. Demarcations between types of prevention are often fuzzy because a given activity can involve several types of prevention. For example, consultation with a teacher about the school-phobic behavior of a six-year-old child is secondary prevention, but if it alters the teacher's knowledge and competencies, it may be primary prevention for future children. Although the labeling issue is not serious in this case, it illustrates the terminological confusion in this area. A single concept of prevention that strives to include all three past usages of the term (primary, secondary, and tertiary) would be a useless catch-all. Such a broad use does not offer an alternative to the medical model. Instead, it includes it! The goals and actions of tertiary, and most secondary, prevention are identical to those of the medical model. We need to discontinue either the nonunitary usage of the term prevention, or the basic concept of the medical model; they simply duplicate each other.

The best way to arrive at a meaningful ideological alternative to the medical model is to narrow the term prevention to exclude most medical model activities. That would make it a clear-cut alternative. The practical question is "just where does that point occur?" That is like asking, "What's black, what's white, and how broad is grey?" Tertiary prevention belongs 100 percent to the medical model as defined here. By contrast, little if any of primary prevention does. Secondary prevention is in a more ambiguous position. Earlier, the point was made that secondary prevention itself is not unitary. Although it seeks, globally, to prevent mild disorder from becoming prolonged and severe, it can do so through a cross-sectional approach that identifies and treats current episodes of disorder as promptly as possible or, longitudinally, by emphasizing early identification and intervention with the young when the first signs of prospectively serious disorder appear. Cross-sectional, adult-oriented secondary prevention clearly falls within the scope of the medical model. By contrast, early secondary prevention allows one to try new approaches not previously part of that model. To us, prevention in mental health should refer only to primary and early secondary prevention. This offers a genuine contrast to the medical model and an important conceptual alternative for future mental health planning.

There is an irony in our view. Historically, most of mental health's effort has gone into tertiary and late secondary prevention. The mental health fields evolved as society distinguished between ordered and disordered behavior, became concerned with the unfortunate human and social consequences of the latter, and tried to correct these disorders. Thus, mental health's mandate came from psychopathology. That view still predominates. The more disturbed the individual, the more people believe that they must turn to mental institutions and mental health professionals for help. We are seen as the doctors of disordered psyches. Yet as a result both of our broadening views of dysfunction and the difficulty of treating established pathology, we are growing more aware of the limitations, perhaps even the futility, of that role. We are beginning to appreciate, in theory at least, the attractiveness of approaches that can cut down the flow of disorder and short-circuit mild cases before they become serious. Achieving such ends requires us to examine and modify the social causes of dysfunction and to identify and intervene early in the course of a developing problem.

SOCIAL SYSTEM PREVENTIVE APPROACH

The mental health field is slowly retreating from the dominant view that the source of most human dysfunction can be found in an individual's psychodynamic history (Lennard & Bernstein, 1969). Reality demands this retreat. Associations between social systems characterized by squalor, poverty, lack of opportunity, and helplessness and the presence of all kinds of serious psychological problems force us to entertain the possibility that social systems predispose or cause disordered behavior. Today more than ever before we question the view that symptoms are related to a person's internal makeup rather than reflecting particular social contexts. The distinction is important since, as Lennard and Bernstein (1969) suggest, immediate actions and long-range planning in mental health are shaped by one's stance with respect to it.

Human growth and psychological development take place in many specific contexts, within relatively few social systems. The impact of these contexts and systems, though not always apparent, is nevertheless profound. Too often we take system structures as givens, with little more than passing thought about their hidden assumptions and latent, but potentially basic, shaping effects. Sarason (1971) uses the term "regularities" to describe a program's or setting's ways of doing things. Presumably, regularities are as they are to help settings meet their objectives. Whether or not they do, is a more complex matter. How often, for example, do we question the underlying, influential notion that high school students develop best intellectually and personally in settings that must be attended from 8:30 A.M. to 3:30 P.M., five days a week, with homework each evening, and with roughly equal time and effort divided between English, social studies, math, science, and a language?

Social systems and interaction contexts are hardly neutral in their effects. They shape people importantly and either contribute to, or hinder, sound development. This fact should be recognized explicitly and studied systematically, so that findings can be used to strengthen human development. The alternative is to let established ways reign by default even if their impact is random rather than informed.

This general orientation highlights the need for three types of thrusts. First we must develop clearer understandings of the nature of social systems and how they affect us in basic ways (Barker & Gump, 1964; Barker & Schoggen, 1973). Thus far there has been greater concern about the behaviors that occur within systems than about the defining qualities of the systems themselves (Lennard & Bernstein, 1969). We need also to understand the influential dimensions of social environments and organizational structures and how these vary among settings (Kelly, 1969). An example of such work is Lennard and Bernstein's (1969) comparison of interactions in the family with those in psychotherapy, and normal versus disturbed family interactions.

After influential dimensions of social environments have been identified (Moos, 1973; Moos & Insel, 1974; Price & Moos, 1975; Trickett & Moos, 1973), we can study critical questions about their effects. Barker and Gump (1964), for example, show that "undermanned" (thinly populated) school environments, in contrast to "overmanned" (crowded) ones, have students who: engage in more, and more varied, activities;

are less aware of individual differences; and have sharper identity and greater visibility. Mental health should strive to identify forces in the system or environment that contribute to, or impair, psychological well-being—indeed how to create or engineer settings that produce positive outcomes (Sarason, 1972).

However important system effects are, they vary among individuals. Some people thrive in one type of environment while others do better in very different environments. For example, Allinsmith and Grimes (1961) showed that compulsive-anxious children did much better in highly structured, as opposed to relatively unstructured, school environments, even though the reverse was true for other children. Very recently, Reiss and his coworkers (Reiss & Dyhdalo, 1975; Reiss & Martell, 1974) have reported on the effects of open versus self-contained environments. Beyond their many significant "main-effects" findings, they also found several intriguing and challenging person-environment interactions. For example, children from open-space classes were found to persist more on difficult tasks than children from self-contained classes, and there was a closer relation between persistence and high academic achievement for open-space educated children. However, looking only at nonpersistent (distractible) children, those from self-contained classes had much higher educational achievement than those from open-space environments—an important person-environment interaction, with far-reaching practical implications. An ideal educational climate for child A can be exactly the opposite for child B. Thus, we need to do a third type of investigation —ecological studies of the consequences of various person-environment matches (Insel & Moos, 1974; Kelly, 1966; Moos,

1973). Ironically, ecological-match questions that seem so important for abnormal psychology have been studied far more extensively among lower organisms than humans (Edney, 1974).

If we can discover the growth-producing or development-inhibiting aspects of social settings, we will have a sound base for modifying systems to facilitate people's adjustment (Cowen & Zax, 1967; Lennard & Bernstein, 1969). Even so, we still face the questions of: "Just how should we modify social systems?" and "What *exactly* are the mental health relevant consequences of such modifications?" To change systems effectively we not only require much basic system information, but we must also contend with many practical problems. Once established, systems resist change (Sarason, 1972; Sarason et al., 1966). Power structures form, vested interests are protected, and people involved in the system are threatened by change. Rooted systems die hard and, even if mental health specialists clearly understood the theory and practice of system-change, it would not occur smoothly or easily.

Fairweather (1967) believes that establishing procedures to "bring about social change in a systematic orderly and rational manner" (p. 4) is a prime social need. He proposes "experimental social innovation," a blend of service and research techniques as a way to achieve these objectives. Fairweather advocates both naturalistic and laboratory research designed to solve socially significant problems that affect man's well-being. Experimental social innovation is designed to deal with visible sore spots in contemporary society. Key social institutions and settings—for example, schools, mental hospitals, prisons, and the ghetto—are his targets. He urges social scientists and mental health specialists to become interested in the problems of such settings

and to use behavior science's knowledge and technology to help solve them.

Fairweather describes the steps involved in experimental social innovation and suggests ways of implementing each. The cycle begins by defining a significant social problem. Next comes naturalistic observation to identify the factors related to the problem's occurrence in a natural context, and to formulate alternatives for resolving it. This key step implies that there are many ways of resolving any social problem and that current approaches may fail to grasp essential issues and/or to have considered worthwhile alternatives. After alternatives have been clarified, the next step is to set up an experiment comparing them. Although specific methods for such experiments differ for different situations, all should meet the scientific requirements of systematic variation, control, and comparison. Since research evaluating the effectiveness of innovative methods is always embedded in real social settings, much time is needed to assess process and outcome variables properly. Studies in experimental social innovation assume that investigators are responsible for the well-being of the people in the system during the research. The scope of many experiments in social innovation is likely to be sufficiently broad to require a multidisciplinary effort.

Fairweather's earlier work (1964) on low discharge and high recidivism rates among chronic mental hospital patients is a good example of his approach to experimental social innovation. Naturalistic observation helped to formulate a plan for restructuring hospital wards to increase discharge rates and lower recidivism. This new alternative was compared experimentally to a traditional ward regimen. The outcomes of the two approaches were compared. Another example of experimental social innovation, in a very different area, has been reported by a team working in elementary schools (Cowen et al., 1975). This group was interested in how school mental health services were delivered as well as their effects on children's educational and personal well-being. Naturalistic observation suggested that many youngsters referred for help in early adolescence had long histories of school maladjustment. This led to the development of an early-detection, early-secondary prevention model that was compared experimentally to traditional school mental health services. The evaluation was objective and longitudinal. Evidence of the greater effectiveness of the preventive model led to its more widespread adoption within the system.

Experimental social innovation and some direct social action programs share common objectives, but, whereas the former use systematic observation and research to compare alternatives, the latter often rely on intuitive reactions. Fairweather (1967) makes the point that experimental social innovation, as defined, "is needed to compare the effects of . . . proffered solutions *prior* to their adoption and implementation by society's members" (1967, p. 5). By contrast Caplan's (1964) social-action proposals for primary prevention, although reasonable theoretically, are largely assumed to be worthwhile. Fairweather's emphasis is less on *specific* programs than on a rational-empirical methodology for solving social problems.

Family and School

If psychological problems have key roots in unfortunate life conditions and unhappy human interactions, system modification should aim at maximizing the health-building qualities of significant systems and interactions. This view spotlights the special importance of childhood. Two socializing agencies, the family and the school, have powerful impact on early psychological development. Most of the young child's waking hours are spent in one or the other. A child's view of life as friendly or hostile, rewarding or frustrating, challenging or restricting, the directions and goals he establishes, and his way of interacting, are all shaped by home and school.

In diagnostic studies of adult patients, clinicians often identify stressful forces in the person's history and can see clear relationships between those forces and current dysfunction. Even though such relationships have been repeatedly shown in research studies of the causes of pathological states, we have neglected looking at the opposite side of the coin, that is, forces and experiences that promote *healthy* development. Abnormal psychology's focus has always been on the pathological. However, because that approach seems to have limited payoff, we must shift our focus toward averting disorder rather than trying to contain it after it has become blatant. To do so requires an understanding of how family and school affect psychological development—both healthy and pathological.

Few doubt that the family is the most important influence on a child's psychological development. The family's central role in providing necessary human supplies for long time periods, its close day-to-day interactions, and the intimacy and depth of the emotional ties among its members are powerful moulding influences. The family must either enhance or limit a child's development. The human infant's total helplessness and dependency at birth requires that he be cared for by others. While this ensures the infant's physical survival, those who care for the child play

© J. Brian King 1975

Sound family relations enhance a child's
psychological development.

an even more significant role in his psychological development.

Lennard and Bernstein (1969) studied family interactions and their impact on psychological development. Their research compared family with psychotherapeutic contexts, German with American family contexts, and disturbed with normal family contexts. Their work focused on certain key dimensions of family interaction and identified some consequences of variation on these dimensions. One dimension of concern was the extent to which a child initiates behavioral interactions himself. Lennard and Bernstein argue that being able to engage only in *responsive* behavior limits a child's development. They found that families of normal children encouraged self-initiated behavior more than the families of schizophrenic children. Another important shaping dimension is the extent to which family interactions encourage age-appropriate socialization and learning by providing the child with information, defining roles, and clarifying behavior

standards and expectancies for him. They found deficiencies in such socialization opportunities to be related to pathological outcomes. Level of discord is another important family interaction dimension. Interactions that are stressful for the child, reduce communication, encourage withdrawal from the system, or curtail needed sources of support, all favor negative psychological outcomes.

While no attempt is made here to classify all family interaction dimensions, such dimensions do exist and knowing their consequences is important for preventing disordered behavior. We need to learn more about basic dimensions of family interaction and their relation to healthy or pathological outcomes must be charted. As such knowledge is developed, effective ways of using it will also be needed. An important start in this direction can be found in Jacob's (1975) recent comprehensive review of interaction patterns in normal and disturbed families.

Because the current mental health delivery system is geared to troubled people, it largely bypasses family-directed prevention options. But there are ways to promote well-being before disaster strikes. Pregnancy and well baby clinics offer one such mechanism. Another is through the (ostensibly, nonpsychological) contacts that families have with society's caregivers: physicians, teachers, clergymen. Mental health specialists should help social agents to understand more clearly the relations between social structures or human interactions and a person's behavior so that such information can be applied more effectively. Is it not just as important for a pediatrician to explain to mothers that a child's psychological development is helped by making age-appropriate decisions, as it is for him to explain that the infant can start eating solid cereals at age one month?

Despite the family's critical moulding influence, it is more difficult to work preventively with families than through schools. Families are separated and difficult to reach. Schools, by contrast, are large, geographically consolidated settings with unified administrations. Although it is not easy to introduce programs to maximize effectiveness and reduce dysfunction in schools, it is probably less difficult than trying to do the same thing with 1000 separate families. In Western society, schools shape people continuously for long periods during their formative years (Bardon, 1968; Hunt, 1968). They are especially important environments to study in order to explore and evaluate alternative structures for promoting healthy child development. Thus, schools, particularly in the primary grades, are attractive targets for programs designed to produce more effective learning and sound personal development (Allinsmith & Goethals, 1962; Bower & Hollister, 1967; Lambert, 1965; Sarason, 1971; Sarason et al., 1966). Schools, incidentally, are also good entry points for establishing family contacts (Cowen, 1967).

The questions about schools that must be answered have a familiar ring. They are much like ones already posed for social environments in general: "What are the key impact dimensions of the school environment?"; "How do variations on these dimensions affect children's learning and development?"; "How can school environments be changed to make them more facilitating for children?" Such questions frame the social system approach to prevention in the schools (Michael, 1968; Sarason, 1971; Trickett & Moos, 1973, 1974; Watson, 1967).

Examples of budding attempts to explore these questions can be cited. Ojemann (1961) distinguished "surface" and "causal" approaches to teaching. Whereas the former emphasizes teaching facts, the latter seeks to help children develop ways of thinking about situations and choosing among alternatives. Ojemann found that causal teaching produced superior generalization of knowledge, better weighing of alternatives, reduction of confusion, and more adequate coping with the environment. These qualities promote psychological growth and educational mastery.

Studies done at the Bank Street College of Education (Biber, 1961; Minuchin et al., 1969; Zimiles, 1967) have raised important questions about relations between the school environment and child development. Biber emphasizes that schools are not just places where knowledge is imparted; they are complicated social structures. They house different class environments, learning atmospheres, values, and objectives—all important influences on the child's learning and personal development.

Minuchin et al. (1969) and Zimiles (1967) report an experimental comparison of two learning models: "modern" versus "traditional." The former emphasizes developing processes of thinking and learning while the latter focuses on mastery of factual content. A school's educational approach was defined by three factors, the extent to which it: (a) used the surrounding environment as part of the educational experience; (b) focused on current social events and problems and used new communication techniques; and (c) was willing to experiment with new teaching approaches. Their contrast analyses of four socioeconomically comparable schools that fell at different points on a modern-traditional continuum revealed some important intellectual, interpersonal, self-concept, and attitude differences in the children educated in such settings. Children from the modern school had more: differentiated self-perceptions, acceptance of negative impulses, investment in their status as children, and openness in their sex-role concepts. Cognitively, children from modern schools, in comparison to those from traditional schools, were more independent in their thinking and pursued ideas more seriously. They focused more on connections between facts, on new discovery, and on productive thinking. However, they did not differ on group intellectual test scores suggesting that standard tests are not sensitive to some differential consequences of the two environments.

The authors concluded that schools profoundly affect children's lives and functioning, but that their impact is moderated by home influences and by the interaction between home and school. Another important conclusion they reached is that school environments can change characteristics once thought to be related to childhood developmental stages. Moreover they found that schools had different consequences for different children. The Bank Street project shows that a definable, structural school variable, that is, "modern versus traditional," is related to different psychological and educational outcomes.

Some steps seem essential if the school social system is to be changed. One is to develop systematic ways of observing what goes on and to classify the influential variables of the school environment. How that can best be done depends on value judgments about which variables are the most significant. Based on many studies of varied social institutions and environments ranging from mental hospital wards to industrial and educational settings, Moos (1973) and Insel and Moos (1974) propose that when you try to define social environments several key dimensions nearly always recur. Environments have: *relational* properties that reflect people's involvement and affiliation with each other; *goal orientation* dimensions, such as their task-orientation or competitiveness; and *maintenance* qualities, such as their rule-clarity and orderliness. Using this framework, Trickett and Moos (1974) developed a Class Environment Scale to measure nine basic dimensions of junior high and high school class environments. These investigators showed that classes vary substantially on these dimensions and that different class environments are associated with different perceived satisfactions and mood states in students (Trickett & Moos, 1973, 1974). Can we, using such an approach, learn to create class environments that promote children's well being and effective learning from the start? The goal is certainly worthwhile.

Gump (1969) developed an observational framework to describe the complex world of third-grade classrooms. This framework permitted careful study of relationships between classroom events and children's subsequent behavior. Gump's approach is a useful tool for evaluating the school's potential for enhancing psychological and intellectual development.

Hollister (1965, 1967) reminds us that mental health has been so heavily oriented to pathology that the English language still lacks a word that is the opposite of "trauma." He proposes that we use the word "stren" to describe a psychologically strengthening experience. Finkel (1974) shows that this concept can be operationalized and subjected to empirical study. Hollister urges that schools incorporate the notion of strens into their thinking and that they strive to create such experiences for all children. As a psychiatrist, he seeks to foster sound "ego-processes"—particularly those of assimilation, differentiation, and integration, and to identify school climates and approaches that serve that end. Not only have we lacked vocabulary to describe health-building processes, we have not even had good measures of children's strengths and resources. Recent development of competency measures for young school children (for example, Gesten, 1974) offers a tool for schools to use to measure their success in building resources in children.

Susskind's (1969) studies approach the challenge of system analysis and modification in the schools. Susskind correctly noted that both educational and psychological theory emphasize the importance of curiosity for effective learning (Suchman, 1967). Teachers speak positively and consistently about encouraging children to be curious. Children show their curiosity by the questions they ask in class. Accordingly, Susskind observed 32 third- to sixth-grade social studies classes, three times each, and recorded both children's and teachers' questions. Despite the fact that his observations were made in *non*-inner-city schools at times that, theoretically, encouraged question-asking behavior, Susskind found that the average number of questions asked by teachers in a single 30-minute class period was 50.6, whereas children collectively averaged only 1.8 questions. This indicates that the system had simply failed to produce curiosity behavior. An entire class of children asked, on the average, less than five percent of the number of questions asked by the average teacher. This was far less than teachers had estimated would be asked or considered ideal. In addition, content analysis showed that the teachers more often asked "lower-order" (that is, fact and memory-centered) as opposed to "higher-order" (drawing on thought and experiences) questions.

Susskind's data challenge the assumption that the school encourages curiosity in children. His study also provides a model for studying prevailing, but sometimes obscure, regularities of the school structure. Moreover, his findings help to formulate changes designed to overcome the system's inadequacies. Thus, Susskind "trained" a small group of teachers to change their question-asking and discussion-leading behaviors to encourage greater student curiosity. In a relatively short time he found changes in teachers' questioning (for example, shifts from "lower-order" to "higher-order" questions) and greater student participation. A system change to correct a flaw had been identified. The result was to free up children's curiosity behavior.

In a recent significant series of papers Kelly and his associates (Kelly, 1966, 1967, 1968, 1969, 1970; Trickett et al., 1971) argue in favor of an ecological approach, emphasizing person-environment pairings to determine the kinds of social environments that best support sound development. They propose that changes in some members of a system affect both other members and the functioning of the system itself, and, conversely, that system change affects everyone who is part of it. Kelly's group used high school environments as laboratories for its empirical studies. They (Trickett et al., 1971) analyzed role-characteristics and demands placed on key members of the complex social system of the high school such as superintendents and principals, teachers, mental health professionals, and pupils.

A system's attributes, for example, its size (Barker & Gump, 1964) as well as how its critical roles are spelled out, influence people's adaptation to it. Barker and Gump found that "undermanned" (thinly populated) school settings, in contrast to "overmanned" (crowded) ones, produced students who: get into more varied activities; are less sensitive; have sharper identity and greater visibility. Similarly, Kelly (1968) studied how one important aspect of a high school environment—its stability, measured by annual student turnover rates, related to exploratory behavior. He hypothesized that exploratory behavior would be adaptive in a fluid environment but inappropriate, or even maladaptive, in a constant one. Kelly's research in this area supports this proposition. The significance of person-system couplings suggests the following new roles for school mental health specialists: describing and understanding social systems and the jobs and interactions of people within them, and social engineering that optimizes the effects of environments.

By emphasizing the importance of school structures and practices in shaping children's development, we do not mean to imply that these are the only aspects of the school situation to be considered in developing its fullest health-producing potential. Any such analysis would be incomplete without including the teacher as a key determinant of how children grow.

NEA

Teachers play a key role in how a child grows (Photograph courtesy National Educational Education Association Publishing, Joe di Dio.)

The sources of teacher influence are broader than just the knowledge he imparts; they include his personal style, his own adjustment, and how he goes about teaching. Justifiably, much has been written about these sources of influence (Clarizio, 1969a; Sarason, Davidson, & Blatt, 1962; Wilhelms, 1967). Wilhelms argues that to be truly effective, teaching must go well beyond passing along knowledge. He suggests that sensitivity to other people, the ability to accept human variability and to transmit knowledge in a way that respects individual differences, are at the core of effective teaching. Sarason, Davidson, and Blatt (1962) share this view. They see the teacher not as a technician who merely spoons out knowledge, but as someone who must continually apply psychological principles effectively. These authors regret that teacher education has typically emphasized the knowledge that teachers must "deliver" instead of understanding of the learning process and development. They call for teacher education that will stress understanding the child and his personal growth.

Some have argued persuasively that the school curriculum should be used to promote children's psychological strength and mental health. Ojemann (1969) illustrates this view by applying the concept of causal thinking to curriculum. He found that teachers could increase children's awareness of the complexity and dynamics of human behavior; reduce anxiety, punitiveness, and antidemocratic tendencies; and lead students to more tolerant views of teacher roles and functions. Ojemann holds that introducing psychological awareness into the curriculum provides children with resources they need to handle later experiences and crises. An important related development is the emergence of behavioral science, or psychology, curricula and awareness-oriented discussion approaches for primary grade children (Long, 1968; Roen, 1967). Such approaches assume that mental health concepts can be communicated meaningfully to young children, and that doing so adds a significant dimension to the educational experience. Learning about onself, how to deal with problems and to interact effectively with others may be as important as learning about world geography, Aztec art, and Byzantine culture. Roen (1967) reports the positive effects of a behavior science program for fourth graders. Human service, or helping practices in which young schoolchildren provide service to other people in need, is another potential way to foster personal development. This approach assumes that children can better acquire altruistic behavior by engaging in it rather than by simply talking or reading about it.

Recently acquired knowledge in the area of behavior modification has been applied successfully in schools (Clarizio, 1971; MacMillan, 1973; Woody, 1969). Thus far, this effort has focused on limiting socially or educationally maladaptive behavior in a medical-model tradition. Even more exciting applications of this approach can be envisioned. Schools offer the behavior modifier unparalleled opportunities to build and strengthen positive characteristics, such as, curiosity, inventiveness, prosocial and altruistic behavior. Behavior modifiers have already done considerable work using parents, teachers, and peers as change agents (Guerney, 1969). Such programs appropriately recast mental health professionals as trainers, consultants, and resource people (Sarason & Ganzer, 1969).

The decision to focus on home and school in discussing system-directed preventive approaches assumes that these settings shape early psychological development most significantly. To prevent dysfunction it seems essential that we concentrate on ways to maximize home and school contributions to positive human outcomes. This is not to deny the importance of other social forces. Legal, enforcement and welfare agencies, church groups, detention homes, and community centers also play important roles in shaping human well-being. How such settings are defined and structured, how they approach people, how they render service, and how they can be changed all need to be understood. Such an understanding in fact is vital to any attempt to prevent psychological dysfunction.

PEOPLE-CENTERED PREVENTIVE APPROACHES

We have just made a strong case for understanding and modifying social systems as a way of preventing behavior disorder. That is fine for the future, but as of right now, there are still many more emotional problems than can be handled by available resources. So, even if mental health does shift toward prevention, it will probably never become *exclusively* system-oriented and impersonal. That being the case, we must still make critical choices to allocate scarce resources optimally among many possible people-centered functions. Cowen (1967) has argued that the potential payoff from such contacts was a good metric to use in making such difficult decisions. Doing so, of course, requires that value judgments be made but this is always so when needs exceed resources. Given the past failures of mental health delivery systems and the magnitude of today's problems, our value judgment is that person-centered applications must focus on: young people (early childhood orientation); critical stress points in people's lives (crisis intervention); and approaches that have the widest possible impact (consultation with community caregivers).

Crisis Intervention

Much emphasis has been placed on the importance of psychological crises and their handling for positive mental health (Caplan, 1964; McGee, 1974; Specter & Claiborn, 1973). Crises are brief, transitional periods of acute disturbance. Because they typically involve situations that are psychologically important to the individual, they require adaptations that can centrally affect his well-being. Lindemann (1944) developed many important ideas about crisis as a result of his contact with victims of the tragic Coconut Grove nightclub fire in Boston. He was impressed both with the range of people's reactions to the trauma and the fact that, for some, serious negative consequences could be short-circuited through appropriate intervention during the critical period following the tragedy. From this experience, he drew broad implications for a theory of prevention.

All people experience crises. In a crisis state we are likely to feel acutely uncomfortable, preoccupied and emotionally upset, uncertain about where to turn and what to do, and open to the influence of others. Several people (Lindemann, 1944; Cumming & Cumming, 1966) have identified a specific set of reactions to crisis: turmoil that disrupts or immobilizes body functions and thinking, preoccupation with the past, and, finally, attempts to gather resources to readjust.

The crisis experience is so intense that it often has major consequences for a person's adjustment. But, as Caplan (1961,

1964) has said, crisis involves opportunity as well as danger. Whereas failure to deal effectively with a crisis makes future adjustment more difficult, successful crisis resolution builds future psychological strength. Because crises are significant crossroads, the importance of which go far beyond just the brief moment when they occur, the mental health professions should develop ways of dealing with them more effectively.

Although a person's psychological make-up determines whether certain experiences do in fact lead to crisis states, and, if so, how severe they are, some events are likely to produce crises for all of us. Such events involve the loss or threat of loss of basic supplies, heightened demands on the individual, and prospective thwarting of valued goals (Caplan, 1964). Cumming and Cumming (1966) believe that disasters that occur suddenly and disrupt our lives produce the most drastic crisis reactions. The death of a loved one is a classic example of such a crisis. Job change, retirement, and moving to a psychologically unknown, unpredictable setting are all situations that can threaten the flow of life's supplies and hence cause crisis.

Crisis can also be viewed developmentally. Many common situations such as the birth of a new sibling, starting school, and certain medical procedures produce crises for children. Some theorists (such as, Erikson, 1959) see the personality as developing through a series of differentiated and unique stages each separated from earlier ones by transitional periods of developmental crises. Because such growth crises are gradual and predictable, they differ from sudden crises such as bereavement or disaster, for which one typically cannot prepare. From a developmental standpoint, effective crisis resolution can expand a person's role repertoire and strengthen his ego by forcing him to learn a new set of adaptations. Successful crisis-coping can also increase a person's confidence in his ability to control his environment and add to his knowledge of himself.

Mental health specialists can play an important role in crisis situations by helping to forestall maladaptive behavior. Because the person in crisis is upset, preoccupied, and has "tunnel vision," he can neither well perceive alternatives nor their potential consequences. If successful crisis resolution depends on the choices people make during brief critical periods, their indecision and susceptibility to influence allow professionals to be very helpful by identifying constructive alternatives.

Even more exciting possibilities, many developmentally oriented, can be envisioned for mental health specialists in crisis work. Since psychological growth can be seen as involving stages of disrupted psychological balance and its subsequent restoration (Cumming & Cumming, 1966; Bower, 1964) why cannot mental health professionals develop controlled crisis-resolution training to help people "exercise their psychological muscles" for restoring balance—a skill which should ultimately serve to improve adjustment? Cumming and Cumming (1966) propose just such a program, that is, giving individuals a series of graded crisis experiences to work through under sheltered conditions that favor a positive outcome. Successful crisis-coping under protected circumstances can provide people with resources and know-how ("psychological mucles") which allow them to handle real-life crises effectively. Cumming and Cumming argue that guided crisis-coping leads to significant growth in ego strength, even for people with limited initial endowments or with histories of severe environmental stress.

"Anticipatory guidance" or "emotional innoculation" (Caplan, 1965) is another approach to training in crisis-coping. This technique can be used for predictable individual stresses or hazardous life circumstances (for example, imminent elective surgery, separation from a parent, starting school). The person is encouraged to anticipate the impending experience and the unpleasant feelings associated with it, vividly. As negative feelings surface a counselor offers support, guidance, consideration of alternatives, and rehearsal of prospective options. In other words, by arousing limited stress under controlled conditions adaptive responses that offer immunity against the impending real stress can be developed. Opportunities to cathart, to express distorted fantasies, and to receive support under psychologically sheltered circumstances are all important aspects of this process.

Early Childhood Focus

Some argue (Smith & Hobbs, 1966) that fully half of *all* our mental health resources (personnel, facilities, etc.) should go to work with children, a sharp departure from past practice. This proposal rests on the key assumptions that childhood is crucial to later development and that children are more flexible and changeable than adults. These assumptions imply that investing professional time and program development for children will yield valuable payoffs—the earlier the investment, the greater the payoff.

We know a fair amount about how prevalent maladjustment is in children. The extensive survey on this topic done by a Task Force of the Joint Commission on Mental Illness and Health in Children (Glidewell & Swallow, 1969) indicated that 30 percent of all elementary school children have school adjustment problems.

And for 10 percent of the school population, such problems are severe enough to require immediate professional help. School adjustment problems are surely plentiful even in the very young.

The next critical question concerns the stability of early detected childhood dysfunction. If it is true both that untreated early problems persist and young children have the potential to change readily, all-out efforts at early intervention are vital. But if most childhood problems resolve themselves, then system-change and intervention are much less necessary. The data on this question are conflicting. The Onondaga County School Studies (1964) found considerable instability in young children's early adjustment problems. Youngsters with difficulties in first grade were not necessarily the same ones who had troubles in third grade. Similarly, one review (Clarizio, 1969b) suggested that the correspondence between childhood and adult dysfunction was at best modest. Clarizio concluded that the evidence that disturbed children become disturbed adults is weak. He argues that only the more extreme child maladjustments persist into adulthood, and that aggressive, antisocial problems are more likely to endure than shy, timid, withdrawn childhood problems.

Beyond these doubts about the persistence of childhood dysfunctions, some have argued that child treatment has had no better outcomes than treatment of adults. The Joint Commission Report (1961) described child treatment as largely ineffective and found little support for the view that it keeps people out of mental hospitals. Although less specific in his attack, Caplan (1964) also suggests that the child guidance movement has failed. He doubts the value of traditional child-intervention approaches. Indeed, he argues that crisis intervention is a more hopeful preventive strategy than treatment, for all age groups. Levitt's surveys of the effectiveness of psychotherapy with children (1957, 1963, 1971) led to pessimistic conclusions, consistent with the position taken by the Joint Commission and Caplan. Although these concerns about the effectiveness of child treatment approaches may be justified, they may point more to the limits of existing methods than the inappropriateness of the target group.

In any case, that is not the whole story. Data from several sources, particularly follow-up studies of children seen in clinics, and studies of the early history of emotionally disturbed adults, suggest another view. The most comprehensive of these is a series of follow-up studies done in St. Louis, Missouri, covering a 30-year span (O'Neal & Robins, 1958a, 1958b; Robins, 1966). These investigators tracked down a sample of 524 people, all above 80 in IQ, who had been evaluated clinically (as children) in the 1920s, as well as a sample of 100 problem-free matched controls. Even though 30 years had passed since the initial evaluations, more than 90 percent of the clinic sample was located. For the combined categories of psychosis, sociopathy, and alcoholism, adult incidence figures for the early "problem" group were very high (about 60 percent)—a figure three times greater than the comparable one of the control group. The data also showed that adult schizophrenics had histories of more pathological, antisocial symptoms, more areas of disturbed function, and more arrests and hospitalizations than did their problem-free controls.

Robins' excellent report (1966) examined the diagnostic category of sociopathic personality in detail. In her study, children who were seen in the clinic did less well than controls on virtually all later criteria of antisocial behavior used. Patients exceeded controls on one key criterion—subsequent history of five or more adult antisocial symptoms—tenfold. The clinic sample also had four times as many "disabling" adult symptoms as controls. The latter included higher arrest rates, poorer job achievement, more instances of hospitalization, more frequent symptoms, greater alienation from friends and relatives, and higher frequency of adult family disruption (divorce, incidence of behavior problems in offspring, use of welfare services, and the like). At least for this patient group, whose childhood antisocial behavior was serious enough to have warranted clinic referral and evaluation, disturbed children *did* turn out to be disturbed adults. Whereas antisocial behavior in childhood predicted adult sociopathy with about 50 percent accuracy, the absence of childhood antisocial behavior virtually assured the absence of adult sociopathy. Robins' (1966) data also suggested that the more severe the childhood dysfunction, the poorer the later adult adjustment.

Another restrospective study (Bower, Shellhamer, & Dailey, 1960) compared the high school records of schizophrenics and nonschizophrenic controls. The schizophrenic group was found to have had poorer school achievement and poorer judged mental health status in high school. Still other studies have also used school records to evaluate the stability of childhood symptoms. Stennett (1965), using screening techniques developed by Bower et al. (Bower, 1965, 1969; Bower & Lambert, 1961), identified nearly 25 percent of a sample of fourth, fifth, and sixth graders as having moderate to severe emotional handicaps. Follow-up of this group, several years later, showed that the vulnerable children did not self-correct; instead, they fell even further behind their peers. Westman, Rice, and Bermann (1967), in a retrospective study spanning 18 years, found a very high correlation (.88) between maladjustment ratings based on direct observation of nursery school children and later use of mental health services and facilities. Again, early difficulties predicted later ones; moreover, later dysfunctions were found to be of the same type as the earlier ones. Studies by Feldhusen, Thurston, and Benning (1969, 1970) similarly showed that children identified as aggressive or disruptive by their sixth- and ninth-grade teachers, were, five years later, achieving significantly less well in school than their nonidentified peers.

A series of research studies done at the University of Rochester (Cowen, 1971; Cowen et al., 1966; Cowen et al., 1975) also deals with this question. These investigators identified first-grade children with school adjustment problems on the basis of a combination of: teacher reports, classroom observation, social work interview with mothers, and group psychological screening. By the end of the third school year, the early detected sample was doing significantly less well than nonidentified peers: in school achievement; on self, peer, and teacher ratings; and on several behavior measures such as attendance and frequency of illness. Follow-up, four years later, at seventh-grade level (Zax et al., 1968) showed that the early detected, vulnerable group continued through the elementary years to do less well educationally than peers. A recent 11–13 year follow-up study (Cowen et al., 1973) established that about twice as many early identified problem children developed noteworthy psychiatric problems as compared to problem-free peers.

A number of these studies support Allinsmith and Goethals' (1962) statement that while some child adjustment problems self-correct, early dysfunction often persists in one or another form. Still the case is not "open and shut." Indeed, contrary findings from some studies suggest that the matter is quite complicated. There is more to be learned about the types of early problems that endure and those that do not. Rather than lumping varied children's problems together under a label "maladjustment," we need to establish specifically how various behaviors, both positive and negative, evolve over time. The safest conclusions to be drawn from existing data are that: (a) some early childhood problems are significant danger signs for the future; (b) severe early dysfunctions are most likely to endure and to have unfortunate later consequences; (c) other things being equal, aggressive, acting-out problems are more likely to persist than problems of shyness or withdrawal and under-socialization.

Both because we cannot say for sure that early pathology definitely predisposes people to later pathology and because past efforts to correct childhood maladjustment have been less than fully successful, an early childhood focus must still be taken, in part, on faith. Doing so rests on: (1) the belief that a person's psychological development depends heavily on important shaping settings and social systems such as home and school; and (2) the fact that it is increasingly difficult for people to change as their life styles become entrenched. In good measure these are the reasons that Smith and Hobbs (1966) recommended that a far greater proportion of mental health budget and resources be allocated to young children.

Consultation

One study in the Joint Commission series (Gurin, Veroff, & Feld, 1960) reported findings about the help-seeking behavior of troubled people that were both eye-opening and deflating to the mental health field. About 25 percent of the respondents in this interview survey indicated that they had at some time felt the need for help with a personal problem. Roughly 15 percent sought such help. Of this number, however, fewer than 20 percent took their problems to mental health professionals. The largest single group of requests for help (42 percent) went to clergymen and the next largest (29 percent) to family physicians. These data are limited to people who both recognized a psychological problem and sought help for it. Still others with equally serious problems do not label them as emotional difficulties for any of a number of reasons. Thus the mandated mental health professions (psychiatry, psychology, and social work) do *not* provide most of the help to people with personal problems. This fact raises several challenging questions about how most psychological problems actually do get resolved and what mental health professionals might do to increase the effectiveness of this process.

Virtually everyone at some time experiences stress, adjustment difficulties, or psychological problems. For many fortunately, their social ties, provide outlets for dealing with such problems. Most people are close enough to family, friends, neighbors, or coworkers to allow them to resolve difficulties in everyday living by talking to others before their problems become entrenched. The majority of people know exactly where to turn to find comfort or wisdom in the face of adversity. Such natural contact lines are often effective precisely *because* they are accessible and comfortable. This is a socially valuable first line of defense for resolving problems promptly. Fortunately, many people are effective as informal helpers because of their experiences and sensitivity rather than as a result of specific professional training. If everyone had such help available in their everyday environments, we might not need large numbers of mental health specialists.

That, however, is not always the case. Some people just do not have good helpers to turn to, and the problems that others take to would-be helpers are simply "too hot to handle." In such cases the troubled individual may seek help from other professionals—but not necessarily mental health professionals. All communities have professionals (physicians, lawyers, clergymen, or educators) whose jobs bring them into close trusting contacts with people. Lindemann (1944) and Caplan (1964) call such agents *caregivers*, reflecting the fact that they often promote personal well-being and help people to resolve problems. Caregivers are an important social force in the fight against human distress. They get into this position, sometimes involuntarily, either because people respect and trust them or because they are the only ones around to help a person with problems.

Other troubled people who lack contact even with caregivers follow still a different route in trying to find peace. Many people with *no* mental health background or training whatsoever nevertheless have daily contacts with people that expose them to others' distress. Policemen, welfare workers, cab drivers, hairdressers and barbers, truant officers, bartenders, and shop owners are all good examples. Kelly (1964) used the term *urban agents* to designate these people, noting that they play different roles at different social strata. People's

contacts with urban agents are usually neither planned nor formal, but the urban agent is in an especially good position to provide *immediate* support or counsel. Such support at critical moments can forestall the need for formal help. Too, an urban agent who knows his community can refer troubled individuals promptly to existing helping resources. Thus, the urban agent can be a significant frontline mediator between the distressed individual and the community's formal helping structures.

There are important differences between caregivers and urban agents. Caregivers are professionals even though their primary training is not in mental health. Urban agents are not professionals. Because professional education in many fields today recognizes the complex role of emotional factors in diverse areas of human function, physicians, teachers, and clergymen are more likely than ever before to have had exposure to mental health concepts. Also caregivers, as contrasted with urban agents, represent specific professional groups whose recognized competencies in other fields identify them as people who *might* also be able to offer effective help with psychological problems.

Only for a very few types of urban agents (for example, welfare and enforcement agents) can it be said beforehand that they will almost surely have contact with people in personal distress. Most other urban agents simply stumble across problems. Because a storekeeper, bartender, or hairdresser has frequent and prolonged contacts with people, he is in a position to hear about their problems. His job makes it possible for this to happen, without guaranteeing it. Hence, only a small fraction of prospective urban agents, possibly those with special sensitivity and responsiveness, take on significant helping roles. Urban agents are, thus, less identifi-

A friendly bartender can be a help-agent to someone experiencing personal distress.

able and accessible to mental health planners and administrators than caregivers. Whereas in area X a friendly bartender or cab driver may assume this role, in area Y it may be the beautician or druggist.

Some are concerned that teachers and physicians, much less police officers and welfare agents, are not well enough trained in mental health to be trusted with fragile human psyches. That argument misses the point. Today's reality is that there are not enough professionals around to meet the need for help. Even if there were, many people still cannot accept the fact that their problems are psychological, or they will not take them to mental health professionals. To say smugly that this state of affairs is "bad" simply denies reality. The mental health professions will use their person-resources best by joining, rather than repressing, reality. That means developing approaches that strengthen the hand of those who inevitably have frontline involvement with emotional distress. This is an exciting opportunity for mental health consultation.

Society has become increasingly sophisticated about the nature, and potential impact, of mental health problems. The media pay more attention to this area today than ever before. Courses in mental health are not uncommon in high school; indeed, some are found at the elementary level. Even so, caregivers are not *primarily* trained in mental health and urban agents have even less of such training. The preparation such people have for their life's work focuses on topics largely unrelated to people's psychological functioning. But, psychological problems often are not presented in ways that respect the preparation and training of the person whose help is being sought. More often, the urgency a person feels and his sense of comfort with a prospective helper govern when, and how, his problems are raised. That is why caregivers and urban agents inevitably become enmeshed in the people's personal problems. What they do from that point on reflects their mental health attitudes, prior background and experience, individual styles and personalities. For better or worse, caregivers have influenced, and will continue to influence, many people's emotional well-being. In some ways they are in a better position to be helpful than professionals. They often encounter dysfunction earlier, under less artificial circumstances, and in more trusting, confidence-breeding atmospheres. None of these factors should be dismissed lightly. Each can add to the effectiveness of prospective helpers.

Mental health consultation is an approach born of realism. It rests on several current mental health assumptions: (a) resources are insufficient to meet needs; (b) early intervention promises more positive outcomes than late intervention; (c) it is better to build health-promoting structures than to fight entrenched disorder; (d) psychological problems are interwoven with other complex problems of living; and (e) many such problems are brought to people who are not trained to deal with them. Consultation methods well illustrate how changing times and changing conceptions of psychological problems generate new approaches.

Basically, consultation is a process whereby mental health professionals try to help less knowledgeable contact persons to deal with psychological problems (Haylett & Rapoport, 1964). Since much has been written about consultation (Altrocchi, 1972; Caplan, 1964, 1970; Kern, 1969; Mann, 1973; Mannino, MacLennan & Shore, 1975; Schwab, 1968; Zusman & Davidson, 1972), its core aims can be readily identified. These include: providing information, suggesting alternatives in situations that go beyond the backgrounds and competencies of consultees, extending awareness of mental health factors in situations that the consultee experiences in his everyday work, and developing a relationship that helps the consultee to deal more securely and effectively with the mental health problems he encounters.

Consultation is a broad, generic term. The approach has varied objectives and proceeds differently depending on a consultee's needs. Consultation can take place in individual and group forms. It can deal with clinical case material, program elements, or administrative issues. It can emphasize either client problems or the consultee's problems in working with them (Haylett & Rapoport, 1964). But whatever its specifics, a basic aim of consultation is to share the mental health professional's knowledge and expertise and, thus, to increase his impact.

Mental health consultation has broad potential. Its prospectively wide reach is attractive at a time when the need to expand services is great. For example, consulting with a group of 10–12 pediatricians about the psychological problems of their everyday practice could potentially benefit thousands of people. Pediatricians are particularly influential caregivers. They interact with children and families during crises. They have extensive contact with individuals and community organizations that set child-care policy. They often occupy important community positions that enable them to shape administrative, social, and legislative action about children's services.

Other exciting examples of consultation's potential can be cited. Sarason and Ganzer (1969) describe the use of social reinforcement techniques for modifying behavior, noting that this approach can be easily learned and applied even by people with limited backgrounds. They propose a set of consultative roles for mental health professionals working within a behavior modification framework, including: training, serving as resource people, and helping to identify problems and to develop ways for modifying socially maladaptive behavior. Behavioral engineering approaches have much potential. As Sarason and Ganzer note, 10 teachers trained in behavior modification could positively affect the development of 300 youngsters annually.

In addition to expanding mental health's scope, consultation can reach dysfunction early and in settings that encourage effective intervention. Crisis intervention could, for example, be strengthened by effective consultation since many good opportunities for crisis-coping arise through contacts with caregivers and urban agents (Singh, Tarnower, & Chen, 1971).

Another facet of consultation bears mention. One report in the Joint Commission series (Robinson, DeMarche, & Wagle, 1961) indicates that major sections of this country (for example, rural areas, small urban centers, and geographically isolated regions with low population density) lack mental health personnel and services. People who live in such areas find mental health facilities either totally unavailable or so hard to get to that they are not considered as sources of help. But the people still need help and the task of providing it falls, by default, to caregivers such as physicians, nurses, clergymen, and educators. In such areas consultation can support well-intentioned people who must deal each day with pressing problems that strain their limited mental health backgrounds. Many caregivers who are involuntarily placed in such roles thirst for help, and even a small amount of consultation can be extremely valuable to them. There have been growing numbers of reports recently of effective consultation programs in areas lacking mental health (Griffith & Libo, 1968; Huessy, 1966; Kiesler, 1969; Spielberger, 1967).

Thus far the discussion of mental health consultation has been based on a traditional view of its purposes. This stresses expanding services by strengthening the hand of those who deal with problems, producing new kinds of help-agents, and bringing mental health knowledge to underdeveloped regions. Another valuable application of consultation can be noted. Consultation can play a role in carrying out our earlier suggestion that some of mental health's effort should be redirected toward engineering social environments that favor sound psychological development and prevent dysfunction. To do this we need consultants who can advise people about social environments, how they relate to psychological development, and how they can be modified. Kelly (1970) and Trickett et al. (1971) call for consultation that stresses the interactions between people and the characteristics of their environment as a stepping stone to

truly preventive programs. They argue, for example, that tomorrow's most exciting opportunities for school mental health professionals lie in social system analysis and modification rather than in direct child services. Much the same can be said for mental health professionals working in courts, prisons, and other influential community agencies. An even more striking challenge is for mental health professionals to become involved in planning and engineering new communities.

NONPROFESSIONALS AND PROFESSIONALS: FUTURE DIRECTIONS

A dominant theme in this chapter is that evolving mental health programs require new manpower sources and new uses of current manpower. The need for new mental health manpower is dictated by more than the obvious fact of current professional manpower shortages. The very nature of some emergent programs *demands* innovative manpower use. There are also circumstances in which mental health services can be provided better by nonprofessionals than by professionals. Although there have been numerous accounts of the use of nonprofessionals in mental health in recent years (Arnhoff, Rubenstein, & Speisman, 1969; Cowen, 1967; Ewalt, 1967; Gartner, 1971; Grosser, Henry, & Kelly, 1969; Guerney, 1969; Harris, 1966; Reiff & Riesman, 1965; Sobey, 1970), it is still worth considering some characteristics of this development, and some issues that it raises.

The Early Use of Nonprofessionals

Among the first programs involving nonprofessionals in mental health roles were those using college undergraduates as volunteers in mental hospitals (Holzberg, 1963; Holzberg, Knapp, & Turner, 1967; Umbarger et al., 1962). The joint Harvard University-Metropolitan State Hospital program is an early example. In the seven years between that program's start and the time it was written up (Umbarger et al., 1962) more than 2000 student volunteers took part in a variety of patient services. These included companionship programs on adult and children's wards, ward-improvement programs, working as case aides, and working in specialty area programs such as teaching music or foreign languages. Greenblatt and Kantor, in the introduction to Umbarger et al.'s volume (1962), reason that the students' commitment, interest, and enthusiasm were factors that brought about positive change in patients, and they speculate that students may be more effective change-agents than traditional hospital personnel, including professional staff.

Another influential hospital program, starting in 1958, was the Connecticut Valley State Hospital Companion Program (Holzberg, 1963; Holzberg et al., 1967). This project extended the earlier Harvard program by including a formal evaluation of program effects both for patients and student volunteers. The following quote reflects the group's view about program effects:

The relationship (between student and patient) has had many beneficial consequences for both. The patient seems to borrow some of the optimism and courage of his companion and the companion gains wisdom and charity that is personally enlarging. Above and beyond this, it has opened another channel of communication between the hospital and its patients and the outside community. [Holzberg et al., 1967, p. 108]

Whereas there were only a few pioneering student volunteer programs in the mid-1950s, current surveys indicate that there are now such programs in nearly 1000 colleges and universities and perhaps as many clinical settings. Although student volunteer programs were originally justified on logical or impressionistic grounds, recent efforts have been made to evaluate them objectively (for example, Rappaport, Chinsky, & Cowen, 1971). The pressing need to help chronic patients and the fact that patients, students, and hospitals all seem to be helped by these programs are the vital factors in their multiplying.

Rioch and her coworkers (Rioch 1967; Rioch, Elkes, & Flint, 1965; Rioch et al., 1963) describe a very different, though conceptually related, program using nonprofessionals as mental health workers. That project, beginning in 1960 in response to social need, trained housewives as psychotherapists. The program was based on two assumptions: (1) that all communities have large pools of untapped talent including housewives who have much to offer as interpersonal helpers; and (2) that personal experience is as important to one's helping potential as is the traditional training and preparation of mental health professionals. Hence, Rioch et al. recruited a pilot group of middle-aged housewives and gave them broad training, considerable support and supervision, and lots of practical experience to prepare them as therapists. After training, the women were placed in schools, out-patient clinics, and mental hospitals, where they served in responsible positions. Evaluation of their job performance by outside observers showed that they had acquired good clinical proficiency. In fact, their scores on the Psychiatric Board Examination indicated that they had assimilated as much knowledge as beginning psychiatrists. Magoon,

Golann, & Freeman (1969) reported a follow-up evaluation of the initial housewife-trainee group, three years later. They collected data from employers, supervisors, coworkers, and from the women themselves. Not only did they find that the women had continued to work for three years after training ended, but all evaluation sources agreed that they had done a very effective job in roles once thought to be exclusively professional.

Rioch's decision to train women as psychotherapists reflected a value judgment about the importance of that role. The pilot project's most important contribution, however, was to show that nonprofessionals can do well at mental health jobs previously regarded as professionally sacrosanct. Rioch's program attracted much attention and stimulated other groups to train housewives and other helper groups for a variety of mental health activities.

Although the move to nonprofessionalism is not yet firmly grounded in research, several studies offer food for thought. Poser (1966), for example, compared the effectiveness of experienced mental health professionals and untrained female undergraduates as leaders of groups of chronic male schizophrenics, hospitalized for an average of 14 years. Poser's design included three matched groups involving nearly 350 chronic patients: those led by naive, 18-year-old coeds; those led by mental health professionals; and no-treatment controls. Treatment subgroups in the two active conditions each included ten patients, seen for an hour, five times a week, for five months. Group leaders were free to do whatever they wanted in trying to foster patient interaction.

A comprehensive pre-post battery including perceptual, verbal, and psychomotor tests was given to all patients to assess program effects. Treated patients as a group improved more than controls. Surprisingly, patients seen by *students* improved significantly more than those seen by professional therapists. While Poser's design has limitations, for example, using tests rather than behavioral criteria such as discharge rates, and the fact that student leaders happened incidentally to be attractive young females, his findings offer little support for the view that mental health professionals have special expertise in treating chronic disordered behavior. In this study variables other than formal training seemingly led to positive changes in patients. That these "other" variables may have included the charm or sex-appeal of an 18-year-old coed is not the point. The fact is that highly change-resistant, "sick" patients improved—an improvement that was maintained in a small subgroup followed-up for three years. Although Poser's data have limited generalizability, similar findings have been reported by other investigators (Carkhuff & Truax, 1965a, 1965b; Rappaport, Chinsky, & Cowen, 1971). Even if his study shows nothing more than the fact that nonprofessionals, under very special conditions, can bring about a better adaptation in chronic schizophrenics, it still makes an important contribution. Whatever the limits of Poser's work, it argues for the need to explore further the effectiveness of nonprofessionals as change agents, with different target groups and in a variety of settings.

Current Nonprofessional Roles

The nonprofessional thrust in mental health is now quite diverse with respect to who the helpers are, the groups they serve, what they do, and where. The interest and enthusiasm that the movement generated led to active exploration of new ways of delivering mental health service. The following section highlights the scope and complexity of this development.

A wide range of nonprofessional groups has been used in mental health roles (Cowen, 1967; Gartner, 1971; Sobey, 1970). Workers have varied markedly in background and education, age, socioeconomic status, and social position. Mental health programs have been reported using college, high school, and elementary students as help-agents, as well as housewives, indigenous neighborhood workers, retired people, offenders and delinquents, hospital attendants, parents, teachers, and welfare or enforcement workers. Helpees have been equally varied. They range from institutionalized mental patients, to clinic, agency, or court clientele, schoolchildren, inner-city residents, and women seen in pregnancy or well-baby clinics.

A decision to use nonprofessionals often reflects a willingness to accept experiential and life-style variables as substitutes for extensive formal training. In practice, the amount of training given to nonprofessionals in various programs has ranged from none to nearly two years (Rioch, 1967). Factors that govern the type of training provided include: the trainers' biases, the roles envisioned for the worker, and how agency and client needs are seen. Some programs using nonprofessionals rely largely on a committed human relationship, some stress a segment of professional training (as, for example, psychotherapy), some depend on workers' styles and their know-how in providing a range of helping services, and some call for specific training to be applied in specific ways. The latter is well illustrated in various behavior modification programs using nonprofessionals.

Some observers (Albee, 1969a; Arnhoff, Rubenstein, & Speisman, 1969; Reiff, 1967) warn that merely to generate an army of nonprofessionals is less important than how they are used. Expansion, they feel, should be a product, rather than a shaper, of conceptualization. Arnhoff, Jenkins, and Speisman (1969) report that the most typical use of nonprofessionals has been in a "technical, assisting relationship to traditional mental health professionals . . ." (p. 149). Such usage breaks up the professional's job and trains relatively unskilled people to carry out the less demanding professional roles. Theoretically, this should allow professionals to spend more time doing the demanding ones. However, if the activities themselves are ineffective, it would serve little purpose to train 100,000 more people to do them. Merely providing overburdened professionals with relief so they can drop low-prestige traditional roles would hardly resolve today's pressing mental health problems. Indeed, the most exciting potentials of nonprofessionals may be realized in the new, preventive roles that they can assume, or in the extent to which the development permits professionals to take a new look at mental health problems through new conceptualization, program development, and research.

The use of indigenous nonprofessionals (Reiff & Riessman, 1965) illustrates an innovative approach that does something beyond breaking up a job and extending existing professional roles. The role's significance lies in the fact that the poor do not typically define their problems psychologically and feel alienated from typical mental health services. There has been little common ground between mental health professionals and the poor. Consequently there are few entry points for those professionals who wish to deal with problems of ineffectiveness in the ghetto. The indigenous nonprofessional *is* an inner-city person. He has been there. His language,

Robert Reiff was innovative in the use of nonprofessionals in the mental health field.

Debits and Credits of Nonprofessionals

The groping, trial-and-error nature of new manpower uses in mental health cannot be overemphasized. Although the development arose out of social need, it has lacked a sound empirical base. We do not know how effective nonprofessionals really can be; which personality, attitude, and experience variables make for successful functioning; how best to train them; or how optimally to match helpers, target groups, functions, and settings. As experience with such programs increases, we get a clearer picture of their problems and of the most helpful program elements (Cowen, 1967; Gartner, 1971; Goldberg, 1969; Grosser et al., 1969). But because the people behind the development of many of these programs are often highly committed and involved, impartial evaluation is difficult. Right now it can certainly be seen as a logical development, but one that still has not taken final form.

Nonprofessional programs often create administrative headaches. Many of them carve out new roles that lack prior precedent. That can cause complex, burdensome problems in: overhauling tables of organization, finding advancement opportunities and career ladders, and locating permanent budget. Pursuing such issues can create political or personal problems and challenge vested interests. Indeed, more than a few well conceived and executed nonprofessional programs have succumbed to such mundane, nonacademic hazards. Because some programs that have used nonprofessionals have had brief existences, some trainers have felt that training programs should be general enough to allow for easy role shifts if insurmountable practical problems force specific programs to close down.

approach, way of operating, and life style are all very much like those of the people he serves. He can handle concrete problems as they arise. He can communicate easily with his fellows and win their trust. He is, thus, an ideal bridge between the mental health professional and the community. He is not limited to, or burdened by, the ways of the professional. He can provide individual services or promote community action and can help powerless people develop a sense of being able to do something about their own destinies. The use of indigenous nonprofessionals in the inner-city extends the reach of helping services where they are badly needed and makes it possible to deal with problems in the contexts in which they occur. These are innovative new roles rather than mere extensions of established professional ones.

Resistances to programs using nonprofessionals are considerable. These may come from consumers fearful of getting "second-best" from a nonprofessional or from professionals who are afraid that nonprofessionals may replace them. Professional concerns are often stated in terms of the nonprofessional's alleged lack of background and qualifications and the possibility that they may seriously harm the people they see. But given the magnitude of today's mental health problems, we are in greater social jeopardy from what has *not* been done, than from what *has* been or might be done. Although nonprofessionals, like professionals, will surely make mistakes, the fact remains that mental health has so far failed more by omission than by commission.

Although, admittedly, problems in the use of nonprofessionals as mental health workers remain, direct observation and some research show that in many cases they help the people they serve. That nonprofessional programs "work" has made people wonder about why, and how, this happens. Just as the programs and their objectives vary, so do the explanations of their success. "Know-how," "style-match," and having shared similar experiences, as noted above, have all been cited as specific factors that contribute to the indigenous nonprofessional's success (Reiff & Riessman, 1965). Capitalizing on shared experience to win acceptance is not restricted to work in the inner-city. Other helping approaches, such as Recovery, Inc., for ex-hospital patients, Synanon for drug addicts, and AA for alcoholics, rest on a similar concept. In all these programs the fact that the helper has had experiences that relate closely to the helpee may place him in a better position to understand those he serves. The helping program is built around, and harnesses, this factor.

Such characteristics as involvement, enthusiasm, and dedication have also been cited (Cowen, 1967; Gartner, 1971) to explain the success of programs using nonprofessionals. These attributes are especially important in drab, pessimistic institutional settings such as state hospitals where few people dare hope that patients will get better. Since patient disorders in such settings are often difficult to treat, and there is a history of low cure-rates, many staff members often seek primarily to maintain patients and to avoid upsetting incidents. An enthusiastic nonprofessional in such a setting can be both a model for patients and a link to an exciting world with which they have lost touch. The nonprofessional is, so to speak, a breath of fresh air in an otherwise stagnant atmosphere.

Related to the "enthusiasm" hypothesis is the fact that nonprofessionals often approach helping situations with more optimistic "expectancies" than professionals. They see mental hospital patients as people rather than as incurably sick objects; they may even expect to be answered when they speak to a patient. While positive expectancies alone are not enough to draw *all* patients into social interaction, some patients may indeed be positively influenced by the expectations of a committed outsider. To the extent that nonprofessionals anticipate "normal" behavior in patients, a force exists to encourage such behavior.

Nonprofessionals do not always share the "certainties" that professionals often have about how distressed people are helped. Most professionals operate according to fixed ground rules that govern helper-patient interactions, even though it is not clearly established that these actions are the most effective ones. Nonprofessionals engage more in trial-and-error behavior. For whatever reason, they often do things in new, different ways and, in the process, help to expand techniques of effective intervention. For example, a housewife-aide may happily sew a button on a schoolchild's shirt or an indigenous nonprofessional may talk to his client on the street, at home, or at a bar. Professionals are hesitant about such contacts, viewing them as unprofessional, improper, or perhaps even dangerous. But in full candor, we are still a long way from understanding clearly which actions and behaviors genuinely help people in distress. Indeed, most of the things we have tried out are biased in that they are restricted by professional "do's and don't's." Our knowledge about right and wrong interventions stands to increase from the flexible exploration that nonprofessionals bring to human interactions.

The social distance hypothesis is another way of explaining how nonprofessionals help people (Cowen, 1967; Rioch, 1966). Many who need help but who see themselves as social underdogs or victims may find it easier to talk to people whom they see as closer to themselves in the social hierarchy. Such groups include inner-city residents, schoolchildren, and hospital patients. To be sure the social distance hypothesis applies only to some people. Others, doubtlessly, are better helped by a person respected as having status and authority.

Beyond the value of any specific program, the nonprofessional development has broad social potential. It extends the scope of human services to the formerly unreached. It can free professionals to do badly needed new jobs. Some nonprofessional programs can help resolve more than one social problem at the same time. This is the case when the helper himself is victimized by a personal or social problem.

As a simple example, many middle-class housewives feel noncontributory because they have too much leisure time. For such women, getting involved in meaningful human service has the dual value of helping the target persons and creating a personal sense of meaningfulness in them. Even clearer examples are the teenager who is on his way toward becoming a chronic social problem, or the retired person who is ignored by those around him and whose main goal may simply be to avoid being burdensome to others. Using such persons effectively in human service work can both reduce their problems and those of the people they serve. Riessman (1965) calls this the helper-therapy principle. He asserts that being genuinely helpful to a person in distress is among the most therapeutic experiences that a human being can have.

The Changing Professional

An important challenge for professionals is to find new approaches to problems of disordered behavior. Some of these approaches will call for nonprofessional help-agents. In such programs, professionals will have the important job of identifying, recruiting, and training the nonprofessionals and monitoring their work to maximize program effectiveness. The professional will also become a consultant, a supervisor, and a resource person. He will also serve as the liaison person with host agencies and do administrative, organizational, and, perhaps, political work that good programs may need to survive.

Some professionals find new nonprofessional programs threatening. They fear that service will deteriorate, that people may be harmed, or that professional responsibility will be bypassed. But even widespread use of nonprofessionals should not abridge professional responsibility, though it could well change professional roles along the lines specified. For example, a typical school mental health professional who treats three children a week, can, in the same amount of time, train and supervise five nonprofessionals. They, in turn, may see 50 children per week and thereby increase his social impact manyfold.

Newly evolving professional roles surely present problems. They remain poorly defined and, because the professional's service involvement is indirect, the consequences of his actions are less observable. Moreover, the fact that professionals have had little prior academic training or experience to prepare them for the necessary new roles also presents problems. It is, therefore, important to develop model programs that explore new prevention approaches and to modify training to equip professionals better to carry out needed new functions (Goldston, 1965; Iscoe & Spielberger, 1970). It will surely take time to change past rooted ways of professional function.

SOME PROBLEMS OF PREVENTION

This chapter began by reviewing classic uses of the term "prevention" in mental health. Limits in past usage and some of the semantic problems it creates were identified. This led to a proposal that primary and early secondary prevention be viewed as the core of prevention in mental health, since most secondary, and all tertiary, prevention are restorative rather than truly preventive. Throughout, we have argued that the best approach to disordered behavior is to forestall it in the first place.

An objective reader could, justifiably, say that this chapter glorifies prevention.

It would be misleading to end the discussion without identifying some weak spots in the pure prevention view. The concept of prevention in mental health, much less its defining operations, is still murky. Professionals neither fully understand nor agree upon its objectives nor on how to reach them. While a broad outline of primary prevention can be sketched, its details and the specific roles it implies for professionals remain vague. So, one must justify prevention on the basis of logic and theory, reaction to the shortcomings of past approaches, and faith. The present transitional era is exciting for its new discoveries and its potential, but the danger exists that one set of faiths may be "horse-traded" for another. We are still without the hard empirical data needed to justify prevention.

Many who have thought seriously about current mental health problems and future needs are so awed by their enormity as to react with pessimism and defeatism. Clearly, we still lack good cookbooks for setting up preventive programs. This is threatening to professionals (and others) who need immediate, direct verification of relationships between their activities and patient outcomes. Developing sound preventive programs will surely require much trial and error and bold exploration. Professionals with set ways who are threatened by a shift from known activities that have been rewarding in the past do not find this an attractive prospect.

Some future-oriented prevention programs are likely to require at least a generation from the time they are designed and set up to evaluation. This poses problems. It means that the professional's helping activities will be much less direct than in the past. He will have to give up the chance to see personally the immediate effects of *his* words, *his* behaviors, and *his* interventions in reducing another person's distress. These are the satisfactions that often stimulate many people to go into mental health careers in the first place. Also the fact that prevention is targeted to the future well-being of groups and communities detracts from its allure. In the past, both professionals and laymen have been concerned with immediate, visible distress. The more serious the disorder, the more bizarre the behavior, the stronger the need to correct it *now*. The fact that a presently nontroublesome, perhaps even hardly observable, symptom *might* indicate that a full-blown schizophrenic reaction could occur years from now could easily be ignored. And, because mental health's goal has long been to contain or reverse evident problems, that is where mental health money and resources have gone. The deep roots of this orientation discourage administrators, legislators, fund-granting organizations, professionals, and the lay public from mounting preventive programs.

Moral arguments against prevention have also been raised. Some critics see prevention as intrusive, meddling, invading human privacy, or even as shaping

people in the image of Orwell's *1984* (Bower, 1965). Recent controversy over sex education or the appropriateness of certain books in the schools are examples of this. Both Bower (1965) and Eisenberg (1962) remind us, however, that society makes many decisions about "common good"—for example, mandatory education. Both argue that it is not only defensible but necessary that valid knowledge about human well-being be applied. Eisenberg draws an analogy between prevention in mental health and certain environmental health interventions—water fluoridation, innoculation for polio and smallpox, and the like. Past discussions of moral and ethical issues in mental health fail to stress sufficiently that as long as people live in environments with psychological consequences and interact with each other, the way those environments are set up will inevitably shape those who are exposed to them. In other words, some values always *do* and *will* affect others. The main choice is whether behavior shall be shaped randomly by human values or by values based on knowledge of the effects of certain forces on human development and well-being.

SUMMARY

1. Prevention can be divided into primary, secondary, and tertiary types. Because primary and early secondary prevention provide genuine alternatives to the medical model, they are more clearly preventive approaches. Tertiary and late secondary prevention are in keeping with traditional mental health approaches.

2. One primary preventive approach (the system-centered approach) is concerned with creating environments that facilitate adaptation provide coping skills, and, hence, optimize development. This approach calls for much work, in many settings, to identify factors that support good sound growth and development.

3. System-oriented prevention studies are being done in institutions, schools, the family, and the like.

4. People-centered approaches are the second major group of preventive possibilities. Such approaches seek to build competencies and strengths in individuals, as innoculations against future problems. These approaches include: a focus on people in crisis, young children, and consultation with community caregivers who are in a position to help others experiencing adaptive problems.

5. Crises, brief transitional periods of acute disturbance, require adaptations that can centrally affect a person's well-being. While crises can endanger adjustment, they also offer opportunities for building inner strengths to bolster resistance against the ravages of future upset. Some crises occur randomly; others occur developmentally and are predictable. Both types can benefit from suitable intervention.

6. We still lack clear evidence that child maladjustment necessarily relates to adult maladjustment, though for some types of early conditions this is very likely. For this reason an early childhood focus is still, in part, an act of faith, justified mostly by the knowledge that is easier for younger people to change than older ones.

7. The need for mental health consultation stems in part from the realization that most people with emotional problems turn to other than mental health professionals for help. Such help is sought from *caregivers*, professionals in fields other than the mental health whose work brings them in regular contact with people in distress. Clergymen, physicians, lawyers, and educators are examples of caregivers.

8. Many distressed people turn informally to *urban agents*—policemen, hairdressers, bartenders, and the like—for assistance.

9. Mental health consultation with caregivers and urban agents accepts reality. It seeks to upgrade the skills of individuals who, in the normal discharge of their everyday functions, are called on to help others with personal problems.

10. Many new preventive programs rely heavily on nonprofessionals both for needed manpower and to gain entry to groups normally unwilling to approach traditional helping agencies.

11. Nonprofessionals have been shown to function effectively as: (a) companions and therapists to mental patients; (b) outpatient therapists; and (c) indigenous workers in a variety of settings.

12. There are many problems involved in using nonprofessionals, as, for example, how effectively they can function. Using nonprofessionals often creates administrative problems in traditional settings and both consumers and other professionals may resist using them.

13. But nonprofessionals also offer many advantages. The indigenous nonprofessional, having had similar life experiences to those he works with, can better understand and communicate with his helpees. Nonprofessionals may often be enthusiastic and optimistic about chances for helping patient groups on which jaded professionals have given up. The nonprofessional can approach problems flexibly in ways that are not

possible for tradition-ridden professionals. And some nonprofessionals may themselves be helped by being placed in a helping role.

14. Preventive approaches call for a change in the professional roles, giving up some direct service in favor of recruiting, training, and supervising those who give direct service. Such new roles will create problems since few professionals have yet been trained to assume them.

15. The concept of prevention is still far from clear; hence, its value must be justified, at least in part, on faith.

CHAPTER 18

Programs in Action:
I. The Schools

Contemporary society is shocked by awareness of serious social and adaptive problems: explosive inner-city riots, antisocial acting-out in high school dropouts, teenage drug addicts, the appalling conditions of many of our institutions, and the bombing of public buildings. Today, such events are "close to home" thanks to the drama of prompt public media reports. Reactions to such frightening unrest range from a repressive "law and order" cry to a super-humanitarian surge toward developing crash programs to wipe out specific social blights. However well motivated these programs are, they suffer from being drastic, crisis-born counter-measures rather than well-planned, long-term approaches.

Crash programs for "overwhelming" a problem start with several strikes against them because the conditions they seek to overcome are already entrenched and basic to people's adaptive styles. Even if that were not so, programs to deal with a specific problem such as addiction rest on the shaky assumption that the condition has *specific* determinants and can be treated by *specific* interventions. That assumption ignores the more likely possibility that a given adverse set of personal/social conditions can result in many different kinds of maladaptations. If so, effective early identification and prevention could reduce the occurrence of many of the disorders that comprise abnormal psychology. Such a view demands that we look carefully at the primary institutions and social settings that shape human development. We should think about designing environments that help most people to adapt. And we should find ways to use social settings to identify and deal more effectively with dysfunction.

The view that mental health should direct more of its effort to prevention has implications for what abnormal psychology texts should include. In the past such volumes have always been built around negative "end-states" (psychosis, neurosis, antisocial personality, addiction, and the like). A preventive orientation dictates that emphasis be placed on the social institutions and settings that shape behavior in the first place. Home and school, therefore, become as important foci as paranoid schizophrenia, anxiety neurosis, or addiction.

This chapter and the next illustrate how a "settings" approach can forestall disordered behavior. Several evolving programs in the schools and the inner-city are described, both to "model" the alternate approach and to apprise the reader of important current developments. The schools and the inner-city are chosen as the proving grounds for this approach for several reasons. Each area affects many people, reflects pressing social problems, and has attracted much recent interest. Keep in mind, though, that the same approach can profitably be extended to other areas and settings. Service agencies such as pregnancy and well-baby clinics or child-care centers are specific examples. The planning of new communities is a much broader one.

There is a sharp gap between abstractions about *ideal* conceptual models in mental health and actual programs-in-action. Conceptual blueprints can be drawn up without worrying too much about life's realities. Getting a live program going, however, is another story. Such programs must meet visible service needs and will be constrained by political, budgetary, manpower, and resource factors. Hence, even the more pioneering, imaginative emergent mental health programs are narrower in scope, more oriented to individuals "at risk," and less system-directed than

a theoretical "ideal" (Glasscote & Fishman, 1974). This discrepancy between theory and fact reflects two obvious points. First, concrete programs cannot ignore the realities of their surrounding world or the needs and pressures of the settings in which they unfold. Second, shifting from known, tried approaches to disorder to theoretically sound, but ill-charted, new ones will at best be a slow process.

Emergent programs, reported in the following pages, are thus not more than a "baby-step" away from the classically defined medical model. More basic preventive steps, such as those designed to engineer "total" educational environments to optimize the child's educational and personal development, are conceivable and have, in fact, been attempted. Whether or not, for example, one agrees with the thrust or efficacy of the Summerhill experiment (Neill, 1960), it is a serious attempt to create an educational environment with such objectives.

THE DEVELOPMENT OF PROBLEMS IN SCHOOLS

If a child does not make minimal educational progress, or if, in trying to do so, he violates the behavioral standards established by the school or his teachers, he is seen as a school-adjustment problem. Children may be seen as having adjustment problems either because of unfortunate prior life experiences or because they lack the skills needed to cope with the school's social and educational demands. Although mental health specialists tend to think first about how emotional problems cause educational failure, the opposite also happens. Thus, reasonably well-adjusted children who fail, for whatever reason, to learn can easily develop psychological problems.

Such children may be ridiculed by peers, teachers and family, feel anxious and self-doubting, and see themselves as personally inadequate. As educational problems become more chronic and apparent to others, such feelings may lead to more serious adjustment difficulties. Hence, there is an evident reciprocity between educational and psychological problems; early educational failings can cause psychological problems, just as psychological difficulties can disrupt the learning process.

Most maladjusted school behaviors are relatively minor. The teacher can handle many of these with her everyday repertoire of classroom management skills. Remarks such as: "Johnny, stay in your seat!", "Mary, when the 'Robins' read, you must join them", or "We don't throw things in class," are typical examples of teacher handlings. Most teachers expect that such minor problems will occur and have routine practices for dealing with them. Indeed, some (Glidewell & Swallow, 1969) note that because teachers expect "misbehavior" and "limit-testing" when children start school, many see the first school year as a "honeymoon" period. Considerable latitude is permitted and only mild rebukes are made for objectionable behavior. However, as "misbehaviors" accumulate, or get more extreme, as they interfere with class objectives, and as they block the child's normal educational development, the teacher comes to see the situation as one which requires "outside" help.

Like anyone else, teachers have different tolerance levels, personality styles, and ways of dealing with children's behavior. Also, schools have different resources for dealing with "problem" children. Hence, there are few automatic rules about when, and from whom, help for children's school adjustment problems will be requested. When a decision is reached that outside help is needed, various helping resources, each more "drastic" than direct classroom handling, can be sought. If a teacher, for example, felt that the child's problems stemmed from a poor home situation, she might contact the parents hoping that they could help to eliminate the maladaptive behavior. The teacher's concern is less with the means than the fact that Johnny shape up in class. A teacher may also seek help for a difficult child within the school. There, the principal, the school psychologist (Fein, 1974), or social worker can be called on. So, identifying and communicating about a problem is often a first step in formally labeling a child as "trouble."

If the actions of any one, or combination, of these agents fail and the child continues to adapt poorly in class, a further level of labeling and action can occur. It may be assumed that since the child cannot be influenced by important people to "shape up," environmental change is needed. Often, by then, many people have given up on the child and even though environmental change is tried, it is done largely for the sake of feeling that, "We tried." The child may be moved to another class in the same school in the hope that he will, miraculously, do better with a new teacher and classmates. Or he may be transferred to a new school with the hope that this will let him get off to a fresh start.

More drastic outcomes such as suspension, exemption, or expulsion occur later in this sequence. Such actions dramatically label the child as one who cannot "cut it" in school. For many youngsters this is effectively the end of the formal education road. Separating the child from his normal educational environment can seriously curtail his educational and personal development. Labeled a "misfit," his future development is limited to whatever resources the community-at-large happens to have available

TABLE 18.1
Approaches to School Problems

EXTENT OF SCHOOL PROBLEM	TYPE OF PROBLEM	INTERVENTION AGENT	TYPE OF INTERVENTION
Minor	Restlessness, minor misbehavior, limit testing	Teacher	Mild rebukes
Moderate	Accumulation and exaggeration of minor misbehaviors	Principal, parent, school mental health worker	Influence of important figures outside the class
Severe	Continued poor class adaptation	School administrator	Change of class, suspension, expulsion

for such cases. Some victims of the process wander aimlessly, perhaps with limited individual tutoring. Some become dropouts or delinquents. And some go the treatment route, ending up in clinics or hospitals. All this suggests that prevention is preferable to early detection, early detection and intervention to later detection and intervention and that procedures that do not remove the child from school are preferable to more drastic isolating ones.

The school-related mental health programs to be described differ from each other with respect to the stage, in a failure sequence, at which they deal with a child's difficulties. At one extreme, programs are cited for youngsters who are so disturbed that schools have given up on them and disqualified them from further participation. At the other extreme are more nearly preventive programs for youngsters either not yet "at risk" or in whom relatively minor signs of dysfunction have been detected early. Between these extremes we find a series of secondary preventive programs targeted to children whose school experiences, though not disasterous, fall far short of being fulfilling. The latter type

of program is reviewed more fully in other sources (Quinn & Wegener, 1972; Zax & Specter, 1974).

SCHOOL PROGRAMS: DISTURBED CHILDREN

Project Re-ED

Background and Rationale

Project Re-ED (Hobbs, 1966, 1967, 1969; Lewis, 1967) is an important model for helping schoolchildren with serious, longstanding, emotional disabilities. The Joint Commission on Mental Illness and Health (1961) appointed a task force under Hobbs to survey mental health developments abroad, hoping to identify effective models that could be used in this country. Our country's affluence has sometimes encouraged the development of treatment approaches that reflect that affluence, without necessarily being either logical or effective. Among the intriguing programs that this task force discovered was "re-education" of school-age children with serious emotional problems, examples of which are the French educateur and the Scottish educational psychologist. Accordingly, the Joint Commission recommended that "centers for the re-education of emotionally disturbed children be 'established' using different types of personnel than are customary" (p. xiii). Beginning in 1961, Hobbs and his coworkers have developed and evaluated several experimental "re-education" programs in Tennessee and North Carolina.

Re-ED is predicated on several simple facts. It is, for example, estimated that there are about one and a half million children in this country whose emotional problems are so serious that they cannot live under normal family, school, and community circumstances. Many are seen in psychiatric hospital treatment units, some are hidden away at home, and others end up in state hospitals, detention homes, or institutions for delinquents. Hobbs (1966) challenged two key assumptions about how to change the behavior of emotionally disturbed children: (1) that psychotherapy is the approach of choice for them and (2) that they need at least two years of intensive care to change meaningfully. Project Re-ED, by emphasizing a child's actual behaviors and making a given social system work rather than traditional intrapsychic factors, offers a genuine alternative for children who cannot function in regular schools.

Setting and Children

Project Re-ED is educationally rather than psychotherapeutically oriented, assuming that effective education is the best of all therapies. A therapeutic milieu that serves a child 24 hours a day is seen as preferable to several hours of psychotherapy a week. Re-ED established two residential experimental schools, with family-like living arrangements and a therapeutic milieu. Each has an affiliated nearby summer camp facility. The child's separation from his family is minimized in several ways while he is with Re-ED. For example, he is typically admitted to the program only on a short-term (six months) basis. Not only are plans for his release already made when he is accepted for the program, but the matter is given central attention during his entire stay. While with Re-ED the child's ties with his natural environment are maintained by having him spend weekends at home whenever possible, and through continuous contact between project staff and family, schools, and referral agencies.

The Re-ED process starts when a referral source (school, social services or community agency, or family) identifies a severe school problem that cannot be handled through available community resources. Re-ED is defined as an addition to existing resources rather than as a separate, independent treatment facility. Program children range from ages 6–12, averaging around 10, and include a variety of diagnoses. All have failed to make it in regular school settings. Some are so aggressive or self-destructive that they cannot be handled in open community settings. Many Re-ED children have either been hospitalized, or would have to be without the program.

The Teacher-Counselor

Re-ED's aim is "to provide an engaging goal-oriented educational climate during all the child's waking hours" (Lewis, 1967, p. 354). To further that goal, the project has created the new professional role of the teacher-counselor, closely resembling the French educateur. Teacher-counselors are selected from among effective classroom teachers who have interest in, and talent for, this difficult work. They must be people who can handle mental health concepts and vocabulary and have the skills of an effective recreation leader, handyman, personal counselor, and parent substitute. Teacher-counselors live and work with disturbed children all day, every day in a natural environment.

Teacher-counselors are given three academic quarters of combined didactic and practicum training, leading to an M.A. in Special Education. Formal academic work is aimed at providing an understanding of emotionally disturbed children and acquiring skills in school remediation, counseling, recreation, and camping. Field experience provides the teacher-counselor familiarity with clinical practice, small group teaching methods, and how family, school, and community liaison services work. In selecting teacher-counselors, Re-ED strongly emphasizes such human qualities as warmth, good interpersonal relationships, the ability to give and receive affection, tolerance for stress, and a strong commitment to young children and

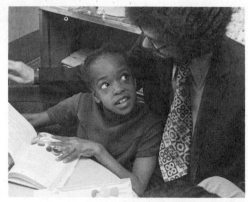

NEA

A teacher possessing the human qualities of warmth and the ability to give and receive affection can help disturbed children. (Photograph courtesy National Education Association Publishing, Joe di Dio.)

to the program's philosophy. Re-ED stands or falls with the effectiveness and dedication of the teacher-counselor.

Re-ED's basic structural unit includes two teacher-counselors, a liaison-teacher, and eight children for whom they have full responsibility. The teacher-counselors set goals for the children, plan programs, evaluate progress, and maintain continuous contact with the child's home base to pave the way for his early, smooth return. One of the two teacher-counselors is responsible for the program's daytime formal teaching aspects and the other for non-school areas such as counseling, recreational, and group activities. Sometimes these roles are interchanged. The two, however, stay in close touch to review objectives, share day-to-day planning, and develop consistent educational approaches. In planning for the child, goals are selected that are realistic for the social context to which he will return and can be achieved fairly quickly in an educational setting. Since all Re-ED children have experienced prior school failure, school achievement goals are frequent and specific.

Re-ED activities are not confined to school. There are camping trips, field trips, group projects, and income-producing activities. Beyond the goals established for particular children, a high priority is placed on group activities and helping children to live and interact with peers more effectively.

Other Personnel

Mental health professionals associated with the program are primarily consultants. They evaluate children during the admission process and help to deal with difficult problems and to determine whether goals are being met for individual children. Thus, the basic, day-to-day responsibility for the program rests with the teacher-counselor. But expert talent is available when difficult problems arise.

Initially, Re-ED's staff had one full-time mental health professional—a social worker. But social worker's traditional clinical role was played down in favor of program co-ordination for Re-ED children. The social worker maintained close relations with key representatives of the child's family, school, and referring agency to insure that the child might return to his normal environment under favorable circumstances. The social worker arranged for such things as parent counseling, individual academic and reme-dial programs in the child's home school, and special club membership for him. Such planning is first done when the child is ac-cepted in Re-ED, is periodically revised during his stay, and is followed-up after the Re-ED experience ends.

The "liaison-teacher" is another unique Re-ED specialist. He or she has the same training as the teacher-counselor and is usu-ally recruited from their ranks. The liaison teacher is concerned with all facets of the child's *school* experience. Before the child is accepted for Re-ED, the liaison-teacher gathers information about his school back-ground and problems. This information is used to set initial objectives for the child. While the child is in the program, the liai-son-teacher remains in touch with his home school through teacher conferences, gets regular assignments for him, and encour-ages him to have as much contact as pos-sible with his peers. When plans for the child's discharge are well along, the liaison-teacher discusses with his classroom teach-er his educational progress in Re-ED, fur-ther remedial work needed, anticipated problems in behavior and school adapta-tion, and program changes in the home school that might ease the transition. After the child goes home, the liaison-teacher

stays in touch with his teacher to monitor progress and problems. This unique role reflects Re-ED's emphasis on having close ties between the program and the child's regular social environment.

Basic Program Concepts

Re-ED is guided by several basic ideas (Hobbs, 1966). Every hour of the day should be used to facilitate learning and promote adaptation. An intensive, total ed-ucational experience should be provided over a short time period. The natural cli-mate of education rather than psychother-apy's artificial one is the best change vehi-cle. Trust, confidence, and understanding are the best helping tools. Children should be trained for competence. It is preferable to try to control symptoms and specific neg-ative behaviors rather than to dig to root out psychodynamic sources of dysfunction. Children should be encouraged to express feelings and helped to acquire skills in im-pulse management. A sense of group and community participation should be fostered. Children should gain some measure of "joy" from life.

There is no assurance that all these objec-tives are met for all Re-ED children. Still, they offer a clear alternative to the em-phases of more "drastic" approaches such as psychiatric hospital treatment units, de-tention homes, shelters, and state hospital settings for the disturbed child who cannot get by in the normal school environment.

Evaluation Studies

Re-ED's early justification came both from its seeming logic and favorable clinical im-pressions of its effectiveness. From the start, however, the project has seen the need for more rigorous evaluation. For an average child, Re-ED costs about $4000, or $20–$25 per day (Hobbs, 1966). Those figures are much lower than average figures for "per instance" custodial care, because the latter requires much more time. The daily Re-ED cost figure is less than one-third of the per day cost for inpatient psychiatric facilities. However, even though Re-ED can be justified on economic grounds, its advocates prefer to evaluate program effects along human dimensions.

In an early evaluation, Hobbs (1966) compared the preenrollment status of Re-ED's first 93 children to their status six months after discharge. Parent, teacher, the Re-ED staff, and agency data were used for this evaluation. He reports a most impressive 80 percent success rate. Specifically, children in the initial sample showed decreased bedwetting, fears, tantrums, and nightmares, increased social maturity, and improved school adjustment. The parents of these children showed a decrease in the discrepancy between their ideal standards and actual perceptions of Re-ED children.

An even more comprehensive, careful Re-ED evaluation has been reported—an outcome study of the first 250 program children (Weinstein, 1969, 1970, 1971). These studies evaluated Re-ED children at four points: enrollment, discharge, and follow-ups afer six and eighteen months. Although the initial evaluations were done without control groups, two control groups were added later (Weinstein, 1970). One included disturbed children matched to Re-ED children for age and sex. These children were identified by principals of the schools from which Re-ED children came as being as disturbed as a referred child but having to stay in the school because a referral could not be worked out. The second control group consisted of an age and sex-matched group of normal children.

The study used a variety of measures and evaluators, including Re-ED staff, parents, teachers, peers, and community personnel.

Also, several laboratory and special situational tests were used to assess specific functions that the program might have changed. Only a few key findings are presented here.

Based on several measures, about 75 percent of the Re-ED children showed moderate to considerable improvement following program participation. Parents and referring agencies were slightly more favorable in their judgment of outcome than the Re-ED staff. Disturbed controls failed to improve; indeed, in some ways, they got worse. At the 18-month follow-up point, *all* Re-ED alumni were in regular schools and only one had a special class placement. Re-ED parents saw their children as having improved by displaying fewer inappropriate behaviors, fewer symptoms, and being more relaxed and less aggressive. Teachers saw Re-ED youngsters as less distressed personally, less disruptive in class, harder working, and as having established better peer relationships after being in the program. Their school work also improved although it was still somewhat below grade norms. Re-ED children improved, too, on several self-concept measures.

Re-ED children, after the program, saw themselves as more like what their parents expected them to be and felt less rejected by their parents. Findings based on special situational tests (Weinstein, 1970) showed that Re-ED children decreased significantly more in impulsivity than disturbed controls during the seven-month period between enrollment and discharge. Finally, a measure reflecting the extent to which a child sees other people's responses to him to be determined by his own behavior, rather than by forces beyond his control, found Re-ED children to be significantly more internally oriented after the program.

Available returns from Re-ED are thus positive. The model seems to deal effectively with a difficult problem in the mental health field—the "total" school casualty. The program uses effective education as a therapeutic force and identifies a new type of helper who seems especially qualified for this difficult challenge. Re-ED also deals realistically with current shortages of mental health professionals by using them sparingly in consultation.

Re-ED is not a sinecure. It is limited to a very small fraction of the population, that is, extreme instances of interpersonal and educational failure, within the 6–12 age range. It does not, nor does it pretend to, approach either primary prevention or generalized early secondary prevention. Rather, it is an effective approach, based on innovative conceptualization and programming, for seriously disturbed young children identified as total school failures and otherwise destined to become seriously human casualties.

The Elmont Project

Background and Rationale

Like Project Re-ED, the Elmont project (Donahue, 1967; Donahue & Nichtern, 1965; Nichtern et al., 1964) seeks to help children with severe emotional handicaps— such as childhood schizophrenia and organic impairments—disabilities that are sufficiently crippling to keep them from being educated effectively in a normal school setting. The concerns that motivated the Elmont project were much the same as those behind Re-ED. The children in question were to be excluded from school and the only available alternatives removed them even further from educational opportunities, isolated them, and made their problems even worse. The Elmont project shared Re-ED's central beliefs that: education should be a therapeutic force, each child's program should be tailored to his deficits and needs,

a child's normal living pattern should not be disrupted, and he should be returned as soon as possible to the normal educational environment. The two programs differ in specifics rather than in objectives or target groups. Re-ED is a statewide residential program. The Elmont project is a day-program started by, and contained within, a particular community.

The Community Setting

Elmont is a small community of 50,000 in Nassau County, Long Island. It is not especially wealthy. Its overcrowded schools housed about 9000 children, 6000 at the elementary level. Elmont's special school services, including medical, speech and hearing, psychological, reading skills and special subject skills, were not abundant. Over time the Elmont schools identified a number of children with emotional problems serious enough to keep them from profiting from regular classes. Since, philosophically, the district accepted responsibility for providing proper education for *all* children, it faced a serious conflict about how best to serve these disabled youngsters.

District planners visualized an ideal program—one that was custom-made for each child based on his particular condition and needs, and with his own private teacher. A very special program was envisioned that required a warm, interested, therapeutic personal relationship without separating the child from his family or community. But neither budget, space, nor personnel for such a program was available. So the project staff took the problem back to the community to develop a workable plan, jointly. A local synagogue was found with suitable space and the Elmont Kiwanis Club contributed money for materials and supplies. The remaining and most critical problem, however, was to find a teaching staff. The

Elmont group solved this problem in a novel, imaginative way.

The "Teacher-Mom"

The inadvertent heroine in the Elmont program was a new breed of nonprofessional—the "teacher-mom." Lack of budget for regular teachers forced the project staff to re-examine its assumptions. Ultimately, it decided what the children really needed were dedicated people with empathy, warmth, and the capacity to give, rather than professional skills. If women with such qualities could be found, the staff was convinced that they could acquire the necessary technical skills later. With limited publicity and searching, project staff identified a small group of women who had the qualities of ideal "moms" and who were willing to give several mornings a week to the program. Two mothers were assigned to each child, alternating days. The total number of mothers varied with program size, with a low of 12 and a high of 38.

Most professional services for the project were put on a limited, consultative basis. A primary grade teacher from the district was assigned part-time to the project to instruct "moms" in teaching methods and to help work out individual study programs for the children. She also coordinated provision of materials, supplies, and transportation, and supervised the teaching of the mothers. A physician and several school mental health professionals were used as consultants. The school psychologist spent one half-day every other week with the project and the psychiatrist visited it three or four times a year. Twice a year teacher-moms participated in child evaluations with the teacher-consultant, psychiatrist, psychologist, and school administrators to consider progress of specific children, problems in running the program, and plans for returning children to their classes.

The Program

Children in the Elmont program ranged in age from six to eight. On the average they stayed in the program for two years (a range of from six months to five years). When the child's discharge was foreseen, he began to spend short trial periods in his regular class.

Individual sessions involving the teacher-mom and a single disturbed child were the program's educational backbone. The specific aims and content of each child's educational plan were based on a combination of information. Inputs from the project teacher and the consulting mental health professionals were included. The teacher-mom had much freedom in working with a child. If, for example, a child was not "with it" or got tense, she could discontinue academic work in favor of play activities, talking with the child, taking him for a walk, or just having him sit on her lap. Even though there were general goals for each child, playing it by ear was the rule rather than the exception. Novel activities were frequently improvised simply because they made sense. The teacher-mom was an active, decisive agent in the child's experience who made frequent on-the-spot judgments, based both on her helping reflexes as well as on her understanding of the background of a particular case.

Despite its focus on individual education, the Elmont program maintained a small core of group activities and contacts such as daily "good-morning" exercises conducted by the teacher-in-charge. These included raising the flag and a short group reading-discussion session based on material that the teacher put on the board, or some "show-and-tell" time. Each morning there was a brief (15–20 minute) group activity period in arts and crafts, music, story-telling, or recreation, and communal snack time. Other group functions included riding to and from school together, occasional birthday and holiday parties, and playground activities.

The project's main goal was to return children to their normal classes as soon as possible. The two most important indicators of progress were the child's being able to get along better with peers and teacher-moms, plus evidence that the child could do age-appropriate academic work. Elmont children were returned gradually to the classroom. When the staff believed a child to be ready, a psychologist worked out arrangements for a trial placement. He tried to pave the way for a smooth transition and successful adaptation. Such arrangements often included providing extra instruction in specific subject areas and much individual attention. Children often began their return by attending their regular class for only a half-day a week. If that worked out well, in-school time was gradually increased according to the child's adjustment.

Program Evaluation

The Elmont program can be evaluated in several ways. Cost-analysis data indicate that the program was very inexpensive. Indeed, it only cost $38 a year per child more than the regular education costs for a child in the Elmont school district. This was so because, thanks to the volunteer services of teacher-moms, teaching costs, typically the most expensive item in highly individualized programs, were eliminated. Since space was also provided free, the program's main expense came from the supervising teacher, transportation, and its consulting services.

The Elmont program was evaluated, though not rigorously. Program children were tested several times using standard intelligence and personality measures. The data, rather than being analyzed statistically, were used to formulate impressionistic observations. Program evaluators reported an increase in IQ for more than half the Elmont children, as well as gains in impulse control and frustration tolerance, more favorable self-images, and a better grasp of reality based on responses to projective tests. But such changes do reflect clinical judgment rather than solid empirical findings.

Interviews were conducted and questionnaires were given to many people who took part in the project, including school personnel, school board members, community leaders, and parents. In general, such feedback was positive, especially from people who were deeply invested in the program. Parent responses, though variable, were, on balance, positive. Teacher-moms remained with the program. They felt positively about it, were proud to be associated with it, and believed that being in it had helped them personally and their family relationships.

The project's most important finding may be the fact that 11 of the first 21 children returned successfully to their regular classes where they made satisfactory educational and personal progress. Given their severe initial problems, these children were very likely to be disabled for their entire lifetime. Thus, being able to return them to a normal classroom is an important achievement.

SCHOOL PROGRAMS:
LOW-RISK CHILDREN

Re-ED and Elmont worked with a small percent of the most extreme cases of school failure. School mental health consultation (Beiser, 1972; Faust, 1968; Fullmer & Bernard, 1972; Lawrence, 1971; Mannino, 1969; Newman, 1967) is a much more general approach aimed at improving the performance of children in general. This approach will be considered before going on to specific programs for children at less than grave risk.

Iscoe, Pierce-Jones, Friedman, and Mc-Gehearty (1967) described an ambitious school mental health consultation program involving 14 experimental and 14 control schools. Advanced Ph.D. candidates in school psychology were trained in consultation and assigned to program schools for one half-day a week. They did case consultation on classroom problems of children, helped teachers and administrators with management problems, and dealt with school crises of specific children. The project used varied measures to determine how extensively consultation was used, the types of problems such services covered, and how effective they were.

Program findings are reported for 28 schools and about 750 teachers and administrators who were potential users of the consultation. About 40 percent of the sample actually used the service. Roughly 70 percent of the child consultations were for boys. Two-thirds of the children brought up for consultation had only minor problems; the other third was judged to have moderate to severe disabilities. The highest frequency category (45 percent of the problems) brought to the consultant was concern about the child's emotional status, motivation, or learning ability. Another 15 percent of the problems had to do with the teacher's concerns about his or her professional skills, and 14 percent more with the teacher's personal anxieties. About 7 percent of the problems dealt with the teacher's role-uncertainties or interpersonal problems. Teachers used consultation differently. For example, younger, less experienced teachers used consultants more than older, more experienced ones. Iscoe et al. conclude that the consultative program led to positive out-

Yale University Office of Public Information

Seymour B. Sarason, advocate of moving mental health consultation to the community setting.

comes in the participating schools and systems.

Sarason and his colleagues at the Yale Psycho-Educational Clinic (Sarason et al., 1966) describe another type of school mental health consultation. The innovative Psycho-Educational Clinic provided consultation to many community settings, especially those dealing with children and youth. In working with an agency, clinic personnel established close enough liaison with it so that they become accepted as part of the setting's way of operating. This reduced the danger of being seen as a "foreign body" and made it easier to identify and deal with important problems of agency organization and structure. The latter was the clinic's focus rather than individual case consultation. To the extent that a consultant is accepted as part of an agency's operation, he is in a position to identify and deal with organizational and structural issues.

In describing their work in schools, Sarason et al. (1966) consider such issues as gaining entry into a system, establishing a climate of trust and confidence, helping teachers to change perceptions of problems and to consider alternative ways of handling them, supporting teachers who are on the right track but who need an outside boost, and specific teacher concerns about "unmanageable" children. The Yale group accepted the challenge of translating psychological concepts and behavioral science knowledge into action and capitalized on the school's special potential for building resources in children.

Sarason (1971) found that many highly influential school practices ("regularities") are so basic that they are simply taken as givens without so much as a pause to examine their impact. Awareness of this fact opens a vast area for potentially fruitful school mental health consultation and change.

The St. Louis and Austin Projects

The St. Louis school mental health project (Gildea, 1959; Gildea, Glidewell, & Kantor, 1967; Glidewell et al., 1957; Glidewell & Stringer, 1967; Rae-Grant & Stringer, 1969) was among the first systematic preventively oriented school programs. In 1947 the St. Louis group began to conduct therapy groups for the parents of children judged by teachers to be experiencing school adjustment problems (Gildea, 1959). Because the groups, led by social workers, seemed effective, the program was expanded by adding parent groups led by less extensively trained lay leaders. To nourish this development, the St. Louis Mental Health Association developed a group discussion program having lay leaders trained in seminars and workshops by mental health professionals. After training, the leaders ran discussion groups with mothers in schools, through

mother's clubs, and with PTAs. With the help of the St. Louis Health Department the service was expanded to nearby county areas. Gross appraisal of the new program's effects, based primarily on teachers' judgments of children's current school function, suggested that about 80 percent of the children of parents seen in groups had improved in adjustment, whereas 80 percent of comparable children whose parents were *not* seen failed to improve (Gildea, Glidewell, & Kantor, 1967).

Although encouraged by their early findings on the effectiveness of parent discussion groups, project staff recognized some biases in its main outcome criterion: that is, reports of child change had been made by nonneutral teachers to parent group leaders whom they knew. To overcome this shortcoming, the project began in 1956 to develop a battery of objective child adjustment measures to evaluate the parent intervention programs (Rae-Grant & Stringer, 1969). Symptom check lists, sociometric measures, projective tests, and maternal attitude measures were used. A major study with 30 third-grade classrooms in 15 schools and a total of 830 children was carried out to compare the two new school mental health programs and a "no-treatment" control group. The first of the two new approaches was the volunteer lay education program; the second, called the School Mental Health Services, included the volunteer program plus professional mental health consultation provided by the St. Louis Health Department. Comparison of the effectiveness of the two experimental groups with the controls did not show significant differences. In fact, teachers judged all children's (experimental and control) behavior to have become worse during the project period. The authors (Gildea, Glidewell & Kantor, 1967) attribute this finding to the teachers' increased sensitivity and sophistication about psychological dysfunction. Participating mothers, however, reported that their children had fewer symptoms and that they themselves had more favorable attitudes following the program. Those changes, however, were clearer for middle-income than for low-income mothers, and for boys, as compared to girls (Glidewell, Gildea, & Kaufman, 1973).

During the early phases of the research, an instrument called the Academic Progress Chart (APC) was developed to chart the child's school progress objectively (Stringer, 1959). This seemed to provide a promising, efficient, and inexpensive way of detecting emotional dysfunction early in school children. Retrospective application of the APC showed most disturbed schoolchildren could have been identified when they started school and that at least 60 percent of the children referred to school mental health services could have been picked up from one to eight years earlier (Glidewell & Stringer, 1962).

These findings turned the group's attention away from trying to deal with manifest problems toward early detection and prevention of dysfunction and an emphasis on promoting positive mental health. A project of the St. Louis group, called "Mothers as Colleagues in School Mental Health Work," seeks to implement this focus. In this program, systematic contact is made with mothers of all schoolchildren, efforts are made to detect problems very early, and school mental health personnel are used as resource people for mothers. Interviews with mothers emphasize children's resources rather than their pathology, introduce them to concepts of positive mental health, and identify the consultant as someone to be called on in time of need. The professional mental health consultant is available to teachers and other school personnel. The new project assumes that school helping services are most effective when people feel the need for them and that a focus on the early years and nonentrenched disorders will yield the greatest payoff. Using this new approach has increased requests for consultation by teachers and other school staff.

The St. Louis project is not the only one to try to improve children's school adjustment by working with parents. Hereford (1963) reported a project in Austin, Texas, for which the St. Louis experience was a model. Hereford's program trained 22 lay leaders to conduct parent discussion groups. Leaders met with groups of about 15 parents in a series of six 2-hour meetings that focused on parent-child relationships. An evaluation study compared the program's effectiveness for parents who participated in the discussion groups (and their children) and three control groups: (a) parents who attended one or more lectures by mental health professionals on parent-child relationships; (b) parents who signed up but never attended; and (c) parents who neither registered for, nor attended, the program. More than 1000 parents and their children were involved in this study. Parent attitude change was measured by pre-post comparisons of the four groups on a parent-attitude survey and data from parent interviews. Although children did not *directly* participate in the program, they were still evaluated on peer sociometric measures and on a teacher behavior rating form.

Both the attitude scale and the interview data showed positive changes in parent attitudes and behavior. Parents who participated in the discussion groups improved significantly more than the three control groups. Even more striking, *children* of the discussion group parents improved significantly more in sociometric attractiveness than children from the three parent control groups. The author reasons that the latter improvements were due to the attitude and behavior changes in parents which presumably modified parent-child relations in ways that helped children to improve these relations with peers. Hereford's findings suggest that parent education can be a useful tool for primary prevention.

The California State Education Department Program

The work of Bower and his associates (Bower, 1965, 1969; Bower & Lambert, 1961; Bower, Tashnovian, & Larson, 1958) at the California State Department of Education is among the most ambitious attempts to develop methods for the early detection of emotional handicap in schoolchildren. This program was carried out in 75 California school districts, each having one or more school mental health professionals. Professionals identified fourth-, fifth-, and sixth-grade children experiencing moderate to severe emotional handicaps. The home classes of identified children were studied without the teachers' knowing, specifically, why this was being done. Screening data were collected for 5500 children and detailed information was provided by nearly 200 teachers for 207 children (162 boys and 45 girls) identified as emotionally disturbed. Teachers provided data about the children's intelligence, reading, achievement scores, attendance, age-grade relationships, and father's occupation, and they rated their physical and psychological status. Two additional tests were given in all 200 classrooms to measure the child's self-image and his peer-sociometric status.

This investigation showed clearly that children identified by clinicians as emotionally handicapped were quite different from their nonhandicapped peers. For example, the emotionally handicapped group did significantly less well than the nonhandicapped on group IQ, reading, and arithmetic tests. These differences were greatest

at the upper grade levels and were not due to differing socioeconomic backgrounds. On the sociometric measure, the emotionally handicapped were seen more negatively by peers more often than the nonhandicapped. Teachers rated 87 percent of the children identified by clinicians as emotionally handicapped as among the most poorly adjusted in their classes. Bower (1969) notes that teachers' judgments about maladjusted child behavior corresponded closely to those of clinicians, and that young children's perception of their peers are surprisingly accurate.

The importance of Bower's work lies in its pioneering development of "a means to identify children who are vulnerable to or handicapped by emotional disturbance—before the problem is one for the mental institution, the court or the hospital" (1969, p. 250). Early identification · provides a foundation for effective early remediation and secondary prevention. The screening techniques first developed by the California group have, as we shall see, been used and extended by other groups and have made possible earlier correction of school adjustment problems.

The Pace I.D. Center Project

The Pace I.D. Center in San Mateo County, California, (Brownbridge & Van Vleet, 1969) developed a comprehensive program for early identification of school dysfunction and early interventions for children with behavior problems. Preliminary screening of about 6000 kindergarten through fourth-grade children in 19 San Mateo County schools was carried out using teacher-submitted data on the AML Behavior Checklist, a measure originally piloted by Bower's group. The AML is an 11-item rating scale with five aggressive-acting out (A) items; five moodiness (M) items; and one learning problem (L) item. The teacher rates all 11 items on 5-point frequency scales ranging from seldom (1) to always (5). Four school maladjustment scores—A, M, L, and Total—are derived.

Children with AML scores in the top 10 percent (N = 626) were identified as possible candidates for the PACE project, eliminating those over ten years of age and those who had family members on a social agency roster in San Mateo County. Thus, none of the youngsters in the study came from a hard core, multi-problem family. The 354 children who remained were divided into experimental (E) and control (C) subgroups matched for grade and sex. The groups were set up so that 90 percent of the children were kindergarteners or first or second graders. Due to such factors as moving or incomplete data, at the end of the project there were 130 matched pairs of children (N = 260) for whom all data were available. Project evaluation was based on an individually administered test battery plus the results of several group intelligence tests.

The PACE Program used social workers extensively to work with schools and families and in the communities of children who had early adjustment problems. Workers first got to know the children's teachers, clarified the program's purposes for them, and tried to get a clear understanding of the child's educational and behavioral problems. These objectives were met through teacher conferences, the continuous availability of the social worker, and direct child observation. As specific goals for children were clarified, social workers took on additional roles. They helped school people to identify situations in which children could experience success and coordinated planning to improve communication and bring together those concerned about the child's welfare. They expedited direct services for children, and served as consultants for school personnel who lacked mental health know-how.

Social workers also sought to establish meaningful contacts with the families of PACE children, both to build bridges between home and school, and to stimulate a joint effort toward achieving shared goals for the child's well-being. Parents were seen at home, in the schools, at the PACE headquarters, in coffee shops, and for lunch meetings. Evening appointments were not uncommon as part of the serious effort to involve fathers in the program. The depth of social work contacts with families varied. Such contacts tended to be superficial, supportive, and educationally oriented with the families of low-risk children. However, with the families of high-risk youngsters, social work interventions were frequent, intensive, and active. Thus, the child's problems, as well as family circumstances, shaped the social worker's contacts with the family.

Social workers were involved in a variety of community activities in the PACE program. They participated in agency planning and evaluation conferences for individual children and in PTA meetings. They ran parent discussion groups. They promoted group membership in activities appropriate for PACE children. They encouraged participation of community groups in educational programs, supported the development of special education facilities, and organized a Head Start program for Spanish-speaking families.

PACE social workers had feedback through consultation. Bi-weekly staff meetings provided a chance to review their clinical activities and to identify areas in which they needed more information. Several child psychiatrists with considerable school experience also provided intensive case consultation.

The main outcome findings of the three-year PACE project were complex. PACE children, on the basis of the AML scores were rated initially as more maladjusted than nonPACERS on the study's criterion measures. This validates the screening procedures used. Although PACE children generally improved through participation in the program, their improvement varied from measure to measure. It was, for example, clearer on clinical measures of emotional disturbance than on educational criteria, and clearer for girls than for boys. On some measures significant E versus C differences were due to less slippage among Es, suggesting that for some children, the program helped primarily to avoid further setbacks.

Although it is accurate to say that PACERS, as a group, improved, the statement must be qualified. About one-third of the children either improved spontaneously or after only minimal social work intervention. For another third, although adjustment improved, it remained changeable. Those children needed further intensive support. The last third were still at high-risk when the program ended and needed much more help from the schools and community agencies. Project staff believed that the program was most effective with the two latter groups and that those were the children who showed the most improvement or the least regression.

PACE staff identified program factors that they considered to be the most important in producing positive changes in target children. One was the low case load that permitted intensive but flexible interventions for the identified children. A second was the ability to tailor programs to a specific child's problems and needs. A third was the consultative support provided by the PACE Center. A final factor was the coordination of services among schools, families, and the community. Based on this experi-

ence, PACE staff has developed a further proposal for a prevention service and training center to extend the program.

The Rochester Primary Mental Health Project

Background and Rationale

The Rochester Primary Mental Health Project (PMHP) (Cowen, 1971; Cowen & Lorion, 1975; Cowen et al., 1975; Zax & Cowen, 1967), like the St. Louis project described above, has developed in a slow evolutionary way since the late 1950s. PMHP emphasizes early detection and prevention of school maladjustment, and uses nonprofessional child-aides as direct help-agents with school children who are having problems.

The Rochester project started as a result of two recurrent observations. Often, teachers complained that disproportionate amounts of their class time was taken up by three or four youngsters out of a group of 25 or 30. Not only did these youngsters do poorly themselves, but the fact that they required so much of the teacher's time adversely affected the rest of the class. This

The use of direct help-agents for children with problems can work to prevent school maladjustment.

caused the teacher to feel unhappy about the job she was doing.

A second relevant observation was that referrals for school mental health services seemed to increase sharply during the late elementary period, just before the transition to high school. And, typically, the resources to help with such surfacing problems were unavailable. Close examination of the records of the referred youngsters frequently identified repetitive, sometimes serious earlier signs of behavior problems. These had not been dealt with sooner, either because resources were not available or because people hoped that they would "go away" with time. In many cases, the early difficulties simply got worse as the years went by.

These two observations led to a decision to concentrate resources for early detection and prevention in the primary grades, even if it meant being short of services in the upper grades. The hope was that by doing this effectively, later more serious problems could be reduced. A psychologist and social worker were thus assigned full-time to the primary grades of a single elementary school and an early detection-prevention program was mounted. Two adjacent demographically comparable schools were used as control schools so that program outcomes could be assessed objectively.

During PMHP's initial stage, all first-grade children were screened early in the year, using personality, intellectual, and behavioral measures. The social worker interviewed all mothers of first-grade children to open lines of communication and to convey the image of an interested, friendly school. The interview also helped the social worker to learn about the child, and family attitudes and interactions. Based on psychological screening, social work interviews, classroom observations, and teacher reports, the psychologist and social worker classified each child as "Red-Tag" or "Non-Red-Tag."

Red-Tag children were those who already showed, or seemed prone to have, moderate to severe school adjustment problems. All other children were called Non-Red-Tag. About one of every three children was classified as "Red-Tag," not very different from the composite 30 percent school maladjustment figure reported by Glidewell and Swallow (1969) based on their national review.

The early PMHP program changed professional roles from providing direct service to children, to consulting and resource functions with teachers and other school personnel. Professionals did classroom observations both so that they could make helpful suggestions to teachers and to get first-hand impressions of children who were having problems. Observation, screening, and family background data were used to set goals and to decide on ways to work with children. A special after-school activity program was set up for children, who, in the teachers' judgment, needed more individual help and attention than the class could provide. Regular parent and teacher meetings were held to consider aspects of psychological development and learning that were thought to be relevant to these groups.

Program Evaluation

The first PMHP program lasted for three years (first through third grade) for several independent year samples. To evaluate its effectiveness, program children were compared to controls at the end of the third school year on about 20 criterion measures. These included school record indexes (for example, nurses' referrals, days absent, report card grades, and achievement-aptitude discrepancy scores), achievement tests (reading and arithmetic), and personality and behavior measures (teacher, peer, and self ratings). Cowen et al. (1966) found that program children were better off than controls on all but one of these measures. Differences between groups were significant on seven (fewer absences, higher grades, higher reading comprehension, better achievement in relation to basic aptitude, higher adjustment rating by teacher, lower anxiety scale scores and lower lie scale scores). This suggested that the experimental preventive program had been effective educationally and interpersonally.

The research also compared Red-Tag and Non-Red-Tag children on the same test battery at the end of third grade. On 14 of 20 comparisons, Red-Taggers were found to be significantly worse off than Non-Red-Taggers. Follow-up of these Red-Tag children at seventh grade (Zax et al., 1968) showed that without special programming for them in the later elementary years, their problems had remained seriously handicapped.

Thus, two main conclusions emerged from PMHP's initial research studies. The experimental prevention program seemed to have positive effects and children with early-identified dysfunction, left alone, did poorly in the first several school years and were already quite impaired by third grade. This encouraged further efforts to develop preventive techniques and launched PMHP's second stage.

Child Aides

Having learned that children with serious school adjustment problems and poor prognoses could be readily identified, the key question became: "What could be done to help them?" Potential answers to this question ran up against the problem of the severe professional manpower shortages that have always made it so difficult to bring effective help to children with crippling school handicaps. PMHP's solution was to use nonprofessionals as help-agents

for primary graders with adjustment problems.

The first group that PMHP recruited and trained as "child-aides" consisted of housewives. Any community has a large reservoir of womanpower in those mothers who have raised their own children and are anxious to find challenging productive uses of their time. PMHP assumed that life style, personality, and successful child-rearing experience might be more important in helping needy schoolchildren than the usual educational credentials of advanced professional training.

Hence, a group of housewives, judged to be warm, outgoing and genuinely interested in children, was recruited and trained for six weeks to prepare them as child-aides in the schools (Zax et al., 1966; Zax & Cowen, 1967). Since it was assumed that the women's personal qualities and experience would be their main assets in helping children, the training program did not try to cram great amounts of knowledge into them. Training touched briefly on several content areas such as personality development, children's behavior disorders, and parent-child relationships to orient aides to the problems they would be handling and to help relieve anxiety about their prospective roles. Clinical training was provided through films, case materials, and classroom observation plus discussions of those experiences. School personnel provided some training in teaching methods, but most of their learning took place on-the-job through conferences, discussion, and supervision. The PMHP professionals' role emphasized consultation and supervision. He served as a mental health "quarterback" (Cowen, 1967) whose impact and reach was greatly extended by using aides.

The child-aide program worked as follows. The teacher referred a child if he seemed to be unable to keep up with the class educationally or if he presented a behavior problem. At an initial meeting, the teacher, prospective aide, and mental health consultant exchanged information, pinpointed the problem, and considered alternative ways of dealing with it. Aides usually saw children in the school, but outside of class, for two 30–40 minute sessions per week. Periodic conferences including teachers, aides, and professionals were held to evaluate progress and reset goals. The program's aim was to return the child to normal classroom function as soon as possible.

The aide intervention has both educational and emotional goals. Referred children include the hyperactive and disruptive, the shy, timid, and withdrawn and those with learning problems. Aides differ in their personalities, styles, and interests, differences that are often reflected in their approach to children. A committed human relationship between an aide and a child or group of children is at the program's core.

Because the program is sponsored by a school, educational progress is a key objective. However, it is often necessary for the aide to spend much time establishing a sound relationship with a child before educational activities can be undertaken. Aides engage in a broad range of activities with children including working with expressive media, play with games and toys, reading and story telling, recreational activities, and talking and conversation. How an aide and a given child interact depends on the child's problem, the objectives set for him, the stage of the relationship, and the aide's style.

Evaluation of the aide program (Cowen, 1968; Dorr & Cowen, 1973) shows that it is effective. Moreover, the model of the child-aide program has been a springboard for developing similar programs using many different nonprofessional groups. These include college students (Cowen, Carlisle, & Kaufman, 1969; Cowen, Zax, & Laird,

1966), retired persons (Cowen, Leibowitz, & Leibowitz, 1968), indigenous neighborhood teenagers and mothers, and fourth graders (Cowen & Lorion, 1975).

Child-aides usually work half-time. Five such aides, at a cost considerably less than that of a single professional, see about 50 children—a significant increase in helping services. But the use of such personnel is not justified solely on manpower or budgetary grounds. Nonprofessionals are, in many instances, as, or more, effective than professionals.

Recent Directions and Comment

PMHP's first two (pilot) stages, described above, lasted 11 years. During that period the project was always in a single school at any one time. But when the approach was shown to be both sensible and effective, the idea of expanding it to many more schools arose. This was a challenge. The program had to abandon its past sheltered context and move into the cold, hard, unprotected world of reality. There, it had to compete with other programs and vested interests for budget, resources, and space. An important factor that made this possible was the formation of a committee of interested, committed citizens in support of the project. Through this group's efforts in public education and fund raising, PMHP succeeded in expanding to 25 schools in four school districts in the Rochester area. Because these schools differ considerably in size, affluence, personnel, and location (urban versus suburban), a variety of different program forms and personnel uses under a common guiding philosophy has evolved.

PMHP began this expansion by training school mental health professionals both in the rationale and "nuts-and-bolts" of early detection and prevention. Nearly 100 child-aides were also recruited and trained. A typical staffing pattern for a pair of PMHP schools calls for portions of the time of a school psychologist and social worker, depending on a district's resources, and ten child-aides. This deployment expands effective helping services geometrically. PMHP's most recent utilization survey (Cowen et al., 1974) reports that intensive (an average of 30 helping contacts per child) helping services were brought to 833 young schoolchildren in a single year. Such expansion is needed in the light of the overall school maladjustment figure reported by Glidewell and Swallow.

Parallel to its local expansion, PMHP has also started working with other school districts around the country to develop similar programs shaped to fit *their* needs, problems, and resources. A dozen or so programs of this type are now in operation. Thus, having shown PMHP to be a viable, effective alternative, a current thrust is to adapt and disseminate the model in other settings.

The growing interest in early detection and prevention of school adjustment problems around the country is apparent at many levels: for example, planning bodies, state education departments, and legislatures. But sustained, systematic work in this area is still limited. Sometimes the product of such effort is very complex and difficult to interpret (Kellam et al., 1975), if not downright discouraging (Marmorale & Brown, 1974). But experiences such as PMHP's showing that early detection-prevention programs are both possible and yield good results, argue for investing more in this area in the future.

PMHP's most important emphases are structural rather than substantive: (1) its focus on young, flexible modifiable children whose problems are not yet entrenched; (2) its emphasis on systematic *early* detection and screening to locate vulnerable children as soon as possible; (3) its use of nonprofessional help-agents to support early identification with concrete follow-up for

large numbers of primary graders who desperately require such help in order to cope with school demands; and (4) changing the role of school mental health professionals in ways that support prompt, geometric expansion of effective help for maladapting primary graders.

PMHP does not argue that its substantive approaches are inviolable. There may well be better ways of screening or ways in which aides can be of greater help to maladapting children. In fact, several PMHP offshoot programs have explored the use of just such variants (for example, behavior modification) with encouraging results (Sandler, Duricko, & Grande, 1975). PMHP's most important message is that systematic early detection and dramatically expanded effective intervention are essential to deal with the documented, rampant problems of early school maladaptation. Indeed, PMHP's experience argues for even more fundamental approaches to school adjustment as, for example, trying to engineer school environments that produce healthy development and effective learning in the first place.

The Sumter Child Study Project

The Sumter Child Study Project (Newton & Brown, 1967) differs in several important ways from other programs thus far reviewed. First, it is a mass-oriented, primary preventive effort, and second, it is targeted primarily to preschool children. The Sumter group reasons that prevention is a better strategy for dealing with disordered behavior in children than typically used approaches including discipline, treatment, education, and even inaction. They emphasize the need to build strengths and resources in children and to foster coping mechanisms for normal life crises. Their approach is influenced by Bower's work in early identification of school dysfunction

cited above and by the efforts of the Welles-
ley group (Klein & Ross, 1958) in crisis
intervention. School entry is seen as a potential crisis. The project tries to identify
critical factors in this normal life crisis and
to determine the best interventions to ease
the transition from home to school.

The project, based in Sumter, South Carolina, covered a county district of about
75,000 that lacked extensive mental health
facilities. Its first aim was to develop a psychological screening procedure to predict
how children would cope with school entry
and future school stress. This preschool
check-up, administered six months before
the child started school, involved two 45-
minute sessions. The first session consisted
of structured observations and testing by
the psychologist and a simultaneous interview with the child's mother by a social
worker. In the second session, team members discussed the data gathered during the
first session and formulated case impressions.

The project's second purpose was to develop interventions to increase the child's
adaptive skills and his ability to cope with
stress. Interventions were determined individually for each child based both on the
preschool evaluations and data from his
early school experience. A final aim was to
evaluate the effectiveness of the various interventions by following children's progress
during the early school years.

The project was housed in six schools,
three experimental and three control, covering a broad socioeconomic band. The
sample for the first project year included
515 children who would shortly fill 19 first-
grade classes in the six schools. An intervention was defined as an activity designed to
develop and reinforce skills in coping with
stress. Interventions were either mass-oriented (that is, for the entire sample or
specific subsamples), or individual-oriented.
The preschool check-up was offered to all

children scheduled to enter the three experimental schools. About 70 percent of the
sample took advantage of the offer. The
authors found that screening yielded important information about the child's maturity,
competence, needs, and problems. It provided a good framework for planning group
and individual interventions.

Four group interventions were used. For
immature children with reading problems
or weakness in other adaptive skills, a six-
week preschool summer program was prescribed. Teachers in this program developed
experiences to augment their children's social skills and to strengthen specific competencies. Both teachers and parents of
program children reacted favorably to the
experience.

A group intervention was used for a second cluster of children with speech and
communication problems (10–13 percent of
the sample). At the time, the Sumter area
lacked facilities for such children and depended on a traveling state clinic that did
not reach the area until the fall. The professional team, working directly with parents,
developed individual remedial programs for
the children during the summer. The results
of this program were encouraging and led
to the school's hiring two speech therapists.

A third group of children was seen to be
deficient in social skills and group experiences. In these cases, program personnel
met with parents to encourage greater participation by the children in informal neighborhood play groups, church programs, and
family outings. The project also stimulated
a joint effort by a number of parents to
bring undersocialized children together in
activity groups.

The final group intervention was specifically designed for children who needed a
preschool experience but whose parents
either could not afford it or had insoluble
transportation problems. The project, together with the City Recreation Depart-

ment, developed a new preschool program and established a recreational center in a deprived project-school area. The City Recreation Department provided personnel, funds, and resources for the program. Project staff promoted communication with the families and consulted with the Recreation Department about the problems of this age group.

Individual interventions began during the prescreening cycle. Psychologists, for example, helped children directly to clarify their perceptions of school. Social workers dealt with parent concerns about their children's development. During screening, the professional noted the child's resources as well as his problems and discussed these in follow-up interviews attended by 98 percent of the parents. Where problems (for example, the need for a medical check-up) were identified, specific follow-up suggestions were made. The vast majority of *all* interventions, individual and group, were targeted to a subsample of 25–30 percent of the experimental children.

The Sumter Project has reported some research findings. For example, the team made 4-point school adjustment-prognosis ratings for all children (1 = exceptional, 2 = typical, 3 = weak, 4 = trouble). An estimate of screeners' sensitivity and the validity of the screening process was obtained by comparing those judgments to later performance criteria. Children rated one or two did significantly better than those rated three or four on most criteria. They completed twice as many first-grade reading requirements and only 3 percent of them, compared to 29 percent of the threes and fours, failed to receive reading primers. Children rated one or two also had significantly fewer absences and only 6 percent of them compared to 34 percent of the threes and fours, were not promoted.

Other comparisons between the two groups were based on observations and test data from the initial screening. Those with prognostic ratings indicating good adjustment significantly exceeded those rated as potentially maladjusted on each of the following measures: reality basis for feelings about school, initiative, coping effectiveness, age-appropriateness of responses, acceptance of one's self-concept and body image, and curiosity behavior. The two groups were comparable intellectually except for a somewhat higher proportion of suspected defectives in the maladjusted group. Although each of the characteristics noted above differentiated the two adjustment groups, they are not independent of the overall prognostic rating. More likely, such differences were what influenced the initial screening judgments. However, group differences in reading achievement, attendance, and promotion are independent of the initial screening rating and suggest that the early prognostic judgment had substantial predictive validity.

Based on their findings, the Sumter group concludes that mental health professionals can profitably invest time in preschool check-ups of emotional status and that the information obtained through such procedures is very useful to parents and schools. The high initial response rate of parents (70 percent) and extremely low rate of missed follow-up appointments (2 percent) support this view. Moreover, the positive attitudes expressed by parents, their heavy use of program facilities and their requests for further services indicate that the initial time investment builds a solid base of communication and positive feelings about the project that facilitate later help-seeking behavior by families.

The Sumter findings to date validate their screening procedures rather than demonstrate the educational or behavioral effectiveness of the program's interventions. Gathering and analyzing effectiveness data are planned for the future. Based on clinical observation, the authors believe that the program interventions have helped children to achieve new, situationally more appropriate roles, to develop more adequate interpersonal relationships and to grow through effective confrontation and management of stress situations and crises.

Emerging school mental health programs discussed in this section are targeted both to children already at risk and to populations-at-large. They include school mental health consultation, early detection and screening, early secondary prevention, and new deployments of professionals and nonprofessionals. These programs all seek to identify and correct dysfunction as soon as possible in order to maximize the child's educational and personal growth.

BUILDING SKILLS

Most of the programs so far considered are for children with problems of varying severity. Thus, they begin with identified dysfunction, which they seek to minimize in hopes of forestalling later, more serious problems. The underlying issue, however, can be recast! Perhaps the very best way to avoid unfortunate outcomes is to forget symptoms altogether and to concentrate on helping children to build strengths. As mental health professionals have come more and more to perceive this alternative, efforts to develop programs based on such objectives have increased.

The more general approaches use educational environments and curricula in ways that will produce positive educational and adaptive outcomes in children. Work on the development of curricula to encourage causal thinking (Muss, 1960; Ojemann, 1969), analyses of modern versus traditional educational atmospheres (Minuchin et al., 1969) and the open-classroom environment all exemplify this thrust.

But there are also more focused, goal-

World Wide Medical Press

To help a child to maximize his potential educational and personal growth is the aim of all school mental health programs.

directed examples of this same approach. Two questions that inspire this development are "Which particular skills and behaviors are essential to effective learning?" and "How can these be taught?" Roughly, five steps are involved in pursuing work in this area. First, the critical behavior or skill to be studied is determined on clinical, rational, or empirical grounds. Second, the behavior's preprogram occurrence is assessed. Third, ways are designed to increase the target behavior. Fourth, the direct consequences of the intervention are assessed. And finally, indirect consequences of the intervention can also be studied, that is, related skills or adaptive behaviors that the program may, incidentally, improve.

Susskind's work, cited in Chapter 17, illustrates this approach. In this case, children's curiosity behavior was the target. Preliminary study showed that curiosity behavior did not often occur in class, even though teachers thought it did. The "intervention" was to educate teachers in techniques designed to encourage curiosity behavior in children. Follow-up showed that this, indeed, did happen.

Spivack and Shure (1974) model another approach to this area in their pioneering effort to develop a program to teach young children effective problem-solving skills. They reasoned that for such skills to be acquired, children must be active learners, and must gain both a cognitive understanding and a sense of mastery of the process. Children who succeed in doing so should be able to generalize problem solving to more personal situations—in other words, to cope more effectively and to improve overt behavior and adjustment.

Spivack and Shure's comprehensive training program was based on a series of games and dialogues, between children and adults, used to teach word concepts and cognitive skills. Training scripts covered prerequisite abilities such as listening and attending as well as the prime problem-solving skills themselves. Daily lessons, always put in an interesting "game" form, varied in length from 5–20 minutes. The entire program required 10–12 weeks. Typically, it was presented to small (N=6–8) mixed-sex groups which included both responsive and not-so-responsive children.

The program's evaluation was based on a comparison of several hundred youngsters from Philadelphia's inner-city schools, half of whom (experimentals) participated in the program and half (controls) who did not. Both experimental and control children had been classified as adjusted, impulsive, or inhibited based on teaching ratings.

The program was found to have significantly strengthened children's cause-and-effect thinking and to have decreased their superfluous and irrelevant responses. This was just as true for children of low-average intelligence as for bright ones. The program was more effective for *problem*-children— especially the inhibited, socially withdrawn type—than for adjusted children. In addition to strengthening problem-solving skills, the program also changed priorities in problem-solving strategies, moving them away from aggressive solutions and towards nonforceful ones. Equally, if not more important, the program resulted in improved behavioral adjustment in such areas as: concern for others, taking the initiative, and autonomy. Once again the initially most maladjusted children profited the most. Analyses were reported suggesting that the gain in problem-solving skills was, indeed, the critical factor that led to improved behavioral adjustment. Finally, the problem-solving and adjustment gains from the program held up six months later at the time of follow-up.

Spivack and Shure's work is important both in its own right and for what it models. They have developed a method for strengthening problem-solving competence in children. This particular competence seems to have great importance for strengthening the child's adjustment in other critical areas. Thus, without dealing directly with symptoms or maladaptive behaviors, Spivack and Shure reduced such difficulties through competence training. In their words, the children's most instrumental acquisition was learning to "conceptualize relevant alternative solutions to real life problems" (1974, p. 106).

CONCLUSIONS

A chapter on schools and school mental health programs is atypical in an abnormal psychology text. Its inclusion in this volume reflects the biases that: preventing disorder and dealing with dysfunction before it becomes rooted are desirable long-range objectives, much of mental health's effort should be directed to the young child and his environment, and schools play a vital role in psychological development.

As one looks at the individual programs that have been reviewed, not to mention their overall profile, one can see a beginning recipe for tomorrow's school mental health workers. One important role will be as a social engineer or systems analyst as contrasted with simply applying band-aids to bleeding psyches. Schools must come more to be seen as places to promote effective learning and health, than as places to undo troubles. The school mental health worker must focus more on early dysfunction and on primary, and the earliest possible secondary, prevention designed to forestall it. Much of his effort should be directed to the very young child. All this contrasts noticeably with past emphases on well-entrenched symptoms in older children, on one-to-one diagnosis and treatment or on exclusion.

To implement a preventive thrust, the school mental health professionals must be educators, consultants, and resource people for parents, teachers, other school personnel, and for a corps of nonprofessional helpers that will have to be created to overcome current shortages in the mental health fields. The helping professions must emphasize consultative and preventive functions for the many rather than just individual diagnosis and treatment for the few. Only through such changes can a mental health helping structure, capable of dealing with the serious social problems of disordered human behavior and of maximizing human effectiveness, evolve. And, by any system of logic, the schools must figure centrally in such an evolution.

SUMMARY

1. School problems may arise because of adjustment problems or, conversely, failure in school may cause adjustment problems.

2. Many school adjustment problems are minor and are routinely handled by teachers. Teachers tolerance for misbehavior is high in the child's early school years. The school system typically allows for many different ways of handling children's behavior problems. Teachers manage many problems in the classroom. When they cannot do so themselves, they can turn to parents, the principal, or school mental health professionals for help. Exclusion from class is a last resort.

3. Exclusion and its consequences often mark the end of a child's formal education. Thus, prevention and early detection of problems seem greatly preferable to permitting the child to enter a progressive cycle of separation from formal schooling.

4. Some school programs are designed for the already seriously disturbed child. Project Re-ED is one such program that provides a total educational and living setting on weekdays. The Elmont project is another. It provides close tutorial and emotional support for disturbed children through the use of nonprofessionals outside of the regular classroom.

Both have the basic goal of returning the child to the regular classroom as soon as possible. Both report success in helping children who are typically among the most difficult to treat.

5. Some prevention programs are directed primarily at children who show relatively minor signs of school maladjustment. These include consultation programs involving teachers and school administrators, programs directed primarily toward parents, and programs aimed at the children themselves.

6. One of the pioneer secondary prevention school programs was developed in St. Louis beginning in 1947. It focused on the mothers of poorly adjusted schoolchildren who were seen in therapy and discussion groups. Limited results with this approach led the St. Louis group to shift its focus toward early detection and prevention.

7. A program sponsored by the California State Education Department in the late 1950s developed techniques for identifying early signs of emotional handicap in school children.

8. The Pace I.D. Center in California created an early identification and prevention program for youngsters in kindergarten through second grade. Social workers in this program provided service to the teachers and families of problem children. Outcome studies of this program indicated mixed results.

9. The Rochester Primary Mental Health Project was set up in the late 1950s to identify problem children as early as first grade. In its preventive phase, it trained nonprofessionals to work with needy children outside of the classroom on referral from teachers. The success of this program has led to its expansion and its serving as a model for other programs.

10. The Sumter Child Study Project in South Carolina identified potential problems in preschoolers and tailored group interventions for four types of problems. Some positive program effects were demonstrated.

11. Several programs have demonstrated success in building skills such as the ability to think causally, to exercise curiosity, and to solve problems in school children.

12. The potential, long-range benefits of preventive approaches were emphasized. Such programs require a shift in professional mental health roles toward engineering healthy environments, consultation, and the recruitment, training, and supervision of nonprofessionals.

CHAPTER 19

Programs in Action:
II. The Inner City

Major American cities are changing dramatically. One-sixth of the nation's people now live in 14 of its largest cities (Roberts, 1967a). This has come about because of rapid population shifts among racial and ethnic subgroups. For example, the black population in America doubled between 1920–1965. It is expected to double again by 1985 (Pfautz, 1969). Today blacks make up 25 percent of the population of most American cities of 100,000 or more. In the District of Columbia about 75 percent of the total population and 97 percent of all public schoolchildren are black. Similar population shifts have occurred with other minorities (for example, Spanish-speaking groups) in other parts of the country. Whites are leaving urban centers for the suburbs. As a result, the combined population of New York and Chicago shrank by more than one million in the decade 1950–1960, with proportional decreases in the numbers of white children enrolled in the public schools. Indeed, the proportion of black children who now attend predominantly black schools often exceeds 90 percent in major cities.

These facts support the observation that "in less than a generation, Negro Americans have been transformed from a regional, rural, and agricultural population to an essentially national, urban, and industrial population" (Pfautz, 1969, p. 59). In 1910 more than 80 percent of all black Americans lived in the South. Today the comparable figure is well under 50 percent. More than one-third of all American blacks are now crowded into the ghettos of twelve of our largest cities (Miller & Woock, 1970; Roberts, 1967a). Such shifts came about because blacks, unhappy with poverty, squalor, and degradation, set out to find a better existence—defined in terms of better jobs, living conditions, and opportunities. They have not found it. Measured in terms of employment, income, integration, or life opportunities, there has been precious little improvement in the lot of most black Americans. Indeed, for many life's conditions have become worse, and geographic change has meant only that problems were moved from rural to urban settings with consequent changes in their *specific* nature—not their severity.

As a result of urbanization, the black American's problems are more a matter of public conscience today than before. Developments such as the Supreme Court desegregation decision of 1954, civil rights legislation, and government support of social philosophies that stress equality create an image of how things "should be" and, as such, a target for those who know, from direct experience, that they are not that way. Vocal black leadership has emerged, struggling to end the inferior status of blacks in America. But even so, daily newspaper headlines and stories about outbreaks of conflict and urban violence remind us

© J. Brian King 1975

With the population growth in the nation's cities has come an increasing demand for urban mental health programs.

that adverse conditions of black Americans both result from and contribute to major current social problems.

Mental health professionals have traditionally seen disordered behavior as a problem within the individual. Today, such a causal view is severely limiting. Far more emphasis must be placed on the social conditions that predispose to disorder and, if there is to be constructive change, the insulated mental health professional must move closer to the real world.

Several studies were cited in Chapter 16 showing that psychological problems are closely associated with race and poverty. Ryan's report (1969) on mental health facilities and personnel in Boston, and who they serve, vividly underscores this point. Two recent sociology volumes (Finney, 1969; Kosa, Antonovsky, & Zola, 1969) suggest that interrelations among culture change, mental health, and poverty are so basic that no one of them can be fully understood without taking the others into account. The point has repeatedly been made that the poor have the highest rates of severe psychiatric disorder (Fried, 1969; Kosa, Zola, & Antonovsky, 1969); the same can be said for the physical health of this group (Lerner, 1969). The mental health professions have, justifiably, been accused of not having contributed materially to the resolution of these problems (Albee, 1969b; Arnhoff, 1969). The glaring human problems of the inner-city are more likely to be resolved by changing past assumptions about how to approach such problems, rather than by simply providing more of the same service and manpower that has been available in the past. To illustrate the point: Boston is among America's best endowed cities with respect to traditional mental health facilities and manpower. Some have described it as the world's most densely saturated mental health training area. Even so, Ryan's (1969) report makes it clear that Boston's poor are woefully lacking in mental health resources.

It is easier for mental health professionals to recognize this situation than to do something about it. One serious drawback to constructive action stems from the complex social roots of psychological problems among the poor. Though many mental health professionals "sense" relationships between unfortunate living conditions and unfavorable human outcomes, they are unclear about specific causes and effects. Unfortunate living conditions that are psychological irritants include unemployment, poor housing, and lack of opportunity. Dealing with such conditions calls for social and political action and institutional change —areas in which most mental health professionals have little experience or expertise. Lacking the know-how to work in these areas, professionals can readily tune them out. Thus, although most mental health experts accept the view that improving man's lot is a positive goal, their traditional training and experience do not prepare them to be helpful with constructive institutional and social change. They are more comfortable and secure as interviewers, diagnosticians, and psychotherapists.

Given this gap, mental health specialists either repress "the whole mess" or throw up their hands in despair because the problem seems so enormous. One writer tries, sardonically, to make this point using an analogy. He recalls a night club scene from the Broadway show *Cabaret*, set in Germany during the Nazi rise, in which call girls, totally insulated from the world outside, continue to go full tilt about the business of attracting clientele "while outside there grows the unmistakable sound of approaching horror" (Albee, 1969b, p. 222). Albee's message is that mental health professionals cannot afford to repress the compelling realities of the world around them—in this case

the psychologically troubled world of the urban ghetto.

What can the mental health professional do to help reduce disordered behavior in the inner city? He must start by recognizing the problems of living in such settings and how little past mental health approaches have been able to do about them. Such a perspective necessarily forces consideration of alternatives. The deep and complex roots of urban problems require that we abandon past assumptions about our own professional "preciousness" (Sarason et al., 1966). Resolving the complex social problems of the inner-city calls for the efforts of many different groups and specialists. It cannot be achieved alone, even by the best intentioned or most highly informed mental health professional. But mental health professionals must be responsive to human need. They cannot ignore the real problems of the inner city. Some professionals who have tried seriously to understand urban life have at least been able to identify ways of engaging problems. Lerner's work (1972) on therapy in the ghetto is a case in point. She argues compellingly that interventions with the poor must be built around their needs and realities, and that paternalistic approaches that work for other groups will fail with them. That is an example of a significant first step. Others are needed.

The rest of this chapter considers several promising steps taken by mental health professionals to engage inner-city problems. The approach, as in the chapter on schools, is illustrative rather than exhaustive. Focusing on just a few programs, each different from the others in the problems it addresses and in its methods, may help to identify promising pathways for reducing ineffectiveness, misery, and dysfunction in the ghetto. The programs cited range from specific to broad and from person-oriented to group oriented. They also fall at different points along a hypothetical continuum anchored at one extreme by "repair" and at the other by "primary prevention."

DEVELOPMENTAL PROGRAMS

Factors Contributing to Deficit in Inner-City Children

Many recent contributions consider the early development of inner-city children and describe programs designed to make such development optimal (Chess & Thomas, 1969; Deutsch, Katz, & Jensen, 1968; Hellmuth, 1969a, 1969b; Hess & Bear, 1968; Horowitz & Paden, 1973; Jason, 1975; Miller & Woock, 1970; Roberts, 1967b). Diverse topics are covered in these reviews, including physical, cognitive, personality, language, and motivational development, family structure and influences, early stimulation, compensatory education, and inner-city schools. While these writings focus on black children, they also apply to other disadvantaged minorities. The literature in these areas is substantial, rapidly growing, and sometimes inconsistent—qualities that do not make for a crisp, authoritative summary. Nevertheless, it may be helpful to draw a loose sketch of the early development of inner-city children.

The Coleman report describes a massive, nationwide survey dealing with the equality of educational opportunity for racial groups (Coleman, 1966). A stark fact that anchors the report's finding is that about 85 percent of black students scored below whites on measures of educational function and achievement. There is a need to understand this finding. Divergent hypotheses have been advanced. Some emphasize home and family factors and the slum child's environment, whereas others, citing the "defeatism" that pervades ghetto schools (Clark, 1967),

stress the failings of inner-city schools. Still others remind us that the criteria (for example, IQ or achievement tests) used to assess educational progress may be inappropriate for inner-city children (Roberts, 1967a). There is much merit in each of these arguments. The controversy about whether educational achievement differences between racial groups reflect innate ability differences is still alive (Dreger, 1973; L'Abate, Oslin, & Stone, 1973; Miller & Woock, 1970). Jensen (1969) represents the view that there are true "racial differences," whereas Pettigrew (1967) takes the opposing position.

If slum children do less well in school than their nonslum peers, it is important to establish the factors behind such an outcome. For example, perceptual and attentive skills are important to effective school

- Kenneth B. Clark, psychologist and educator, has written about "defeatism" in ghetto schools.

functioning—particularly reading. Deutsch (1968) and Marans and Lourie (1969) report that inner-city children have disrupted, atypical development in these areas. Marans and Lourie believe that ghetto-reared children experience more perceptual *under*-stimulation and *over*stimulation than nonghetto children. Understimulation shows up in different ways for different age children. An infant left unattended for hours in his crib, or a young child who has no books, games, or toys is understimulated. A child who lacks stimulation is more likely to have trouble perceiving and assimilating the real world. Marans and Lourie (1969) use the term "overstimulation" to describe overexposure to intrusive, competing stimuli. Overstimulation may result from crowded living conditions, where people constantly come and go and there are high noise levels from multiple sources. They suggest that such conditions blur incoming stimuli and make it hard for the child to get appropriate feedback or to differentiate relevant from irrelevant inputs.

Behind these views is the belief that slum children often have inappropriate perceptual inputs which restrict development of adaptive perceptual skills. Deutsch (1968) suggests that many inner-city children may have to be trained to acquire the skills needed for attending to relevant stimuli. She believes that this can be achieved, first by teaching the child to attend, then by appropriate organization of stimuli, and finally through direct verbal explanation. White (1968) presents data suggesting that the first five months of life are very important for certain types of perceptual development and that structured visual input can influence when and how visual-motor responses are acquired.

Because language facilitates thought development and the acquisition of reading skills, it is very important to later school achievement. Thus, language development

among ghetto children has attracted much attention recently (Cazden, 1968; Bereiter, 1968; John & Goldstein, 1969; Marans & Lourie, 1969). Although current data suggest that ghetto children have "impaired" language development, such groups are actually quite variable (Sigel & Perry, 1968). One study, in fact, found that inner-city children were superior in a specific area of language development (Entwisle, 1969). Another point to keep in mind is that "proper" language development is usually defined in terms of prevailing white middle-class standards. This overlooks the fact that nonstandard black English is itself a well-structured, internally consistent system (Baratz, 1973; Jason, 1975).

Early language acquisition is closely related to the child's home and family situation. Those who believe that ghetto children are deficient in language tried to explain it on the basis of the language and communication "styles" of inner-city households, as, for example, the use of dialect that differs from the schools' middle-class English (Ramsey, 1969). Marans and Lourie (1969) argue that inner-city parents are often not good language identification models, either in actual behavior or values—at least, not by white middle-class standards. They speculate that language models in inner-city homes emphasize body language, facial expression, and abbreviated communications rather than words and sentences, and that such emphases impair the child's language development. They suggest that underdeveloped verbal skills interfere with a child's ability to handle his inner feelings and thus predispose him to frustration and overt eruptions of anger. Much of the foregoing is speculative rather than fact. But if language deficit is indeed widespread among slum children, this would hamper the acquisition of other adaptive skills needed for effective school performance.

Hess and Shipman's (1968) research suggests that maternal style relates to how dis-advantaged children approach cognitive tasks. Children performed poorly on such tasks, especially when their mothers used many imperatives and failed to provide mediating words or verbal cues to help them to use language to label and order stimuli. Slum children have been described as more responsive to authority than ra-tional explanation—a factor that inhibits reasoning skills. This view has led to an emphasis on teaching mediating, ordering, and information processing skills, rather than just facts, in programs that address the cognitive deficiences of the disadvantaged.

The early personality and motivational development of inner-city children has also been a topic of considerable interest (Ausu-bel & Ausubel, 1967; Christmas, 1973; Langner, 1967; Marans & Lourie, 1969; Pro-shansky & Newton, 1968). Such develop-ment is best understood in the context of social living conditions and of family struc-tures among black Americans. The black child all too soon becomes aware that many whites place a negative value on his skin color. Awareness of a disfavored social sta-tus promotes self-doubt, self-rejection, am-bivalence, and damaged esteem (Proshan-sky & Newton, 1968). Those feelings can easily lead to anxiety, hostility, a sense of social isolation, alienation, distrust, and helplessness. Several authors (Ausubel & Ausubel, 1967; Marans & Lourie, 1969) have hypothesized that the combination of feeling socially wronged, having loose fam-ily ties, limited home-emphasis on teaching of impulse control, and a punitive, authori-tarian disciplinary orientation increases de-linquency and antisocial acting-out among blacks.

Related factors affect the motivational de-velopment of the black child (Ausubel & Ausubel, 1967; Proshansky & Newton, 1968). Lack of opportunity is one such fac-tor. Another is the fact that many black families either place a low value on educa-tion or lack educated peer or adult models. And finally if the black child's early life ex-periences do not equip him for school work, he is more likely to fail. Nothing is quite so effective in discouraging motivation as failure. The child who cannot "cut it" in school, through no fault of his own, is not motivated to seek further education. And in our society education is a stepping stone to achievement and status. Zigler and But-terfield's (1969) work suggests that moti-vational influences on behavior start early and are very important for children. Refined analyses of their data showed that the intel-lectual improvement of disadvantaged chil-dren following a nursery school experience was due more to motivational than cogni-tive gains.

Certain family determinants also play an important role in the black's personality and motivational development (Jackson, 1973; H. Lewis, 1967; Rodman, 1969). Familial bonds, for several reasons, may be weaker among blacks than whites. Since illegiti-macy rates are higher among blacks (H. Lewis, 1967), they have fewer stable family structures. Moreover, lack of opportunity limits the black male's chances of getting and holding good jobs. That undercuts his role of family "breadwinner," leads to his devaluation as a family member, and ulti-mately perhaps to separation from the fam-ily. Inner-city families are thus more likely to be matriarchal and/or broken. Mothers, even those with very young children, must work to survive even if that loosens ties with children and familiness. Thus, many inner-city households may be fluid groupings of several generations and families in enlarged, changing collectivities with shifting, prag-matically determined lines of responsibility. Grandparents, neighbors, or only slightly older siblings often care for very young children, who may be required to do things that tax their capacities (Ausubel & Ausubel, 1967; Marans & Lourie, 1969). These demands may be for self-care activities such as dressing and feeding oneself, or homemaker functions such as housecleaning and shopping. A three or four-year-old child might thus be called on to cross busy intersections, carry heavy bundles, and hang on to change. A child-care situation in which a six-year-old must take care of a two-year-old illustrates a demand for early responsibility.

In trying to sketch a broad developmental profile for inner-city children, our oversimplified discussion has ignored the enormous variability within black and white groups and the overlap between groups. It thus overlooks the issue of why two children raised under comparably adverse conditions develop differently. It also overweights psychological factors. Birch (1969) warns against such an emphasis and urges that physical and health factors also be considered in trying to understand the development of socially disadvantaged children. Examining prenatal determinants, prematurity, and obstetric care, as well as such post-natal factors as diet and malnutrition, health care and illness, Birch concludes that "a serious consideration of available health information leaves little or no doubt that children who are economically and socially disadvantaged in an ethnic group exposed to discrimination are exposed to massively excessive risks for maldevelopment" (p. 286). Birch makes the further point that such risks have serious direct and indirect consequences for the child's ability to learn. An example of a direct danger is the poor development of physical systems that subserve learning. Indirect consequences include reduced environmental responsiveness, distractibility, loss of learning time, and interference with learning during critical developmental periods. A hungry or sick child cannot profit maximally from educational opportunities.

The discussion so far overemphasizes deficit development among the disadvantaged at the expense of positive factors such as emerging group identity, pride, and a sense of shared effort in pursuing human rights. Proshansky and Newton (1968) warn against such an exclusive orientation. The special resources of the disadvantaged should be kept in mind, not to balance a hypothetical scoreboard, but to indicate that they can potentially be harnessed in dealing with their problems (Rappaport et al., 1975). For example, although earlier we used the negative term "forced precocity" in speaking about ghetto children, one could equally well use a positively valued term such as "independence" for the same behavior and think of it as a resource.

Special Remedial Programs

Harsh conditions of inner-city living make people more vulnerable to adaptive problems. But whatever these are, they do not typically appear in the form of high referral rates to mental health professionals. In fact, there is growing doubt about whether they show up in total prevalance rates for mental disorder (See & Miller, 1973). Among the clearer indications of emerging difficulties, however, are the problems many inner-city children have in adapting to school (Gordon, 1968).

How might the school experience of inner-city children be improved? Several possible solutions have been proposed (Stendler-Lavatelli, 1968). A first obvious, but complex, one is the primary preventive step of improving basic living conditions (such as, housing, employment, opportunity) in the ghetto, on the assumption that improving man's general well-being will also improve his adaptation. Second, inner-city schools must create environments that take the child's prior life experiences into careful account. Third, early identification and intervention programs that provide training and experience for children with background deficiencies are needed to help them cope more effectively, and realistically, with later demands.

These approaches can all be attempted at the same time. Of the three, mental health professionals are currently best qualified for early intervention and least for primary prevention. The section to follow illustrates programs that try to improve the disadvantaged child's coping and adaptive skills.

Broad-Gauge Compensatory Education

Compensatory education is a term used to describe a variety of educational enrichment programs, usually at the preschool level. Such programs assume that disadvantaged children have developmental defects or lack certain skills needed for educational progress (Gottfried, 1973; Jason, 1975). Gordon (1968) suggests that these programs are both remedial, because they fill cultural, social, and academic gaps, and preventive, because they short-cut educational failure. Compensatory education is motivated by social concerns about underdeveloped human potential and the human toll that results from being disadvantaged. But beyond that, Hunt (1968) argues that both psychological theory and recent research findings support the view that compensatory education is worthwhile and important. He rejects the assumption that intelligence is rigidly fixed, that child development is predetermined, and that preverbal experience is unimportant for later learning. Each of these would, in the past, have been considered a serious barrier to compensatory educational programs.

Head Start has been the most ambitious national effort to promote early education for the disadvantaged (Hellmuth, 1969b; Payne et al., 1973). Head Start's broad ob-

jectives are to enhance the educational, psychological, and physical development of disadvantaged children and the well-being of their families and their community. In practice, Head Start centers have developed very different emphases and programs—some educational, others stressing community service. Some provide socialization training and enriched experience, others feature perceptual and language training. Many Head Start programs also emphasize outreach to families and to the community. Head Start's enormity and complexity are well reflected in the fact that New York City's program included more than 25,000 youngsters in nearly 300 Head Start centers (Ginsberg & Greenhill, 1969) and a total program staff of more than 10,000.

Because Head Start includes so many and such different programs, it is next to impossible to evaluate it as an entity. However, several themes come up fairly often in descriptions of various Head Start programs: teaching children process-like skills rather than simple facts (Omwake, 1969); belief in the importance of following-up Head Start children (Egbert, 1969); and the conviction that manipulative, self-corrective toys, controlled environment, and home teaching programs (for example, Weikart & Lambie, 1969) are useful educational approaches (Gordon, 1969). Although many people believe that Head Start has helped children to acquire specific skills such as reading (Ramsey, 1969), we still lack a clear final picture of what the program has accomplished.

A recent sympathetic, but nevertheless realistic, review (Payne et al., 1973) recognizes many of the concerns expressed about Head Start's diverse programs and objectives. Examples include an overemphasis on intellectual achievement in comparison to such noncognitive goals as "changes in attitude, emotional stability, social maturity, task-involvement, initiative" (Gordon, 1969,

p. 13), failure to consider long-term as well as immediate effects, and the need to evaluate Head Start's impact on family, school, and community agencies, as well as on the child. While serious critics have little trouble identifying Head Start's flaws, they argue that on balance its goods outweigh its bads and that it should be maintained and strengthened (Payne et al., 1973).

In contrast to the broad array of programs that comprise Head Start and make it so difficult to evaluate, we next consider several early enrichment programs with more specific objectives and fewer obstacles to evaluation. A recent volume by Stanley (1972) presents in-depth summaries of five of these programs.

The Illinois Program

Bereiter and Englemann (1966, 1968) describe an approach that bypasses several of the typical assumptions made about the early development of disadvantaged children. These investigators view the deficits of disadvantaged preschoolers in the same way as skill deficits in the nondisadvantaged. They try to provide these children with the necessary prerequisites on a straight teaching basis. Since the disadvantaged child's language and reasoning skills may be weak, the program emphasizes these two areas, using a straightforward learning experience with few conventional nursery school activities.

The Illinois program is conducted with groups of about 15 four-year-olds. The school day is built around three focused 20-minute lessons in language, reading, and number work. Language acquisition, particularly rudimentary language that allows the child to learn other things, is the program's most central goal. In oversimplified terms, language training proceeds as if English were to be learned as a second language.

The training requires only one assumption —that the child can imitate. Language training starts with, and builds on, two simple identity statements, "This is a ———" and "This is not a ———." After these identities are mastered, the program moves to a slightly more complex structure: "This ——— is ———," using negative and plural variations, comparatives, subclass nouns, and different types of predicates. After this second training phase has been completed, children can expand rapidly to active verbs, different tenses, and pronouns. Then they go on to logical "if-then" statements involving concepts such as: "all," "only," "some," "and," and "or." The goal is to develop a language of deductive reasoning, based on prior acquisition of statement forms and concept types. Teaching generalizable rules is handled through patterned drill and correction.

Teaching rests on variants of five basic strategies: Verbatim Repetition (This block is red); Yes-No Questions (Is this block red?); Location Tasks (Show me a red block); Statement Projection (Tell me about this piece of chalk); and Deduction (This chalk is not red; do you know what color it is?). These tasks form a rough hierarchy of difficulty. Whereas the early emphasis is on the simple strategies, later the balance swings to deduction. Repetition, discipline, and drill are used heavily throughout. The pace is fast and children are required to put forth continued effort. Casual guessing is discouraged and prompt correction, including pronunciation, is emphasized. Arithmetic is also taught as if it were a language—in a highly verbal way, using generalizable rules.

Early reports on the effectiveness of Bereiter and Englemann's program have been encouraging (Bereiter, 1968). Children acquire color names, master prepositional usage, and use proper, formal grammatical patterns within several months. Children in the first program group were found to be performing at or above grade level in arithmetic, their best subject, reading, and spelling. The IQ of this group increased from 95 to 105 during the kindergarten year; for a second group, IQ jumped from 95 to 112. This second group had two control groups —one that participated in instructional games and another that had a traditional nursery school experience. Prior schooling and pupil-teacher ratios were comparable for experimentals and controls. Program children exceeded controls in reading, spelling, and arithmetic, significantly so on all but the latter.

Bereiter and Englemann's program has its advocates and critics (Stendler-Lavatelli, 1968). Those who like it point to the program's simplicity, logic, apparent workability, and empirical findings. Concerns have been voiced about the program's "narrowness" and rote-drill emphasis. Some people fear that even though program children can acquire situation-appropriate responses, these will not endure or generalize to the more complex, demanding school situation. The ultimate answer to this challenge must come from long-term follow-up of the educational and personal development of those in the program. It would be shortsighted, however, to reject the program before long-term evaluations are done, if only because it addresses a profound social-educational problem not well handled by existing approaches. This is no time to look such a gift horse in the mouth.

Institute for Developmental Studies Program

The early enrichment program of the Institute of Developmental Studies (IDS) in New York (Deutsch & Deutsch, 1968; Stendler-Lavatelli, 1968) rests on the twin assumptions that the environment plays a vital role in cognitive development and that slum environments offer less adequate stimuli than middle-class ones for such development. Hence the program uses an enriched, therapeutic curriculum for five years—two preschool and the first three school years. It features training in language, arithmetic, science, reading, and concept formation. Language training is basic. It pervades all of the child's classroom activities. Training in vocabulary, concept development, and listening are considered essential for acquiring reading skills. Skill acquisition follows a three-stage sequence. In the first (sensorimotor), the child has contact with concrete objects. In the second (perceptual), he learns contrasting shapes, colors, and sounds, and in the third (ideation-represen-

Robert de Villeneuve

A slum environment can be confining.

tational), he deals abstractly with things and concepts without concrete stimuli or perceptual props.

Recognizing that the development of slum children is variable, the program's planning takes the individual child's status into account. Thus, IDS staff has developed methods for identifying precise, relatively narrow areas of slowdown in specific children. Cultural enrichment is provided by frequent field trips to museums, parks, libraries, and zoos.

Although the IDS program is housed in a typical school setting, it uses fairly unique self-teaching materials. Its Listening Center permits small groups of children to hear tapes of their teacher, other people, and a variety of different language excerpts that are not typical in their daily environment. A Language Master, a two-tracked tape recorder, is used to provide children immediate feedback and direct comparison of their teacher's and their own verbal productions. The program also uses an Alphabet Board with cut-out letter-shaped recesses into which the child learns to place appropriate letter forms to help develop visual discrimination. And finally, a "talking typewriter" (Moore & Anderson, 1968) is used to encourage development of reading skills.

Evaluation of the IDS program was based on comparisons between its students, nearly all black slum children from Harlem, and two control groups with similar backgrounds. One of the latter entered first grade without prior educational experience whereas the other had had a standard kindergarten experience. Both general and specific tests were used to compare the groups. On standard intelligence measures program children scored higher than the matched controls after the first year. These differences were even greater after the second year.

The IDS staff was concerned with noncognitive as well as cognitive change, particularly in self-concept. Literature references often suggest that disadvantaged children have poorer self-images and more negative self-attitudes than the nondisadvantaged, though serious methodological failings of studies in the area have been noted (Christmas, 1973). One study (Whiteman & Deutsch, 1968) found that the higher the slum child scored on a measure of environmental impoverishment, the poorer was his self-concept. One of IDS's important objectives was to enhance self-concept and to overcome negative self-attitudes in these children. Play and reading activities were built around black families, and props, such as full-length mirrors and photographs of the children, were used to foster self-awareness and positive identity. Impressionistic evaluation of self-concept change was favorable, not only for program children, but also in terms of positive "spill-over" for other members of their families.

The Peabody Early Training Project

The Peabody Early Training Project (Gray & Klaus, 1965, 1968) sought to prevent school retardation among culturally deprived children by building good motivation and aiding cognitive development. The program involved an intensive 10-week summer preschool experience. One group of disadvantaged children spent three consecutive summers in such a program and another spent two summers in it. Home visitors were used throughout the year to keep mothers and children continually involved in activities started in the summer programs and to make suggestions to facilitate the child's personal and educational development. The home visit part of the program continued through first grade. Program children were compared to two demographically comparable control groups.

The subjects were all deprived urban black children. Deprivation was defined in terms of poor housing, parent occupation and education (eighth grade or below), and income well below the then-established national poverty figure of $3000 per year. Children were trained in groups of about 20, each with a teacher and several adult (black and white, male and female) assistants—a highly favorable adult-pupil ratio.

Motivational and skill training were the key program objectives. Motivation training was aimed at fostering attitudes and behaviors considered important for school success such as an achievement orientation, learning to delay gratification and to persist, developing school-related interests, and identifying with adult role-models. Reinforcement and shaping techniques, based on loose guidelines rather than specific formal schedules, were used to promote such development. Skill training focused on perceptual, concept, and language development. A rich learning environment was provided to encourage the child to process information in keeping with his abilities.

Experimental and control children were compared on a number of intellectual measures, based on pre-post change during the 27-month preschool project period. On one IQ measure (the Binet) program children improved an average of nine points, from 86 to 95, while controls dropped an average of six points—a statistically significant difference. Similar findings were reported for other intelligence measures. Moreover, program children significantly exceeded controls on standard school entrance tests, including reading-readiness on which they did nearly as well as nondisadvantaged children. However, Gray and Klaus (1968) found that some of the improvements had eroded by the time first-grade achievement tests were given.

Infant Stimulation

The rapid spread of enrichment programs for the preschool disadvantaged has increased awareness of the potential and the limits of such programs. One limit is the fact that follow-through seems vital if program gains are to be maintained (Egbert, 1969). Another comes from recognizing the deep-seated nature of developmental problems among the disadvantaged. This has led to an exploration of even earlier programs of infant stimulation for this group (Gottfried, 1973; Jason, 1975; Stendler-Lavatelli, 1968). This section presents examples of such programs.

Caldwell (1968) developed an infant stimulation program based on the assumption that the first three years critically shape the disadvantaged child's cognitive and personal development. She established a small educational day-care unit that accommodated about 25 culturally deprived youngsters, divided into three age groups starting with six-month-old infants. The children attended this intensive program 6–9 hours daily, five days a week.

The broad aim of Caldwell's program was to improve children's personal and social development. But it also had more specific goals such as strengthening children's sense of trust in adults, enhancing their self-image, instilling an achievement orientation, improving social skills, and providing feelings of mastery, curiosity, intellectual independence, and a capacity to delay gratification. Caldwell suggests that these goals could be met through a proper learning climate and by teachers who have a broad guiding orientation, rather than through specific learning activities. The program's sensory, perceptual, and cognitive training all emphasized watching, listening, classifying, ordering, coordinating and relating, memorizing, conceptualizing, and problem-solving. "Culturally relevant knowledge" was promoted by continually exposing the child to new words, events, and experiences.

Program evaluation was restricted by an uneven flow of children and because a control group was not selected until 18 months after the program started. Nevertheless, children who were in the program for three or four months showed a significant mean IQ gain of six points. This was encouraging because, in that age-span, disadvantaged children often show IQ decreases in their natural environments. Program children were also reported to have gained in social competence (Caldwell, 1968).

Schaefer's (1968) approach to infant stimulation involved home tutoring as the active ingredient. This program assumed that verbal stimulation, during the language acquisition period, could accelerate the intellectual development of disadvantaged children. Inner-city black male children in Washington, D.C., all 14 months old, were identified through door-to-door solicitation. For a child to be included in the program, the family had to meet at least two of the following three criteria: income under $5000; mother's education less than 12th grade; and mother's occupational level semi-skilled or lower. Mothers also had to be interested in the program. Sixty-four identified children were divided into matched experimental and control groups.

Children started the program at age 15 months and stayed in it until they were 36 months old. Home visits were made by college-trained tutors, five days a week, for an hour a day. Each tutor, on the average, worked with four children. Typically, two tutors worked with a single child, alternat-

ing weeks. Tutors established close personal relationships with the children and provided them with a variety of enriching experiences and verbal stimulation. A full range of curriculum items was used, including sorting and classifying activities, building objects, games, and musical activities. Tutors also served as part-time mothers by reading, talking, and playing games with children, and taking them for walks and small trips.

The intellectual status of experimental and control subjects at ages 14, 21, 27, and 36 months was compared. IQ scores for the E group held roughly constant (14 month IQ = 105; 36 month IQ = 106), whereas the C group fell sharply (14 month IQ = 108; 36 month IQ = 89). Thus, experimental children had significantly higher post-program IQ scores, due mostly to the marked drop in controls. Program children also significantly exceeded controls on perceptual tests and ratings of task-oriented behavior at age 36 months. Home observations suggested that additional, incidental changes also took place during the program. For example, the children's interests expanded and mothers of program children became more involved. But since there were no home observations for controls, those impressions are difficult to evaluate. Follow-up data suggested that the IQ scores of program children dropped when the program ended, but that language skills held up.

A series of studies in Rochester, New York (Jason, Clarfield, & Cowen, 1973; Jason & Kimbrough, 1974; Specter & Cowen, 1971), describes a ghetto-based infant stimulation program for very young children with serious early developmental problems. This program was first established for infants identified, through routine well-baby examinations in a Neighborhood Health Center, as having slow early language and social development in the absense of physiological or neurological signs.

The program has gone through several stages and much expansion. Initially, it was based on four main elements: (1) establishing a committed human relationship with the children; (2) environmental enrichment using games, toys, and activities; (3) language modeling and reinforcement; and (4) shaping prosocial behavior. College student volunteers worked with the children. Children were seen 2–3 times a week for about five months. Initial evaluations, lacking control groups, showed consistent, significant increases (averaging 15 points) in the developmental quotients of program children. But, follow-up reports after the program ended showed that these gains began to erode quickly—a finding similar to ones reported by other investigators in this area.

Recent modifications of this program were designed to maintain the early gains shown in the initial program. For example, the program has been broadened to include specific behavior modification approaches modeled directly in the home. Parent discussion groups have been formed so that the program's aims and methods can be communicated directly. Videotapes of program sessions have been used to facilitate this process. Inner-city nonprofessionals, as well as college students, have been trained to work with the children. Continuing children's groups have been formed so that infant stimulation "alumni" can be worked with after they finish the original program. The most recent program evaluation (Jason & Kimbrough, 1974) shows that the experimental children improved significantly on IQ measures compared to a matched, nonprogram control group.

Collectively, these infant stimulation programs show that the intellectual and social behavior of very young disadvantaged children can be improved dramatically in short time periods. But, if such programs are no more than isolated entities, their positive effects will be sharply limited. They must work more closely with families. They must continue over long time periods. And they must be attentive to the realities of ghetto life. The last point is vital. Symptomatic solutions to the broad, deeply rooted problems of inner-city living are likely to fail.

The Woodlawn Program

The Woodlawn program (Kellam et al, 1975) unlike the preceding ones, deals with young ghetto children already in the schools. It is considered here, rather than in Chapter 18, because its main focus is on problems of the black, inner-city ghetto. Woodlawn is a black ghetto area in South Chicago which went through rapid and dramatic transition between 1950 and the mid-1960s. By the end of that period, the area had taken on most of the characteristics of an urban slum. Its population was 98 percent black, housing was inadequate and overcrowded, unemployment and public assistance rates were high, and income levels were low. Relationships between the schools and the community were poor.

Having established that school failure was a rampant problem in Woodlawn, the program's main goal was to help young children get off on the right foot in school. That meant improving the children's school performance and strengthening their sense of personal well-being.

It is difficult to summarize the Woodlawn program because it was complex, changed continually, and had significant community-based components. Its main constancy was its clear focus on the school as a social system. In general, Woodlawn emphasized consultation with teachers and school administrators, weekly classroom meetings with children and teachers, and meetings to inform parents about the program and to enlist their support. These interventions took place during the second semester of the first school year. The Woodlawn program rarely stood pat. As an example, in the program's first year classroom meetings included only a small number of children with obvious problems. In later years, they included *all* children and sometimes even parents.

The results of the Woodlawn program were tracked through a series of objective evaluations. The 12 public schools in the area were initially divided by "coin-flip" into six experimental (program) and six control schools. Periodic evaluations compared these groups on measures of intellectual status, personality, and behavior. An instrument called the "Teachers Observation of Classroom Adjustment" (TOCA) was developed to assess children's social adaptation using four-point scales in the areas of social contact, accepting authority, maturity, cognitive achievement, and ability to concentrate. Specific defining items were provided for all five areas, and a global adaptation rating was used. TOCA ratings were made on the basis of information received about each child through a standardized interview with his teacher.

Several measures were used to assess children's psychological well-being. These included direct clinical observation, a mother's symptom inventory completed by all first grade mothers, and a brief self-report measure called "How I Feel."

Even though the Woodlawn project did not always yield firm evidence of the program's effectiveness, it still produced informative findings. As an example, for program children success in school increased psychological well-being and failure decreased it. Woodlawn also found that early school maladaptation related to later symptomatology and that early symptomatology predicted later social dysfunction. Throughout, the authors stress the close relation between effective school performance and personal well-being. School failure made the black ghetto child more vulnerable to symptoms. And strengthening the relation between school adaptation and personal well-being did not increase the numbers of children with severe symptoms in the program schools.

Woodlawn was an ambitious, persistent, self-critical project. Although its central findings fail to validate clearly its early intervention procedure, they are nevertheless useful. Moreover, there were important "secondary" program benefits, such as bridging the wide gap between ghetto homes and schools and encouraging community involvement. Woodlawn's program model and its emphasis on the links between effective school adaptation and sound personal development among ghetto children should not be ignored. The program is an important attempt to deal with a knotty social problem. Its goal—to engineer school experiences that maximize the ghetto child's adaptation and personal development—and its methods can advance future work in this area.

COMMUNITY ACTION PROGRAMS IN THE INNER-CITY

Background Considerations

Enrichment programs are for young inner-city children. Their thrust is preventive; they seek to short-circuit tomorrow's problems. But other grave here-and-now problems in the inner city demand attention. Generally speaking, because past efforts of the middle-class mental health establishment have not reached such problems, there is plenty of room for innovative programs in this area. The rest of this chapter considers several action-oriented programs aimed at identified, but unsolved, problems of the inner city.

The Residential Youth Center

Rationale and Program

Goldenberg (1968, 1969, 1971) developed and evaluated a new type of short-term residential setting—the Residential Youth Center (RYC)—to promote the growth of inner-city youth with adaptive problems. The RYC program assumes that we cannot produce positive change in the poor simply by focusing on individuals; rather we must develop settings that foster positive change.

RYC planners considered and rejected several key assumptions of prior programs. For example, the Job Corps assumes that the problems of the poor are best solved in settings other than those that produce them. By contrast, the RYC believes that problems of the urban poor are best solved on their own turf. The traditional view is that mental health professionals are the best qualified people to bring needed services to the poor. This assumption, too, was rejected in favor of the view that knowledgeable, committed, indigenous nonprofessionals are the most appropriate change-agents. Finally, RYC discarded the widely held notion that a helping agency's structure and operating policies should be in professional hands in favor of the view that a setting's core staff and residents should have the main decision-making powers.

The RYC was located in the heart of the inner-city within easy walking distance of the homes of prospective residents. Its building was a converted neighborhood rooming house that looked just like other neighborhood houses. The Center emphasized survival, coping, and self-help in the face of realistic life circumstances and prob-

lems, rather than psychodynamics. Staff were chosen on the basis of knowledge of the inner city, prior experience with the poor, a flexible orientation to change, and commitment to project aims, rather than for their educational backgrounds and degrees. The staff consisted mostly of young people (mean age, under 30) who had been born and raised in the inner city. Educationally, most, though not all, were high school graduates.

The RYC had what is called a "horizontal" administrative organization. Thus, each staff member, from director of janitor, had responsibility for decisions and interventions with a certain number of residents and their families. Although there were staff meetings to discuss specific youths and their problems and to formulate recommendations, final responsibility was always vested in the staff person assigned to a particular enrollee. The Center's horizontal administrative structure required that duties which are part of the setting's normal operation be shared. Thus, all staff members had to do kitchen work on the cook's day off and to sleep in when "live-in" counselors were off duty. Similarly, key administrative responsibilities typically reserved for "top brass" were distributed among staff members on the basis of their experience, interest, and ability. Staff growth and change were primary objectives at the RYC.

The RYC was set up as a community facility rather than as a regimented institutional setting. Every effort was made to create a home-like atmosphere with no restrictions on visiting hours and with open access to and from the surrounding community. The Center's key "change agents" were indigenous neighborhood nonprofessionals, each of whom had direct responsibility for a certain number of residents and their families. Since many of the resident youths had given up on education, personal and vocational development were major goals. Center staff developed effective contacts with community vocational manpower and personnel programs to help prepare residents for full-time employment in an area of their choice.

All staff members counseled residents, formally and informally, individually and in small groups, as a central part of the program. In other words, such counseling was not restricted to specific times and places. The RYC also provided ample opportunity for academic and other learning experiences.

Residents participated actively in the Center's operation and governance. A Resident House Council had responsibility for program development, formulating rules of self-government, and fostering Center-community interactions. This self-government was designed to encourage meaningful peer interactions and to give residents a stake in making decisions. Self-help and personal goal setting were also emphasized heavily and active steps were taken to dispel the view that the Center was an easy "handout." Residents had to support the Center financially as much as they could. They were expected, for example, to pay rent up to 30 percent of their weekly salaries, with a ceiling of $15 per week.

The RYC was geared to a capacity of 25 youths. Enrollees had histories of chronic educational, social, vocational, and personal failure. Admission was voluntary. When the Center admitted its first group of 20 residents, ranging in age from 16–21, a comparable group of 20 control youths was identified for purposes of program evaluation. The average "length of stay" of RYC enrollees was five months. Residents and controls were compared pre and post on a series of behavior and attitude measures. Post-testing was done 9–12 months after the program started.

Evaluation

The main criteria used to evaluate the RYC program were the behaviors that defined the failures of residents before they entered it. For example, employment of residents increased from 54 to 93 percent during the evaluation period; for controls it decreased from 60 to 50 percent. The 39 percent employment gain for residents compared to the 10 percent loss for controls yielded a differential net gain of 49 percent. Attendance at work also improved comparably for residents compared to controls. Residents increased their income by an average of $20 per week (80 percent) over the evaluation period while controls lost an average of $8 per week (29 percent). Thus, the differential net income gain favoring residents was 109 percent, or $28 per week.

Another key set of criteria used was contact with the police. Arrests among residents decreased by 49 percent in the post-project period, whereas controls showed a 22 percent increase—a net difference of 71 percent favoring residents. In absolute figures this meant that residents averaged under one arrest each during the six-month post-RYC period; by contrast, controls exceeded two arrests each for the same period. Residents showed a 54 percent decrease in number of days spent in jail, while controls had an 84 percent increase; the net differential of 138 percent again favored the residents. The consistent pattern of differences favoring the residents on the measures taken is the most impressive evidence of the program's worth. These data are particularly meaningful because the criteria are important and objective behavioral measures.

Residents and controls were also compared on attitudes. Whereas the residents' feelings of alienation decreased significantly in the pre-post comparison period, those of the controls increased significantly; thus, at the post-point residents felt significantly less alienated than controls. Residents' authoritarianism scores also dropped significantly while controls stayed the same on this measure. At the post-point residents had significantly lower authoritarianism scores than controls. The reverse was true on a measure of trust. Whereas residents remained the same on this measure, controls became significantly less trusting during the evaluation period. A ten-scale semantic differential measure of the "World I Live In" yielded significantly more positive changes in outlook for residents than for controls. There were no differences between the groups on the Machiavellianism scale, a measure of how much people think they can manipulate their world, or on a social desirability measure. The absence of social desirability differences between the groups suggests that other significant attitude differences were *not* due to a need by residents to produce "proper" responses. Collectively, the attitude findings also support the view that the RYC program brought about significant, positive changes in the target youths.

Cost is another way to evaluate program effects. The RYC program had an initial annual budget of about $150,000. Since the facility houses 25 youths with an average stay of 5½ months each, about 50 youths a year can be served at an average cost of $3000 per resident. It is instructive to contrast this figure to other cost accounting data. For example, it is estimated (Duggan, 1965) that the cost of processing a single youth through juvenile court is roughly $4000, and that a community's total support cost for a single high school dropout who reaches the welfare rolls exceeds $30,000. Thus, for those who are not impressed by RYC's human changes, its value (savings) can also be figured in dollars and cents. The

documented success of the original RYC has led to the establishment of similar centers in other communities.

Reinforcement and Modeling Procedures with Delinquents

The frameworks of operant conditioning, behavior modification, and modeling (Sarason, 1968; Sarason & Ganzer, 1969; Schwitzgebel, 1964, 1967; Slack, 1963) have generated other innovative approaches to delinquency among inner-city youths. Slack's work in this area began with the incidental observation that delinquents who were hired as paid research interviewees on a project seemed both to enjoy and profit from the experience. This prompted Schwitzgebel (1964) to set up a storefront called the "Street Corner Research Laboratory" in a community area with a high delinquency rate. Neighborhood youth between the ages of 15 and 20 with arrest and jail records were contacted on street corners, in pool rooms, and through gang acquaintances and offered the paid job of talking into a tape recorder. Different reinforcements, such as warm welcoming greetings or food, were used to encourage attendance and punctuality. The youths worked anywhere from one to three hours weekly for nine months, often perceiving the job as a "soft touch." Two years after the project ended, participating delinquents had fewer offenses and less time in reform school or jail than comparable nonproject controls.

Schwitzgebel's later study (1967) compared two experimental delinquent youth groups averaging 16 years in age with a control group. Once again youths were engaged as employees under the guise of learning more about their attitudes and ideas. Experimental subjects completed roughly 20 tape-recorded interviews during a three-month period while controls completed only two. Positive reinforcers such as money, cigarettes, and candy were given to one experimental group for prosocial behavior (such as, cooperativeness, helping others, tactfulness). The second experimental group received negative verbal reinforcements or inattention following hostile or aggressive remarks about others. There were significant increases in positive statements about people, punctuality, and behavioral indications of cooperativeness and employability in the positive reinforcement group. But, the negatively reinforced group failed to reduce its hostile or aggressive statements.

Slack's (1963) Project SCORE used a similar approach. SCORE is a low cost program designed to reduce offenses among hard-core teenaged delinquents in metropolitan areas. It used reinforcers such as money, food, clothing, and a prestigious meeting place in ways designed to reduce crime. A SCORE worker was able to serve 30–50 youths. Slack hired youths as partners in the "business" of crime reduction, paying them for such activities as making tape recordings or speeches, acting, or attending meetings. His relation to the teenagers was much like that of a scientist to a subject. The youth was told that he was a worker whose job it was to discover the cause and cure of juvenile crime. He was paid for things he actually did, such as construction work, painting, or conducting meetings. He saw himself as an applied scientist doing the job of producing "clean man" (that is, crime-free) days for a community. SCORE was financed by community agencies and private sources concerned with crime reduction. It operated from storefronts or lofts. The worker promoted activities (for example, running a small business or newspaper) that could compete with delinquent behavior. Immediate reinforcement was a primary action principle and red-tape or

delay of gratification was avoided.

Sarason and his associates (Sarason, 1968; Sarason & Ganzer, 1969) describe an approach used with institutional delinquents that applied *modeling* principles to social influence and behavior modification. These investigators reasoned that if delinquents could watch socially acceptable behavior-models engage in positive role behaviors and have a chance to practice these behaviors, it would enlarge and strengthen their repertoire of prosocial responses. They worked with 15–18-year-old male first offenders, most diagnosed as neurotic or with personality trait disturbances, in a detention center in the State of Washington. This center accommodated short-term residents, living together in cottage units of 20–25 for an average of six weeks.

Specific modeling scripts, revelant to real-life situations for the offenders, and close rapport between the models and the target youths were needed for the approach to work. Specially trained psychology graduate students served as models. They spent time getting to know the offenders and their needs, desires, goals, and problems. Based on these contacts, the research team developed about 20 scripts in relevant areas such as coping with authority, planning ahead, handling negative pressure from peers, and interacting in positive, social ways with others.

The actual training sessions, which were either tape recorded or videotaped, included two models and four youths. Sessions began by having one model introduce the scene. Both models then acted it out with the boys observing. One youth then summarized and explained the scene, after which the models discussed and commented on it, replaying the recording. After that, a pair of youths enacted the same scene, which was also replayed. The same procedure was followed with the other pair.

Finally, the group developed session summaries and comments on its broader applicability.

There were three subject groups in the project. The first went through the entire modeling procedure as described above. The second role-played the situations without prior modeling, and the third was a control group with no experimental manipulations. The three groups were matched for age, IQ and severity-chronicity of prior delinquencies. The experimental and control groups were compared on self-report measures and staff behavioral ratings. The latter included a 25-item Behavior Rating Scale, requiring judgments of specific behaviors, such as lying and table manners, and a gross weekly Behavior Summary assessing seven areas such as peer relations, authority relations, and work performance. Experimental subjects showed more positive behavior and attitude changes than controls on these measures. These differences were sharper for subjects who had modeling plus role-playing than for those who had role-playing alone.

Workers cited in this section see delinquency as being due to inadequate learning experiences. Delinquent youths are thought of as people who have failed to acquire certain forms of adaptive behavior and socially accepted responses. Thus viewed, the challenge is to create situations in which appropriate learning can occur. Many people believe that modeling and behavior modification procedures have much to offer in this regard. A growing body of data supports this view.

New Careers

The New Careers program has been a socially significant development (Fishman et al., 1969; Pearl & Riessman, 1965; Riessman & Popper, 1968). This broad program is designed to deal with concrete problems of the urban poor. It includes specific features that address mental health issues. New Careers programs, which were pioneered in Washington, D.C., New York, Boston, and New Haven in the early and middle 1960s (Riessman & Popper, 1968), have since spread to many communties around the country.

Earlier chapters emphasized the close connection among the poor between everyday problems of living and those that middle-class professionals include under the umbrella of "mental health." For example, there is a widespread conviction that unemployment is the root problem of the poor (Kennedy, 1968). For many poor people, not having a job and a chance in life are the well-springs from which other problems flow. Riessman and Popper (1968, p. 6) argue strongly that employment is everyone's right: "in an affluent, automated society the number of persons needed to perform . . . tasks equals the number of persons for whom there are no other jobs." Although automation and advances in technology have eliminated many jobs, they have also opened up new possibilities for dealing with human adjustment problems by freeing manpower for a concerted attack on areas of social need in health, education, and welfare.

The New Careers movement seeks to provide poor people with an opportunity in life by giving them jobs that extend human services to other poor people who need them—reaching the heretofore unreachable. New Careers also enables poor people to experience educational growth and personal advancement, reorganizes service agencies to meet needs of their clientele better, and frees professionals to supervise, consult, and create new programs.

By mandate, New Careers' programs must provide permanent jobs for the unemployed, including the uneducated and unskilled, establish job ladders that allow the skilled and talented to advance, and create human service jobs that can contribute to society's well-being (Pearl & Riessman, 1965). New Careers provides both the opportunity to enter a system without prior qualifications and the possibility of advancing in it (MacLennan, 1969).

New Careers' programs are not built along traditional mental health lines to serve such "disordered" clinical groups as schizophrenics, alcoholics, or children with learning disabilities. They are designed to provide mental health benefits for help-agents as well as for target populations. Riessman (1965) formally recognizes that potential in describing the "helper-therapy" principle, that is, the growth and therapeutic value that the helper experiences by virtue of genuinely helping other human beings in need.

The Howard University Institute for Youth Studies (IYS) Program

The Howard University Institute for Youth Studies (IYS) program (Fishman et al., 1969; Klein, 1967; MacLennan, 1969; MacLennan et al., 1966) is one of the first, largest and most influential of the New Careers' programs. It was established in Washington, D.C., primarily for unemployed school dropouts—largely multiproblem, delinquent youth, ages 16–21. The problems that IYS addresses reflect New Careers' objectives. IYS is concerned with the high unemployment rates and chronic alienation of ghetto youth, unmet needs for a variety of human services in the inner-city, and the ever-widening chasm between "haves" and "have nots" in urban society.

The IYS trained youth for human service activities in small groups, paid them from the start, and provided salary increases for

Robert de Villeneuve

Inner-city youth frequently are discouraged by their "have not" status in a consumer-oriented society and may react accordingly.

on-the-job progress. Training sought to provide skills needed for specific jobs. Most of IYS training was for human service in health and mental health, recreation, education, child care, social service, and enforcement.

Training was built around "core" groups (Klein, 1967) designed to help the trainee to learn more about himself, his immediate community, and the world at large. These meetings had the further aims of teaching trainees to relate job problems to broader contexts, to acquire skill in observation and recording, to use supervision, to get to know community services, and to learn interpersonal skills. Thus, although training had specific objectives, it was flexible enough to allow shifts to other roles and settings if that became necessary. Core group training, was supplemented with small-group counseling, additional specific training, direct educational experience, and discussions with peers that emphasized real-life problems and reflected job experiences and feedback.

The IYS program and others like it are more complex than simply "picking up" a group of disadvantaged individuals and giving them some training. However difficult the latter goal is to achieve, it is among the program's least complex problems. Success or failure of such programs depends very much on how well anchored they are in the real world, the appeal and stability of the jobs they create, advancement ladders available to trainees, and the permanence of program funding.

IYS staff, in conjunction with various community agencies, worked out appropriate job opportunities, arrangements for on-the-job training, and assurances that bona fide employment would be available for trainees. Much effort went into these steps. Eventually, 11 separate human service training programs were established. The project's main evaluation report (Fishman et al., 1969) is based on nine programs for which relatively complete data were available at the time. These programs trained enrollees for jobs such as child day-care aides, teacher aides, welfare aides, recreation aides, counselors, and the like.

Fishman et al. (1969) report training details, curricula, and descriptions of job functions for the various programs. Analysis of the job specifications set up by prospective employers shows that providing direct human services was the most important function. Such activities accounted for more than 75 percent of the trainees' work time. The remaining portions were assigned primarily to clerical or maintenance activities.

Training for the 11 programs varied from a minimum of three months of full-time training for most jobs to a maximum of nine months of full-time training for counselor interns. Daily training included two hours with the core group, four hours of experience at the agency, and two hours of special skill-training to facilitate job entry. When training ended, certificates attesting to successful completion of the program were issued jointly by the IYS staff and employing agency.

Fishman et al.'s (1969) evaluation report was based on 132 of the initial group of trainees for whom complete data were available. The group, as intended, included delinquents, dropouts, the unemployed or underemployed, and unwed mothers. This was assured by using minimal screening criteria for admission to the program: for example, merely being able to complete an application form, absence of only gross physical defect or current communicable disease, no current criminal case pending, and, for dropouts, having been out of school for at least one year. Trainees came to the program from many sources. The largest single group (55 percent) was referred by government and community agencies. About 70 percent were under 21, 63 percent were married, and 99 percent were black. Roughly equal numbers of males and females, high school graduates and dropouts, and District of Columbia natives and outside the District youths were accepted. More than 90 percent were unemployed when they enrolled and about 35 percent had had one or more previous arrests. Of the 132 who started the training program, 106 (approximately 80 percent) successfully completed it, an encouraging finding by itself.

A follow-up survey of trainees was done six months to two and a half years after the training ended. Its purpose was to determine how well program objectives had been met by assessing current occupational, social, and educational status. The data were obtained from structured interviews with ex-trainees and supervising agency personnel. The most striking finding was that 87 percent of the group was gainfully employed, in comparison to a 90 percent unemployment figure when the project started. The average length of employment was eight months. A number of trainees (47 percent) had shifted jobs one or more times. More than half of these shifts were due to factors beyond the trainees' control. Many resulted from better job opportunities or higher salary. But given the trainees' poor life situations when they started the program, their subsequent overall work record was good.

Only about one-third of the trainees went on for further formal education, that is, completing high school equivalency courses, precollege or college training, or adult education programs. High school graduates did more, educationally, than dropouts. The training program, therefore, did not equalize opportunities as much as had been hoped. While most (80 percent) of the trainees expressed a *wish* to further their education (nearly 50 percent verbalized a desire to complete a college degree), this happened only gradually during the follow-up time period.

Data pertaining to delinquent, antisocial behavior were also collected in the follow-up. Whereas before the program 35 percent (37) of the trainees had been apprehended for 79 delinquent acts, only eight trainees committed a total of 15 delinquent acts in the follow-up period. Although the "post" time period was shorter than the pre period and the trainees were older and thus less vulnerable to delinquency, the substantial decrease in delinquency rate supports the view that the program achieved one of its central objectives.

Both observations and hard data suggest that the IYS program was socially utilitarian and effective (Fishman et al., 1969). The people who ran the program attributed its success to the staff's commitment and the faith and positive expectations they communicated to trainees about their ability and potential. The program's flexibility—reflected in its adaptive professional roles, redeploying resources as needed—individualized approach, and differential responses to trainees were also important to its suc-

cess. Finally, developing meaningful jobs, insuring their continuity, and serving a vital liaison function between trainees and agencies increased the program's effectiveness.

The value of the IYS and similar programs goes beyond their concrete attributes and specific locations. The potential ripple effects of such programs and the growing visibility of these models through conferences, publications, and publicity may ultimately be as important as the programs themselves. The New Careers' approach has become more visible in public and professional eyes. It is seen as a potentially useful way to deal with difficult social problems that are more and more a matter of public conscience. Legislation (the Economic Opportunity Act of 1964, the Subprofessional Career Act of 1966, and the Emergency Employment Act of 1967) establishing a nationwide network of such programs has been enacted. MacLennan (1969) believes that the original New Careers' program piloted a fruitful model that stimulated much good thinking and planning in manpower development and utilization, delivery of human services, and social intervention. The approach, in addition to "upgrading" the poor, takes needed institutional change into account. The New Careers' approach has grown considerably and applications quite different from, and beyond, the original IYS model have been reported in schools, correctional work, enforcement, social work, and industry (Riessman & Popper, 1968).

The Neighborhood Service Center

Background and Rationale

The Neighborhood Service Center (NSC) concept grew out of the Mobilization for Youth (MFY) project, an early demonstration program to reduce poverty, delinquency, and social disorganization in the urban slum (Weissman, 1969). The MFY target area was a large Puerto Rican ghetto of more than 100,000 people from New York City's Lower East Side. This major program was established to help low-income people make contact with various services and help opportunities. The MFY project was first staffed by social caseworkers whose major job was to settle differences between the poor and welfare, housing, legal, and school agencies. A second role was to promote change in the way agencies operated in order to encourage social action for community problems. It was felt that in this way the poor might better be served, and also that participating in social action is constructive and therapeutic for the poor.

NSC's later flowering was due to the efforts of the Mental Health Services group at the Lincoln Hospital—part of the Albert Einstein Medical Center (Peck & Kaplan, 1969; Riessman, 1967) in the South Bronx area of New York City. This group pioneered new methods for delivering mental health and other services to urban disadvantaged groups. Later, the NSC concept was expanded to a broader multi-service center (Peck & Kaplan, 1969) in which one element, the Neighborhood Mental Health Unit, assumed the functions formerly handled by the NSC.

The South Bronx region, with more than one-third of a million inhabitants, was one of New York City's three worst slum areas. Poverty and unemployment rates were high and alienation and many other serious social problems were common. Before 1963, that area had no formal mental health services. Extensive demographic and sociological data have been presented (Riessman, 1967; Peck & Kaplan, 1969) comparing the South Bronx both to the borough of the Bronx and to New York City at large. For all criteria used, the South Bronx was in bad shape. Admission rates to public mental

Robert de Villeneuve

Transplanted minorities often experience poverty and social disorganization in urban ghettos and are much in need of neighborhood services.

hospitals, homicides, and suicides were very high in this area. Divorce and separation rates, delinquency figures, and the incidence of venereal disease among youth under 21 years of age were twice as high in the South Bronx as in the city at large. Virtually all sociological variables showed the same trends. Mean education levels for the area were substantially lower and welfare and unemployment rates substantially higher than for the city as a whole. As might be expected, mean income was very low, and nearly 40 percent of the South Bronx population was living in deteriorated or dilapidated dwellings. Peck and Kaplan (1969) rightly described the area as a "community in crisis."

Mental health services in the South Bronx had virtually no entry points and little leverage or effectiveness. Poor people, for many reason, just did not use mental health services (Reiff, 1967; Riessman, 1967). In part this was ideological. Low-income people rarely define or see problems as psychological. Nor are they comfortable with traditional middle-class mental health settings or the ways in which mental health professionals usually work. Thus, even the limited services available to the poor failed to match their expectancies or styles. The NSC tried to remedy these problems by recognizing the close relationship between a community's social organization and the psychological make-up of its people (Peck & Kaplan, 1969).

The Lincoln Hospital NSC Program

The original Lincoln Hospital NSC, established in 1965, was set up to serve a five-square-block area with a population of about 50,000. The NSC, located in a street level storefront, was manned by a staff consisting of a single mental health professional as director and some half-dozen indigenous neighborhood nonprofessionals. Two more centers were later opened in the same area. The three centers had somewhat different emphases and operating styles with respect to their community action orientation and their relationships with other agencies.

The NSCs had several central goals (Riessman, 1967). They tried to attract new clientele and develop services designed to meet their specific needs. They worked to increase social cohesion in the neighborhood by forming groups designed to reduce the poor's sense of powerlessness and to increase their involvement in community action. They initiated institutional change, especially better coordination of community services for the poor.

The first NSC emphasized direct services to the poor. It was felt that there was great need for such services and that effective service would increase people's comfort, reduce strain, and prevent the negative consequence of cumulative distress. It was also believed that providing needed concrete services was the best way to encourage the formation of cohesive community action groups. The Center's direct service included providing information, escorting clients to agencies, filling out forms and writing letters, expediting, integrating, and coordinating agency services, making referrals, and follow-up. These services were not necessarily directly related to mental health problems. The Center also offered specific mental health services, including counseling and providing "psychosocial first aid," which were often embedded in more concrete services. However useful and successful such individual services were, the NSC viewed them merely as entry points for later more important activities.

The NSC's second key objective was to work informally with people in the community to stimulate a self-help orientation that could create social pressure (Peck, Kaplan, & Roman, 1966) against vested institutional structures. The concern here was more to get people involved and to increase their stake in the community than with any specific changes that might be made in agencies. Seeking self-improvement was assumed to be dignifying and therapeutic and to reduce apathy. The NSC's structure and its use of indigenous nonprofessionals furthered these objectives. The Center's social action functions included voter registration campaigns, block clean-up programs, and organizing complaints against local agencies that were not meeting the needs of the poor. In addition there were antiviolence and antidrug activities, active concern with political and social issues, and collaborative activities with area school, welfare, and housing organizations to make needed improvements.

Riessman (1967) identified six steps in working toward key community action objectives. These ranged in involvement and complexity from acceptance of individual services to large-scale community action programs. The starting point for all later steps was to recruit and train nonprofessional mental health aides, the program's backbone. Applicants were first attracted with the help of formal and informal community agents and through meetings and announcements in the mass media. Large and small group meetings, as well as individual contacts, were used as screening mechanisms to identify prospective aides whose experience, life style, and interests seemed to suit them for such work. Warmth and empathy, ability to communicate, flexibility, self-awareness, sensitivity, the ability to handle stress, and relevant prior life experiences were stressed. Aides had to be able to function effectively as a communication "bridge" between professionals and the people of the neighborhood.

The initial aide training, led by professionals, emphasized community surveys, door-to-door interviews, visiting neighborhood settings and agencies, and sitting in on intake conferences. Role-playing techniques were used heavily. After this first training period ended, aides spent several weeks in the NSC dividing their time equally between providing direct services and additional training based on actual experiences. Training at the NSC continued even after the job started. About 20 percent of the work week was devoted to discussing case material, direct supervision, and acquiring new skills.

When aide training ended and the Center was fully staffed and operational, the emphasis shifted to providing *some* direct services and expediting others. During this second period, information was built up about community resources, pressure points and action channels, how to cut red tape, how to interview, and how best to be a friendly neighbor. A third program phase at the Center featured small informal meetings, led by aides, for community residents who had received individual services. These

meetings were to explore and gather information. They were designed to identify needs, develop leadership, and to begin to organize small neighborhood task forces to deal with specific problems.

A fourth phase involved a transition to organized group activity. Meetings led by aides formed groups to deal with such problems as fuller use of neighborhood health services, distributing surplus food, and registering children for nursery school programs. Phase five sought to relate NSC task forces to other local community groups working toward similar objectives. The sixth and final phase, institutional change, involved coordinating NSC neighborhood groups with those of related programs throughout the city. Such coalitions aim ultimately at improving welfare, housing, employment opportunities, and living conditions for the urban disadvantaged.

This final goal is more complex than earlier ones because it can involve direct attacks on well-established social institutions. NSC's goal of improving services for the poor can readily bring it into conflict with existing agencies. Its emphasis on organizing poor people makes community institutions obvious targets for attack. Because the NSC has access to mass media and sources of publicity, its bite can sting. In practice, however, the NSC has focused more on mobilizing self-determining groups among the apathetic and alienated from which institutional change can flow naturally, rather than on specific institutional change.

The NSC's strongest emphases have been on community action and primary prevention, but it has also developed secondary and tertiary programs. One of the three NSCs, for example, developed an after-care program for patients discharged from the Bronx State Hospital (Peck & Kaplan, 1969). The specific nature of a program can influence the types of aides recruited, how they are trained, and what they do on-the-job. A center, for example, that emphasizes secondary or tertiary preventive goals would need to train its personnel in such areas as diagnosis, counseling, group leadership and group dynamics approaches, and the like.

It is not easy to evaluate the mental health impact of an NSC program directly for two reasons. First, mental health problems in the ghetto do not typically appear in pure middle-class forms. More often they are simply part of the everyday problems of living and survival. Hence it is difficult even to get a "head-count" of mental health problems. Second, since primary prevention has long-range implications, it is very hard to identify specific relationships between NSC interventions and outcomes. Ultimately, the outcome is seen most clearly in the types of demographic and sociological data first used to describe the South Bronx. If one really believes that virtually anything done to improve man's lot can be a step toward primary prevention of emotional problems, the NSC's specific impact cannot be separated from the effects of housing programs, changes in school organization and structure, or the creation of new employment opportunities.

For these reasons, NSC's main short-term evaluation has been based on clinical impressions, cost analysis, and "utilization" figures rather than on client-effectiveness data. Reports by Riessman (1967) and Peck and Kaplan (1969) are optimistic and suggest that the NSC is a viable, useful model that merits further development. Relatively speaking, NSC is an economical operation. Total annual cost of a center, including professional, nonprofessional, and secretarial salaries, storefront rental, and operating expenses was estimated at under $50,000 per

year. Since a single NSC served a subcommunity of 50,000 people, its per capita cost was about one dollar a year. Data from two centers indicated very high use-rates, especially so since the target area residents were people who had previously avoided agencies and community services. In their first six months these centers provided direct services for 6,620 new cases, an average of over 500 new individual clients, per center, per month. Since the average family size of clients served was about four, each NSC may have reached nearly 25,000 people indirectly. These estimates exclude people who participated in NSC's community action and education programs. Thus centers had a wide "reach." Beyond that, Riessman's (1967) assertion that nonprofessionals are effective in providing and expediting services, crisis intervention, dealing with otherwise unapproachable pathological situations, mobilizing community action, and bridging the gap between professionals and neighborhood residents supports the conclusion that the NSC model is a sensible approach to ghetto problems.

But it would be misleading in the extreme to imply that such programs come about easily or live uneventfully. Because they depart so much from traditional ways, they require unusual effort and persistence to get rooted. And then, survival can follow a rocky course. For example, even though the innovative Lincoln Hospital Mental Health Services programs, of which NSC was part, won an excellence award from the American Psychiatric Association in 1968, one year later they were in utter turmoil. Disastrous conflicts had erupted involving professionals, nonprofessionals, community residents, government agencies, the hospital, and the medical school (Kaplan & Roman, 1973) and stayed active for several years.

A Competency Alternative for the Poor

The problems of the poor can be seen through a very different set of spectacles. Rather than just cataloging their "deficits" and trying, as we have so often done in the past, to "remedy" them, one can seek out strength and competency bases and do everything possible to support their further development. This, essentially, is the position taken by a group of workers who have founded the Community Psychology Action Center (CPAC) in Champaign-Urbana, Illinois (Rappaport et al., 1975).

Their approach carefully avoids "blaming the victim" (Ryan, 1971) or fitting the poor into "the system." Instead it accepts a group's existing cultural values and seeks to "amplify" that culture by extending identified competencies to new areas. Traditional problem areas are ignored and an all-out effort is made to maximize resources that, in the past, have traditionally been overlooked. Behind this effort is the goal of creating settings that foster independence rather than dependence.

The CPAC is located physically in a black neighborhood in Champaign-Urbana. Its first step was to promote dialogue with black community representatives to get a better understanding of the turf and its resources. The aim of this dialogue was not to spot problems, but to identify people with positive program ideas and the competencies to support them. For example, a black community health nurse was instrumental in developing a special type of infant (ages six weeks to two years) day-care center for one-parent families. The center is not just to "baby sit" for, or even "enrich," these disadvantaged infants. It allows a number of single parents—youths with strengths and talent in many cases—to pursue further ed-

ucation and/or employment. The center's administrative control rests with the community people who staff it. University students and community residents work side-by-side and contribute to each other's development.

Similarly, a black graphic artist from the community helped to establish a communications and information center. The center's press and public information center both train young black residents in specific job functions and print a newspaper dealing with matters of interest to the local community. In conjunction with the latter, a reporting course that teaches ways of gathering information has been developed.

The CPAC is a very real alternative. It bypasses "problems" and strives to parlay existing competencies into an even broader network of strengths. Even though the two proving grounds are worlds apart, there are important similarities between CPAC's approach and Spivack and Shure's program, cited in Chapter 18, for teaching problem-solving skills to young school children. Both of these programs force us to consider more seriously the possibility that developing strengths in people may be the very best way to deal with their problems. The next several decades must take this possibility into more serious account.

CONCLUSION

The powerful role of adverse life circumstances in causing disordered behavior is becoming more apparent. This highlights the need for primary prevention programs to improve employment opportunities, housing conditions, physical health and well-being, and life opportunities among the poor. Mental health professionals have only limited knowledge in these areas. But, if

TABLE 19.1
Comparison of Developmental and Community Action Programs

	TARGET POPULATION	TYPES OF APPROACHES
Developmental Programs	Infants Preschoolers Primary-graders	Infant stimulation programs Compensatory education programs Enrichment programs
Community Action Programs	Delinquent youth Underprivileged young adults Urban slum dwellers	Residential communities New careers programs Modeling programs Neighborhood service centers

they are to be truly responsive to human psychological need, they must engage such problems with greater flexibility. This means developing new solutions to chronic problems, rather than simply trying to apply what professionals know best to situations where such approaches are inapplicable or ineffective.

School maladaptation and failure are widespread, critical problems for the disadvantaged. And educational achievement and success may be the only stepping stone for many of the poor to a good adjustment in later life. Much has been written about the reasons for the school failure of the disadvantaged. Although satisfactory explanations are still lacking, empirical data show clearly that the disadvantaged child has cognition, linguistic, perceptual, and motivational deficits that impede later school performance. Although primary prevention may someday eliminate such deficits, we cannot just sit back and wait for that to happen. Mental health professionals have some knowledge and skills that can now be applied to the problems of the poor.

Programs for the preschool disadvantaged, stressing enrichment and training for specific deficits, have short-term positive effects on cognitive and noncognitive development. But specific, time-limited enrichment programs that lack family and community involvement or follow-through do not produce *lasting* positive results. Such programs must be pushed back as far as possible in time, on the assumption that the earlier the intervention the less serious the deficit, and the easier it will be to correct it. For that reason, many new infant stimulation programs with the inner-city disadvantaged have appeared.

Action programs for inner-city youth and adults have also increased. These programs share an emphasis on actual behavior rather than psychodynamics, developing ways of delivering service that fit the needs and life styles of the poor, and the concrete problems of living as they occur in the inner-city. In addition, many inner-city programs emphasize institutional and community change and the imaginative use of new helping personnel, particularly indigenous nonprofessionals.

Inner-city problems, including those having to do with mental health or the development of pathological behavior, are not likely to be solved in the near future. But they sound challenges that we cannot afford to ignore.

SUMMARY

1. American cities are changing dramatically. Rapid population shifts have brought large numbers of racial and ethnic minorities to the city. This has created inner-city ghettos with a variety of serious personal and social problems. Traditional mental health approaches have done little to alleviate these problems.

2. New ways of dealing with ghetto problems must be developed by mental health specialists in concert with other social scientists.

3. Inner-city children have been found to have motivational and cognitive problems that put them at a disadvantage with respect to traditional school experiences.

4. Special compensatory education programs to enhance the early school adjustment of ghetto youngsters have been developed as one approach to these problems.

5. Project Head Start, developed with federal funds on a national level, works with preschoolers. There has been great variation among individual Head Start programs. Although this makes it impossible to evaluate Head Start as a total entity, most observers feel that the program is worth maintaining.

6. The Illinois Program views the deficits of disadvantaged preschoolers as skill deficits. Correction is attempted through direct teaching. Early reports on the program's effects are positive.

7. The preschool program for the disavantaged of the Institute for Developmental Studies in New York stresses the need for adequate environmental stimulation. An enriched curriculum is used for two preschool years and the first three school years. Evaluation of the program indicates that it is producing favorable results.

8. The Peabody Early Training Project focuses on building motivation and aiding cognitive development in a ten-week summer preschool experience. Positive program effects have been reported.

9. Several infant stimulation programs for the disadvantaged have been set up. These programs show that intellectual and social behavior can be dramatically improved in short periods of time. However, without family involvement and program continuity, these gains tend to erode.

10. Inner-city community action programs address existing problems as expressed. They avoid psychodynamic formulations. They use approaches that are congenial to the life styles of the poor, and they emphasize flexible uses of nonprofessional help-agents.

11. The Residential Youth Center is a residential setting for delinquents and socially maladjusted neighborhood youths. Residents participate in its maintenance and administration. Favorable program results were found on many basic criteria.

12. Several programs featuring the modeling and reinforcement of adaptive behavior have been set up for inner-city delinquents. A growing body of data attests to the value of these approaches.

13. New Careers programs deal with the employment problems of the disadvantaged. Lack of fulfilling employment is seen to be a cause of many behavioral problems. New Careers programs provide an opportunity for the disadvantaged to enter a human service occupation at their existing skill and educational levels. The program provides advancement ladders. Reports of the results of the Howard University Institute for Youth Studies Program are favorable.

14. The Neighborhood Service Center (NSC) program was designed to help the disadvantaged to cope with the problems of the urban slum. Besides direct service for existing problems, these centers also seek to stimulate social action to get agencies and administrators to better meet the needs of the poor. The NSC programs established by Lincoln Hospital in the Bronx, New York, were impressionistically considered to be successful.

15. The great need for continued efforts to develop programs to deal with inner-city problems was stressed.

CHAPTER 20

Summary and Prospects

This book emphasizes that, in perspective, abnormal psychology has always been a changing, evolving field. It has had long static periods but there have also been instances of dramatic reconceptualization and change that some have called "mental health revolutions." These revolutions have been marked by both rapid theoretical ferment and change in practice. Although several had great impact on many aspects of the field, most were slow and gradual, with little accompanying fanfare. A new major mental health revolution now seems to be in process. Its prospective impact is so great that Hobbs (1964) calls it the third mental health revolution. This ranks it in importance with Pinel's sweeping reforms in the hospital care of the mentally ill and Freud's far-reaching influence.

We have tried to show that prior mental health revolutions were ushered in by broadening redefinitions of the field of abnormal psychology. In early times the first predecessors of mental health professionals were concerned only with the most extreme behavior deviations. Such deviations were then thought to be caused by spirits and demons and were treated by "religious" leaders who cast exorcising spells to free the victims. Later, when natural causes of psychological aberration were better understood, physicians with mechanistic causal views took over treatment. They used potions, drugs, and varied other physical therapies.

The first major mental health "revolution" under Pinel featured sweeping humanitarian change in hospital care for the profoundly sick. But it neither redefined the nature of disordered behavior nor did it lead to major theoretical advances. By contrast, Freud's contributions markedly expanded our theoretical horizons. When his work began, mental health professionals were still singlemindedly concerned with extreme behavior disorders. In fact, neither Freud nor most of his early disciples were traditional mental health professionals. They were concerned specifically with hysteria, a condition not previously within mental health's scope. Although this mystifying problem had attracted charlatans, faith healers, general medical practitioners, and eventually neurologists, it had not previously interested psychiatrists. Freud's success in understanding and treating this and other psychoneurotic disorders eventually won the interest and acclaim of the mental health field and resulted in a redefinition of its scope. Through his efforts, the behavioral aberrations we now call the neuroses—more subtle and less disabling conditions than the psychoses—were first accepted as part of the proper domain of an expanded abnormal psychology.

Freud's views about how the neuroses developed had other important consequences. His theories, for example, were extended and applied to the psychoses. His focus on the nature of psychological development paved the way for even more important expansions of mental health's scope. Psychosomatic medicine was one such expansion. For many years, emotional factors were suspected to play a central role in many physical illnesses, but advances in physical medicine and physiology in the nineteenth century had established one-sided physicalistic explanations of medical problems. Not until Freud convinced professionals that he could treat behavior and emotional disorders effectively were his theories extended to physical illness. Eventually, psychosomatic disorders came to be seen as problems that mental health work-

ers, particularly psychiatrists, could treat. Since then, many substantive theories of psychosomatic medicine have been developed and these broadened views have attracted researchers from many fields, including psychology.

The concept of character or personality disorder developed gradually over a period of years. Despite the fact that it did not evolve with a flourish, the concept, which embraced both subtle behavior disorders and dramatic conditions earlier considered to be religious or legal concerns, broadened the mental health fields enormously. When the helping fields accepted character disorders as part of the realm of the psychologically abnormal, they also took on service responsibilities for many, many more people. This step paved the way for a further broadening of the field's scope, since it was but one short step from character problems to those of the school dropout, the juvenile delinquent, the occupationally maladjusted, the irresponsible parent, and people without a life purpose.

The combination of this further scope-broadening step and the growing persistence of unresolved mental health problems led to the field's most recent revolution. Among today's most serious unresolved problems are: failure to have found a cure for profound disorders such as schizophrenia; limited effectiveness of therapeutic techniques; inequities in the delivery of mental health services; the many unmet mental health needs of the general population; and acute shortages of mental health manpower (Cowen, 1973). The last problem is a nearly inevitable consequence of the fact that each new expansion of abnormal psychology's scope has committed professionals to provide more services for many more thousands of people, in a variety of new settings. Because professional schools grind out their products so slowly and increase in number even more slowly, future projections of need-manpower ratios are pessimistic (Albee, 1959, 1963, 1967).

The combination of broadening scope and increasing service demands on the one hand, and the vexing presence of unresolved mental health problems on the other. makes it necessary to reexamine our conceptual footings. Alternatives in theory and practice are needed as part of the search for solutions to the complex problems of disordered behavior. These are the forces behind the third mental health revolution—a transformation that is still in an early, formative stage.

Historically, disordered behavior has been approached largely from a medical-model framework. The medical model's most fundamental assumption, and most serious failing, is that physical and psychological dysfunction have similar onsets and natures. Psychological problems in fact differ from physical ones in that they usually have deeper roots, develop more slowly over time, and are more affected by significant people, experiences, and settings. Practically, the shaky assumption of a parallelism between physical and psychological problems has meant that people who follow the medical model deal with psychological problems only after they exact a heavy toll and are entrenched. At such times dysfunction is difficult to treat and the potential interventions are often inadequate. Dismal failures in the past treatment of schizophrenia reflect this discrepancy.

Also, since the flow of psychological problems has exceeded helping resources, those who use the medical model, must, by default, be socially passive. The mental health professional typically sets up shop and waits, usually not very long, for people with serious problems to find him. The failing here is two-fold. The specialist rarely sees people at a time when treatment can be most effective, and he sees only those who have the orientation and means to seek help. Because the scope of the professional's work is so selective, many, many needy people fall beyond the reach of mental health helping resources.

Our intent is not to condemn the medical model. There are many ways in which it has served well in the past and will continue to do so in the future. Some psychological dysfunctions have organic bases. Others, whose etiologies are still unknown, may eventually be found to have similar causes. Encapsulated dysfunction in otherwise healthy people can also be well handled within this model. However successful alternative approaches prove to be, we shall not soon be a society without psychological problems. Certainly the ethic of concern for the individual assures continuity in treating the suffering—a central thrust of the medical model.

However understandable the evolution and ascendancy of the medical model is in our past efforts to cope with disordered behavior, however necessary it is that aspects of it survive, and however much we can improve it in the future, it fails to deal satisfactorily with many nonpostponable problems facing mental health today. Hence it can no longer stand alone as a guiding framework for long-range planning. A preventive approach, designed to cut down the flow of disorders, is a necessary and compelling alternative that must be pursued more actively.

As the two terms "medical model" and "preventive model" have been traditionally used, they are all-embracing and their operations overlap considerably. Only primary and early secondary prevention offer clear conceptual alternatives to the practices of the medical model. Primary prevention is concerned with the impact on development of influential environments and settings, such as homes and schools. It emphasizes social system modification as a way of optimizing psychological development. It seeks to build strengths and resources in people rather than to combat pathology. Primary prevention's scope and operations are broader and more demanding than those for which mental health professionals are now trained. Yet professionals must participate in such programs, helping both to frame pertinent questions and to develop programs that reflect their knowledge and skills. To do so requires that mental health professionals extend their frames of reference, sacrifice some of the privacy of their offices and consulting rooms, and interact with other community specialists in pursuing the shared objective of human well-being.

A preventive orientation to disordered behavior does not rule out intervention with individuals. Carefully thought out choices, however, must be made among many different types of individual interventions if the reach and impact of helping services are to be maximized. Guidelines for choosing have been suggested. Crisis intervention is a potentially high impact form of intervention because individuals in crisis can be readily influenced and reactions to crisis serve as a force either for psychological growth or regression. Other things equal, interventions with young, flexible organisms are more promising than later ones. Consultation with caregivers and urban agents, people whose social roles bring them into front line contact with the psychologically distressed, is also a potentially valuable activity for professionals. By recognizing the realities of human help-seeking behavior and by strengthening the hand of those who are cast in help-giving roles, consultation can greatly expand helping services.

Implementing prevention will bring mental health professionals closer to their com-munities—a movement that is in keeping with the expanding definition of abnormal psychology. More and more these days we hear of emergent fields such as community psychology, community psychiatry, and community mental health. Granted that such terms are still defined sketchily (Cowen, 1973) as reflected in Newbrough's (1969) tongue-in-cheek statement: "Community mental health has become a term which refers to all activities carried out in the community in the name of mental health" (p. 70). Granted there is the danger that much of what we call community mental health is little more than modern packaging of ancient products. Nevertheless, the community approach holds that disordered behavior reflects important environmental stresses, not just intraindividual, intrapsychic dynamics, and that to deal effectively with them, we must place greater emphasis on environmental engineering and modification.

The community thrust values prevention, recognizes the heavy formative impact of primary social institutions on people, and uses community settings and resources to cope with established disorder. Community psychology promises to be a genuine mental health revolution both because it involves, as Freud's work did, a scope-broadening redefinition of the mental health fields, and because it challenges established practices in ways that are as basic as Pinel's humanitarian hospital reforms.

A preventive approach to disordered behavior calls for new roles and ways of using mental health personnel. For example, nonprofessional help-agents must be used more to meet service needs. This development started as a result of professional manpower shortages and the desire to extend helping services to many needy people, but it has gone beyond that. Clearly situations have been identified in which a nonprofessional can help as effectively as a professional. Moreover, new helping roles uniquely suited to the skills and life experience of certain nonprofessionals have been articulated. As an example, specific roles have been found for indigenous nonprofessionals that bridge the heretofore large gap between middle-class professionals and the serious problems of ghetto residents. In the past, professionals have been insensitive to, or ineffective in dealing with, inner-city problems. Even when such problems are understood, the professional has often had problems of communicating with, and being accepted by, those he hoped to help. Other needed professional roles include supporting and helping caregivers and urban agents who must deal with psychological distress in their everyday activities.

The required new professional roles range from recruitment, training, and supervision of nonprofessionals to expediting social action and political organization. Since professionals in the past have not typically been trained for many of these roles, some will obviously require retraining.

Because these new modes of professional activity remain unclear, they are threatening and their acceptance requires faith. This is particularly the case when the role puts the professional into contact with settings and individuals who neither share his views nor are ready to accept the changes he proposes. For example, the disadvantaged understandably define and perceive many of their problems in material, rather than "psychological," terms. Hence, to be appealing, programs initiated for such groups by a "shrink" must consider how the poor define their needs.

A number of innovative school and inner-city programs have been cited to illustrate how new, community-based approaches to disordered behavior are developing. The content of these programs, and the level at which they address problems, do not closely resemble past, traditional mental health services. Indeed, to the extent that some rely on before-the-fact, mass-oriented, preventive efforts, some observers do not even consider them to be mental health programs.

Schools were chosen for emphasis because the experiences children have in schools are, outside of the family, the most important shaping influence on development. Schools either enhance or hinder children's development. Analyzing the effects of school environments on children's development and engineering environments that optimize growth are necessary to build psychological resources in people and to prevent ineffective behavior. Emergent school mental health programs vary considerably. Some, for example, are geared to prevention and others to already evident, sometimes extreme, problems. Still, they share several common elements. All are directed toward young children, and all seek to identify dysfunction as soon as possible.

Approaches that minimize removing the child from his natural environment or labeling him as a misfit are emphasized, as is the view that educational experience, rather than psychotherapy, is the prime vehicle for personal and intellectual growth. In addition, such programs emphasize the child's complex, transactional world and try to promote communication and mutual support in the interest of his well-being. Finally, many programs feature imaginative uses of nonprofessional help-agents and constructively recast professional mental health roles.

America's inner cities harbor many festering social problems. Though many associations between adverse living conditions (inadequate housing, limited employment opportunities and income) and dramatic signs of maladaptation have been shown, the disadvantaged understandably feel less of a need for psychological services than they do for programs to improve their poor social conditions. Thus far, mental health professionals have had only limited reach and effectiveness in the inner city. To make a greater future contribution professionals must deal more realistically with problems as they are expressed, rather than simply transplanting the same services they provide to their middle-class clientele.

School maladaptation and failure have been very common problems for inner-city children. This may be due to conditions of living, familial patterns, the organization of the school experience, or some combination of these factors. Whatever the reason, school failure is very costly, since an effective school experience is a critical gateway for so many important later-life adaptations. The empirical demonstration of cognitive, linguistic, perceptual, and motivational deficit among very young inner-city youngsters has led to the development of infant stimulation and early compensatory educational programs to increase the likelihood of effective school adaptation. Community-based, action-oriented programs for youth and adults have also been developed to deal with certain inner-city problems. Although these programs vary in scope and objectives, they share common features. Most emphasize concrete behavior and mastery rather than psychodynamic causes. They use organizational structures and service delivery approaches that are appropriate to the life styles of the groups served. They include in their scope the possibility of institutional and community change, and many feature new imaginative uses of helping personnel.

It is not easy to predict the ultimate form that the current mental health revolution will take. Each past broadening of mental health's scope has resulted in the acquisition of new problems that had "belonged" to other groups which had made little headway with them. Illustratively, the mental health field took on new mandates and was filled with new hope after Freud's seemingly startling advances in understanding human behavior. The excitement that his work generated, and the resulting view that virtually all problems of disordered behavior "belonged" to mental health, led to the reclassification of behavior problems to new domains.

At this time, however, it is still too early to know how successful the mental health fields will be in carrying out their greatly expanded mandate. The pell-mell collection of causes, new missions, and concerns has taken place over a relatively short time-period and has grown largely out of pressing social need. It has not been a logical or systematic process deriving from advances in theory or research. Today, most mental health professionals are overburdened and quite unclear about where and how to use their professional expertise. A crucial need is to appraise realistically the effects of what professionals do and to redetermine their special roles alongside those of other groups who also serve people and share concern about man's welfare. A new, more comprehensive framework for understanding and coping with disordered human behavior is, indeed, emerging. Its early, primitive explorations point to exciting future possibilities. But, in the last analysis, it remains to be shown empirically whether this evolving order will be more effective than its predecessors in resolving the extraordinarily challenging, resistant problems of disordered behavior.

References

Abood, L. G. A chemical approach to the problem of mental disease. In D. D. Jackson (Ed.), *The etiology of schizophrenia*. New York: Basic Books, 1960. Pp. 91–119.

Abraham, K. Notes on the psycho-analytical investigation and treatment of manic depressive insanity and allied conditions (1911). In B. D. Lewin (Ed.), *On character and libido development*. New York: Norton, 1966. Pp. 15–34. (a)

Abraham, K. A short study of the development of the libido, viewed in the light of mental disorders (1924). In B. D. Lewin (Ed.), *On character and libido development*. New York: Norton, 1966. Pp. 71–150. (b)

Ader, R. Effects of early experience and differential housing on behavior and susceptibility to gastric erosions in the rat. *Journal of Comparative and Physiological Psychology*, 1965, *60*, 233–238.

Ader, R. The influence of psychological factors on disease susceptibility in animals. In M. L. Conalty (Ed.), *Husbandry of laboratory animals*. London: Academic Press, 1967.

Ader, R., Beels, C. C., & Tatum, R. Blood pepsinogen and gastric erosions in the rat. *Psychosomatic Medicine*, 1960, *22*, 1–13.

Ader, R., & Friedman, S. B. Differential early experiences and susceptibility to a transplanted tumor in the rat. *Journal of Comparative and Physiological Psychology*, 1965, *59*, 361–364.

Aichhorn, A. *Wayward youth*. New York: Viking, 1935.

Albee, G. W. *Mental health manpower trends*. New York: Basic Books, 1959.

Albee, G. W. American psychology in the sixties. *American Psychologist*, 1963, *18*, 90–95.

Albee, G. W. Give us a place to stand and we will move the earth. In J. G. Harris

(Ed.), *Mental health manpower needs in psychology*. Lexington, Ky.: University of Kentucky, 1966. Pp. 15–25.

Albee, G. W. The relation of conceptual models to manpower needs. In E. L. Cowen, E. A. Gardner, & M. Zax (Eds.), *Emergent approaches to mental health problems*. New York: Appleton-Century-Crofts, 1967. Pp. 63–73.

Albee, G. W. The relation of conceptual models of disturbed behavior to institutional and manpower requirements. In F. N. Arnhoff, E. A. Rubenstein, & J. S. Speisman (Eds.), *Manpower for mental health*. Chicago: Aldine, 1969. Pp. 93–111. (a)

Albee, G. W. We have been warned. In W. Ryan (Ed.), *Distress in the city*. Cleveland, Ohio: Case-Western Reserve University Press, 1969. Pp. 213–222. (b)

Alexander, F. Psychological aspects of medicine. *Psychosomatic Medicine*, 1939, *1*, 7–18.

Alexander, F. *Psychosomatic medicine*. New York: Norton, 1950.

Alexander, F., Eisenstein, S., & Grotjahn, M. *Psychoanalytic pioneers*. New York: Basic Books, 1966.

Alexander, F., & Selesnick, S. T. *The history of psychiatry*. New York: Harper & Row, 1966.

Alexander, F., & Szasz, T. S. The psychosomatic approach in medicine. In F. Alexander & Helen Ross (Eds.), *Dynamic psychiatry*. Chicago: University of Chicago Press, 1952. Pp. 369–400.

Allinsmith, W., & Goethals, G. W. *The role of schools in mental health*. New York: Basic Books, 1962.

Allinsmith, W. & Grimes, J. W. Compulsivity, anxiety, and school achievement. *Merrill-Palmer Quarterly*, 1961, *7*, 247–261.

Allport, G. W. *Personality: A psychological interpretation*. New York: Holt, 1937.

Alt, E. Insured psychiatric care. *Public Health Reports*, 1959, *74*, 687–691.

Altrocchi, J. Mental health consultation. In S. E. Golann & C. Eisdorfer (Eds.) *Handbook of community mental health*. New York: Appleton-Century-Crofts, 1972. Pp. 477–508.

American Psychiatric Association Committee on Nomenclature and Statistics. *Diagnostic and statistical manual—mental disorders*. Washington, D.C.: American Psychiatric Association, 1952. (DSM-I)

American Psychiatric Association Committee on Nomenclature and Statistics. *Diagnostic and statistical manual—mental disorders*. Washington, D.C.: American Psychiatric Association, 1968. (DSM-II)

"The A. P. A. ruling on homosexuality." *New York Times*, Dec. 23, 1973, p. 9e.

Arieti, S. Introductory notes on the psychoanalytic therapy of schizophrenics. In A. Burton (Ed.), *Psychotherapy of the psychoses*. New York: Basic Books, 1961. Pp. 69–89.

Arnhoff, F. N. The Boston Mental Health Survey: A context for interpretation. In W. Ryan (Ed.), *Distress in the city: Essays on the design and administration of urban mental health services*. Cleveland, Ohio: Case-Western Reserve University Press, 1969. Pp. 144–162.

Arnhoff, F. N., Jenkins, J. W., & Speisman, J. C. The new mental health workers. In F. N. Arnhoff, E. A. Rubenstein, & J. C. Speisman (Eds.), *Manpower for mental health*. Chicago: Aldine, 1969, Pp. 149–165.

Arnhoff, F. N., Rubenstein, E. A., Shriver, B., & Jones, D. R. The mental health fields: An overview of manpower growth and development. In F. N. Arnhoff, E. A.

Rubenstein, & J. C. Speisman (Eds.), *Manpower for mental health*. Chicago: Aldine, 1969. Pp. 1–37.

Arnhoff, F. N., Rubenstein, E. A., & Speisman, J. C. *Manpower for mental health*. Chicago: Aldine, 1969.

Arnhoff, F. N., & Speisman, J. C. Summary and conclusions. In F. N. Arnhoff, E. A. Rubenstein, & J. C. Speisman (Eds.), *Manpower for mental health*. Chicago: Aldine, 1969. Pp. 185–197.

Ash, P. The reliability of psychiatric diagnoses. *Journal of Abnormal and Social Psychology*, 1949, *44*, 272–276.

Atthowe, J. M., Jr., & Krasner, L. Preliminary report on the application of contingent reinforcement procedures (token economy) on a "chronic" psychiatric ward. *Journal of Abnormal Psychology*, 1968, *73*, 37–43.

Ausubel, D. P. Causes and types of narcotic addictions: A psychosocial view. *Psychiatric Quarterly*, 1961, *35*, 523–531.

Ausubel, D., & Ausubel, P. Ego development among segregated Negro children. In J. I. Roberts (Ed.), *School children in the urban slum*. New York: Free Press, 1967. Pp. 231–2601.

Ayllon, T. Intensive treatment of psychotic patients by stimulus satiation and food reinforcement. *Behavior Research and Therapy*, 1963, *1*, 53–61.

Ayllon, T., & Azrin, N. H. The measurement and reinforcement of behavior of psychotics. *Journal of the Experimental Analysis of Behavior*, 1965, *8*, 357–384.

Ayllon, T., & Azrin, N. H. *The token economy—motivational systems for therapy and rehabilitation*. New York: Appleton-Century-Crofts, 1968.

Ayllon, T., & Michael, J. The psychiatric nurse as a behavioral engineer. *Journal of the Experimental Analysis of Behavior*, 1959, *2*, 323–334.

Back, K. W. *Beyond words*. New York: Russell Sage Foundation, 1972.

Baer, D. M. Some remedial uses of reinforcement contingency. In J. M. Shlien (Ed.), *Research in psychotherapy*, Vol. 3. Washington, D.C.: American Psychological Association, 1968. Pp. 3–20.

Bales, R. F. Cultural differences in rates of alcoholism. *Quarterly Journal of Studies on Alcohol*, 1946, *6*, 480–499.

Bandura, A. Psychotherapy based upon modeling principles. In A. E. Bergin & S. L. Garfield (Eds.), *Handbook of psychotherapy and behavior change*. New York: Wiley, 1971. Pp. 653–708.

Baratz, J. C. Language abilities of Black Americans. In K. S. Miller & R. M. Dreger (Eds.), *Comparative studies of Black and Whites in the United States: Quantitative studies in social relations*. New York: Seminar Press, 1973. Pp. 127–183.

Bardon, J. I. School psychology and school psychologists. *American Psychologist*, 1968, *23*, 187–194.

Barendregt, J. T. A cross-validation study of the hypothesis of psychosomatic specificity, with special reference to bronchial asthma. *Journal of Psychosomatic Research*, 1957, *2*, 109–114.

Barker, R. G., & Gump, P. *Big school, small school*. Stanford, Ca.: Stanford University Press, 1964.

Barker, R. G., & Schoggen, P. *Qualities of community life*. San Francisco: Jossey-Bass, 1973.

Bateson, G., Jackson, D. D., Haley, J., & Weakland, J. H. Toward a theory of schizophrenia. *Behavioral Science*, 1956, *1*, 251–264.

Bebout, J., & Gordon, B. The value of encounter. In L. N. Solomon & B. Berzon (Eds.), *New perspectives on encounter groups.* San Francisco: Jossey-Bass, 1972.

Beck, A. T. *Depression.* New York: Harper & Row, 1967.

Becker, J. Achievement-related characteristics of manic-depressives. *Journal of Abnormal and Social Psychology,* 1960, *60,* 334–339.

Becker, J., Spielberger, C. D., & Parker, J. B. Value achievement and authoritarian attitudes in psychiatric patients. *Journal of Clinical Psychology,* 1963, *19,* 57–61.

Becker, W. C. A genetic approach to the interpretation and evaluation of the process-reactive distinction of schizophrenia. *Journal of Abnormal and Social Psychology,* 1956, *53,* 229–236.

Bednar, R. L., & Lawlis, G. F. Empirical research in group psychotherapy. In A. E. Bergin & S. L. Garfield (Eds.), *Handbook of psychotherapy and behavior change.* New York: Wiley, 1971.

Beiser, A. R. *Mental health consultation and education.* Palo Alto, Ca.: National Press Books, 1972.

Benne, K. D. History of the T-group in the laboratory setting. In L. P. Bradford, J. R. Gibb, & K. D. Benne (Eds.), *T-group theory and laboratory method.* New York: Wiley, 1964.

Bereiter, C. A nonpsychological approach to early compensatory education. In M. Deutsch, I. Katz, & A. R. Jensen (Eds.), *Social class, race, and psychological development.* New York: Holt, Rinehart and Winston, 1968. Pp. 337–346.

Bereiter, C., & Englemann, S. *Teaching disadvantaged children in the preschool.* Englewood Cliffs, N.J.: Prentice-Hall, 1966.

Bergin, A. E. The evaluation of therapeutic outcomes. In A. E. Bergin & S. L. Garfield (Eds.), *Handbook of psychotherapy and behavior change: An empirical analysis.* New York: Wiley, 1971. Pp. 217–270.

Bergin, A. E. & Suinn, R. M. Individual psychotherapy and behavior therapy. In M. R. Rosenzweig & L. C. Porter (Eds.), *Annual Review of Psychology,* 1975, *26,* 509–556.

Bergler, E. Personality traits of alcohol addicts. *Quarterly Journal of Studies on Alcohol,* 1946, *7,* 356–361.

Berne, E. *Games people play.* New York: Grove Press, 1964.

Biber, B. Integration of mental health principles in the school setting. In G. Caplan (Ed.), *Prevention of mental disorders in children.* New York: Basic Books, 1961. Pp. 378–397.

Bigelow, N. The involutional psychoses. In S. Arieti (Ed.), *The American handbook of psychiatry,* Vol. I. New York: Basic Books, 1959. Pp. 540–545.

Bindrim, P. Nudity as a quick grab for intimacy in group therapy. *Psychology Today,* 1969, *3,* 24–28.

Birch, H. C. Health and the education of socially disadvantaged children. In S. Chess & A. Thomas (Eds.), *Annual progress in child psychiatry and child development.* New York: Brunner-Mazel, 1969. Pp. 265–291.

Bleuler, E. *Dementia praecox or the group of schizophrenias.* New York: International Universities Press, 1950.

Bloom, G. L. The "medical model," miasma theory and community mental health. *Community Mental Health Journal,* 1965, *1,* 333–338.

Böök, J. A. Genetical aspects of schizophrenic psychoses. In D. D. Jackson (Ed.), *The etiology of schizophrenia.* New York: Basic Books, 1960. Pp. 23–26.

Boring, E. G. *A history of experimental psychology*. New York: Appleton-Century-Crofts, 1950.

Bowen, M. A family concept of schizophrenia. In D. D. Jackson (Ed.), *The etiology of schizophrenia*. New York: Basic Books, 1960. Pp. 346–372.

Bower, E. M. Primary prevention in a school setting. In G. Caplan (Ed.), *Prevention of mental disorders in children*. New York: Basic Books, 1961. Pp. 353–377.

Bower, E. M. The modification, mediation and utilization of stress during the school years. *American Journal of Orthopsychiatry*, 1964, *34*, 667–674.

Bower, E. M. Primary prevention of mental and emotional disorders. In N. M. Lambert (Ed.), *The protection and promotion of mental health in schools*. Bethesda, Md.: U.S. Dept. of Health, Education and Welfare, Public Health Service Publication No. 1226, 1965. Pp. 1–9.

Bower, E. M. *Early identification of emotionally handicapped children in school*. (2nd ed.) Springfield, Ill.: Thomas, 1969.

Bower, E. M., & Hollister, W. G. (Eds.) *Behavioral science fronters in education*. New York: Wiley, 1967.

Bower, E. M., & Lambert, N. M. *A process for in-school screening of children with emotional handicaps*. Sacramento, Ca.: California State Department of Education, 1961.

Bower, E. M., Shellhamer, T. A., & Dailey, J. M. School characteristics of male adolescents who later became schizophrenic. *American Journal of Orthopsychiatry*, 1960, *30*, 712–729.

Bower, E. M., Tashnovian, P. J., & Larson, C. A. *A process for early identification of emotionally disturbed children*. Sacramento, Ca.: California State Department of Education, 1958.

Bowlby, J. *Maternal care and mental health*. Geneva, Switzerland: World Health Organization, 1952.

Brady, J. V. Ulcers in "executive" monkeys. *Scientific American*, 1958, *199*, 95–100.

Brady, J. V., Thornton, D. R., & Fisher, D. O. Deleterious effects of anxiety elicited by conditioned pre-aversive stimuli in the rat. *Psychosomatic Medicine*, 1962, *24*, 590–595.

Braginsky, B. M., Braginsky, D. D., & Ring, K. *Methods of madness: The mental hospital as a last resort*. New York: Holt, Rinehart and Winston, 1969.

Brecher, E. M. *Licit and illicit drugs*. Boston: Little, Brown, 1972.

Brecher, E. M. Marijuana: The health questions. *Consumer Reports*, 1975, *40*, 143–149.

Bredemeier, H. C. The socially handicapped and the agencies: A market analysis. In F. Riessman, J. Cohen, & A. Pearl (Eds.), *Mental health of the poor*. New York: Free Press, 1964. Pp. 98–112.

Brenner, C. *An elementary textbook of psychoanalysis*. New York: Doubleday Anchor Books, 1955.

Breutsch, W. L. Neurosyphilitic conditions. In S. Arieti (Ed.), *The American handbook of psychiatry*, Vol. II. New York: Basic Books, 1959. Pp. 1003–1020.

Brill, N. Q., & Storrow, H. A. Social class and psychiatric treatment. In F. Riessman, J. Cohen, & A. Pearl (Eds.), *Mental health of the poor*. New York: Free Press, 1964. Pp. 68–75.

Brosin, H. W. Psychiatric conditions following head injury. In S. Arieti (Ed.), *The American handbook of psychiatry*, Vol. II. New York: Basic Books, 1959. Pp. 1175–1202.

Brownbridge, R., & Van Vleet, P. (Eds.) *Investments in prevention: The prevention of learning and behavior problems in young children.* San Francisco: Pace ID Center, 1969.

Burrow, T. The group method of analysis. *Psychoanalytic Review,* 1927, *14,* 268–280.

Burton, A. (Ed.) *Encounter.* San Francisco: Jossey-Bass, 1969. (a)

Burton, A. Encounter, existence, and psychotherapy. In A. Burton (Ed.), *Encounter.* San Francisco: Jossey-Bass, 1969. (b)

Buss, A. H. *Psychopathology.* New York: Wiley, 1966.

Caldwell, B. M. The fourth dimension in early childhood education. In R. D. Hess & R. M. Bear (Eds.), *Early education.* Chicago: Aldine, 1968.

Cameron, N. A theory of diagnosis. In P. Hoch & J. Zubin (Eds.), *Current problems in psychiatric diagnosis.* New York: Grune & Stratton, 1953. Pp. 33–45.

Cameron, N. Paranoid conditions and paranoia. In S. Arieti (Ed.), *The American handbook of psychiatry,* Vol. I. New York: Basic Books, 1959. Pp. 508–539.

Cameron, N. *Personality development and psychopathology.* Boston: Houghton-Mifflin, 1963.

Cameron, N., & Magaret, A. *Behavior pathology.* Boston: Houghton-Mifflin, 1951. Pp. 21–52.

Cannon, W. B. *Bodily changes in pain, hunger, fear and rage.* New York: Appleton, 1920.

Caplan, G. *Prevention of mental disorders in children: Initial explorations.* New York: Basic Books, 1961.

Caplan, C. *Principles of preventive psychiatry.* New York: Basic Books, 1964.

Caplan, G. Opportunities for school psychologists in primary prevention of emotional disorders of children. In N. M. Lambert (Ed.), *The protection and promotion of mental health in schools.* Bethesda, Md.: U.S. Dept. of Health, Education and Welfare, Public Health Service Publication No. 1226, 1965. Pp. 9–22.

Caplan, G. *Theories of mental health consultation.* New York: Basic Books, 1970.

Carkhuff, R. R., & Truax, C. B. Training in counseling and psychotherapy: An evaluation of an integrated didactic and experiential approach. *Journal of Consulting Psychology,* 1965, *29,* 333–336. (a)

Carkhuff, R. R., & Truax, C. B. Lay mental health counseling: The effects of lay group counseling. *Journal of Consulting Psychology,* 1965, *29,* 426–431. (b)

Casriel, D. *A scream away from happiness.* New York: Grosset & Dunlap, 1972.

Cautela, J. R. Treatment of compulsive behavior by covert sensitization. *Psychological Record,* 1966, *16,* 33–41.

Cazden, C. B. Some implications of research in language development for preschool education. In R. D. Hess & R. M. Bear (Eds.), *Early education.* Chicago: Aldine, 1968. Pp. 131–142.

Chafetz, M. E., & Demone, H. W., Jr. *Alcoholism and society.* New York: Oxford University Press, 1962.

Chein, I., Gerard, D. L., Lee, R. S., & Rosenfeld, E. *The road to H.* New York: Basic Books, 1964.

Chess, S., & Thomas, T. (Eds.) *Annual progress in child psychiatry and child development.* New York: Brunner-Mazel, 1969.

Christmas, J. J. Self concept and attitudes. In K. S. Miller & R. M. Dreger (Eds.), *Comparative studies of Black and Whites in the United States: Quantitative studies in social relations.* New York: Seminar Press, 1973. Pp. 249–272.

Clarizio, H. F. (Ed.) *Mental health and the educative process.* Chicago: Rand McNally, 1969. (a)

Clarizio, H. F. Stability of deviant behavior through time. In H. F. Clarizio (Ed.), *Mental health and the educative process*. Chicago: Rand McNally, 1969. Pp. 68–74. (b)

Clarizio, H. F. *Toward positive classroom discipline*. New York: Wiley, 1971.

Clark, A. W., & Yeomans, N. T. *Fraser House: Theory, practice and evaluation of a therapeutic community*. New York: Springer, 1969.

Clark, K. B. Defeatism in ghetto schools. In J. I. Roberts (Ed.), *School children in the urban slum*. New York: Free Press, 1967. Pp. 559–610.

Cleckley, H. *The mask of sanity*. St. Louis: Mosby, 1941.

Cleckley, H. Psychopathic states. In S. Arieti (Ed.), *American handbook of psychiatry*, Vol. I. New York: Basic Books, 1959. Pp. 567–588.

Cohen, M. B., Baker, G., Cohen, R. A., Fromm-Reichmann, F., & Weigert, E. V. An intensive study of twelve cases of manic-depressive psychosis. *Psychiatry*, 1954, *17*, 103–137.

Colarelli, N. J., & Siegel, S. M. *Ward H: An adventure in innovation*. Princeton, N.J.: Van Nostrand, 1966.

Coleman, J. C. *Abnormal psychology and modern life*. (4th ed.) Chicago: Scott, Foresman, 1972.

Coleman, J. S. (Ed.) *Equality of educational opportunity*. Washington, D.C.: U.S. Dept. of Health, Education and Welfare, 1966.

Conger, J. J. The effects of alcohol on conflict behavior in the albino rat. *Quarterly Journal of Studies on Alcohol*, 1951, *12*, 1–30.

Cowen, E. L. Emergent approaches to mental health problems: An overview and directions for future work. In E. L. Cowen, E. A. Gardner, & M. Zax (Eds.), *Emergent approaches to mental health problems*. New York: Appleton-Century-Crofts, 1967. Pp. 389–455.

Cowen, E. L. The effectiveness of secondary prevention program using nonprofessionals in the school setting. *Proceedings, 76th Annual Convention, American Psychological Association*, 1968, *2*, 705–706.

Cowen, E. L. Emergent directions in school mental health: The development and evaluation of a program for the early detection and prevention of ineffective school behavior. *American Scientist*, 1971, *59*, 722–733.

Cowen, E. L. Social and community interventions. In P. Mussen & M. Rosenzweig (Eds.), *Annual Review of Psychology*, 1973, *24*, 423–472.

Cowen, E. L., Carlisle, R. L., & Kaufman, G. Evaluation of a college student volunteer program with primary graders experiencing school adjustment problems. *Psychology in the Schools*, 1969, *6*, 371–375.

Cowen, E. L., Dorr, D. A., Izzo, L. D., Madonia, A. J., & Trost, M. A. The Primary Mental Health Project: A new way of conceptualizing and delivering school mental health services. *Psychology in the Schools*, 1971, *8*, 216–225.

Cowen, E. L., Gardner, E. A., & Zax, M. (Eds.) *Emergent approaches to mental health problems*. New York: Appleton-Century-Crofts, 1967.

Cowen, E. L., Izzo, L. D., Miles, H., Telschow, E. F., Trost, M. A., & Zax, M. A preventive mental health program in the school setting: Description and evaluation. *Journal of Psychology*, 1963, *56*, 307–356.

Cowen, E. L., Leibowitz, E., & Leibowitz, G. The utilization of retired people as mental health aides in the schools. *American Journal of Orthopsychiatry*, 1968, *38*, 900–909.

Cowen, E. L., & Lorion, R. P. New directions in school mental health: A secondary prevention program. In H. H. Barten & L. Bellak (Eds.), *Progress in community mental health*, Vol. 3. New York: Brunner-Mazel, 1975. Pp. 197–230.

Cowen, E. L., Lorion, R. P., Kraus, R. M., & Dorr, D. Geometric expansion of helping resources *Journal of School Psychology*, 1974, *12*, 288–295.

Cowen, E. L., Pederson, A., Babigian, H., Izzo, L. D., & Trost, M. A. Long-term follow-up of early detected vulnerable children. *Journal of Consulting and Clinical Psychology*, 1973, *41*, 438–446.

Cowen, E. L., Trost, M. A., Lorion, R. P., Dorr, D., Izzo, L. D., & Isaacson, R. V., *New ways in school mental health: Early detection and prevention of school maladaptation*. New York: Human Sciences Press, 1975.

Cowen, E. L., & Zax, M. The mental health fields today: Issues and problems. In E. L. Cowen, E. A. Gardner, & M. Zax (Eds.), *Emergent approaches to mental health problems*. New York: Appleton-Century-Crofts, 1967. Pp. 3–29.

Cowen, E. L., & Zax, M. Early detection and prevention of emotional disorder: Conceptualizations and programming. In J. W. Carter (Ed.), *Research contributions from psychology to community mental health*. New York: Behavioral Publications, 1969. Pp. 46–59.

Cowen, E. L., Zax, M., Izzo, L. D., & Trost, M. A. Prevention of emotional disorders in the school setting: A further investigation. *Journal of Consulting Psychology*, 1966, *30*, 381–387.

Cowen, E. L., Zax, M., & Laird, J. D. A college student volunteer program in the elementary school setting. *Community Mental Health Journal*, 1966, *2*, 319–328.

Creighton, C. *Illustrations of unconscious memory in disease, including a theory of alternatives*. London: Lewis, 1886.

Cumming, J., & Cumming, E. *Ego and milieu: Theory and practice of environmental therapy*. New York: Atherton, 1966.

Daly, C. U. (Ed.) *Urban violence*. Chicago: University of Chicago Press, 1969.

Davison, G. C. Appraisal of behavior modification techniques with adults in institutional settings. In C. M. Franks (Ed.), *Assessment and status of the behavioral therapies and associated developments*. New York: McGraw-Hill, 1969. Pp. 220–278.

Dekker, M. D., Pelser, H. E., & Groen, J. Conditioning as a cause of asthmatic attacks. *Journal of Psychosomatic Research*, 1957, *2*, 97–108.

DeMille, R. L. Learning theory and schizophrenia: A comment. *Psychological Bulletin*, 1959, *56*, 313–314.

Denker, P. G. Results of treatment of psychoneuroses by the general practitioner. *New York State Journal of Medicine*, 1946, *46*, 2164–2166.

Deutsch, C. P. Environment and perception. In M. Deutsch, I. Katz, & A. R. Jensen (Eds.), *Social class, race, and psychological development*. New York: Holt, Rinehart and Winston, 1968. Pp. 58–85.

Deutsch, C. P., & Deutsch, M. Brief reflections on the theory of early childhood enrichment programs. In R. D. Hess & R. M. Bear (Eds.), *Early education*. Chicago: Aldine, 1968. Pp. 83–90.

Deutsch, M., Katz, I., & Jensen, A. R. (Eds.) *Social class, race, and psychological development*. New York: Holt, Rinehart and Winston, 1968.

Ditman, K. S. The use of LSD in the treatment of the alcoholic. In R. Fox (Ed.), *Alcoholism: Behavioral research, therapeutic approaches*. New York: Springer, 1967. Pp. 256–271.

Dohrenwend, B. P., & Dohrenwend, B. S. *Social status and psychiatric disorder*. New York: Wiley, 1969.

Dole, V. P., & Nyswander, M. E. Methadone maintenance and its implication for theories of narcotic addiction. In A. Wikler (Ed.), *Research publications: Association for Research in Nervous and Mental Disease*, Vol. XLVI. Baltimore: Williams & Wilkins, 1968. Pp. 359–366.

Dollard, J., & Miller, N. E. *Personality and psychotherapy.* New York: McGraw-Hill, 1950.

Donahue, G. T. A school district program for schizophrenic, organic and seriously disturbed children. In E. L. Cowen, E. A. Gardner, & M. Zax (Eds.), *Emergent approaches to mental health problems.* New York: Appleton-Cenutry-Crofts, 1967. Pp. 369–386.

Donahue, G. T., & Nichtern, S. *Teaching the troubled child.* New York: Free Press, 1965.

Dorcus, R. M., & Shaffer, G. W. *Textbook of abnormal psychology.* Baltimore: Williams & Wilkins, 1934.

Dorcus, R. M., & Shaffer, G. W. *Textbook of abnormal psychology.* (4th ed.) Baltimore: Williams & Wilkins, 1950.

Dorr, D. & Cowen, E. L. Nonprofessional mental health workers' judgments of change in children. *Journal of Community Psychology*, 1973, *1*, 23–26.

Dreger, R. M. Intellectual functioning. In K. S. Miller & R. M. Dreger (Eds.), *Comparative studies of Black and Whites in the United States: Quantitative studies in social relations.* New York: Seminar Press, 1974. Pp. 185–229.

Duggan, J. N. An example of secondary prevention activities in the schools: Talent searching in a culturally deprived population. In N. M. Lambert (Ed.), *The protection and promotion of mental health in schools.* Bethesda, Md.: U.S. Dept. of Health, Education and Welfare, Public Health Service Publication No. 1226, 1965. Pp. 48–52.

Dunbar, H. F. *Emotions and bodily changes.* New York: Columbia University Press, 1935.

Dunbar, H. F. *Psychosomatic diagnosis.* New York: Hoeber-Harper, 1943.

Duvall, H. J., Locke, B. Z., & Brill, L. Follow-up study of narcotic drug addicts five years after hospitalization. *Public Health Reports*, 1963, *78*, 185–193.

Ebaugh, F. G., & Tiffany, W. J., Jr. Infective-exhaustive psychoses. In S. Arieti (Ed.), *The American handbook of psychiatry*, Vol. II. New York: Basic Books, 1959. Pp. 1231–1247.

Edney, J. J. Human territoriality. *Psychological Bulletin*, 1974, *81*, 959–975.

Egbert, R. L. Follow through: Fulfilling the promise of Head Start. In J. P. Hellmuth (Ed.), *Disadvantaged child*, Vol. II. New York: Brunner-Mazel, 1969. Pp. 571–580.

Eisenberg, L. If not now, when? *American Journal of Orthopsychiatry*, 1962, *32*, 781–793. (a)

Eisenberg, L. Possibilities for a preventive psychiatry. *Pediatrics*, 1962, *30*, 815–828. (b)

Ellsworth, R. B. *Nonprofessionals in psychiatric rehabilitation.* New York: Appleton-Century-Crofts, 1968.

Engel, B. T., & Shapiro, D. The use of biofeedback training in enabling patients to control autonomic functions. In J. Segal (Ed.), *Mental health program reports—5.* Washington, D.C.: U.S. Government Printing Office, 1971. Pp. 349–376.

Engel, G. L. Studies of ulcerative colitis: I. Clinical data bearing on the nature of the somatic process. *Psychosomatic Medicine*, 1954, *16*, 496–501. (a)

Engel, G. L. Studies of ulcerative colitis: II. The nature of the somatic process and the adequacy of psychosomatic hypotheses: A review. *American Journal of Medicine*, 1954, *16*, 416–433. (b)

Engel, G. L. *Psychological development in health and disease.* Philadelphia: Saunders, 1962.

Entwisle, D. R. Developmental sociolinguistics: Inner-city children. In S. Chess & A. Thomas (Eds.), *Annual progress in child psychiatry and child development.* New York: Brunner-Mazel, 1969. Pp. 202–216.

Erikson, E. H. *Identity and the life cycle.* New York: International Universities Press, Psychology Issues Monograph No. 1, 1959.

Ewalt, P. L. *Mental health volunteers.* Springfield, Ill.: Thomas, 1967.

Eysenck, H. J. The effects of psychotherapy: An evaluation. *Journal of Consulting Psychology*, 1952, *16*, 319–324.

Eysenck, H. J. The effects of psychotherapy. In H. J. Eysenck (Ed.), *Handbook of abnormal psychology.* New York: Basic Books, 1961. Pp. 697–725.

Eysenck, H. J. The effects of psychotherapy. *International Journal of Psychiatry*, 1965, *1*, 97–178.

Fairweather, G. W. (Ed.) *Social psychology in treating mental illness: An experimental approach.* New York: Wiley, 1964.

Fairweather, G. W. *Methods for experimental social innovation.* New York: Wiley, 1967.

Fairweather, G. W., Sanders, D. H., Maynard, H., & Cressler, D. L. *Community life for the mentally ill: An alternative to institutional care.* Chicago: Aldine, 1969.

Fairweather, G. W., Sanders, D. H., & Tornatzky, L. *Creating change in mental health organizations.* New York: Pergamon, 1974.

Falconer, W. *A dissertation on the influence of the passions upon disorders of the body.* London: Dilly, 1796.

Farberow, N. L., & Shneidman, E. S. (Eds.) *The cry for help.* New York: McGraw-Hill, 1961.

Faris, R. E. L., & Dunham, H. W. *Mental disorders in urban areas.* Chicago: University of Chicago Press, 1939.

Faust, V. *The counselor-consultant in the elementary school.* Boston: Houghton-Mifflin, 1968.

Fein, L. G. *The changing school scene: Challenge to psychology.* New York: Wiley, 1974.

Feldhusen, J. F., Thurston, J. R., & Benning, J. J. Aggressive classroom behavior and school achievement. *Journal of Special Education*, 1969, *4*, 431–439.

Feldhusen, J. F., Thurston, J. R., & Benning, J. J. Longitudinal analysis of classroom behavior and school achievement. *Journal of Experimental Education*, 1970, *38*, 4–10.

Felix, R. H. *Mental illness: Progress and prospects.* New York: Columbia University Press, 1967.

Fenichel, O. *The psychoanalytic theory of neurosis.* New York: Norton, 1945.

Ferraro, A. Psychoses with cerebral arteriosclerosis. In S. Arieti (Ed.), *The American handbook of psychiatry*, Vol. II. New York: Basic Books, 1959. Pp. 1078–1108. (a)

Ferraro, A. Senile psychoses. In S. Arieti (Ed.), *The American handbook of psychiatry*, Vol. II. New York: Basic Books, 1959. Pp. 1021–1045. (b)

Finkel, N. J. Strens and traumas: An attempt at categorization. *American Journal of Community Psychology*, 1974, *2*, 265–275.

Finney, J. C. (Ed.) *Culture change, mental health and poverty.* Lexington, Ky.: University of Kentucky Press, 1969.

Fishman, J. R., Denham, W. H., Levine, M., & Shatz, E. O. *New careers for the disadvantaged in human services: Report of a social experiment.* Washington, D.C.: Howard University Institute for Youth Studies, 1969.

Foley, J. P., Jr. The criterion of abnormality. *Journal of Abnormal and Social Psychology,* 1935, *30,* 279–291.

Fontana, A. F. Familial etiology of schizophrenia: Is a scientific methodology possible? *Psychological Bulletin,* 1966, *66,* 214–227.

Ford, D. H., & Urban, H. B. *Systems of psychotherapy: A comparative study.* New York: Wiley, 1963.

Fort, J. P., Jr. Heroin addiction among young men. *Psychiatry,* 1954, *17,* 251–259.

Foucault, M. *Madness and civilization.* New York: Random House, 1965.

Fox, R. Disulfiram (Antabuse) as an adjunct in the treatment of alcoholism. In R. Fox (Ed.), *Alcoholism: Behavioral research, therapeutic approaches.* New York: Springer, 1967. Pp. 242–255.

Frank, J. D. *Persuasion and healing.* Baltimore: Johns Hopkins University Press, 1961.

Freud, A. *The ego and the mechanisms of defense.* New York: International Universities Press, 1946.

Freud, A., & Burlingham, D. *Infants without families.* New York: International Universities Press, 1944.

Freud, S. *The interpretation of dreams.* New York: Random House, 1950.

Freud, S. *On dreams.* New York: Norton, 1952.

Freud, S. Mourning and melancholia (1917). In E. Jones (Ed.), *Collected papers,* Vol. IV. London: Hogarth, 1956. Pp. 152–170. (a)

Freud, S. Psycho-analytic notes upon an autobiographical account of a case of paranoia (1911). In E. Jones (Ed.), *Collected papers,* Vol. III. London: Hogarth, 1956. Pp. 390–470. (b)

Freud, S. *Group psychology and the analysis of the ego.* New York: Bantam Books, 1960.

Freud, S. The aetiology of hysteria (1896). In S. Freud, *Early psychoanalytic writings.* New York: Collier Books, 1963. Pp. 175–204. (a)

Freud, S. Sexuality in the aetiology of the neuroses (1898). In S. Freud, *Early psychoanalytic writings.* New York: Collier Books, 1963. Pp. 205–228. (b)

Freud, S. On psychotherapy (1904). In S. Freud, *Therapy and technique.* New York: Collier Books, 1963. Pp. 63–76. (c)

Freud, S. My views on the part played by sexuality in the aetiology of the neuroses (1905). In S. Freud, *Sexuality and the psychology of love.* New York: Collier Books, 1963. Pp. 11–19. (d)

Freud, S. The dynamics of the transference (1912). In S. Freud, *Therapy and Technique.* New York: Collier Books, 1963. Pp. 105–116. (e)

Freud, S. On narcissism: An introduction (1914). In S. Freud, *General psychological theory.* New York: Collier Books. 1963. Pp. 56–82. (f)

Freud, S. The unconscious (1915). In S. Freud, *General psychological theory.* New York: Collier Books, 1963. Pp. 116–150. (g)

Freud, S. Neurosis and psychosis (1924). In S. Freud, *General psychological theory.* New York: Collier Books, 1963. Pp. 185–189. (h)

Freud, S. Analysis terminable and interminable (1937). In S. Freud, *Therapy and technique.* New York: Collier Books, 1963. Pp. 233–272. (i)

Freud, S., & Breuer, J. *Studies on hysteria.* New York: Avon Books, 1966.

Fried, M. Social differences in mental health. In J. Kosa, A. Antonovsky, & I. K. Zola

(Eds.), *Poverty and health: A sociological analysis.* Cambridge, Mass.: Harvard University Press, 1969. Pp. 113–167.

Friedman, S. B., & Ader, R. Parameters relevant to the experimental production of "stress" in the mouse. *Psychosomatic Medicine*, 1965, *26*, 27–30.

Friedman, S. B., & Glasgow, L. A. Psychologic factors and resistance to infectious diseases. *Pediatric Clinics of North America*, 1966, *13*, 315–335.

Fromm-Reichmann, F. *Principles of intensive psychotherapy.* Chicago: University of Chicago Press, 1950.

Fromm-Reichmann, F. Intensive psychotherapy of manic-depressives. In D. M. Bullard (Ed.), *Psychoanalysis and psychotherapy.* Chicago: University of Chicago Press, 1959. Pp. 221–226.

Fullmer, D. W., & Bernard, H. W. *The school counselor-consultant.* Boston: Houghton-Mifflin, 1972.

Garfield, S. L. Research on client variables in psychotherapy. In A. E. Bergin & S. L. Garfield (Eds.), *Handbook of psychotherapy and behavior change: An empirical analysis.* New York: Wiley, 1971. Pp. 271–298.

Garmezy, N. Process and reactive schizophrenia: Some conceptions and issues. In M. M. Katz, J. O. Cole, W. E. Barton (Eds.), *The role and methodology of classification in psychiatry and psychopathology.* Washington, D.C.: U.S. Government Printing Office, 1968. Pp. 419–466.

Garmezy, N. Children at risk: The search for the antecedents of schizophrenia. Part I. Conceptual models and research methods. *Schizophrenia Bulletin*, 1974, 8, 14–90.

Gartner, A. *Paraprofessionals and their performance.* New York: Praeger, 1971.

Gazda, G. M. Group psychotherapy: Its definition and history. In G. M. Gazda (Ed.), *Innovations to group psychotherapy.* Springfield, Ill.: Thomas, 1968.

Gesten, E. L. A Health Resources Inventory: The development of a measure of the personal and social competence of primary grade children. Unpublished Ph.D. dissertation, University of Rochester, 1974.

Gibson, R. W. The family background and early life experience of the manic-depressive patient. *Psychiatry*, 1958, *21*, 71–90.

Gildea, M. C.-L. *Community mental health.* Springfield, Ill.: Thomas, 1959.

Gildea, M. C.-L., Glidewell, J. C., & Kantor, M. B. The St. Louis school mental health project: History and evaluation. In E. L. Cowen, E. A. Gardner, & M. Zax (Eds.), *Emergent approaches to mental health problems.* New York: Appleton-Century-Crofts, 1967. Pp. 290–306.

Ginsberg, S., & Greenhill, M. New York City Head Start: Pluralism, innovation, and institutional change. In J. Hellmuth (Ed.), *Disadvantaged child*, Vol. II. New York: Brunner-Mazel, 1969. Pp. 399–420.

Glasscote, R. M., and Fishman, M. E. *Mental health for preschool children: A field study.* Washington, D.C.: National Association for Mental Health, 1974.

Glasscote, R. M., Sanders, D., Forstenzer, H. M., & Foley, A. R. *The community mental health center: An analysis of existing models.* Washington, D.C.: American Psychiatric Association, 1964.

Glidewell, J. C., Gildea, M. C.-L., & Kaufman, M. K. The preventive and therapeutic effects of two school mental health programs. *American Journal of Community Psychology*, 1973, *1*, 295–329.

Glidewell, J. C., Mensh, I. N., Domke, H. R., Gildea, M. C.-L., & Buchmueller, A. D. Methods for community mental health research. *American Journal of Orthopsychiatry*, 1957, *27*, 38–54.

Glidewell, J. C., & Stringer, L. A. Progress Report III, OM-188 St. Louis County Health Department, August, 1962.

Glidewell, J. C., & Stringer, L. A. The educational institution and the health institution. In E. M. Bower & W. G. Hollister (Eds.), *Behavior science frontiers in education*. New York: Wiley, 1967. Pp. 384–400.

Glidewell, J. C., & Swallow, C. S. *The prevalence of maladjustment in elementary schools: A report prepared for the Joint Commission on the mental health of children*. Chicago: University of Chicago Press, 1969.

Goffman, E. *Asylums*. New York: Doubleday, 1961.

Goldberg, C. S. Nonprofessionals in human services. In C. Grosser, W. E. Henry, & J. G. Kelly (Eds.), *Nonprofessionals in the human services*. San Francisco: Jossey-Bass, 1969. Pp. 12–39.

Goldenberg, I. I. The Residential Youth Center: The creation of an assumptions-questioning rehabilitative setting. In *Criminal corrections in Connecticut: Perspectives and progress*. West Hartford, Conn.: Conn. Planning Committee on Criminal Administration, 1968. Pp. 40–59.

Goldenberg, I. I. *Prospectus and guidelines for residential youth centers*. Washington, D.C.: U.S. Dept. of Labor, Office of Special Manpower Programs, 1969.

Goldenberg, I. I. *Build me a mountain: Youth, poverty and the creation of new settings*. Cambridge, Mass.: M.I.T. Press, 1971.

Goldstein, K. Functional disturbances in brain damage. In S. Arieti (Ed.), *The American handbook of psychiatry*, Vol. I. New York: Basic Books, 1959. Pp. 770–794.

Goldston, S. E. (Ed.) *Concepts of community psychiatry: A framework for training*. Bethesda, Md.: U.S. Dept. of Health, Education and Welfare, Public Health Service Publication No. 1319, 1965.

Gordon, E. W. Programs of compensatory education. In M. Deutsch, I. Katz, & A. R. Jensen (Eds.), *Social class, race, and psychological development*. New York: Holt, Rinehart and Winston, 1968. Pp. 381–410.

Gordon, E. W. Introduction. In J. Hellmuth (Ed.), *Disadvantaged child*, Vol. II. New York: Brunner-Mazel, 1969. Pp. 8–14.

Gottesman, I. I., & Shields, J. Contributions of twin studies to perspectives on schizophrenia. In B. A. Maher (Ed.), *Progress in experimental personality research*, Vol. 3. New York: Academic Press, 1966. Pp. 1–84.

Gottfried, N. W. Effects of early intervention programs. In K. S. Miller & R. M. Dreger (Eds.), *Comparative studies of Black and Whites in the United States: Quantitative studies in social relations*. New York: Seminar Press, 1973. Pp. 273–293.

Gray, S. W., & Klaus, R. An experimental pre-school program for culturally deprived children. *Child Development*, 1965, *36*, 887–898.

Gray, S. W., & Klaus, R. The early training project and its general rationale. In R. D. Hess & R. M. Bear (Eds.), *Early education*. Chicago: Aldine, 1968. Pp. 63–70.

Greenblatt, M. Electro-encephalographic studies of homicidal psychopaths. In P. Sorokin (Ed.), *Explorations in love and altruistic behavior*. Boston: Beacon Press, 1950.

Greenblatt, M., & Levinson, D. J. Mental hospitals. In B. Wolman (Ed.), *Handbook of clinical psychology*. New York: McGraw-Hill, 1965. Pp. 1343–1359.

Griffith, C. R., & Libo, L. M. *Mental health consultants: Agents of community change*. San Francisco: Jossey-Bass, 1968.

Grosser, C., Henry, W. E., & Kelly, J. G. (Eds.), *Nonprofessionals in the human services*. San Francisco: Jossey-Bass, 1969.

Guerney, B. G. *Psychotherapeutic agents: New roles for nonprofessionals, parents and teachers.* New York: Holt, Rinehart and Winston, 1969.

Gump, P. V. Intro-setting analysis: The third grade classroom as a special but instructive case. In E. P. Willems & H. L. Raush (Eds.), *Naturalistic viewpoints in psychological research.* New York: Holt, Rinehart and Winston, 1969. Pp. 200–220.

Gurin, G., Veroff, J., & Feld, S. *Americans view their mental health: A nationwide interview survey.* New York: Basic Books, 1960.

Haase, W. The role of socioeconomic class in examiner bias. In F. Riessman, J. Cohen, & A. Pearl (Eds.), *Mental health of the poor.* New York: Free Press, 1964. Pp. 241–247.

Haley, J. An interactional description of schizophrenia. *Psychiatry,* 1959, *22,* 321–332.

Hall, C. S., & Lindzey, G. *Theories of personality.* (2nd ed.) New York: Wiley, 1968.

Harris, J. G. (Ed.) *Mental health manpower needs in psychology.* Lexington, Ky.: University of Kentucky, 1966.

Harris, T. A. *I'm OK—You're OK.* New York: Harper & Row, 1967.

Hartocollis, P. Some phenomenological aspects of the alcoholic condition. *Psychiatry,* 1964, *4,* 345–348.

Haylett, C. H., & Rapoport, L. Mental health consultation. In L. Bellak (Ed.), *Handbook of community psychiatry and community mental health.* New York: Grune & Stratton, 1964. Pp. 319–339.

Heath, R. G. A biochemical hypothesis on the etiology of schizophrenia. In D. D. Jackson (Ed.), *The etiology of schizophrenia.* New York: Basic Books, 1960. Pp. 146–156.

Hellmuth, J. (Ed.) *Disadvantaged child,* Vol. I. New York: Bruner-Mazel, 1969. (a)

Hellmuth, J. (Ed.) *Disadvantaged child,* Vol. II. New York: Brunner-Mazel, 1969. (b)

Henderson, D. K., & Gillespie, R. D. *A textbook of psychiatry* (6th ed) New York: Oxford University Press,1944.

Henry, G. W. *Essentials of psychiatry* (3rd ed.) Baltimore: Williams & Wilkins, 1938.

Hereford, C. F. *Changing parental attitudes through group discussion.* Austin, Texas: University of Texas Press, 1963.

Herron, W. G. The process-reactive classifications of schizophrenia. *Psychological Bulletin,* 1962, *59,* 329–343.

Hess, R. D., & Bear, R. M. (Eds.) *Early education.* Chicago: Aldine, 1968.

Hess, R. D., & Shipman, V. C. Maternal influences upon early learning: The cognitive environments of urban pre-school children. In R. D. Hess & R. M. Bear (Eds.), *Early education.* Chicago: Aldine, 1968. Pp. 91–103.

Heston, L. L., & Denney, D. Interactions between early life experience and biological factors in schizophrenia. In D. Rosenthal & S. S. Kety (Eds.), *The transmission of schizophrenia.* New York: Pergamon, 1968.

Hobbs, N. Mental health's third revolution. *American Journal of Orthopsychiatry,* 1964, *34,* 822–833.

Hobbs, N. Helping disturbed children: Psychological and ecological strategies. *American Psychologist,* 1966, *21,* 1105–1115.

Hobbs, N. The reeducation of emotionally disturbed children. In E. M. Bower & W. G. Hollister (Eds.), *Behavior science frontiers in education.* New York: Wiley, 1967. Pp. 339–354.

Hobbs, N. Re-education, reality and community responsibility. In J. W. Carter (Ed.), *Research contributions from psychology to community mental health.* New York: Behavioral Publications, 1969. Pp. 7–18.

Hollingshead, A. B., & Redlich, F. C. *Social class and mental illness: A community study.* New York: Wiley, 1958.

Hollister, W. G. The concept of "strens" in preventive interventions and ego-strength building in the schools. In N. M. Lambert (Ed.), *The protection and promotion of mental health in schools.* Bethesda, Md.: U.S. Dept. of Health, Education and Welfare, Public Health Service Publication No. 1226, 1965. Pp. 30–35.

Hollister, W. G. Concept of strens in education: A challenge to curriculum development. In E. M. Bower & W. G. Hollister (Eds.), *Behavioral science frontiers in education.* New York: Wiley, 1967. Pp. 193–205.

Holt, R. R. A review of some of Freud's biological assumptions and their influences on his theories. In N. S. Greenfield & W. C. Lewis (Eds.), *Psychoanalysis and current biological thought.* Madison: University of Wisconsin Press, 1965. Pp. 93–124.

Holtzman, W. H., & Sells, S. B. Prediction of flying success by clinical analysis of test protocols. *Journal of Abnormal and Social Psychology,* 1954, *49,* 485–498.

Holzberg, J. D. The companion program: Implementing the manpower recommendations of the Joint Commission on Mental Illness and Health. *American Psychologist,* 1963, *18,* 224–226.

Holzberg, J. D., Knapp, R. H., & Turner, J. L. College students as companions to the mentally ill. In E. L. Cowen, E. A. Gardner, & M. Zax (Eds.), *Emergent approaches to mental health problems.* New York: Appleton-Century-Crofts, 1967. Pp. 91–109.

Horowitz, F. D., & Paden, L. Y. The effectiveness of environmental intervention programs. In B. M. Caldwell & H. Ricciuti (Eds.), *Review of child development research,* Vol. 3. New York: Russel Sage Foundation, 1973.

Horton, D. The functions of alcohol in primitive societies: A cross-cultural study. *Quarterly Journal of Studies on Alcohol,* 1943, *4,* 199–320.

Huessy, H. R. (Ed.) *Mental health with limited resources: Yankee ingenuity in low-cost programs.* New York: Grune & Stratton, 1966.

Hunt, G. H., & Odoroff, M. E. Follow-up study of narcotic drug addicts after hospitalization. *Public Health Reports,* 1962, *77,* 41–54.

Hunt, H. A. The American school system: A possible locus for a national mental health program. *Psychology in the schools,* 1968, *5,* 35–40.

Hunt, J. McV. Traditional personality theory in the light of recent evidence. *American Scientist,* 1965, *53,* 80–96.

Hunt, J. McV. Environment, development and scholastic achievement. In M. Deutsch, I. Katz, & A. R. Jensen (Eds.), *Social class, race, and psychological development.* New York: Holt, Rinehart and Winston, 1968. Pp. 293–336.

Insel, P. M., & Moos, R. H. Psychosocial environments: Expanding the scope of human ecology. *American Psychologist,* 1974, *29,* 179–188.

Isaacs, W., Thomas, J., & Goldiamond, I. Application of operant conditioning to reinstate verbal behavior in psychotics. *Journal of Speech and Hearing Disorders,* 1960, *25,* 8–12.

Iscoe, I., Pierce-Jones, J., Friedman, S. T., & McGehearty, L. Some strategies in mental health consultation: A brief description of a project and some preliminary results. In E. L. Cowen, E. A. Gardner, & M. Zax (Eds.), *Emergent approaches to mental health problems.* New York: Appleton-Century-Crofts, 1967. Pp. 307–330.

Iscoe, I., & Spielberger, C. D. (Eds.) *Community psychology: Perspectives in training and research.* New York: Appleton-Century-Crofts, 1970.

Jackins, H. *Elementary counselors manual.* Seattle: Personal Counselors, Inc., 1962.

Jackins, H. *The human side of human beings.* Seattle: Rational Island Publishers, 1965.

Jackson, D. D. A critique of the literature on the genetics of schizophrenia. In D. D. Jackson (Ed.), *The etiology of schizophrenia.* New York: Basic Books, 1960. Pp. 37–87.

Jackson, D. D. Schizophrenia. *Scientific American,* 1962, *207,* 65–78.

Jackson, J. J. Family organization and technology. In K. S. Miller & R. M. Dreger (Eds.), *Comparative studies of Black and Whites in the United States: Quantitative studies in social relations.* New York: Seminar Press, 1973. Pp. 405–445.

Jacob, T. Family interaction in disturbed and normal families. *Psychological Bulletin,* 1975, *82,* 33–65.

Janov, A. *The primal scream.* New York: Dell, 1970.

Jason, L. Early secondary prevention with disadvantaged preschool children. *American Journal of Community Psychology,* 1975, *3,* 33–46.

Jason, L., Clarfield, S. P., & Cowen, E. L. Preventive intervention with young disadvantaged children. *American Journal of Community Psychology,* 1973, *1,* 50–61.

Jason, L., & Kimbrough, C. A preventive educational program for young economically disadvantaged children. *Journal of Community Psychology,* 1974, *2,* 134–139.

Jaynes, J. The routes of science. *American Scientist,* 1966, *54,* 94–102.

Jellinek, E. M. Some principles of psychiatric classification. *Psychiatry,* 1939, *2,* 161–165.

Jellinek, E. M. Phases of alcohol addiction. *Quarterly Journal of Studies on Alcohol,* 1952, *13,* 673–684.

Jensen, A. R. How much can we boost I.Q. and scholastic achievement? *Harvard Educational Review,* 1969, *39,* 1–123.

Jervis, G. A. The mental deficiencies. In S. Arieti (Ed.), *The American handbook of psychiatry,* Vol. II. New York: Basic Books, 1959. Pp. 1289–1314.

John, V. P., & Goldstein, L. S. The social context of language acquisition. In J. Hellmuth (Ed.), *Disadvantaged child,* Vol. II. New York: Brunner-Mazel, 1969. Pp. 355–469.

Joint Commission on Mental Health of Children. *Crisis in child mental health: Challenge for the 1970's.* New York: Harper & Row, 1969.

Joint Commission on Mental Illness and Health. *Action for mental health.* New York: Basic Books, 1961.

Jones, E. *The life and work of Sigmund Freud,* Vol. I. New York: Basic Books, 1953.

Jones, M. *The therapeutic community.* New York: Basic Books, 1953.

Jones, M. *Beyond the therapeutic community.* New Haven, Conn.: Yale University Press, 1968.

Kalish, H. I. Behavior therapy. In B. B. Wolman (Ed.), *Handbook of clinical psychology.* New York: McGraw-Hill, 1965. Pp. 1230–1253.

Kallman, F. J. Genetic aspects of psychoses. In Milbank Memorial Fund, *Biology of mental health and disease.* New York: Hoeber-Harper, 1952. Pp. 283–302.

Kallman, F. J. The genetic theory of schizophrenia: An analysis of 691 twin index families. *American Journal of Psychiatry,* 1946, *103,* 209–322.

Kallman, F. J. *Heredity in mental health and disorder.* New York: Norton, 1953.

Kanfer, F. H., & Saslow, G. Behavioral analysis: An alternative to diagnostic classification. *Archives of General Psychiatry,* 1965, *12,* 529–538.

Kantor, R. E., Wallner, J., & Winder, C. L. Process and reactive schizophrenia. *Journal of Consulting Psychology,* 1953, *17,* 157–162.

Kaplan, S. R., & Roman, M. *The organization and delivery of mental health services in the ghetto: The Lincoln Hospital experience.* New York: Praeger, 1973.

Karpman, B. Psychopathy in the scheme of human typology. *Journal of Nervous and Mental Diseases*, 1946, *103*, 276–288.

Kazanjian, V., Stein, S., & Weinberg, W. L. *An introduction to mental health consultation*. Washington, D.C.: U.S. Dept. of Health, Education and Welfare, Public Health Monograph No. 69, 1962.

Kellam, S. G., Branch, J. D., Agrawal, K. C., & Ensminger, M. E. *Mental health and going to school: The Woodlawn program of assessment, early intervention, and evaluation*. Chicago: University of Chicago Press, 1975.

Kellam, S. G., Branch, J. D., Agrawal, K. C., & Grabill, M. E. Woodlawn Mental Health Center: An evolving strategy for planning community mental health. In S. E. Golann & C. Eisdorfer (Eds.), *Handbook of community mental health*. New York: Appleton-Century-Crofts, 1972.

Kelley, E. L., & Fiske, D. W. *The prediction of performance in clinical psychology*. Ann Arbor, Mich.: University of Michigan Press, 1951.

Kelly, J. G. The mental health agent in the urban community. In Symposium No. 10, *Urban America and the planning of mental health services*. New York: Group for Advancement of Psychiatry, 1964. Pp. 474–494.

Kelly, J. G. Ecological constraints on mental health services. *American Psychologist*, 1966, *21*, 535–539.

Kelly, J. G. Naturalistic observations and theory confirmation. *Human Development*, 1967, *10*, 212–222.

Kelly, J. G. Towards an ecological conception of preventive interventions. In J. W. Carter (Ed.), *Research contributions from psychology to community mental health*. New York: Behavioral Publications, 1968. Pp. 75–97.

Kelly, J. G. Naturalistic observations in contrasting social environments. In E. P. Willems & H. L. Raush (Eds.), *Naturalistic viewpoints in psychological research*. New York: Holt, Rinehart and Winston, 1969. Pp. 183–199.

Kelly, J. G. The quest for valid preventive interventions. In C. D. Spielberger (Ed.), *Current topics in clinical and community psychology*. New York: Academic Press, 1970. Pp. 183–207.

Kennedy, R. F. Government, jobs and new careers. In F. Riessman & H. I. Popper (Eds.), *Up from poverty*. New York: Harper & Row, 1968. Pp. 18–24.

Kern, H. M. The new emphasis on mental health consultation. In L. Bellak & H. H. Barten (Eds.), *Progress in community mental health*, Vol. 1. New York: Grune & Stratton, 1969.

Kessler, M., & Albee, G. W. Primary prevention. In M. R. Rosenzweig & L. C. Porter (Eds.), *Annual Review of Psychology*, 1975, *26*, 557–591.

Kety, S. S. Biochemical theories of schizophrenia: Part I. *Science*, 1959, *129*, 1528–1532. (a)

Kety, S. S. Biochemical theories of schizophrenia: Part II. *Science*, 1959, *129*, 1590–1596. (b)

Kety, S. S. The relevance of biochemical studies to the etiology of schizophrenia. In J. Romano (Ed.), *The origins of schizophrenia*. Amsterdam: Excerpta Medica Foundation, 1967. Pp. 35–41.

Kety, S. S. Rosenthal, D., Wender, P. H., & Schulsinger, F. The types and prevalence of mental illness in the biological and adoptive families of adopted schizophrenics. In D. Rosenthal & S. S. Kety (Eds.), *The transmission of schizophrenia*. New York: Pergamon, 1968. Pp. 345–362.

Kiesler, F. More than psychiatry: A rural program. In M. F. Shore & F. V. Mannino

(Eds.), *Mental health in the community: Problems, programs and strategies*. New York: Behavioral Publications, 1969. Pp. 103–120.

King, G. F., Armitage, S. G., & Tilton, J. R. A therapeutic approach to schizophrenics of extreme pathology: An operant-interpersonal method. *Journal of Abnormal and Social Psychology*, 1960, *61*, 276–286.

Kinsey, A. C., Pomeroy, W. B., & Martin, C. E. *Sexual behavior in the human male*. Philadelphia: Saunders, 1948.

Kinsey, A. C., Pomeroy, W. B., Martin, C. E., and Gebhard, P. H. *Sexual behavior in the human female*. Philadelphia: Saunders, 1953.

Klein, D. C., & Ross, A. Kindergarten entry: A study of role transition. In M. Krugman (Ed.), *Orthopsychiatry and the school*. New York: American Orthopsychiatric Association, 1958. Pp. 60–69.

Klein, M. *Contributions to psychoanalysis, 1921–1945*. London: Hogarth, 1950.

Klein, M. H., Dittman, A. T., Parloff, M. B., & Gill, M. M. Behavior therapy: Observations and reflections. *Journal of Consulting and Clinical Psychology*, 1969, *33*, 259–266.

Klein, W. L. The training of human service aides. In E. L. Cowen, E. A. Gardner, & M. Zax (Eds.), *Emergent approaches to mental health problems*. New York: Appleton-Century-Crofts, 1967. Pp. 144–161.

Kleiner, R. J., & Parker, S. Goal striving, social status and disorder: A research review. In S. K. Weinberg (Ed.), *The sociology of mental disorders*. Chicago: Aldine, 1967. Pp. 55–66.

Knapp, P. H., & Nemetz, S. J. Personality variations in bronchial asthma. *Psychosomatic Medicine*, 1957, *19*, 443–465.

Knight, R. P. The psychodynamics of chronic alcoholism. *Journal of Nervous & Mental Diseases*, 1937, *86*, 538–548.

Kolb, L. C. *Noyes' modern clinical psychiatry*. (7th ed.) Philadelphia: Saunders, 1968.

Kosa, J., Antonovsky, A., & Zola, I. K. (Eds.) *Poverty and health: A sociological analysis*. Cambridge, Mass.: Harvard University Press, 1969.

Kosa, J., Zola, I. K., & Antonovsky, A. Health and poverty considered. In J. Kosa, A. Antonovsky, & I. K. Zola (Eds.), *Poverty and health: A sociological analysis*. Cambridge, Mass.: Harvard University Press, 1969. Pp. 319–340.

Kraepelin, E. *Clinical psychiatry*. (Abstracted from 7th German edition by A. R. Diefendorf) New York: Macmillan, 1923.

Krasner, L. The operant approach in behavior therapy. In A. E. Bergin & S. L. Garfield (Eds.), *Handbook of psychotherapy and behavior change*. New York: Wiley, 1971. Pp. 612–652.

Kretschmer, E. *Physique and character* (2nd ed.). London: Routledge & Kegan Paul, 1936.

Kringlen, E. Hereditary and social factors in schizophrenic twins: An epidemiological clinical study. In J. Romano (Ed.), *The origins of schizophrenia*. Amsterdam: Excerpta Medica Foundation, 1968. Pp. 2–14.

Kuhn, T. S. *The structure of scientific revolutions*. Chicago: University of Chicago Press, 1962.

L'Abate, L., Oslin, Y., & Stone, V. W. Educational achievement. In K. S. Miller & R. M. Dreger (Eds.), *Comparative studies of Black and Whites in the United States: Quantitative studies in social relations*. New York: Seminar Press, 1973. Pp. 325–354.

Laing, R. D. *The politics of experience*. New York: Ballantine, 1967. (a)

Laing, R. D. The study of family and social contexts in relation to the origin of schizophrenia. In J. Romano (Ed.), *The origins of schizophrenia*. New York: Excerpta Medica Foundation, 1967. (b)

Lambert, N. M. (Ed.) *The protection and promotion of mental health in the schools.* Bethesda, Md.: U.S. Dept. of Health, Education and Welfare, Public Health Service Publication No. 1226, 1965.

Landis, C. A statistical evaluation of psychotherapeutic methods. In L. E. Hinsie (Ed.), *Concepts and problems of psychotherapy*. New York: Columbia University Press, 1937. Pp. 155–165.

Lang, P. J. Experimental studies of desensitization psychotherapy. In J. Wolpe, A. Salter, & L. J. Reyna (Eds.), *The conditioning therapies*. New York: Holt, Rinehart and Winston, 1964. Pp. 38–53.

Lang, P. J. Fear reduction and fear behavior: Problems in treating a construct. In J. M. Shlien (Ed.), *Research in psychotherapy*, Vol. 3. Washington, D.C.: American Psychological Association, 1968. Pp. 90–102.

Lang, P. J., & Buss, A. H. Psychological deficit in schizophrenia II: Interference and activation. *Journal of Abnormal Psychology*, 1965, 70, 77–106.

Lang, P. J. & Lazovik, A. D. The experimental desensitization of a phobia. *Journal of Abnormal and Social Psychology*, 1963, 66, 519–525.

Lange, J. *Crime and destiny*. New York: Boni, 1930.

Langner, T. S. Socioeconomic status and personality. In J. I. Roberts (Ed.), *School children in the urban slum*. New York: Free Press, 1967. Pp. 180–214.

Langrod, J., Brill, L., Lowinson, J., & Joseph, H. Methadone maintenance: From research to treatment. In L. Brill & L. Lieberman (Eds.), *Major modalities in the treatment of drug abuse*. New York: Behavioral Publications, 1972. Pp. 107–142.

Lawrence, M. M. *The mental health team in the schools*. New York: Behavioral Publications, 1972.

Lazarus, A. A. Group therapy of phobic disorders by systematic desenitization. *Journal of Abnormal and Social Psychology*, 1961, 63, 504–510.

Lazarus, A. A. Behavior therapy in groups. In G. M. Gazda (Ed.), *Basic approaches to group psychotherapy and counseling*. Springfield, Ill.: Thomas, 1968.

Leighton, D. C. Distribution of psychiatric symptoms in a small town. *American Journal of Psychiatry*, 1956, *112*, 716–723.

Leighton, D. C. *The character of danger*. New York: Basic Books. 1964.

Lemkau, P. V. Mental hygiene. In S. Arieti (Ed.), *American handbook of psychiatry*, Vol. 2. New York: Basic Books, 1959. Pp. 1948–1959.

Lemkau, P. V. The planning project for Columbia. In M. F. Shore & F. V. Mannino (Eds.), *Mental health and the community: Problems, programs and strategies.* New York: Behavioral Publications, 1969. Pp. 193–204.

Lennard, H. L., & Bernstein, A. *Patterns in human interaction*. San Francisco: Jossey-Bass, 1969.

Lerner, B. *Therapy in the ghetto: Political impotence and personal disintegration.* Baltimore: Johns Hopkins University Press, 1972.

Lerner, M. Social differences in physical health. In J. Kosa, A. Antonovsky, & I. K. Zola (Eds.), *Poverty and health: A sociological analysis*. Cambridge, Mass.: Harvard University Press, 1969. Pp. 69–112.

Lester, D., & Greenberg, L. A. Nutrition and the etiology of alcoholism: The effect of sucrose-saccarin on fat on the self-selection of ethyl alcohol by rats. *Quarterly Journal of Studies on Alcohol*, 1952, *13*, 553–560.

Levis, D. J., & Carrera, R. Effects of ten hours of implosive therapy in the treatment of outpatients: A preliminary report. *Journal of Abnormal Psychology*, 1967, *72*, 504–508.

Levitt, E. E. The results of psychotherapy with children: An evaluation. *Journal of Consulting Psychology*, 1957, *21*, 189–204.

Levitt, E. E. Psychotherapy with children: A further evaluation. *Behavior Research and Therapy*, 1963, *1*, 45–51.

Levitt, E. E. Research on psychotherapy with children. In A. E. Bergin & S. L. Garfield (Eds.), *Handbook of psychotherapy and behavior change: An empirical analysis*. New York: Wiley, 1971. Pp. 474–494.

Levy, L., & Rowitz, L. *The ecology of mental disorder*. New York: Behavioral Publications, 1973.

Lewis, H. The changing Negro family. In J. I. Roberts (Ed.), *School children in the urban slum*. New York: Free Press, 1967. Pp. 397–405.

Lewis, N. D. C. *A short history of psychiatric achievement*. New York: Norton, 1941.

Lewis, W. W. Project Re-ED: Educational intervention in discordant child rearing systems. In E. L. Cowen, E. A. Gardner, & M. Zax (Eds.), *Emergent approaches to mental health problems*. New York: Appleton-Century-Crofts, 1967. Pp. 352–368.

Liddell, H. S. Conditioned reflex method and experimental neurosis. In J. McV. Hunt (Ed.), *Personality and the behavior disorders*, Vol. I. New York: Ronald Press, 1944. Pp. 389–412.

Liddell, H. S. Effects of corticosteroids in experimental psychoneurosis. In Milbank Memorial Fund, *The biology of mental health and disease*. New York: Hoeber-Harper, 1952. Pp. 591–594. (a)

Liddell, H. S. Experimental induction of psychoneuroses by conditioned reflex with stress. In Milbank Memorial Fund, *The biology of mental health and disease*. New York: Hoeber-Harper, 1952. Pp. 498–507. (b)

Lidz, T. General concepts of psychosomatic medicine. In S. Arieti (Ed.), *The American handbook of psychiatry*, Vol. I. New York: Basic Books, 1959. Pp. 647–658.

Lidz, T., Cornelison, A. R., Fleck, S., & Terry, D. The intrafamilial environment of schizophrenic patients: II. Marital schism and marital skew. *American Journal of Psychiatry*, 1957, *144*, 241–248.

Lidz, T., & Fleck, S. Family studies and a theory of schizophrenia. In T. Lidz, S. Fleck, & A. R. Cornelison (Eds.), *Schizophrenia and the family*. New York: International Universities Press, 1965. Pp. 362–376.

Lidz, R. W., & Lidz, T. The family environment of schizophrenic patients. *American Journal of Psychiatry*, 1949, *106*, 332–345.

Lieberman, M. A., Yalom, I. D., & Miles, M. B. Impact on participants. In L. N. Solomon & B. Berzon (Eds.), *New perspectives on encounter groups*. San Francisco: Jossey-Bass, 1972.

Lieberman, M. A., Yalom, I. D. & Miles, M. B. *Encounter groups: First facts*. New York: Basic Books, 1973.

Lief, A. (Ed.) *The commonsense psychiatry of Dr. Adolph Meyer*. New York: McGraw-Hill, 1948.

Lindemann, E. Symptomatology and management of acute grief. *American Journal of Psychiatry*, 1944, *101*, 141–148.

Little, K. B., & Shneidman, E. S. Congruencies among interpretations of psychological and anamnestic data. *Psychological Monographs*, 1959, *73*, No. 6, Whole No. 476.

Lolli, G. Alcoholism as a disorder of the love disposition. *Quarterly Journal of Studies on Alcohol*, 1956, *17*, 96–107.

London, P. *The modes and morals of psychotherapy*. New York: Holt, Rinehart and Winston, 1964.

Long, B. E. Teaching psychology to children. *American Psychologist*, 1968, *28*, 691–692.

Lorenz, M. Expressive behavior and language patterns. *Psychiatry*, 1955, *18*, 353–366.

Lorion, R. P. Socioeconomic status and traditional treatment approaches reconsidered. *Psychological Bulletin*, 1973, 79, 263–270.

Lorion, R. P. Patient and therapist variables in the treatment of low-income patients. *Psychological Bulletin*, 1974, *81*, 344–354.

Lovaas, O. I. Some studies on the treatment of childhood schizophrenia. In J. M. Shlien (Ed.), *Research in psychotherapy*, Vol. 3. Washington, D.C.: American Psychological Association, 1968. Pp. 103–121.

Lowen, A. *Physical dynamics of character structure*. New York: Grune & Stratton, 1958.

MacKinnon, D. W. The structure of personality. In J. McV. Hunt (Ed.), *Personality and the behavior disorders*, Vol. I. New York: Ronald Press, 1944. Pp. 3–48.

MacLennan, B. W. New Careers: Program development and the process of institutional change. In M. F. Shore & F. V. Mannino (Eds.), *Mental health and the community: Problems, programs and strategies*. New York: Behavioral Publications, 1969. Pp. 179–190.

MacLennan, B. W., Klein, W. L., Pearl, A., & Fishman, J. R. Training for new careers. *Community Mental Health Journal*, 1966, 2, 135–141.

MacMillan, D. L. *Behavior modification in education*. New York: Macmillan, 1973.

Magoon, T. M., Golann, S. E., & Freeman, R. W. *Mental health counselors at work*. New York: Pergamon, 1969.

Maher, B. A. *Principles of psychopathology*. New York: McGraw-Hill, 1966.

Malzberg, B. Important statistical data about mental illness. In S. Arieti (Ed.), *The American handbook of psychiatry*, Vol. I. New York: Basic Books, 1959. Pp. 161–174.

Mann, P. A. *Psychological consultation within a police department: A demonstration of cooperative training in mental health*. Springfield, Ill.: Thomas, 1973.

Mannino, F. V. *Consultation in mental health and related fields: A reference guide*. Washington, D.C.: U.S. Government Printing Office, Public Health Service Publication No. 1920, 1969.

Mannino, F. V., MacLennan, B. W., & Shore, M. W. *The practice of mental health consultation*. Washington, D.C., Dept. of Health, Education and Welfare, Publication No. (ADM) 74–112, 1975.

Marans, A. E., & Lourie, R. Hypotheses regarding the effects of child-rearing patterns in the disadvantaged child. In J. Hellmuth (Ed.), *Disadvantaged child*, Vol. I. New York: Brunner-Mazel, 1969. Pp. 17–41.

Margolin, S. G. Genetic and dynamic psychophysiological determinants of pathophysiologic processes. In F. Deutsch (Ed.), *The psychosomatic concept in psychoanalysis*. New York: International Universities Press, 1953.

Marmorale, A. M. & Brown, F. Mental health intervention in the primary grades. *Community Mental Health Journal, Monograph Series*, 1974, *No. 7*, 63 pp.

Maslow, A. H. Cognition of the particular and of the generic. *Psychological Review*, 1948, *55*, 22–40.

Maslow, A. H., & Mittleman, B. *Principles of abnormal psychology*. New York: Harper, 1951.

Masserman, J. H. *Principles of dynamic psychiatry.* Philadelphia: Saunders, 1946.

Masserman, J. H., & Carmichael, H. Diagnosis and prognosis in psychiatry. *Journal of Mental Science,* 1938, *84,* 893–946.

Masserman, J. H., Yum, K. S., Nicholson, M. R., & Lee, S. Neurosis and alcohol: An experimental study. *American Journal of Psychiatry,* 1944, *101,* 389–395.

Masters, W. H., and Johnson, V. E. *Human sexual inadequacy.* Boston: Little, Brown, 1970.

Maughs, S. A concept of psychopathy and psychopathic personality: Its evolution and historical development. Part I. *Journal of Clinical and Experimental Psychopathology,* 1941, *2,* 329–356. (a)

Maughs, S. A. concept of psychopathy and psychopathic personality: Its evolution and historical development. Part II. *Journal of Clinical and Experimental Psychopathology,* 1941, *2,* 465–499. (b)

McCary, J. L. *Human sexuality.* (2nd ed.) New York: Van Nostrand, 1973.

McCord, W., & McCord, J. *The psychopath: An essay on the criminal mind.* Princeton, N.J.: Van Nostrand, 1964.

McCord, W., McCord, J., & Gudeman, J. Some current theories of alcoholism: A longitudinal evaluation. *Quarterly Journal of Studies of Alcohol,* 1959, *20,* 727–749.

McDermott, J. F., Harrison, S. I., Schrager, J., & Wilson, P. Social class and mental illness: Observations of blue collar families. *American Journal of Orthopsychiatry,* 1965, *35,* 500–508.

McGee, R. K. *Crisis intervention in the community.* Baltimore: University Park Press, 1974.

Mednick, S. A. A learning theory approach to research in schizophrenia. *Psychological Bulletin,* 1958, *55,* 316–327.

Mednick, S. A. Learning theory and schizophrenia: A reply to a comment. *Psychological Bulletin,* 1959, *56,* 315–316.

Mednick, S. A. Breakdown in individuals at high risk for schizophrenia: Possible predispositional perinatal factors. *Mental Hygiene,* 1970, *54,* 50–63.

Mednick, S. A., & McNeil, T. F. Current methodology in research on the etiology of schizophrenia: Serious difficulties which suggest the use of the high-risk group method. *Psychological Bulletin,* 1968, *70,* 681–693.

Mednick, S. A., Mura, E., Schulsinger, F. & Mednick, B. Perinatal conditions and infant development in children with schizophrenic parents. *Social Biology,* 1971, *18* (Sept. supplement), 103–113.

Mednick, S. A., & Schulsinger, F. A longitudinal study of children with a high risk for schizophrenia: A preliminary report. In S. G. Vanderberg (Ed.), *Methods and goals in human behavior genetics.* New York: Academic Press, 1965. Pp. 255–275.

Meehl, P. E. Schizotaxia, schizotypy, schizophrenia. *American Psychologist,* 1962, *17,* 827–838.

Mehlman, B. The reliability of psychiatric diagnoses. *Journal of Abnormal and Social Psychology,* 1952, *47,* 577–578.

Mendelson, M., Hirsch, S., & Webber, C. S. A critical examination of some recent theoretical models in psychosomatic medicine. *Psychosomatic Medicine,* 1956, *18,* 363–373.

Menninger, K. *Man against himself.* New York: Harcourt Brace Jovanovich, 1938.

Mental Deficiency Committee of Royal Medico-Psychological Association Report. *Journal of Mental Science,* 1937, *82,* 247–257.

Michael, D. N. *The unprepared society: Planning for a precarious future.* New York: Basic Books, 1968.

Michael, R. P., & Gibbons, J. L. Interrelationships between the endocrine system and neuropsychiatry. In C. Pfeifer & J. Smythies (Eds.), *International review of neurobiology.* New York: Academic Press, 1963.

Michaels, J. J. A psychiatric adventure in comparative pathophysiology of the infant and adult. *Journal of Nervous and Mental Diseases,* 1944, *100,* 49–57.

Michaels, J. J. Character structure and character disorders. In S. Arieti (Ed.), *American handbook of psychiatry,* Vol. I. New York: Basic Books, 1959. Pp. 353–377.

Miller, H., & Baruch, D. W. A study of hostility in allergic children. *American Journal of Orthopsychiatry,* 1950, *20,* 506–519.

Miller, H. L., & Woock, R. R. *Social foundations of urban education.* Hinsdale, Ill.: Dryden Press, 1970.

Miller, N. E. Psychosomatic effects of specific types of training. *Annals of the New York Acadmey of Sciences,* 1969, *159,* 1025–1040.

Miller, S. M., & Mishler, E. G. Comparison of experience and behavior of lower and higher status groups: Findings and hypotheses. In F. Riessman, J. Cohen, & A. Pearl (Eds.), *Mental health of the poor.* New York: Free Press, 1964. Pp. 16–38.

Minuchin, P., Biber, B., Shapiro, E., & Zimiles, H. *The psychological impact of school experience.* New York: Basic Books, 1969.

Mirsky, I. A. Psychoanalysis and the biological sciences. In F. Alexander & H. Ross (Eds.), *Twenty years of psychoanalysis.* New York: Norton, 1953. Pp. 155–176.

Mishler, E. G., & Waxler, N. *Interaction in families: An experimental study of family processes and schizophrenia.* New York: Wiley, 1968.

Mishler, E. G., & Scotch, N. A. Sociological factors in the epidemiology of schizophrenia. *Psychiatry,* 1963, *26,* 315–357.

Mogar, R. E. Research in psychedelic drug therapy: A critical analysis. In J. M. Schlien (Ed.), *Research in psychotherapy,* Vol. III. Washington, D.C.: American Psychological Association, 1968.

Moore, O. K., & Anderson, A. R. The Responsive Environments Project. In R. D. Hess & R. M. Bear (Eds.), *Early education.* Chicago: Aldine, 1968. Pp. 171–190.

Moos, R. H. Conceptualizations of human environments. *American Psychologist,* 1973, *28,* 652–665.

Moos, R. H., & Insel, P. M. *Issues in social ecology: Human milieus.* Palo Alto, Ca.: National Press Books, 1974.

Moreno, J. L. Group psychotherapy and psychodrama. In W. S. Sahakian (Ed.), *Psychotherapy and counseling: Studies in technique.* Chicago: Rand McNally, 1969.

Morgan, C. T., & Stellar, E. *Physiological psychology.* New York: McGraw-Hill, 1950.

Mowrer, O. H. Learning theory and the neurotic paradox. *American Journal of Orthopsychiatry,* 1948, *18,* 571–610.

Mulder, D. W. Psychoses with brain tumors and other chronic neurological disorders. In S. Arieti (Ed.), *The American handbook of psychiatry,* Vol. II. New York: Basic Books, 1959. Pp. 1144–1162.

Muss, R. E. The effects of a one and two-year causal learning program. *Journal of Personality,* 1960, *28,* 479–491.

Myers, J. K., & Roberts, B. H. *Family and class dynamics in mental illness.* New York: Wiley, 1959.

Naranjo, C. Present centeredness: Technique, prescription, and ideal. In J. Fagan & I. L. Shepherd (Eds.), *Gestalt therapy now*. Palo Alto, Ca.: Science and Behavior Books, 1970. Pp. 47–69.

Nathan, P. E., Andberg, M. M., Behan, P. O., & Patch, V. D. Thirty-two observers and one patient: A study of diagnostic reliability. *Journal of Clinical Psychology*, 1969, *25*, 9–15.

Neill, A. S. *Summerhill: A radical approach to child-rearing*. New York: Hart, 1960.

Newbrough, J. R. Community mental health: A movement in search of a theory. In A. J. Bindman & A. D. Spiegel (Eds.), *Perspectives in community mental health*. Chicago: Aldine, 1969. Pp. 70–78.

Newman, R. G. *Psychological consultation in the schools*. New York: Basic Books, 1967.

Newton, M. R., & Brown, R. D. A preventive approach to developmental problems in school children. In E. M. Bower & W. G. Hollister (Eds.), *Behavior science frontiers in education*. New York: Wiley, 1967. Pp. 503–527.

Nichols, R. S. The influence of economic and administrative factors on the type and quality of care given to persons with psychological disease. *Working Papers in Community Mental Health*, 1963, *1*, 1–34.

Nichtern, S., Donahue, G. T., O'Shea, J., Marans, M., Curtis, M., & Brody, C. A community educational program for the emotionally disturbed child. *American Journal of Orthopsychiatry*, 1964, *34*, 705–713.

Nowlis, H. H. *Drugs on the college campus*. New York: Doubleday Anchor Books, 1969.

Noyes, A. P. *Modern clinical psychiatry*. (2nd ed.) Philadelphia: Saunders, 1939.

Noyes, A. P., & Kolb, L. C. *Modern clinical psychiatry*. (6th ed.) Philadelphia: Saunders, 1963.

Nyswander, M. E. Drug addictions. In S. Arieti (Ed.), *American handbook of psychiatry*, Vol. I. New York: Basic Books, 1959. Pp. 614–622.

Ojemann, R. H. Investigations on the effects of teacher understanding and appreciation of behavior dynamics. In G. Caplan (Ed.), *Prevention of mental disorders in children*. New York: Basic Books, 1961. Pp. 378–397.

Ojemann, R. H. Incorporating psychological concepts in the school curriculum. In H. P. Clarizio (Ed.), *Mental health and the educative process*. Chicago: Rand McNally, 1969. Pp.360–368.

Omwake, E. Head Start: Measurable and immeasurable. In J. Hellmuth (Ed.), *Disadvantaged child*, Vol. II. New York: Brunner-Mazel, 1969. Pp. 531–544.

O'Neal, P., & Robins, L. N. The relation of childhood behavior problems to adult psychiatric status: A 30-year follow-up of 150 subjects. *American Journal of Psychiatry*, 1958, *114*, 961–969. (a)

O'Neal, P., & Robins, L. N. Childhood patterns predictive of adult schizophrenia: A 30-year follow-up. *American Journal of Psychiatry*, 1958, *115*, 385–391. (b)

Onondaga County School Studies, Interim Report No. 1. Persistence of emotional disturbances reported among second and fourth grade children. Syracuse, N.Y.: N.Y. State Department of Mental Hygiene, 1964.

Orne, M. T. On the social psychology of the psychological experiment: With particular reference to the demand characteristics and their implications. *American Psychologist*, 1962, *17*, 776–783.

Pasamanick, B., Roberts, D. W., Lemkau, P. W., & Krueger, D. B. A survey of mental disease in an urban population: Prevalence by race and income. In

F. Riessman, J. Cohen, & A. Pearl (Eds.), *Mental health of the poor.* New York: Free Press, 1964. Pp. 39–48.

Pasamanick, B., Rogers, M. E., and Lilienfeld, A. M. Pregnancy experience and the development of behavior disorder in children. *American Journal of Psychiatry,* 1956, *112,* 613–618.

Patterson, C. H. Is psychotherapy dependent upon diagnosis? *American Psychologist,* 1948, *3,* 155–159.

Patterson, C. H. *Theories of counseling and psychotherapy.* New York: Harper & Row, 1966.

Paul, G. L. *Insight versus desensitization in psychotherapy.* Stanford, Ca.: Stanford University Press, 1966.

Paul, G. L. Insight versus desensitization in psychotherapy two years after termination. *Journal of Consulting Psychology,* 1967, *31,* 333–348. (a)

Paul, G. L. Strategy of outcome research in psychotherapy. *Journal of Consulting Psychology,* 1967, *31,* 109–118. (b)

Paul, G. L. Chronic mental patient: Current status—future direction. *Psychological Bulletin,* 1969, *71,* 81–94.

Paul, G. L., & Shannon, D. T. Treatment of anxiety through systematic desensitization in therapy groups. *Journal of Abnormal Psychology,* 1966, *71,* 124–135.

Payne, J. S., Mercer, C. D., Payne, R. A., & Davidson, R. G. *Head Start: A tragicomedy with epilogue,* New York: Behavioral Publications, 1973.

Pearl, A., & Riessman, F. *New careers for the poor.* New York: Free Press, 1965.

Peck, H. B., & Kaplan, S. R. A mental health program for the urban multi-service center. In M. F. Shore & F. V. Mannino (Eds.), *Mental health and the community: Problems, programs and strategies.* New York: Behavioral Publications, 1969. Pp. 123–142.

Peck, H. B., Kaplan, S. R., & Roman, M. Prevention treatment and social action: A strategy of intervention in a disadvantaged urban area. *American Journal of Orthopsychiatry,* 1966, *36,* 57–69.

Perls, F. S. *Gestalt therapy verbatim.* Lafayette, Ca.: Real People Press, 1969.

Pettigrew, T. Negro American intelligence. In J. I. Roberts (Ed.), *School children in the urban slum.* New York: Free Press, 1967. Pp. 32–63.

Pfautz, H. W. The American dilemma: Perspectives and proposals for white Americans. In C. U. Daly (Ed.), *Urban violence.* Chicago: University of Chicago Press, 1969. Pp. 57–72.

Phillips, L. Case history data and prognosis in schizophrenia. *Journal of Nervous and Mental Disease,* 1953, *117,* 515–525.

Plaut, T. F. A. *Alcohol problems: A report to the nation.* New York: Oxford University Press, 1967.

Pollin, W., & Stabenau, J. R. Biological, psychological and historical differences in a series of monozygotic twins discordant for schizophrenia. In D. Rosenthal & S. S. Kety (Eds.), *The transmission of schizophrenia.* New York: Pergamon, 1968. Pp. 317–332.

Poser, E. G. The effect of therapist training on group therapeutic outcome. *Journal of Consulting Psychology,* 1966, *30,* 283–289.

Price, R. H., & Moos, R. H., Toward a taxonomy of impatient treatment environments. *Journal of Abnormal Psychology,* 1975, *84,* 181–188.

Pritchard, R., & Rosenzweig, S. The effect of war stress upon childhood and youth.

Journal of Abnormal and Social Psychology, 1942, 37, 329–344.

Proshansky, H., & Newton, P. The nature and meaning of Negro self-identity. In M. Deutsch, I. Katz, & A. R. Jensen (Eds.), *Social class, race, and psychological development.* New York: Holt, Rinehart and Winston, 1968. Pp. 178–218.

Quinn, R., & Wegener, L. M. *Mental health and learning.* Washington, D.C.: Department of Health Education and Welfare, Publication No. (HSM 72–9146), 1972.

Rado, S. Psychoanalysis of pharmacothymia. *Psychoanalytic Quarterly,* 1933, 2, 1–23.

Rae-Grant, Q., & Stringer, L. A. Mental health programs in schools. In M. F. Shore & F. V. Mannino (Eds.), *Mental health and the community: Problems, programs, and strategies.* New York: Behavioral Publications, 1969. Pp. 83–99.

Ramsey, W. Head Start and first grade reading. In J. Hellmuth (Ed.), *Disadvantaged child,* Vol. II. New York: Brunner-Mazel, 1969. Pp. 289–298.

Rappaport, J., Chinsky, J. M., & Cowen, E. L. *Innovations in helping chronic patients: College students in a mental institution.* New York: Academic Press, 1971.

Rappaport, J., Davidson, W. S., Wilson, M. N., & Mitchell, A. Alternatives to blaming the victim or the environment: Our places to stand have not moved the earth. *American Psychologist,* 1975, 30, 525–528.

Raush, H. L., & Raush, C. L. *The halfway house movement: A search for sanity.* New York: Appleton-Century-Crofts, 1968.

Reddy, W. B. Screening and selection of participants. In L. N. Solomon & B. Berzon (Eds.), *New perspectives on encounter groups.* San Francisco: Jossey-Bass, 1972.

Reich, W. *Character analysis.* (3rd ed.) New York: Noonday Press, 1949.

Reich, W. *Selected writings.* New York: Noonday Press, 1960.

Reiff, R. Mental health manpower and institutional change. *American Psychologist,* 1966, 21, 540–548.

Reiff, R. Mental health manpower and institutional change. In E. L. Cowen, E. A. Gardner, & M. Zax (Eds.), *Emergent approaches to mental health problems.* New York: Appleton-Century-Crofts, 1967. Pp. 74–88.

Reiff, R., & Riessman, F. The indigenous nonprofessional: A strategy of change in community action and community mental health programs. *Community Mental Health Journal,* Monogr. No. 1, 1965.

Reinberg, A. The hours of changing responsiveness or susceptibility. *Perspectives in Biology and Medicine,* 1967, 11, 111–127.

Reiss, S., & Dyhdalo, N. Persistence, achievement and open-space environments. *Journal of Educational Psychology,* 1975, 67, in Press.

Reiss, S., & Martell, R. Educational and psychological effects of open space education in Oak Park, Ill.: Final Report to Board of Education, District 97, Oak Park, Illinois, 1974.

Richter, C. P. The phenomenon of unexplained sudden death in animals and man. *Psychosomatic Medicine,* 1957, 19, 191–198.

Rieff, P. *Freud: The mind of the moralist.* New York: Viking Press, 1959.

Riessman, F. The "helper" therapy principle. *Social Work,* 1965, 10, 27–32.

Riessman, F. A neighborhood-based mental health approach. In E. L. Cowen, E. A. Gardner, & M. Zax (Eds.), *Emergent approaches to mental health problems.* New York: Appleton-Century-Crofts, 1967. Pp. 167–184.

Riessman, F., Cohen, J., & Pearl, A. (Eds.), *Mental health of the poor.* New York: Free Press, 1964.

Riessman, F., & Miller, S. M. Social change versus the "psychiatric world view." *American Journal of Orthopsychiatry,* 1964, 34, 29–38.

Riessman, F., & Popper, H. I. *Up from poverty: New career ladders for nonprofessionals.* New York: Harper & Row, 1968.

Rioch, M. J. Changing concepts in the training of psychotherapists. *Journal of Consulting Psychology,* 1966, *30,* 290, 292.

Rioch, M. J. Pilot projects in training mental health counselors. In E. L. Cowen, E. A. Gardner, & M. Zax (Eds.), *Emergent approaches to mental health problems.* New York: Appleton-Century-Crofts, 1967. Pp. 110–127.

Rioch, M. J., Elkes, C., & Flint, A. A. *National Institute of Mental Health pilot project in training mental health counselors.* Washington, D.C.: U.S. Dept. of Health, Education and Welfare, Public Health Service Publication No. 1254, 1965.

Rioch, M. J., Elkes, C., Flint, A. A., Usdansky, B. S., Newman, R. G., & Silber, E. National Institute of Mental Health pilot study in training of mental health counselors. *American Journal of Orthopsychiatry,* 1963, *33,* 678–689.

Roback, A. A. *The psychology of character.* (3rd ed.) London: Routledge & Kegan Paul, 1952.

Roberts, J. I. (Ed.) *School children in the urban slum.* New York: Free Press, 1967. (a)

Roberts, J. I. Cognitive factors and environment. In J. I. Roberts (Ed.), *School children in the urban slum.* New York: Free Press, 1967. Pp. 17–28. (b)

Robins, L. N. *Deviant children grown up.* Baltimore: Williams & Wilkins, 1966.

Robinson, R., DeMarche, D. F., & Wagle, M. K. *Community resources in mental health.* New York: Basic Books, 1961.

Rodman, H. Family and social pathology in the ghetto. In S. Chess & A. Thomas (Eds.), *Annual progress in child psychiatry and child development.* New York: Brunner-Mazel, 1969. Pp. 292–307.

Rodnick, E. H., & Garmezy, N. An experimental approach to the study of motivation in schizophrenia. In M. R. Jones (Ed.), *Nebraska symposuim on motivation.* Vol. V. Lincoln: University of Nebraska Press, 1957. Pp. 109–184.

Roen, S. R. Primary prevention in the classroom through a teaching program in the behavioral sciences. In E. L. Cowen, E. A. Gardner, & M. Zax (Eds.), *Emergent approaches to mental health problems.* New York: Appleton-Century-Crofts, 1967. Pp. 252–270.

Rogers, C. R. *Counseling and psychotherapy.* Boston: Houghton-Mifflin, 1942.

Rogers, C. R. *Client-centered therapy.* Boston: Houghton-Mifflin, 1951.

Rogers, C. R. A theory of therapy, personality and interpersonal relationships as developed in the client-centered framework. In S. Koch (Ed.), *Psychology: A study of a science,* Vol. 3. New York: McGraw-Hill, 1959. Pp. 184–256.

Rogers, C. R. The group comes of age. *Psychology Today,* 1969, *3,* 27–31.

Rogers, C. R., & Dymond, R. F. (Eds.) *Psychotherapy and personality change.* Chicago: University of Chicago Press, 1954.

Romano, J. Introduction. In J. Romano (Ed.), *The origins of schizophrenia.* Amsterdam: Excerpta Medica Foundation, 1967. P. 1.

Rosanoff, A. J. The etiology of child behavior difficulties. *Psychiatric Monographs,* 1943, *1.*

Rosen, E., Fox, R., & Gregory, I. *Abnormal psychology.* (2nd ed.) Philadelphia: Saunders, 1972.

Rosen, J. N. *Direct analysis: Selected papers.* New York: Grune & Stratton, 1953.

Rosen, J. N. *Direct psychoanalytic psychiatry.* New York: Grune & Stratton, 1962.

Rosenbaum, M. Group therapy and psychodrama. In B. Wolman (Ed.), *Handbook of clinical psychology.* New York: McGraw-Hill, 1965. Pp. 1254–1274.

Rosenhan, D. L. On being sane in insane places. *Science,* 1973, *179,* 250–258.

Rosenhan, D. L., & London, P. Character. In P. London & D. Rosenhan (Eds.), *Foundations of abnormal psychology.* New York: Holt, Rinehart and Winston, 1968. Pp. 251–289.

Rosenthal, D. Problems of sampling and diagnosis in the major twin studies of schizophrenia. *Journal of Psychiatric Research,* 1962, *1,* 116–134.

Rosenthal, D., Wender, P. H., Kety, S. S., Schulsinger, F., Welner, J., & Østergaard, L. Schizophrenics' offspring reared in adoptive homes. In D. Rosenthal & S. S. Kety (Eds.), *The transmission of schizophrenia.* New York: Pergamon, 1968. Pp. 377–392.

Rosenthal, M. S. New York City. Phoenix House: A therapeutic community program for the treatment of drug abusers and drug addicts. In L. Brill & E. Harms (Eds.), *Yearbook of drug abuse.* New York: Behavioral Publications, 1973. Pp. 83–102.

Rosenthal, R. On the social psychology of the psychological experiment: The experimenter's hypothesis as unintended determinant of experimental results. *American Scientist,* 1963, *51,* 268–283.

Rosenthal, R. *Experimenter effects in behavioral research.* New York: Appleton-Century-Crofts, 1966.

Rotter, J. B. The future of clinical psychology. *Journal of Consulting and Clinical Psychology,* 1973, *40,* 313–321.

Roueche, B. *Alcohol: Its history, folklore, effect on the human body.* New York: Grove, 1960.

Rowe, H. P., & Robinson, D. B. Psychiatric conditions associated with metabolic, endocrine, and nutritional disorders. In S. Arieti (Ed.), *The American handbook of psychiatry,* Vol. II. New York: Basic Books, 1959. Pp. 1260–1288.

Rubenstein, R., & Lasswell, H. D. *The sharing of power in a psychiatric hospital.* New Haven, Conn.: Yale University Press, 1966.

Ryan, W. (Ed.) *Distress in the city: Essays on the design and administration of urban mental health services.* Clevand, Ohio: Case-Western Reserve University Press, 1969.

Ryan, W. *Blaming the victim.* New York: Random House, 1971.

Sager, C. J., Waxenberg, S. E., Brayboy, T., Slipp, S., & Waxenberg, B. Dimensions of family therapy. In L. Bellak & H. H. Barten (Eds.), *Progress in community mental health,* Vol. I. New York: Grune & Stratton, 1969. Pp. 137–166.

Sameroff, A. J., & Zax, M. Perinatal characteristics of the offspring of schizophrenic women. *Journal of Nervous and Mental Disease,* 1973, *157,* 191–199. (a)

Sameroff, A. J., & Zax, M. Schizotaxia revisited: Model issues in the etiology of schizophrenia. *American Journal of Orthopsychiatry,* 1973, *43,* 744–754. (b)

Sanders, R., Smith, R. S., & Weinman, B. S. *Chronic psychosis and recovery.* San Francisco: Jossey-Bass, 1967.

Sandler, I. N., Duricko, A., & Grande, L. Effectiveness of an early secondary prevention program in an inner-city elementary school. *American Journal of Community Psychology,* 1975, *3,* 23–32.

Sanford, N. The prevention of mental illness. In B. Wolman (Ed.), *Handbook of clinical psychology.* New York: McGraw-Hill, 1965. Pp. 1378–1400.

Sanua, V. D. Sociocultural aspects of psychotherapy and treatment: A review of the literature. In L. E. Abt & L. Bellak (Eds.), *Progress in clinical psychology,* Vol. VIII. New York: Grune & Stratton, 1966. Pp. 151–190.

Sanua, V. D. Socio-cultural aspects. In L. Bellak & L. Loeb (Eds.), *The schizophrenic syndrome*. New York: Grune & Stratton, 1969. Pp. 256–310.

Sarason, I. G. Verbal learning, modeling and juvenile delinquency. *American Psychologist*, 1968, *23*, 254-266.

Sarason, I. G., & Ganzer, V. J. Concerning the medical model. *American Psychologist*, 1968, *23*, 507–510.

Sarason, I. G., & Ganzer, V. J. Developing appropriate social behaviors of juvenile delinquents. In J. R. Krumboltz & C. E. Thoresen (Eds.), *Behavioral counseling: Cases and techniques*. New York: Holt, Rinehart and Winston, 1969. Pp. 178–193. (a)

Sarason, I. G., & Ganzer, V. J. Social influence techniques in clinical and community psychology. In C. D. Spielberger (Ed.), *Current topics in clinical and community psychology*, Vol. 1. New York: Academic Press, 1969. Pp. 1–66. (b)

Sarason, S. B. *The culture of the school and the problem of change*. Boston: Allyn-Bacon, 1971.

Sarason, S. B. *The creation of settings and the future societies*. San Francisco: Jossey-Bass, 1972.

Sarason, S. B., Davidson, K., & Blatt, B. *The preparation of teachers: An unstudied problem in education*. New York: Wiley, 1962.

Sarason, S. B., Levine, M., Goldberg, I. I., Cherlin, D. L., & Bennett, E. M. *Psychology in community settings*. New York: Wiley, 1966.

Savage, C. Psychedelic therapy. In J. M. Shlien (Ed.), *Research in psychotherapy*, Vol. III. Washington, D.C.: American Psychological Association, 1968. Pp. 512–520.

Schaefer, E. E. Intellectual stimulation of culturally deprived infants. Unpublished paper, 1968.

Schaffer, L., & Myers, J. K. Psychotherapy and social stratification: An empirical study of practice in a psychiatric out-patient clinic. *Psychiatry*, 1954, *17*, 83–93.

Scheff, T. J. *Being mentally ill: A sociological theory*. Chicago: Aldine, 1966.

Scheidlinger, S. Innovative group approaches. In L. Bellak & H. H. Barten (Eds.), *Progress in community mental health*, Vol. I. New York: Grune & Stratton, 1969. Pp. 123–136.

Schilder, P. The psychogenesis of alcoholism. *Quarterly Journal of Studies of Alcohol*, 1941, *2*, 277–283.

Schlagenhauf, G., Tupin, J., & White, R. B. The use of lithium carbonate in the treatment of manic psychoses. *American Journal of Psychiatry*, 1966, *123*, 201–207.

Schmale, A. H., Jr. Relation of separation and depression to disease: A report on a hospitalized medical population. *Psychosomatic Medicine*, 1958, *20*, 259–277.

Schofield, W. *Psychotherapy: The purchase of friendship*. Englewood-Cliffs, N.J.: Prentice-Hall, 1964.

Schutz, W. C. *Joy*. New York: Grove, 1967.

Schwab, J. J. *Handbook of psychiatric consultation*. New York: Appleton-Century-Crofts, 1968.

Schwitzgebel, R. R. Delinquents with tape recorders. In F. Riessman, J. Cohen, & A. Pearl (Eds.), *Mental health of the poor*. New York: Free Press, 1964. Pp. 582–588.

Schwitzgebel, R. R. Short-term operant conditioning of adolescent offenders on socially relevant variables. *Journal of Abnormal Psychology*, 1967, *72*, 134–142.

See, J. J., & Miller, K. S. Mental health. In K. S. Miller & R. M. Dreger (Eds.), *Comparative studies of Black and Whites in the United States: Quantitative studies in social relations*. New York: Seminar Press, 1973. Pp. 447–466.

Selling, L. S. *Men against madness*. New York: Greenberg, 1940.

Shakow, D., & Rapaport, D. The influence of Freud on American psychology. *Psychological Issues*, Vol. IV, No. 1. New York: International Universities Press, 1964.

Shapiro, A. K. Placebo effects in medicine, psychotherapy and psychoanalysis. In A. E. Bergin & S. L. Garfield (Eds.), *Handbook of psychotherapy and behavior change*. New York: Wiley, 1971. Pp. 439–473.

Shapiro, D. *Neurotic styles*. New York: Basic Books, 1965.

Shapiro, D. S., Maholick, L. T., Brewer, E. D. C., & Robertson, R. N. *The mental health counselor in the community: Training of physicians and ministers*. Springfield, Ill.: Thomas, 1968.

Sheldon, W. H. Constitutional factors in personality. In J. McV. Hunt (Ed.), *Personality and the behavior disorders*, Vol. I. New York: Ronald Press, 1944. Pp. 526–549.

Shlien, J. (Ed.) *Research in psychotherapy*, Vol. 3. Washington, D.C.: American Psychological Association, 1968.

Shoben, E. J., Jr. Psychotherapy as a problem in learning theory. *Psychological Bulletin*, 1949, *46*, 366–392.

Shoben, E. J., Jr., Toward a concept of the normal personality. *American Psychologist*, 1957, *12*, 183–189.

Shore, M. F., & Mannino, F. V. (Eds.) *Mental health and the community: Problems, programs and strategies*. New York: Behavioral Publications, 1969.

Sigel, I. E., & Perry, C. Psycholinguistic diversity among "culturally deprived" children. In S. Chess & A. Thomas (Eds.), *Annual progress in child psychiatry and child development*. New York: Brunner-Mazel, 1969. Pp. 196–201.

Simmons, D. J., & Diethelm, O. Electroencephalographic studies of psychopathic personalities. *Archives of Neurology and Psychiatry*, 1946, *55*, 410–413.

Simon, B., O'Leary, J. L., & Ryan, J. J. Cerebral dysrhythmia and psychopathic personalities: A study of 96 consecutive cases in a military hospital. *Archives of Neurology and Psychiatry*, 1946, *56*, 677–685.

Singer, M. T., & Wynne, L. C. Differentiating characteristics of parents of childhood schizophrenics, childhood neurotics, and young adult schizophrenics. *American Journal of Psychiatry*, 1963, *120*, 234–243.

Singer, M. T., & Wynne, L. C. Thought disorder and family relations of schizophrenics: III. Methodology using projective techniques. *Archives of General Psychiatry*, 1965, *12*, 187–200. (a)

Singer, M. T., & Wynne, L. C. Thought disorder and family relations of schizophrenics. IV. Results and implications. *Archives of General Psychiatry*, 1965, *12*, 201–212. (b)

Singer, M. T., & Wynne, L. C. Principles for scoring communication defects and deviances in parents of schizophrenics: Rorschach and TAT scoring manuals. *Psychiatry*, 1966, *29*, 260–288.

Singh, R. K. J., Tarnower, W., & Chen, R. *Community mental health consultation and crisis intervention*. Palo Alto, Ca.: National Press Books, 1971.

Skinner, B. F. *The behavior of organisms: An experimental analysis*. New York: Appleton-Century-Crofts, 1938.

Skinner, B. F. *Science and human behavior*. New York: Macmillan, 1953.

Slack, C. W. SCORE: A description. In *Experiment in culture expansion*. Sacramento, Ca.: California Dept. of Corrections, 1963. Pp. 59–64.

Slavson, S. R. Analytic group psychotherapy. In W. S. Sahakian (Ed.), *Psychotherapy and counseling: Studies in technique*. Chicago: Rand McNally, 1969.

Smith, H. C. *Sensitivity to people.* New York: McGraw-Hill, 1966.

Smith, J. J. A medical approach to problem drinking. *Quarterly Journal of Studies on Alcohol,* 1949, *10,* 251–257.

Smith, M. B., & Hobbs, N. The community and the community mental health center. *American Psychologist,* 1966, *21,* 499–509.

Sobey, F. *The nonprofessional revolution in mental health.* New York: Columbia University Press, 1970.

Soskin, W. F. Bias in postdiction and projective tests. *Journal of Abnormal and Social Psychology,* 1954, *49,* 69–74.

Specter, G. A., & Claiborn, W. L. *Crisis intervention.* New York: Behavioral Publications, 1973.

Specter, G. A., & Cowen, E. L. A pilot study in stimulation of culturally deprived infants. *Child Psychiatry and Human Development,* 1971, *1,* 168–177.

Spielberger, C. D. A mental health consultation program in a small community with limited professional mental health resources. In E. L. Cowen, E. A. Gardner, & M. Zax (Eds.), *Emergent approaches to mental health problems.* New York: Appleton-Century-Crofts, 1967. Pp. 214–236.

Spielberger, C. D., Parker, J. B., & Becker, J. Conformity and achievement in remitted manic-depressive patients. *Journal of Nervous and Mental Diseases,* 1963, *137,* 162–172.

Spitz, R. Anaclitic depression. In A. Freud, H. Hartmann, & E. Kris (Eds.), *Psychoanalytic study of the child,* Vol. II. New York: International Universities Press, 1946. Pp. 313–342.

Spitzer, R. L., & Wilson, P. T. A guide to the American Psychiatric Association's new diagnostic nomenclature. *American Journal of Psychiatry,* 1968, *124,* 41–51.

Spivack, G., & Shure, M. B. *Social adjustment of young children.* San Francisco: Jossey-Bass, 1974.

Srole, L., Langner, T. S., Michael, S. T., Opler, M. K., & Rennie, T. A. C. *Mental health in the metropolis.* New York: McGraw-Hill, 1962.

Stainbrook, E. Psychosomatic medicine in the nineteenth century. *Psychosomatic Medicine,* 1952, *14,* 211–227.

Stampfl, T. G., & Levis, D. J. Essentials of implosive therapy: A learning-theory-based psychodynamic behavioral therapy. *Journal of Abnormal Psychology,* 1967, *72,* 496–503.

Stanley, J. C. (Ed.) *Preschool programs for the disadvantaged: Five experimental approaches to early childhood education.* Baltimore: Johns Hopkins University Press, 1972.

Stendler-Lavatelli, C. B. Environmental intervention in infancy and early childhood. In M. Deutsch, I. Katz, & A. R. Jensen (Eds.), *Social class, race, and psychological development.* New York: Holt, Rinehart and Winston, 1968. Pp. 347–380.

Stennett, R. G. Emotional handicap in the elementary years: Phase or disease. *American Journal of Orthopsychiatry,* 1965, *35,* 444–449.

Stoller, F. H. Marathon group therapy. In G. M. Gazda (Ed.), *Innovations to group psychotherapy.* Springfield, Ill.: Thomas, 1968.

Strauss, H. Epileptic disorders. In S. Arieti (Ed.), *The American handbook of psychiatry,* Vol. II. New York: Basic Books, 1959. Pp. 1109–1143.

Strecker, E. A., & Ebaugh, F. G. *Practical clinical psychiatry* (5th ed.) New York: Blakiston, 1940.

Stringer, L. A. Academic progress as an index of mental health. *Journal of Social Issues,* 1959, *15,* 16–29.

Strupp, H. H., & Bergin, A. E. Some empirical and conceptual bases for coordinated research in psychotherapy: A critical review of issues, trends, and evidence. *International Journal of Psychiatry*, 1969, 7, 18–90.

Suchman, J. R. The pursuit of meaning: Models for the study of inquiry. In E. M. Bower & W. G. Hollister (Eds.), *Behavioral science frontiers in education.* New York: Wiley, 1967. Pp. 481–497.

Sullivan, H. S. *The interpersonal theory of psychiatry.* New York: Norton, 1953.

Sullivan, H. S. *Clinical studies in psychiatry.* New York: Norton, 1956 (a)

Sullivan, H. S. *The psychiatric interview.* New York: Norton, 1956. (b)

Sullivan, H. S. *Schizophrenia as a human process.* New York: Norton, 1962.

Susskind, E. C. Questioning and curiosity in the elementary school classroom. Unpublished Ph.D. dissertation, Yale University, 1969.

Szalita, A. B. Psychodynamics of disorders of the involutional age. In S. Arieti (Ed.), *The American handbook of psychiatry*, Vol. III. New York: Basic Books, 1966.

Szasz, T. S. Psychoanalysis and the autonomous nervous system. *Psychoanalytic Review*, 1952, 39, 115–151.

Szasz, T. S. The myth of mental illness. *American Psychologist*, 1960, 15, 113–118.

Szasz, T. S. *The myth of mental illness.* New York: Hoeber-Harper, 1961.

Taft, R. The ability to judge people. *Psychological Bulletin*, 1955, 52, 1–23.

Taft, R. Multiple methods of personality assessment. *Psychological Bulletin*, 1959, 56, 333–352.

Thompson, G. N. Acute and chronic alcoholic conditions. In S. Arieti (Ed.), *The American handbook of psychiatry*, Vol. II. New York: Basic Books, 1959. Pp. 1203–1221.

Trickett, E. J., Kelly, J. G., & Todd, D. M. The social environment of the high school: Guidelines for individual change and organizational redevelopment. In S. E. Golann & C. Eisdorfer (Eds.), *Handbook of community psychology.* New York: Appleton-Century-Crofts, 1971.

Trickett, E. J., & Moos, R. H. The social environment of junior high and high school classrooms. *Journal of Educational Psychology*, 1973, 65, 93–102.

Trickett, E. J., & Moos, R. H. Personal correlates of contrasting environments: Student satisfaction in high school classrooms. *American Journal of Community Psychology*, 1974, 2, 1–12.

Tuke, D. H. *Illustrations of the influence of the mind upon the body in health and disease, designed to elucidate the action of the imagination.* London: Churchill, 1872.

Turner, R. J., & Cumming, J. Theoretical malaise and community mental health. In E. L. Cowen, E. A. Gardner, & M. Zax (Eds.), *Emergent approaches to mental health problems.* New York: Appleton-Century-Crofts, 1967. Pp. 40–62.

Ullman, A. D. The psychological mechanism of alcohol addiction. *Quarterly Journal of Studies on Alcohol*, 1952, 13, 602–608.

Ullmann, L. P., & Krasner, L. *Case studies in behavior modification.* New York: Holt, Rinehart and Winston, 1965.

Ullmann, L. P., & Krasner, L. *A psychological approach to abnormal behavior.* (2nd ed.) Englewood Cliffs, New Jersey: Prentice-Hall, 1974.

Umbarger, C. C., Dalsimer, J. S., Morrison, A. P., & Breggin, P. R. *College students in a mental hospital.* New York: Grune & Stratton, 1962.

Volkmann, R., & Cressey, D. R. Differential association and the rehabilitation of drug addicts. *American Journal of Sociology*, 1963, 64, 129–142.

Wallace, J. An abilities conception of personality: Some implications for personality measurement. *American Psychologist*, 1966, 21, 132–138.

Ward, C. H., Beck, A. T., Mendelson, M. Mock, J. E., & Erbough, J. K. The psychiatric nomenclature: Reasons for diagnostic disagreement. *Archives of General Psychiatry*, 1962, 7, 198–205.

Watson, G. (Ed.) *Change in school systems.* Washington, D.C.: National Training Laboratories, National Educational Association, 1967.

Watson, R. I. *The great psychologists—Aristotle to Freud.* New York: Lippincott, 1963.

Weakland, J. H. The "double-bind" hypothesis of schizophrenia and three-part interaction. In D. D. Jackson (Ed.), *The etiology of schizophrenia.* New York: Basic Books, 1960. Pp. 373–388.

Wegrocki, H. J. A critique of cultural and statistical concepts of abnormality. *Journal of Abnormal and Social Psychology*, 1939, 34, 166–178.

Weikart, D. P., & Lambie, D. Z. Preschool intervention through a home teaching program. In J. Hellmuth (Ed.), *Disadvantaged child*, Vol. II. New York: Brunner-Mazel, 1969. Pp. 435–500.

Weinstein, L. Project Re-Ed schools for emotionally disturbed children: Effectiveness as viewed by referring agencies, parents and teachers. *Exceptional Children*, 1969, 35, 703–711.

Weinstein, L. *Personal communication.* January 30, 1970.

Weinstein, L. *The evaluation research: The effectiveness of the Re-Ed intervention.* Unpublished manuscript (1971).

Weiss, J. H. Effects of professional training and amount and accuracy of information on behavioral predictions. *Journal of Consulting Psychology*, 1953, 27, 257–262.

Weissman, H. H. Priorities in social services for the slum neighborhood. In M. F. Shore & F. V. Mannino (Eds.), *Mental health and the community: Problems, programs, and strategies.* New York: Behavioral Publications, 1969. Pp. 149–171.

Westman, J. C., Rice, D. L., & Bermann, E. Nursery school behavior and later school adjustment. *American Journal of Orthopsychiatry*, 1967, 37, 725–731.

White, B. L. Informal education during the first five months of life. In R. D. Hess & R. M. Bear (Eds.), *Early education.* Chicago: Aldine, 1968. Pp. 143–169.

White, R. W. *The abnormal personality.* New York: Ronald, 1948.

Whiteman, M., & Deutsch, M. Social disadvantage as related to intellective and language development. In M. Deutsch, I. Katz, & A. R. Jensen (Eds.), *Social class, race, and psychological development.* New York: Holt, Rinehart and Winston, 1968. Pp. 86–114.

Wikler, A. A psychodynamic study of a patient during experimental self-regulated re-addiction to morphine. *Psychiatric Quarterly*, 1952, 26, 270–293.

Wikler, A. *Opiate addiction.* Springfield, Ill.: Thomas, 1953.

Wikler, A. Interaction of physical dependence and classical and operant conditioning in the genesis of relapse. In A. Wikler (Ed.), *Research publications: Association for Research in Nervous and Mental Disease*, Vol. XLVI, Baltimore: Williams & Wilkins, 1968. Pp. 280–287.

Wild, C., Singer, M. T., Rosman, B., Ricci, J., & Lidz, T. Measuring disordered styles of thinking in the parents of schizophrenic patients on the Object Sorting Test. Part I. In T. Lidz, S. Fleck, & A. R. Cornelison (Eds.), *Schizophrenia and the family.* New York: International Universities Press,, 1965. Pp. 400–422.

Wilhelms, F. T. Actualizing the effective professional worker in education. In E. M. Bower & W. G. Hollister (Eds.), *Behavioral science frontiers in education.* New York: Wiley, 1967. Pp. 359–378.

Willems, E. P., & Raush, H. L. *Naturalistic viewpoints in psychological research*. New York: Holt, Rinehart and Winston, 1969.

Williams, R. H. (Ed.) *The prevention of disability in mental disorders*. Washington, D.C.: U.S. Dept. of Health, Education and Welfare, Public Health Service Publication No. 925, 1962.

Williams, R. J. Biochemical individuality and cellular nutrition: Prime factors in alcoholism. *Quarterly Journal of Studies on Alcohol*, 1959, *20*, 452–463.

Wittman, P. A scale for measuring prognosis in schizophrenic patients. *Elgin State Hospital Papers*, 1941, *4*, 20–33.

Wolff, H. S. Life stress and bodily disease: A formulation. In *Proceedings of the Association for Research in Nervous and Mental Disease*, Vol. 29. Baltimore: Williams & Wilkins, 1950.

Wolpe, J. *Psychotherapy by reciprocal inhibition*. Stanford, Ca.: Stanford University Press, 1958.

Wolpe, J. Behavior therapy in complex neurotic states. In J. M. Shlien (Ed.), *Research in psychotherapy*, Vol. 3. Washington, D.C.: American Psychological Association, 1968. Pp. 130–139.

Woody, R. H. *Behavioral problem children in the schools*. New York: Appleton-Century-Crofts, 1969.

Wootton, B. *Social science and social pathology*. New York: Macmillan, 1959.

World Health Organization. *International classification of diseases, 6th Revision*. Geneva, Switzerland: World Health Organization, 1968.

Wynne, L. C., Ryckoff, I. M., Day, J., & Hirsch, S. I. Pseudomutuality in the family relations of schizophrenics. *Psychiatry*, 1958, *21*, 205–220.

Yablonsky, L. *Synanon: The tunnel back*. Baltimore: Penguin Books, 1967.

Zax, M., & Cowen, E. L. Early identification and prevention of emotional disturbance in a public school. In E. L. Cowen, E. A. Gardner, & M. Zax (Eds.), *Emergent approaches to mental health problems*. New York: Appleton-Century-Crofts, 1967, Pp. 331–351.

Zax, M., & Cowen, E. L. Research on early detection and prevention of emotional dysfunction in young school children. In C. D. Spielberger (Ed.), *Current topics in clinical and community psychology*, Vol. 1. New York: Academic Press, 1970.

Zax, M., Cowen, E. L., Beach, D. R., Rappaport, J. & Lard, J. D. Follow-up study of children identified early as emotionally disturbed. *Journal of Consulting and Clinical Psychology*, 1968, *32*, 369–374.

Zax, M., Cowen, E. L., Izzo, L. D., Madonia, A. J., Merenda, J., & Trost, M. A. A teacher-aide program for preventing emotional disturbance in primary grade school children. *Mental Hygiene*, 1966, *50*, 406–414.

Zax, M., Cowen, E. L., Rappaport, J., Beach, D. R., & Laird, J. D. Follow-up study of children identified early as emotionally disturbed. *Journal of Consulting and Clinical Psychology*, 1968, 32, 360–374.

Zax, M., & Specter, G. A. *An introduction to community psychology*. New York: Wiley, 1974.

Zax, M., & Stricker, G. *Patterns of psychopathology*. New York: Macmillan, 1963.

Zigler, E., & Butterfield, E. C. Motivational aspects of changes in IQ preformance of culturally deprived nursery school children. In S. Chess & A. Thomas (Eds.), *Annual progress in child psychiatry and child development*. New York: Brunner-Mazel, 1969. Pp. 137–151.

Zigler, E., & Phillips, L. Social effectiveness and symptomatic behaviors. *Journal of Abnormal and Social Psychology*, 1960, *61*, 231–238.

Zigler, E., & Phillips, L. Psychiatric diagnosis: A critique. *Journal of Abnormal and Social Psychology*, 1961, *63*, 607–618. (a)

Zigler, E., & Phillips, L. Social competence: The action-thought parameter and vicariousness in normal and pathological behavior. *Journal of Abnormal and Social Psychology*, 1961, *63*, 137–146. (b)

Zigler, E., & Phillips, L. Social competence and the process-reactive distinction in psychopathology. *Journal of Abnormal and Social Psychology*, 1962, *65*, 215–222.

Zilboorg, G., & Henry, G. W. *A history of medical psychology*. New York: Norton, 1941.

Zimiles, H. Preventive aspects of school experience. In E. L. Cowen, E. A. Gardner, & M. Zax (Eds.), *Emergent approaches to mental health problems*. New York: Appleton-Century-Crofts, 1967. Pp. 239–251.

Zusman, J., & Davidson, D. L. *Practical aspects of mental health consultation*. Springfield, Ill.: Thomas, 1972.

Zwerling, I., & Rosenbaum, M. Alcoholic addiction and personality. In S. Arieti (Ed.), *American handbook of psychiatry*, Vol. I. New York: Basic Books, 1959.

Name Index

Subject Index and Glossary

Alcoholism *(Continued)*
  as learned behavior, 386
  LSD therapy, 391
  as medical problem, 379
  physiological theories of, 380-381
  psychological theories of, 382–388
  as self-destruction, 383–384
  treatment of, 388–391
Alzhesimer's disease, 93
Ambivalent, feeling both positively and negatively
    at the same time toward someone or some-
    thing, 143
Amenorrhea, 299
American Psychiatric Association, 12
  Ruling on Homosexuality (1973), 369
AML Behavior Checklist, 527
Amnesia, partial or total loss of memory, 282–283
  in dissociative hysteria, 259–261
Amphetamine, a drug that heightens wakefulness,
    394–395
Amytal, 394
Anal personality, 327
Anal stage, 130, 131–132
Analytic group psychotherapy, a form of group
    psychotherapy based on psychoanalytic
    principles involving free association by the
    patients in a group format, 436
Anesthesias, the loss of physical sensation in some
    part of the body, 113
Anethopaths, 346
Angina, 299
Angular transverse temporal gyrus, 82
Animal magnetism, a supposed invisible force that
    one person was thought to be capable of
    exercising over another. The term was first
    popularized by Anton Mesmer, 49, 113
Animism, the belief that natural and psychological
    phenomena are caused by spirits, 30–31, 43
Anna O., case of, 117–119
Anorexia, loss of appetite or aversion to food
Anosmia, loss of the sense of smell, 258
Antabuse, a drug that causes noxious physical
    symptoms when combined with alcohol.
    Used to prevent impulsive drinking, 390–
    391
Anticipatory guidance, crisis-coping method in
    which an individual is given an opportunity
    under psychologically sheltered conditions
    to express and work through feelings as-
    sociated with an anticipated life stress, 495
Antidepressant, 229
Antisocial personality, a personality disorder char-
    acterized by behavior that repeatedly con-
    flicts with society, is lacking in loyalty, is
    callous and irresponsible, 338–340, 344–356

Anxiety, 280–283
  and alcohol, 385–386
  avoidance of, 170–171
  as conflict of instincts, 125
  as drive, 204
  and the ego, 126–127
  hierarchy of, 422–423, 426
  from incongruency, 275
  in mother, and infant tension, 166
  and psychoneurosis, 255
Anxiety attacks, relatively brief, acute panic-like
    states seen in anxiety neurotics, 256
Anxiety neurosis, neurosis marked by general
    anxiety and tension and sometimes periods
    of panic, 256–258
Anxiety reaction, 288
Anxiety-relief response, 423
Aphasia, impairment of language ability due to
    brain damage, 119
Apomorphine, 390
Arteriosclerosis, a hardening of the walls of a
    blood vessel, 99
Assertive response, 421
Assimilative projection, a person's assuming that
    other people or animals feel the same as he
    does, 245–246
Association, of thought, 140–142
Associational psychology, 44
Asthenic body type, 326–327
Asthenic personality, a personality disorder mani-
    festing a low energy level, lack of en-
    thusiasm, a tendency to tire easily, and an
    inability to enjoy things, 336
Asthma, recurrent difficulty in breathing accom-
    panied by a wheezing cough, 299, 313–315
  and biological rhythms, 321–322
Astrology, 43
Atarax, 424
Ataxia, inability to coordinate voluntary bodily
    movement, 258
Atherosclerosis, a thickening of the blood vessel
    walls due to the deposit of fats, 99–100
Athletic body type, 326–327
Attention, and schizophrenia, 144–145
Attitudes, abstract and concrete, 83–84
Aurae, 103
Autism, a detachment from reality in which the
    inner life is dominant over the external,
    144
Auto-eroticism, taking oneself as a sex object, 242
Automatisms, 116
Autonomic nervous system, a part of the nervous
    system that regulates involuntary functions,
    301
Aversive therapy, 389–390